ESTABLISHING THE FOUNDATION
OF COLLABORATIVE NETWORKS

IFIP – The International Federation for Information Processing

IFIP was founded in 1960 under the auspices of UNESCO, following the First World Computer Congress held in Paris the previous year. An umbrella organization for societies working in information processing, IFIP's aim is two-fold: to support information processing within its member countries and to encourage technology transfer to developing nations. As its mission statement clearly states,

> IFIP's mission is to be the leading, truly international, apolitical organization which encourages and assists in the development, exploitation and application of information technology for the benefit of all people.

IFIP is a non-profitmaking organization, run almost solely by 2500 volunteers. It operates through a number of technical committees, which organize events and publications. IFIP's events range from an international congress to local seminars, but the most important are:

- The IFIP World Computer Congress, held every second year;
- Open conferences;
- Working conferences.

The flagship event is the IFIP World Computer Congress, at which both invited and contributed papers are presented. Contributed papers are rigorously refereed and the rejection rate is high.

As with the Congress, participation in the open conferences is open to all and papers may be invited or submitted. Again, submitted papers are stringently refereed.

The working conferences are structured differently. They are usually run by a working group and attendance is small and by invitation only. Their purpose is to create an atmosphere conducive to innovation and development. Refereeing is less rigorous and papers are subjected to extensive group discussion.

Publications arising from IFIP events vary. The papers presented at the IFIP World Computer Congress and at open conferences are published as conference proceedings, while the results of the working conferences are often published as collections of selected and edited papers.

Any national society whose primary activity is in information may apply to become a full member of IFIP, although full membership is restricted to one society per country. Full members are entitled to vote at the annual General Assembly, National societies preferring a less committed involvement may apply for associate or corresponding membership. Associate members enjoy the same benefits as full members, but without voting rights. Corresponding members are not represented in IFIP bodies. Affiliated membership is open to non-national societies, and individual and honorary membership schemes are also offered.

ESTABLISHING THE FOUNDATION OF COLLABORATIVE NETWORKS

IFIP TC 5 Working Group 5.5 Eighth IFIP Working Conference on Virtual Enterprises
September 10-12, 2007, Guimarães, Portugal

Edited by

Luis M. Camarinha-Matos
New University of Lisbon, Portugal

Hamideh Afsarmanesh
University of Amsterdam, The Netherlands

Paulo Novais
University of Minho, Portugal

Cesar Analide
University of Minho, Portugal

 Springer

Establishing the Foundation of Collaborative Networks

Edited by L. Camarinha-Matos, H. Afsarmanesh, P. Novais, and C. Analide

p. cm. (IFIP International Federation for Information Processing, a Springer Series in Computer Science)

ISSN 1571-5736/1861-2288 (Internet)

ISBN 978-1-4419-4475-7   e-ISBN 978-0-387-73798-0

Printed on acid-free paper

9 8 7 6 5 4 3 2 1

springer.com

TABLE OF CONTENTS

PRO-VE '07 – 8th IFIP Working Conference on VIRTUAL ENTERPRISES
Guimarães, Portugal, 10-12 September 2007

Program Chair - Luis M. Camarinha-Matos (PT)

Program track co-chairs:
- Hamideh Afsarmanesh (NL) - VO Breeding Environments
- Willy Picard (PL) - Professional Virtual Communities
- Xavier Boucher (FR) - Evolutionary Supply Chains and VOs
- Klaus-Dieter Thoben (DE) - Industrial CNO Applications

Organization Chair - Paulo Novais (PT)
Co-chair - Cesar Analide (PT)

REFEREES FROM THE PROGRAMME COMMITTEE

Hamideh Afsarmanesh (NL)
Cesar Analide (PT)
Samuil Angelov (NL)
Dimitris Assimakopoulos (FR)
Américo Azevedo (PT)
Eoin Banahan (UK)
José Barata (PT)
Ron Beckett (AU)
Peter Bertok (AU)
Kirsimarja Blomqvist (FI)
Xavier Boucher (FR)
Jim Browne (IE)
Luís M. Camarinha-Matos (PT)
Jorge Cardoso (PT)
Wojciech Cellary (PL)
Maria Manuela Cunha (PT)
Sophie D'Amours (CA)
Heiko Dirlenbach (DE)
Schahram Dustdar (AT)
Elsa Estevez (AR)
Joaquim Filipe (PT)
Myrna Flores (CH)
Cesar Garita (CR)
Ted Goranson (US)
Paul Grefen (NL)
Fernando Guerrero (ES)
Sergio Gusmeroli (IT)
Jairo Gutierrez (NZ)
Tarek Hassan (UK)
Vltaka Hlupic (UK)
Raimo Hyötyläinen (FI)

Tomasz Janowski (MO)
James Joshi (US)
Toshiya Kaihara (JP)
Iris Karvonen (FI)
Fumihiko Kimura (JP)
Alexandra Klen (BR)
Bernhard Koelmel (DE)
Kurt Kosanke (DE)
Adamantios Koumpis (GR)
George Kovacs (HU)
John Krogstie (NO)
Nada Lavrac (SI)
Celson Lima (FR)
José Machado (PT)
Karsten Menzel (IE)
Istvan Mézgár (HU)
Arturo Molina (MX)
Ugo Negretto (DE)
Laszlo Nemes (AU)
José M. Neves (PT)
Ovidiu Noran (AU)
Paulo Novais (PT)
Adegboyega Ojo (MO)
Eugénio Oliveira (PT)
Martin Ollus (FI)
Angel Ortiz (ES)
Luis Osório (PT)
Kulwant Pawar (UK)
Adam Pawlak (PL)
Willy Picard (PL)
Michel Pouly (CH)
Kenneth Preiss (IL)

Goran Putnik (PT)
Ricardo Rabelo (BR)
Heri Ramampiaro (US)
Yacine Rezgui (UK)
Rainer Ruggaber (DE)
Hans Schaffers (NL)
Weiming Shen (CA)
Waleed W. Smari (US)
Riitta Smeds (FI)
António L. Soares (PT)
Jorge P. Sousa (PT)
Volker Stich (DE)
Klaus-Dieter Thoben (DE)
Lorna Uden (UK)
Agostino Villa (IT)
Antonio Volpentesta (IT)
Peter Weiß (DE)

FOREWORD

Establishing the foundation of Collaborative Networks

*The need for computer-assisted collaboration, which originally manifested decades ago in manufacturing to establish small business-oriented networks of organizations in forms of supply chains or extended enterprises, is by now extended into a large number of other areas. While today production and service provision constitute the main areas of application for Collaborative Networks (CNs) worldwide, during the last decade virtual scientific laboratories, inter-enterprise collaborative engineering, crisis management, virtual institutes and virtual learning communities among others, are also rising within the wide spectrum of application areas in need of CNs. These developments emphasize the urgency for **establishing a sounder foundation for collaborative networks**, namely in terms of theoretical principles and formal models, capturing the concepts, entities, behaviors, and operations of the CNs, and developing technology-independent infrastructure architecture, tools and methodologies.*

Further to the shorter-term, goal-oriented, and opportunity-based virtual organizations, nowadays a variety of long term "strategic" association / coalition of organizations have emerged. These associations, earlier called clusters or clubs, act as the breeding environments for virtual organizations, and provide the necessary conditions and mechanisms to prepare their members towards dynamic and fluid establishment of potential opportunity-based virtual organizations. A good collection of active VO Breeding Environments (VBEs) and Professional Virtual Communities (PVCs) can be found in various regions of the world. Europe with its considerable number of SMEs and micro organizations have particularly realized the benefits it can gain from establishing such networks, and have been investing in both its research and practice.

As a new scientific discipline, research on different aspects of CNs is gaining momentum. Nevertheless, while a large number of research projects and pilot cases address many aspects of the collaboration networks, a large number of new challenges are identified everyday, in need of innovative solutions. Namely, the research on CNs is still young and spread among several disciplines, including computer science, computer engineering, communications and networking, management, economy, social sciences, law and ethics, etc., thus requiring holistic approaches. Such holistic framework shall combine business models, conceptual models, governance principles and methods, as well as supporting infrastructures and ICT-based services. Considering that today the computing and networking technologies provide the needed base for establishment of collaborative platforms, emphasis within the CN research is expanding towards understanding of collaboration promotion mechanisms and CN governance principles, as well as establishing new value systems, performance assessment methodologies, trust establishment, and measurement of the benefits and risks of collaboration.

*By representing a good synthesis of the work in the CN area, PRO-VE plays an active role in the promotion of these activities. In this context, PRO-VE is well recognized as the most focused scientific and technical conference on Collaborative Networks, offering a major opportunity for the presentation and discussion of the latest research developments and industrial practice case studies. In line with the vision of **IFIP** and **SOCOLNET** societies, the PRO-VE Conference offers a forum for collaboration and knowledge exchange among experts from different regions of the world. With the steady growth of the PRO-VE community, this platform has offered a base for consolidation of research results, as well as for **development and dissemination of the foundation of Collaborative Networks**.*

The PRO-VE '07 held in Guimarães, Portugal, is the 8th event in a series of successful conferences, including PRO-VE '99 (held in Porto, Portugal), PRO-VE 2000 (held in Florianopolis, Brazil), PRO-VE 02 (held in Sesimbra, Portugal), PRO-VE '03 (held in Lugano, Switzerland), PRO-VE '04 (held in Toulouse, France), PRO-VE '05 (held in Valencia, Spain), and PRO-VE '06 (held in Helsinki, Finland).

This book includes a number of selected papers from the PRO-VE '07 Conference, providing a comprehensive overview of recent advances in various CN domains. There is a special emphasis on the CN topics related to trust aspects, performance and value systems, VO breeding environments, VO creation, e-contracting, collaborative architectures and frameworks, professional virtual communities, interoperability issues, business benefits, and case studies and applications in industry and services.

The book itself is the result of cooperative and highly distributed work among the authors of the articles and the International Program committee members of this conference, thus constituting a valuable tool for all those interested in the emerging applications, research advances, and challenges of the collaborative networks. We would like to thank all the authors both from academia/research and industry for their contributions. We appreciate the dedication of the PRO-VE Program Committee members and other reviewers who helped both with the selection of articles and contributed with valuable comments to improve their quality.

The editors,

Luís M. Camarinha-Matos
Faculty of Science and Technology, New University of Lisbon, Portugal

Hamideh Afsarmanesh
Faculty of Science, University of Amsterdam, The Netherlands

Paulo Novais and Cesar Analide
Engineering School, University of Minho, Portugal

PART 1

TRUST ASPECTS IN COLLABORATION

1

TOWARDS ESTABLISHING TRUST RELATIONSHIPS AMONG ORGANIZATIONS IN VBES

Simon Samwel Msanjila, Hamideh Afsarmanesh

University of Amsterdam, NETHERLANDS
msanjila@science.uva.nl, hamideh@science.uva.nl

Organizations compete in acquiring competitive resources, knowledge, and competencies. However, in the current market, when an opportunity is brokered, organizations need to collaborate, more than competing, by sharing the acquired resources, knowledge, and competencies to respond to the opportunity which none of them could handle otherwise. This means organizational strategies must now adapt to the notion of collaboration with others. One important organizational strategy necessary in the virtual organization breeding environment (VBE) is focused on the organizational preparedness that is required to enhance the chances of participating in virtual organizations (VOs). A crucial aspect of preparedness is the establishment of trust relationships with other member organizations to smoothen the sharing of resources, knowledge, and competence, and in turn facilitate the organizations' collaboration. In this paper we address approaches and mechanisms for establishment of trust relationships among member organizations in VBEs.

1   INTRODUCTION

The word "trust" as used daily by individuals refers to the opinion of somebody about another person. It is not only an estimation of another's intention, but also the possible competencies of others that are needed to establish trust relationships among people. Gambetta [Gambetta, D. 1988] provided a definition of trust, which has been widely used, as *the subjective probability by which an individual "A" expects another individual "B" to perform a given action on which A's welfare depends*. Trust is a subject, which is studied by researchers in various disciplines from which different definitions are generated [Msanjila, S.S. et al 2007-1].

In VBE environments, trust relationships must be addressed from three points of view, including: the VBE member organizations, the external stakeholders, and the VBE administration. VBE members are organizations and not individuals, and VBE focuses on preparing its members for involvement in VOs [Afsarmanesh, H. et al 2005]. Therefore, while this work can benefit from the general past research on trust relationships among individuals, their results cannot be directly applied.

Trust among organizations in VBEs is a complex subject, which must be addressed considering the interdisciplinarity, heterogeneity and contradictions among interests and goals of involved organizations [Msanjila, S.S. et al 2007-2]. In our study, *identification and tuning of trust elements, modeling of trust relationships, assessment of trust level, and establishment and promotion of trust relationship* constitute the main focus of the *management of trust* among organizations in VBEs. These specific topics are addressed considering the following three main trust objectives in VBEs, namely for creating trust and establishing trust relationships: (1) among VBE member organizations, (2) of the VBE member

Msanjila, S.S., Afsarmanesh, H., 2007, in IFIP International Federation for Information Processing, Volume 243, Establishing the Foundation of Collaborative Networks; eds. Camarinha-Matos, L., Afsarmanesh, H., Novais, P., Analide, C.; (Boston: Springer), pp. 3–14.

organization to the VBE administration, and (3) of the external organization to the VBE. In [Msanjila, S.S. et al 2007-3] we addressed the identification of trust elements for organizations; in [Msanjila, S.S. et al 2007-1] we addressed the modeling of trust relationships among organizations, in [Msanjila, S.S. et al 2007-2] we addressed the assessment of trust level of organizations. This paper focuses on the establishment of trust relationships among organizations in VBEs by applying the trust models/elements as characterized in our previous work.

The remaining part of this paper is organized as follows: section 2 provides the definitions of base concepts. Section 3 describes the problem area and presents research questions. Section 4 addresses the antecedents and importance of trust. Section 5 addresses the establishment of trust relationships among organizations. Section 6 discusses the tradeoffs between risks and trust in VBEs. Section 7 addresses the importance of validity of information. Section 8 concludes the paper.

2   DEFINITIONS OF MAIN CONCEPTS

This section presents the definitions of the base concepts applied in this paper. These definitions are listed in Table 1 [Msanjila, S.S. et al 2007-1].

Table 1: definitions of important concepts

Concept	Definition
Trust actors	Refer to the two organization parties involved in a specific trust relationship. The first party is the organization that needs to assess the trustworthiness of another and is referred to as the trustor. The second party is the organization that needs to be trusted, and thus its trust level will be assessed and is referred to as the trustee.
Trust objective	Refers to the purpose for which the trust relationship establishment among the involved organizations is required. Examples of trust objectives include the following: for inviting an organization to join a VO, for appointing or selecting an organization as the VO coordinator, etc.
Trust perspective	Represents the specific "point of view" of the trustor on the main aspects that must be considered for assessing the trust level of the trustee.
Trust requirement	Represents the essentials (cardinals) that characterize and guide on how the respective trust perspective can be realized. Thus, trust requirements are the fundamental cardinals that guide or suggest what must be met in order for the respective trust perspective to be realized. For instance, "financial stability" is an example requirement that must be met to support the economical perspective, similarly "compliance with community standards" is a requirement for the social perspective, etc.
Trust criteria	Represents the measurable trust elements that characterize a respective trust requirement. Therefore, for each organization, the values of its trust criteria (related to a requirement) can be used to make an objective fact-based judgment on whether the respective requirement is met. Each trust criteria constitutes a value structure and the metric, which defines the acceptable structure and meaning for its data, such as scalars, vectors, arrays, list of strings, etc.
Trust level	Refers to the intensity level of trust for a trustee in a trust relationship, based on the assessment of values for a set of necessary trust criteria. Clearly enough, the criteria for the trust level assessment of organizations are varied and wide in spectrum depending on the purpose (e.g. depending on the requirements, the perspective, and the objective of trust establishment). When trust level is assessed for a certain specific purpose, such as for inviting a member to a VO, and the assessment is based on specific trust criteria for that the purpose, we call the results, specific trustworthiness of the trustee.
Trust relationship	A relationship is a state of connectedness among people or organizations or is a state involving mutual dealing among parties. Trust relationship refers to the state of connectedness between a trustor and a trustee whose intensity is characterized and based on the fact-based assessment of trust level.

3   PROBLEM AREA AND RESEARCH QUESTIONS

Trust is defined differently in different disciplines and research. Among others, the three following definitions are dominant:

1. *Trust is the willingness of a trustor to be vulnerable to the actions of another party based on the expectations that the trustee will perform a particular action important to the trustor irrespective of the ability to monitor or control the trustee [Mayer, R. C. et al 1995].*
2. *Trust is the belief in the competency of an entity to act dependably, securely and reliably within a specified context [Grandison, T., et al 2000].*

3.Trust is a psychological condition comprising the trustor's intention to accept vulnerability based upon expectation of trustee's intentions and behavior [Rousseau, D.M. et al 1998].

Traditionally, trust is subjective and thus the evaluation has been opinion-based. However, trust among organizations is the base for any collaborative transaction in which they get involved. Thus specifically for SMEs, their survivability may depend on getting involved in such collaborations. Therefore, opinion-based trust (subjective) is too risky and fact-based trust (objective) is required to be created among organizations to facilitate goal oriented collaborations.

The diversity among these definitions makes it difficult to properly characterize trust and its concepts. There are many theories on trust, some of which diverge from each other only in their identification of the grounds on which they are based [Rousseau, D.M. et al 1998]. Despite the difficulties in solidifying the definition of trust, in practice, trust is a base for collaboration among individuals as well as among organizations. Research addressing the subject of collaboration among organizations had reported that the effectiveness of VBE operation depends on the right balance of trust level among organizations [Msanjila, S.S. et al 2007-1].

Trust among organizations, as it is applied in VBEs, is defined as the objective-specific confidence of a trustor to a trustee based on the results of fact-based assessment of trust level of the trustee [Msanjila, S.S. et al 2007-3].

Therefore, objective based trust creation refers to the process of creating trust among organizations based on the results of the fact-based assessment of their trust levels. Only measurable or numeric data are applied for the assessment and the resulted trust levels can be supported with some formal reasoning applied during the assessment of trust level, which in turn enhances the reasoning of the established trust relationships [Msanjila, S.S. et al 2007-2]. While the importance of trust relationships is palpable for collaboration among organizations, the following three research questions must be addressed:

1. *Can trustworthiness (trust level) of an organization be measured? How complex is trustworthiness? Does it have a quantitative value, and if so, what is the metric? Furthermore, is it one number or a set of numbers? If not quantitative, then is it a qualitative value, such as good/bad, high/low?*

In [Msanjila, S.S et al 2007-2], we presented an approach for measuring trust level of organizations in terms of values of a set of trust-related criteria. We argued that trustworthiness is complex and can neither be measured with a single value nor interpreted with a single metric. The levels upon which the data about certain trust criteria in an organization meet the specified ratings represent its trust level.

2. *Does every organization have the same objectives and perspectives for establishing trust relationship with others?*

In VBEs, trust must be thoroughly characterized to ease the understanding about the motivations from which organizations prefer to establish trust relationships with others. *Antecedents and importance* of trust relationships among member organizations must be studied. This paper addresses this question.

3. *How can establishment of trust among organizations in VBE be achieved and enhanced?*

This paper addresses this question by providing approaches for establishing and promoting trust relationships among organizations in VBEs.

4   ANTECEDENTS AND IMPORTANCE OF TRUST IN VBES

In this **section we** address the antecedents and importance of trust relationships among organizations in VBEs. We first address the antecedents.

4.1   Antecedents for establishing trust relationships among organizations

Trust antecedents are cardinal elements that may have positive or negative effects (impacts) on the effectiveness of the established trust relationships among organizations. In this work three antecedents are identified for organizations that are also partially studied in other research [Rtanasingam, P. 2004], namely: *the shared values, the previous interactions, and the practiced behaviors.*

Shared values occur when the trustor and the trustee have common understanding on important issues that might influence the creation of trust to each other, such as missions, goals, policies, interpretation of right or wrong etc. [Morgan, R.M. et al 1994]. Shared values can range from business objectives to the internal management processes and approaches. In business environments, it is more difficult to have shared values when the two organizations are competing than when they are complementing each other [Clay, K. et al 2000]. Typically, when two organizations have some common understanding, they both feel that there will not be unexpected results during the cooperation/collaboration, and thus it is easier to establish trust relationship between them. As an aspect of preparedness, the VBE must ensure member organizations do have some shared values.

Previous fruitful interactions between the trustor and the trustee either directly or indirectly (through other intermediate organizations) enhances the effectiveness of the established trust relationships. The interactions can be formal as well as informal, i.e. sharing meaningful and up-to-date information. Interactions can also involve individuals working in the two organizations. Although, there may be no existing business interactions, but the existence of previous interactions will enable fluid and smooth the establishment of trust relationship.

Practiced (moral and/or ethical) behaviours basically refer to acting against the *opportunistic behaviour*. Opportunistic behaviour refers to taking immediate advantage, often unethically, of any circumstance that may generate possible benefit. Opportunistic behaviour in competitive market seems natural because the focus of organizations in such environments is to acquire customers without caring the long-term relationships with other organizations. However, in collaborative networks, organizations must collaborate with others to serve the same customer. Opportunistic behaviour has a negative impact on the effectiveness of trust relationships. It has its roots in transaction cost literature and is defined as *self-interest seeking with guile* [Mukherjee, A. 2003]. In this paper we refer to opportunistic behaviour as *ungentle action taken by VBE members for the purpose of benefiting themselves unethically more than others (e.g. quitting the collaboration once they gain, or if they expect for the risks of the collaboration to arise).*

4.2   Importance of establishing trust relationships among organizations

The stability of a VBE requires delicate balance of trust level among the involved organizations in various specific trust relationships [Msanjila, S.S. et al 2007-1]. As explained earlier, VBEs are characterized as multi-actor environments, where each actor has autonomy, interests, and goals that might be contradicting to those of others. Interdisciplinary and heterogeneity nature among several aspects, such as business domains and technological aspects, are some issues that increase the complexity for creating trust among organizations in VBEs. A catalyser for enhancement of cooperation among member organizations in VBEs is the establishment of their trust relationships. That is why the past research pointed out that trust is the most salient factor for cooperation networks to achieve their objectives [Morgan, R.M. et al 1994]. Trust relationships among organizations are more important for industry-based VBEs that function under the pressure from global economy, the growing value of information, and the increasing uncertainties surrounding their businesses [Msanjila, S.S. et al 2007-1].

Several advantages can be gained once trust relationships among member organizations are properly established and managed. Among others the key advantages include: (1) Motivating member organizations to accept responsibilities in case of uncertain or incomplete information, (2) Facilitating the achievement of common goals by encouraging information exchange, knowledge sharing, tools sharing, etc., among member organizations, (3) Encouraging member organizations to avoid opportunistic behaviours during collaboration, (4) Easing the process of creating and launching VOs, (5) Creating competitive advantage by facilitating the reduction of governance, internalization (acquisitions), and transaction costs among organizations, (6) Enabling open communication, and reduces conflicts, (8) Speeding up the contract negotiation process among partners.

5 ESTABLISHING TRUST RELATIONSHIPS

In this section we address the establishment of trust relationships among organizations in VBEs. We first present some existing related approaches.

5.1 Existing approaches for trust relationship establishment

There are several approaches for establishing trust relationships which are applied for different actors in various kinds of environments. These approaches are applied to the establishment of trust relationships either among individuals, among actors in specific domain (e.g. in health service provision), or among entities in a specific technology (e.g. agent technologies). Although the following few cannot be directly applied for trust relationships among organizations, they do have relevance: role-based, reputation-based, interaction-based, and risk-based approaches.

Role based approach: Role-based trust relationships are established to facilitate responsibilities related to roles of organizations in collaborative networks. This approach is mostly used for establishment of trust relationships among systems representing organizations and those systems are either using multi agent systems or peer-to-peer interactions on Internet based relationships [Huynh, D. et al 2004]. Each peer, node or agent represents a single organization in the dynamic community interacting through the Internet. The approach was developed as a solution to the trust relationship problems in the decentralized and dynamic working environments [Field, S. et al 2003]. With this approach, an organization cannot take more than one role and it is trusted only for a specific known role. This approach can be applied to create trust of the member organizations to the VBE administrator. Thus the VBE administrator is trusted to take the VBE related administrative tasks.

Reputation based approach: At individual level, reputation is an overall quality or character as seen or judged by people within a community. There are two possible sources for reputation information of an organization for establishing trust relationship with others. First is the *Witness reputation* that refers to the reputation information collected by the trustor or the trustor's associated (friends) organizations [Huynh, D. et al 2004]. In this case the trustor must observe the required character for the trustee or at least its associated organizations must observe. In VBEs, where organizations collaborate virtually, the adaptation of this approach is hardly feasible. And second is the *Certified reputation* that refers to the reputation information collected by the trustee and made available to the trustor. The trustee can provide its information such as the detailed organization's profile to the trustor to enhance its trust level [Yu, B. et al 2003]. The trustee can also request its friend/authorized organizations to provide positive information (e.g. accreditation document) to the trustor that can be used to enhance its trust level. The main problem for this approach is that there is high risk of using biased information and thus the resulted trust relationships are risked to failure. The validation of such information is also difficult since the bad reputation is usually hidden.

Interaction based approach: Past experiences obtained from direct interactions among organizations enhance the chance of successfully establishing their trust relationships. Yet, member organizations sometimes need to collaborate with others, which they had never collaborated with before, and even they do not know them physically. Thus this approach cannot apply in every case in VBEs.

Consumer-opinion based approach: This approach is applied to establish trust relationships among customers and suppliers/producers. It is based on expressed opinions, ranking or comments provided by customers on the quality of products/services they purchase/use. While buying/using products/services, the customers are typically requested by a website to comment (rank) the quality of the same product/service (e.g. a television or a hotel room, etc.) from a number of producers/providers. Then, the comments (ranks) are usually organized by that site in a scorecard format. The results from the scorecard are then made available to future customers, for smoothing the creation of trust to certain producers/providers. In most cases, this approach is applicable to online businesses and thus the proof of data validity might be difficult.

Risk based approach: This approach focuses on reducing possible risks that may exist during the collaboration. As such organizations can trust each other and thus collaborate because of the confidence that limited risks may be encountered. However, in practice risks are unexpected results and cannot be predicted to when they will arise. Thus it is hard to practically avoid risks. It is even difficult in VBEs where virtual collaboration and cooperation are the key approach for co-working.

5.2   Establishing trust relationships among organizations in VBEs

To properly establish trust relationships among organizations in VBEs, which will be fruitful, several steps must be followed. We suggest four main steps: assessment of trust level of organizations, validation of trust level results, presentation and interpretation of trust levels, and creation of trust among organizations.

Step 1: Assessment of trust level of organizations
The fundamental step during the establishment of trust relationships among organizations is assessing their trust level. This step aims at ensuring that the involved organizations do have acceptable trust levels and also their trust levels are rightly balanced. In VBEs the assessment of trust level of organizations is performed for three purposes namely for ensuring that: (1) the trust of a VBE membership applicant meet the minimum trust level acceptable in the VBE, namely the base trust level, (2) all member organizations conform to the base trust level specified in the VBE, and (3) the specified trustworthiness for an objective is met by all involved partners. In our approach for the assessment of trust level, the measurements are not

absolute rather comparative. The trust levels are valid for given: rating, involved organizations, and set of trust criteria preferred by the trustor. The assessment of trust level of organizations is addressed in detail in [Msanjila, S.S. et al 2007-1].

Step 2: Validations of trust level results

The assessment of trust level applies the values of trust criteria provided and made available in the VBE by the respective organizations. The source of information can be either the organization's businesses or participations in VOs. A priori to confirming the resulted trust levels of organizations the information applied for each organization must be validated. By validating the applied information the resulted trust levels will also be validated. In this paper we suggest some sources of evidences that can prove the validity of information made available in the VBE by each organization. The information validity evidence is addressed in section 7.

Step 3: Presentation and interpretation of trust levels

Our approach for the assessment of trust level is based on set of trust criteria that are selected by either the VBE administrator or the trustor. Thus the resulted trust levels are also expressed in terms of these trust criteria. Understanding and properly interpreting trust levels described in terms of values for a set of trust criteria will be complex and difficult to most decision makers, such as managers, directors, etc. who are not trust experts. Therefore, trust levels must be presented in a format which is as understandable as possible. However, an assistance of trust experts, in specific domain or environment, to interpret the trust levels will be helpful to decision makers. In this study we have suggested a qualitative means for representing the comparative trust levels in five ratings namely: strongly less trustworthy, less trustworthy, *average trustworthy, more trustworthy, and strongly more trustworthy.* Figure 1 shows the relations among these qualitative trust levels.

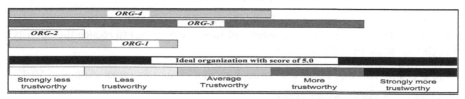

Figure 1: Trust-meter for representing trust levels among organizations

Step 4: Creation of trust among organizations and initiation of their trust relationships

When the valid trust level results are confirmed the organizations with acceptable trust level can be identified. To create trust among organizations each one must be convinced that others are trustworthy enough to establish trust relationships with them. Thus each organization needs enough information that will support under-standing other organizations. However, the perceptions of trust and thus the preferred trust perspective are not uniform and can vary among the organizations. The *challenge question is which information and at what level of details should be provided to each specific organization?*

In our approach the creation of trust for the trustor organization to a trustee organization is based on the performance information of the trustee organization. Based on its preferred trust perspective the trustor organization shall be provided with detailed information enough to create the required trust. The detail of the information provided will also differ due to the following five aspects:

- **Who**: The role of the actors during and after the establishment of their trust relationships
- **When**: The period when the information is gathered and provided
- **What**: The kind and the content of the information collected and provided
- **How**: The sources of information and the mechanisms for its collection and provision
- **Why**: The specific purpose for requesting the information and thus the trust objective.

When trust among the involved organizations is successfully created trust relationships among them can be initiated. Various forms for initiating established trust relationships are in practice, but the most popular one is the *contracting*. At this stage organizations trust each other and they thus guarantee each other, through the contract, that they can now start collaborating for the current common goals.

There are two kinds of trust relationships that can be established among organizations, namely: *Short-term and Long-term trust relationships*. Short-term trust relationships are established to facilitate co-working among organizations that will exist for a relatively short period of time, e.g. collaboration in VOs. Long-term trust relationships are established to facilitate co-working among organizations that will exist for a relatively long period of time, e.g. cooperation in VBEs.

6   RISKS AND TRUST RELATIONSHIPS

Risk refers to potential negative impact to an asset or value that may arise from present process or future event. Generally, risk is related to the potential losses, which can be caused by a risky transaction, and mainly addresses its probability.

6.1   Risks that can occur during cooperation in VBEs

Various types of risks exist in VBEs while member organizations are cooperating. These risks (Table 2) must be addressed and strategic response to reduce the severity of such risks must be put in place.

Table 2: Some risks that can occur during cooperation among organizations in VBEs

Risk type	Description and sources
Strategic risks	Several different strategic risks may be associated with operating in different types of business or industry domains. These include risks arising from: acquiring business opportunity, changing customers, changes of customer's demands, changes of operating environments, and emerged new innovative results from research and developments. Organizational strategies must be flexible to accommodate the changes. Rigid strategies can result risks such as failure of an organization to properly integrate and collaborate with others due to unacceptable or outdated strategies [Anargiridou, D. C. 2006].
Operational risks	Operational risks may exist due to direct or indirect loss resulted from inadequate or failed internal processes, employees, or systems. Failure of an organization to achieve agreed results due to its internal problems causes risk of failure to the entire consortium configured for collaboration, and thus failure in achieving the common goals.
Legal issues and cross border risks	These are risks that may exist due to changes of government or local authorities, rules, regulations and laws. Usually business organizations are not involved in proposing legal issues and thus they have no influence. In the VBE however, organizations might belong to different legal systems and even from different countries. Changes of legal issues in one country where some members are located might cause risks for their cooperation with others and vice versa for others.
	Compliance risks are those associated with the need to comply with laws, regulations or norms. They also apply to the need to act in a manner which other organizations and customers expect, for example by avoiding opportunistic behavior. Since VBEs are not closed border, various standards might exist in different markets. Collaboration among

Compliance risks	organizations operating in markets with different standards might face the risk of failure to comply. In some cases these standards might even be contradicting. Compliance risks are also associated with violation of, or non-conformance with, laws, regulations, norms, and ethical standards. With, the current information and communication technologies (ICTs) and the virtual co-working, assuring compliance becomes more difficult to prove.
Financial risks	These are the risks associated with financial aspects of the collaboration. They refer to the chance that an actual investment's return is lower than expected. This includes the possibility of losing some or all of the original investment due to issues such as customer failure to pay, opportunism of partners in collaboration consortium, etc. Financial risks are measured using the returns for a specific investment. There are various kinds of financial risks, among others they can be related to: credit, liquidity, transactions, interest rate, foreign exchange, etc., risks
Reputation risks	Reputation risk is related to organization's image and instability arising from negative opinions either from other member organizations in the VBE, or from the public. This affects the organization's ability to establish new, or continue with the existing, trust relationships with other organizations. This risk may expose the organization to litigation, financial loss, or loosing its customers. Reputation risk exposure must be dealt with throughout the organization, and requires exercising caution in dealing with its customers and the community.
Technology risks	Risks surrounding ICTs, such as network failure, lack of resources and skills, hacking and viruses, etc., have the potential of a greater negative impact on an organization than in the past. Collaboration and cooperation are both facilitated by computer networks. Several risks exist related to collaboration to which an organization must be prepared to quickly respond. These include: security, privacy, information access, applied technologies complexity related risks, etc.

6.2   Risks avoidance vs. commitment to trust relationships

In investment, it is generally the case that the greater the risk that a person takes, the higher the return that he/she will expect to receive, and the less risk entails lower return. The tradeoffs concerning organizations in relation to risks are about the values that will be received or obtained once a specific risk is accepted. However, the cooperation among organizations in VBEs does not provide a direct return value. The economical benefits of cooperation among member organizations are the increase in their chance of acquiring better and more opportunities, as well as involvement in opportunities brokered with others.

In practice, trust and risks are inversely related - when one increases there is a high chance of the other to decrease. Thus if risks existing in a certain environment increase then organizations operating in such environment feels at risky and can hardly trust each others for collaboration. Similarly, if organizations strongly trust each other then they feel that risks while collaborating can hardly arise.

Considering the style of co-working in VBEs - the virtual cooperation - organizations may interact with others without knowing them physically and thus the feeling of possibility that such risks and even more can arise might be high. A number of risks exist in VBEs as discussed in section 6.1. One strategy that organizations can assume to avoid risks related to collaboration is either not committing themselves into trust relationships or resist establishing such trust relationships by being reluctant in creating trust to others. Such strategy can in fact cause problems related to sharing resources, knowledge, and competency as well as exchanging information necessary for enabling the collaboration.

In VBEs, cooperation is the only potential style of co-working that has so far been proved to be suitable for member organizations in such environments. Trust and trust relationships have illustrated to be the amenable facilitators which smooth the cooperation among organizations in VBEs as well as their collaboration in VOs. The challenging issue for the VBE administrator is to convince the organizations to establish and commit to the trust relationships despite the existing risks.

6.3 Promoting trust relationships among organizations

There are several complexities that member organizations might face when co-operating in VBEs. In addition to the risks addressed in section 6.2 these complexities can also make it difficult to establish trust relationships among organizations. Among others, they include: social, economical, technological, and behavioral complexities. However, once an organization is confident that there are potential benefits related to its involvement in the VBE, there is a high chance of successfully establishing trust relationship with other organizations. Promoting high trust levels for organizations will ease the process of establishing trust relationships among them. In this work we suggest four approaches for promoting trust level of organizations which in turn promotes the participation in trust relationships:

- *Committed participation in VOs*: Every VO does have requirements such as resources, competencies, etc., that each partner must possess. When an organization manages to participate in many VOs it indicates that it has the capabilities and enough trust level for collaboration. The participations in VOs enable it to improve its performance records, e.g. by clearing their bad image, if any, which in turn enhances its trust level.

- *Higher level of VBE membership:* A VBE is managed through the agreed working and operating principles. Therefore, there are some requirements and rules that a VBE member must meet and comply with in order to receive the membership. Three membership levels are defined in the VBE [Afsarmanesh, H. et al 2005] namely: the fully active, the loosely associated, and the external level (very loose) memberships.

- *VBE's market performance and branding (market credibility):* Branding and marketing done by the member organization in external markets not only enhance its trust level but also the reputation of the VBE and hence high chance for brokering opportunities. The organization that performs better in the market, such as bringing many opportunities to the VBE, has a high chance of successfully establishing trust relationships with others.

  Point accumulation and rewarding: With this approach, mechanisms and tools must be developed to assess achievements which in turn form the basis for either awarding points upon being productive or deducing points upon failures. The points are accumulated and later are used as a quick indicator for the trustworthiness of organizations.

7 INFORMATION VALIDITY EVIDENCE

The **information that is made available by a member organization to the VBE for the assessment of** its trust level must be supported with some validity evidences. This section addresses the evidence that can prove the validity of trust related data.

7.1 Witness evidence

These evidences constitute some form of documents generated by third parties that although provide some proof of accuracy for their respective information they cannot be considered as official and authorized proofs. The witnessed evidences can include information obtained from: (1) *Public channels*, (e.g. the magazines, newspapers) and (2) *Private channels*, (e.g. recommendations).

Although these evidences are not as strong as the authorized evidence, in the lack of authorized evidences and depending on the source of evidence, they can provide some assurance to the validity of the provided information. Clearly, the weight of this validity increases if the channels used (the source of the news or the person providing the recommendation) are publicly recognized. For example, reputable news media put extra effort into finding the truth about the story they report, while their report can only focus on certain aspects of the story and does not guarantee to provide a comprehensive coverage. Similarly, a letter of recommendation from A about B only shows a part of B's qualifications, as they are known to party A.

7.2   Authorized certified evidence

The validity of information in this category is based on well-defined and agreed standards that the information must comply, and the validation is usually performed by authorized organizations. Following are the five suggested sources:

Accreditation: Accreditation is defined as an independent act of granting recognition to an organization as a proof that the respective organization meets and maintains the specified standards. For example, for health sector, accreditation is an independent external review process that assesses the quality of health care services in order to encourage improving performance and assuring the public on the quality of the services provided by the organizations [Lichiello et al 2002]. Accreditation standards are traditionally set at what are considered minimum achievable and allowed levels. Accreditation is practiced for *quality, cost, and business processes.*

Financial rating: Financial rating (credit rate) is a published ranking, based on detailed financial analysis performed by a credit bureau focusing on the financial history of an organization, and specifically as its ability to meet payment obligations. Members must validate and get approval of their financial record from authorized organizations that are involved in analyzing: *rating, credit score, in-depth financials, solvency, profitability ratios, bankruptcy prediction, etc.*

Patent: A patent is a set of exclusive rights granted by an authorized party to an organization for a fixed period of time in exchange for the regulated or public disclosure of a certain device, method, process or composition of matter (substance) (known as an invention) which is new, inventive, and industrially applicable. Patents granted for organizations could be evidence on the provided performance data.

License: License is an official or legal permission to do or own a specified thing. A license can be a document, plate, or tag that is issued as proof of official or legal permission such as a business license. In law discipline, a license is an actual permission to an act in a way that would be otherwise unlawful. Intellectual property rights such as a copyright or trademark provide a license as a proof of being allowed to use, reproduce, or create an instance of the licensed work. License can also be used as a proof for validity of the information provided by an organization.

Certificate and awards: A certificate is an official document affirming some fact. For example, a business registration certificate testifies to basic facts regarding the formulation and formal existence of an organization. In computing and especially computer security and cryptography, the word certificate generally refers to a digital identity certificate, also known as a public key certificate. An award is something given to a person or organization to recognize excellence in a certain field. Such proof can also be used as a means of validating the information provided by an organization.

8   CONCLUSION

Creating and managing trust among organizations has illustrated of its potential for smoothing and facilitating their cooperation in VBEs as well as their collaboration within VOs. This paper has addressed the subject: *"establishment of trust relationships among organizations"*. It also presents the antecedents and importance of trust relationships in collaboration. The validity evidences of the information needed for assessing the trust level of organizations, which constitutes the base for establishment of trust relationships, are presented. Also, the risks that exist during the operation stage of the VBE are addressed.

Acknowledgement: This work was supported in part by the ECOLEAD project funded by the European Commission. The authors thank for contributions from partners in the ECOLEAD consortium.

9   REFERENCES

1. Afsarmanesh H., Camarinha-Matos L., A framework for management of virtual organization breeding environments, in Collaborative Networks and their Breeding Environments, Springer, pg. 35-49, 2005.
2. Anargiridou, D. C. A critical examination of the main types of the e-finance risks in Greece and how the Greek web financial organizations could handle them. In Business, Law and Technology: Present and Emerging Trends, [Kierkegaard, S.M. -editor], Vol. 2, ISBN87-991385-1-4, 2006.
3. Clay, K., Strauss, R. Trust, risk and electronic commerce. The 19th century lessons for the 21st century. In the proceedings of the 93rd annual conference on Taxation, national tax association and ecommerce, Mexico, 2000.
4. Gambetta, D. Trust: Making and Breaking Cooperative Relations. Basil Blackwell. 1988.
5. Field, S., Hoffner, Y. Web services and matchmaking. In international journal of networking and virtual organizations. Inderscience enterprises Ltd, Vol. 2, No. 1, pg. 16-32, 2003.
6. Huynh, D., Jennings, N. R., Shadbolt, N. R. Developing an integrated trust and reputation model for open maulit-agent system. In proceedings of 7th workshop on Trust, Privacy, Deception and Fraud in Agent Societies, USA, 2004.
7. Lichiello, P. and Turnock B.J. "Guidebook for Performance measurement". Turning point - Collaboration for a new century in public health. 2002.
8. Mayer, R. C. Davis, J. H., Schoorman, F. D. An integrated model of organizational trust. Academic of Management review. Vol. 20, No. 3, pg. 709-734, 1995.
9. Morgan, R. M., Hunt, A.D. The commitment-trust theory of relationship marketing. In the journal of marketing, Vol. 58, No. 3, pg. 20-38, 1994.
10. Msanjila, S. S., Afsarmanesh, H. Modeling Trust Relationships in Collaborative Networked Organizations. International Journal of Technology Transfer and Commercialisation, Inderscience. ISSN (Print): 1470-6075. To appear in 2007-1.
11. Msanjila, S. S., Afsarmanesh, H. Trust Analysis and Assessment in Virtual Organizations Breeding Environments. International Journal of Production Research, Taylor & Francis. ISSN: 0020-7543, pg. 1-43, April, 2007-2.
12. Msanjila, S. S., Afsarmanesh, H. HICI: An approach for identifying trust elements – The case of technological perspective in VBEs. In proceeding of International conference on availability, reliability and security (ARES-2007), pg. 757-764, Vienna. April 2007-3.
13. Mukherjee, A. A model of trust in online relationship banking. Journal of bank marketing, Vol. 21. No. 1, 2003.
14. Grandison, T., Sloman, M. A survey of trust in Internet applications. In IEEE communications survey and tutorials. Fourth quarter, 2000. Grandison, T., Sloman, M. A survey of trust in Internet applications. In IEEE communications survey and tutorials. Fourth quarter, 2000.
15. Rousseau, D. M., Sitkin, S. B., Burt, R. S., Camerer, C. Not so different after all: A cross-discipline view of trust. Academic management review Vol. 23, pg. 393-404, 1998.
16. Rtanasingam, P. Trust in inter-organizational exchanges: a case study in business-to-business electronic commerce. In the journal of decision support system, pg. 525-544, 2005.

2

FOSTERING R&D COLLABORATION – THE INTERPLAY OF TRUST, APPROPRIABILITY AND ABSORPTIVE CAPACITY

Pia Hurmelinna-Laukkanen[1]
Kirsimarja Blomqvist[2]

[1,2]*Lappeenranta University of Technology, School of Business,*
[1]*University of Oulu, Faculty of Economics and Business, FINLAND*
pia.hurmelinna@lut.fi, kirsimarja.blomqvist@lut.fi

Value creation in the present day markets demands new kind of managerial logic. One manifestation of this can be seen in relation to R&D collaboration: while importance of external knowledge and networks of relationships is undoubtedly increasing as a source of competitive advantage, collaborations still frequently fail. In order to avoid this, companies need to find ways to manage factors that have an effect not only on the outcomes of collaboration but on each other as well. Such important factors include trusting relationships, creating security through means such as contracts and intellectual property rights, and capabilities to absorb relevant knowledge. In this study we will examine these factors and their roles for R&D collaboration among 299 Finnish companies. Our results suggest that these factors are intertwined and that they are closely related to willingness to engage into R&D collaboration and the final outcomes.

1   INTRODUCTION

Due to various changes in the operating environment of companies, value creation in the present day markets demands new kind of managerial logic. One manifestation of this is related to operating in networks and collaboration: while importance of external knowledge and networks of relationships is undoubtedly increasing as a source of competitive advantage, collaborations still frequently fail (e.g., Heimeriks 2002). The difficulties that the parties face in getting what they seek from collaboration are caused by various issues and absence of essential success factors. Several studies cite the critical factors such as clear ground rules, communication and trust (e.g., Hoffmann et al. 2001, Mohr and Spekman 1994, Forrest and Martin 1992), which may be difficult to establish and maintain. Nature of knowledge and its role in R&D collaboration is also very special and may cause challenges. The more dense and connected networks, technologies and communications facilitate the diffusion of knowledge, thus improving the accessibility of knowledge and creating ground for learning. However, it is very difficult for collaborating parties to identify and control which type of knowledge should flow between the parties for increased collaboration performance, and which should be restricted to protect own core capabilities. Especially codified knowledge (or information) can be captured and copied relatively cost-efficiently by competitors (Nelson 1959), which easily creates an appropriability problem: the failure of an innovating firm to capture profits from its innovations (e.g., Arrow 1962, Winter 2006). Consequently, companies somehow need to be able to manage simultaneous knowledge protection and knowledge sharing so that the benefits sought from collaboration and networking are achieved.

Hurmelinna-Laukkanen P., Blomqvist K., 2007, in IFIP International Federation for Information Processing, Volume 243, Establishing the Foundation of Collaborative Networks; eds. Camarinha-Matos, L., Afsarmanesh, H., Novais, P., Analide, C.; (Boston: Springer), pp. 15–22.

In this study knowledge sharing and protection is first discussed in the context of collaborative innovation, and especially R&D collaboration. Next, the dilemma of knowledge protection and sharing is considered through examination of absorptive capacity, appropriability issues, and trust. These issues are selected because of their relevant roles for R&D collaboration intensity, which surely is important considering collaborative innovation in more general, and their interactions. Section four presents the empirical evidence drawn from a dataset collected from 299 Finnish companies, and the final section summarizes the findings.

2   R&D COLLABORATION

Nowadays success in creating competitive advantage through innovation activities depends to a large extent on the effectiveness with which the firm can obtain, create, and transfer knowledge both within the firm and beyond its boundaries (Chesbrough 2003, Tyler 2001, Miles et al. 2005). R&D collaboration enables sharing the risks & costs and access to complementary resources and capabilities (Stuart 2000, Blomqvist 2002). Consequently, inter-organizational collaboration is becoming increasingly important (e.g., Jarillo 1988, Dyer and Singh 1998, Gulati et al. 2000, Ireland et al. 2002) and especially R&D collaboration can notably improve the innovation performance of the firms engaged in such activities.

Managing R&D collaboration requires various capabilities from managers, however. *Collaboration capability* is one of the most important ones. It has been defined as the firm's ability to build and manage relationships based on mutual trust, communication and commitment, and it has been argued to be critical for knowledge creation and R&D collaboration (Blomqvist and Levy 2006). Further, such a capability is needed in varying circumstances: The firm's *ability to leverage knowledge and resources from various actors* is critical for R&D collaboration as well – especially in contemporary and increasingly complex R&D environment where knowledge is dispersed (Tsoukas, 1996). The higher the variety in external relationships is, the higher the potential for getting access to relevant knowledge. In relation to variety, it is not only the quantity of relationships that is important, but also their quality: In addition to the volume of knowledge flows, also diversity of knowledge is central. Therefore, in this research we propose that a firm's ability to build relationships with asymmetric actors (firms of different sizes and with different competences, capabilities, power and cultures, for example; see Blomqvist 2002) is relevant for its R&D collaboration activities. Indeed, firms are seen to learn through partnerships, and those companies with experience with more various types of partnerships may perform better (Kale et al. 2002).

Summarizing the above discussion, we hypothesize that there is a relationship between the firm's R&D collaboration intensity and innovation performance:

H1: R&D collaboration intensity of a firm is positively related to its innovation performance.

3   SHARING AND PROTECTING KNOWLEDGE

Despite all the potential that R&D collaboration holds, collaborations frequently fail, which suggests that managing collaborative activities entails challenging areas. In order to be able to capture benefits from networking and cooperative activities, companies need to find ways to manage many dilemmas. One of them is the paradox of knowledge protection and knowledge sharing. The potential of competitors to capture essential knowledge of a firm and the possibilities of a company to prevent it have an effect on the profit margins and incentives to invest in innovation (van Dijk 2000), which highlights the need to keep knowledge secret and proprietary. Similar needs may be present in R&D collaboration as well, in particular if the risk of opportunism emerges. In fact, prior research has shown that many firms that operate in collaboration with other organizations are worried about knowledge spillovers between the participants (e.g., Baughn et al. 1997, Norman 2002, Helm and Kloyer 2004). These concerns influence many things starting from the firms' propensity to engage in collaborative arrangements: in decision-making related to collaborative activities the benefits that can be captured from incoming knowledge seem to be outweighed by the ability of a firm to prevent out-bound knowledge spillovers (Bönte and Keilbach 2005). On the other hand, knowledge sharing is inherently needed for value creation in R&D collaboration (see also Miles et al. 2005; Blomqvist and Levy 2006).

One approach to dealing with this paradox is examining the interplay of trust, appropriability regime (i.e., the means to protect innovations and intangibles and their profitability), and absorptive capacity of firms and their partners.

3.1   Potential for knowledge flows – absorptive capacity

Being able to avoid the appropriability problem – or at least to diminish its effects – depends on both the firm's internal and external factors. The ability of imitating companies to extract information about the innovation and exploit it so that the relative advantage of the innovator is notably reduced is fundamentally determined by the combined effect of the ability of a firm to prevent imitation, and the absorptive capacity of other firms. (This combination is also called as expropriability; Willman 1992, Heiman and Nickerson 2004).

Cohen and Levinthal (1990, p. 128) define the firm's absorptive capacity as "the ability of a firm to recognize the value of new, external information, assimilate it, and apply it to commercial ends." In R&D collaboration absorptive capacity is needed in order to obtain, incorporate, transform and exploit knowledge (see Zahra and George 2002) so that the collaborating organizations can create new products and services, or new intangibles. Therefore, we hypothesize that the scope of R&D collaboration with various partners and the volume of knowledge flows in such activities are related to absorptive capacity:

H2: Company's absorptive capacity is positively related to the R&D collabora-tion intensity of the firm.

3.2   Appropriability regime of a firm

The problem with competitors' capabilities is that a firm cannot really have a bearing on them as such. Thus, as noted above, one potentially efficient way to approach the appropriability problem is to pay closer attention to building barriers against imitation, i.e., to take notice of the formation of the firm's appropriability regime; the combination of available and effective means of protecting intangibles and innovations, their profitability, and the increased rents due to R&D.

Companies can benefit from having a strong appropriability regime considering that "a real possibility is that the value created by the collaboration from transferring knowledge may be eclipsed by the value of the knowledge expropriated" (Heiman and Nickerson 2004, p. 402). Utilizing a range of mechanisms makes it possible for innovators to earn (temporary) monopoly rents and other quasi rents. Such appropriability mechanisms include the tacit nature of knowledge, lead time, human resource management, practical and technical means of concealment, and institutional protection consisting of intellectual property rights (IPRs such as patents, copyright, and trade secrets), contracts and labor legislation (see, e.g., Hurmelinna-Laukkanen and Puumalainen, 2007, for references). These mechanisms can be utilized effectively in managing knowledge protection. However, while preventing knowledge flows may be essential in some situations, in others, such as in R&D collaboration, loosening or giving up protection and sharing knowledge generates more value (see Pisano 2006). Therefore, the appropriability strategy of a firm needs to be build so that protection will not be overly emphasized (it may not be even needed if other's absorptive capacity is weak) and so that the appropriability mechanisms actually foster knowledge sharing when it is needed.

The appropriability regime can have an important role in relation to collaboration. Previous research indicates that when a firm is able to protect its knowledge, it more willingly engages in collaboration (Kuivalainen et al. 2003). Using contracts, for instance, enables companies to "minimize their external dependencies and protect themselves against opportunism" (Yli-Renko et al. 2001, 530), which provides a safer starting point for companies. Subsequently, we can formulate the following hypothesis:

H3: The strength of the firm's appropriability regime is positively related to its R&D collaboration intensity.

3.3   Trusting relationships

Despite the companies' efforts to protect themselves, knowledge leakages are bound to happen, and other firms are going to be able to absorb such knowledge, at least to an extent. Therefore, there is an inherent risk related to R&D collaboration. In such a situation trust and trusting relationships become essential. In a modern society trust may be increasingly important for actors to be able to make decisions and act. A comprehensive, consistent, transparent, integrated and legitimated institutional system has been seen to provide stability and predictability which makes trust relationships easier (Deakin et al., 1997 referred in Möllering 2006, 149).

Trust may not evolve without a trusting behaviour, open communication and some type of risk taking. An actor's willingness to trust may be related to perceived risk, his/her ability and willingness to risk-taking as well as the perception of the other party's trustworthiness (Blomqvist 2005). Trust can be seen as a social governance mechanism complementing, or even substituting legal governance (Blomqvist et al. 2005). Trust has a critical role in R&D collaboration, as it can increase the effectiveness and efficiency of collaboration through enhanced coordination, communication and commitment. Trust may enhance shared norms and knowledge protection through mutual interest for continuous cooperation.

Based on this, we hypothesize that trusting relationships are relevant considering firm's orientation towards R&D collaboration:

H4: Trust is positively related to the R&D collaboration intensity.

4 EMPIRICAL EVIDENCE

4.1 Sample and data collection

The hypotheses were tested using a data set drawn from a survey conducted in Finland in 2004. The data were collected by means of a structured questionnaire, using the key-informant technique. The initial population comprised Finnish companies from eight industrial sectors engaged in R&D. The sample used consisted of firms operating in different industrial sectors, which provides a fair degree of generalizability. All firms with at least 50 employees from selected industry sectors were included in the sample frame. A total of 1,140 firms were identified from the Blue Book Database, and 881 of them were found to be eligible. Of these firms, 200 refused to participate. The pretested survey questionnaire with an introductory letter was mailed to the 681 remaining companies, followed by a reminder e-mail. We received responses from 299 companies, representing a satisfactory effective response rate of 33.9% (299/881). Non-response bias was checked on a number of variables by following the suggestions of Armstrong and Overton (1977), and did not appear to present a problem.

4.2 Measures

Following the Oslo manual (1997), *innovation performance* was measured as the share of sales from new or substantially improved products that were launched during the past three years (percentage of total sales).

The measure for evaluating the *R&D collaboration intensity* was composed as a mean of 8 likert-scaled (1-5) items illustrating how much the firm conducted R&D activities with suppliers, customers, universities and competitors, and the volume of knowledge flows in joint R&D with other organizations and the firm. The composite measure showed a good reliability with Cronbach alpha value[1] at .73.

Absorptive capacity was measured as a combination of 4 items. Two of them described the extent to which companies gathered and exploited knowledge in terms of actively observing, adopting and exploiting the best practices in the firm's own industry and in other industries respectively, and two assessed how soon the firms became aware of other's R&D activities (alpha =.64)[2].

The perceived strength of *appropriability regime* in protecting innovation was assessed on the following question: "How significant have the following mechanisms been during the past three years in protecting product innovations from imitation by (potential) competitors?" A list of 17 different mechanisms followed, and the respondents rated the significance of each one on a five-point scale (1 = slightly significant, 5 = very significant). The Cronbach alpha value was .87.

Trust measure was composed as a mean of 4 Likert-scaled items describing the the importance of trust building for performance, ability to build fast trust, and the

---

[1] Cronbach's alpha is an index of reliability associated with the variation accounted for by the true score of the "underlying construct". The higher the score, the more reliable the generated scale is. The value of 0.6 has been seen as an acceptable reliability coefficient.

[2] This measure was preferred since R&D intensity, which often is seen as sign of absorptive capacity (see, e.g., Tu et al. 2006, Cohen and Levinthal 1990), does not seem to be suitable indicator in every industry (e.g., Palmberg 2002).

role of trusting relationships as a factor diminishing harmful imitation of products and processes of a firm (alpha =.66).

4.3   Analysis and results

A correlation matrix was computed in order to identify the hypothesized relationships between the R&D collaboration intensity, Innovation performance, absorptive capacity, appropriability regime, and trust (see Table 1).

Table 1. Correlation matrix

Variable	Mean (SD)	1	2	3	4	5
1. Innovation performance#	23.78 (21.23)	1.00				
2. R&D coll. intensity	1.97 (0.59)	.183**	1.00			
3. absorptive capacity	3,91 (0.96)	.061	.164**	1.00		
4. Appropriability regime	2.43 (0.69)	.246**	.313**	.117	1.00	
5. Trust	3.80 (0.69)	.029	.230**	.182**	.365**	1.00

**=sig. < .01, *=sig. < .05, a =sig. < .10 (n = 299), # Logarithmic transformation

The relationship between the R&D collaboration intensity and innovation performance was the focus of the first hypothesis, H1. The results indicate a significant positive relationship between the variables. Therefore, support can be found for hypothesis 1.

We also found a direct positive association between the absorptive capacity and R&D collaboration intensity. Hence, our hypothesis 2 is supported. Similarly, the strength of the appropriability regime and the R&D collaboration intensity are positively related, supporting hypothesis 3. Finally, the correlation between trust and R&D collaboration intensity is positive and significant, providing support for our hypothesis 4.

5   DISCUSSION AND CONCLUSIONS

This study examined factors that foster R&D collaboration. We considered, in particular, the roles of trust, absorptive capacity and appropriability regime. Theoretical consideration suggests that they all are important factors behind the readiness and ability of companies to engage into R&D collaboration. In our empirical analysis we found that the more companies are able to protect their know-how and the more they can trust on their partners, the more willing they are to engage into R&D collaboration and to share knowledge through such activities (H3 and H4). Similarly, also the absorptive capacity is positively related to R&D collaboration (H2 was supported).

Considering, in particular, that R&D intensity is positively related to innovation performance, managers should pay special attention to the linkages of absorptive capacity, trust and appropriability regime. For instance, it seems that when trust resides in a relationship, knowledge can flow more freely, which may improve the absorptive capacity of participating firms. These interactions can be very relevant. In terms of consequences for R&D collaboration, for example, breaching a trusting relationship may be more costly than breaching a contract, infringing IPRs, or violating some other form of protection. On the other hand, abusing the partner's rights also damages trust. Thus, acknowledging the different elements is needed.

There are some limitations related to this study. Considering the empirical part, the measures used may not be fully optimal. Adding more variables might reveal various relationships that are now left out. In further research an in-depth analysis of the interplay of the key variables in inter-organizational relationships would also be valuable. The processes how firms balance contracts, intellectual property rights and trust, for example, could improve understanding of governance and outcomes of collaborative innovation. However, this study provides one point of view on the topic of R&D collaboration, and it certainly offers a point of departure for future studies.

6   REFERENCES

1.   Armstrong SJ, Overton TS. Estimating non- response in mailed surveys. Journal of Marketing Research 1977; 18: 263-264.
2.   Arrow K. "Economic welfare and the allocation of resources for invention". In The Rate and Direction of Inventive Activity: Economic and Social Factors, R. Nelson, ed. New York: Princeton University Press, 1962.
3.   Baughn CC, Stevens JH, Denekamp JG, Osborn RN. Protecting intellectual capital in international alliances. Journal of World Business 1997; 32, 2: 103-117.
4.   Blomqvist K. Partnering in the dynamic environment: The role of trust in asymmetric technology partnership formation. Doctoral thesis, Acta Universitatis Lappeenrantaensis 122, 2002.
5.   Blomqvist K. "Trust in a Dynamic Environment – Fast Trust as a Threshold Condition for Asymmetric Technology Partnership Formation in the ICT Sector". In Trust in Pressure, Investigations of Trust and Trust Building in Uncertain Circumstances, Edward Elgar Publishing, Inc., 2005.
6.   Blomqvist K, Hurmelinna P, Seppänen R. Playing the Collaboration Game Right – Balancing Trust and Contracting. Technovation 2005; 25, 5: 497-504.
7.   Blomqvist K, Levy J. Collaboration Capability – A Focal Concept in Collaborative Knowledge Creation and Innovation in Networks. International Journal of Management Concepts and Philosophy 2006; 2, 1: 31-48.
8.   Bönte W, Keilbach M. Concubinage or marriage? Informal and formal cooperations for innovation. International Journal of Industrial Organization 2005; 23: 279-302.
9.   Chesbrough H. The Logic of Open Innovation: Managing Intellectual Property. California Management Review 2003; 45, 3: 33-58.
10.   Cohen WM, Levinthal DA. Absorptive capacity: A new perspective on learning and innovation. Administrative Science Quarterly 1990; 35, 1: 128-152.
11.   Dyer JH, Singh H. The Relational View: Cooperative Strategy and Sources of Interorganizational Competitive Advantage. The Academy of Management Review 1998; 23, 4: 660-679.
12.   Forrest JE., Martin M.JC. Strategic Alliances between large and Small Research IntensiveOrganizations: Experiences in the Biotechnology Industry. R&D Management 1992; 22, 1; 41-53.
13.   Gulati R, Nohria N, Zaheer A. Strategic Networks. Strategic Management Journal 2000; 21, 3: 203-215.
14.   Heiman BA, Nickerson JA. Empirical evidence regarding the tension between knowledge sharing and knowledge expropriation in collaborations. Managerial and Decision Economics 2004; 25: 401-420.
15.   Heimeriks K. Alliance capability, collaboration quality, and alliance performance: an integrated framework, Eindhoven Centre for Innovation Studies, Working Paper 02.05, 2002.
16.   Helm R, Kloyer, M. Controlling contractual exchange risks in R&D interfirm cooperation: an empirical study. Research Policy 2004; 33: 1103-1122.
17.   Hoffmann WH, Schlosser R. Success Factors of Strategic Alliances in Small and Medium-sized Enterpises – An Empirical Survey. Long Range Planning 2001; 24: 357-381.
18.   Hurmelinna-Laukkanen P, Puumalainen K. The nature and dynamics of appropriability – Strategies for appropriating returns on innovation. R&D Management 2007; 37, 2: 95-112.
19.   Ireland RD, Hitt MA, Vaidyanath D. Alliance Management as a Source of Competitive Advantage. Journal of Management 2002; 28: 413-44
20.   Kale P, Dyer JH, Singh H. Alliance Capability, Stock Market Response, and Long-Term Alliance Success: The Role of the Alliance Function. Strategic Management Journal 2002; 23,8: 747-767.

21. Kuivalainen O, Kyläheiko K, Puumalainen K, Saarenketo, S. "Knowledge-based view on internationalization: Finnish telecom software suppliers as an example". In Management of Technology: Growth through Business, Innovation and Entrepreneurship, M. Von Zedtwitz, G. Haour, T. Khalil, L. Lefebvre, Eds., Oxford: Pergamon Press, 2003.

22. Miles R, Snow C, Miles G. Collaborative entrepreneurship. How groups of networked firms use continuous innovation to create economic wealth? Stanford, CA: Stanford University Press, 2005.

23. Mohr J, Spekman R Characteristics of Partnership Success: Partnership Attributes, Communication Behaviour, and Conflict Resolution Techniques. Strategic Management Journal 1994; 15: 135-152.

24. Möllering G. "Trust, institutions, agency: towards a neoinstitutional theory of trust". In Handbook of Trust Research, R. Bachmann, A. Zaheer, eds. 2006.

25. Nelson, RR The simple economics of basic scientific research. Journal of Political Economy 1959; 67: 297-306.

26. Norman, P. Protecting knowledge in strategic alliances. Resource and relational characteristics. Journal of High Technology Management Research 2002; 13: 177-202.

27. OECD. Oslo Manual – proposed guidelines for collecting and interpreting technological innovation data. Paris, OECD, 1997.

28. Pisano G. Profiting from innovation and the intellectual property revolution. Research Policy 2006; 35, 8: 1110-1121.

29. Palmberg C. The many faces of absorptive capacity in low-tech industries – The case of glue-lam timber and foodstuffs. The DRUID summer conference, 6-8 June, Copenhagen, 2002.

30. Tsoukas H. The firm as a distributed knowledge system: A constructionist approach. Strategic Management Journal 1996; 17: 11-25.

31. Tu Q, Vonderembse MA, Ragu-Nathan TS, Sharkey TW. Absorptive capacity: Enhancing the assimilation of time-based manufacturing practices. Journal of Operations Management 2006; 24: 692-710.

32. Tyler B. The Complementarity of Cooperative and Technological Competencies. A Resource-based Perspective. Journal of English Technology Management 2001; 18: 1-27.

33. Stuart T. Interorganizational alliances and the performance of firms: A study of growth and innovation rates in a high-technology industry. Strategic Management Journal 2000; 21: 791-811.

34. Van Dijk M. Technological regimes and industrial dynamics: The evidence from Dutch manufacturing. Industrial and Corporate Change 2000; 9, 2: 173-194.

35. Willman P. Playing the long game; Reaping the benefits of technological change. Business Strategy Review 1992; 3, 1: 89-98.

36. Winter S. The logic of appropriability: From Schumpeter to Arrow to Teece. Research Policy 2006; 35, 8: 1100-1106.

37. Yli-Renko H, Sapienza H, Hay M. The role of contractual governance flexibility in realizing the outcomes of key customer relationships. Journal of Business Venturing 2001; 16: 529-555.

38. Zahra SA, George G. Absorptive capacity: A review, reconceptualization, and extension. Academy of Management Review 2007; 27, 2: 185-203.

3

TRUST BUILDING IN COLLABORATIVE NETWORKED ORGANIZATIONS SUPPORTED BY COMMUNITIES OF PRACTICE

Leandro Loss
Federal University of Santa Catarina, Department of Automation and Systems
GSIGMA – Intelligent Manufacturing Systems Group, BRAZIL
loss@gsigma.ufsc.br
Claudio Henrique Schons
Federal University of Santa Catarina, Department of Information Science, BRAZIL
claudioschons@cin.ufsc.br
Rosane Maria Neves, Iliane Luft Delavy
Federal University of Santa Catarina, Department of Knowledge Management Engineering,
BRAZIL
roneves@univali.br, ilianedmaster@gmail.com
Iny Salete Chudzikiewicz, Ana Maria Cordeiro Vogt
Uniandrade University, BRAZIL
iny@uniandrade.br, ana@uniandrade.br

In view of the competitive scenario in which organizations are currently inserted, it is necessary for them to adopt a philosophy of continuous learning, aiming at improving their products and processes, besides encouraging an environment that allows knowledge exchange and innovation. On the one hand CNOs aim at increasing competitiveness through the flow of knowledge aggregated to products and processes in a formal environment. On the other hand, CoPs rise up as a mechanism that permeates new structures of communication, encouraging institutional learning and knowledge sharing, combining common values to their members in informal environments. The aim of this article is to propose the use of CoPs within CNOs to promote trust among members, aiding and encouraging the practices of knowledge sharing.

1   INTRODUCTION

Currently Small and Medium-sized Enterprises (SMEs) have been counting on an always increasing source of technological resources, aiming at the optimization of processes, better business prospecting, ameliorating the information flow and improving organizational processes in general. However, SMEs working only by themselves do not have productive capacity to compete with large companies as far as cost reduction, time to market, better quality products, and services are concerned.

Collaborative work in the form of a network among organizations allows for interactivity, increased capacity and control in order to select the desired profiles and contents. Because of their always increasing importance in society those networks can find, in technological resources, a powerful ally in the search for better performance, increased information flow and better means of gathering people and

Loss, L., Schons, C.H., Never, R.M., Delavy, I.L., chudzikiewicz, I.S., Vogt, A.M.C., 2007, in IFIP International Federation for Information Processing, Volume 243, Establishing the Foundation of Collaborative Networks; eds. Camarinha-Matos, L., Afsarmanesh, H., Novais, P., Analide, C.; (Boston: Springer), pp. 23–30.

groups with common interests, reaching beyond physical limitations. However, one must not consider only the technological aspect. Despite the fact that networks allow access and distribution of information as well as the promotion and socialization of knowledge by bringing together and confronting ideas, it is important consider that in order to create a suitable context for knowledge sharing it is not enough to provide means of contacting actors, by real or virtual channels. It is essential to create conditions for a confrontation of experiences (Jonassen, 1996).

For this contact to occur, it is fundamental that the entities involved, regardless of being people or organizations, trust each other. Trust is an element fostered by common interests, worries or concerns that appears in a group of a single area of knowledge that wishes to share experiences for the solution of problems, as well as the exchange of ideas and practices aiming at preserving and improving its capabilities and competences. In this sense, Communities of Practice (CoPs) may contribute with the construction of trust among members of the group.

Stewart (1997) emphasizes the fact that CoPs have special characteristics and defines them as groups that learn and emerge from their own initiative – people who, due to professional and social demands, cooperate directly with each other and learn from each other. Terra (2001) claims that "part of what we 'know' comes from our acceptance of the knowledge validated by other communities and that 'Communities of Practice' is a term that refers to the ways through which people work in groups and/or are naturally drawn to each other". The members of a CoP become responsible for disseminating knowledge and mapping it out, creating a network of interactions that allows for the construction of trust. It fits with the general idea of CNOs.

This paper brings a comparison between CNOs and CoPs in order to highlight their overlaps and differences. It is argued that CoPs can be used as a supporting mechanism in the process of trust building among CNOs' members. The research question is "can CoPs promote the trust building among members taking part in a CNO environment?". It is structured in the following way: in section 2 it is presented a characterization of trust in CNOs environment; in section 3 a brief overview about the concepts of CoPs is presented; in section 4 it is depicted the overlaps and differences between CNOs and CoPs; section 5 presents how the authors see CoPs as a instrument for trust building in CNOs, finally in section 6 the conclusions are presented.

2   CHARACTERIZATION OF TRUST BUILDING IN CNOS

The need to be competitive and the characteristics of open markets are forcing organizations to concentrate on their core business. One option to SMEs is to merge their core competences through alliances and to use the available resources of other enterprises to execute the tasks that are not covered by one single enterprise, when required (Karvonen et al. 2004).

One way of joint work among organizations, even among competitors, is by means of collaborative networks. According to Camarinha-Matos, (2006) a Collaborative Networked Organization (CNO) is built by a range of entities that can be individuals or organizations, usually autonomous, geographically distributed, and heterogeneous when considering their environments and their culture. The CNO's main characteristic is that its operations are supported by computer networks. However, the high costs involved and the lack of knowledge in a wide range scope could make such resource unfeasible (Camarinha-Matos, 2006). The main rationale behind a CNO is that it covers three core areas that are related among themselves: i) Virtual organization Breeding Environment (VBE); ii) Virtual Organization (VO); and iii) Professional Virtual Community (PVC).

These three areas shall provide the basis for competitiveness, world excellence, and agility for the organizations involved, through business identification and exploitation, promoting innovation and increasing their participants' knowledge. Despite the importance of these topics, this paper is mainly focused in the fields of VBEs and VOs. PVCs will be better explored in the next opportunity.

The paradigm behind the CNO discipline changes the way in which the commercial, industrial, and cultural activities are organized (Soares et al. 2003). According to Vallejos (2006), among many factors such as technological support, via an Information and Communication Technology Infrastructure (ICT-I), rules, and procedures when working collaboratively **trust** is a key factor. That means that a VBE, being a long-term network, presents the adequate environment for the establishment of cooperation agreements, common infrastructures, common ontologies and especially, the development of trust between its members, which is the necessary precondition for creating successful VOs. In their work, Vallejos (2006) describe a case where trust was built among the CNO's partners via simultaneous travels to events that were thematically relevant to all members. It allowed the creation of a feeling of belonging to the group.

Laaksonen (2006) measured, from a different perspective, mutual and inter-organizational trust in a particular case – the Finnish paper industry. They classified suppliers by the type of the relationship into different categories and explored the development of such relationships. They presented one model for building trust where the central elements were trust and mutual dependency. According to those authors these elements were also potential key factors within a successful partnership relationship.

Another point of view can be found in the research done by Urze (2006). This approach is related to economic sociology and sociology of organizations. It relies on the case study of an industrial network, developed in the north of Portugal, where patterns of relationships were identified among the organizations as well as how, and to what extend, trust interferes in business relationships. The author concludes that the meaning of trust in business refers precisely to the issues of price, quality, and delivery time. It means that a supplier is trustful when s/he is able to prove that s/he knows how to deal with those factors accordingly. Urze (2006) also points out that trust relationship among enterprises in a network is favored by long lasting links where there are several opportunities to test that trust. However Sako (1992) emphasizes that the trust that was slowly and carefully built can be quickly destroyed if something unexpected happens.

Msanjila (2006) go deeper in the study of trust among organizations arguing that in small-sized CNOs, members know each other and are able to built trust. However in large-size VBEs new approaches and mechanisms are required to be designed for measuring/assessing the trustworthiness level of organizations. Msanjila (2006) also approach the technical aspect of the matter, such as confidentiality, integrity, authentication, access control and non-repudiation, as well as the human side of trust and the important factors in trust building.

In the current paper the authors argue that the process of trust building in CNOs can be stimulated by CoPs. The next section is dedicated to study the concepts of CoPs.

3 GENERAL CONCEPTS ABOUT COPS

Knowledge has been increasingly seen as a vital resource for the survival of organizations. It adds value to products, services and processes, taking an active role in the deal, and when attached to a business, confers more competitiveness to organizations, through the adoption of different practices and organizational functions. Thus, many organizations are realizing that knowledge needs to be managed, in the sense of establishing politics to promote collaborative practices to enhance that knowledge. Raja et al (2006) observe that organizations have been viewing their employees' knowledge as their most valuable trump. However few of them are currently managing their knowledge in a wider context. Communities of practice (CoPs) can help organizations fill in that blank, through knowledge sharing and the creation, in conjunction with ICT-Is, of virtual learning environments. It is understood that CoPs can be used to integrate specialists, even from different functional areas in a company, who dedicate to a matter of specific interest.

Brown (1991) claim that CoPs represent self-organized groups composed by coworkers who possess complementary knowledge and who communicate with each other to share the same practices, interests and professional goals. Following that line of thought, Coakes (2006) add that such groups can be local or geographically dispersed, they are motivated by common interests and are willing to develop and share tacit and explicit knowledge.

Therefore, CoPs allow organizations to share knowledge and help them become more competitive by increasing their performance (Smith, 2003). According to those authors, people engaged in CoPs share experiences and knowledge in order to promote innovation. CoPs can be understood as resources to improve organizational performance, as they allow members to share their professional experiences and thus, better understand their work (Scarbrough, 2002).

CoPs can be either formal or informal, and are based on learning practices through social participation (Wenger, 2006). Each member participates actively and constructs identities of relationship in the community. For Wenger (2006), CoPs present three different dimensions from other types of communities: joint enterprise, members' mutual commitment, and resources sharing, in other words, members work with the same tools, techniques and technologies and create a common language. An important characteristic is that relations of interactivity among members do not have to be necessarily personal, as the advance of the technologies of ICT-Is allows members to relate to each other and participate by virtual means (Wenger, 2006).

Another characteristic is that shared knowledge is ruled by norms of reciprocity and by the trust among community members (Scarbrough 2002). Because they are based on trust, CoPs are difficult to build, but easy to destroy. One of the success factors for communities of practice is voluntary association (Coakes, 2006). The need to take part in the community must come from individuals, i.e., s/he must feel like sharing knowledge and learning something new.

The process of communication is facilitated by the use of specialized forms of language and/or specific conversation idioms to keep the information flowing among members. Therefore, Scarbrough (2002) observe that some basic expressions and matters are previously known and technical jargons are widely used.

The way a certain theme or matter is dealt with somehow helps to establish the members' identities. Wolf (2006), however, point out that glossaries, taxonomies and ontologies provide support for the understanding of the essencial contents. Davenport (1998) also highlight the important role played by a common language among participants, as its absence would entail misunderstandings and mistrust among members.

4   OVERLAPS AND DIFFERENCES BETWEEN CNOS AND COPS

As already mentioned, trust is intimately related to the success or failure of CNOs and CoPs, as it is the element that supports collaboration and the exchange of information and knowledge. However, it is important to consider the differences and overlaps between those two areas in order to have integration and sustainability. These aspects are dealt with in this section.

4.1   Overlaps

CNOs, when they appear as Virtual Organizations, as well as CoPs, may emerge in temporary arrangements and have at least one coordinator. Both CNOs and CoPs may work in different domains. The basic assumption for their operation is the wish to cooperate and collaborate. When their goals are achieved they are dissolved. It means that they have a well-defined life-cycle.

CNOs and CoPs can be geographically dispersed, they follow a clear and well-defined set of rules for their efficient operation and, finally, their members can participate simultaneously in more then one CNO or CoP.

4.2   Differences

While one of the prerequisites for the efficient operation of a CNO is based on an ICT-I architecture and on a formal organizational structure, CoPs may exist without a formal structure and without any computational support, although, interaction is facilitated when such support is provided. Whereas CNOs are multidisciplinary and demand some level of preparedness from their participants, CoPs are focused on a specific segment and require prior basic knowledge of the subject.

CNOs are adaptable according to a market niche and are focused on the high quality of the products, as well as on client satisfaction. CoPs are directed to their members' specific interests and, as that, are adaptable to their needs, focused on knowledge sharing and on trust building. Table 1 summarizes the overlaps and differences between CNOs and CoPs.

Table 1 – Characteristics of CNOs and CoPs. Source: the authors.

Collaborative Networked Organizations	Communities of Practice
Work with strong computational support	May use some computational infrastructure for support
Settled on temporary arrangements	Settled on temporary arrangements
Emerge in many forms and in different domains	Emerge in many forms and in different domains
Multidisciplinary	Focused on one specific issue
Some level of preparedness is necessary	Knowledge in the area is required
*Try to build **trust** among the actors participating in a certain collaboration opportunity*	*Provide **trust** building among their members*
Adaptable according to the market's needs	Adaptable according to the group's needs.
Focused on high quality products and client satisfaction	Focused on knowledge sharing and trust building
There is at least one coordinator	There are moderators
Once their objective is achieved they will no longer exist	Once their objective is achieved they will no longer exist
May be geographically dispersed	May be geographically dispersed
Are formally settled	Are usually informally settled
There is a clear set of rules to follow	There is a clear set of rules to follow
Members may participate in several CNOs	Members may participate in several CoPs

5   COPS FOR TRUST BUILDING IN CNOS

Of all the overlapping and divergent traits presented, the key factor that gives CNOs and CoPs impulse and that is their very basic purpose is **trust**. According to Lewis (1985) and Jones (1998), trust can be built through cognitive and affective elements. Cognitive elements are linked to reason, i.e., the network members' sense of responsibility and specific competencies. It is important to highlight the transparency of competencies and the aims for each network member producing, through systematic thought, a philosophy that every single member is important and able to benefit the group as a whole. Wolf (2006) believe that CoPs can foster the development of a horizontal communication hierarchy, encouraging flow of knowledge in a wide social context, aiming at the collective participation of their members. It may also contribute for CNOs knowledge sharing.

The promotion of social relationships is vital to the affective elements responsible for building trust. The first step towards that direction is to promote events, or personal meetings among the members, aiming at encouraging a collective spirit of interactivity and participation.

CoPs may help to develop trust building among members of CNOs either cognitively or affectively. The former occurs because the members of the CNOs have common interests by sharing skills, competences and resources. The latter, by improving the flow of knowledge, as well as it is based on levels of interpersonal relationships (virtual or not). For Kimble et al (2000), trust and identity are built through personal communication, so that CoPs may encourage the interaction among CNO actors either local or distributed way.

According to Raja et al (2006), trust is more easily developed in local environments, where network members share the physical space. That is because contact in daily relationships and personal communications allows for better identification and perception as far as affective elements are concerned. Smith (2003), concurring to that idea, claim that trust must be developed mainly through personal contact. Raja et al (2006) also call attention to the fact that also in a virtual context, where members are geographically dispersed, it is possible to foster trust among network members.

The existence of mechanisms, communication channels, and rules that support the practices of interactivity in CNOs may have a strong basis on the relationship of their members. This relationship shall be cultivated by CoPs. The initiatives for the participation and volunteer contribution from members shall promoted by group leaders inside the CoPs.

6   CONCLUSIONS AND NEXT STEPS

CoPs can improve trust building among CNOs as they allow for homogeneity ("horizontality") among members. It occurs because, according to Turner (1999), CoPs facilitate the information flow horizontally, effectively collaborating to the network of relations. Wenger (2006) complements that idea when claiming that CoPs are not limited by formal structures; they create connections among their members, sorting out the organization's hierarchical structure and promoting autonomy and informality.

Another interesting aspect is that in informal environments (typical of CoPs), affective elements are more easily introduced than cognitive elements. In CNOs one can notice high cognitive values and a smaller rate of affective values. Thus the importance of establishing contact among members, as mentioned above.

CoPs may contribute to CNOs when they enhance the use of collaborative networks in favor of affective elements to make the experience exchange in the network less formal, thus improving the trust building process in its two tiers: through affective and cognitive elements. Therefore one can understand that CoPs can encourage better relations among CNO members and consequently promote interpersonal trust.

As it happens within CNOs, trust is a prerequisite for the development of a CoP and for the knowledge flow among the organization members (Davenport, 1998). The challenge for managers is to find the means to actually develop values to promote trust in practice, aiming at collective participation in knowledge sharing.

At last, one must highlight the existence of a continuous cycle, where the higher the trust level, the higher the participation, engagement and commitment of each networked member. In this sense the interactivity and the collaborative feeling. One can perceive, at that stage, the presence of autonomy, as members watch for each other and solve their own problems. The network becomes, thus, an organic cell, with the capacity for self-organization.

6.1 Acknowledgments

This work has been partially supported by the Brazilian councils of research and scientific development – CNPq (www.cnpq.br) and CAPES (www.capes.gov.br). It has been developed in the scope of the Brazilian IFM project (www.ifm.org.br).

7 REFERENCES

1. Brown, L.S.; Duguid, P., 1991. Organizational learning and communities of practice: Towards a unified view of working, learning and innovation. Organization Science, n°1. pp. 40-57.
2. Camarinha-Matos, L. M. e Afsarmanesh, H.; 2006. Collaborative networks: Value creation in a knowledge society. Em Wang, K., Kovács, G. L., Wozny, M. J., e Fang, M., editors, PROLAMAT, volume 207 of IFIP, páginas 26–40. Springer.
3. Coakes, E.; Clarke, S. 2006. The Concept of Communities of Practice. IN: Coakes, E.; Clarke, S. Encyclopedia of Communities of Practice in Information and Knowledge Management.
4. Davenport, T.; Prusak, L. 1998. Working Knowledge: How Organizations Manage What They Know. Boston: Harvard Business School Press.
5. Jonassen, D.; 1996. O uso das novas tecnologias na educação a distância e a aprendizagem construtivista. INEP. ano 16, n.70.
6. Jones, G. R.; George, M..;1998. The experience and evolution of trust: Implications for cooperation and teamwork. Academy of Management Review, 531-546.
7. Karvonen, I.; Jansson, K.; Salkari, I.; Ollus, M.; 2004. Challenges in the Management of Virtual Organizations. In: Balanced Automation Systems and Services BASYS´04. Vienna Austria. Proceedings. Austria Ed. Springer. p. 255-264.
8. Kimble, C.; Li, F.; Barlow, A. 2000. Effective Virtual Teams Through Communities Of Practice. Research Paper N° 2000/9. Management Science.
9. Laaksonen, T.; Kulmala, H. I.; 2006. Coordinating Supplier Relations: The Role of Interorganizational Trust and Interdependence. In: PROVE-06, Eds. Camarinha-Matos, L.; Afsarmanesh, H.; Ollus, M.; Boston: Springer, pp. 191-198.
10. Lewis, J.D., & Weiger, A. 1985. Trust as a social reality. Social Forces. Vol.63, n.4, 967-985.
11. Msanjila, S. S.; Afsarmanesh, H. 2006. Assessment and Creation of Trust in VBEs. In: PROVE-06, Eds. Camarinha-Matos, L.; Afsarmanesh, H.; Ollus, M.; pp. 161-172.
12. Raja, J. Z.; Huq, A.; Rosenberg, D. 2006. The Role of Trust in Virtual and Co-Located Communities of Practice. IN: Coakes, E; Clarke, S. Encyclopedia of Communities of Practice in Information and Knowledge Management. Idea Group Inc. ISBN 1-59140-558-0.
13. Sako, M.; 1992 Prices, Quality and Trust. Cambridge, Cambridge University Press, 1992.
14. Scarbrough, H.; Swan, J. 2002. Knowledge Communities and Innovation. IN: Huysman, M. Baalen, P. Communities of Practice. The European Institute for the Media. ISBN 9053527540.
15. Smith, H. A.; Mckeen, J. D., 2003. Creating and Facilitating Communities of Practice. IN: Holsapple, C.W. Handbook on Knowledge Management. Springer-Verlag Berlin Heidelberg.
16. Stewart, T. 1997. Intellectual Capital: The new wealth of organizations. Currency.
17. Soares, A. L., de Sousa, J. P., e Barbedo, F.; 2003. Modeling the structure of collaborative networks: Some contributions. Em Camarinha-Matos, L. M. e Afsarmanesh, H., editors, PROVE'03, volume 262 of IFIP Conference Proceedings, pp. 23-30. Kluwer.
18. Urze, P. 2006. Industrial Network Trust Bond: A Sociological Perspective. In: PROVE-06, Eds. Camarinha-Matos, L.; Afsarmanesh, H.; Ollus, M.; Boston: Springer, pp. 199-210.
19. Vallejos, R. V.; Wolf, P.; 2006. Virtual Collaboration in the Brazilian Mould and Die Industrie. In: Kazi, A.S., and Wolf, P. (eds) Real-Life Knowledge Management: Lessons from the Field, KnowledgeBoard, ISBN: 952-5004-72-4.
20. Terra, J. C., Gestão do conhecimento: o grande desafio empresarial, Negócio Editora, Segunda edição, 2001.
21. Turner, Chris. O que são Comunidades de Prática?, IN:SENGE, P. et al. A Dança das Mudanças. Rio de Janeiro:Campus, 1999.
22. Wenger, E., SNYDER, W. M. (2006). Communities of Practice: The Organizational Frontier. In: Harbard Business Review on Organizational Learning.
23. Wolf, Patricia; Kazi, Abdul Samad (2006). Communities of Practice – A Case Study from the Automotive Industry. IN: Wolf, Patricia; Kazi, Abdul Samad (eds). Real-Life Knowledge Management: Lessons from the Field. KnowledgeBoard, ISBN: 952-5004-72-4.

PART **2**

PERFORMANCE AND VALUE SYSTEMS

Ingo Westphal
Bremen Institute of Industrial Engineering and Applied Work Science
win@biba.uni-bremen.de
Klaus-Dieter Thoben
Bremen Institute of Industrial Engineering and Applied Work Science
tho@biba.uni-bremen.de
Marcus Seifert
Bremen Institute of Industrial Engineering and Applied Work Science
sf@biba.uni-bremen.de
GERMANY

Management activities need an appropriate information basis. This applies also to the management of Virtual Organizations (VO). A potential source for this information is Performance Measurement. But traditional Performance Measurement (PM) methodologies and indicators are designed to assess the performance of single companies or static networks. Specific challenges and requirements of VOs are not addressed in an appropriate way. An essential aspect is for instance the collaboration performance, which has in many VOs a vital impact on the success. The objective of this paper is to provide an approach for addressing collaboration performance in the performance measurement of a VO. Therefore the main perspectives of collaboration performance and examples for potential indicators are described.

1   INTRODUCTION

Collaboration is today an established option to deal with the increase in product and service complexity, dynamic of changes, requirements upon responsiveness and still high quality demands. It helps to overcome the limitations of a single enterprise, especially of small and medium sized enterprises, regarding competences, capacities and financial resources. According to our understanding collaboration creates an environment in which enterprises and human actors temporarily or permanently can merge their processes for performing joint business in non-hierarchic way. A special type of collaboration is represented by Virtual Organizations (VO). Kürümlüoglu et al. define a VO as a set of co-operating (legally) independent organizations, which to outside world provide a set of services as if they were one organization, supported by a computer network [Kürümlüoglu et al. 2005].

However, collaboration is no general guarantee for success. Research has shown that many collaborative organisations were not able to accomplish the set goals [Bamford et al. 2004; Bullinger et al. 2003; Dürmüller 2002]. Deficits in the management of the collaboration constitute one category of the identified reasons for failure.

An essential prerequisite for an effective management is a sound information basis. Performance Measurement (PM) is an important source for this information.

Westphal, I., Thoben, K.-D., Seifert, M., 2007, in IFIP International Federation for Information Processing, Volume 243, Establishing the Foundation of Collaborative Networks; eds. Camarinha-Matos, L., Afsarmanesh, H., Novais, P., Analide, C.; (Boston: Springer), pp. 33–42.

We understand PM as the systematic approach to plan and conduct the collection and monitoring of data regarding the accomplishment of defined tasks and corresponding objectives [ECOLEAD 2005]. Several research activities dealt with Performance Measurement and various approaches like EFQM, Balanced Scorecard, Six Sigma or the Performance Prism have been developed. Overviews about PM research are given e.g. by Sandt [2005] or by Graser et al. [2005]. So what could be the reasons that existing PM approaches do not provide a sufficient information basis for the management of collaborations? One potential reason is that they are difficult to apply in a non-hierarchic network of independent partners. A second potential reason could be that the existing approaches do not cover all aspects needed for the management of the collaboration.

The need for an extension respectively customisation of PM to the specific requirements of a network was already identified e.g. by Gunasekaran [2001], Leseure [2001] or Hieber [2002]. However this research work was focused on static networks like supply chains with a more hierarchic character and even for supply chains there are still unsolved challenges regarding PM [MacBeth 2005]. The requirements of dynamic VOs are not addressed in the exiting approaches. In particular the consideration of interaction between independent VO members in merged processes is a specific challenge of PM in Virtual Organizations (VOPM).

This leads to the other potential reason for a lack of management information: The insufficient application of PM. PM in a network is also a collaborative process. If there is resistance against a common PM this is a symptom that shows that the planned PM activities do not match the actual status of collaboration capabilities and willingness.

So the objective of this paper is to widen available PM approaches to meet the specific requirement of VO management in a better way. It will focus on the aspect of collaboration performance that is one of the essential differences between VOs and single companies as well as static hierarchic networks.

A defined structure of the main aspects of collaboration performance in VOs supports a better understanding of this performance perspective and the related communication. This is not only beneficial for managing the operation phase of a VO but also for the consortium formation in the creation phase. So the considerations can contribute to current research activities regarding VOs and other collaborative network organisations.

2   PM REGADING INTERACTIONS BETWEEN COMPANIES

As already stated in the introduction, the vast majority of research work upon Performance Measurement is focussing on perspectives like cost, quantities, time, and quality. These perspectives are used to assess the accomplishment of defined objectives. To obtain information about potential future results new perspectives were added mainly in the early 1990s. A well known and established example is the Balanced Scorecard of Kaplan and Norton [Kaplan et al. 1992] that adds the perspectives customer, processes, learning/growth to the traditional financial perspective. In addition some approaches consider also intangible aspects like human capital, strength of brands or established customer relationships that are relevant for the company's value that moved more and more in the centre of attention in the middle of 1990s. Examples are the Skandia Navigator [Skandia 2007] developed decisively by Edvinsson in 1993, the Intangible Assets Monitor of

Sveiby in 1996 [www.sveiby.com] or the Intellectual Capital Monitor of Stewart [1999]. These examples have shown that also "soft-facts" can be assessed in a performance measurement based on values.

However there was still a gap regarding the performance of interaction between partners. Approaches that intended to fill this gap are looking at this type of performance mainly from two viewpoints: Either they tend to assess the actual interaction between partners or the general capability of a company to cooperate, which is important for self-assessment and partner selection.

Works that are focussed on the assessment and control of interaction are for example Beamon [1999], Leseure [2001], Gunasekaran et al. [2001], Supply Chain Operations Reference Model (SCOR) [www.supply-chain.org], Hieber [2002], Schweier [2004], Sivadasan et al [2002] or Simatupang and Sridharan [2004]. Performance perspectives suggested by these approaches are for instance equity, flexibility, reliability, responsiveness, partnership, collaboration efficiency, generic cooperation performance, absorption of complexity in collaboration, information sharing, decision synchronisation or incentive alignment (sharing of risks, costs and benefits).

More recent works like from Höbig [2002] or Seifert [2006] are looking at the performance of interactions between partners from the viewpoint of assessing a company's capability and preparedness for cooperation.

Höbig analysed in his work the general cooperation capabilities of production enterprises. The main criteria are: Communication capability, peparedness for future developments, adaptability, stability, reliability, and customer orientation. For each of these criteria, generic high-level indicators are defined.

Seifert analyses in his approach different combinations of partners to accomplish a production task. The assessment of the different consortiums is based on the values the potential partners have achieved for defined performance indicators. As the approach is build upon the SCOR model and the corresponding indicators it covers also some aspects of interactions between partners.

Regarding the practical application of the approaches cited above for a particular VO there are some weaknesses respectively shortcomings. At first, there is a lack of clear descriptions what is included in the performance perspective of interaction. In addition the approaches have some gaps with regard to the complete set of relevant perspectives of performance in the interaction of network partners that goes beyond a very generic level and is not just describing interactions.

Thus the following chapter aims at a suitable definition and an overall picture of the performance perspectives that cover the interaction of partners in a VO.

3 MEASURING COLLABORATION PERFORMANCE IN VO

Main subjects of this chapter is to clarify the term of collaboration performance in VOs and the development of an approach to structure the different sub-perspectives of collaboration performance in VOs.

The first step is to describe performance measurement in VOs (VOPM). Following the interactions of VO members are characterised and a definition for collaboration performance in VOs is provided. The characteristics and the definition are used to structure the potential perspectives of collaboration performance. The perspectives are obtained from literature and the practical experiences of existing networks.

3.1   VO Performance Measurement – VOPM

Performance Measurement is an essential task of VO Management. It supports the accomplishment of defined objectives by clarifying them and providing transparency about the degree of accomplishment.

The following graphic should give an overview over the different types of performance that has to be measured by VOPM.

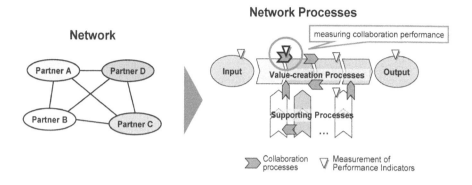

Figure 1 – Types of measurement points

The different types are:

1. Performance of the VO as a whole (output/results received by the customers and the VO's stakeholders).
2. Performance of the VO member and suppliers regarding their contributions to the value-creation process and the supporting processes (enablers).
3. Performance of VO members' collaboration ("lubrication").

While the fist two types of measured performance are generally the same as in single companies and static, hierarchical networks the third type of performance data is particularly important for the management of collaborative activities. It considers the effectiveness and efficiency of interactions between the independent network partners when they merge their processes to accomplish the common task in non-hierarchic way. We understand this as *collaboration performance*.

3.2   Collaboration Performance in VOs

The importance of collaboration performance for VO management can be explained with the aid of two plausible incidences.

Even if all VO members have the general capabilities to accomplish the defined task according to the defined objectives it is not guaranteed that this is practically achieved. There are effects that obstruct the full development of capabilities in the merged processes. For instance one of the partners has specific know-how to solve a certain problem but he hesitates to provide this to other companies in the network. A second example is that only low priority is given to the VO-activities in case of short capacities. Collaboration has to deal with these effects to ensure effective and efficient work in the VO.

Another reason for the necessity of collaboration is the fact that it is almost impossible to regulate all issues and all potential situations when a VO is created. Consequently unforeseen and not regulated problems will occur during the operation phase of a VO. This gap in agreed regulation has to be filled by the VO members with new agreements and actions, in many cases under tough time constraints. Without effective collaboration this could jeopardise the overall success of the VO.

In the following paragraph the need for concrete types of collaboration performance should be derived from the main characteristics of VOs. Input for the considerations comes from literature and from practical experiences in the ECOLEAD project[1].

The main characteristics are [ECOLEAD 2005]:

- Independency of partners.
- Dynamic.
- Uniqueness.
- Temporary limitation.

According to the *independency of partners* there is no higher authority that can take the final decision and force VO members into doing something. Only concrete contractual agreements can be demanded from the partners. So it is essential to reach common decisions and agreements. This requires the willingness to do so, the ability to achieve compromises, and competences in problem solving. To support compromises and problem solving the partners have to communicate effectively.

Another characteristic of VO that occurs in many cases is the *dynamic* in VO creation process and sometimes even during the operation phase. This leads usually to restrictions regarding detailed formal agreements. Especially if the VO has to fulfil complex tasks there will be many issues that remain un-discussed and un-regulated. On the one hand this requires common decisions and agreements like described above. On the other hand there is necessity for flexibility to react on dynamic changes, ability to compensate problems, responsiveness and for reliability that avoids additional changes caused by VO members.

VOs are *unique* organisations. Usually they will not come together in the same constellation when they dissolved. Thus they can not be build on experiences from the past. When the VO is created many things are new and uncertain. To handle this uncertainty the partners have to be collaborative in terms of compromises, conflict solving, flexibility, and reliability. Furthermore it is necessary that the partners take the initiative to advance the work and to share information as they can not rely on well proven process patterns.

Finally it has to be considered that a VO has a *temporary limitation*. This influences the effort that is acceptable for preparing the VO during the creation phase. It has to be ensured that there is an amortisation of this effort before the VO dissolves. This leads again to incomplete agreements and regulations that require corresponding collaboration performance. The temporary limitation requires also initiatives of the VO members to make the best use of the limited time.

---

[1] ECOLEAD is a research project with more than 20 international partners funded by the European Commission. The consortium itself can be regarded as VO. In addition there are project partners that represent different network organisations from various industries.

One conclusion that can be drawn from the considerations above is that collaboration performance can be divided in a pro-active and a re-active part. Pro-active collaboration aims at enhancement in the accomplishment of objectives. This can also be reached by active avoidance of problems and critical situations. In contrast, re-active collaboration tries to handle already occurred problems and critical situations. Initiating activities and information sharing are examples for pro-active collaboration while flexibility and responsiveness belong to the category of re-active collaboration.

3.3   Integration of Collaboration Performance in VOPM

To obtain corresponding data for the management of the VO the aspect of colla-boration performance has to be integrated into the VO Performance Measurement (VOPM). In the introduction it was shown that several PM approaches are available. The Balanced Scorecard (BSC) is an established and well known approach that provides the opportunity to be extended by performance perspectives that are relevant for specific applications. Moreover the BSC approach analysis the relationships between indicators, e.g. how quality aspects influence the customer satisfaction and future profit. This gives the opportunity clarify the influence of collaboration per-formance on the other perspectives. Therefore the BSC approach is chosen to be extended by the aspect of collaboration performance.

The following graphic gives an overview over the integration of the collabo-ration perspective and its sub-perspectives in the initial BSC. (The learning and growth perspective and the sub-perspective capital are in most cases less relevant for VOs as they have usually no own capital and their lifetime is limited.)

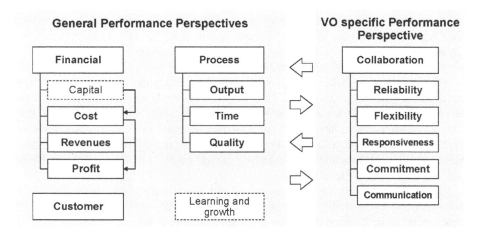

Figure 2 – Performance perspectives in VOPM

As depicted in the graphic the collaboration performance is closely connected to the other performance perspectives. On the one hand, some performance indicators can be assigned to the general perspectives as well as to the collaboration performance perspective, e.g. on-time delivery can be used for the time perspective and for the reliability perspective. On the other hand, collaboration can support the performance regarding the general perspective. For instance, a good responsiveness of VO members could reduce cycle times and improve on-time delivery.

The detailed description of all sub-perspectives of collaboration would go far beyond this paper. Therefore description is focused on the perspective of commitment. Reliability, flexibility, responsiveness and communication are already discussed in other approaches, e.g. SCOR or Höbig [2002]. Although this was done with another intention than measuring collaboration performance and the considerations need some extension (e.g. the aspect of confidentiality in the perspective of reliability) a general notion about these perspectives is given. In contrast the perspective of commitment is a specific core element of collaboration performance and needs some more explanation.

The perspective of commitment is introduced to summarise aspects of collaboration performance that are strongly related to the attitude towards the VO and the interaction with other VO members. It considers contributions to the VO that are not formally defined but come from the motivation of partners.

At first sight, commitment seems to be a "soft" aspect of collaboration performance that is difficult to measure. However, if commitment is divided into further sub-perspectives its meaning becomes clearer and potential performance indicators become perceptible. The graphic below presents sub-perspectives of commitment.

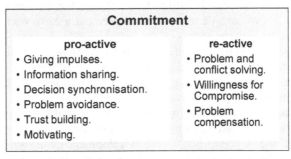

Figure 3 – Sub-perspectives of the VOPM perspective commitment

On this more concrete level of collaboration performance suitable performance indicators become more obvious. Some examples:

- Number of problems in a defined period caused by late or missing information from partners (information sharing).
- Degree of participation in meeting or conference calls - % of all agreed meetings, % of full-time participation (Decision synchronisation).
- Frequency of adjusting/coordinating the planning with related VO members (decision synchronisation).
- Number of problems between VO members that could not be solved between the members but need escalation to the VO management (problem/conflict solving).
- Relation between deviations from planning regarding the input and remaining deviations regarding the output – based on other performance indicators like on-time delivery (problem compensation).

Like for other performance perspectives a VO has to decide which indicators should be applied, not least because of limited resources and time. The selection of indicators is done according to the specific conditions of a particular VO. If, for instance, the VO members know each other well and have collaborated in previous VOs the need to measure trust building will be low.

Most of the indicators for collaboration performance do not provide absolute values that are objectively comparable. Rather there is a strong dependence between the indicator value and the particular composition of VO members. For instance the openness for information sharing of partner A could be very good if he interacts with partner B but, according to bad experiences in the past, very limited in the interaction with partner D. However, these "atmospheric disturbances" are exactly what should be measured by the VOPM to enable an active management of collaboration by the VO management.

4   IMPLICATIONS FOR VO MANAGEMENT

The gap in existing performance measurement approaches regarding collaboration performance is generally filled with the developed structure of collaboration pers-pectives. This gives the opportunity to the VO manager to monitor the collaboration in his VO and to take actions if corresponding indicators show unsatisfactory results. In industrial practice this can be utilised to enhance the awareness regarding the needed commitment of each partner and to implement a early warning system that indicates frictions between partner.

The developed structure of collaboration performance can also improve the selection of partners for a VO, either by regarding performance indicator values from VOs in the past or by assessing the general capabilities regarding the different collaboration performance perspectives.

Besides the application of this structure in a VO it could also provide new ideas for other networks of interacting partners, e.g. for supply chains.

Nevertheless, the intention behind the development of the suggested structure was to provide a starting point for the assessment of collaboration performance in VO. One the one hand, this implies that the perspectives and indicators have to be further improved, e.g. according to new experiences. On the other hand, it means, that even if many indicators for the collaboration perspectives are applied it has to be regarded that they will not be able to draw a complete and objective picture of the collaboration performance. To identify an appropriate set of indicators that provide good transparency about the collaboration performance in a particular VO without causing unreasonable effort is still a challenge.

5   CONCLUSIONS

Existing approaches for Performance Measurement do not meet all specific requirements of VO management. In particular the aspect of collaboration performance, which is essential for the success of a VO, is not considered in a sufficient way. However, research work has already provided several components dealing with interaction between network partners. These components were taken up and joined up with the specific requirements of VOs. Necessary adaptations and extensions were made. The result is a general structure for the performance perspectives and sub-perspectives of collaboration performance in VO. "Commitment" was introduced as new sub-perspective of collaboration performance that completes the perspectives that were already discussed in literature. The perspective of commitment summarises aspects of collaboration performance that are mostly informal and strongly related to the attitude towards the VO and the interaction with other VO members.

One of the next challenges is to provide a support for the VO management to identify, which of the various indicators for collaboration performance are relevant and suitable for the particular VO.

6 ACKNOWLEDGEMENTS

The paper is mainly based on work performed in the project ECOLEAD (FP6-IP 506958; www.ecolead.org) funded by the European Commission within the IST-Programme of the 6th Framework Research Programme. The authors would like to grant acknowledgements to the ECOLEAD consortium, especially to the participants of work-package 3 ("VO Management").

7 REFERENCES

1. Bamford, James; Ernst, David; Fubini, David G.: Wie man Weltklasse Joint Venture startet. In: Harvard Business Manager, 26th Volume, May 2004.
2. Beamon, Benita M.: Measuring supply chain performance. In: International Journal of Operations and Production Management, Vol. 19, No. 3, 1999.
3. Bullinger, Hans-Jörg; Kiss-Preußinger, Elke; Spath, Dieter (eds.): Automobilentwicklung in Deutschland – wie sicher in die Zukunft. Study of Fraunhofer IAO, PROMIND, MVI Group, Stuttgart 2003.
4. Dürmüller, Christoph: Checkliste für erfolgreiche Allianzen. In: New Management, No. 6, 2002.
5. ECLOEAD Project, Work Package 3, Deliverable 3.11, www.ecolead.org, 2005.
6. Graser, Falk; Jansson, Kim; Eschenbächer, Jens; Westphal, Ingo; Negretto, Ugo: Towards Performance Measurement in Virtual Organisations - Potentials, Needs, and Research Challenges. In: Proceedings Pro-VE 2005.
7. Gunasekaran, A.; Patel, C.; Tirtiroglu, E.: Performance measures and metrics in a supply chain environment. International Journal of Operations & Production Management, Bradford, Vol. 21, Iss. 1/2, pg. 71, 2001.
8. Hieber, Ralf: Collaborative performance measurement in logistics networks : the model, approach and assigned KPIs. In: Logistik-Management, Nürnberg, Vol. 4, No. 2, 2002.
9. Höbig, Michael: Modellgestützte Bewertung der Kooperationsfähigkeit produzierender Unternehmen. Fortschritt-Berichte VDI Reihe 16 Nr. 140, VDI Verlag, Düsseldorf 2002.
10. Kaplan, Robert S.; Norton, David P. The Balanced Scorecard - Measures that Drive Performance, Harvard Business Review, January-February, 1992.
11. Kürümlüoglu M., Nøstdal R., Karvonen, I.: Base concepts. In Camarinha-Matos, L., Afsarmanesh, H., Ollus, M. (eds.), Virtual organizations. Systems and Practices, Springer-Verlag, 2005.
12. Leseure, M.; Shaw, N.; Chapman, G.: Performance measurement in organisational networks: an exploratory case study. In: International journal of business performance management. - Milton Keynes, Genève, Vol. 3, No. 1, 2001.
13. Macbeth, D.-K. (2005) Performance Measurement in Supply Chains. Presentation of the IMS-NOW SIg Meeting in Glasgow on Feb 24, 2005.
14. Sandt, Joachim: Performance Measurement – Übersicht über Forschungsentwicklung und –stand. In: Zeitschrift für Controlling & Management, Vol. 49, No. 6, 2005.

15. Schweier, Hendrick: Aspekte eines Controlling logistischer Netzwerke. In: Gericke, J.; Kaczmarek, M.; Neweling, S.; Schulze im Hove, A., Sonnek, A.; Stüllenberg, F.: Management von Unternehmens-netzwerken. Verlag Dr. Kovač, Hamburg, 2004.

16. Seifert, M.: Unterstützung der Konsortialbildung in Virtuellen Organisationen durch prospectives Performance Measurement, Bremen 2007.

17. Simatupang, T.M.; Sridharan, R.: A benchmarking supply chain collaboration: An empirical study. In: Benchmarking, An International Journal, Vol. 11, No. 5, 2004.

18. Sivadasan, S.; Efstathiou, J.; Frizelle, G.; Shirazi, R.; Calinescu, A.: An information-theoretic methodo-logy for measuring the operational complexity of the supplier-customer systems. International Journal of Operations & Production, 22, 80-102, 2002.

19. Skandia: Visualizing Intellectual Capital in Skandia. http://www.skandia.com/en/includes/documentlinks/annualreport1994/e9412Visualizing.pdf, accessed 15.02.2007.

20. Stewart, T.A.: Intellectual Capital: The new wealth of organizations. Currency Doubleday, London 1999.

5	# A CONCEPTUAL MODEL FOR VIRTUAL BREEDING ENVIRONMENTS VALUE SYSTEMS

David Romero[1], Nathalie Galeano[1], Arturo Molina[2]

[1]*CYDIT - ITESM Campus Monterrey, Monterrey, MEXICO*
david.romero.diaz@gmail.com, ngaleano@itesm.mx
[2]*VIYD - ITESM Campus Monterrey, Monterrey, MEXICO*
armolina@itesm.mx

Virtual Breeding Environments (VBEs) represent networks of disperse organisations, that will exploit specific collaboration opportunities through the creation of Virtual Organisations (VOs) supported by information and communication technologies (ICTs). This type of Collaborative Networked Organisation (CNO) should be able to generate different types of values (economical, social, cultural, etc) to its members and stakeholders. In this sense, the definition of a value system represents a useful network management tool for the recognition, measurement and configuration of value generation objects and activities inside the network. This paper presents a conceptual model that integrates the different value generation objects, from the different stakeholders, to describe a VBE value system that supports managerial activities in the network such as value co-creation and performance measurement.

1   INTRODUCTION

Virtual Organization Breeding Environments (VBEs) are long-term cluster/associations of autonomous, geographically dispersed and heterogeneous organizations. The VBE aims to prepare its member's organizations and support institutions, and enhance their readiness for potential involvement in collaboration opportunity-based Virtual Organizations. A Virtual Organization (VO) is defined as a temporally association of (legally) independent organizations that come together to share skills and resources to achieve a common goal, such as preparing a proposal (or a bid), or jointly performing the tasks needed to satisfy a market/society opportunity by co-producing products/services for the customer, and whose cooperation is supported by computer networks (Camarinha-Matos and Afsarmanesh, 2006).

This paper will present a conceptual model for defining a VBE value system considering the main elements that should be identified in order to manage different strategies to co-create value for the customers and wealth for all VBE stakeholders. A proposal for define a performance measurement system for the evaluation of value creation process in a VBE is also presented in this article.

Romero, D., Galeano, N., Molina, A., 2007, in IFIP International Federation for Information Processing, Volume 243, Establishing the Foundation of Collaborative Networks; eds. Camarinha-Matos, L., Afsarmanesh, H., Novais, P., Analide, C.; (Boston: Springer), pp. 43–52.

2   BASIC CONCEPTS ON VALUE SYSTEMS

For a complete definition of a Value System it is important to understand the term value, the types of values that are involved in a value system, and how these values can be measured and evaluated.

Value: Two scientific disciplines that have been studying this concept for several years: economy and sociology. Each discipline has developed a different concept of value. On one hand, economists define value as "the worth of a product or service (often measured in terms of money) to someone", and on the other hand, sociologists define value as "the shared beliefs on moral/ethical principles that govern the behaviour of individuals and organisations in society" (Macedo et al, 2006).

For the purpose of this paper, economic values will be understood in relation to the production factors: land, labour, capital and knowledge, involved in value creation, considering tangible and intangible perceptions of what is valuable. Furthermore, ethical values will be comprehended as the set of accepted conduct standards that regulate the behaviour of organisations in value exchange among them and their customers in the market.

Value systems: underline the value-creation system through which an organisation or group of organisations produce value. Therefore, a value system is the identification, structure and measurement of a set of values that an actor holds, exchanges and creates for specific purposes. Moreover, value systems are based on the notion that "each product/service offered requires a set of activities carried out by a number of actors forming a value-creation system, that use tangible and intangible resources for creating value for customers" (Parolini, 1999).

Value systems are important in terms of regulation role for guarantee social cohesion and understanding between actors and their transactional mechanisms to assure an equality utility in value exchange; value systems are also important in terms of performance measurement to monitor how different actors, activities and resources work together to co-produce value (Afsarmanesh and Camarinha-Matos, 2005).

Performance Measurement: Measuring value creation in a value system requires a performance management cycle that plan, sets expectations and continually monitors performance.

Performance measurement in value systems is usually focused on economic values, including tangible and intangible resources, involved in a value creation process. The purpose of performance measurement is to assess whether progress is being made towards the desire goals and whether activities are performed efficiently to create value. Performance measurement serves to identify how actors are carrying out their activities and using their resources in a value-creation system to deliver a product/service to the customer.

VBE Value System: Form the definitions presented we can derive a definition of a VBE Value System as follows: The Value System is the identification, structure and measurement of a set of values that a VBE creates, holds, and exchanges. Since value is multidimensional, the Value System in a VBE should consider economic, ethical and cultural values; it also considers the identification and measurement of what is valuable for all VBE stakeholders.

3 VBE VALUE SYSTEM CONCEPTUAL MODEL

The main purpose of the Value System is to identify the value added of the VBE, which can be measured, through the Performance Measurement System, in terms of tangible (economic benefits productivity related) and intangible values or benefits (strategic, social, among others). Value systems are a useful network management tool for the recognition, measurement and configuration of value generation objects and activities inside the breeding environment.

Therefore, VBE value systems should be able to recognize how their different stakeholders such as members, support institutions, administrators, opportunity brokers, VO planners and VO coordinators combine their knowledge, resources and activities in a value-creation system capable of creating different types of values, for instance: economical and ethical values.

3.1 VBE Value System and its Elements

Three important elements integrate the conceptual model proposed for a VBE value system (Figure 1): first, the value generation objects as the different types of capitals hold by the breeding environment itself and by its members; second, the performance measurement system evaluating the value co-creation process; and third, the ethical values guiding the value exchange among actors (customers and stakeholders). Additionally, VBE value system elements support the trust building process among actors by providing an inventory of the value generation objects inside the breeding environment, and also through an ethical code as a set of functional rules to assure the ethical viability of business operation.

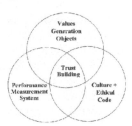

Figure 1 – VBE Value System Model

Figure 2 presents the relationship among the first two VBE value system elements: the value generation objects and the performance measurement system. The VBE value system combines the value generation objects (detailed in section 3.2) represented by financial, intellectual and social capitals of VBE members with the value generation objects of the breeding environment itself (also known as VBE platform) to co-create value in the development of collaborative business opportunities. Furthermore, value co-creation processes is measured to encompass the assessment of performance and results achieved by VBE actors; five dimensions are defined: financial, productivity, strategic, social and trust. The performance measurement system (detailed in section 3.3) evaluate at different levels: VBE members, VOs and the VBE itself. Additionally, some monitoring and reporting tools could be based on actual valuation models such as Balance Scorecard model (BSC) or European Foundation for Quality Management Model (EFQM).

Finally according to the results of the performance indicators, incentives and sanctions can be identified for each VBE member.

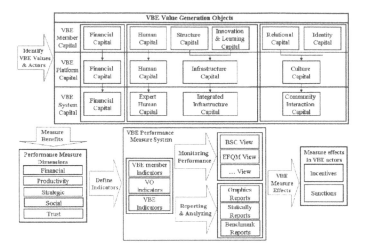

Figure 2 – Relationship between VBE Value Generation Objects and VBE Performance Measurement System

3.2   VBE Value Generation Objects: Capitals in Organisations

Value Generation Objects, or Capitals, identify the main values and benefits, such as economic success and other types of valuable benefits (productivity, strategic, social, trust) for breeding environment stakeholders. VBE members participate in the breeding environment by converting their competences and knowledge into tangible and intangible deliverables that are valuable for other VBE members, stakeholders and VO customers. In a successful breeding environment every VBE member contributes and receives value in ways that sustain their own success and the success of the VBE as a whole system.

The value generation objects in a VBE are identified as the sum of:

- VBE member's value generation objects that represent the capitals that each member has and generates by itself.
- VBE platform value generation objects that represents the methodologies, ICT and supporting tools for the breeding environment. This platform by itself offers different types of values.

The total VBE system value generation objects are constituted by the synergy of the capitals of each VBE members and capitals of the VBE platform.

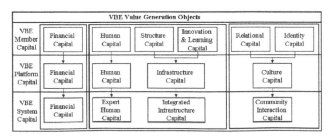

Figure 3 – VBE Value Generation Model

VBE value generation objects or capitals may fall into several categories; two major types of values are identified in organisations: tangible and intangible values. Three types of capitals can be identified in organisations: financial, intellectual and social capitals. The financial capital is related to all physical assets (that generates tangible values), meanwhile intellectual and social capitals are related to all the knowledge and relational based assets (that generates intangible and tangible values).

The components of VBE value generation model are presented in Tables 1 to 3:

Table 1 – VBE Member Capitals

Financial Capital: It refers to the financial resources (e.g. cash, bank accounts, physical assets) that an organisation uses to achieve objectives. It can be also understood as any kind of representation of financial value.	
Intellectual Capital:	**Social Capital:**
• **Human Capital.** Assets of knowledge (explicit or tacit) of the organisation staff useful to create value through their competences (skills, talent, capabilities and knowledge). • **Structure Capital.** Knowledge that an organisation materializes, systematizes and internalizes in form of physical resources: information and communication technologies, production technologies, work processes, management system, and quality standards. • **Innovation & Learning Capital.** The possibility to maintain the success of an organisation in a long term by developing or improving competences to increase and fortify the efficiency of the manufacturing processes or services development.	• **Relational Capital.** It refers to the relations and logistic channels that an organisation maintains with his clients, suppliers or other organisations (e.g. supply chain, collaborative networks, and relations in the VBE), and the value that these types of relation generates. • **Identity Capital.** It refers to the mix of recognition and history of the organisation used to influence the perception and activities of employees, customers and other organisations. It has the ability to create the image of vision of the organisation as parts of its culture.

Table 2 – VBE Platform Capitals

Financial Capital: It refers to the financial resources that a VBE as a Platform uses to achieve objectives (e.g. cash, insures, bank accounts, physical assets such as tools, equipment, inventories).	
Intellectual Capital:	**Social Capital:**
• **Human Capital.** Composed by the VBE administrator, VO broker, VBE advisor, VBE service provider and VBE ontology provider with their skills, talent, capabilities and knowledge. • **Infrastructure Capital.** It includes the technologies (e-catalogue, value and performance measure systems, and VBE management system), methods and processes (e-brokering, trust building and management, VO creation process, VBE administration) and physical resources that support the VBE.	• **Social and Cultural.** It refers to the working and sharing principles of a VBE represented in his strategies, philosophy, culture and ethical code (e.g. rules, policies, agreements, and contracts).

Table 3 – VBE System Capitals

Financial Capital: It refers to the sum of the financial capital of the VBE members that will be shared in the VBE and VBE platform.	
Intellectual Capital:	**Social Capital:**
• **Expert Human Capital.** It is the result of sharing and combining the Human Capital competences (skills, talent, capabilities and knowledge) of the VBE members' staff with other VBE member's or VBE staff. This will lead to conform expert teams able to increment the VBE actors' capacity of using knowledge (know-how) to common objectives (e.g. add value to a product/process). • **Integrated Infrastructure Capital.** It is the result of sharing and combining resources (e.g. technologic and financial resources) between VBE members to increment their capacity to develop new products or services.	• **Community Interaction Capital.** It refers to the VBE strategies focus on the exploitation of VBE members' relations and logistics channels. These strategies according to the changes and necessities of the market to create competitive advantages. Also to the relations and working & sharing principles of a VBE and their VBE members that create a moral responsibility, positive intentions, understanding, respect and equity between the VBE and VBE members in collaborative opportunities.

3.3   Performance Measurement System

VBE Performance Measurement System is formed by a set of indicators that translate the value co-creation process into "numbers". The ability to quantify VBE results is the first step for improving the overall performance of the VBE members and therefore the value co-creation process in the breeding environment.

The indicators defined in the performance measurement system should be the base to define and create incentives and sanctions in the breeding environment.

The performance measurement system provide the strategic information to VBE members about how VBE platform capitals and VBE member's capitals work together to co-produce value. The performance measurement system will permit to the VBE actors and mainly the VBE members to calculate the value of their relationships inside the breeding environment, and this information will be useful for taking the right and strategic collaborative business decisions. The breeding environment indicator system will make easier to monitor the progress of VBE value co-creation.

To monitor the VBE performance, the performance measurement system the Balance Scorecard (BSC) model can be used. BSC (Kaplan and Norton, 2004) is a model that shows the balance between the present and the future of an organisation, including its internal and external perspectives. It permits the organisations to analyze their final results (financial and non financial) and at the same time to monitor the progress of the construction of intangible assets for which the organisation needs to create more value. The measures depend on the indicators, which need to be aligned to the activities originated by the organisation strategy.

Figure 4 presents a VBE generic strategic map based on the BSC concepts, as a proposal for supporting the performance measurement system in a breeding environment. It is important to mention that depending on the focus, strategy and the main goals of each VBE this map should change accordingly.

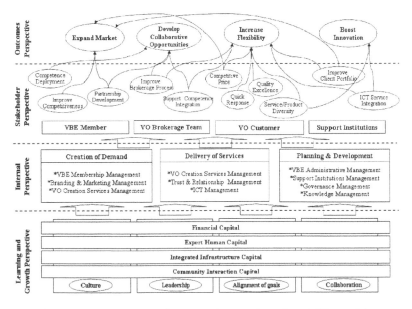

Figure 4 – VBE Generic Strategic Map based on BSC model

Four perspectives can be identified from the VBE generic strategic map:

- **Outcomes Perspective:** Constitute the final outcomes that are the result of the actions taken by the breeding environment. The measurement of outcomes indicates how the strategies have lead to results for the organisation. Four main outcomes are generally expected in profit-driven VBEs: Expand market for its members, support the exploitation and development of collaborative opportunities, boost innovation, and increase flexibility of its members.
- **Stakeholder Perspective:** In this perspective, the organisation identifies the market segments in which it wants to compete. Some of the most common indicators for this perspective are: the VBE stakeholders' satisfaction, and retention, number of VBE new stakeholders and collaborative opportunities. In the VBE there are four main stakeholders: VBE members, VO brokerage team (opportunity broker, VO planner or integrator and VO coordinator), VO customer and support institutions.
- **Internal Processes Perspective:** In this perspective the processes which must be precisely executed and improved continuously are identified. These processes help the VBE to develop a value proposition for: obtain and maintain members, create VOs, and satisfy the expectations of all its stakeholders. Main processes in a VBE include: 1) those related with the delivery of services of the VBE, such as: VO creation services management, trust and relationship management, and ICT management; 2) those related with the creation of demand in terms of collaboration opportunities exploitation, such as: VBE members management, branding and marketing management, and VO services management; and 3) those related with the planning and development of the VBE such as: VBE administrative management, support institutions management, governance management, and knowledge management.
- **Leaning and Growth Perspective:** It refers to the infrastructure that the VBE must construct to create growth in long term. This infrastructure is supported by the value generation objects that are present in a VBE, including: VBE community interaction capital, VBE integrated infrastructure capital, VBE expert human capital and VBE financial capital. All of them, supported by the VBE culture, leadership, collaboration and alignment of goals among the VBE and its members.

The monitoring of Performance Indicators in a VBE can be guided by this model. Tables 4 to 6 show a proposal that aligns main VBE indicators previously proposed in each perspective.

Table 4 – Example of Outcome Perspective Indicators

Elements	Goal Indicators
Expand Market	• Annual VBE sales
Develop Collaborative Opportunity	• Annual number of VOs created
Boost Innovation	• Annual number of new products/services developed in the VBE
Increase Flexibility	• Annual number of products/services developed in the VBE • Number of members in the VBE • Number of services available for VBE members

Table 5 – Example of Stakeholders Perspective Indicators

Elements		Indicators
VBE member	Competence deployment	• Number of services available for the VBE members • Number of competencies available in the VBE
	Partnership development	• Annual incomes to VBE as result of VOs creation • Annual number of business/collaborative opportunities identified
	Improve competitiveness	• Annual number of new products/services developed in the VBE
VO Brokerage team	Improve brokerage process	• Annual % of business/collaborative opportunities answered over the opportunities identified
	Support competences integration	• Average number of participations of a VBE member in VOs
VO Customer	Competitive price	• Customer satisfaction evaluation
	Quality excellence	• Customer satisfaction evaluation • % collaborative opportunities rejected by the customer for quality reasons
	Quick Response	• % collaborative opportunities attended on time
	Service/product diversity	• Annual number of patents registered • Annual number of new products/services developed in the VBE • Annual investment in research & development
Support institutions	Improve client portfolio	• Number of members in the VBE
	ICT services integration	• Number of services offered to VBE members • Annual number of new services developed for VBE members

Table 6 – Example of Internal Perspective Indicators

Elements	Internal Indicators
Strategic and Marketing Management	• Annual investment in marketing & branding • Annual number of business/collaborative opportunities identified • Level of satisfaction of VO Customers
VBE Membership Management	• Annual number of participations of a VBE member in VOs • Annual VBE incomes derived from memberships • Number of competencies available in the VBE
VO Creation Services Management	• Annual incomes to VBE as result of VO services offer • Number of VO creation services available in the VBE
Trust Management	• Number of trustable relations in the VBE
ICT Management	• % of coverage of services demanded by VBE members • Annual cost of maintenance of VBE infrastructure
Governance Management	• Annual number of conflict resolutions in the VBE
Knowledge Management	• Number of accesses to the VBE knowledge/ontology sources
Support Institution Management	• Number of support institutions in the VBE
VBE Accountability Management	• Annual expenses in VBE operation

Together with the identification of the indicators in each perspective, its relation among perspectives should be analyzed. This means that there is a direct relation between the internal perspective, stakeholder perspective and outcome perspective indicators. The internal perspective indicators (those that are measured in the VBE business processes) should support the improvement and achievement of goals related with the stakeholder perspective indicators (which are defined according to the stakeholders' interests). In the same way, the stakeholder perspective should support the achievement of goals and improvement of the outcome perspective indicators.

3.4   VBE ethical values

The third VBE value system element is the ethical values described in terms of VBE ethical code and culture.

The VBE members culture (shared values: strategy structure, systems, style, staff and skills) represents the "glue" which holds a breeding environment together. The willingness of potential VBE members to accept and capitalize on new ways of working, including participating in VOs will depend in part on the prevailing organisational culture. The VBE culture can be defined as "the collection of relatively uniform and enduring values, beliefs, customs, traditions and practices that are shared by VBE members, learned by new member's recruits, and transmitted from one generation of members to the next one" (Adapted from Rezgui et al, 2005).

VBE culture derives from basic assumptions of the values held by VBE members which shape breeding environment objectives, structures, and processes, and which are promoted and shared both directly/indirectly through a range of mechanism. While VOs are a temporary structure, its human resources are drawn from different VBE members, each with their own (possible conflicting) cultures. The lack of a shared culture may create difficulties for the effective operation of a VO. This is partly due to reduced opportunities for interaction between employees, particularly face-to-face interaction, which provide opportunities for new employees or VBE members of the VO to learn about e.g. company values, history, and folklore. Asynchronous communications, which are typical of the VO, mitigate the development of sense of community, although the use of synchronous electronic meetings spaces may help to develop a community with sense of shared culture (Adapted from Rezgui et al, 2005).

A good practice that should guide the operation of the VBE is then, the definition of an ethical code that includes some of the culture elements mentioned before. The Institute of Business Ethics in UK defines an *ethical code* as a "management tool for establishing and articulating the corporate values, responsibilities, obligations, and ethical ambitions of an organisation and the way it functions". It provides guidance to employees and organisations, on how to handle situations which pose take a dilemma between alternative right courses of action, or when faced with pressure to consider right and wrong. Having an ethical code is not enough, however. It can only be effective and practically useful with committed dissemination, implementation, monitoring and embedding at all levels so that behaviour is influenced in the VBE.

4   CONCLUSIONS

A VBE Value System includes the following main elements:

- The identification of the value generation objects or capitals that a VBE and its members have,
- The Performance Measurement System, which will measure the value generation and will be the base for define the VBE incentives and sanctions schemas, and
- The definition of its ethical/cultural values, represented in the culture and ethical code.
- A value system is an important managerial tool for a VBE, because a value system:
- Identify the main elements that generate value in a VBE, in order to focus the VBE operation on these elements.

- Identify the forms of value (measured in terms of capitals) in each VBE member, making them available to combine with other forms of value of other VBE members to create superior forms of value.
- Support improvement of the overall performance of VBEs and VBE members by providing VBE actors with meaningful performances indicators to evaluate and manage their strategies and processes with the objective to achieve their operational and financial goals.
- Identify the capacity in each VBE member to generate meta-value by combing its capitals with other VBE members (VO Creation).
- Identify the total value generated by a VBE, to evaluate the increase or decrease of value in the VBE during its life-cycle, and compare the success of a VBE with other VBEs and other forms of networks.
- Involve social values (behaviour, ethics and culture) with operational performance in order to create a common functioning environment to better respond in business collaboration.
  Support the decisions about adding and retreating members by evaluating their performance through a pre-established indicator system.

5 ACKNOWLEDGMENTS

The information presented in this document is part of the results of the ECOLEAD Project (European Collaborative Networked Organizations Leadership Initiative), funded by the European Community, FP6 IP 506958. Document D21.4a - "VBE characterization of Value System and Metrics" presents in detail results about this topic.

6 REFERENCES

1. Afsarmanesh, H. and Camarinha-Matos, L.M. (2005). A Framework for Management of Virtual Organization Breeding Environments. In L.M. Camarinha-Matos et al (Ed.), Collaborative Networks and their Breeding Environments. International Federation for Information Processing (IFIP), Volume 186 (pp. 35-48). New York: Springer Publisher.
2. Camarinha-Matos, L.M. and Afsarmanesh, H. (2006). Collaborative networks: Value creation in a knowledge society. In K. Wang et al (Ed.). Knowledge Enterprise: Intelligent Strategies in Product Design, Manufacturing and Management. International Federation for Information Processing (IFIP), Volume 207 (pp. 26-40). New York: Springer Publisher.
3. Institute of Business Ethics - UK. Retrieved on March, 2007, from: http://www.ibe.org.uk/ codesofconduct.html
4. Macedo, P., Sapateiro, C., Filipe, J. (2006). Distinct Approaches to Value System in Collaborative Networks Environments. In L.M. et al (Ed.). Network-Centric Collaboration and Supporting Frameworks. International Federation for Information Processing (IFIP), Volume 224 (pp. 111-120). Boston: Springer Publisher.
5. Parolini, C. (1999). The Value Net Tool for Competitive Strategy. John Wiley & Sons Ltd.
6. Rezgui, Y., Wilson, I., Olphert and Damodaran, L. (2005). Socio-Organisational Issues. In L.M. et al (Ed.), Virtual Organisations: Systems and Practices. Springer Science+Busineess Media Inc.

<table>
<tr><td>6</td></tr>
</table>

TOWARDS A CONCEPTUAL MODEL OF VALUE SYSTEMS IN COLLABORATIVE NETWORKS

Luis M. Camarinha-Matos
New University of Lisbon, Quinta da Torre – 2829 Monte Caparica, PORTUGAL
cam@uninova.pt

Patrícia Macedo
Escola Superior de Tecnologia de Setúbal, Instituto Politécnico de Setúbal, PORTUGAL
pmacedo@est.ips.pt

Decision making and thus the individual and joint behavior in a collaborative network depend on the underlying value system. Therefore the identification and characterization of the value system of the network and its members is fundamental when attempting to improve the collaborative process. However the concept of value system is not formally defined yet and there is not even an agreement in research community about its intuitive definition. Departing from a formal definition of value and evaluation, this paper proposes a formal conceptual model for value system and discusses its application in collaborative networks management.

1   INTRODUCTION

In psychology and sociology values have typically been conceptualized as shared beliefs about desired behaviors and end-states (Rokeach,1973). *Value* has also been defined as the "relative worth, utility, or importance: degree of excellence". This definition highlights the fact that an object's value depends on the referential that is used in its evaluation. Inside an organization, cultural and socialized values are used as referential for evaluations. Therefore, the choices and processes of an organization are directly influenced by its values. The set of values hold by an individual or society define its *value system*. The decision-making process in a collaborative network is naturally influenced both by the common *value system* of the network and the individual *value system* of each partner. Therefore the identification and characterization of these *value systems* is an important issue when attempting to improve collaborative processes. As partners have different *value systems*, they might have different perceptions of outcomes, which might lead to non-collaborative behavior and inter-organizational conflicts. Consequently, the development of a common *value system* is a significant element for the sustainability of collaboration. The definition of a *value system* is also an important aspect in the collaborative network operation, because it will allow the identification of the main elements that generate value in the network, and the diverse perspectives to evaluate them (Alle, 2000).

Value systems have been studied for a long time and diverse applications of the concept have been developed in several scientific areas, such as: education (Cooley, 1977), organizational management (Krishnan, 2005), and   information systems design (Goguen, 2003, Shneiderman, 1998). Various authors have also referenced the *value system* topic in their collaborative networks studies, (Katzy, 1998, Liu, 2005, Tan, 2004), (Afsarmanesh, 2005, Filipe, 2003, Gordijn, 2000, Jamieson,1986,

Camarinha-Matos, L., Macedo, P., 2007, in IFIP International Federation for Information Processing, Volume 243, Establishing the Foundation of Collaborative Networks; eds. Camarinha-Matos, L., Afsarmanesh, H., Novais, P., Analide, C.; (Boston: Springer), pp. 53–64.

Rezgui, 2004). However, from the analysis of these works, it can be concluded that there is no consensus about what a *value system* is, what elements belong to it, and how they are characterized.

The involvement of different types of stakeholders in a collaborative network, representing different interests and concerns of organizations, raises the risk of misunderstandings. It is therefore important to formalize the *value system* concept in order to promote a shared understanding. Moreover, formal conceptual models allow for a sounder analysis and provide a basis for the design of inter-organizational information systems that better support collaborative networked organizations (CNO). Therefore, this paper intends to give a contribution to a better understanding of this concept.

2   *VALUE SYSTEM* CONCEPTUAL MODEL

2.1   Value and evaluation base concepts

First a set of concepts about value and evaluation are introduced in order to allow a better understanding of the value system formal definition.

In literature the term *value* is used in diverse ways and for distinct purposes, often with an unclear meaning. *Value* in its plural form usually refers to beliefs as "*an enduring belief that a specific mode of conduct or end-state of existence is personally or socially preferable to an opposite or converse mode of conduct or end-state of existence*" (Rokeach,1973). Theories about *value*s as a shared belief have been developed in Sociology and Psychology. *Value* in its singular form can also be used with different meanings. For instance, the concept of *value* involved in the mechanism of exchange is defined as: "*how much is given in exchange of a product or service*". This concept was first developed in the economic theories, where all products and services have an associated price that is the reference *value* used for the exchange. In sociological studies, Piaget (Piaget,1965) and Homans (Homans,1958) developed theories about the dynamics of *value* exchange, where the notion of *value* is extended from the specific association *value-price* and *value-cost* to a wider notion, under which, the term value is associated to "anything that can give rise to an exchange"(Piaget,1965). Also in this sense, values are not only material objects, but may also be actions, ideas, emotions, social habits, etc. For Piaget, the economic value is a quantitative value while social interactions comprise essentially qualitative values exchange. The concept of value as the utility of a product or service, considers that value comes from the qualitative characteristics of a product or service.   Under this perspective, the theory of Value Analysis has developed methods for defining the value of a product, depending on its internal qualities.   An object has value to the degree it fulfils its concept (Mefford,1997). Finally, the concept of value as meaning considers that something can have value not depending on its utility but depending on its significance. The meaning of a product, service or attitude depends a lot from the social and cultural context.

In an attempt to cope with the various perspectives mentioned above, the following general definition of *value* is proposed.

Value *is the relative worth, utility or importance of something.*

In order to explain this definition of *value* and how it embraces various meanings of *value*, the concepts of *evaluation object, evaluator,* and *evaluation* have to be introduced. An *evaluation object* can be anything that is valuable for the evaluator. (e.g. resources, processes, behaviors, relationships, beliefs, information etc.) The *evaluator* is the entity that performs the *evaluation*. This entity can be an individual person, a social group (organization, government, virtual organization), or an instrument. *Evaluation* is the act of judging, measuring or calculating the quality, importance, or amount of something.

Judgment, measurement and calculation are made essentially through two basic forms: in an objective way, by applying rules and formulas to the data that characterize the evaluation object, and in a subjective way, by using mental perception about the importance, the quality or the quantity of something. In other words, the *value* of something depends on the function used to evaluate it. This function can be:

- A **numeric function** that assigns a number to an evaluation object. This number represents the *value* of this object in one dimension and the function implements the calculation formula of an indicator, an estimation method, or a measurement function of an instrument. The measurement process involves estimating the ratio between the magnitude of a quantity and the magnitude of a unit of the same type (e.g. length, time, mass, etc.). A measurement is the result of such process expressed as the product of a real number and a unit, where the real number is the estimated ratio. In order to define a function that implements an act of measurement, properties like monotonic, replicability and finite additivity should be studied.
- A **qualitative function** that represents a mental process or a qualitative judgment. This function assigns a qualitative *value* to something, as illustrated in Fig. 1. The properties of monotonic and replicability should also be satisfied by qualitative functions.

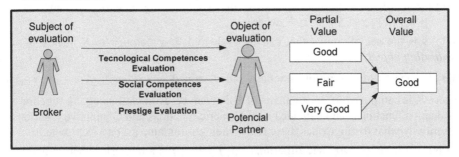

Figure 1 – Example of qualitative judgment

When making an evaluation, we are often evaluating not the overall object but a specific characteristic of this object. Therefore, it is relevant to provide a way to specify the evaluation of a particular property of an object. For instance, products, services and behaviors have several characteristics and each characteristic can be evaluated independently. When making a global evaluation, we are evaluating several characteristics and aggregating the corresponding individual *values* in order to reach a global *value*.

To better clarify this notion, two other terms are introduced: evaluation dimension and evaluation perspective.

> **Evaluation dimension** – *Characteristic of an object that is evaluated.*

The different characteristics of an object may have different degrees of importance to the actor that performs the evaluation (Note: Sociologists usually use the term "priority" to denominate the concept of degree of importance of a dimension). This idea is represented by associating, to each evaluation dimension, a weight that represents its degree of importance.

> **Degree of importance** – *Level of importance of an evaluation dimension for a given evaluator.*

Depending on the objective of the evaluation, a different set of evaluation dimensions can be considered to evaluate an object, as illustrated in Figure 2. The set of selected evaluation dimensions to evaluate an object are denominated as *evaluation perspective*. Examples of possible perspectives:

- The **business perspective**, where a set of characteristics related to the business is considered.
- The **social perspective**, where a set of characteristics related to social, moral and cultural aspects is considered.
- The **cooperation perspective**, where a set of characteristics related to cooperation relationships, such as: adaptability, affinity, reliability, and agility, are considered.

The evaluation dimensions that compose a perspective can have different degrees of importance.

> **Evaluation perspective** – *A selected set of evaluation dimensions and the corresponding weights chosen to evaluate an object from a given point of view.*

The following propositions are an attempt to formalize the above ideas using algebraic expressions.

(E1) *Value* of x is defined as the result of evaluating x with the function f
$$y = f(x) : x \in S \wedge f \in F \text{ where:}$$

(E2) S is the set of things that can be evaluated. *if x belongs to S then x is an* **evaluation object**.

(E3) F is the set of **evaluation functions** and is defined as $\forall f \in F, \exists x \in S_f : y = f(x)$,

where S_f is composed of the elements of S that can be evaluated using the function f. Evaluation functions can be divided into: Numeric functions and Qualitative functions. Essentially what distinguishes these two is their co-domain. $F = QF \cup NF$ where:

- NF is the set of **numeric functions**. If $f \in NF$, f is a numeric function defined as: $f : S_f \to \Re$ where $S_f \subset S$ The *value* resulted from the evaluation of x using the numeric function f is a real number. In some cases the result of the evaluation is expressed as the product of a real number and a unit.
  $$y[u] = f(x) : f \in NF \wedge y \in \Re \wedge x \in S_f$$
  where u is the unit of measurement (e.g. 3[ms^{-2}] , 10 [kg]).
- QF is the set of **qualitative functions**. If f belongs to QF then f is a Qualitative function defined as: $f : S_f \to Y$
  where $S_f \subset S$ and $Y = \{y1, y2..yn\}:$ y$_i$ is a qualitative ordinal.

The value resulted from the evaluation of x using the qualitative function f is a *qualitative value*.

(E4) The set of **evaluation dimensions** can be defined as $D = \{d_1, d_2, ... d_n\}$ where for each dimension it is possible to define an evaluation function that evaluates it. The operator Φ is introduced, in order to express the statement: *the function f allows the evaluation of the characteristic d: $f_i \Phi d_i$ where $d_i \in D \wedge f_i \in F$*

(E5) An **evaluation perspective** can be defined as $pe =< dv, wv >$ where:

- dv is the dimensions-vector of x that is defined as: $dv_x = [d_1, d_2, ... d_n] : d_i \in D$.

  This vector expresses the set of characteristics of an object that are evaluated.
- wv is the weights -vector and is represented as:

$wv = [w_1, ... w_n] : w_i \in [0..1] \wedge \sum_{i=0}^{n} w_i = 1$ and $wv[i]$ is the degree of importance of $dv_x[i]$

Each element of the vector represents the degree of importance of the corresponding characteristic specified in dv. Note: The vector should be normalized in order to allow comparing the importance of a particular characteristic by distinct evaluators. For each element of the dimensions vector, a function has to be defined/ selected in order to evaluate the corresponding characteristic of the object. So, for each *dimensions-vector* an ***evaluation-vector*** can be specified as:

$fv_d = [f_1, f_2, ... f_n] : f_i \in F$ where $i \in [1..n] \wedge fv_d[i] \Phi dv_x[i]$

In order to represent the fact that an object can be evaluated through different perspectives, the operator Ξ is defined *as:*

$x \Xi pe$, meaning x is evaluated through the perspective pe, where

$x \in S \wedge pe \in P$ and P is the set of perspectives.

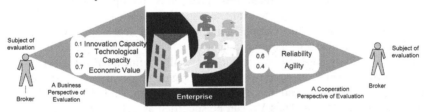

Figure 2 – Different evaluation perspectives

Application example: Different evaluation perspectives

This example does not intend to specify which dimensions should be used to evaluate a partner. It simply tries to illustrate the application of the evaluation perspective concept as it was defined in (E5).

Suppose that a CNO manager wants to evaluate a partner (an enterprise). Distinct evaluation perspectives can be defined. In the case illustrated in Figure 2 a Business Perspective and a Cooperation Perspective are shown. Depending on the purpose of the evaluation the manager selects the evaluation perspective.

dv_1=[*Innovation Capacity, Technological Capacity, Economic Value*]
wv_1=[0.1,0.2,0.7]
Evaluation Business Perspective $= pe_{business} <dv_1, wv_1>$
dv_2=[*Reliability, Agility*]
wv_2=[0.6,04]
Evaluation Cooperative Perspective $= pe_{cooperation} = <dv_2, wv_2>$

2.2   A definition of *value system*

Before defining the concept of *value system* it is necessary to introduce some auxiliary definitions:

A **system** is an assemblage[1] of inter-related elements comprising a unified whole. Any element which has no relationship with any other element of the system cannot be a part of that system. So a *system* can be formalized as a duple:

(E6) $SYS=<EL,RE>$ where EL is set of elements and RE is the set of relationships among the elements of EL.

(E7) *Value objects subsystem (OS)* is a system composed of the objects that can be evaluated and can be defined as a duple: $OS = <S, RS>$ where:

- S is the set a valuable things
- RS is the set of relationships among the elements of S, which can be essentially of two types: composition and specialization.

(E8) *Evaluation subsystem (ES)* is a system composed of all elements that represent "mechanisms" of evaluation (functions, dimensions and perspectives) and can be defined as a duple:

$ES=<EF, RE>$ where EF represents all the elements that belong to the evaluation subsystem and is defined as a triple: $EF =< F, D, P >$ where:

- F is the set of evaluation functions; D is the set of evaluation dimensions and P is the set of evaluation perspectives.
- RE is the set of relationships among the elements of EF. These relationships can be categorized as:
  o Composition-relation – One function is defined by aggregation of two or more functions.
  o Evaluates-relation – The relation is specified by the operator Φ, that specifies that a function can be used to evaluate a specific dimension.
  o Priority-relation – The relation that specifies the degree of importance of a characteristic in an evaluation perspective.

Using these auxiliary concepts, we can now formally define a *value system*.

(E9) A *value system (VS)* is composed of an aggregation of two subsystems, the value objects subsystem and the evaluation subsystem, and the set of relations established between them. Thus VS can be specified as a duple $VS =< EVS, RVS >$ where:

- $EVS =< OS, ES >$ is the aggregation of the two subsystems that compose the *value system*. OS is the set of valuable things for an organisation and ES represents the set of mechanisms used for their evaluation under different perspectives, where each perspective is composed of a weighted set of dimensions of evaluation.
- RVS represents the set of relationships between the two sub-systems. According to the systems theory, if there is a relation between two elements of different sub-systems, this implies that these two subsystems are related. These two subsystems are related by two categories of relationships:
  o Value-relation – What relates a function and an object is the value resulting from evaluating the object using that function.
  o Perspective-relation – The relation that is defined by the operator Ξ, that specifies that an object is evaluated through a given evaluation perspective.

---

[1] assemblage -a collection of things or a group of people or animals, in Cambridge Dictionary.

This definition of *value system* can be applied to a CNO. Considering that a CNO is composed of several organisations, it is possible to define the *value system* for each organization and the *value system* for the network as a whole.

The *value system* of a CNO is defined as:

(E10) $VS_{CNO} = < EVS_{CNO}, RVS_{CNO} >$ where EVS_{CNO} is composed of the two subsystems:

- Value objects subsystem *(OS_{CNO})*, containing the set of CNO valuable things such as financial resources, human resources, processes, information, relationships with external entities, brands.
- Evaluation subsystem *(ES_{CNO})*, containing the set of evaluation functions (F_{CNO}); the set of characteristics that are going to be evaluated for each object (D_{CNO}), and the set of evaluation perspectives used in the CNO (P_{CNO}).

Each CNO should define the order and prioritization of the dimensions of evaluation that will be used during its life-cycle. The set of functions, dimensions and perspectives of evaluation should be defined during the CNO set-up and all partners should know and agree on them. The change of one of these elements during the CNO operation should be done with the agreement of all partners.

For some CNO processes not just the specification of the CNO *value system* is relevant, but also the specification of the *value system* of each partner can be useful. For example, in the partner's selection process, in order to choose the partner that best fits a coalition in terms of shared common beliefs, it is necessary to know both the *value system* of the candidate members and of the planned CNO.

Application example: Definition of order and prioritization of *core-values* in a CNO

This example does not intent to specify which "core values" should belong to the Value System of any CNO. It simply illustrates how the set of "core values" can be specified according to the proposed modeling approach. The shown "core values" are based on the findings of a survey concerning the definition of value systems performed by ECOLEAD (Romero,2006).

The definition of the set of evaluation dimensions that are important to the members of the CNO and that guide all actions should be specified during its configuration. This notion of order and prioritization of *"core values"* can be mapped onto our conceptual model by the evaluation perspective. Imagine that a CNO defines that the most relevant attributes for the network are: *Quality, Reliability, Flexibility, Innovation* (see Figure 3). These four attributes do not have the same degree of importance. Thus the CNO should specify the degree of importance of each attribute and all members of the CNO should be aware that all decisions and behaviors should be in accordance to this perspective of evaluation.

For each dimension of evaluation (each attribute) an evaluation function should be defined in a collaborative way. The definition of methods to evaluate agility, quality, reliability and flexibility are not standard, and several studies proceed in theses areas.

In the proposed conceptual model the specification of the "core values" can be done as represented above. The *value system* (VS_{CNO1}) is composed of an aggregation of two subsystems the value objects subsystem (OS_{CNO1}) and the evaluation subsystem (ES_{CNO1}), and the set of relations established between them (RVS_{CNO1}).

$VS_{CNO1} = < EVS_{CNO1}, RVS_{CNO1} >$ where $EVS_{CNO1} = < OS_{CNO1}, ES_{CNO1} >$.

- All resources, activities, beliefs and behaviour that have value to the CNO_1 are elements of the subsystem OS_{CNO1}.
  - { *Quality, Innovation, Flexibility, Reliability* } $\subset D_{CNO1}$ - Evaluation dimensions of the CNO_1.
    - $pe_{core} = < dv, wv > \in P_{CNO1}$ All the evaluation functions (F_{CNO1}), evaluation dimensions

(D_{CNO1}), evaluation perspectives (P_{CNO1}), and the set of relations established among the elements of these three sets define ES_{CNO1}.

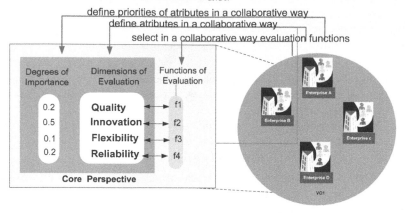

Figure 3 – Core-values definition in a CNO

- The perspective pe_{core} is used to evaluate the network   where $dv=[$ *Quality* , *Innovation, Flexibility, Reliability*$]$ and (e.g.) $wv=[0.2,0.5, 0.2,0.1]$.
- $\{f_1,f_2,f_3,f_4\} \subset F_{CNO1}$ - These evaluation functions belong to the elements of *the* subsystem ES_{CNO1}. $fv=[f_1,f_2,f_3,f_4]$ is a functions' vector that contains the evaluation functions selected to evaluate the four evaluation dimensions defined in dv. Just as an example, the following functions are considered:

$f_1 : S_{x1} \rightarrow \Re_0$ $f_1=$ *percentage of services and materials deliverable without any complain.*

$f_2 : S_{x1} \rightarrow \Re_0$ $f_2=$ *number of industrial patents*

$f_3 : S_{x1} \rightarrow \Re_0$ $f_3=$*average time to develop or change a logistic process*

$f_4 : S_{x1} \rightarrow \Re_0$ $f_4=$ *percentage of time without process faults.*

RVS$_{CNO1}$ is composed of the relations among the two subsystems. The relation that specifies that the CNO$_1$ is evaluated through the evaluation perspective pe_{core} belongs to RVS$_{CNO1}$.

2.3   Related work

One of the aims of the proposed conceptual model is to offer a framework that embraces, in a coherent way, diverse assumptions about *value* and *value system*. In this subsection the proposed conceptual model is compared to related work.

Goguen and Linde have developed, since 1978, several studies about *value* and *value system* in organizations (Goguen,1994) (Goguen, 2003).They introduced a method for using discourse analysis to determine the *value system* of an organization from a collection of stories told by members of the organization among themselves on informal occasions. The evaluative material collected from the stories is classified and represented using a formal structure called a *value system* tree. A *value system* tree (Goguen, 1994) serves as a formal summary of the interpretation that the analysts gave to data that has been collected. It is possible with the conceptual model proposed above to represent a *value system* tree, but the formal model proposed by Goguen has several limitations: it only considers one type of relationship between values (hierarchical relationship); it does not make a distinction between the value and the characteristic that is evaluated; it does not represent the evaluation function.

Romero et al. (Romero, 2006) have proposed a *multi-value system* model for VO Breeding Environments as part of the business model. The *multi-value system* includes the definition of different values: economic, social, and knowledge; and the identification of the stakeholders' participation in the value generation process. The work presented by these researchers does not include a formal specification of *value system*, neither a clear definition of value. They classify values in: financial, social and knowledge, but some times they also use the term value with the meaning of valuable object. This model for *value system* does not include the concept of different degrees of importance and is focused essentially on the identification of value transactions.

Another contribution to the study of *value systems* comes from the Distributed Artificial Intelligence discipline, which has developed some theories about *value systems* using agents (Filipe, 2003), (Antunes, 2000), (Rodrigues, 2005). Filipe (Filipe, 2003) proposed an approach based on organizational agents where it is assumed that an agent it responsible for its values. The agent's preferences with respect to norms are defined in its *value system*. In this approach an agent can represent a member of an organization or an organization itself. The norms that define the preferences are formally represented using Deontic Logic. This approach to *value systems* limits the specification to the definition of preferences and does not include the notion of evaluation functions and evaluation dimensions.

The work done by (Rodrigues,2005) is based on the Piaget theories (Piaget,1965) on values exchange and is concerned with the dynamics of values in interactions. The focus of our conceptual model is not the representation of value exchange mechanisms, but rather the definition of evaluations functions and dimensions, thus providing the base elements to specify value transaction between actors.

Gordijn, Yao-Huan Tan and Kartseva (Gordijn, 2000), (Tan, 2004), (Kartseva, 2004) have developed a methodology and an ontology called e3-value in order to define *value models* that support the business processes. This ontology has introduced the concepts of *value object* and *value activity*. It defines an *actor* as an independent entity that adds *value* to the system with the performance of *value activities*. An actor is an economic or legal entity that is engaged in business transactions and exchanges *value objects*. A *value object* is defined as a service, thing, or consumer experience that is of *value* to one or more actors. Each *value object* has one or more valuation properties that are characterized by a name and a unit that indicates the scale of evaluation. The e3-value model was developed to support e-commerce business and is essentially focused on the economic value of objects and on activities and actors that create economic value (Gordijn, 2000). One important issue in collaboration sustainability is the agreement about the shared values (Afsarmanesh,2005), but as the e3-value model does not support the idea of value system as the ordering and prioritization of values, it is not possible with such model to analyze if the members of a CNO share the same values. Another relevant point in CNO management is the agreement among CNO members about the method used to evaluate each object property. This aspect cannot be supported directly with the e3-value model, because it does not consider the specification of evaluations functions, neither the specification of the relationships between functions and characteristics to be evaluated.

3   FUTURE WORK AND RESEARCH ISSUES

The proposed conceptual model of a *value system* for CNOs includes a set of complex entities; some of them may require the adoption of soft modeling perspectives and techniques in order to allow a proper understanding and management. One interesting possibility is to develop a hybrid system, where some entities of the model are represented using crisp techniques and others using soft computing ones. Soft computing methods can exploit the tolerance for imprecision, uncertainty and partial truth (Berthold,2003). Therefore such methods are promising candidates to deal with aspects related to qualitative evaluation and priority of values. For these two aspects fuzzy logic, which derived from the fuzzy sets theory, seems to be a promising approach. Its objective is to allow degrees of inclusion/relevance of each element in a given set. It means to allow one element to belong in a given set in a bigger or smaller intensity, also known as degree of membership or degree of truth. For instance, to calculate the overall value of an object using a specific evaluation perspective, we can use fuzzy rules to combine the partial values and their weights of importance to infer an overall value

When partners have different *value systems*, which typically leads to different perceptions of values, non-collaborative behaviors are likely to develop. Consequently, the development of a common *value system* in a CNO context is an important step to support the sustainability of a collaborative behavior over time (Abreu, 2006). In order to overcome this problem, mechanisms to reason about the compatibility among *value systems* should be developed. The first step is to specify forms of comparison or identification of relationships between *value systems* of different members. Causal modeling seems to be a good tool to deal with this. This method has naturally grown due to a need for a sketching technique to support and facilitate reasoning about cause and effect. It builds upon a binary relationship, called an *influence relationship*, between two entities that represent named quantitative or qualitative value or value set. Whereby changes in the influencing entity are conveyed as changes in the influenced entity (Greenland, 2002) .

Example: Analysis of influence between values

The causal modelling method may be used to model:

- Causal relations among organizational values– this will allow to analyze the influence among values. For example it is possible to specify, for a university, that the value of *Knowledge* influences positively the value of *Prestige*.
- Inter-relations of influence between values of distinct members. An university and an industry are two types of organization that are expected to give different priorities to their evaluation dimensions. In spite of this, it is possible that a sustainable collaborative relationship is established between them. So different *influence relationships* between values systems do not mean that their level of alignment is low.

In the example illustrated in Fig. 4 three inter-relations of influence are represented:

- *Industry-prestige* influences positively the *University-prestige*. If a University collaborates with a prestigious industry then the value of prestige of the university tends to increase.
- *University-prestige* influences positively the *Industry-prestige*. If an industry collaborates with a prestigious university then the level of prestige of the industry tends to increase.
- *University-Knowledge* influences positively the *Industry-Technological Capacity*. If an industry collaborates with a university with a high degree of knowledge then the university tends to "transfer" its knowledge to industry in form of best-practices, developing the technological skills of industry worker and consequently the technological

capacity level will increase.

    The degree of importance of each value is also relevant and should be represented. In the example represented in Fig. 4, the industry does not consider the technological capacity as a priority. So, in spite of the positive causal inter-relationship between *University -Knowledge* and *Industry-Technological Capacity*, this inter-relationship does not contribute to the alignment of the two *value systems*, because Industry will not value the knowledge contribution from the university.

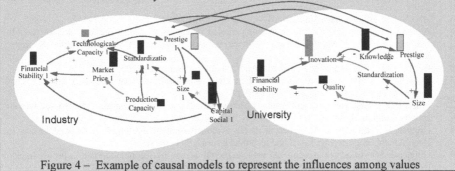

Figure 4 – Example of causal models to represent the influences among values

    The processes of analyzing and formulating policies for CNOs are an important and critical issue, which must consider the influence and causal effect, which may lead to their effectiveness or ineffectiveness. In the process of formulating policies, all important values of all stakeholders must be considered. The causal analysis can be applied in order to understand the causal effects in each partner of applying some policies depending on the *value system* of each partner.

    Another research issue that is very important is the development of a methodology to define a *value system* for a CNO in a collaborative way. As mentioned above, one of the difficulties about *value system* definition is the ambiguity about the meaning of values and evaluation characteristics so, this methodology has to be supported by collaborative negotiation and meaning negotiation. The work done in the areas of meaning negotiation (Moor, 2006), meaning evolution, and ontology's alignment (Kotis, 2004) may give some hints in order to define a proper methodology for common *value system* definition in CNOs.

4   CONCLUSIONS

The characterization and understanding of *value systems* is a key condition for improving the sustainability of collaborative networks. In this context and considering the notions of *value system* suggested in different disciplines, an attempt to provide a comprehensive formal conceptual framework was made. The conceptualization of *value system* is expected to promote a shared understanding among the different stakeholders of the network. This framework is also suggested as the baseline for further research and development in the area, namely in what concerns the issue of alignment or compatibility of *value systems*.

Acknowledgments – This work as supported in part by the ECOLEAD integrated project funded by the European Commission.

5   REFERENCES

1.   Abreu A, Camarinha-Matos LM. On the Role of Value Systems and Reciprocity in Collaborative Environments. In: Spring, ed. IFIP, Volume 224, Network-Centric Collaboration and Supporting Frameworks: Boston Springer, 2006.
2.   Afsarmanesh H, Camarinha-Matos LM. A framework for Management of Virtual Organization Breeding environments. In: Collaborative Networks and their Breeding Environments: Springer, 2005.
3.   Alle V. Reconfiguring the Value Network. Journal of Business Strategy 2000;21.
4.   Antunes L, Coelho H, Faria J. Improving choice mechanisms within the bvg architecture. In: Lesprance CCaY, ed. Agent Theories, Architectures, and Languages - ICMAS 2000; 2000: Springer - Verlag, 2000: 209-304.
5.   Berthold MR. Intelligent Data Analysis: An Introduction: Springer, 2003.
6.   Cooley CR. Cultural Effects in Indian Education: An Application of Social Learning Theory. Journal of American Indian Education 1977;17.
7.   Filipe J. The organisational semeiotics normativa paradigma In: Collaborative Networked Organizations. London: Springer, 2003: 261-272.
8.   Goguen J. Requirements Engineering as the Reconciliation of Technical and Social Issues. In: Requirements engineering: social and technical issues, 1994: 162-199.
9.   Goguen J. Semiotics, compassion and value-centered design. In: Keynote lecture, in Proceedings of the Organizational Semiotics Workshop, University of Reading; 2003; UK, 2003.
10. Gordijn J, J.M. Akkermans, Vliet JCv. Value based requirements creation for electronic commerce applications. In: In Proceedings of the 33rd Hawaii International Conference On System Sciences; 2000, 2000.
11. Greenland S, Brumback B. An overview of relations among causal modeling methods. international journal of epidemiology 2002.
12. Homans GC. Social Behavior as Exchange. American Journal of Sociology 1958; 63:597-606.
13. Jamieson M, A. T, . TA. Refocusing collaboration technologies in the construction Value System. In: JCIB W78 Conference Construction on the Information Superhighway, 1986; Slovenia, 1986: 279-289.
14. Kartseva V, Gordijn J, Akkermans H, . A Design Perspective on Networked Business Models: A Study of Distributed Generation in the Power Industry Sector. In: 12th European Conference on Information Systems; 2004, 2004.
15. Katzy B. Value System Redesign. ACM SIGGROUP Bulletin archive, 1998;19: 48-50.
16. Kotis K, Vouros GA. The HCONE Approach to Ontology Merging. In: The Semantic Web: Research and Applications. First European Semantic Web Symposium (ESWS 2004); 2004, 2004: 137-151.
17. Krishnan VR. Leader - Member Exchange, Transformational Leadership, and Value System. EJBO Electronic Journal of Business Ethics and Organization Studies 2005;10.
18. Liu P-Y. A study based on the Value System for the interaction of the multi-tiered supply chain under the trend of e-business. In: The 7th international conference on Electronic Commerce; 2005, 2005.
19. Mefford D, Meffortd V. Values Usage Exercise (VUE) A Tool For Raising Values Awareness ConcerningThe Professional - Personal Values Interface. In: Conference on Professional Ethics. Washington, 1997.
20. Moor AD, De Leenheer P, Meersman M. DOGMA-MESS: A Meaning Evolution Support System for Interorganizational Ontology Engineering. In: 14th International Conference on Conceptual Structures (ICCS 2006); 2006; Aalborg, Denmark: Springer-Verlag, 2006: 189-203.
21. Piaget J. Essay sur la Th´eorie des Valeurs Qualitatifs en Sociologie Statique. Paris: Librairie Droz, 1965.
22. Rezgui Y, Wilson I, Olphert W, Damodaran L. Socio-Organizational issues. In: Collaborative Networked Organizations: Springer 2004, 2004: 187-198.
23. Rodrigues MR, Luck M. Analysing Partner Selection Through Exchange Values. In: MABS; 2005: J.S. Sichman and L. Antunes, 2005: 24-40.
24. Rokeach M. The nature of human values. New York: Free Press. 1973.
25. Romero D, Galeano N, Giraldo J, et al. Ecolead WP2, D21.4 Characterization of VBE Value System and Metrics, 2006.
26. Shneiderman B. Designing the User Interface: Strategies for Effective User Interface Interaction, 3rd ed: Addison Wesley Longman, 1998.
27. Tan Y-H, Thoen W, Gordijn J. Modeling Controls for Dynamic Value Exchange in Virtual Organizations. In; 2004, 2004.

PART 3

COLLABORATION NETWORK ANALYSIS

7	# NETWORK ANALYSIS BY THE CODESNET APPROACH

Dario Antonelli, Agostino Villa

Politecnico di Torino – Corso Duca degli Abruzzi, 24 – 10129 – Torino, ITALY
dario.antonelli@polito.it, agostino.villa@polito.it

The paper approaches the problem of analyzing complex industrial bodies like the clusters of enterprises in order to evaluate their performances. The analysis is based on a formal model of a cluster of SMEs, represented in terms of its structure, its organization and its interactions with the outside. The paper aims at giving a comprehensive presentation of the evaluation approach to network organization developed in the EU-funded Coordination Action CODESNET (COllaborative DEmand & Supply NETwork), as well as of the "analysis road map" developed on the SME network model itself. A case study derived by an Italian industrial district is used to validate the proposed analysis approach.

1 INTRODUCTION

Analysis and evaluation of the different Industry Networks is becoming valued in European countries for pursuing effective industrial politics aiming to develop Small-Mid Enterprises (SMEs) (European Commission, 2002 and 2003). Analysis of a complex industrial structure as a cluster of collaborative enterprises has to be established on a formal unambiguous model (Albino & Kuhtz, 2004; Samarra, 2003). The setup and application of such a model is the basis of CODESNET project. CO-DESNET is the acronym of a Coordination Action (CA) project, supported by the European Commission, started in 2004 under the coordination of Politecnico di Torino. The aim of this project and of other European projects like ECOLEAD, is to create a favorable environment for the development of SME networks. CODESNET is focused on the collaboration between industry and academia as a prerequisite for a successful evolution of the network organization in a stable paradigm. ECOLEAD aims at giving theoretical foundation for collaborative networks and at exploiting the potential of ICT infrastructures to make the collaboration feasible.

The model developed by CODESNET describes a cluster of SMEs in terms of structure, organization and interactions with the external socio-economic context (Villa & Cassarino, 2004; Villa, 2006). This viewpoint aims at representing how efficiently the multi-SME industrial body can operate, how effectively it can be managed and how conveniently it could interact with the external markets of goods, supplies and labor.

Antonelli, D., Villa, A., 2007, in IFIP International Federation for Information Processing, Volume 243, Establishing the Foundation of Collaborative Networks; eds. Camarinha-Matos, L., Afsarmanesh, H., Novais, P., Analide, C.; (Boston: Springer), pp. 67–74.

The final goal is to have a tool which could help in evaluating some performance indicators of a collaborative SME cluster (Gajda, 2004; Evans & Wolf, 2005), such as to recognize a "best practice" in terms of good performance either in operating (efficient and high quality production & servicing), or in managing the network (balanced distribution of responsibilities and good organization), or in negotiating with markets (e.g., good market penetration).

In practice, the aim of the CODESNET project is to help industrial managers and administrators along three main lines (Villa, 2006):

I.   to understand the current state of a cluster or network of SMEs (e.g., how the SMEs are connected together; which type of organization is managing the network; how large is the presence of a SME network in its final market);

II.   to recognize problems affecting the cluster/network life or development (e.g., how much conflicting the network organization could be; how the present organization of a SME network can be modified in order to enforce its robustness);

III.   to estimate the SME cluster/network potentials in the future (e.g., how much profitable to join a network may be for a SME operating in a similar industrial sector and in the same region; how relevant are the technological innovations planned in a network).

The idea surrounding the CODESNET analysis approach rests upon the following considerations. Any SME network can be analyzed according to *three complementary viewpoints*:

1.   analyze the production and logistic network which are connecting the collaborative SMEs, i.e.
       • analyze the distribution of production operations among SMEs; the type of logistic organization; the production capacities of SMEs;
       • estimate how the network organization can enhance the production volumes of the different SMEs, the amount of personnel employed at the different SMEs, the transport capacities over the internal logistic network.

2.   analyze the governance organization, i.e.
       • analyze the management responsibility assigned to each SME and the amount of information that each SME can use for management purpose (i.e. how the decisional power is assigned), the types of internal agreements and control mechanisms, and the types of agreements with external bodies;
       • estimate the characters of the organization chart at the network level, the functionality of the coordination body, if any, and the coordination strategies.

3.   analyze the network interactions with outside, i.e.
       • analyze the types of commercial agreements with clients/suppliers, the types of strategies to manage, at the network level, both production resources and labor, the types of politics to plan, at the network level, innovation programs;
       • estimate the dynamic evolutions of the market penetration, the labor employment, the risk-capital acquisition.

These three viewpoints respectively correspond to three specific basic functions which the SME network usually performs, namely: (1) *produce*; (2) *manage*; (3) *negotiate* with suppliers, customers, potential financiers and potential employees.

In analyzing a SME network, the above listed analysis objectives can be obtained if a sufficient set of information can be collected. Two types of facts are necessary:

descriptions of existing SME networks, among which to identify the most effective and robust networks, to be considered "best practice" units;

1. scientific reports and papers presenting models of networks and discussing issues of network design, management and validation (by which industrial managers and designers could derive both personal suggestions as well as information about RTD groups to be contacted for consultancy and joint projects).

The two sets of data, namely a catalogue of scientific papers (named in the following *Virtual Library*) and an archive of SME networks descriptions (named *Virtual Laboratory*), are the keystones on which the analysis method, developed in the CODESNET project, is based.

Section 2 will deal with the "Analysis Road Map" by which an end-user can consult the CODESNET web site, by surfing from a SME network representation to related scientific papers.

Section 3 will outline how the papers' archive and the SME networks catalogue, both in a standardized format, have been arranged into the dedicated web portal (www.codesnet.polito.it) in order to be easily consulted by expert end-users.

Last section will give a survey of the set of SME networks catalogued, by showing which main features and main management/organization aspects could be found through a navigation in the CODESNET web site.

2 THE ANALYSIS ROAD MAP

CODESNET web portal has been arranged as an "Analysis Support System - ASS" for expert users (also called Innovation Support System – ISS, for its potential use as support of managers and designers to approach innovation programs for SME networks.

Two crucial points have been approached in designing the Analysis Support System:

1. the complexity in organizing and assuring maintenance of the SME descriptions' archive and the scientific papers' catalogue;
2. the necessity of assuring an easy exploitation of the Analysis Support System by some industrial end-user.

Typically, the utilization of an archive and catalogue concerning SME networks is expected by an industrial manager and/or technicians who should approach some innovation problem in his own industrial body. Then, searching in the archive and catalogue, he aims to rapidly fetch either a description of another SME network in which his own problem has been solved through some new approach, or a description of a solving procedure. The Analysis Support System has then been organized in such a way to help this way of searching.

The *three complementary viewpoints*, corresponding to the three components of any network, namely the Operation Structure, the Organisation Arrangement and the

Interactions with Socio-Economic Context, have been adopted as the three "Main CODESNET Issues" concerning *network design, management* or *evaluation*, and have been used as key-drivers in the search within the SME networks' archive and the papers' catalogue. Each main issue plays the role of "analysis viewpoint/ approach" for an industrial user.

In a nutshell, the idea characterizing the Analysis Support System organization approach is that, once an industrial user has selected the customized "analysis viewpoint", he can then search for the registered SME networks, stored as "best practices" for the issue and the viewpoint selected, or he can search for the registered model/procedure (i.e., technical paper) facing that issue.

A scheme of the Analysis Support System driving the industrial user is sketched in Figure 1, showing the list of the "Main CODESNET Issues" for analysis purpose, organized according to the above mentioned three components of a network.

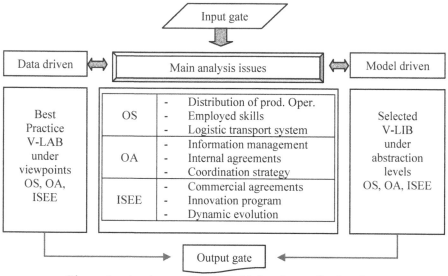

Figure 1 – A scheme of the ISS driving the professional user

From these considerations one can see the double interest of industrial end-users in the CODESNET analysis methodology here proposed:

- for each type of standard problem, to have the possibility of analyzing data sets which describe benchmark SME networks in which the values of the Performance Indicators are optimal: these SME networks are denoted innovative networks, referred to as "best practice";
- for each type of standard problem, to have the opportunity of analyzing dedicated solution procedures and technologies which specifically approach the main issue under examination.

Then, the selected list of "Main Issues" becomes the hinge of the interaction between data archive and model catalogue, for an analysis procedure to be applied according to the following steps.

Analysis Procedure Steps:

1. An end-user enters the ASS through the list of "Main Issues" (described through a brief and easy presentation);
2. the end-user selects the "Main Issue" of his own interest;
3. starting from the selected "Main Issue", the end-user will be addressed, depending on his choice,
   a. towards the data set which describes the benchmark SME network for the considered "Main Issue";
   b. towards the list of models which approach that "Main Issue", together with the problem solution procedures and tools;
4. in case the direction (3-b) is selected, the end-user is finally addressed to the scientific papers related to the "Main Issue" at the beginning.

Figure 2 – Analysis Procedure

3   OUTLINE OF THE VIRTUAL LIBRARY AND VIRTUAL LABORATORY

The organization of scientific papers into the Virtual Library catalogue (stored in a standard format denoted V-LIB in the CODESNET web site) and of SME networks' presentations in the Virtual Laboratory archive (V-LAB) has been based on the same concept above stated, meaning the "Main CODESNET Issues".

In practice, the most qualifying attributes of a SME network can be recognized through the V-LAB format, where the nine main questions (named Main CODESNET Issues, points I to III of the Introduction) can be answered.

Depending on which main qualifying attributes of the analyzed SME network are recognized in the V-LAB format, either proper models (for network simulation, design or performance evaluation) or methods (for network management) or procedures (for network innovation and skill improvement) can be found in the archive of scientific papers, stored in the Virtual Library.

Table 1 shows the potential links suggested to the CODESNET web portal end-user. Starting from the consultation of a V-LAB format, and having interest in a particular component of the SME network (either the "Operational Structure" or the "Organisational Arrangement" or the "Interaction with the Socio-Economic Environment"), an end-user can find three typical questions for the SME network component he/she has chosen: these questions are listed in the left-side column of Table 1.

The three questions related to a SME network component can give suggestions to the end-user to search for further technical information and/or scientific models/ procedures concerning either the structure type of the network under examination (together with the internal logistics), or the governance methods and interaction agreements, or the innovation programs and required personnel skills (to be nego-tiated with external markets). These last information can be found in the papers catalogued in the Virtual Library.

The portal design and maintenance facilities keep on increasing the numbers of V-LABs and V-LIBs included and maintaining and improve the links between them. The future evolution of the CODESNET project will be the European Virtual Institute on Innovation in Industrial Networks, composed by an international Association of academic institutions, research centers and enterprises.

Table 1. Links suggested to the CODESNET web portal end-user.

Questions in the V-LAB …	…correspond to main attributes of a Network …	3.1 …and to the following topics in the V-LIB
Re. to the "Operational Structure":		
1. distribution of production operations & volumes, 2. different skills employed, 3. which logistic network is used.	a) **type**: supply chain; industry network; scientific park; development agency;… b) **logistics** (internal service or outsourcing)	I **model** of the product processing & transports; - simulation, - network design - performance evaluation
Re. to the "Organizational Arrangement":		
4. attribution of management responsibilities; 5. internal agreements, or control mechanisms; 6. organization chart or coordination strategy.	c) Existence of **leading firm**(s); d) **Governance**: type (political committee; support agency; management centre).	II **organizational chart** of the governance committee: - enforce cooperation - assure coordination
Re. to the "Interaction with the Socio-Economic Environment":		
7. negotiate commercial agreements with external bodies; 8. network innovation program; 9. dynamic evolution of the network.	e) **Personnel skill level** and qualification; f) **Innovation programs** through interactions with universities and RTD centres.	III **skill competence profile**: how to improve skill; IV. **innovation plans**: - design, - evaluate effectiveness

4 ANALYSIS CONSIDERATIONS FROM THE VIRTUAL LABORATORY

A typical analysis of the SME networks and clusters catalogued in the Virtual Laboratory has been done in order to focus main features of the different industrial bodies presently stored in the web portal. To perform such an analysis, a selected set of V-LAB formats have been considered. Four characteristics were investigated:

   a. the type of industrial body, i.e., either a Supply Chain, or a Network/District, or a Scientific Park, or a Development Agency;

b. the type of governance, i.e., through either a Cluster/Network Committee, or a Leading Firm, or a Support/Coordination Agency, or through Individual Agreements;
c. the requests for personnel skills, i.e. in terms of high-level skills, or specialised skills, or many skills without any special request;
d. the presence of innovation programs.

First, the numbers of enterprises included in the different types of bodies seem to belong to specific value ranges. Scientific Parks include more frequently from 10 to 100 enterprises, depending on the dimensions of the enterprises: in case of larger enterprises, the number is lower, thus showing a specific goal or scope of the park, like promoting a balanced network of (usually) high-specialization firms. Alternatively, in case of smaller enterprises, the role of the scientific park appears to be that of promotion and support agency.

The industrial districts range from ten to hundredth firms. This pattern of firm groupings, however, does not seem to be sufficiently motivated: it could be a characteristic of the set of collected networks. Indeed, the aim of the consortium was to have clear information on some industrial districts, mainly in the Italian and French countries: this can make the sample excessively polarized.

A clear pattern occurs for Supply Chains, which ranges from hundreds to thousands of components. This is a typical organisation in several supply chains operating in a specific industrial sector producing mass customised products (as for automotive or electronic goods).

Regarding Development Agencies, a specific French organization, only a few similar data are available. However, their main features are really interesting for a comparison with the Scientific Park as they present similar mission.

A second analysis has been centered on the kind of governance (i.e., Organizational Arrangement), which has been classified either as Cluster/Network Committees, or by the presence of a Leading Firm, or by a Support/Coordination Agency. Considering this second character, the difference among the types of analyzed industrial bodies seems to be more recognizable.

Among the considered networks, the presence of a committee is usual: this feature has also been detected in a number of other similar districts. A smaller number of networks show evidence of leading firms: usually this pattern can be found in districts producing customized goods (e.g., jewels), where leaders are firms which also denote the district trade mark. Presence of individual agreements linking the component firms rarely occurs in the set of analyzed districts: however, in several industrial sectors, this percentage should be greater than the detected one.

Considering the Supply Chains, both the presence of coordination committees, and of Support Agencies and of Leading Firms can be found: no special type of governance can be recognized. However, a different situation between a supply chain managed by either a committee or a support agency, on one side, and that controlled by a leading firm, is related to the type of production and the dimensions of enterprises there included: in the former case, firms of similar dimensions agree in having a coordination structure for managing the production flows as well as the interactions with markets; in the latter, the leader drives all the chain, being usually the enterprise at the end of the chain and the final product supplier.

In case of Scientific Parks, a prevalence of Support Agencies can be seen, with respect to presence of leaders. The first situation is the usual one both in Italian parks, and in the French "poles of competitiveness". Finally, in the few Development Agencies here detected, only coordination committees are present.

Good suggestions come by considering the requested skills of personnel employed in the analyzed industrial bodies. A variety of skill types - i.e., high-level skills, or specialised skills, or many skills without any special request – can be found both in the Supply Chains and in the industrial districts: this sparse pattern depends on the usual Operation Structures of these two organisations, meaning lines or networks for mass production of consumer goods, calling for any type of skill, from workers to designers (a few) and to managers. On the contrary, Scientific Parks only call for high-level skills, thus justifying their function of promotion and support agency already recognised by considering both the number of enclosed firms and the usual types of governance.

Finally, other complementary good considerations can be done by summarising the numbers of different industrial bodies which have started innovation programs or not. The percentages can be seen in the following small (but interesting) table:

Table 2. Links suggested to the CODESNET web portal end-user.

Innovation	Supply Chains	Districts/networks	Scientific Parks	Support Agencies
Yes	27%	33 %	70 %	N.A.
No	73 %	66 %	30 %	N.A.

The last data, referred to Support Agencies, are too small to be significant.

For the other ones, the estimated percentage of industrial bodies launching innovation programs or having innovation actions under development gives a clear answer to the initial question: "is the action of supporting chains and networks a good social-political strategy for Europe?" The answer now is clear: these industrial bodies, are not yet equipped with a robust organization for an effective and stable governance and they need to be supported to guarantee their survival in the worldwide markets.

5   REFERENCES

1. Alberti F. The governance of industrial districts: a theoretical footing proposal. Liuc Papers n. 82, Serie Piccola e Media Impresa 5, January 2001.
2. Albino V., Kühtz S., Enterprise input–output model for local sustainable development—the case of a tiles manufacturer in Italy, Resources, Conservation and Recycling, 2004, 41, 165-176.
3. European Commission, Regional Clusters in Europe, Observatory of European SMEs 2002/ No 3, Enterprise Publication, http://europa.eu.int/comm/enterprise.
4. European Commission, SMEs and Cooperation, Observatory of European SMEs 2003/ No 5, Enterprise Publication, http://europa.eu.int/comm/enterprise.
5. Evans P., Wolf B., Collaboration Rules, Harvard Business Review, the High Performance Organization, July-August 2005.
6. Gajda R., Utilizing Collaboration Theory to Evaluate Strategic Alliances, The American Journal of Evaluation, Volume: 25, Issue: 1, Spring, 2004, pp. 65-77.
7. Samarra A., Lo sviluppo nei distretti industriali, Percorsi evolutivi fra globalizzazione e localizzazione, Carocci, 2003, Roma (in Italian).
8. Villa A., Cassarino, I, "Management of a multi-agent demand & supply network", Proc. IFAC Conference on Advanced Control Strategies for Social and Economic Systems, Vienna, 2004.
9. Villa A., "Reinforcing industrial districts: need for a structured approach", Keynote paper, 12th IFAC Symp. on Information Control Problems in Manufact., St. Etienne, Vol.1, pp. 55-66, 2006.

8 | ASSESSMENT OF COLLABORATIVE NETWORKS STRUCTURAL STABILITY

Vera Tolkacheva[2], Dmitry Ivanov[1], Alexander Arkhipov[2]

[1]Chemnitz University of Technology, GERMANY
dmitri.ivanov@mail.ru
[2]Saint Petersburg State University of Technology and Design, RUSSIA
a_arkhipov@sutd.ru
vera_tolkacheva@mail.ru

Subject of this contribution is to develop a framework for assessment of collaborative networks (CN) structural stability on the stage of the CN design. CN design is a critical source of competitive advantage given that as much as 80% of total product cost may be fixed by these decisions. The importance of the stable CN structuring is evident. The elaborated framework aims to develop a technique for simultaneous CN structuring and its stability assessment based on parametric analysis of possible participants and integral stability assessment. This procedure is based on the application of special Index of Structure Consolidation (ISC), which makes it possible to estimate the project stability. The index shows mutual interest between CN partners and the coordinator. This index should be taken into account while taking decision about the final structure of the network and its application claims for fuzzy logic introduction. It makes it possible to increase the quality of decision-making about the CN configuration under the terms of uncertainty.

1 INTRODUCTION

CN design is a critical source of competitive advantage given that as much as 80% of total product cost may be fixed by these decisions (Harrison et al., 2005). The importance of the stable CN structuring is evident. One of the CN structuring challenges is a combined formation of the CN structural-functional-informational configuration and estimation of the CN execution stability. An important point of such simultaneous formation consists in ensuring of the business-processes continuity, information availability, and system stability. To answer this challenge, we introduce a framework for assessment of collaborative networks (CN) structural stability on the stage of the CN design.

2 LITERATURE ANALYSIS

CN functioning is challenged by high uncertainty. This leads to perturbations and deviations during the CN execution. Stability is an appropriate category for the increasing quality of the CN modelling and decision making under the terms of uncertainty. In general case stability analysis consists in investigation of influence of the CN execution parameters deviations on the final CN goals. Stability analysis is especially useful in the situations, which are characterized by high level of uncertainty, which does not allow producing deterministic or stochastic models. The stability analysis allows proofing execution plan feasibility, selecting a plan with the sufficient stability degree from a set of alternative plans, determining CN execution bottle-necks and steps for their strengthening.

Tolkacheva, V., Ivanov, D., Arkhipov, A., 2007, in IFIP International Federation for Information Processing, Volume 243, Establishing the Foundation of Collaborative Networks; eds. Camarinha-Matos, L., Afsarmanesh, H., Novais, P., Analide, C.; (Boston: Springer), pp. 75–82.

The concept of 'stability' plays a fundamental role in the systems theory. The sense of this term in general is equal for different types and classes of systems. It consists in limited reaction of a system (bounded output) on scale-limited (bounded input) entering impacts (controlled and non-controlled). In the systems and control theories is usually used a term BIBO (Bounded Input Bounded Output)-Stability. In mathematics, stability theory deals with the stability of the solutions of differential equations and dynamical systems (Rouche et al., 1977). Stability can be estimated by means of different approaches such as Nyquist, Hurwitz, Routhor with Cross-over Modell von McRuer.

In production and logistics, the issue of plan stability has attracted increased attention and interest in recent years. This is mainly due to an increasing integration of planning systems both within and across companies in supply chain management Heisig, (2006). (Fox et al., 2006) proposes a framework for using plan stability metric in the plan adaptation issues. The authors demonstrate empirically based on the local search strategy that the proposed plan repair strategy achieves more stability than replanning without stability consideration. (Groson et al., 2005) consider the order stability issues in supply chains with the focus on coordination to avoid the bullwhip effect. These experiments follow the standard protocol of the Beer Distribution Game. Approach, described in (Kulba, 2006), introduces the term of structural-technological reserve for increasing stability of manufacturing systems and proposes a Petri-net based solution method.

A special feature of the CN stability analysis consists in adjustment actions elaborated by managers (not by machines) in a combination of centralized and *decentralized* management. The CN differs from a physical system. The latter is remarkable for its planning mechanisms, which have some elements of subjectivism. That is why it becomes necessary to broaden the sense of 'stability' term while CN considering. In paper (Ivanov et al., 2006), we introduced a framework of CN stability analysis and presented a conceptual model of CN stability analysis and its dynamical interpretation. In this paper, we put the emphasis on a specific aspect of the CN stability analysis – analysis of collaboration stability. The elaborated framework aims to develop a technique for simultaneous CN structuring and its stability assessment based on parametric analysis of possible participants and integral stability assessment. This procedure is based on the application of special index of structure consolidation (ISC), which makes it possible to estimate the project stability.

3   FRAMEWORK FOR COLLABORATIVE NETWORK SYNTHESIS

At the CN configuration stage the aim of a CN coordinator is to synthesize alternative structures of CN and range them due to their preference. This procedure is carried out on the base of two structured setss: the set of potential executors and the set of alternative project structures.

Project structuring. At this step the goal of coordinator consists in project description and structuring according to the proper level of decomposition. In complex projects different operations have different importance for the final result. That is why the importance level of each operation must to be taken into account. When coordinator is in charge of several projects, there may be situations, when the same competency is needed for different projects at the same time. These projects should not be considered independent, because they compete for the same resource. In order to analyse such "linked" projects together we propose to present them as a joined structure scheme that we call technological network. The model of technological network is an oriented graph. Its heads are considered competencies that are necessary for project realisation, and its edges serve to show the logic sequence of operations. Weights of each head reflect the volume of the competency that is needed for projects performance (e.g., the total working time to execute a concrete technological operation on a concrete machine). Finally, in the end of this step coordinator obtains properly structured projects that are considered technological network.

Executors structuring. Using common information breeding environment, coordinator analyses possible executors for his technological network. Each potential participant is characterised by several competencies as well as by additional characteristics (an ability to perform their obligations in the specified terms, a presence of free resources to accomplish the order in full, a proper quality level of delivered products, a price per unit, a level of additional costs, a risk level of order execution failure).

Executors structuring is carried out in two phases: i) analysing the whole set of information breeding environment members, coordinator selects potential participants for his project due to their competencies; ii) coordinator analysis additional characteristics of selected potential executors for the each stage and ranges them. This procedure was thoroughly described in recent works (Ivanov et al, 2006). First of all, it is necessary to consecutively allocate Pareto-optimal groups of alternative executors and give a rank to each group. Then applying the special method, proposed by authors, which is based on the concept of "curves of indifference", coordinator ranges the members of each determined group. By the end of this step coordinator has several alternative executors for each project stage that are ranged due to their preference level.

CN synthesis. There are different approaches to CN synthesis that depend on whether a technological network and a number of possible executors are fixed or not. In this paper we consider, that projects are independent (they do not compete for the same resources), the structure of technological network is fixed and coordinator is provided with all necessary information about potential members.

Coordinator should built different alternative variants of CN structures, assess them and select the most preferable. According to different requirements to the result, several procedures may be applied: i) full number of combinations of executors for each project stage; ii) formation of the sole CN structure from the preset reduced number of best executors for each separate stage (local optimization); iii) reduced number of CN alternative combinations.

The third procedure seems to be the most advantageous. This method provides us with common search scheme, whose limiting cases are the procedures described above – full number of combinations and local optimization. Introduction of restrictions on executor ranks is important, because it allows coordinator to reduce the space of search considerably. Synthesis of CN alternative variants is carried out by introduction of executors (from the obtained subset) in the next CN variant according to their rank. The result of this procedure is the set of CN alternative structures ranged due to their preference level. This is the most flexible form of result as it lets the coordinator operatively maneuver in case various sorts of failures or deviations during project performance occur. Thus, the result of the given step is the synthesis of either one CN structure that is most preferable for the coordinator, or the sequence of CN structures ordered due to their preference level.

4   INTEGRAL STABILITY ASSESSMENT OF THE CN STRUCTURE

Now coordinator should carry out the analysis of the constructed CN. First of all it is necessary to evaluate the internal "affinity", "durability" of the synthesized CN. As CN members are independent active subjects and their aims may change under market environment, the assessment of potential reliability (structure stability) seems to be much more complicated. There may be situations, when CN members are willingly to go out of the project, and coordinator – to change the executor. An active behavior of CN participants together with their insufficient consolidation in the frameworks of CN can lead to project failure that, obviously, is extremely undesirable for the coordinator, responsible for its realization.

In this paper we propose an approach to the CN reliability assessment, which is based on the application of special index of structure consolidation (ISC). This index shows mutual interest between CN partners and the coordinator and makes it possible to estimate how successful the project will be. This index should be taken into account while taking decision about the final structure of the collaborative network. To determine the ISC we offer the following algorithm.

1. The evaluation of coordinator's interest in i-executor

Let us consider, that i-executor is described with the parameter vector $p_i=(p_{i1},p_{i2}, ..., p_{in})$. We introduce the concept of i-executor utility and believe that it additively depends on values of parameters mentioned above:

$$P_i = \lambda_1 \cdot p_{i1} + \lambda_2 \cdot p_{i2} + ... + \lambda_n \cdot p_{in}, \qquad (1)$$

where P_i – i-executor utility function;

$p_{i1}, p_{i2}, ..., p_{in}$ – i-executor normalized parameters;

$\lambda_1, \lambda_2, \lambda_n$, – coefficients of parameter importance, determined by the coordinator.

We assume that coordinator is able to explain what values of executor's parameters he wants to see. The vector of such desirable parameters we call "ideal" vector p^0. So, we can determine the ideal utility function P_i^0.

The index U_i of coordinator's interest in i-executor we establish as follows:

$$U_i = P_i / P_i^0 \quad i= 1, 2, ... , n \qquad (2)$$

It is obviously that this index may alter in the interval [0, 1].

2. The evaluation of i-executor's interest in project by the coordinator

From the point of view of the coordinator the executor's interest in project is defined by two factors: i) the level of capacity utilization while order execution (K_{Mi}); ii) the expected revenue (C_i), i.e. the cost of the contract between the executor and the coordinator.

The utility (S_i) of participation in the project for the i-executor we determine as follows:

$$S_i = \lambda_c \cdot C_i + \lambda_k \cdot K_{Mi} , \qquad (3)$$

where λ_c and λ_k – coefficients of parameter importance, determined by the coordinator.

Let us determine the vector of "ideal" values of parameters C_i and K_{Mi} and, accordingly, the ideal value of utility function S_i^0. The latter is established for a case when executor has the maximal level of capacity utilization ($K_{Mi} = 1$) and the expected revenue is "normative" for him ($C_i = C_{norm.}$).

The evaluation of i-executor's interest in project participation by the coordinator (Z_i) is determined as follows:

$$\mathbf{Z_i} = \mathbf{S_i} / \mathbf{S^0_i} \tag{4}$$

3. The evaluation of mutual interest between the coordinator and i-executor

The evaluation of mutual interest between the coordinator and i-executor is determined as minimum of $\mathbf{Z_i}$ and $\mathbf{U_i}$:

$$\mathbf{U_{0i}} = \min (\mathbf{U_i}, \mathbf{Z_i}), i = 1, 2, \ldots, n \tag{5}$$

The received estimations describe separate CN participants, therefore we name them individual. On the basis of these individual estimations we construct the integrated estimation of CN participants' interest in cooperation, i.e. we determine the index of structure consolidation (ISC).

4. The index of structure consolidation (ISC) determination

To determine the ISC the following procedure is proposed. Let us construct the "petal" diagram. Every axis, starting with the center, is set with the certain executor (and, accordingly, with the certain competency) and scaled from 0 to 1. This scale shows the relative importance of the particular competency for the project. Then it is necessary to mark 1-points for each axis and connect them. The square of the obtained polygon (F_{max}) shows maximal value of CN participants' mutual interest in collaboration. It is the "ideal" case, when CN structure is absolutely "compatible". After that we mark U_{0i} estimations (5) on each axis accordingly and connect the obtained points. The square of the obtained polygon (F) shows real value of CN participants' mutual interest in collaboration. The index of structure consolidation (ISC) is determined as follows:

$$ISC = F / F_{max} \tag{6}$$

The value of ISC may alter in the interval [0, 1]. It is necessary to set it to the subjective opinion of coordinator about the "affinity" of CN structure. This procedure claims for fuzzy logic application. The coordinator characterizes the CN structure "affinity" with several linguistic variables, e.g. weak, medium, and strong. Then the coordinator sets the certain zone of the interval [0, 1] with each linguistic variable. In case of three variables (weak, medium, and strong) the interval [0, 1] of ISC altering should be divided into three zones by boundary points q_1 and q_2 ($q_1 < q_2$). The further actions of coordinator will be different depending on which zone contains the ISC determined previously (6).

If ISC $< q_1$, the level of mutual interest is extremely low, CN is potentially unstable and the risk of project failure is very high. The coordinator is recommended to change the CN structure or elaborate additional motivation measures.

If ISC $> q_2$, the level of mutual interest is very high, CN is stable and the risk of project failure is extremely low. The coordinator is recommended to finally select this variant of the CN structure.

If $q_1 < ISC < q_2$, the level of mutual interest is medium, the situation is extremely uncertain. It is necessary to carry out additional analysis, reconsider the structure of accepted requirements, priorities and other elements of the applied selection model.

If necessary, the proposed method is applied also for next modified CN structure till the coordinator receives the CN structure that is satisfactory for him.

5　ILLUSTRATION

Let us assume that based on CN configuration models and algorithms (Ivanov et al., 2004, 2005, 2006, 2007), a CN structure is configured. While analysing CN structure we focuses on the evaluation of its internal "affinity"or "durability". It is necessary to estimate CN structure stability applying the Index of Structure Consolidation (ISC). Let us assume that the level of structure consolidation can be one of three: low, medium and high. Therefore, boundaries for these three options are set as follows: q1=0,3 and q2=0,6. After that we determine the level of mutual interest between the coordinator and each executor (1,2,3,4,5). The result is presented in table 1.

Table 1 - Level of mutual interest between the coordinator and each executor

The level of interest	Executors			
	A	B	D	F
The level of coordinator's interest in executor (U_i)	0,95	0,98	0,99	0,98
The level of executor's interest in project (Z_i)	0,96	0,8	0,75	0,75
The level of mutual interest between the coordinator and the executor (U_{0i})	0,95	0,8	0,75	0,75

To determine the ISC it is necessary to construct the "petal" diagram (fig.1) using data presented in table 2. The level of comparative importance of the project stage (ricom) is determined as follows:

$$r_i^{\text{отн}} = r_i / r_i^{\max} \qquad (7)$$

For the stage with maximum level of importance ($r_i^{\max}$) $r_i^{\text{com}} = 1$.

The estimation of comparative mutual interest between the coordinator and the executor (U^{com}_{0i}) is carried out as follows:

$$U^{\text{com}}_{0i} = r_i^{\text{com}} * U_{0i} \qquad (8)$$

Table 2 - Mutual interest between partners

Indices	Executors			
	A	B	C	D
The importance of the project stage (r_i)	0,2	0,34	0, 24	0,22
The mutual interest between the coordinator and the executor (U_{0i})	0,95	0,8	0,75	0,75
The comparative importance of the project stage (r_i^{com})	0,59	1	0,71	0,65
The comparative mutual interest between the coordinator and the executor (U^{com}_{0i})	0,56	0,8	0,53	0,49

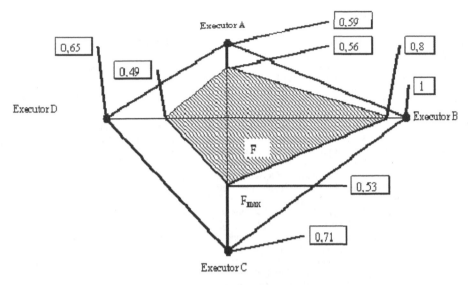

Figure 1. ISC determination

Finally, we obtained the result: F_{max} = 1,0725, F = 0,70305, **ISC = 0,66.** It is clear, that ISC > q_2. It means that the level of mutual interest is very high. From the coordinator's point of view CN structure is stable enough and the risk of project failure is extremely low. The coordinator is recommended to finally select this variant of the CN structure. It is reasonable to consider this variant of CN structure most preferable.

6   CONCLUSIONS

Stability analysis is an efficient tool to analyze CN under the terms of uncertainty. In this paper, we put the emphasis on a specific aspect of the CN stability analysis – analysis of collaboration stability. The elaborated framework aims at developing a technique for simultaneous CN structuring and its stability assessment based on parametric analysis of possible participants and integral stability assessment. This procedure is based on the application of special index of structure consolidation (ISC), which makes it possible to estimate the project stability. The index shows mutual interest between CN partners and the coordinator. This index should be taken into account while taking decision about the final structure of the network and its application claims for fuzzy logic introduction. Numerical eexperiments illustrated efficiency of the proposed methods and algorithms. The elaborated framework makes it possible to increase the quality of decision-making about the CN configuration under the terms of uncertainty.

7   ACKNOWLEDGMENTS

The research described in this paper is partially supported by grants from Russian Foundation for Basic Research (RFFI) and German Research Foundation (DFG). The author thanks the contribution from their partners in such projects.

8   REFERENCES

1.   Camarinha-Matos, L., Afsarmanesh, H. and A. Ortiz (eds.) (2005). Collaborative Networks and Their Breeding Environments, Springer.
2.   Croson, R., H. Donohue, E. Katok and J. Sterman, Order Stability in Supply Chains: Coordination Risk and the Role of Coordination Stock, MIT Press, 2005.
3.   Fox, M., A. Gerevini, D. Long and I. Serina, Plan Stability: Replanning versus Plan Repair, in: Proceedings of the ICAPS'2006, 2006.
4.   Heisig, G. Planning Stability in Material Requirements Planning Systems, Gabler Verlag, 2006.
5.   Ivanov, D., A. Arkhipov, V. Tolkacheva and B. Sokolov, Stability Analysis in the Framework of Decision Making Under Risk and Uncertainty, in: Network-centric collaboration and supporting frameworks, L.M. Camarinha-Matos, H. Afsarmanesh, M. Ollus (eds.), Springer, 2006, pp. 211-218.
6.   Ivanov, D., Arkhipov A., Sokolov B. (2004): Intelligent Supply Chain Planning in Virtual Enterprises. In: Virtual Enterprises and Collaborative Networks, edited by L.Camarihna-Matos, Kluwer Academic Publishers, 2004: 215-223.
7.   Ivanov, D. DIMA – Decentralized Integrated Modeling Approach. Interdisziplinäre Modellierung von Produktions- und Logistiknetzwerken (2007), Verlag der GUC, Chemnitz, 2007
8.   Ivanov, D., B. Sokolov (2007) Intelligent planning and control of manufacturing supply chains in virtual enterprises, accepted IJMTM, 2007.
9.   Ivanov, D., Käschel, J., Arkhipov, A., Sokolov, B., and Zschorn L. (2005): Quantitative Models of Collaborative Networks, In: Collaborative Networks and Their Breeding Environments, edited by L.Camarihna-Matos, H. Afsarmanesh, A. Ortiz, Springer, 2005, pp. 387-394.
10.   Kulba, V., B. Pavlov', and O. Zaikin, Stuctural-technological reserve for increasing stability of manufacturing systems', in: Proceedings of the 12th IFAC Symposium on Information Control Problems in Manufacturing, St. Etienne, France, 2006, Vol. 2, pp. 93-98.
11.   Rouche, N., P. Habets and M. Laloy, Stability Theory by Liapunov's Direct Method, Springer, 1977.

9   A DECISION SUPPORT FRAMEWORK FOR COLLABORATIVE NETWORKS

Ovidiu Noran
Griffith University, AUSTRALIA
O.Noran@griffith.edu.au

Collaborative Networks (CNs) enhance the preparedness of their participants to promptly form Virtual Organisations (VOs) that are able to successfully tender for large scale and distributed projects. However, the CN efficiency essentially depends on the ability of its managers to match and customise available reference models but often, also to create new project activities. Thus, given a particular VO creation project, the CN managers must promptly infer 'what needs to be done' (discover the project processes) and how to best communicate their 'justified beliefs' to the CN members involved. This paper proposes a framework for a decision support system that can help managers and enterprise architects discover/update the main activities and aspects that need to be modelled for various enterprise task types, with special emphasis on the creation of VOs. The framework content is also explained 'by example', in the context of a real-world scenario.

1   INTRODUCTION

Collaborative Networks (CNs) allow their members to promptly create virtual organisations (VOs) able to bid for projects that exceed the competencies of the individual CN participants. Although most CNs maintain pools of reference models, VO projects often require their customisation and sometimes, the creation of new specific project processes altogether. This involves understanding the current situation, choosing the right alternative from a set of plausible scenarios, planning the transition from present to future states, knowledge and choice of the available technologies and other useful artefacts and importantly, communicating and justifying the decisions to the rest of the CN organisation(s) involved. Many modern support systems such as Executive Dashboards, although based on Decision Support Systems (DSS) principles (Volonino and Watson, 1990-91), focus on presenting information, rather than on actively assisting in the decision-making process.

This paper describes a decision support system framework based on analysing the interactions between CN members involved in a (VO or not) project in the context of their lifecycles, using elements of main architectural frameworks (AFs).

2   A META-METHODOLOGY FOR COLLABORATIVE NETWORKS

Previous research (Noran, 2004a, 2004b, 2005) has attempted to find a set of steps ('meta-methodology') that would assist in the creation of process models customised for various CN projects. This forms the theoretical basis of the DSS framework.

Noran, O., 2007, in IFIP International Federation for Information Processing, Volume 243, Establishing the Foundation of Collaborative Networks; eds. Camarinha-Matos, L., Afsarmanesh, H., Novais, P., Analide, C.; (Boston: Springer), pp. 83–90.

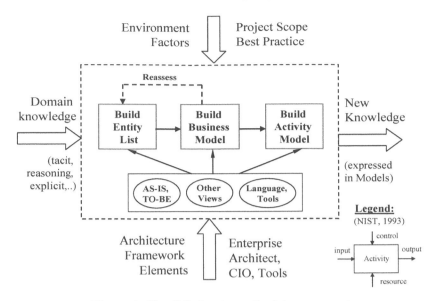

Figure 1. Simplified meta-methodology concept

The main deliverable of the meta-methodology is a model of the tasks performed in order to accomplish the VO project. However, in order to be able to obtain this model, the user has to represent several other aspects choosing appropriate tools, reference models and modelling frameworks (MFs) containing views, languages, etc. The meta-methodology requires existing domain knowledge (see **Figure 1** left) that is *transformed* into new, explicit knowledge and is eventually internalised by other stakeholders (Kalpic and Bernus, 2006) thus closing the knowledge lifecycle.

This paper describes a way to harness the meta-methodology concept, rather than to provide a full description of the meta-methodology research and development. The interested reader can find all these details in (Noran, 2004a, 2004b, 2005).

3   THE DECISION SUPPORT SYSTEM FRAMEWORK

Knowledge is continuously *produced* (or 'converted' (Nonaka and Takeuchi, 1995)) in the organisations as a consequence of decision-making processes (Holsapple and Whinston, 1996). The proposed system intends to promote this conversion and help management make 'semi-programmed' decisions (Simon, 1977) difficult to encode in a program but possible to *facilitate* by a DSS (Keen and Scott_Morton, 1978).

3.1   Requirements

A successful executive decision support system is likely to become widely used (Wheeler et al., 1993). Therefore, the system should be *scalable* from desktop to enterprise-wide level (Power, 2002). The system should also be *interactive*, allowing the decision maker to use own insights to modify the solutions provided by the system (Turban, 1995). This will promote user buy-in, ownership and the use of natural knowledge management skills and talents (Holsapple and Whinston, 1996).

The system should help detect existing problems, be able to model them for clarification, provide the means to consider options (by simulation of various scenarios until a suitable solution is obtained) and help with implementation of change (Finlay, 1994; Hättenschwiler, 1999).

Importantly, the proposed support system should deliver *guidance* in defining the change processes needed to migrate from the present to the selected future state and in *uttering* those processes and aspects in an intelligible form for the target audience.

3.2   Proposed Architecture of the Support System

The close link between decision-making and knowledge management has been manifest throughout the research pertaining to the support system requirements. This has suggested a rule-based knowledge base approach for the system repository and an expert system-type paradigm for the entire support system architecture.

The adopted concept has been assessed against previous research in the area. Thus, most knowledge-based DSS framework elements described by Sprague (1980), Sprague and Carlson (1982) and Marakas (1999) are present in the design of this system. Among other components, this system comprises a database (in the form of a knowledge base, if the components are represented as facts and rules), a model base (containing reusable reference models, which are extracted and classified from AFs and previous projects[1]) and a dialog generation mechanism (provided by an inference or similar engine type see **Figure 2**).

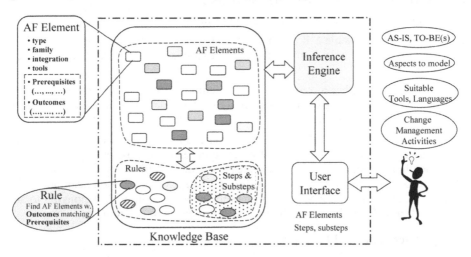

Figure 2. Decision support system architecture and outcomes of a consultation

Figure 2, left presents the rule-based knowledge base approach applied to the repository, where the rules for element selection, ordering (for ranked lists), etc share the knowledge base with the facts. The rules could take the form of typical IF/THEN-type statements specific to the inference engine involved (as exemplified in (Noran, 2005)). Simon's (1977) so-called *programmable, semi-programmed* and

---

[1] e.g. using ISO15704:2000 Annex A (ISO/TC184, 2000) as described in (Noran, 2006)

non-programmable decisions are reflected in this DSS by static/dynamic facts and by the user choices (e.g. by accepting or overriding of the highest ranked elements).

The proposed system assists in all decision-making phases identified by Simon (1977), i.e. intelligence gathering (via AS-IS modelling), design (via TO-BE modelling of several scenarios), choice (via WHAT-IF simulation) and review (through analysis of the various scenario results). The decision maker should be able to understand the alternatives, make the choice and explain the decisions to other echelons by selecting suitable modelling formalisms (assisted by the system).

The inference engine can be selected off-the-shelf (e.g. from a 'shell') as long as it meets the specifications (rule-based, platform independent, etc) and performance requirements resulting from the architectural design of the decision support system.

3.3   Main Rules of the Support System

Main Rule 1: Identify a list of entities relevant to the EA project. If projects are set up to build the target entity (entities), include them in the list;

Main Rule 2: Create a business model showing the relations between the life cycles of the listed entities. Re-assess the need for each entity in the diagram, and the *extent* of the life cycle set to be represented for each entity;

Main Rule 3: Using the life cycle diagram of each target entity, infer a set of activities describing the creation of each entity and the roles played in it by other entities. Detail the activities to the necessary level.

The following rules apply to each of the main rules:

Rule a: Identify a suitable MF if applicable/mandated. Choose the aspects to model, using the chosen MF and other aspects in the repository as checklist. Resolve aspect dependencies.

Rule b: Choose whether to represent the present (AS-IS) state. Choose whether to represent AS-IS and TO-BE states separately or combined. Model AS-IS when not fully understood or when the TO-BE will be derived from it (no radical change)

Rule c: Choose modelling formalism(s) depending on the aspect(s) selected, intended audience and modelling best-practice criteria, such as: previously used in the modelling, specialisation, prerequisites, potential multiple uses, part of a set, language set integration. Choose modelling tool depending on formalism and best practice, such as rigorously defined (preferably using a metamodel), belonging to an integrated suite, feasibility, availability, staff proficiency in that tool, etc.

3.4   Other Rules and Features

Rules are provided to resolve dependencies, seek solutions, order the AF elements (for the ranked lists) using the best practice criteria previously described, etc. Other rules provide default choices and generic elements if no preferences are entered. Examples: GERA[2] MF, plain English text, 'dumb' (i.e. language unaware) graphical editors, Rich Pictures. Solutions are found and dependencies are resolved using techniques specific to the inference engine selected (e.g. pattern matching, etc). The user can reject system suggestions and mark the override points for later reference.

---

[2] Generalised Enterprise Reference Architecture (ISO/TC184, 2000)

3.5 Implementation

Small-scale pilot implementations of the proposed DSS rules have been attempted using expert system shells such as JESS (Friedman-Hill, 2003). These efforts have typically involved a (thin) client–server paradigm and platform-independent applet/servlet technologies. Results have been encouraging thus far and are to be published.

4 TESTING THE FRAMEWORK: A CASE STUDY

4.1 Background and Specific Features of VO Formation

Schools A and B within the Faculty FAC wish to form a VO, called *Unified School* (US) in the TO-BE state shown in **Figure 3**. This would ensure a unique corporate image and consistency in the product delivered and the policies governing the future VO campuses at locations L1, L2 and L3. The individual campuses are set to retain much of their internal decisional and organisational structure except for the highest layer, which will be replaced by the VO governance structure. The function of CN is performed by the Faculty FAC. The lead partner for the VO project is school A. The VO is *on-going* and importantly, the partners cease to operate independently during the life of US. Since the support system is still being tested, a facilitator with knowledge of AF elements will *assist* the use of the system by the stakeholders and will note all decisions made by the system and the stakeholders. The audience of the support system deliverables is the management of U, FAC, A and B.

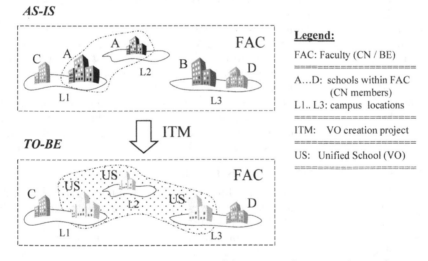

Figure 3. AS-IS and TO-BE states of the proposed VO creation project

4.2 Framework Application

Main Rule One: Identify the Entities Relevant to the VO formation

Rule a: Using stakeholders' domain knowledge, elicit relevant entities participating in the VO task; decide whether to represent a full or restricted set of life cycle phases. **Motivation:** Other aspects not relevant for this early stage. ***Rule b:*** Choose to represent both AS-IS and TO-BE states in a unified representation. **Motivation:** there is no obvious gain in having two lists with most list members identical. ***Rule c:*** Choose text representation as the modelling formalism. Choose a plain text editor or whiteboard as 'tool'. **Motivation:** formalism and tool must preserve simplicity. The list of entities constructed in this step is shown in the legend of **Figure 4**.

Main Rule Two: A Business Model of Entity Roles in a Life Cycle Context

Rule a: adopt the GERA MF. Model the management/service, decisional and organisational aspects for the entities participating in the project. **Motivation:** no user preference for a particular framework, hence default MF chosen. The aspects selected were elicited from stakeholders from the checklist of aspects in the repository. *Life cycle representation context is mandatory.* ***Rule b:*** represent both AS-IS and TO-BE states. Represent management/service states combined and decisional/organisational states separately. **Motivation:** The stakeholders felt they did not fully understand the present state. No tangible advantage was seen in showing separate AS-IS/TO-BE business models; more interest shown in the decisional structure. Organisational structure was the *only representation able to discern between several TO-BE states* - hence show separate AS-IS and TO-BE. ***Rule c:*** choose modelling formalisms ranking highest in efficiency for the aspects selected by rule a: for life cycle and management/service, choose a GERA MF-based formalism. Choose the GRAI[3]–Grid formalism for decisional and organisational aspects and a plain graphical editor for modelling. **Motivation:** GRAI-Grid ranks high in respect to other languages due to its specialisation, potential multiple use (e.g. organisational aspect) and lack of prerequisites. Recommended modelling tool (IMAGIM (GRAISoft, 2002) overridden by user with 'plain graphical editor' due to tool complexity and lack of skills.

The business model (**Figure 4**) is now constructed using stakeholder knowledge. This illustrates entity roles in fulfilling the VO project, in the context of the life cycle and management/production (M/P divisions in **Figure 4**) aspects. Several entities influence various life cycle phases of US directly or via other entities - notably ITM, the project set up specifically to build US.

The AS-IS and TO-BE decisional and organisational models are then built to enable a better understanding of the problems that triggered the VO project (e.g. narrow/paternalistic management, improper information flows) and allow discerning between various TO-BE scenarios. These models are presented in (Noran, 2007).

Main Rule Three: The Set of Activities describing the VO Creation

This rule is performed by 'reading' the life cycle diagram of the US and ITM in the context of their relations with other entities (**Figure 4**). The set of activities obtained is decomposed using aspects selected from the chosen MF and repository, ranked and suggested by the system and approved by the user during the consultation. ***Rule a:*** choose functional and life cycle aspects; use other views to *detail* the activities. **Motivation:** the main deliverable is an activity model, hence functional. However, to be understood and enacted, the activities must be detailed using other necessary aspects and views – here, management/service, human/machine and software/hardware aspects. ***Rule b:*** choose to represent AS-IS and TO-BE states, in a unified representation. **Motivation:** the activity model is expressing a *transition* from AS-IS to TO-BE, thus both should be represented. Separate views did not justify the consistency-maintaining overhead. ***Rule c:*** choose the IDEF language set

---

[3] Graphs with Results and Methods Interrelated (Doumeingts, 1984)

(NIST, 1993); select the AI0Win tool (KBSI, 2007). **Motivation:** The Unified Modelling Language (Rumbaugh et al., 1999) ranks higher than IDEF0 due to an underlying metamodel and wider tool support; however, availability of the AI0Win tool and IDEF0 skills have motivated the user to override the proposed ranking.

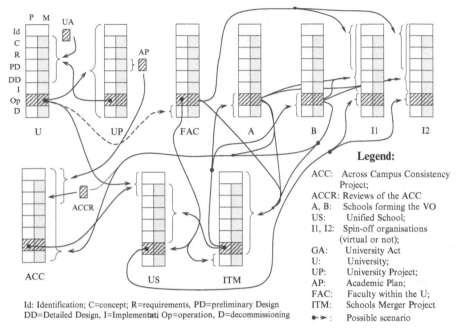

Id: Identification; C=concept; R=requirements, PD=preliminary Design
DD=Detailed Design, I=Implementatj Op=operation, D=decommissioning

Legend:
ACC:	Across Campus Consistency Project;
ACCR:	Reviews of the ACC
A, B:	Schools forming the VO
US:	Unified School;
I1, I2:	Spin-off organisations (virtual or not);
GA:	University Act
U:	University;
UP:	University Project;
AP:	Academic Plan;
FAC:	Faculty within the U;
ITM:	Schools Merger Project
●→➤ :	Possible scenario

Figure 4 Business model expressing entity roles in accomplishing the EE project

4.3 Notes on the Creation of the Activity Model

The functional model can be initiated by creating one main activity for each VO (and VO setup project if applicable) life cycle phase. The modelling formalism chosen will also assist in developing the model. For example, IDEF0 requires inputs, controls, outputs and mechanisms to be defined for these activities (see **Figure 1** lower right). Therefore, the system will prompt the IDEF0 user to represent what is used in each activity, what controls it, what is produced and who/what executes it.

Each activity should then be decomposed to a level understood by the envisaged audience, showing aspects used in previous steps and/or present in the chosen MF and contained in the repository, such as human/machine, hardware/software.

Not all aspects are relevant to all life cycle phases. For example, early life cycles (e.g. Identification, Concept) require few or no aspects, and the human/automation boundaries may only be relevant in the Preliminary/Detailed Design phases.

Detailed descriptions of the activity model creation and structure, which is beyond the purpose of this paper and available space are contained in (Noran, 2007).

5 CONCLUSIONS

CN management involves complexity, politics, tacit knowledge and uncertainty. A DSS can help managers understand and isolate problems, examine scenarios, predict outcomes and thus make *informed decisions.* The proposed support system framework has several additional distinctive features: it is supported by an original and tested theoretical concept; it is based on a life cycle paradigm, appropriate for the dynamic nature of organisations; it uses mainstream AF elements (while neutral in respect to any AF); and finally, it suggests areas that need to be represented in the change process via suitable models that enable management to communicate their 'justified true beliefs' (Nonaka and Takeuchi, 1995) to the rest of the organisation.

6   REFERENCES

1.   Doumeingts, G. La Methode GRAI. Doctoral Thesis, University of Bordeaux, Bordeaux, France, 1984
2.   Finlay, P. N. Introducing Decision Support Systems. Manchester: Blackwell publishing, 1994
3.   Friedman-Hill, E. Jess in Action: Java Rule-based Systems. Cherokee Station, New York, NY: Manning Publications Co., 2003
4.   GRAISoft. IMAGIM software product, (PDF document). GRAISoft. Available: http://www.graisoft. com, 2002
5.   Hättenschwiler, P. Neues anwenderfreundliches Konzept der Entscheidungsunterstützung. Gutes Entscheiden in Wirtschaft, Politik und Gesellschaft. Zurich: vdf Hochschulverlag AG, 1999
6.   Holsapple, C. W., Whinston, A. B. Decision Support Systems: A Knowledge-Based Approach. Minneapolis/St. Paul: West Publishing, 1996
7.   ISO/TC184. "Annex A: GERAM", ISO/IS 15704: Industrial automation systems - Requirements for enterprise-reference architectures and methodologies, 2000
8.   Kalpic, B., Bernus, P. Business process modeling through the knowledge management perspective. Journal of Knowledge Management, 10(3), 2006
9.   KBSI. AI0Win Software Product, (White Paper). Knowledge Based Systems, Inc. Available: http://www.kbsi.com/Software/KBSI/AI0WIN.htm, 2007
10. Keen, P. G. W., Scott_Morton, M. S. Decision Support Systems: An Organizational Perspective. Reading, MA: Addison-Wesley, Inc, 1978
11. Marakas, G. M. Decision support systems in the twenty-first century. Upper Saddle River, N.J.: Prentice Hall., 1999
12. NIST. Integration Definition for Function Modelling (IDEF0) (183: Federal Information Processing Publication): Computer Systems Laboratory, National Institute of Standards and Technology.1993
13. Nonaka, I., Takeuchi, H. The Knowledge-Creating Company. How Japanese companies create the dynamics of innovation. Oxford: Oxford University Press, 1995
14. Noran, O. A Meta-methodology for Collaborative Networked Organisations. Doctoral Thesis, School of CIT, Griffith University, 2004a
15. Noran, O. "A Meta-methodology for Collaborative Networked Organisations: A Case Study and Reflections". In P. Bernus, et al. (Eds.), Knowledge Sharing in the Integrated Enterprise: Interoperability Strategies for the Enterprise Architect. Toronto/Canada: Kluwer Academic Publishers, 2004b
16. Noran, O. "A Meta-methodology Prototype for Collaborative Networked Organisations". In L. Camarinha-Matos (Ed.), Collaborative Networks and Breeding Environments (Proceedings of the 6th IFIP Working Conference on Virtual Enterprises - PROVE 05) (pp. 339-346). Toulouse/ France: Springer Verlag, 2005
17. Noran, O. "Using Reference Models in Enterprise Architecture: An Example". In P. Fettke, P. Loos (Eds.), Reference Modeling for Business Systems Analysis. Hershey, USA: Idea Group, 2006
18. Noran, O. "Discovering and modelling Enterprise Engineering Project Processes". In P. Saha (Ed.), Enterprise Systems Architecture in Practice (pp. 39-61) Hershey, USA: IDEA Group, 2007
19. Power, D. Decision support systems: concepts and resources for managers (Vol. 2007). Westport, Conn.: Quorum Books, 2002
20. Rumbaugh, J., et al. The Unified Modelling Language Reference Manual. Reading, MA: Addison-Wesley, 1999
21. Simon, H. The New Science of Management Decision (3rd ed.). Englewood Cliffs, NJ.: Prentice-Hall, 1977
22. Sprague, R. H. A Framework for the Development of Decision Support Systems. Management Information Systems Quarterly, 4(4), 1-26, 1980
23. Sprague, R. H., Carlson, E. D. Building Effective Decision Support Systems. Englewood Cliffs, NJ: Prentice-Hall, Inc, 1982
24. Turban, E. Decision support and expert systems: management support systems. Englewood Cliffs, N.J: Prentice Hall, 1995
25. Wheeler, F. P., et al. Moving from an executive information system to everyone's information system: lessons from a case study. Journal of Information Technology, 8(3), 177-183, 1993

PART **4**

VO BREEDING ENVIRONMENT ENABLERS

David Romero[1], Jorge Giraldo[1], Nathalie Galeano[1], Arturo Molina[2]

1CYDIT - ITESM Campus Monterrey, Monterrey, MEXICO
david.romero.diaz@gmail.com, giraldodiaz@gmail.com, ngaleano@itesm.mx
2VIYD - ITESM Campus Monterrey, Monterrey, MEXICO
armolina@itesm.m

Designing and managing an effective corporate governance structure for Virtual Breeding Environments (VBEs) is a challenging process. Therefore, a governance model is required to define operational rules, bylaws and principles that will govern the behaviour of the members of a VBE during its life cycle. VBE governance will help to define who can make what decisions, who is accountable for which effects, and how each of the VBE actors must work to operate the VBE management process effectively. This paper presents first attempts in the definition of guidelines for Governance Rules and Bylaws in VBEs.

1   INTRODUCTION

Virtual Breeding Environments (VBEs) represent a group of organisational entities that have developed preparedness for cooperation, in case a specific collaborative opportunity arises or is identified by one member (acting as a broker). Therefore, such form of organisation, also known as a source network, is considered as a pre-condition for effective establishment of dynamic virtual organisations. Furthermore, VOs are temporary alliances of organisations that come together compromising their resources and skills in order to respond collaboratively to a competitive market opportunity, and its interaction is supported by computer networks (Camarinha-Matos and Afsarmanesh, 2006).

This paper describes main elements involved in VBE governance through a set of guidelines for defining the breeding environment governance, including internal operational rules and bylaws. Some of these elements include: membership, incentive and sanction system, ethical code, VBE culture, administrative functions in order to identify priorities, roles and responsibilities, and bases for decision making in managing sphere during VBE lifecycle stages.

Romero, D., Giraldo, J., Galeano, N., Molina, A., 2007, in IFIP International Federation for Information Processing, Volume 243, Establishing the Foundation of Collaborative Networks; eds. Camarinha-Matos, L., Afsarmanesh, H., Novais, P., Analide, C.; (Boston: Springer), pp. 93–102.

2   BASIC CONCEPTS ON GOVERNACE

The governance word derives from Latin origins that suggest the notion of "steering". It refers to the "use of institutions, structures of authority and even collaboration, to allocate resources and coordinate or control activities in societies or economies". In general terms governance occurs in three broad ways: a. through top-down methods that primarily involve governments and the state bureaucracy, b. through the use of market mechanisms where market principles of competition are employed to allocate resources while operating under government regulation, and c. through networks involving public-private partnerships or with the collaboration of community organisations.

Good governance structures encourage organisations to create value (through entrepreneur, innovation, development and exploration) and provide accountability and control systems commensurate with the risk involved (Kumar, 2005).

Governance refers to the act of affecting government and monitoring (through policy) the long-term strategy and direction of an organisation. In general, governance comprises the traditions, institutions and processes that determine how power is exercised, how citizens are given a voice, and how decisions are made on issues of public concern (Graham et al 2003). VBE governance is specifically aimed at facilitating and improving processes of business opportunities approaching, as well as guaranteeing the sustainability and correct performance of all stakeholders involved. It is concerned with the questions: how the value chain itself is moving, how it can be reconfigured and where possible new synergies can be found (Gilsing, 2000).

There are several governance models, some of them related to the governance of a nation, while others are related to the governance of an organisation. Some aspects that governance models respond are mainly related to next questions: what to do, how to do it, who should do it and how it should be measured (GGB, 2002).

Principles are the values that govern a person or organisation's behaviour. In this case they will be defined as the result of a vision, something that a VBE, wants to reach. They constitute the main guidelines for breeding environments on a macro level. Key elements of good governance principles include honesty, trust and integrity, openness, performance orientation, responsibility and accountability, mutual respect, and commitment to the organisation.

Rules refer (formally or informally) to various types of guidelines (i.e. direction, standard, method, operation) or standard (i.e. definition, fact, law, code, truth, etc.). Maintaining the VBE as a sustainable organisation requires the performance of some important processes which will be created, monitored and controlled through definition and application of operational rules for each one.

Bylaws are generally understood as the document adopted by an organisation to regulate its affairs; formally referred to as the rules of operation. Bylaws should include the following: organisation mission, membership policy, meeting information (attendance requirements, number that constitutes quorum), organisation board (number of members, responsibilities, special roles, officers and their responsibilities, length of terms), committees and their functions, fiscal year accounting procedures, indemnification, bylaws amendment procedures, and dissolution of organisation.

3   GUIDILINES FOR DEFINE VBE GOVERNACE

This section presents an approach to guide the creation of VBE governance rules, involving both operational and behavioural structures. The relationships among governance concepts are presented in the Figure 1.

The top level defines the strategic plan for VBE governance, establishing the principles as a result of a vision, where objectives that the VBE wants to reach are depicted. The definition of rules includes both behaviour and function related rules. Behaviour rules, such as ethical code, and VBE culture, are related to social values. VBE governance can be supported by ICT tools that facilitate the implementation of related rules and principles.

Rules and bylaws for breeding environment should be initially defined by a VBE manager together with VBE members and VBE advisor. During VBE operation the VBE manager and VBE members can propose rules, laws and bylaws that must be considered during the creation of VOs. Definition of rules and bylaws will depend on the specific sector of the VBE. However, there should be a procedure that defines the creation and inclusion of new rules; new rules must be evaluated according to bylaws defined.

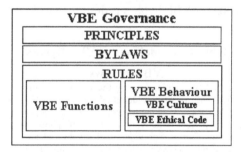

Figure 1 – VBE Governance Model

3.1   VBE Principles

Since principles are described as values that govern the stakeholders' behaviour within an organisation, they are most referred to the social attitudes which will obviously impact its operational performance.

Some general principles will be enumerated in Table 1 order to establish the social model that should be part of VBE governance body:

Table 1 – Guidelines for VBE Principles

Honesty	Acting with loyalty, with good faith for all stakeholders benefit.
Trust and integrity	Being part of the VBE gives rights to members, but also allocates some duties where trusted collaborative network is the fundamental key.
Openness	The value of sharing information and collaborate in business opportunities will reflect the openness of VBE members.
Performance orientation	The good performance in the VBE related area, as well as high quality levels and social attitudes allow companies to keep the membership and deserve rewards, and invitations to participate in new opportunities.

Responsibility and accountability	Respond with assigned tasks, actively participate in coordinated work.
Mutual respect	The coordination for collaborative work will have diverse opinions for creation or development of any task, those opinions must be carefully analysed and respected during agreements. Not only cultural and ethical issues are involved in mutual respect, but also technical elements.
Commitment to the VBE	Understand that the breeding environment growth together with the improvement of the company.

3.2   VBE Bylaws

Principles and rules represent a general and global schema under which a VBE will control and monitor the performed activities along its lifecycle. The definition of Bylaws for a VBE represents the formal documentation of principles and rules that govern VBE members' behaviour.

Structured governance bylaws for any VBE will define regulations for its affairs; however, those regulations must aim to a common objective in order to guarantee reaching of goals and achievements depicted in VBE mission and vision. The specific mission and vision for each VBE should be developed during the definition of its business model.

Main proposed section for VBE bylaws is described in Table 2:

Table 2 – Guidelines for VBE Bylaws

VBE Bylaws	
Rights and Duties policies	During the VBE creation process, the actors of the VBE and their roles must be identified. The main actors identified are: VBE member, VBE administrator, VO broker, VO planner and the VO coordinator. Other participating stakeholders to support the performed activities are the VBE advisor, supporting institutions (i.e. common tools/services provider, SMEs, industrial association, chambers of commerce, regional development agencies, universities, government entities) and a common ontology provider. It is important to characterize the management board of the VBE as well as define its responsibilities. The board can be formed in first instance by the VBE manager, brokers, some VBE members, and the VBE advisor; and it could be modified according to the internal policies of each VBE, these policies should be formally described in the bylaws document.
Membership policies	*Qualification criteria and associated processes:* Define what kinds of organisations will form the VBE, how to evaluate them in order to reward or sanction its performance. Policies to accept new members or retreat old ones must be clearly defined. The acceptation of new members in the VBE requires a prior evaluation of the organisation that includes the following issues, among others: profile, record of performance, products, processes, delivery time, quality, etc. Before the establishment of VBE, the potential members must be aware of the working policies, like membership agreements which would content: Benefits, potential incomes for participating on the VBE, duties, subscription process, and qualification criteria, among others. Every process necessary to clarify roles of each involved party for different activities should be detailed.
	Membership control and governance: Specific policies and rules must be also defined for the maintenance and control of VBE membership. It includes the creation of an Incentive and Sanctions System that will act as an enabler for managing activities, allowing the manager to make decisions about sanctioning, retrieval or rewarding members.
Incentives	The definition of a system of incentives is important for attracting and maintaining partners and members. In general, for business related contexts, the key incentives to participate in a VBE are business benefits and knowledge

Sanctions	VBE members could be also punished if they fail to adhere to the defined rules and principles in the VBE (i.e. not adhering of VBE code of ethics, not adhering to the VBE contracts and agreements, low performance of the VBE member according predefined goals of performance indicators, not being truthful on their reporting to the VBE, etc.). Similarly some rules must be established for accepting and retreating VBE members (i.e. the selection process should include quality tests, samples and performance indicators). For retreating any member it must be considered the type and effect of the fault committed, thus an order for faults and their sanctions must be structured.
Security Issues	Policies to safeguard the confidentiality of gained information and obtained knowledge must be defined prior to operations of the VBE; these aspects should be included in the ethical code, and will be part of the incentive and sanctions system since the information management from a member gives drivers to make decision about it (retreats, renewals). Members are obligated not to disclose confidential or private corporate knowledge or information to competitors. The definition of the confidentiality is really important within the VBE (What kind of information about their company partners must share with the other partners of the VBE?), between the VBE and the Clients (Who can have access to the information of the clients? Is the client allowed to know who the different partners of the VO are?), and between Clients and VBE.
ICT use guidelines	This element is related to the use of technology as a mean to disclose and share the information, respecting the policies and rules, according to the ethical and behavioural code (see Section 3.4).
Conflict resolution policy	Possible conflicts and disputes presented among members will be worked out by the board, headed by the VBE manager with the support of a VBE advisor, in presence of involved parties. In case of not solving the problem according to internal VBE bylaws, it will proceed to take the case into the legal statements. The most relevant cases that could introduce conflicts to the VBE are: breach to a contract, disclose of confidential information, use VBE means for approaching particular interests external to the VBE, intellectual property rights (in case of patents), among others.
Financial policies	Even for non-profitable VBEs, it is necessary to build a sustainable organisation; it means that policies for payments and an accounting structure must be defined in order to guarantee a potential growth at economic level.
Amendments to bylaws	Bylaws are subject to amendment at any regular meeting of the Management Board. Notice of proposed changes in the rules should be circulated to all VBE members with a considerable time in advance of the meeting at which they are to be acted upon. Changes in the bylaws require consensus. Any changes in the bylaws approved by the management board should take effect according to the rules defined.
Intellectual property rights policies	Intellectual property rights must be defined when the VBE will be launched. Definition of owner of rights (sharing patents, selling or licensing patents) is a task for VBE manager advised by a supporting institution (preferably an external member of the VBE).

Guidelines described above represent a general approach to guide the process of defining principles and bylaws in a VBE, however bylaws that will govern the internal structure and functioning of the VBE will depend on the specific sector where it will perform its activities for (i.e. a service VBE will necessarily have to manage different processes than a manufacturing VBE, and the principles/bylaws defined should be guided and supported by this processes).

Other important issues to bear in mind, when defining VBE principles and Bylaws are: representation of those global and common activities for any VBE creation and/or operation, administration processes (accountability), management roles nomination and renewal processes, contract enforcement policy, and purchasing and management of outsourced services.

3.3   VBE Rules

VBE rules can be divided in two groups: rules related to the behaviour of VBE actors and rules related to functions or processes of the VBE (see Figure 2). Next sections will depict some guidelines for defining these types of rules.

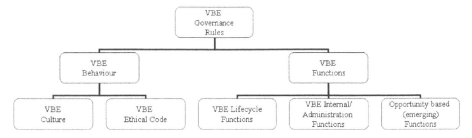

Figure 2 – VBE Governance Rules (operating/functioning)

3.3.1   VBE Behaviour

General rules must be defined within a frame that involves behavioural rules, which includes the VBE culture and ethical code. Ethical behaviour support trust building process which will guarantee the social and operational sustainability of the breeding environment.

VBE Culture

The culture of a group can be defined as: "a pattern of shared basic assumptions that the group learned as it solved its problems of external adaptation and internal integration, that has worked well enough to be considered valid and therefore, to be taught to new members as the correct way to perceive, think, and feel in relation to those problems" (Schein, 1992). Among other factors, the primary requirements for a proper collaboration culture in a VBE can be associated to the guidelines presented in Table 3:

Table 3 – Guidelines for VBE Culture

Commitment	In order to be trusty, a level of commitment is required. This can be measured based on previous work like accuracy of service times of an enterprise with its clients or with its partner's previous alliances.
Leadership	Organisations should focus on their core competences to achieve market leadership. This idea can be generalized for a VBE, where enterprises collaborate to obtain a recognized level of quality. The vision of being one of the best should be constant in the environment and to differentiate from competition should be also a common mission.
Trust	Trust is a basic element in VBE culture. Trust can be developed via formation of alliances, consortiums, associations, value chain integration, among others.
Self-Learning	Self-learning related to the ability of organisations and individuals to learn by their selves. Self-learning supports VBEs sustainability.
Long-term and Global Vision	A VBE should have a defined long term vision, which will guide its activities according to the strategy defined by the organisation. The activities performed in the VBE should be aimed at results and profitability in long maintaining VBE operation. This vision should consider the global market aspect, especially for the development of dynamic VOs.
Effective Communication	VBE members must use proper communication ways and tools. Communication includes aspects related with information sharing and knowledge sharing.

Innovation	The ability to be creative in products, process and services is the base of innovation. VBE actors should involve innovation in the execution of its activities. Innovation should be present during VO creation, operation and dissolution.

In conclusion VBE culture comprises all organisation's beliefs, knowledge, attitudes, and customs. Culture may result in part from managers' beliefs/thoughts, but it also results from VBE members beliefs (opinions/approaches). It can be supportive or unsupportive and positive or negative and it also can affect members' ability or willingness to adapt or perform well.

VBE Ethical Code

An ethical behaviour (accepted standards of conduct) expected from members of VBE will determine in certain way the feasibility for a member to form part of a VBE. Some important deontological values to be evaluated during all VBE operation (PVC ethical value based – general values) are:

- Sharing attitude: All collaborative business forms requires a special thinking for sharing knowledge, opportunities, contacts, resources, etc.
- Awareness for win-win development of business opportunities, where organisation does not only want to obtain benefits from others, but also to give and share things with others (no opportunistic behaviour).
- No discrimination, "knowledge" and "collaboration attitude" based enterprise valuing (enterprise recognition).
- Enterprise strategic advantage through collaboration.
- Recognition of merits for self-organizing leadership (for instance, the member which brings in the business opportunity is empowered to lead the virtual organisation build up).

3.3.2   VBE Functions/Operational Rules

These rules support both operational and administrative processes along all VBE lifecycle stages. Table 4 proposes a general guide to establish the most important operational rules for a VBE that support right activities execution.

Table 4 – Guidelines for VBE Operational Rules

General Management and Support Process	
Rule	**Description**
VBE management processes (how the VBE will be managed, decision making principles)	The decision making rules should be established by a VBE management board where manager and advisor will play a relevant role as experts and enablers for definition of concerned rules.
Administration processes (Accountability)	Accounting processes will be responsibility of a statement created to support in financial issues, and monitored by VBE manager.
Management roles nomination and renewal processes	Assignment of responsibilities and roles, for different actors and members, as well as tasks to be performed and their management represent one of most important elements in VBE lifecycle.
Policies for code of conduct - Ethical Code	Defined policies and norms related to these behavioural aspects should be described as an independent document; these rules also embody the social value for VBE.
Conflict resolution policy - Dispute Management	For both, ethical and technical disputes among VBE members (or any stakeholders) and the definition of manners how they will be worked out must be depicted.

Contract enforcement policy	The policies for sanctioning those members that does not apply contracted terms with VBE are described in the incentive and sanctions system.
Purchasing and management of outsourced services	Define specific rules for outsourced services; these rules must be in accordance with general principles and bylaws.
ICT principles and security policies	Allocating the roles and rights for each member; and access level for ICT tools and responsibility in its utilization.

Business Process Management

Rule	Description
Collaborative Opportunity qualification (scope compatibility control)	According to the characteristics of VBE to be created, it is necessary to evaluate the competences of potential partners, and identify the scope of process and performance, naming rules that constrain the qualification of collaborative opportunities development.
Commercial processes	Policies related to sales, and establishment of business relationships, contacting, and how to disclosure obtained information, are issues to define related to commercial processes.
Marketing	Rules related to marketing activities, success projects progressing, brand, recognition and prestige. VBE launching will need publicity campaigns and use of different communication channels to introduce the concept into the market and industry. Rules to govern the marketing should be defined for each VBE.
Responsibility	The rules to define and allocate roles and responsibilities for all VBE actors correspond to proper bylaws in each VBE. A general description about responsibility management and assignment.
VO constitution process	How to select and evaluate partners, contracting process, and operation principles definition are some rules to establish for VO constitution process.

Membership Management

Rule	Description
Membership qualification criteria and associated processes	Selection of partners that will be members of the VBE. Qualification and evaluation criteria in order to avoid partial and unfair preferences.
Membership agreements (benefits and dues) and subscription process	Before becoming member, each organisation must know benefits, liabilities and rights when participating in a VBE.
Member profiles management	Requirements and functionalities to be governed are described in a profile and competency management System, and rules to update information in the system
Members' internal evaluation processes	Some rules to assess the performance of the member as well as social elements that affect VBE work; must be defined. Metrics to measure performance, trust and value generation, will address the conformation of an internal evaluation process.
Membership control and governance	The incentive and sanction system defined through the identified metrics will facilitate decision making about memberships concession or retirement.

Knowledge Management

Rule	Description
Information sharing	Rules related to exchanging information, and sharing experiences and business opportunities.
Community Body of Knowledge management processes	Collecting, maintaining and enriching the knowledge body are the main goals to be achieved through definition of rules that focus on them.
Internal projects for Knowledge creation	The challenge is to identify where the knowledge is created, and from there to generate applications or models to keep, and enlarge it. Rules related to this process should also be defined.
Intellectual Property Rights management rules	IPR is an important issue to be considered when the VBE is operating. Define the owner of rights (sharing patents, selling or licensing patents) is a task for VBE manager advised by a supporting institution (preferably an external member of the VBE).

Members' general interaction	Cultural values combined with ethical attitudes, and supported by a good technical performance, allow members to generate an identity where they will follow and operational rules, breeding a good interaction environment.

Most tasks for defining VBE governing are given to VBE manager and VBE advisor (for instance a specialized professional in laws, or an experienced support institution as consulter in network management). The VBE manager is in charge to administrate all tasks for the right daily performance of the VBE (assignment & reassignment of responsibilities, conflict resolution, making common VBE policies, etc.). The definition of specific governance rules will depend on many criteria as VBE type, amount of members, past performance records, among others.

3.4 Governance and ICT support tools

The need for a collaborative space where rules and principles can be published and improved, and where vision, strategies and decisions can be shared, makes to think about some web-tool which could help to solve this problem. A CSCW (Computer Supported Collaborative Work) tool could be one solution to share and promote governance rules and principles. Nevertheless, further research is required in this subject.

4 CONCLUSIONS

The VBE Governance can be defined as the people, policies and processes that provide the framework within which managers make decisions, negotiations and accommodations between parties involved and take actions to optimize functionalities, relationships and performance. In general all outcomes related to the spheres of responsibility inside the Virtual Breeding Environment.

The VBE bylaws will need to be written down in document that will contain the ground rules by which a breeding environment will be run. Bylaws normally establish such matters as the titles and duties of the VBE actors, the timing and procedures for collaborative opportunities, and the manner for conducting the VBE administration.

5 ACKNOWLEDGEMENT

The research presented in this document is a contribution for the ECOLEAD Project, funded by the European Community, FP6 IP 506958. The authors wish to acknowledge the support of the Innovation Center in Design and Technology from ITESM - Campus Monterrey.

6 REFERENCES

1. Camarinha-Matos, L.M. and Afsarmanesh, H. (2006). In K. Wang et al (Ed.). Knowledge Enterprise: Intelligent Strategies in Product Design, Manufacturing and Management. International Federation for Information Processing (IFIP), Volume 207 (pp. 26-40). New York: Springer Publisher.

2. GGB   (2002).   "Governance   International".   Retrieved   on   March,   2007,   from:
    http://www.governanceinternational.org/english/about.html
3. Gilsing, Victor (2000). "Cluster Governance". DRUID PhD-conference, Copenhagen.
4. Graham, John; Amos, Bruce and Plumptre, Tim (2003). "Principles of Good Governance in 21st
    Century". Policy Brief. IOG Canada.
5. Kumar, Poonam (2005). "Driving Globalisation without its discontents – Roles of Corporates
    Proceedings of Corporate Governance challenges in a disparate world". London, England.
6. Schein, Edgar H. (1992). "Organizational Culture and Leadership". 2nd Edition, San Francisco CA,
    USA. Retrieved on March, 2007, from: http://www.12manage.com/methods_schein_three_levels_
    culture.html

Antonio P. Volpentesta, Salvatore Ammirato
Università della Calabria, ITALY
volpentesta@deis.unical.it, *ammirato@deis.unical.it*

A Technological District (TD) is a form of Collaborative Network in a limited geographical area, where a variety of economic entities (enterprises, research centres, public administrations) are involved in high-intensive research activities and distributed scientific-technological processes, including knowledge sharing and technological innovation. In this paper, we hypothesize a TD scenario where a Virtual Breeding Environment (VBE) defines main working and sharing principles in order to enable collaboration between its members. One important goal is that of increasing chances and preparedness of TD members in the constitution of Virtual Organizations (VOs). We introduce a VBE organisational framework for a TD and we propose an approach to identify configurations of a VO addressed to carry out an innovation project.

1   INTRODUCTION

The territorial dimension of scientific research and technological transfer activities is absolutely significant in a knowledge economy development on local basis. This is shown by several examples (e.g.: Silicon Valley and Bangalore) which exhibit some common characteristics:

- presence of Universities or Research Centres able to transfer knowledge to the local territory;
- an industrial structure able to absorb and utilize such knowledge;
- presence of dynamic local governments and category associations;
- a system of SMEs that, as "technological partner" becomes the contact point between research institutions and large enterprises
- consolidated fund rising activities.

This has led to the concept of Technological District (shortly, TD), i.e. a regional cluster of learning firms and institutions (universities, consultants, research centres, spin-offs), working in complementary technologies, in terms of the quality of all of the communication networks within which technological information is shared and transmitted from one firm to another, (Antonelli, 2000). The development of a plurality of dissimilar but complementary cooperative relationships in a collaborative network is the key source of innovation. Empirical evidences are given in (Patrucco, 2003; Quintana-García and Benavides-Velasco, 2005).

In a TD, value creation is strictly cooperative and collaborative while value capture is essentially competitive. This kind of strategic interdependence is known as "coopetitive system of value creation" (Nalebuff and Brandenburger, 1997). The incentive to collaborate derives from the fact that the success of a firm doesn't necessarily mean the failure of the others and different forms of cooperation may be adopted in order to enhance, at the same time, individual and common interests.

An emerging experience of TD is represented by the Logistics and Production TD in the area around the Gioia Tauro (Calabria, Italy) seaport.

Volpentesta, A.P., Ammirato, S., 2007, in IFIP International Federation for Information Processing, Volume 243, Establishing the Foundation of Collaborative Networks; eds. Camarinha-Matos, L., Afsarmanesh, H., Novais, P., Analide, C.; (Boston: Springer), pp. 103–110.

Economic activities in the area of Gioia Tauro can be classified along 3 levels:

1. commercial transit (core functions): essentially based on transhipment activities carried out by 2 main terminal operators ("Medcenter Container Terminal" and "BLG Automobile Logistcs Italia");
2. seaport services (support functions). They can be grouped in: transport and shipping services (e.g.: shipping companies and linear agents), cargo handling at the terminals (e.g.: cargo controlling or warehousing companies), services dedicated to the maritime customers of the seaport (e.g.: reparation, cleaning of ships) and port authority services (management of property assets, safety regulations, environmental protection, etc) ;
3. hinterland industries (secondary functions): these activities generate added value to the goods through transformation and semi-product manufacturing processes (the containerised goods are removed from the containers, transformed, packaged again, controlled, labelled, etc.). At the time being, these activities have very limited extension but the territory shows a good growth potential; as matter of fact, a plethora of SMEs of different manufacturing industries (especially woodworking, agrifood and packaging) as well as insurance and bank companies (focused on transportation and ship insurance, trade financing, etc.) are located in the Gioia Tauro area.

The depicted economic structure and the presence in Calabria of logistic and production research centres (labs at University of Calabria and at University of Reggio Calabria, CNR centres,...) concur to the establishment of favourable conditions for a TD. In 2005, the National and Local Governments established a "Framework Program Agreement", in order to foster a "Logistic and Production TD" in the area of Gioia Tauro. The objective is pursued through the promotion of innovation projects (shortly, IPs) in *advanced supply chain management, cross-docking and materials handling management, coordination of finishing and packaging activities (quality control, product assembly, finished goods packaging), demand chain and order fulfilment management (cost-effective pick up, delivery and reverse logistics), control of pallets and container pooling activities.*

In this paper, we present some results emerging from research activities developed in one of these projects, namely "LogNET-LOGICA". A framework, based on a Virtual Breeding Environment (briefly, VBE)[1] structure, is introduced in order to enable collaborative innovation processes in a TD; particular emphasis is addressed to the problems of:

- characterizing a TD network where Virtual Organisations (shortly, VOs) may emerge;
- identifying competencies in partners and organisational structures of a VO specifically addressed to carry out an IP.

Similar problems have been already faced in previous action research projects, e.g. the "Virtual Factory" project (Schuh et al, 1998), and a process theory of

---

[1] In (Camarinha-Matos and Afsarmenesh, 2005a) a VBE is defined as "an association or pool of organizations and their related supporting institutions that have both the potential and the interest to cooperate with each other, through the establishment of a "base" long term cooperation agreement. When a business is identified by one member, a subset of the VBE members can be rapidly selected to form a virtual organisation"

competency rallying, grounded in a study of successful VOs, has been given in (Katzy and Crowston, 2001). Main contribution of our work consists in providing a mechanism to identify and marshal competencies in a TD, that is, to structurally determine what competencies and from which partner companies are required to carry out a specific IP.

2 REQUIREMENTS FOR A TD-VBE MODEL

In a TD, strong and long-lasting relationships among actors often leads to rigid specialization situations and the TD governance structure becomes very similar to a traditional hierarchy, losing flexibility and global competitiveness. Such a situation determines the need to establish "weak connections" among partners to facilitate the possibility of a TD actor to frequently be a member of different value chains.

In order to achieve the required level of organizational flexibility, the temporariness of collaboration assumes a strategic importance: a TD actor could choose time to time the most appealing cooperation with other actors and provide its expertise in many different temporary organizations. A TD-VBE, i.e. a VBE whose members are economic actors of a TD, can realize and improve coopetitive dynamics among TD actors in order to carry out IPs. In a TD-VBE, instead of the prevailing fixed and long-term partner relationship, short-term and dynamic coalition among TD actors becomes the main stream. A TD-VBE management model may be based on:

Flexible "weak connections" networks. In a TD the division of labour is cognitive based. Each TD actor carries out well defined activities in a value chain and, at the same time, it continuously develops know how and products/process/organization innovation. In a TD-VBE, dynamic actor aggregations, based on flexible weak connections, may be created, time to time, to provide innovative solutions for business opportunities. Under this perspective, a TD-VBE can potentially be regarded as a permanent laboratory of research and innovation.

TD knowledge management. In a TD, the knowledge capital (know how, best practices, relations among TD actors consolidated by practice, etc.) constitutes an important source of competitive advantage in global markets. In a TD-VBE, through an effective knowledge management, each innovation, even if realized by a single actor, rapidly becomes property of the whole district and, thus, shared with other TD actors.

Strong competition among TD actors. Making a TD actor rapidly informed about real capabilities of any others, a TD-VBE determines positive competitive effects among actors that could be involved in a same value chain stage. In other words, the local B2B market turns out to be highly transparent: the best production supplier, the most effective services supplier, the cheapest and the most innovative logistic provider are known by everyone in the TD.

The introduction of a TD-VBE is a necessary context for effective creation of VOs as confirmed by recent surveys (Katzy and Sung, 2003). Such studies highlight that most projects assume the existence of a stable source network (a VBE) from which short-term cooperation in VOs emerges. Furthermore, most of the reported projects do not provide information on the VBE model even when the source network is considered the indispensable factor for the creation of VOs.

A TD-VBE may provide most of the advantages described in (Camarinha-Matos and Afsarmanesh, 2005b) but, of course, it needs to be properly managed during its entire life cycle (i.e.: creation, operation and metamorphosis). In next sections, we focalize our attention only on a base functionality in the TD-VBE operation stage: the VO management[2].

3   MANAGING A VO IN A TD-VBE

In what follows we describe main organizational variables for the management of collaborative innovation processes in a TD-VBE. In particular we consider market-driven innovation that could happen when a solution for a new business problem is requested by some TD actors and this request is needed to be converted into an IP. A suitable combination of technical expertises are needed to be found in the TD-VBE in order to match the problem with a technology. An IP is a project carried out by a VO specifically addressed to innovate a product, a method of production, a form of business organization or simply uses for existing products.

TD Actors/Relationship

One of the critical aspects for the success of a TD consists in the pre-existence on the TD territory of specialised actors involved in scientific and technological knowledge management processes. The presence and role of research centres in a TD represents the main difference between classical Industrial Districts (IDs), which rapidly spread in Italy and Japan since the seventies, and TDs. In the Italian experience, IDs did not developed around Universities and they do not present high tech vocation (in contrast with the Cambridge and Silicon Valley experiences). Of course, other fundamental TD actors, that can be connected through a number of different types of relationships (e.g. client-supplier, knowledge sharing, collaborative design, etc) are represented by enterprises in the TD. Strongly dependent on the local dimension of the TD, a set of factors can condition the TD development and TD the actors relationship (availability of specialized and cheap human resources; diffused entrepreneurial spirit; strong connections with the outlet markets; effective choices in regional and national policy).

TD-VBE Roles

In the TD-VBE four main roles are present:

TD-VBE member. A TD actor may become a TD-VBE member once showing its readiness to contribute in TD-VBE activities and its willingness to be involved in possible VOs. Each of them assumes a set of responsibilities in business relationships with other TD-VBE members and has a set of rights/authorizations needed to enjoy supporting tools and services provided by the TD-VBE service centre.

TD-VBE service centre (TD-SC). In a TD-VBE, multiple value activities are performed by different TD-VBE members that work together in a value network, i.e. a web of relations needed to generate economic value through complex value exchanges among involved actors. This value network requires a variety of supporting information services. Such services may be provided by a TD-VBE Service Centre (shortly, TD-SC) in order to promote cooperation among TD-VBE

---

[2] A detailed list of base functionalities required at any VBE life cycle stage is provided in (Camarinha-Matos et al. 2005a).

members, to fill skill/competency gaps in the TD-VBE, to make available value added services and organizational/technological standards, to define an "ethical code" and behavioural rules in collaboration processes, to improve coordination among TD-VBE members and to transfer knowledge patterns from research centres to enterprises. Furthermore, the TD-SC acts as an aggregator of TD-VBE members for the development of High-Tech programmes; in particular, it identifies the network of all possible configurations of a VO addressed to carry out an IP.

Collaboration catalyst. It is a TD-VBE member that markets TD competencies and assets, negotiates with (potential) customers and identifies new business opportunities. It launches through the TD-SC a request to collaborate in an IP. Successively, it evaluates and selects a configuration of potential collaborators among the ones proposed by the TD-VBE service centre.

Potential collaborator. It is a TD-VBE member that has declared its willingness to collaborate in an IP. In order to asses technical feasibility of innovative ideas it may launch through the TD-SC a new request to collaborate in an innovation subproject and may respond to some others. A potential collaborator participates to the negotiation phase aimed to form a VO only if it belongs to the collaboration configuration selected by the catalyst.

TD-VBE activities

Main TD-VBE activities and roles are represented in tab.1

Table 1 – Activities and roles in a TD-VBE

Activity	Responsible	Participants
Customer Relationship Management	Collaboration catalyst	TD-SC
Identifying a collaboration business opportunity	Collaboration catalyst	
Launching a request to collaborate in an IP	Collaboration catalyst.	TD-SC
Building a potential collaboration network	TD-SC	TD-VBE members, potential collaborators
Identifying the candidate VO-configurations sub-network	TD-SC	
Managing the development of feasibility studies for any IP	TD-SC	Potential collaborators
Evaluating potential collaboration configurations	Collaboration catalyst	TD-SC, potential collaborators
Selecting a collaboration configuration	Collaboration catalyst	
VO formation negotiation	Collaboration catalyst	Selected potential collaborators, TD-SC

VO activities and roles

The success of a VO depends on a balanced provision of management competencies, co-ordination roles and an effective innovation process management. A set of roles and activities should be taken into account for the VO management:

Roles:

the VO partner is a selected potential collaborator that operates in the VO according to a "cooperation agreement" stipulated in the negotiation phase. Each VO partner is responsible for a step in the VO value chain and develops a dedicated interface with the VO to interact with other VO partners. It offers technological know how, resources and expertise to the VO as well as it is exposed to ideas and demands that would have not been apparent operating outside the VO;

the <u>VO broker</u> has the responsibility to market the VO and to retail its competencies. Besides organizing the response to a customer request, the VO broker acts as a promoter to develop and multiply a market opportunity through interaction with involved stakeholders;

the <u>VO coordinator</u> is a TD-VBE member that has been selected by the VO partners in order to organize and coordinate decisional processes in the VO life cycle. It supervises the operations of the VO offering time, project management, and budget control. Additionally the VO coordinator could manage the knowledge engineering process, e.g. replacing partners who do not perform satisfactorily;

the <u>VO service provider</u> enables and supports VO life cycle processes by providing VO partners with technological and information tools and standards, best practices and successful communication models.

Activities

Main activities and roles in the VO life cycle phases are represented in tab.2.

Table 2 – VO life cycle activities and roles

Activity	Responsible	Participants
VO creation		
"Cooperation agreement" stipulation + VO coordinator selection	VO broker	VO partners
Resources analysis and sub-processes definition	VO coordinator	VO partners
Risk analysis	VO coordinator	VO broker
Mapping VO activities on VO members + Virtual Process Breakdown	VO coordinator	VO partners
Selection and integration of elementary critical processes	VO coordinator	VO service provider
Formal definition of process responsibility and authority	VO coordinator	VO partners
Information system design	VO coordinator	VO service provider
Legal aspects and quality standards definition	VO coordinator	VO broker + VO service provider
VO operation		
VO launching	VO coordinator	VO Broker
Virtual process coordination + Risk management + Business process management and monitoring + Quality control and logistic management	VO coordinator	VO service provider
VO dissolution		
Information storing and sharing among partners	VO broker	VO coordinator + VO service provider
Result evaluation	VO broker	VO coordinator + VO partners
Intellectual knowledge property management	VO coordinator	VO broker + VO service provider + VO partners

4   IDENTIFYING VO CONFIGURATIONS IN A TD-VBE

In a TD-VBE, the nature of collaborations is characterized by a high rate of innovation based on continuous knowledge sharing and research results dissemination. When an IP is required to be collaboratively decided on, the classical sequential approach to the identification of partners and configuration of a VO cannot always be applied, (Volpentesta and Muzzupappa, 2005). A more effective approach may be based on building a network of candidate VO configurations, on evaluating them and on selecting the most adapt for the development of the required

IP. The first part of this process is based on a top-down phase and a bottom-up phase3. The top-down phase consists of two sequential steps:

- building a "potential collaboration network". In such a network a weak relationship between two TD-VBE members is established whenever one of them expresses its interest in collaborating on an IP (or sub-project) proposed by the other one;
- identifying the sub-network of all candidate VO-configurations. A candidate VO-configuration is a structured minimal cluster (TD-VBE economic entities and their weak inter-relationships) capable, in principle, to collaboratively develop a feasibility study for the IP identified by the catalyst.

The second phase consists of the bottom-up development of feasibility studies for the IP carried out by potential collaborators in the candidate VO-configurations sub-network.

Building a potential collaboration network. This step starts as soon as the catalyst launches an initial request for collaboration on an IP p^* (shortly, RFC(p^*)) and it takes place in a lapse of time established by the TD-SC. At any moment a TD-VBE member could select an RFC(p), amongst the ones forwarded by the TD-VBE Service Centre, and decide to announce its intention to collaborate on p (in such a case, it may launch other requests for collaboration on some subprojects of p). More precisely, when a TD-VBE member decides to collaborate on p, it becomes a potential collaborator through sending to the TD-SC an expression of interest to respond to RFC(p), conditional on obtaining responses to RFC(p_i), where p_i is a subproject of p, $i=1,..,n$.

Multiple executions of this task, carried out by different TD-VBE members, induce a recursive formation of a potential collaboration network that is represented through a conceptual data model at the TD-SC side.

Identifying the candidate VO-configurations sub-network. In this step TD-SC analyses the potential collaboration network in order to select only those potential collaborators and expressions of interest that could be an integral part of a VO-configuration. In this task the TD-SC could be supported by a Decision Support System based on results presented in Volpentesta (2007) where the logical structure underneath a VO-configuration has been theoretically and algorithmically characterized. On one hand, the logical structure of a VO defines a top-down decomposition of the initial IP in gradually less complex subproject; on the other hand, it identifies potential collaborators and the requirements of their knowledge exchanges and collaborations in a VO-configuration.

Managing the development of feasibility studies. In this step the TD-SC is required to manage the process of recursive composition of feasibility study tasks carried out by potential collaborators along the candidate VO-configurations sub-network. A feasibility study task consists of an analytical and experimental investigation description about an innovative product or a business process in compliance with requirements set out in the RFC(p) which the potential collaborator is responding to. Of course, a potential collaborator could complete its assigned task

---

[3] Volpentesta and Muzzupappa (2006) have faced the case of collaborative projects for innovative product concept design. They have proposed a process formal model making use of logical structures based on concepts related to direct hypergraphs.

only if it has received all the required responses to RFC(p_i), where p_i is a subproject of p, $i=1,..,n$.

Once this three steps process has been carried out by the TD-SC and potential collaborators, a sub-network of candidate VO-configurations as well as their corresponding feasibility studies have been determined. Successively, the collaboration catalyst evaluates them and selects the most promising one for the formation of a VO.

5   CONCLUSIONS AND FUTURE WORKS

In this paper we have introduced a VBE organisational framework specifically addressed to enable collaborative innovation processes in a Technological District. Most of these processes relies on the identification of an effective configuration of a VO that can convert a market request, based on social needs and customer requirements, into an IP.

Besides, we have proposed an approach to identify a network of candidate VO-configurations and to manage feasibility studies for an IP along this network. An early and partial implementation of the approach has been carried out in the project "LogNET-LOGICA", through involving some research labs of the three universities in Calabria and few enterprises of the TD of Gioia Tauro. However, further research activities should be developed to fully implement and validate such an approach.

6   REFERENCES

1.   Antonelli C. "Collective Knowledge Communication and Innovation: The Evidence of Technological Districts", Regional Studies, 2000, 34:6, 535-547.
2.   Camarinha-Matos LM, Afsarmanesh H, Ollus M. "ECOLEAD: a holistic approach to creation and management of dynamic virtual organizations". In Collaborative Networks and Their Breeding Environments, eds. Camarinha-Matos L, Afsarmanesh H, Ollus M., Boston: Springer, 2005a,.3-16.
3.   Camarinha-Matos LM, Afsarmanesh H. "A framework for management of Virtual Organization Breeding environments". In Collaborative Networks and Their Breeding Environments, eds. Camarinha-Matos L, Afsarmanesh H, Ollus M, Boston: Springer, 2005b, 35-48.
6.   Katzy B, Crowston K. "A process theory of competency rallying in engineering projects". Draft of 06 April 2001, retrieved at http://crowston.syr.edu/papers/virtual-short.pdf, accessed on March 2007.
7.   Katzy B, Sung G. "State of the art of Virtual Organization Modeling". In Proceedings of eChallenges Conference– Building the Knowledge Economy Bologna, Italy, 22-24 October 2003.
8.   Nalebuff BJ and Brandenburger AM. Coopetition. London: HarperCollinsBusiness, 1997.
10.   Patrucco PP. "Institutional Variety, Networking and Knowledge Exchange: Communication and Innovation in the Case of the Brianza Technological District'" Reg Studies, 2003, 37:2, 159-172
11.   Quintana-García C, Benavides-Velasco CA. "Agglomeration economies and vertical alliances: the route to product innovation in biotechnology firms", International Journal of Production Research, 2003, 43:22, 4853-4873
11.   Schuh G, Millarg K, Göransson A. Die Virtual Factory. Stuttgart: Hanser Verlag, 1998.
12.   Volpentesta AP. "Hypernetworks in a directed hypergraph", to appear in European Journal of Operational Research, 2007, doi:10.1016/j.ejor.2007.04.023.
13.   Volpentesta AP, Muzzupappa M, "The formation of collaborative chains for conceptual design". In Collaborative Networks and Their Breeding Environments, eds. Camarinha-Matos L, Afsarmanesh H, Ollus M, Boston: Springer, 2005,.89-96.
14.   Volpentesta AP, Muzzupappa M. "Idetifying partners and organizational logical structures for collaborative conceptual design". In Network-Centric Collaboration and Supporting Frameworks, eds. Camarinha-Matos L, Afsarmanesh H, Ollus M, Boston: Springer, 2006, 224: 397-406.

12

IN SEARCH FOR AN INNOVATIVE BUSINESS MODEL OR HOW TO BE SUCCESSFUL IN THE NOWADAYS BUSINESS ENVIRONMENT

Brane Semolic

INOVA Consulting,
University of Maribor, Faculty of Logistics, Celje, Slovenia
Toolmakers Cluster of Slovenia
brane.semoli@siol.net

Classical organization of work does not support the nowadays needs of global market, competition and knowledge intensive economy anymore. The problem is how to maintain and develop the competitiveness at the global level. The article discusses global trends, new theoretical concepts, related problems and questions with some practical examples.

1 INTRODUCTION

The globalization and the fast technological changes require the organizations to develop competitiveness at the global level. This poses great problems, particularly to small and medium -sized enterprises (Case Study of Slovenia) having available limited resources, such as personnel, money, development – operational capacities or knowledge. Therefore, it is urgently necessary that they focus on selected business areas, where they are likely to develop and reach the global competitiveness. Other products or services required for performing their current or anticipated business activity can be procured outside their own organization on the global market. Generally speaking, the technologically developed companies from developed countries in most cases try to find production partners with cheap manpower for performing activities with lower added value. The organizations from technologically less developed regions try to find the business partners for development and transfer of new technologies into practice in their own companies. Of course, for the organizations from developed and less developed countries and regions there can be several reasons why they try to find business partners outside their own organization. Here, the organizations, wanting to develop by constant innovating in all areas of business activities, are concerned.

2 THE GLOBAL MEGA TRENDS

2.1 The New Age Economy

The fast technological development has brought about not only an expansive and fast development of new products and services but it also has caused that due to new technologies, particularly in the area of information science, telecommunications and

Semolic, B., 2007, in IFIP International Federation for Information Processing, Volume 243, Establishing the Foundation of Collaborative Networks; eds. Camarinha-Matos, L., Afsarmanesh, H., Novais, P., Analide, C.; (Boston: Springer), pp. 111–122.

transport the world has become smaller. Of course the world has not become smaller physically but the possibilities of communication and physical accessibility and the information control of the world have increased and cheapened and are still increasing and cheapening. One of the most important generic technologies is the INTERNET technology which has ensured the beginning of formation of a new economic order just like the steam machine technology had ensured the development of the industrial age.

Since a few recent decades in the area of global division of work we have been facing the changes of the conventional work division pattern based on the assumption that the economically developed countries develop and produce industrial products, whereas the less developed countries provide the raw materials and represent the market for these products. That process of changes started slowly to develop already immediately after the second world war. In the today's developed world economy we already face complex and intertwined situations, where the segmentation of the economic activities and their relocation all over the world take place. New, economically rapidly developing regions appear, which together with old centers of the developed countries form the new complex and intertwined whole of the global economy. The business associations supported by the modern information – communication and transport technology are intensifying between the individual regions. A new work division based on knowledge – oriented economy is being established. The countries and regions having enough knowledge to develop the world competitive offer will enjoy successful economic development, whereas those not managing to do that will have to be satisfied with economic subordination.

2.2 Searching for the new innovative business models

Modern companies are permanently analyzing their business activities and the global market and are searching for business opportunities to improve the competitive capacities of their own company. New forms of network organization of the business activities of the companies appear which organize the individual business activities in the regions favorable from the business point of view with respect to the prices of manpower, special know-how as well as raw materials etc. Trans-national research, development and production networks are being formed and their formation and development are influenced by the extent of development of the business of the involved countries, regions, national and regional government rules and regulations, social and cultural conditions etc. The world becomes a more and more intertwined network consisting of a series of different trans-national networks and specialized economic entities, working in different parts of the world, included in it. Analyses of the geo-economic map show that the business activities can be distributed or concentrated but there is a tendency to organize such activities in the frame of geographically localized clusters.[1] Porter defines a cluster as a geographically proximate group of companies and associated institutions in a particular field, linked by commonalities and complementarities.[2] The industrial clusters can be formed as a result of the spontaneous development of a country of region or as a result of the implementation of the development policy of some country or region. Industrial clusters are often formed in close association with certain industrial branch or sector.

[1] Dicken P. Global Shift, 2003
[2] Porter M.: Cluster and new economics of competition, Harvard Busniess Review, 6, 1998

Companies and organizations operating inside such cluster have the tendency towards closer business collaboration and association. The industrial clusters include companies, banks, educational and research institutions etc (Figure 1). Usually, such associating has a favorable influence on the growth of the innovation capacity of the economy involved and on the increase of its business success. Industrial clusters are aimed at increasing the global competitive capacity of the included part of economy in the selected area of its activities and, consequently, of the entire related geographic area.

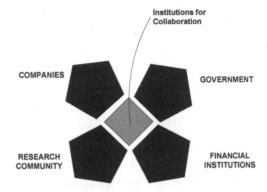

Figure 1: Partners of industrial cluster [3]

The business interest is one of the basic driving forces for formation and development of the industrial cluster. Formation and development of the individual segments of the cluster can be one or several companies wanting in this way to assure better conditions for developing own competitive capacity.

The nowadays companies need to search and maintain their key competence on the global level. This generate permanent problem to all companies worldwide. Especially for a small and medium sized companies (SME's) with limit resources. Clusters bring(s) SME's an opportunity to be more competitive on the global market. Such a small or medium sized company needs to see the cluster as an opportunity how to develop(e) a more innovative and efficient business model. Searching of the companies key competences and related optimization of the company's value chain by the insourcing and outsourcing become one of the most important strategic questions. The cooperation, collaboration, network organization and networking are "buzz" words of a new business concepts. The modern successful companies are not innovative on technologies only. They are permanently searching for innovations on all areas of their own business model. The typical elements of a company's business model are:

    a.   fundamental business assumption,
    b.   client selection,
    c.   specialization and scope of work,
    d.   differentiation,
    e.   stakeholders value creation,
    f.   procurement system,
    g.   production system,
    h.   go to market system,

[3] *Solvell O. Lindquist G, Ketels K.: The Cluster Initiative Greenbook, Stockholm, 2003*

     i.   research and technology development (RTD) system,
     j.   project management system,
     k. organization architecture design (OAD)
     l.   capital intensity,
     m. knowledge management (KM) system

The managers need to permanently analyze (Figure 2) each parameter of their company business model and to find new ways how to be more effective and efficient according to the existing and foreseen technologies and market situation. The harmonized permanent development of all elements of company's business model can secure companies long term effiency and effectiveness.

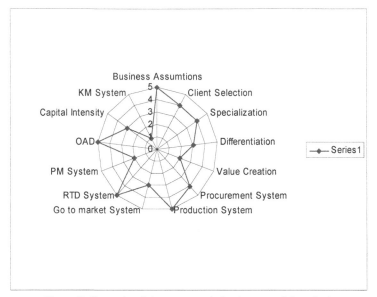

Figure 2: Example of the company's business model analysis

2.3 Changes Obstacles

The organizations must know how to take advantage of the changes brought about by the modern business environment otherwise they may cause much trouble. The extent of changes does not decrease, but it increases. Permanent changes and insecurity are the basic characteristics of the new economic order. In spite of that the changes, in most cases, are not implemented in practice as quickly as it would be desired. Why? Particularly because the execution of changes in own environment is often a difficult task. It is easier to let things happen. However, usually, things do not lead to targets which are so often optimistically written in various development documents and usually related to the international competition and the increase of the competitive capacity of own companies, sectors of economy, industries, regions, countries etc. There are many causes for such situation, including:

- lack of information,
- lack of required knowledge and qualification,
- non-innovative environment,

- wrong beliefs and habits,
- lack of correct motivation,
- lack of entrepreneurial spirit,
- etc.

When analyzing the facts common to all these reasons we find that these are the problems which the modern management must be capable to solve. Here the management as activity and knowledge and the management as personnel performing the tasks are meant.

3   NETWORK ORGANIZATIONS

3.1 Why need for a new business organization

The organizational structure is defined as the sum of methods of how an organization breaks down its operation into the individual business activities and how it coordinates them. The organizational structure is a means by which the management realizes its business targets from the organizational point of view. The process of forming an organization is based on the analysis of the strategic targets and business environment of the organization. The findings so gained help to establish the organizational structure the adequacy of which must be continuously verified. In the present time of changes it may soon happen that the existing organization does no more meet the actual needs of the organization.

The conventional organization of the business activities was based on the high level of the organizational structure and support by the work rules and regulations defined in detail. Modern organization, which has to satisfy the needs of the unstable and fast changing environment is based on the loose management elements such as business targets, strategies and values.

The bases of the theory of companies' organization in the industrial age as set forth by Max Weber, Frederick W. Taylor, Henry Fayol and their contemporaries are based on the bureaucratic model of the organization and business activity structure. The principal characteristics of such organization are the hierarchy, relative impermeability and rigidity. Such a type of organization was adequate for the companies of the industrial age, since the business environment was relatively stable. Today we face the needs of fast development and permanent adaptability, therefore such organization is inadequate. Lately, various forms of network organization have appeared in answer to that problem.

3.2 Enterprise project oriented network- flexible organization

Taking into account that corporations operate within the dynamic environments requiring constant adjustment and development, it is possible to derive that the characteristics of sophisticated corporation are its dynamics, flexibility and quick adjustment, with an everlasting mixture of operative business processes of adjustment and development which require different approaches due to their mutual differences. In order to provide adequate management of business processes of the operation, adjustment and development, it is imperative to be completely familiar with the details of basic principles regarding particular business processes. Closer study of the fundamental properties of described types of business processes reveals that there are actually two types of business processes, namely:

- repetitive – continued business processes and
- non-repetitive – unique type business processes.

Continuous business processes are characteristic for the operative business processes featuring serial, mass production and other similar types of production, where we have to deal with repetitive business processes. From the content and quality aspect such processes remain relatively unchanged. Particular processes differ from each other only in regard to the volume of realization (quantitative dimension) of the already apprehended product/service. Within the network organization it is the matter of carrying out standardized and agreed productions and services, performed by the corporations, participants in the business network. Apart from the mentioned examples, such business processes may be identified also within the business areas (in any company regardless of the characteristics of its basic activity - operation) which provide the required infrastructure necessary for the performance of the basic business management activities of the company.

Unique business processes - *projects*, are present in all companies, whether within the performance of their principal line(s) of business (operative business processes) or within the realization of processes of development and adjustments of the company. These are considered as non-repetitive processes, aimed at realization of single objectives. Essentially this means innovations and innovation processes. In network organization such processes are performed within one corporation, within two of them or within the entire network of participating organizations.

Comparison of functional features and activities of the managerial process required to apprehend particular types of business processes, reveals that they considerably differ from each other. One of the basic differences indicates that in the management of continuous business processes these functions are related to the company resources, while the projects include also external resources, outside the corporation or business network of participating organizations. The term resources here denote all the capacities and other means at the disposition of the manager, employed to realize the set objectives mutually agreed upon. These objectives are situated within certain period of time (week, month, quarter, year), and they are monitored by analyzing the operation of a current period and comparing it with the preceding one. In case of project management one deals with planning, organization, guidance and controlling the resources, aimed at realization of single objectives within the specifically determined period of time. There are numerous differences between the management of continuous business processes and management of projects. Levine underlines the following features of project management, essential for the distinction between the general and project management, and related to the administration of continuous business processes:

- it is not obligatory to employ exclusively the potentials of the company – we may use the potentials of other corporations participating in the project;
- management of the project is a unique process, executed during the period of the performance of the project, which is precisely defined;
- it is necessary to realize precisely defined objectives, also of a single nature and
- Controlling of the project performance is structured according to a particular extent of work or a stage, required to be accomplished, and not according to periods of time as it is the case with the management of continuous activities.

It is perhaps important to mention that the execution of projects usually requires greater "intellectual contribution" from participants, compared to the activities arising from the continuous regular business processes. It is equally important to indicate that the organization of work required for the execution of unique processes – projects is completely different from the organization of continuous business processes. In the first instance we are discussing different forms of project organization, with completely different characteristics and principles compared to the functional organization, which is otherwise usual in the execution of continuous business processes.

It is evident from the above that we are talking about particularities which demand different model of organization and execution of management functions. What we have in mind are above all different manner and approach to planning, organizing, administrating and controlling of business processes, aimed at realization of set objectives.

Basis for the creation of modern organization of a company are strategic business units (SBU), through which the company markets its products and services. Smaller permanent units may be created within the SBU (both within and outside the company) with the task of performing operative duties. For the adjustment and development requirements it is necessary to provide the required organizational background for the creation of temporary project groups, with the task of resolving unique problems.

At the strategic level there is the management of the company, which also has the permanent corporate organizational segment, consisting of the top management with the general administrative support, and temporary groups formed for the performance of projects in regard to the adjustments and development at the level of the whole company. The employed associates have the multifunctional responsibility, which means that they may at the same time be members of one permanent group and members of another project group.

In regard to the levels of authority such modern organization may be asymmetrical, in the sense of divergence, arising from the comparison of operative work within particular SBU.

A great contribution in providing conditions for reducing the number of managerial levels within a company and greater business integration into network organizations must be assigned to the tools of modern information technology which simplifies the communication and the performance of various forms of virtual organization.[4]

By the definition of David Gould[5] a virtual organization can be thought of as a way in which an organization uses information and communication technologies to replace or argument some aspect of the organization. People who are virtually organized primarily interact by electronic means.

Another very important element which must be taken into consideration in the implementation of modern, flexible, project-oriented organization of work within a company (Figure 3) is the cultural environment in which the company functions. What we have in mind is the reflection of general culture, displayed in form of

---

[4] Byrne J., Brand R., in Port O.: The Virtual Corporation, Business Week, (8.2.93), New York, 1993 and Davidov W. H. in Malone M.S. : The Virtual Corporation, Harper-Collins, New York, 1993

organizational culture of a company, and comprises a multitude of values, pre-requisites and confidence which consciously or unconsciously influence the mode of conducting company business. If the organizational culture in the company is at low level, there is great possibility that only organizational changes may not yield worthwhile results. The outcome of an extensive survey, performed several years ago by Denison et al. has indicated that the difference between companies with good business results and those with bad ones in most cases depends upon the propensity of employers, their values and motivation – or in other words, upon the level of the organizational culture of people included in the process. The organizational culture is implicitly related to the strategies of the company, organization and organizational level of the company, and methods of managing the company. Harmony between the organizational culture in a corporation and adequate organization and management enables the company to function rationally and efficiently with minimal, merely formal inspections.

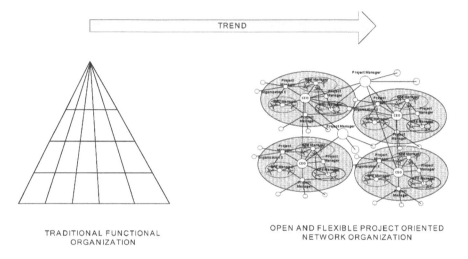

Figure 3: Flexible project oriented network organization is much more effective in nowadays unstable business environment (Semolic B.: Project management, INOVA Consulting, 2005)

4   CASE STUDY – EXPERIENCE FROM SLOVENIA (WWW.SLOVENIJA.SI)

Slovenian economy is mostly presented and powered by the small and medium sized companies. The most presented industrial sectors are automotive, household appliances, machinery, electronics, pharmaceutical and service industries. The global competition and a fast technology development force companies to focus on their key competences and search for a regional and global outsource partners. This process has been started in the nineties and it has characteristics of exponent growth nowadays. To enhance and support the specialization, outsourcing and networking processes, Slovenian government started to support industry clusters and networking projects in the year 2000. This was made according to the results on extensive mapping research, which goal was looking for potential clusters. On the bas is of these results they made

---

[5] *Gould D.: Virtual Organization, daveg@seanet.com, on INTERNET published paper, 2006*

open call for the first pilot cluster initiatives projects on the national level. In this stage the decision for the three pilot cluster project was taken. The proposed projects from the automotive, toolmakers and transport industry were awarded. The results of the first pilot projects followed to open call for a new cluster initiate projects support. This government initiative produced 16 new industrial clusters which included:[6]

- 335 small and medium sized companies,
- 72 big companies,
- 80 research and development institutes and
- 29 supporting organizations (for example: chamber of commerce, regional development agency etc.)

The partners in all clusters started more than 240 joint venture projects. The most common areas of co-operation are:

- Joint R&D projects,
- Joint promotion and related projects
- Joint commercial projects,
- Joint infrastructure development,
- Education and training,
- Etc.

Figure 4: Illustration of Toolmakers Cluster of Slovenia

[6] M.Jaklic and Co.: Final Report, Faculty of Economics, University of Ljubljana, Ljubljana, 2004,

Most of clusters established solid international links and co-operation with the similar or complementary clusters and networks. Figure 4 shows illustrative example of the regional Toolmakers Cluster of Slovenia (www.toolscluster.net).

The performed survey shows that companies see the clustering benefits in improvement of new technologies and know-how acquisition processes, improvement of companies international market visibility, possibility to perform bigger projects, better approach to the international supply/production chains and networks, enhance of company competitiveness etc.

The Figure 5 presents the illustration of the TCS current development project "TCS Laser Engineered Net Shaping (LENS) Living Laboratory (TCS Living Lab). The TCS Living Lab is the virtual dynamic network organization composed by the international group of R&D organizations, product developers and end products and services users. The main purpose of this laboratory is to provide the global cutting edge laser know-how and services to included companies.

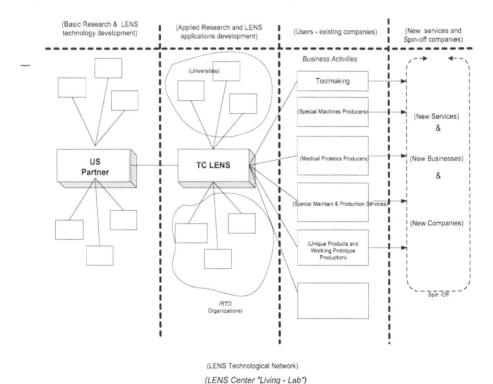

Figure 5: TCS LENS Living Lab

5 CONCLUSIONS

The requirement for continual adjustment is imposed to organizations by the up-to-date environment. Companies are confronted with constantly increasing competitiveness. One of the elementary reasons of increased competitiveness of the business environment is globalization. Mainly the globalization processes impose to companies the requirement for analysis and re-estimation of their strategic orientations as well as modes and forms of operating and activity. The form of company organization is also ranged among areas necessitating radical trans-formation. We can assert that modern organizations have to face with the requirement for continual improvement of their mode or form of organization.

In globalization processes the SMEs (small and medium sized enterprises/companies) are particularly exposed. And just for the said companies it is more and more difficult to achieve competitive advantages due to a great need for concentration of particular types of resources. Formation of network structures appears as a possible solution for SMEs at achievement of competitive capacity in the global business environment. Inter-corporate integration based on a very loose and temporary pooling of the necessary resources at achievement of a certain competitive advantage is the principal characteristic of network connections.

Clusters take a special position among network organizations. Integration and pooling of resources on the regional basis is a very spread form of achieving the competitive capacity at integration of SMEs. In Slovenia SMEs are predominant in the structure of organizations. Due to that the support to integration of SMEs at achieving of their global competitiveness is of significant importance for Slovenia. As it is evident from the presentation of experience in organization of clusters in Slovenia the establishment of network connections between SMEs represents a proper response to difficulties at their achieving of global competitiveness.

REFERENCES

[1] Drucker P.: Managing in the Next Society, St.Martin's Press, New York, 2002,
[2] Lynch, Richard, "Corporate Strategy, 2nd Edition, Prentice Hall, London, 2000.
[3] Kaplan, R S, and Norton, D P, "The Strategy Focused Organization", Harvard Business School Press, 2001.
[4] Murray-Webster R and Thiry M, Gower Handbook of Project Management, 3rd Edition, Chapter 3, "Managing Programmes of Projects", Gower publishing, England, 2000, Ed. Rodney Turner.
[5] Steyn, Pieter G, "Managing Organizations Through Projects and Programmes: The Modern General Management Approach", Management Today, Vol 17, no 3, April 2001.
[6] Steyn, Pieter G, Proceedings of the First Joint IPMA and ICEC Congress, Llubjana, Slovenia, April 2006.
[7] Kotter, John P, "Leading Change", Harvard Business School Press, 1996.
[8] Wyatt, W "Leadership: The Critical Key to Financial Success". Drake Business Review. Volume 1, Issue 1, 2003, pp 21-25.
[9] Dicken P, "Global Shift", Guilford Press, New York, 2003.
[10] Steyn P and Schmikl E, "Progamme Managing Organizational Performance and Improvement", unpublished textbook beta-version, Cranefield College of Project and Programme Management, South Africa.
[11] Semolic B.: A New Economy Trends and Organizational Changes, IPMA & ICEC Expert Seminar, Portorož, 2002,

[12] Semolic B.: The Project Management Organization – "The Quality Breakthrough",
     IPMA&ICEC Expert Seminar, Bled 2003,
[13] Hoffman & Co.: Internationales Projekt-management, DTV, Mainz, 2004.

13

THE ROLE OF UNIVERSITIES DEVELOPING NEW COLLABORATIVE ENVIRONMENTS: ANALYSING THE VIRTUELLE FABRIK, SWISS MICROTECH AND THE TENET GROUP

Myrna Flores*, Claudio Boer*, Charles Huber**,
Adrian Plüss**, Roger Schoch** and Michel Pouly***
*University of Applied Sciences of Southern Switzerland (SUPSI)
Department of Technology and Innovation (DTI)
The CIM Institute for Sustainable Innovation (ICIMSI)
myrna.flores@supsi.ch, claudio.boer@supsi.ch
**University of Applied Sciences of Northwest Switzerland
Institute of Business Engineering (IBE)
charles.huber@fhnw.ch, adrian.pluess@fhnw.ch, roger.schoch@fhnw.ch
***MTO Network/Swiss Federal Institute of Technology, Lausanne (EPFL)
michel.pouly@epfl.ch
SWITZERLAND

In both developed and developing countries, different initiatives are carried out to motivate organisations, mainly companies, to network in new collaborative environments for innovation. In many cases these different initiatives have been promoted by Universities where academic researchers play a very important role by diffusing these networking concepts to local SMEs and by carrying out applied projects to coach firms in the formation of these new collaborative environments. In some occasions, Universities can also join the network to transfer new knowledge during the new product/service development process. The Virtuelle Fabrik and Swiss Microtech in Switzerland and the TeNeT group in India are three successful collaborative environments located in very different settings where the local University has played and still plays an important role for the collaborative environments' continuous evolution and improvement. Therefore, the objective of this paper is twofold: 1) to assess the University key role for developing new collaborative environments and 2) to propose a methodology to benchmark the different initiatives in Universities to develop new collaborative environments.

1   INTRODUCTION

Growing global competition requires companies to be more competitive, improving their productive and business processes to operate in a leaner way. Enterprises are constantly under pressure not only to offer high quality products with competitive prices, but also to be constantly innovative offering new products and services to the international and borderless markets. One current trend is the development of networks within collaborative environments to increase their innovation capability, where usually companies focus on the development and sharing of core compe-tences. As a result, different networking models have emerged, such as Extended Enterprises, Virtual Enterprises and Breeding Environments.

Flores, M., Boer, C., Huber, C., Plüss, A., Schoch, R., Pouly, M., 2007, in IFIP International Federation for Information Processing, Volume 243, Establishing the Foundation of Collaborative Networks; eds. Camarinha-Matos, L., Afsarmanesh, H., Novais, P., Analide, C.; (Boston: Springer), pp. 123–134.

Nevertheless, most of the times research focuses on networks made up mainly of companies, and less attention is paid to the different actors in the territory and the local infrastructure provided to these enterprises by Universities (specially to SME's), which in many cases enable or disable them to be more innovative. Universities play a critical role as a source of fundamental knowledge, therefore should contribute in the formation of new collaborative environments increasing their innovation capabilities and continuous improvement. Universities can in fact be considered as a focal element for the development and dissemination of new knowledge and technologies for the design, development and commercialisation of new products and processes. Therefore, research should also be carried out to analyze and promote different agents in the territory, such as Universities as potential partners to create and be integrated in these new collaborative environments for the transfer of knowledge to foster innovation and promote regional sustainable development. This paper will describe and analyse three case studies where Universities have played an important role to create successful collaborative environments (CE).

2   RESEARCH OBJECTIVES AND APPROACH

The research approach selected was to develop case studies where three different Universities in different locations have enabled the creation of successful collaborative environments. A case study is an examination of a specific phenomenon such as a program, an event, a person, a process, an institution or social group. The bounded system, or case, might be selected because it is an instance of some concern, issue or hypothesis. According to Yin (1994) a case study is an empirical inquiry that investigates a contemporary phenomenon within its real life context, specially when the boundaries between the phenomenon and context are not clearly defined. The **objectives** of the research were to:

- Study how with the support of Universities new collaborative environments can be started by coaching and motivating local companies and entrepreneurs
- Analyze which processes and tools can be proposed by academic partners to enable the network to collaborate sharing information and improving their operative processes.
- Identify how a University collaborates within the collaborative environment transferring new knowledge for innovation.

3   CASE STUDY 1: THE UNIVERSITY OF APPLIED SCIENCES OF NORTHWEST SWITZERLAND (FHNW) AND THE VIRTUELLE FABRIK (VF)

The Virtuelle Fabrik (VF) is the linking together of real companies with the objective of entering new markets or realizing concrete projects that for the individual companies would not be possible in a profitable manner. As the cooperative association offers a broad spectrum of products and services, it is more attractive than the individual SME. With an order orientation, the core competencies of the Virtuelle Fabrik partners are utilized efficiently and flexibly. At present, there are 20 companies in the network, employing a total of 1500 employees. Their core competencies lie in the areas of engineering and services, mechanical processing, precision mechanics, sheet metal processing, metal working, surface treatments, heat treatments, fitting, welding techniques, plastics injection moulding, plastics working, electrical and electronic engineering. In the entire value-added chain, the

VF offers total solutions and services for assemblies and sophisticated components and replacement parts.

Initially, the VF Project was granted financial support by the Swiss CIM (Computer Integrated Manufacturing) Action Program and organized in a process-oriented manner. The time plan for the project was a period of two years (1997 to the end of 1998) and consisted of:

Project Phase I: (1) Analysis and definition, (2) Building of the core network and (3) Prototypical production

Project Phase II: transitioning of the project into independence: it was taken into account that once the project had transitioned into independence, the management processes, main processes, and support processes would continue to function. The basis for management of the project was worked out jointly in a Project Team and voted upon as the project plan. For each process, responsible persons, goals, and resources were defined for the most important activities. Internal project monitoring was conducted each quarter. In the starting phase, the project worked closely with the **Institute for Technology Management (ITEM) at the University of St.Gallen**. The transfer of experience and tools from another VF project, "Euregio Bodensee," went smoothly. In order to coordinate activities between the two networks and allow the mutual exchange of experience, a "VF Forum" was held quarterly. At the end of the two-year period, the network had developed its own dynamics to the extent that it was functioning independently and profitably. **Success Factors** as seen by the partner companies are:

- **The Concept:** The VF is an open, simple, densely woven concept, with rules and roles, which works. With the VF, the required professionalism can become visible.
- **The Structure:** The VF has a flexible structure; the customer deals with only one dedicated customer service representative for all problems and gains the services of the entire value-added chain. The interfaces are fluid.
- **The Market:** The time is ripe for the VF as a business model for the future for the processing of complex tasks in the time allotted. Large-scale customers want to purchase complex goods and services that can be produced reasonably only by value-added chains. This is confirmed by the market's perception and acceptance of virtual companies.
- **The offensive Strategy:** In the entire group of network partners, there is a large proportion of companies that follow expansion strategies and that want to develop the VF accordingly.
- **Innovation Willingness:** The companies in the network have to have enthusiasm for the "new," seek new developments, and be prepared to make the occasional investment even if the potential return is not immediately measurable.
- **Multiplication Effect:** Each company has its own established contacts. If these contacts are pooled, new market opportunities can be targeted. Each member company profits from the networks of the others.
- **Partnership:** The "chemistry" among the partners is good, and their interests point towards the same goals, so they can achieve together what they set out to do. The value of partnership becomes particularly apparent when a company has a project and the others refuse to let the company down, even if they themselves are managing heavy loads. If the relationships are good, you help the partner out. Even those partners that are unable to provide that degree of engagement have to be brought into projects again and again.

- The Culture of Communication: The face-to-face events (conferences for the mutual exchange of experience) have to held frequently enough that thoughts can be exchanged and the "worlds" brought into alignment, so that everyone speaks the same language and follows the same goals. The Executive Committee has the job of making transparent various ways of looking at things, for the network is not looking only to decide by the majority, but rather to examine varying possibilities as well. One of them could turn out to be a potential strength. An Intranet platform was set up to facilitate communication within the VF. Through Intranet communication, all partner companies can post projects and seek possible cooperation partners. One of the ground rules of the VF is that the partner companies must check the Intranet platform at least once a day. This obligation was agreed upon so that projects can be processed as rapidly and efficiently as possible.

- **Know-How:** The VF is a network for knowledge management.
- **1. FHNW key role during the collaborative environment creation phase**
- Project management and administrative tasks (preparation and execution of meetings, animation of work groups, coaching, reporting etc.)
- Know how transfer on networking concepts, prepare, chair and analyse work-shops to create new concepts an processes
- Being a neutral "referee" for the project members
- Identification of the ICT-supportable processes and development of the first web-based intranet platform. This intranet was developed with researchers form the university of applied sciences northwest Switzerland, which is - since the beginning, a partner of the network.
- **2. FHNW role for the Virtualle Fabrik continuous improvement**
- R&D partner for national and international projects (discovering interesting projects, preparation of proposals, taking over R&D activities etc.)
- Active partner of the network as part of the steering-team and in tasks as coaching, administration and new partner acquisition
- Pursue, support and enhance the collaborative ICT-platform
- Combined efforts in publishing scientific papers, books and articles in business magazines.

4   CASE STUDY 2: ECOLE POLYTECHNIQUE FÉDÉRAL DE LAUSANNE (EPFL) AND THE SWISS MICROTECH

The Ecole Polytechnique Fédéral de Lausanne (EPFL) is one of the two Swiss Federal Institutes of Technology. In particular, the Laboratory for Production Management and Processes (LGPP) was created in 1995 in order to answer to the challenges faced by the manufacturing industry in the medium and long-term. The development of collaborative networks has been one of the main objectives in the LGPP's research agenda.

The roots of the Swiss Microtech network can be found in a survey executed in 1998 (Bigoni et al, 1998) by the EPFL on behalf of the Swiss Commission for Technology and Innovation (CTI) of the Swiss federal government which showed the difficulties faced by the screw machining subcontracting branch:

- These small companies were more and more unable to get in touch with large customers of the automobile, electronics and medical branches which drastically reduced the number of their suppliers to those able to provide a complete delivery including engineering, machining, thermal treatments and assembly
- These SME were technically up to date, but their commercial services were lacking and their delivery schedules were too long and not very reliable

Following one of the recommendations of the survey, 10 enterprises belonging to the same professional association decided to start an applied research project aiming to develop a competitor based strategic network and asked for the support of the EPFL to define and lead the project which started in 2000. The first step was the definition of the strategy: the expectations of potential customers were gathered by the way of a questionnaire-based survey followed by interviews with selected potential customers. The definition of the product and market segments to be addressed by the network was directly derived from these results. The structure, roles and business processes were defined and have been tested by simulation during 4 months. Finally, the rules of the game were summarized in a chart to be signed by every partner. The legal framework of Swiss Microtech is an association with lucrative goals. After one and a half year, when the time had arrived to formally create the network, half of the initial project members decided to leave the project. Mistrust and fears were stronger then the desire of collaboration. **An important action of EPFL was to motivate the four most committed members to continue until the creation of Swiss Microtech Enterprise Network, which was officially announced at the end of June 2001. EPFL has been an important facilitator** by taking over the following tasks:

1. During the collaborative environment creation phase
- Preparation and redaction of the funding proposal for the Swiss government
- Project management (preparation and execution of meetings, animation of work groups, coaching, reporting etc.)
- Know how transfer on networking concepts and best practices
- Being a neutral "referee" for the project members
- Enabling the Swiss MICROTECH strategy definition together with clear business processes and organisation.
- **2. EPFL key role for Swiss Microtech continuous improvement**
- R&D partner for national and international projects (discovering interesting projects, preparation of proposals, taking over R&D activities, etc)
- Defining and following students' internships in close collaboration with the network to address specific problems
- Technological surveys and dissemination of results
- Developing new projects to form new collaborative environments in other sectors.

5   CASE STUDY 3: THE INDIAN INSTITUTE OF TECHNOLOGY MADRAS (IITM) AND TENET GROUP

The Indian Institute of Technology, Madras (IIT Madras) is a college of engineering located in Chennai, India. Founded in 1959, it is chronologically the third among the Indian Institutes of Technology established by the Government of India to provide high quality education in **the fields of engineering and technology.**

The TeNeT started in 1994 encouraged by the dream of three professors to develop the rural areas of India: Ashok Jhunjhunwala, Ramamurthi and Gonsalves. The Telecommunications and Computer Networks Group (TeNeT) is a dedicated a R&D network of companies that collaborate closely with IIT professors on the field of telecommunications and computer networking. The mission can be summarized as developing new technologies, fostering research and establishing a man power base in the field of telecommunications and computer networking (Flores, 2006).

The TeNeT group started with a clear vision: To develop new technologies that can be affordable to the rural areas in India by designing and delivering state of the art products that can compete in international markets, which are at the same time specifically suited to developing countries, such as India, in terms of affordability and adaptability. In terms of organisation, TeNeT performs at least one monthly meeting with the partner companies and professors linked to the network to develop new ideas to develop new products. If one idea looks feasible, TeNeT will try to find the adequate partner through the alumni network. After and idea is created (internally or externally), the TeNeT group will evaluate if the competencies are existent within the TeNeT or in IIT. The new technology to be developed should be cost effective and competitive in the global market, focusing on developing countries needs. One key issue about TeNeT is that it has created its own venture capital structure to enable the financing of the new ideas into products. For the TeNeT growth, IIT Madras has provided the infrastructure, such as laboratories and spaces for offices. Up to know, at least six new products have been launched by the TeNeT group.

1. IIT Madras role during the collaborative environment creation phase:

- Identification of market opportunities for new Information and Communication Technologies (ICT) in the rural areas in India
- Discovery and selection of IIT Madras ex-students that could be interested to become entrepreneurs and open start-ups to commercialize the innovations
- Project management and risk analysis for the new product development
- Strong collaboration of IIT Madras researchers and students in the development of the new product. Initially all the start-ups were located inside the campus.
- Searching for seed venture capital for the development of new products

2. IIT Madras role for the TENET group continuous improvement:

- Coaching of the TeNeT group to link the members and perform strategic planning to develop new products as a network
- Coordinating monthly meetings to share ideas and make strategic decisions
- IIT Madras professors act as brokers looking for new ICT market needs and transfer knowledge during the development process.
- Strong dissemination of the TeNeT group by publishing scientific papers.

Table 1. Comparison of the three collaborative environments under analysis

COLLABORATIVE ENVIRONMENT	VIRTUELLE FABRIK	SWISS MICROTECH	TeNeT
UNIVERSITY	FHNW	EPFL	IIT MADRAS
LOCATION	Switzerland	Switzerland	India
GEOGRAPHY	All partners located in the same regional area	All partners located in the same regional area	All partners located in the same regional area
LANGUAGE	German, English occasionally	French, English occasionally	Mainly English, then Tamil and Hindi
INITIAL FUNDING TO DEVELOP THE NETWORK	Swiss Commission for Technology and Innovation (CTI) applied project	Swiss Commission for Technology and Innovation (CTI) applied project	Willingness of professors not paid by a funded research project
FUNDING TO IMPROVE THE NETWORK	Swiss Commission for Technology and Innovation (CTI) and European Commission (FP6)	Swiss Commission for Technology and Innovation (CTI) and European Commission (FP6)	USA venture capital. Some European multinationals like Nokia have also provided funding for R&D
COLLABORATING ENTITIES	Existing companies and FHNW as coach	Existing companies and EPFL as scientific coach	Start-ups and IIT Madras as key partner for knowledge transfer for new developments
COMPANIES	20	7	14
SECTOR	Metal components and parts manufactured by different machining processes	Screw machining enterprises, other machining processes and thermal treatments	Telecommunications new products
SCOPE	Common marketing strategy. Share competences and productive capacity. New Product Development and innovative Solutions	Develop new markets. shorten delivery schedules, increase their flexibility and reduce production costs. Add new services like engineering of parts and logistics	New Product Development coached by IIT Madras. Collective Learning. Technical knowledge Transfer from Universities to companies
MARKET	Solutions - of the concept over the manufacturing up to the care of products within the range of electromechanical building groups to be sold mainly in Europe	90% export mainly to Europe and USA	Initially for rural India; nowadays global mainly other emerging economies (such as Africa and Latin America with the same need for low cost telecommunication technologies).

(continued)

COLLABORATIVE ENVIRONMENT UNIVERSITY	VIRTUELLE FABRIK FHNW	SWISS MICROTECH EPFL	TeNeT IIT MADRAS
COMPETITION AMONG PARTNERS	No direct competition in products on the market but overlap in competences	Yes	No direct competition in products
COLLABORATION MODELS	Breeding Environment enabled by the FHNW and Virtual Enterprise formed by the companies (SMEs)	Breeding Environment enabled by the EPFL and Virtual Enterprise formed by the companies (SMEs)	Breeding Environment enabled by IIT Madras professors and new Virtual Enterprises formed by the companies & IIT Madras according to technological needs
ORGANISATION	Association with responsible units: Steering-Team and Workgroups as much as defined roles: Broker, Order Manager, Coach, In/Outsourcing managers,	Association with lucrative goals. Rules and key roles have been defined: Broker Order Management Coach In/Outsourcing managers	IIT Professors acting as brokers, identifying business opportunities and coaching the network. Strong motivations to file new patents were IIT Madras obtains loyalties.
OPERATIVE PROCESSES	Well defined and shared by all members to manage the complete value chain: Financial Controlling, Marketing and Sales, Development and Member Acquisition, Infrastructure (IT), Training, and Order Processing	Business is done by the members only and each partner is responsible of its own operative processes. Virtual Enterprises are steered by one leading company. The management of the network is supervised by the coach.	Each partner is responsible of its own operative processes.
COLLABORATION ENABLING FACTORS	Common goal to develop new and innovative product(s) Reduction of costs and lead times as a main goal Proximity and Trust Collaborative ICT	Accessing new markets, developing new services and reduction of costs and lead times as main goals Proximity and Trust	Development and sharing of Human Capital New Knowledge Creation Common goal to develop new product(s) Proximity and Trust
INFORMATION & COMMUNICATION TECHNOLOGIES	"Webcorp" developed and provided by FHNW. All partners receive training to use the platform.	Webcorp developed and provided by EPFL in collaboration with FHNW. All partners receive training to use the platform.	Non existent

6   PROPOSED METHODOLOGY TO ASSESS THE UNIVERSITY – COLLABORATIVE ENVIRONMENT (CE)

To analyse the three case studies developed, a four step methodology has been proposed as follows:

1) Identify the types of innovations carried out: To identify how can a University may impact the innovation capabilities of the companies within the collaborative environment (CE), it is necessary to identify the types of innovations that the CE is carrying out. For the analysis, the following levels of innovations will be considered: a) Commercialization of existing technologies new to the domestic market, b) Transfer and customisation of existing technologies new to the domestic or emerging market, c) Changes or Improvements of own products and d) New developments.

2) Classify the types of Collaborative Environment (CE) – University collaborations: Five main types of collaborations have been identified: a) CE Creation and Coaching, b) Information Transfer (students and courses), c) Start-up development (Business plan and business contacts), d) Knowledge enhancement for new product development (joint new product development or acquire loyalties), e) Building Infrastructure (such as ICT platforms, network strategy definition and business roles and rules).

3) Map the Innovation/Network – University Collaboration: Based on the proposed typology of innovations that could be carried out by the network and the proposed classification of possible CE - University interactions, a map can be performed to identify the possible relationship between the innovation activity of the CE and the level of collaboration with the University. Figure 1 shows the map performed for the three case studies under analysis.

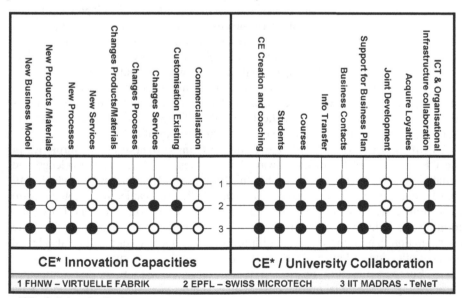

Figure 1. Mapping the CE – University Innovation Capacities and Collaboration

4) Identify the enabling Collaborative Environment – University collaboration factors: One of the main goals of the current research is to identify the possible enabling factors that enabled Universities to develop these new collaborative environments. The high and low frequency of successful Collaborative Environments and University interactions could be the result of many different factors which are present at the national and regional spatial contexts, but also in socio-cultural aspects of companies, such as their decision to invest or not in innovation activities and to trust other partners who in some occasions are competitors. At the same time, Universities internal infrastructure and knowledge transfer mechanisms may motivate or not local companies to consider them as potential partners to coach them and be part of new collaborative environments. The identified enabling factors have been aggregated in four main groups:

1) **Spatial elements**, consider all those factors that are embedded in the nation or region which facilitate the transfer of knowledge to increase the innovative capability of new collaborative environments. **Absorptive capacity**, the ability to learn and innovate by including external information in the learning process, is not only required at companies but also in the Universities. At the same time, the **Innovative Culture**, the need and high motivation to invest in innovation, define innovation targeted policies, learn about new methods to develop new products and being updated of the latest technologies should be a task to be carried out by both companies and Universities to be part of the collaborative environment. This interest to do innovations will actually be the seed that could make these collaborations to emerge. **Proximity** should be seen as a competitive advantage, as actors in the same territory should learn about each other capabilities and look to be closer to target innovations.

2) **University Infrastructure**, refers to all the elements that should be present in Universities to facilitate and encourage collaborations. One key enabler to attract firms is the possibility to use the **laboratories** in Universities which are too costly for companies to sustain and which are necessary for the development of new products and technologies. **Human resources** are also important, in the sense that professors should be motivated and interested to do joint projects with the local networks and motivate them to collaborate. The University should also motivate professors by measuring the impact that their innovations and knowledge transfer activities with local networks. As on most occasions academic researchers don't have experience working in the industry, Universities could define programmes where their professors spend sabbatical periods in the local industries understanding their needs and networking with the business staff as part of the CE.

3) **Information and Knowledge Transfer from Universities to companies in the CE** refers to all the different ways Universities could transfer knowledge and collaborate with companies to enable the formation of new networks which will also be dependent on the absorptive capacity of the companies to be interested to learn from external sources of knowledge (in this case coming from the University forming the collaborative environment). It is important that companies take into consideration that all these sources of information and knowledge will be also based on the motivation and internal strategy from each single company.

4) **Entrepreneurship** regards to the entrepreneur culture of the companies participating in the collaborative environment, being motivated to collaborate with others and start new businesses.

Table 2 shows the comparison of the enabling factors identified in the three collaborative environments:

Table 2. Collaborative Environment (CE) – University collaboration factors

	Virtuelle Fabrik	Swiss Microtech	TeNeT
1) Spatial Elements			
1.1) Absorptive capacity	+++	+++	+++
1.2) Innovative Culture	+++	++	+++
1.3) Proximity	+++	+++	+++
1.4) Informal and Formal Contacts	+++	+++	+++
1.5) Trust	+++	+++	+++
2) University Infrastructure			
2.1) Laboratories	+	+++	+++
2.2) Professors with Industrial Experience	+	+++	+
2.3) Professors motivated to form collaborative environments	+++	++	+++
3) Information and Knowledge Transfer from Universities to companies in CE			
4.1) Students working in company projects	+	+++	+++
4.2) Specialised courses to local industry needs	+	++	++
4.3) Conferences to Industry	+++	++	+++
4.4) Joint R&D Projects	++	+++	+++
4) Entrepreneurship			
4.1) Entrepreneurship Culture	+	+++	+++
4.2) New Business Development Support	++	++	+++
Intensity: +++ High, ++ Medium, + Low			

7 CONCLUSIONS

Industry-University collaboration is increasingly becoming an important topic to spur collaboration for innovation in local networks, specially for many policy makers that aim that these two actors join forces in Collaborative Environments. Nevertheless, as observed from the three case studies presented, it is also quite evident that companies are actually the ones that can push innovations up to their commercialisation and that collaboration is very much dependent on how much open they are to learn and use Universities' knowledge. Companies that don't see any value from the information or knowledge that Universities can provide will not collaborate. On the other hand, some Universities are also much more active providing infrastructures and targeting the needs of the local companies to form these new collaborative environments and to carry out joint developments. In Switzerland the Swiss Commission for Technology and Innovation (CTI) has been a key enabler providing funding to start these collaborative environments. On the other hand, the main encountered problems that academic partners had to form the collaborative environments were:

1. At the beginning, mistrust, specially where members are competitors.
2. Some partners were ready to take but not to give (opportunistic behaviour) .
3. Several organisations did not believe in the collaborative network to innovate or were not able to convince other employees in their own company .
4. Some mistrust against the academic world.

This paper aimed to highlight the importance of Universities to promote and enable the formation of Collaborative Environments by managing applied research projects, diffusing these concepts and coaching companies by presenting three successful case studies: the Virtuelle Fabrik, the Swiss Microtech and the TeNeT group. It is true that working cultures and missions are different, nevertheless both could try to find new mechanisms to make collaborations happen as Universities have played and are playing a key role to create new Collaborative Environments. A methodology was also presented to map the impact of these collaborations including the CE – University Innovation Capacities and identifying four main collaboration factors: 1) Spatial Elements, 2) University Infrastructure, 3) Information and Knowledge Transfer from Universities to companies and 4) Entrepreneurship.

8   REFERENCES

1. Afsarmanesh H, Camarinha-Matos L., A Framework for Management of VO Breeding Environments, In Collaborative Networks and Their Breeding Environments Eds. Camarinha-Matos, Luis M.; Afsarmanesh, Hamideh; Ortiz, Angel, Springer 2005.
2. Bigoni P, Glardon R, Pouly M, Décolletage dans l'arc jurassien, Rappport final CTI, 1998.
3. Flores M., Industry – University Collaborative Networks for New Product Development: The Case of the TeNeT Group in IIT Madras, India presented at the ICE conference, Milan, June 26-27, 2006
4. Flores M., Towards A Taxonomy For Networking Approaches for Innovation presented at the PROVE06 Conference, Helsinki Finland, September 2006.
5. Flores M., Industry – University Collaboration for Innovation and Regional Development: Evidence From Madras, Monterrey, Milan and Lausanne, PhD Thesis, Politecnico di Milano, 2006.
6. Inganäs, M.; Plüss, A. and Marxt C., Knowledge management with focus on the innovation process in collaborative networking companies; in Plüss, A. Network performance management in interaction with network companies, International Journal of Networking and Virtual Organizations, Inderscience Enterprises Ltd, Vol. 3, No 3, p. 283-298, 2006.
7. Plüss A., Network performance management in interaction with network companies, Plüss A. as Editor in Chief, International Journal of Networking and Virtual Organizations, Inderscience Enterprises Ltd, Vol. 3, No 3., 2006.
8. Plüss A., Introduction to Network performance management in interaction with network companies, in International Journal of Networking and Virtual Organizations, Inderscience Enterprises Ltd., Vol. 3, No 3, p. 239-244, 2006.
9. Pouly, M.; Glardon, R. and Huber, C.,Competitor based strategic networks of SME, Knowledge and Integration in Production and Services, Marik, V, Camarinha-Matos, L & Afsarmeanesh, H., Kluwer Academic Publishers, p. 149-156, 2002.
10. Pouly M., Monnier F., Bertschi D., Success and Failure Factors of Collaborative Networks of SME, in "Collaborative Networks and Their Breeding Environments" Eds. Camarinha-Matos, Luis M.; Afsarmanesh, Hamideh; Ortiz, Angel, Springer 2005.
11. Swiss Commission for Technology and Innovation (CTI), http://www.bbt.admin.ch/kti/
12. Yin, R. K., Case Study Research: Design and methods (2nd ed.), Beverly Hills, Sage Publishing.

14 ONTOLOGY ENGINEERING IN VIRTUAL BREEDING ENVIRONMENTS

Dora Simões[1,3], Hugo Ferreira[1], António Lucas Soares[1,2]

INESC Porto[1], Faculty of Engineering Univ. Porto[2], ISCA Univ. Aveiro[3]
dora.simoes@isca.ua.pt, hmf@inescporto.pt, asoares@inescporto.pt
PORTUGAL

This paper proposes a new method for managing the use of ontologies in the context of a Virtual Breeding Environment. This research work focus is on the dissolution phase of a Virtual Enterprise or Collaborative Network, where ontology segmentation techniques are user to enrich the VBE's ontology library. Firstly, an overview of the process of ontology composition and decomposition is given and the ontology library system adopted described. Then, the ontologies' ranking and classification method is described, explaining a set of metrics inspired in social network approaches. Finally, the results of preliminary tests are discussed.

1 INTRODUCTION

Current industrial and technological trends point to the need of SMEs to be able to enter in one or more networks in order to have access to a broader range of market opportunities. The long-term relational structure of cooperating SMEs and the operationalization of market opportunities by collaboration have been conceptualized in some scientific literature as Virtual Breeding Environments (VBE) and Virtual Enterprises (VE), respectively (Bacquet, Fatelnig et al., 2004; Afsarmanesh and Camarinha-Matos, 2005). A VBE is characterised by long-term goal relationships, establishing mutual trust between its members. This is the ideal context for the creation, operation and dissolution of VEs. This process should be as much as possible focused and efficient, in a way that cost and business effectiveness can be achieved. On the other hand we can generalise and consider a VBE not only as being a catalyst of VEs but also of Collaborative Networks (CN) (seen here as a special case of networks whose nodes are mainly SMEs). In the future, VEs and CNs will tend to be formed and to exist for short periods of time, i.e., the time needed to complete a business opportunity. How to structure the information for purposes of supporting the activities of temporary collaborative networks will therefore be a major difficulty in the establishment of the semantic agreements that will be the cornerstone for sharing information and knowledge.

In this paper we propose a method for the management of the knowledge structures required in the formation, operation and dissolution of a VE or CN. More specifically it focuses on the composition and segmentation of domain ontologies supporting information and knowledge management in VEs or CNs. The research focus lies essentially in the dissolution phase, which has not raised as much interest as e.g., the formation phase. It is very important that the knowledge about information structures and its use during a VE or CN operation can be returned to the VBE and reused when needed in a new VE or CN.

Simões, D., Ferreira, H., Soares, A.L., 2007, in IFIP International Federation for Information Processing, Volume 243, Establishing the Foundation of Collaborative Networks; eds. Camarinha-Matos, L., Afsarmanesh, H., Novais, P., Analide, C.; (Boston: Springer), pp. 137–146.

2   PROCESS DESCRIPTION

Assuming that a VBE possesses an Ontology Library System (OLS), during the formation process of a new VE, knowledge that is both relevant and required for supporting the VE's operations is obtained by searching and selecting data sources from this OLS. This is followed by the construction of a global domain ontology using the ontologies retrieved from the OLS (ontology composition). There will come a day when the VE will end, e.g., due to the temporary nature of the business or resulting from market flutuations. The VE will enter then in the dissolution phase. During this dissolution phase it is important to guarantee the storage of new knowledge that has been acquired during the VE's operation so that it may be reused in future (ontology decomposition).

Assuming that ontology decomposition generates meta-data, another task, which is also a goal of this research work, consists in the definition of attributes that allow for the classification of the ontologies within the library, thus supporting the effective search and selection of ontologies that occurs during the formation of news VEs. The systematization of this process is intended to contribute not only to the cyclic, dynamic and agile enrichment of a VBE's library, but also to the competences generated within each VE (see Figure 1).

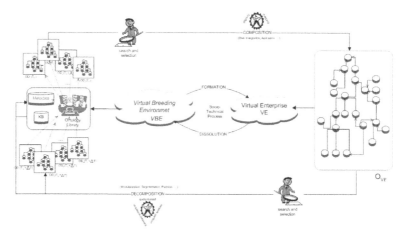

Figure 1 – Outline of Ontology Management System within VBE

The process of ontology management utilized by the OLS of the VBE, involves 5 basic steps:

SEARCH (Search the ontologies in the VBE): The goal is to find some especially relevant ontology for reuse. The search can be made by keyword, metadata, structure-based queries, supported by various evaluation schemes, or any combination of these.

SELECTION (Select the relevant ontologies): The goal is to produce a ranking of domain (concept) ontologies and respective hierarchy based on a set of metrics adopted for ontology evaluation.

COMPOSITION (Compose the ontology of the VE): The goal is to construct a global ontology that will support the VE's operation. It is thus necessary to decide on the use of an integration technique (union, inclusion, mapping, aligning, etc) that will allow for the construction of a global ontology based on the various ontologies or parts of ontologies selected in the previous step. The resulting global ontology will therefore be more representative of the domain of interest.

DECOMPOSITION (Decompose the ontology of the VE): The goal is to break the global domain ontology resulting from the VE's constitution, into several ontologies of complementary domains. This will facilitate the reuse of such knowledge by other EVs. In this case, it is necessary to decide which are the more adequate techniques to be used in the decomposition of the global ontology, so as to enable the extraction of the reused ontologies updated and another ontology segments from others complementary domains of interest.

CLASSIFICATION (Classify and store the ontologies in the VBE): The goal is to classify the ontologies of complementary domains resulting from the segmentation of the previous step and allowing for their adequate storage in the library. Such a classification facilitates the ensuing search that is required when a new VE emerges and consequently a new global domain ontology is created. This task consists in the update of the meta-ontology.

3   ONTOLOGY LIBRARY SYSTEM

According the general orientation given for the specification of an OLS (Ding and Fensel, 2001; Noy and Musen, 2004; Noy, Rubin et al., 2004) and based on the expected capabilities of the approach taken by this work, we can say that the OLS must be supported essentially by the following infrastructural ontological components (Maedche, Motik et al., 2003; Korpilahti, 2004):

Registry – must provide a means for the search and localization of the ontologies in the VBE.

o   Search: mechanisms that support the searching and browsing of the ontologies of the OLS, namely of the Meta-Ontology (MO) are required.

o   Selection: mechanisms that support the evaluation (based on concepts and their relations), verification and consequent ranking of the ontologies found in the OLS (metrics of the evaluation) are necessary.

o   Identification: mechanisms that guarantee the (unique) identification of each domain ontology is essential.

Reuse – must provide a means for the reuse of the ontologies of the VBE.

o   Composition: mechanisms that support the automatic aligning (inclusion or integration) of the several ontology segments that are considered relevant, is required, i.e., editing of the global domain ontology with the aim of supporting the VEs operations.

Evolution – must provide methods that support an adequate and consistent evolution of the ontologies of the VBE.

o   Maintenance: mechanisms that support the addition of new ontology segments and the creation and updating of complementary domain ontologies and respective MO in the OLS are required.

o   Decomposition: mechanisms that support the extraction of the adequate ontology segments from the global ontology resulting from each VE are necessary.

o   Storage: mechanisms that support the adequate classification and registration of the domain ontology segments to be added to OLS are required.

o   Versioning: is a necessary mechanism that allows for the storage and mana-
    gement of all versions controlled copies of the ontology segments in the OLS
    (identification of the several versions of the same ontology segment and the
    information about the relevant updates between each version).

The infrastructure is based on the utilization of an ontology server whose task
consists in storing and maintaining the ontologies (as well as any of its associated
meta-information) of each VE during its operation, and in storing and maintaining
the ontology segments identified and extracted during the extinction of a VE.

As an example suppose that from the formation and operation of the VE1, the
development centre generates the OVE1 (Ontology of the VE). Once VE1's operations
have ceased, two new segments SDO1 and SDO2 are extracted. At this point VE1
contacts the OLS Ontology Registry System (ORS) and stores segments SDO1 and
SDO2. In addition to the segments themselves all their relevant meta-data, described
by the MO, is also recorded. The ORS only stores the meta-data about the extracted
segments. The segments themselves are stored elsewhere in the ontology server.
Note that, after the dissolution of VE1, OEV1 is deleted from the ontology server of
the VBE.

When a new VE is formed, its development centre now referred to as VE2, can
search for the adequate ontology segments it requires. Such segments will allow for
the composition of the global ontology OVE2 that is necessary to support the
operation of this most recent partnership. The search is based on the ontologies
meta-data.

In order to reuse SDO1 for example, the VE2 uses the VBE's ontology composition facilities, making the necessary definitions available to OVE2. Once its
operations terminate, VE2 enters the dissolution phase. In order to preserve the
knowledge acquired during its operation and provide future reuse of such knowledge,
VE2 proceeds with the extraction of the segments judged adequate for such reuse,
namely, the extraction of the original segments that have been updated but also
any additional ones considered of interest to the domain. Once segmentation is
completed, these ontology segments' meta-data is recorded in the ORS and the
ontology segments themselves are recorded elsewhere in the ontology server.

This process is repeated during the life-cycle of each new VE. With the creation
of new VEs and the consequent generation and refinement of the VBEs ontologies,
it is probable that their will be an increase in the number and reuse of ontology
segments. Thus, the process of the decomposition will pass to have several phases,
i.e., one for each ontology segment reused in the development of the global
ontology, more the necessaries to find new segments of interest in complementary
domains.

4   ONTOLOGY REGISTRY

In the ORS, the meta-data (based on the MO) will contain descriptions of all ontology segments stored in the ontology sever. This description consists of information
required for the later selection of ontology segments and hence allow for the
adequate reuse and integration of these segments during the development of new
ontologies. The language used to specify either the ontology segments or the metadata
is OWL (Web ontology Language), which is a W3C recommendation.

4.1   Ranking

The ORS search is based on the identification of pertinent concepts, i.e., relevant terms in the ontology are identified by executing a keyword based search according to a set of conditions (identify concepts by class name, label or definition).

Inspired in works of Buitelaar, Eigner et al. (2004); Alani e Brewster (2005); Alani e Brewster, (2006) and also Alani, Brewster et al. (2006), we define as essentials the following metrics that would be considered in ranking and consequent selection of the ontologies of the OLS, to be applied to ontology segments resulting from the search made to OLS, with base on terms of the interest domain to the VE in formation (involving the metrics: "Covering" (MCB), "Completeness" (MCP), "Representation" (MRP) and "Proximity (MPR)), and with base on structure intended (involving the metrics: "Relationship" (MRL) and "Usage" (MUT)). These last ones have as objective complement the results of Partial Evaluation (AP), supporting a more consistent decision.

Due to space limitations, the metrics above will not be formerly presented. The interested reader is referred to the original article for more information (Alani, Brewster et al., 2006). For completeness sake however, these metrics are briefly described:

Covering (MCB) – This metric quantifies the number of classes of interest in the ontology segment. It is measured by the count of classes that are associated with a given set of labels of those classes which are identified either by exactly or partially matching the searched terms with these labels. A label of a class is considered partially matched with the searched terms if its text includes the searched term.

Completeness (MCP) – This metric measures, for a given set of terms, the degree of detail with which they are represented in the ontology segment. It is measured by the number of relations that the classes of interest (matched) possess. This count is based on the assumption that ontology segments that provide a more complete description of the concepts have greater number of relations. These relations include super-classes, sub-classes, siblings and any other declared or inferred object relation).

Representation (MRP) – This metric quantifies the importance that a concept has in a given ontology segment. It measures the centrality of classes in the ontology segment based on the presumption that if a class has a higher value of *betweenness* in the ontology segment, then this class is central to the domain represented by the ontology.

Proximity (MPR) – This metric measures the proximity between classes related to the terms of interest. Proximity is calculated according to the distance between classes. Such a distance is based on the number of relations (hierarchical and object relations) that separate any two classes. It is based on the assumption that concepts that are far apart from each other have less probability representing the domain of interest in a coherent and detailed manner.

Partial Evaluation (AP) – This is the weighed aggregation of the four metrics (MCB, MCP, MRP e MPR) described above. These metrics are calculated for each ontology segments taking into account the factors that are used to determine their relative importance in ranking the ontology segments.

Definition 1: Let $M = \{M[1], M[2], M[3], M[4]\} = \{MCB, MCP, MRP, MPR\}$, w_i be the weight given to each metric and O the set of ontologies to be ranked. The values measured are normalised to a range [0..1], dividing them by the maximum value of the metrics measured for all ontologies ($M[j]$).

$$AP(o \in O) = \sum_{i=1}^{4} w_i \frac{M[i]}{\max_{1 \leq j \leq |O|} M[j]}$$

In addition to the metrics just described, two new metrics (MRL and MUT) are also included. They are formalised as follows:

Relationship (MRL) – This metric quantifies the extent to which one ontology is linked to others. It is measured by counting the number of ontology segments that are imported by and the number of ontology segments that import the ontology segment that is being evaluated.

Definition 2: Let I = {ontologyImported[o]} e QI = {ontologyThatImport[o]} Thus MRL(O) is the Relationship Measure of the ontology O. φ and λ are the weights given to the ontology segments imported by and that import O, respectively.

$$MRL(O) = \varphi\, I(O) + \lambda QI(O)$$

Usage (MUT) – This metric quantifies the usage that is given to an ontology segment. It is measured by the number of individuals (instances) that are classified as members of the classes of interest. Such concepts are identified by label's exact or partial match with the search terms.

Definition 3: Let S = {Instances[C]} be the set of instances of the class C and n = E(O,T) + P(O,T), where E(O,T) and P(O,T) are the set of classes of the ontology segment O whose labels have respectively been exactly and partially matched with the searched terms (T). Thus, MUT(O) is the Usage Measure of the ontology segment O. λ and δ are the weights given.

$$MUT(O) = \frac{1}{n}\left(\lambda \sum_{i=1}^{E(o,T)} Si + \delta \sum_{j=1}^{P(o,T)} Sj \right)$$

Because it was not possible access the AKTiveRank system (Alani et al., 2006), a Java based system was developed in order to produce the results presented here. The output is generated in the CSV (Comma-Separated Value) format, which can then be easily opened and further processed by many spread sheet applications. In addition to the standard AKTiveRank metrics the MRL(O) and MUT(O) were also implemented. However, these metrics are considered as complementary to the AP result and are analyzed separately during the decision-making in choice of the ontology segment more relevant for particular context of VE in formation.

4.2   Classification

In order to facilitate the advanced query and retrieval of ontology segments, a notation management system will provide a means for domain experts to associate additional data to the ontology segment. Such information, provided in the form of meta-data, will allow for the extensive documentation of the ontology itself. It will include data on such things as: provenance, how the ontology was constructed, recommendations of how to proceed with its extensions, which nomination policy was followed, what are the organizational principles and functions, etc.

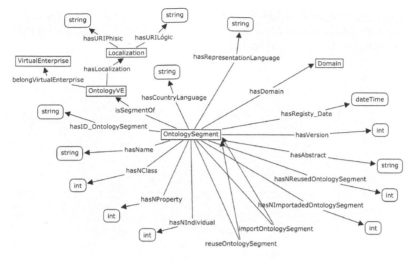

Figure 2 – Conceptual Map of Meta-Ontology

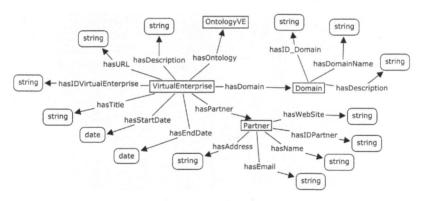

Figure 3 – Conceptual Map of Domain Ontology

In order to facilitate the adequate classification of ontology segments when they are registry in the ORS, the ontology segments will be annotated using the concepts in the MO (presented in form of conceptual map in Figure 2). An additional Domain Ontology (see Figure 3) was also created in order to allow for a more uniform annotation of the ontology segments. Both the MO and Domain Ontology were developed in OWL format.

5 TESTS

In order to test the ranking of the ontologies in the OLS using of the metrics described in section 4.1, two small ontologies that share a percentage of common concepts (labels), but with a relatively different hierarchy structure and set of properties (object property) were used. The ontologies are identified as "community_v2" (O1) and "knowledge_community_v2" (O2). Ontology O2 imports an additional ontology designated as "virtual_network". In both ontologies several instances (individuals) were added. All ontologies were created in the OWL language using the Protégé editor. During the development of these ontologies each class was given a generic designation using a numeric based denomination (C1, C2, etc). In addition to this each class was also assigned a label that identified it (see Figure 4 and Figure 5). This use of labels was done in order to allow for experimentation with the same hierarchy structure but with different sets of labels.

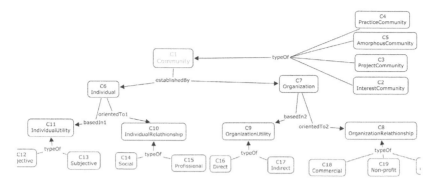

Figure 4 – Conceptual Map of "community_v2.owl" Ontology

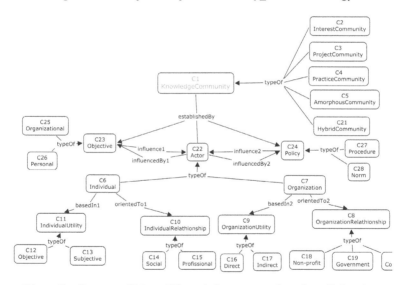

Figure 5 – Conceptual Map of "knowledge_community_v2.owl" Ontology

Table 1 shows the results obtained when calculating the metrics described in 4.1, each of which pertains to a different set of search terms (T). The results of the AP metric were obtained using the following weights: $w_{MCB}=w_{MCP}=0.3$ e $w_{MRP}=w_{MPR}=0.2$ such that $w_{MCB}+w_{MCP}+w_{MRP}+w_{MPR}=1$. The metrics that are considered more relevant to the selection (and therefore ranking) of the ontology are the MCB and MCP metrics. This justifies the choice of assigning larger values to the weights of the MCB and MCP metrics than those of the MRP and MPR metrics. In the case of the MCB, we considered the weights given to the exact matches greater than those given to partial matches (respectively 0.6 to 0.4). Relatively to the MCP, all four parameters (respectively super-classes, sub-classes, relations and siblings) were given equitable weight.

The results show that for all sets of searched terms ontology O2 is always ranked above ontology O1. In other words ontology O2 is considered to be of greater relevance than ontology O1 for this specific search. These results are as expected. Observer that ontology O2 is denser and more complete than ontology O1. It also has a higher frequency of use of the term "community". Because all searches include this term it is natural that O2 be ranked above O1. Note also that even when the set of search terms includes other equally relevant terms ("individual", "organization" and "social") the ranking does not change significantly.

Table 1 – Application of metrics to ontologies O1 and O2

source	MCB	MCP	MRP	MPR	MRL	MUT	AP
T={community}							
./metrics2/community_v2.owl	2,20	1,25000	0,00000	0,40000	0,00	0,80	0,35357
./metrics2/knowledge_community_v2.owl	2,80	2,42857	1,42857	0,90476	0,50	0,34	0,69116
T={community,INDIVIDUAL}							
./metrics2/community_v2.owl	3,60	0,96875	0,62500	0,57143	0,00	0,85	0,37513
./metrics2/knowledge_community_v2.owl	4,20	1,95000	1,46667	0,64815	0,50	0,52	0,52848
T={community,INDIVIDUAL,orGaniZatioN}							
./metrics2/community_v2.owl	5,00	0,86364	0,90909	0,50909	0,00	0,87	0,30107
./metrics2/knowledge_community_v2.owl	6,80	1,50000	3,09688	0,51264	0,50	0,61	0,49582
T={community,INDIVIDUAL,orGaniZatioN, social}							
./metrics2/community_v2.owl	5,60	0,83333	1,15278	0,47222	0,00	0,85	0,30905
./metrics2/knowledge_community_v2.owl	7,40	1,44118	3,29202	0,48206	0,50	0,61	0,48544

In the case of MRL metric both parameters were given an equal weight of 0.5. In respect to the MUT metric greater importance was given to instances belonging to classes that were identified by exact matches than those by partial matches. The value assigned to the metrics of exact and partial matches is respectively 0.6 and 0.4. It is important to reiterate that these metrics serve only as a complementary means of better assessing the ranking of the ontologies provided by do the MCB, MCP, MRP and MPR metrics. The MUT metric will be useful, for example, in case the AP scores between two or more ontologies are either tied or very close. In such cases we would opt for the ontology that demonstrates a greater degree of usage (large values of MUT). The metric MRL, in its turn, will help with the selection, development and hence adaptation of the ontology segments. During this development process larger value of MRL are an indication that the selected ontologies are based on a greater number of reusable (and arguably more stable) ontologies are therefore better candidates for reuse themselves.

6   DISCUSSION AND FUTURE WORK

This paper presented an approach used in the management of multiples ontologies within the context of a VBE. A meta-Ontology and Domain-Ontology were also presented which support the annotation; storage and retrieval of ontologies in the OLS were also presented. A set of metrics for the ranking and selection of ontology segments were also described. These metrics were exemplified by calculating their values with respect to two ontologies in an experiment. The resulting ranking of this experiment was discussed.

In addition to ontology evaluation and ranking, a segmentation algorithm is currently being developed. This algorithm will automate the decomposition and extraction of ontology segments from a global ontology during the dissolution of a VE. These extracted segments allow for the collection, comparison, recording and version control of previously reusable ontology segments. In addition to this it will also allow for the identification and registration of new ontology segments (according to the domains of interest as is specified in Domain Ontology) from ontologies that resulted from the compositions and consequent evolution of a VE's operation.

7   REFERENCES

1.   Afsarmanesh, H. e L. M. Camarinha-Matos (2005). A framework for management of virtual organization breeding environments. Collaborative Networks and their Breeding Environments, (PRO-VE'05), Valencia, Spain, Springer.
2.   Alani, H. e C. Brewster (2005). Ontology Ranking based on the Analysis of Concept Structures. Third International Conference on Knowledge Capture (K-Cap), Banff, Alberta, Canada.
3.   Alani, H. e C. Brewster (2006). Metrics for Ranking Ontologies. WWW2006, Edinburgh, UK.
4.   Alani, H., C. Brewster, et al. (2006). Ranking Ontologies with AKTiveRank. 5th International Semantic Web Conference (ISWC), Georgia, USA.
5.   Bacquet, J., P. Fatelnig, et al. (2004). An outlook of future research needs on networked organizations. Virtual Enterprises and Collaborative Networks (PROVE'O4), Toulouse, France, Kluwer Academic Publishers.
6.   Buitelaar, P., T. Eigner, et al. (2004). OntoSelect: A Dynamic Ontology Library with Support for Ontology Selection. International Semantic Web Conference, Hiroshima, Japan.
7.   Ding, Y. e D. Fensel (2001). "Ontology Library Systems: The key to successful Ontology Re-use." 93 - 112.
8.   Korpilahti, T. (2004). Arquitecture for distributed development of an ontology library. Department of Computer Science and Engineering. Helsinki, Helsinki University of Technology. Master of Science in Technology: 60.
9.   Maedche, A., B. Motik, et al. (2003). An Infrastructure for Searching, Reusing and Evolving Distributed Ontologies. WWW2003, Budapest, Hungary, ACM.
10.   Noy, N. F. e M. A. Musen (2004). "Ontology versioning in an ontology management framework." IEEE Intelligent Systems 19(4): 6.
11.   Noy, N. F., D. Rubin, et al. (2004). "Making Biomedical Ontologies and Ontology Libraries Work." EEE Intelligent Systems 19(6): 78 - 81.
12.   Porter, C. E. (2004). "A Typology of Virtual Communities: A Multi-Disciplinary Foundation for Future Research." Journal of Computer-Mediated Communication (JCMC) 10((1), Article 3).

15 | CAUSAL CROSS-IMPACT ANALYSIS AS STRATEGIC PLANNING AID FOR VIRTUAL ORGANISATION BREEDING ENVIRONMENTS

Heiko Duin

BIBA at the University of Bremen, GERMANY
du@biba.uni-bremen.de

Virtual Organisation Breeding Environments (VBEs) are known as an enterprise network creating virtual organisations (VOs) on occurring business opportunities. Whereas a VO is created dynamically with a limited time horizon, such a VBE is created for medium or long-term existence. Thus, a VBE needs besides operational also strategic planning. Strategic planning for organisations is a topic since the 50ies of last century, but research in the application to networked organisations is very limited. This paper analyses strategic issues, which might occur for VBEs in difference to not-networked organisations followed by the description of an approach, how strategic planning in a VBE could be supported. This approach is based on causal cross-impact analysis and provides a modelling framework for strategic objectives and a simulation component to generate strategic scenarios.

1 INTRODUCTION

Today's manufacturing systems are subject to enormous pressures because of the ever changing market environments showing e.g. discontinuities in trends and globalisation. Manufacturers have responded to these conditions by forming collaborative relationships to suppliers, distributors and even customers (e.g. Jagdev and Thoben, 2001). When two or more enterprises collaborate, they form a collaborative (enterprise) network. Two basic types of collaborative networks are represented by Virtual Organisations (VOs) and by Source Networks (Kürümlüoglu et al., 2005):

- A **Virtual Organisation** (VO) is a temporary consortium of partners from different organisations established to fulfil a value adding task, for example a product or service to a customer. The lifetime of a VO is typically restricted: it is created for a definite task and dissolved after the task has been completed. A synonym for VO is the term *Virtual Enterprise*.
- A Source/**Support Network** is a more stationary, though not static, group of organisational entities which has developed a preparedness to collaborate in case of a specific task/customer demand. Another name for such a network is *Breeding Environment*.

The relationship between these two forms is that the Breeding Environment prepares the instantiation of VOs. It acts as an incubator for a VO. From the VO point of view, the VO is created when a business opportunity occurs. In order to perform the actual value creation task, the VO can be created from scratch (collecting cooperating partners from an "open universe" of enterprises) or through a *VO Breeding Environment* (VBE, see Figure 1).

Duin, H., 2007, in IFIP International Federation for Information Processing, Volume 243, Establishing the Foundation of Collaborative Networks; eds. Camarinha-Matos, L., Afsarmanesh, H., Novais, P., Analide, C.; (Boston: Springer), pp. 147–154.

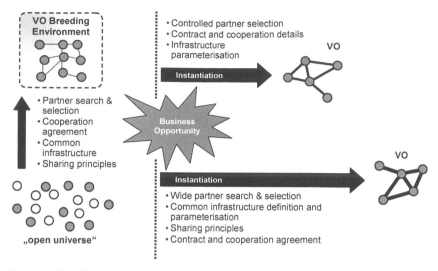

Figure 1: Two Ways to instantiate VOs (after Camarinha-Matos and Afsarmanesh, 2003)

The lifetime of a VO is generally short and depends on the complexity of the value creation process and could be described by the three phases setup, operation and dissolution. In comparison, the lifetime of the VBE is generally long-term. From a perspective of planning, the VO needs operational planning during its operation phase supported by some tactical planning during the set-up and dissolution phase. In difference to a VO the VBE needs strategic planning due its long-term existence. Corporate strategic planning and strategic management is still an subject of research, but has never given much importance to the role networks play (Sturm et al., 2004). A networked organisation like a VBE has some pre-conditions, which may denies the transfer of common strategic planning methods to the network application area.

2   RELATION TO EXISTING THEORIES AND WORK

2.1   State of the Art in VBEs

The concept of having a VBE for the instantiation of VOs is subject of analysis for a couple of years (e.g. Camarinha-Matos and Afsarmanesh, 2006). A VBE can be defined as "*an association of organizations and their related supporting institutions, adhering to a base long term cooperation agreement, and adoption of common operating principles and infrastructures, with the main goal of increasing both their chances and their preparedness towards collaboration in potential Virtual Organizations*" (Camarinha-Matos and Afsarmanesh, 2006).

The life cycle of a VBE includes the stages or phases a VBE goes through. It starts with its creation, continues to its operation and possible dissolution. In fact, a VBE is a long-term alliance, and considering its valuable bag of assets gradually collected in the VBE, its dissolution is an unusual situation. Instead, it is much more probable that the VBE goes through another stage, a so called metamorphosis stage, where it can evolve and change its form and purpose. On the other hand, it is the case that only during the operation stage of the VBE, the VO can be created.

Figure 2 shows a VBE during the operation phase. It continuously creates VOs in different configurations and for different durations. Each of the VOs goes through the three phases of setting it up, operation and dissolution.

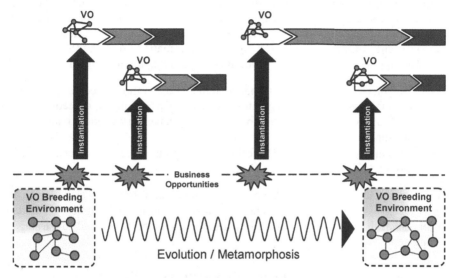

Figure 2: Continuous Instantiation of VOs by a VBE in Operation Phase

Evolution and metamorphosis of the VBE may be driven by random or in a planned and controlled way. Camarinha-Matos and Afsarmanesh do mention a long-term strategy behind the VBE, but the responsibility to develop and implement the strategy has not yet been assigned to one of the roles identified within a VBE. Several roles have already been identified including the member, administrator, opportunity broker, VO planner and coordinator (Camarinha-Matos and Afsarmanesh, 2006).

The *VBE Administrator* is a role performed by a member organisation, which is responsible for the VBE operation and evolution, which includes promotion of cooperation among the VBE members, filling the skill/competency gaps in the VBE by searching and recruiting/inviting new organisations into the VBE and the daily management of the VBE general processes, conflict resolution, preparation of a bag of VBE assets, and making common VBE policies, among others.

The responsibility of the VBE administrator needs to be extended by strategic management tasks, when the long-term evolution and metamorphosis of the VBE should occur in a planned and controlled way.

2.2 State of the Art in Strategic Management

Mintzberg stated that a strategy is best described as a five-tuple, where each dimension starts with a "p" (the 5 P's of strategy): plan, pattern, position, perspective and ploy (Mintzberg, 1994). For the following of this paper, the planning dimension is considered to be central. Planning has two main aspects:

- Identifying the long-term (strategic) objectives of the organisation.
- Setting up a (strategic) action plan to be implemented by the organisation in order to reach the objectives.

Sturm et al outline, that the process of strategic management, which is including the strategic planning, becomes a tedious and time consuming dialog in a network, because the members might have controversial interests and there is a need to find compromises and broadly accepted solutions. The pre-conditions, which makes the execution of a strategy process in a network context to a lengthy procedure are: (1) decentralisation, and volatility of decisions, communications and resources, (2) inconsistency of interests and (3) novelty of coordination processes (Sturm et al., 2004). This applies to open networks, but, this might not apply to VBEs due to:

- An enterprise joining a VBE has to sign an cooperation agreement. Assuming that this agreement regulates the basic responsibilities, procedures and rules of cooperation, the members shouldn't have very controversial understandings.
- The members of the VBE follow a common objective, otherwise they wouldn't join together into a VBE.

From this point of view, the VBE seems not to be that different to other forms of long-term organisations, for whom strategic management is – of course – an issue. And this opens the discussion, which of the traditional methods and tools of strategic planning apply best to VBEs.

3   APPROACH TO STRATEGIC PLANNING IN VBES

In a traditional enterprise, the forms of strategy are (e.g. Jagdev et al., 2004, pp 11-12):

- **Corporate Strategy**: Is the overall business strategy of the enterprise based on the vision and mission. The corporate strategy guide the single business strategies.
- **Business Strategy**: The enterprise divides their activities into Strategic Business Units (SBUs). For each SBU an own strategy is developed and implemented.
- **Functional Strategy**: The functional strategies concern individual business functions and processes, e.g. human resources or marketing.

These three forms of strategy are strictly hierarchical, meaning that the functional strategies are strictly in line with their business strategies and all business strategies are compatible with the corporate strategy. The direction of governance is top down (see Figure 3, left hand side). The right side of Figure 3 provides a comparison with the levels of strategy in a VBE. The corporate level strategies are still top down, but within the VBE, the direction of governance is bottom-up.

The strategies of the single members of the VBE must be compatible with the overall VBE strategy. If not, most probably there is a conflict in the objectives of the VBE compared with some objectives of the respective member. Such conflicts need to be resolved to ensure smooth business operation of the VBE and all its members.

Figure 3: Corporate Strategy and VBE Strategy

Like a traditional enterprise, a VBE has internal resources to be applied in value creating processes (in VOs), and it is operating in an environment (market), which has external factors influencing the success of the VBE. Differentiating external and internal influences leads to the idea of using the *SWOT Analysis* (SWOT = Strengths, Weaknesses, Opportunities, Threats), which is often used to start a strategic analysis process. A SWOT analysis should be followed by another step to process the identified factors and prepare a plan.

Due to the dynamics of the external (e.g. fast changing or disruptive trends) and the internal (e.g. development of skills connected with new member entrance) factors, an approach is needed, which allows the adaptation of plans to changing situations during the course into the future. This is fulfilled by scenario techniques. A well known method to create scenarios is *Cross-Impact Analysis.*

Therefore, the proposed method to develop strategies for a VBE follows two steps:

1. **SWOT Analysis** to identify the internal and external factors.
2. **Cross-Impact Analysis** to inter-relate the factors and to create and simulate scenarios.

As both methods are best applied in group settings, a VBE should establish a *Steering Committee* to support the strategy process. In smaller VBEs, each member can have an own delegate in that committee. For larger VBEs the number of committee members should be limited, but it needs to be ensured, that each of the VBE members has a representative to allow the integration in the strategy process. The steering committee should be chaired by the *VBE Administrator.*

The following chapters show some initial results, when applying this methodology to a generic VBE.

Table 1: Generic SWOT Analysis

Strengths	Weaknesses
• Very fast reaction time on occurring business opportunities • Self-regulation: adapting the number and quality of members to fit requirements • Very good preparedness for business opportunities	• Time consuming processes, if not perfectly coordinated • Members might be competitors • Members prioritise own objectives compared to the VBE strategy
Opportunities	Threats

• Increase of the number of VOs created per time unit
• Competitive advantages by
  o cost leadership
  o innovation leadership
	• Not having the market requested competences/skills in the network
	• Competing VBEs do constitute
	• Customers want to have a single enterprise to deliver the solution

3.1   Application of SWOT Analysis

A SWOT analysis is applied to asses the strengths and weaknesses (internal factors) and the opportunities and threats (external factors) of an organisation (Jagdev et al., 2004). A brainstorming session with colleagues at the institute BIBA revealed the strengths, weaknesses, opportunities and threats of a generic VBE. The most important are listed in Table 1.

3.2   Application of Causal Cross-Impact Analysis

Scenario techniques are based on two principles (e.g. Gausemeier et al., 1998):

- **Systems thinking**: Organisations must perceive their environment as a complex network of inter-related (external as well as internal) factors.
- **Multiple futures**: Organisations should not reduce their strategic thinking to one exact prognosticated future. Instead, alternative future scenarios should be created and considered during strategic planning.

The scenario generation approach adopted by BIBA is based on causal cross-impact analysis (Krauth et al., 1998; Duin, 1995), which has first been developed by Olaf Helmer (Helmer, 1981; Helmer, 1977). Up to now, BIBA included several enhancements to the causal cross-impact analysis method according to requirements identified during various research projects: delayed impacting, threshold impacting, expression variables and a technique for structuring and managing scenarios in a tree. BIBA implemented a cross-impact modelling and simulation software package called CRIMP for Windows, which allows the interactive set-up, simulation and evaluation of causal cross-impact models (Duin et al., 2005; Krauth et al., 1998; Krauth, 1992).

The basic idea of cross-impact analysis is to get a systemic picture of the rough structure of a complex system supporting long-term planning and assessment tasks. In difference to other simulation approaches like system dynamics, causal cross-impact analysis is not used to generate prognostic data, but to analyse effects over and above a business-as-usual scenario provided by the end user.

The end-user (the steering committee, who will commonly develop the model) generates different scenarios by applying action vectors (representing different strategic options) and/or setting uncontrollable events, which might strongly influence the system under consideration.

Causal cross-Impact modelling is based on a discrete time model. The time period under investigation is divided into single time steps called scenes. Each scene represents a time span, e.g. a year, a quarter or a month. The end of the total time period under consideration is called the time horizon.

The basic elements of a causal cross-impact model are trend variables representing the elements of a system (like levels or stocks in system dynamics (Sterman, 2000). For each trend variable the user is asked to provide an estimated business-as-usual development coupled with an uncertainty factor called volatility.

Event variables in a causal cross-impact model describe events which are not under the control of actors of the model, but which might have a strong influence on other variables (trends or events) in the case of their occurrence. The user is asked to provide occurrence probabilities for event variables.

Action variables are under the control of actors and represent their manoeuvring space in decision making. If an actor invests in an action, the variable develops an intensity with which it might influence other system elements (trends or events).

These variables are inter-related by defining cross-impacts between them spawning up the cross-impact matrix as demonstrated in Figure 4. The cross-impact matrix consists of six different areas or sub-matrices: One sub-matrix collects all impacts having a trend variable as source and destination, one for trends on events and so on.

	Trends	Events	List of Variables
Trends	Trends on Trends	Trends on Events	• Number of Competencies covered by VBE • Number of VBE Members • Tender Preparation Time • Market Share • Number of VOs created per Year • Number of Customers • Skills Coverage • Level of Preparedness • Number of Competitors
Events	Events on Trends	Events on Events	
Actions	Actions on Trends	Actions on Events	

Figure 4: Structure of the Cross-Impact Matrix (Duin et al., 2005) and Examples of Variables

Figure 4 also shows some examples for variables involved in the cross-impact matrix and extracted from the SWOT analysis result. A cross-impact is a coefficient, where the absolute value indicates the strength of the impact and the sign indicates its direction. A positive sign means that a deviation in the source variable will cause a deviation in the same direction of the destination variable for the following scene. A negative impact would cause a deviation in the other direction.

Users can generate explicit simulations by setting actions or letting events occur and watching the results of the simulation. Each pattern of action settings and event occurrences defines a specific scenario describing how the target variables are affected in comparison to their business-as-usual development (Figure 5).

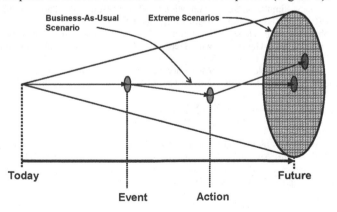

Figure 5: Scenario Funnel with Business-As-Usual Future and another Path

4 CONCLUSION

This paper analysed strategic issues, which occur for generic VBEs in difference to not-networked organisations. This analysis is done by applying SWOT analysis followed by the usage of causal cross-impact analysis and its application to strategic planning. This approach has been applied to a proto-typical generic VBE.

Future research should include the application of the presented approach in different real world VBE contexts to validate the appropriateness of the solution and the generic findings.

5 ACKNOWLEDGEMENTS

The author thanks the partners and the European Commission for support in the context of the PRIME project, funded under contract number FP6-016542.

6 REFERENCES

1. Camarinha-Matos, Luis and Afsarmanesh, Hamideh: Elements of a Base VE Infrastructure. In: Computers in Industry. 51 (2003) 2, pp 139-163.
2. Camarinha-Matos, Luis and Afsarmanesh, Hamideh: Creation of Virtual Organizations in a Breeding Environment. In: Proceedings of INCOM'06: 12th IFAC Symposiumon Information Control Problemsin Manufacturing. 2006. pp 583-592.
3. Duin, Heiko: Object-oriented Scenario Management for Simulation Models. In: Proceedings of IMACS European Simulation Meeting. Gyor 1995. pp 38-44.
4. Duin, Heiko, Schnatmeyer, Martin, Schumacher, Jens, Thoben, Klaus-Dieter and Zhao, Xinhong: Cross-Impact Analysis of RFID Scenarios for Logistics. In: Logistik Management 2005. Wiesbaden 2005. pp 363-376.
5. Gausemeier, Jürgen, Fink, Alexander and Schlake, Oliver: Scenario Management: An Approach to Develop Future Potentials. In: Technological Forecasting and Social Change. 59 (1998) 2, pp 111-130.
6. Helmer, Olaf: Problems in Futures Research: Delphi and Causal Cross-Impact Analysis. In: Futures. 9 (1977) 1, pp 17-31.
7. Helmer, Olaf: Reassessment of cross-impact analysis. In: Futures. (1981) 10, pp 389-400.
8. Jagdev, Harinder S., Brennan, Attracta and Browne, Jimmie: Strategic Decision Making in Modern Manufacturing. Kluwer Academic Publishers. Boston, Dordrecht, London 2004.
9. Jagdev, Harinder S. and Thoben, Klaus-Dieter: Anatomy of Enterprise Collaborations. In: Production Planning and Control. 12 (2001) 5, pp 437-451.
10. Krauth, Johannes: Simulation for the evaluation of CIM Investments as Part of an Enterprise Strategy. In: EUROSIM '92 Simulation Congress Reprints. 1992. pp 295-300.
11. Krauth, Johannes, Duin, Heiko and Schimmel, Annette: A Comparison of Tools for Strategic Simuation and Scenario Generation with Special Emphasis on 'Soft Factors'. In: Simulation Practice and Theory. 6 (1998) 1, pp 23-33.
12. Kürümlüoglu, Mehmet, Nostdal, Rita and Karvonen, Iris: Base Concepts. In: Camarinha-Matos, L.; Afsarmanesh, H.; Ollus, M. (Eds.): Virtual Organizations. Systems and Practices. Springer. New York 2005, pp 11-28.
13. Mintzberg, Henry: The Rise and Fall of Strategic Planning. 1994.
14. Sterman, John: Business Dynamics - Systems Thinking and Modeling for a Complex World. McGraw-Hill. 2000.
15. Sturm, Flavius, Kemp, Jeroen and Wendel de Joode, Ruben van: Towards Strategic Management in Collaborative Network Structures. In: Camarinha-Matos, L.; Afsarmanesh, H. (Eds.): Collaborative Networked Organisations. A Research Agenda for Emerging Business Models. Kluwer Academic Publishers. Boston, Dordrecht, Wien 2004, pp 131-138.

16

ASSESSING THE VALUE OF MEDIATORS IN COLLABORATIVE BUSINESS NETWORKS

Benjamin Rensmann[1], Hans Weigand[1], Zheng Zhao[2], Virginia Dignum[2], Frank Dignum[2] and Marcel Hiel[1]

[1] *Department Information Systems and Management, Tilburg University, NETHERLANDS*
{b.rensmann, h.weigand, m.hiel}@uvt.nl
[2] *Department of Information and Computing Sciences, Utrecht University, NETHERLANDS*
{zheng, virginia, dignum}@cs.uu.nl

One of the basic mechanisms of collaborative business networks is mediation. A literature review is presented that identifies meanings and roles of mediators. Based on the literature a framework is developed that can be used to describe and distinguish different types of mediator services. Core concepts of the framework are the value activities that mediators offer and the functional level of these activities with regard to market transactions. The framework uses the e3-value modelling approach to illustrate the value-creating mediator activities in a business network.

1   INTRODUCTION

With growing complexity in the globalized business world of the 21st century companies increasingly have to depend on temporal or more stable networks of business partners, called by names such as Virtual Organizations, Value Constellations or Collaborative Business Networks (CN). New technologies such as web services are being developed as solutions for the support of such networks (Papazoglou & Ribbers, 2006). However, for the proper development and deployment of those technologies, a structured understanding of the basic principles and mechanisms of business collaborations is needed. One basic coordination mechanism is mediation. Although the relevance of mediators in CN is not disputed, these do still lack the rules and theories that would allow business parties to quickly and systematically assess the added value of involving a mediator in their network.

In this paper we describe a framework that helps demonstrating the values o f mediators in networks of distributed business actors, especially in buyer-seller relationships. The elements of our framework are based on economical and organizational literature. It uses the notion of market transactions to distinguish two different levels of mediator support. We use value modeling to illustrate the values for the mediated parties that result of mediator activities.

The paper is structured as follows. Section 2 provides a short overview of roles and functions of mediators and of the e3-value modeling approach that we use for

Rensmann, B., Weigand, H., Zhao, Z., Dignum, V., Dignum, F., Heil, M., 2007, in IFIP International Federation for Information Processing, Volume 243, Establishing the Foundation of Collaborative Networks; eds. Camarinha-Matos, L., Afsarmanesh, H., Novais, P., Analide, C.; (Boston: Springer), pp. 155–162.

modeling. Section 3 presents our framework. Section 4 gives concluding remarks and an outlook on future work to do.

2   LITERATURE REVIEW

The term "mediator" is used in different fields. Its primary use is in the field of law and dispute resolution, where mediators are independent parties that help to solve disputes of any kind between two parties (Boulle/Nesic, 2001). In computer science mediators are part of a middleware level, conducting tasks of data-information transformation, interface processing and workflow integration (Wiederhold, 1992; Papazoglou & Ribbers, 2006; Schulz & Orlowska, 2004). In the economical and organizational domain the term intermediary is used to describe entities that act as mediating instances between actors in business networks. For the sake of abstraction we will refer to intermediaries also as mediators in the remainder of the paper.

In economic terms mediators create and manage markets to help suppliers and buyers to conduct transactions, i.e. to sell and purchase goods (Spulber, 1996). They fulfill a bundle of tasks that address the failure of the perfect market assumed in classic economic theory (Datta, 2005). Next to price setting and market clearing mediators provide liquidity and immediacy through holding cash on hand and maintaining inventories of goods, doing matching and searching to coordinate the actions of buyers and sellers and providing guarantees and monitoring services to overcome asymmetric information on both sides of a potential transaction. In this view a mediator does not have to be a dedicated organization. Any company, as part of their other business can act as a mediator in a certain market.

Table 2.1 Market functions and the roles of mediators (from (Giaglis/Klein/O'Keefe, 2002) .

Market Function	2.1.1.1 Sub-Functions	2.1.1.1.1.1 **The Role of Intermediaries**
Matching Buyers and Sellers	Determination of Product Offerings	Monitoring, Alerting
	Searching	Reducing Search Costs
	Price Discovery	Facilitating (but increasing price)
Facilitation of Transactions	Logistics	Shipping, Distribution, Warehousing
	Settlement	Facilitating, Monitoring
	Trust	Rating, Guaranteeing
Institutional Infrastructure	Legal	Monitoring, Protecting
	Regulatory	Monitoring, Protecting

The rise of the Internet as an alternative business channel leads to new organizational forms of mediating entities and to new roles assigned to those entities. Although still occupying a mediating function in the economic sense, electronic mediators are confronted with new opportunities and threats due to the different ways of conducting business in the networked world. At an early stage of the discussion the Internet was seen as a major threat to the existence of those mediators and their disappearance was forecasted (Malone/Yates/Benjamin, 1987). Those forecasts did not come true. Instead, new opportunities for mediators were identified and the comeback of traditional mediators that were formerly disintermediated was observed (Chircu/Kauffman, 2000). The extensive dialogue about the roles of electronic mediators that occurred in the context of the disintermediation/ reintermediation discussion produced lots of useful insights regarding the added values of electronic mediators (Bailey/Bakos, 1997).

According to (Bakos, 1998) markets (electronic and otherwise) fulfill three basic functions: Matching of buyers and sellers, facilitation of transactions and provision of the institutional infrastructure. Each of these functions consists of several sub-functions. Mediators typically provide services of the first two functions, but can also play a role in the third function. Table 2.1 gives a brief overview of the functions and sub-functions and the roles that mediators can play in fulfilling them.

2.2 Modelling value exchanges with e³-value

The e3-value modeling approach provides a tool for modeling value exchanges between collaborating entities in a CN and for profitability analysis, helping to determine the value flows for each of the actors (Gordijn/Akkermans, 2003). The core elements of e3-value models are value exchanges, which show the potential transfers of value objects from one actor to another. A value object is of some (economic) value for at least one of the actors. Typical examples for value objects are products, payments and services. Other concepts in e3-value are market segments, value interfaces, value ports and value activities. Market segments represent homogenous groups of actors. A value port is connected to an actor and indicates a potential value exchange connected to the actor. Value ports are grouped into value interfaces. Usually a value interface consists of an ingoing and an outgoing value port, representing the principle of economic reciprocity. Value activities symbolize bundles of operational activities that an actor performs and that create some profit or economic value for at least one of the actors.

3 A VALUE-BASED FRAMEWORK FOR MEDIATORS

The framework that we will present in this chapter is based on typical value activities that mediators carry out to support different phases of a market transaction between two or more actors in a CN. The notion of market transactions is used as a distinguishing feature to identify mediator value activities on two different levels. Furthermore the transfer of goods or services in exchange for a payment, that is usually the subject of a transaction, will be dismantled into its components to provide a better understanding of the involvement of a mediator. The elements of the framework will be expressed using e3-value models, which should serve as a basis for discussion and future development.

3.1 Different mediator levels in market transactions

We define a market transaction as the exchange of goods, services and money between actors in a CN (Lindemann/Schmid, 1999). Typically the following phases describe the steps in conducting a market transaction: Information, Agreement and

Settlement. Whereas the information and agreement phases somehow precede the actual transaction (i.e. the physical transfer of a good or service against a payment), thereby defining the terms of the transaction, the settlement covers the operational conduction of the transfers that are subject to a transaction. Mediators can support a subset of the transaction phases in one or the other way.

The phases of a market transaction represent different aspects that we will use to distinguish different levels of mediator value activities. One aspect is the processing of information to support a transaction; the other is the operational fulfillment of a transaction. Based on this distinction we propose two different levels of value activities that are typically carried out by mediators: Activities on the informational level and on the operational level. The information and agreement phases correspond to the informational level of mediation. They represent the matching function of (electronic) markets as stated in Table 2.1. On the operational level mediators play roles in the settlement phase of a transaction, i.e. the facilitation of a transaction as described in Table 2.1. In the remainder of this section we will explain the mediator value activities in detail and provide corresponding value models to clarify the value exchanges in a CN.

3.1   Mediator value activities on the informational level

The basic value model for the informational level is shown in Figure 3.1. On the left side the market segment of sellers is shown while the buyers are placed on the right side. The mediator actor in the middle contains three value activities, to which we will refer to as mediator value activities on the informational level (dark shaded boxes). The value exchanges that are shown at the bottom of the model indicate the mediated market transaction. The endpoints of the transaction lie in the selling and buying value activities of the seller and the buyer. These two activities usually create value for the respective actors, assuming that transactions are only conducted if some economic value is realized for both parties. The dashed boxes within sellers and buyers represent resources that are used by the actors to create value in a sustainable way. Conversely, the value of a certain activity for an actor can be determined by assessing the impact that this activity has on its resources.

The mediator value activities related to the information phase of a transaction are those of providing supply and demand publicity and supporting the determination of the terms and conditions of the transaction. Mediators provide supply publicity by aggregating supplier's offers and products in e.g. stores, product catalogues (electronic and otherwise), directories or other publishing media. They may gather the necessary knowledge about the supply side of the market through monitoring the product portfolios offered by suppliers, thereby eventually evaluating the products, services and the suppliers. Alternatively the publishing of supply can be interpreted as the provision of the necessary publishing facilities by the mediator.

The value of supply publishing for buyers lies in the reduction of search costs and in the market knowledge buyers obtain through the services of a mediator. However, the value analysis of an informative act is not complete when it considers the value of the information for the receiver only. There is also a return value given to the sender, as the receiver pays attention. How relevant this value is depends on the situation, but it is always there. By exposing supply information sellers receive attention from the buy-side, i.e. from potential customers. The value of this attention is that it adds potential customers to their customer base, which is one of their key resources as being a seller. The potential customer base is an economic resource and should not be identified with a database where the names of these potential customers would be stored.

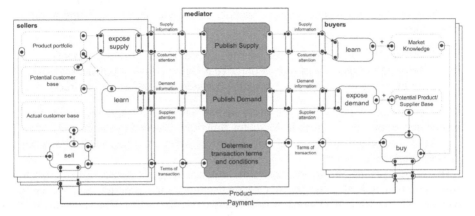

Figure 3.1 Value model of informational mediator value activities.

Mediators also provide relevant expertise about the demand side to suppliers, thus creating demand publicity. This can be done by active market research or through usage of operational data of the mediator (e.g. by analyzing the point-of-sale data of a retailer shop). Additionally mediators often offer facilities for buyers to communicate their demand. Examples are customer platforms like letsbuyit.com. Sellers can use this valuable demand information to design their product portfolio accordingly. By using the demand information in this way suppliers draw their attention towards potential customers. By means of offering products that fit the demand the supplier attention leads to extension of the potential product/and supplier base of customers.

The third value activity in the model (Determine transaction terms and conditions) addresses the agreement phase of a market transaction. There are several mechanisms that are typically offered by mediators, enabling the participating parties to determine the terms and conditions of a transaction to come to an agreement. The simplest mechanisms discover just the price for a product that is part of a transaction. Among these are single-criteria auctions, negotiations and price fixing. More complex procedures are multiple-criteria auctions and negotiations.

The selling and buying value activities use the resources of the respective actor to prepare the actual transaction. For selling this means that a certain product out of the supplier's product portfolio is sold to a customer, and his potential customer becomes an actual customer. The actual customer base constitutes a resource as well as it provides valuable customer contacts for future transactions. The buying value activity uses the resources of market knowledge or potential products and suppliers. The first one contributes to the transaction if the buyer wants to buy something from a certain seller and requests the deal. In case of usage of the latter resource a supplier knows about a certain demand and makes an offer to initiate a deal.

3.2   Mediator value activities on the operational level

On the operational level mediators typically offer support for the actual transfer of the value objects that are subject of a deal, i.e. for the settlement of a transaction. According to (Andersson et al., 2006) a transfer can be viewed as consisting of three components:

- the right to use a certain resource (i.e. a good, a service or a payment)
- provision of custody of that resource (e.g. delivery of the physical good)
- an evidence document describing the transferred right (e.g. a contract)

The provision of custody is the most demanding activity and the other components are usually linked up to it. Mediator functions supporting the custody provision are the provision of financial and logistical services. Figure 3.2 shows the corresponding value model.

The value exchange at the top shows the transfer of rights between the actors in a transaction. It indicates the transfer of ownership of the product from seller to buyer and the transfer of ownership of the payment vice versa. The exchanges of ownership-rights are reflected in the transfers of the actual custody of the product and the payment (and eventually associated evidence documents). The latter transfer can be mediated by banks that offer money transfers from one account to another or by cash on delivery services provided by carriers. Also payment services such as PayPal support the settlement phase by providing custody of the payment.

The role of mediators in transfers of product custody is quite evident. Carriers like TNT and DHL ship and distribute goods, thus facilitating transactions by giving custody of the transferred products to buyers. Furthermore mediators provide stores, maintain warehouses and operate entire logistics chains to enable physical access to products. The delivery of services and digital goods through mediators via electronic networks can also be viewed as providing physical custody of those products.

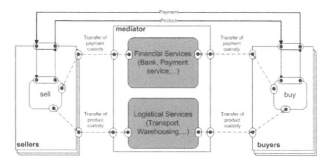

Figure 3.2 Value model of operational mediator value activities.

3.3   Application of the framework

Next to visualizing and categorizing the typical activities of mediators in certain value constellations, the proposed framework should serve as a basis for analyzing specific cases and highlight the role of mediators in real situations. Due to restricted space, a detailed case study to which the framework can be applied will be described in a subsequent work. However, the following example of eBay intends to indicate the usability of the framework to describe typical value activities of a mediator on the informational level.

With a net revenue of 6 billion $ in 2006 eBay is the most successful and probably the most famous online marketplace out there. eBay's main business lies in the provision of an online platform for the sale of goods and services, both by individuals and SMEs. Due to the famous brand and the big customer base, eBay is a good way for sellers to publish their supply to a broad public. By maintaining the online catalogue eBay provides the supply publicity mentioned in the framework. Functionalities like product presentation facilities (adding pictures etc.), search facilities and cross-links to other products of the same seller all contribute to the supply publicity. People pay attention by visiting product pages and become potential customers. At the same time they learn about available products and sellers, which adds to their market knowledge. The publishing of demand is not that distinctive on eBay. The possibility for the seller to track the number of hits on his product-pages is a (rather rudimentary) way to estimate the interest in certain products. Also the possibility to send a comment or ask a question to the seller provides hints for sellers to learn about the buy-side. eBay prescribes the terms and conditions of a trade by way of it's policies. The determination of the price as the most important element of these can be done by way of the auction mechanism of eBay and also via a fixed-price stated by the seller ("Buy-it-now" feature).

The actual transaction (i.e. the transfer of rights of ownership of the product and the payment) is executed directly between buyer and seller. Delivery of custody is done via other mediators, like banks and carriers. However, with PayPal eBay also offers a possibility to handle payments (although PayPal actually does not provide custody of the payment – this is still done via banks or credit card companies).

While the core business of eBay is on the provision of supply publicity and the determination of the price, other mediators focus on different aspects and specialize on certain value activities as described in the framework. Table 3.1 provides an overview of mediators with different aspects.

Table 3. 1 Mediators specializing on different mediation levels.

Mediation Aspects	Informational	¬Informational
Operational	+/+ classic retail stores (example: Wal Mart)	+/– payment companies, banks, carriers (examples: PayPal, DHL)
¬Operational	–/+ e-Marketplaces, search engines, infomediaries (examples: eBay, google, bizrate.com)	–/– direct trades (example: transaction between well known partners)

4   CONCLUSIONS AND FUTURE WORK

In this paper we developed a value-based framework to describe the roles of mediators in collaborative business networks. The framework shows typical media-tor value activities that support the three phases of a market transaction. As a distinguishing feature we proposed two levels on which mediation takes place: The informational level and the operational level.

The framework contributes to a better understanding of the benefits of mediators for the respective actors in a collaborative business network. The value models, which illustrate the mediator value activities on the two levels, can serve as a basis for discussion and as a preparatory step to decide about the best use of a mediator in certain situations. The framework triggers business actors to think about the structure of their business environment (i.e. their CN) and the roles that the various actors take in it. This can lead to the discovery of new business opportunities, if e.g. actors realize that they could utilize their resources to offer a mediator value activity to the network, thus creating profit for themselves. On the other hand emerging threats and existing disadvantages may be identified, due to the observation that mediators handle information in a (for the respective actor) disadvantageous way or that mediators extract too much profit from the network.

The example of eBay indicates the applicability of the framework to specific cases. However, the framework can not only be applied to the e-commerce domain with it's obvious and easily accessible scenarios, but is also intended to support analysis of other kinds of mediators, i.e. any kind of virtual enterprise that mediates between other enterprises. Our main goal for the future is thus to identify suitable and more detailed cases and apply our framework to those, in order to refine and extend it.

5   REFERENCES

1.   Andersson, B., Bergholtz, M., Edirisuriya, A., Ilayperuma, T., Johannesson, P., Grégoire, B., Schmitt, M., Dubois, E., Abels, S., Hahn, A., Gordijn, J., Weigand, H., Wangler, B.: Towards a Reference Ontology for Business Models, In Proceedings of the 25th International Conference on Conceptual Modeling (ER), Tucson, AZ, 2006.
2.   Bailey, J.P., and Bakos, Y.: An Exploratory Study of the Emerging Role of Electronic Intermediaries, International Journal of Electronic Commerce, 1 (1997) 3, pp. 7 – 20.
3.   Bakos, Y.: The Emerging Roles of Electronic Marketplaces on the Internet, Communications of the ACM, 41 (1998) 8, pp. 35 – 42.
4.   Boulle, L. and Nesic, M.: Mediation. Principles, Process, Practice. London et al.: Butterworths, 2001.
5.   Chircu, A.M. and Kauffman, R.J.: Reintermediation Strategies in Business-to-Business Electronic Commerce, International Journal of Electronic Commerce, 4 (2000) 4, pp. 7 – 42.
6.   Datta, P.: Intermediaries as Value Moderators in Electronic Marketplaces. In: Proceedings of the 13th European Conference on Information Systems (ECIS), Regensburg 2005.
7.   Giaglis, G.M., Klein, S., O'Keefe, R.M.: The role of intermediaries in electronic marketplaces: developing a contingency model. Information Systems Journal, 12 (2002) 3, pp. 231 – 246.
8.   Gordijn, J. and Akkermans, H.: Value Based Requirements Engineering: Exploring Innovative e-commerce Ideas. Requirements Engineering Journal, 8 (2003) 2, pp. 114 – 134.
9.   Lindemann, M.A. and Schmid, B.: Framework for Specifying, Building and Operating Electronic Markets. International Journal of Electronic Commerce, 3 (1999) 2, pp.7 – 21.
10.   Malone, T.W., Yates, J., Benjamin, R.I.: Electronic Markets and Electronic Hierarchies. Communications of the ACM, 30 (1987) 6, pp. 484 – 497.
11.   Papazoglou, M.P. and Ribbers, P.M.A.: e-Business. Organizational and Technical Foundations. Chichester: John Wiley & Sons, 2006.
12.   Schulz, K.A., Orlowska, M.E.: Facilitating Cross-Organizational Workflows with a Workflow View Approach. Data & Knowledge Engineering, 51 (2004) 1, pp. 109 – 147.
13.   Spulber, D.F.: Market Microstructure and Intermediation. Journal of Economic Perspectives, 10 (1996) 3, pp. 135 – 152.
14.   Wiederhold, G.: Mediators in the Architecture of Future Information Systems. IEEE Computer, 25 (1992) 3, pp. 38 – 49.

PART 6

VO CREATION

17

A COMPUTER-ASSISTED
VO CREATION FRAMEWORK

Luis M. Camarinha-Matos [1,2], Ana Inês Oliveira [2],
Roberto Ratti [3], Damjan Demsar [4], Fabiano Baldo [5], Toni Jarimo [6]

[1] *New University of Lisbon, PORTUGAL,* cam@uninova.pt
[2] *UNINOVA, PORTUGAL,* aio@uninova.pt
[3] *TXT Solutions, ITALY,* Roberto.ratti@txt.it
[4] *Jozef Stefan Institute, SLOVENIA,* damjan.demsar@ijs.si
[5] *Federal University of Santa Catarina, BRAZIL,* baldo@gsigma.ufsc.br
[6] *VTT Technical Research Centre of Finland, FINLAND,* toni.jarimo@vtt.fi

Computer assistance in the process of creation of virtual organizations (VO) is an important condition for the possibility of having truly dynamic VOs, in response to collaboration opportunities in fast changing market contexts. A realistic approach to materialize agility in VO creation is defined with the assumption of a VO Breeding Environment (VBE) that guarantees the preparedness of its members to quickly get engaged in collaboration processes. A discussion of the process and a set of key functionalities towards a VO creation framework are presented in this context. The approach, architecture, and first results with such tools are described and challenges for future research are identified.

1   INTRODUCTION

The concept of virtual organization (VO) appears as particularly well-suited to cope with very dynamic and turbulent market conditions. This is largely due to the possibility of rapidly forming a consortium triggered by a business opportunity and specially tailored to the requirements of that opportunity. Implicit in this idea is a notion of agility, allowing rapid adaptation to a changing environment. In the heart of this notion is the VO creation process.

Finding the right partners and establishing the necessary conditions for starting a collaboration process have however proved to be costly in terms of time and effort, and therefore an inhibitor of the aimed agility. First a VO planner might face lack of information about the profile and competences of potential partners. The actual capacities and willingness to get involved in a consortium are dynamic and might depend on a negotiation process. Second, collaboration might be hindered by mismatches due to different infrastructures used by different partners, different business cultures and methods of work, different expectations, lack of trust, etc. Overcoming these mismatches is time consuming and therefore an obstacle for rapid consortium formation. Third, the decision on which partner to select for each needed task depends not only on characteristics such as competencies, resources, etc, but also on past performance in collaborative processes, capability to work together with the other partners, and the preferences of the VO planner.

Camarinha-Matos, L., Oliveira, A. I., Ratti, R., Demsar, D., Baldo, F., Jarimo, T., 2007, in IFIP International Federation for Information Processing, Volume 243, Establishing the Foundation of Collaborative Networks; eds. Camarinha-Matos, L., Afsarmanesh, H., Novais, P., Analide, C.; (Boston: Springer), pp. 165–178.

It is therefore necessary to develop an approach and a supporting framework to facilitate the VO creation process in order to make it effective. This article describes the approach developed by the ECOLEAD project and introduces a set of developed tools to support various steps of the VO creation process.

2 PREVIOUS APPROACHES

The VO creation process has received considerable attention in past research work. However, most of the developments were aimed at designing a fully automated process and frequently based on a set of simplistic assumptions.

For example, a large number of works have been published on the application of multi-agent systems and market-oriented negotiation mechanisms for the VO formation. One early example can be found in [19], which assumes a virtual market place where enterprises, represented by agents, can meet each other and cooperate in order to achieve a common business goal. A similar work is found in [14] where a more detailed analysis of the problem of goal decomposition, leading to a hierarchy of VO goals, is done. The work described in [21] identifies the need for yellow pages agents that are responsible to accept messages for registering services. They also consider the notion of Local Area, a concept similar to the Local Spreading center first introduced by the HOLOS system [17, 18]. [11] elaborates further on the application of market-oriented principles, such as the general equilibrium in micro-economics. More recently, [12] describes a game-theoretic approach to support negotiation in VO formation. More recent works have attempted to progress with new negotiation protocols, auction mechanisms, distributed matching processes, learning, etc.

In order to improve the effectiveness of the contracting process and to dynamically form VOs, the need to develop forms of e-contracting has also been identified. Several significant characteristics for the e-contracting process can be found in [3]. Deontic logic [15] is used to describe contract models specifying obligations, permissions, and forbiddances for a specific business process which works in an extremely ideal process. Contracts in CrossFlow and E-ADOME projects describe the agreed workflow interfaces as activities and transitions, based on WfMC's WPDL (Workflow Process Definition Language).

Another line of work is the service-federation approach or implicit VO creation. companies (potential members of the virtual organization) are considered as "service providers", i.e. the potential collaborative behavior of each company is "materialized" by a set of services [1].

Other researchers put the emphasis on formulating the VO creation as an optimization problem. Several researchers present integer programming models where the objective is to minimize total costs which consist of production, operation, and transportation costs, for instance [8, 13, 22]. However, it has been recognized that VO creation is essentially a multi-criteria decision-making problem, including also soft factors such as corporate culture, personal preferences, and learning ability, which are not incorporated in pure cost models. Responding to this challenge, earlier literature presents some multi-criteria models, which however seem to lack one important issue, namely explicit modeling of inter-organizational correlations between partner candidates [4, 16, 20].

For instance collaboration history, trust, and similarity of ICT infrastructure are criteria that need to be considered for a group of organizations rather than for a single organization. On the other hand, several other aspects, in addition to the preferences of the VO planner, are of a dynamic nature in the sense that they depend on the negotiations with potential partners.

3   THE ECOLEAD FRAMEWORK

As mentioned above, when the window of opportunity is short, in order to support the rapid formation of a VO it is necessary that enough information is available about potential partners and that they are ready and prepared to participate in such collaboration. This readiness includes common interoperable infrastructure, common operating rules, common cooperation agreement, and a base trust level among the organizations, among others. Therefore, the approach adopted in ECOLEAD considers that dynamic VOs are mostly created in the context a VO Breeding Environment (VBE). A VBE can be defined [2, 5] as: an association of organizations and their related supporting institutions, adhering to a base long term cooperation agreement, and adoption of common operating principles and infrastructures, with the main goal of increasing both their chances and their preparedness towards collaboration in potential Virtual Organizations. Some of the main aims of the VBE include:

- Establish the base trust for organizations to collaborate in VOs.
- Reduce the cost/time to find suitable partners for configuration of the VOs.
- Assist with the creation, reaching agreements, and contract negotiation for establishment of VOs.
- Assist with the dynamic reconfiguration of the VOs, thus reducing the risk of losses due to some organization failures.
- Provide some commonality for interaction by offering: (i) Base ICT infrastructure (for collaboration), thus reducing the set up times during the VO formation; (ii) Cooperative business rules and common metrics to evaluate member's credibility and performance; (iii) Template contracts for involvement in VOs; (iv) Base ontology for the sector targeted by the VBE.
- In addition to the enterprises, a VBE might include other kinds of organizations (such as consulting/research institutes, sector-associations, governmental support organizations, etc.) and even free-lancer individual workers that represent a one-person small organization. A VO is a temporary organization triggered by a specific business / collaboration opportunity. Its partners are primarily selected from the VBE members. In case there is a lack of skills or capacity inside the VBE, organizations can be recruited from outside. For difficulties of preparedness, trust, etc, this last category will, of course, be the last resort.

When a contract for a new collaboration opportunity is already "guaranteed", the VO creation process can be illustrated by Fig. 1 [7]. The preparatory planning phase includes:

- Collaboration Opportunity Identification and Characterization: this step involves the identification and characterization of a new Collaboration Opportunity (CO) that will trigger the formation of a new VO. A collaboration opportunity might be external, originated by a customer and detected by a

VBE member acting as a broker. Some opportunities might also be generated internally, as part of the development strategy of the VBE.

- Rough VO planning: determination of a rough structure of the potential VO, identifying the required competencies and capacities, as well as the organizational form of the VO and corresponding roles. At this stage it is important to define the partnership form which is typically regulated by contracts and cooperation agreements.

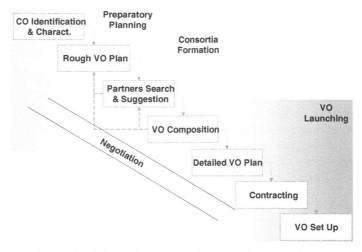

Figure 1 – VO creation process for acquired opportunity

The consortia formation phase departs from the previous characterization and rough planning and mainly includes:

- Partners search and suggestion: perhaps one of the most addressed topics in past research this step is devoted to the identification of potential partners, and their assessment and selection.
- Negotiation: is an iterative process to reach agreements and align needs with offers. It can be seen as complementary to the other steps in the process and runs in parallel with them as illustrated in Fig. 1.
- VO composition: in which the organizational structure and assignment of roles to VO members are made.
- The VO launching phase includes:
- Detailed VO planning: once partners have been selected and collaboration agreements are reached, this step addresses the refinement of the VO plan and its governance principles.
- Contracting: involves the final formulation and modeling of contracts and agreements as well as the contract signing process itself, before the VO can effectively be launched. In other words, this step is the conclusion of the negotiation process.
- VO set up: the last phase of the VO creation process, i.e. putting the VO into operation, is responsible for tasks such as configuration of the ICT infrastructure, instantiation and orchestration of the collaboration spaces, selection of relevant performance indicators to be used, setting up of the VO governance principles, assignment and set up of resources/activation of

services, notification of the involved members, and manifestation of the new VO in the VBE.

In the business domain it is however very often necessary to consider two main phases, as shown in Fig. 2.

1. Quotation/bidding – when a collaboration opportunity is found it is necessary to prepare a bid/quotation in order to try to get a contract with the customer. For the preparation of this bid, it is necessary to make a rough plan of the foreseen VO and to also select the core partners. The bid is often prepared by this initial consortium. In case the bid is unsuccessful, the core consortium dissolves; otherwise we move to the next phase.

2. Final VO creation – In case the bid is successful, the VO's rough plan needs to be revised, based on the specific conditions of the contract with the customer, new additional partners might be necessary, and the VO will be finally detailed and launched.

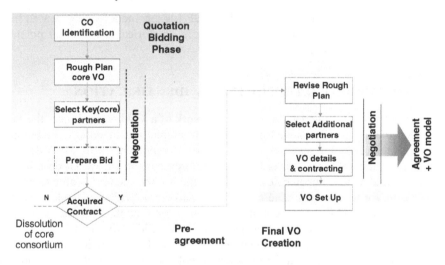

Figure 2 – VO creation process for quotation/bidding

Based on the process and requirements described above, and as a result of extensive interaction with industry end-users, the VO creation framework developed by the ECOLEAD consortium (by different partners, namely UNINOVA, TXT, JSI, UFSC, VTT, and ITESM) is focused on the following tools (Fig. 3):

a) Collaboration opportunity (CO) finder,
b) CO characterization and VO rough planner,
c) Partners' search and suggestion, and
d) Agreement negotiation wizard, which are introduced in the next sections.

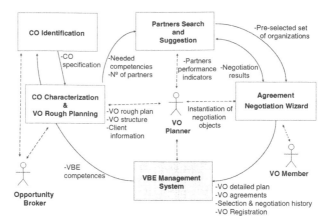

Figure 3 – VO creation support tools

These tools are supposed to interact with a VBE Management System (VMS) from where relevant data (e.g. profiles, competencies, historical data) about potential partners can be collected.

4   COLLABORATION OPPORTUNITY IDENTIFICATION

The coFinder tool is aimed at facilitating the work of a VO broker. It uses the same approach that is usually carried out manually: comparing potential collaboration opportunities (calls for tenders) with the actual competencies of the VBE. The matching in the coFinder tool is based on the comparison of textual descriptions of tenders and VBE competencies. Similar to the broker, the tool is able to browse public calls for tenders available on the Web and extract calls for tenders' descriptions from the HTML pages. coFinder is able to compute their similarity in order to estimate the interestingness of the calls for tenders, identify the most promising ones, and finally propose them to the broker as potential collaboration opportunities. The output of the system is a list of potential collaboration opportunities stored in an XML document.

The collaboration opportunity identification process comprises several steps:

1. First, the user provides information such as a list of tender servers that he intends to use for finding potential collaboration opportunities. In addition, for each server, the user must create a template that is used to identify tenders' descriptions inside the HTML pages. There are two possible ways of creating a template: semi-automatically, by comparing two existing calls for tenders on the server, or manually by editing the HTML code of an existing call for tenders. Another input needed is the competencies of the VBE.
2. After all this information is provided, the coFinder tool crawls all the specified servers and gathers calls for tenders' web pages. It is possible to schedule this process to retrieve new calls for tenders periodically.
3. The next step is parsing. The template previously built is used here to extract tenders' descriptions from their web pages. The information is then stored in a database using the CO XML schema.

4. Once the calls for tenders' description has been extracted and structured, it is possible to identify potential collaboration opportunities by matching tenders' description with the available competencies (an example is shown in Fig. 4). The interestingness factor is computed for each tender. This measure is a weighted sum of the similarity between textual fields describing the call for tenders and textual fields describing VBE competencies.

Figure 4 - Example of a CO

To limit the number of potential collaboration opportunities, a threshold is used for the interestingness measure. The user, at the beginning of the process, sets this threshold. The VO broker will be notified by e-mail only about the potential collaboration opportunities that are above this threshold. It is also possible to browse and search through all the collected tender data, select the tenders suitable for VO creation, or just select the data to be sent by an e-mail to the VO broker. Since all needed data is not always available in the tender data supplied by the server, the system offers the possibility to include some data that the VO broker may collect using other methods (phone calls, email correspondence, etc.). Such data can be useful in further steps of VO creation.

5   CO CHARACTERIZATION AND VO ROUGH PLANNING

This section describes the second tool of the VO Creation framework, the CO Characterization and VO Rough Planning (COC-Plan) tool. Once a Collaboration Opportunity is identified, it should be better described and represented in a structured way in order to support the VO broker during the CO definition and characterization process. In this stage, the preparation of a detailed structure of the VO process is also needed. The objective of the module is twofold:

1. To characterize the CO, by completing the CO description form initialized by the coFinder module. In particular, the CO description form is completed with the name of the VO broker, the needed competencies and the required contractual conditions, while the product/service to be provided by the collaborative VO is decomposed into a tree of sub-entities.

2. To roughly plan the VO, by selecting the collaboration modality of the VO to be created and activating the corresponding modeling tool (editors) and high-level planning.

The approach used consists in characterizing the CO in terms of product (definition of assemblies, components and even services according to an extended-product definition), project (activities, sub-activities and even products according to an extended-product definition), competencies required, and VO Rough Plan. This is done through an editor, with enhanced and innovative features for importing/exporting from both proprietary (like MS Project) and Open Source planning tools (i.e. GANTTProject). The characterized CO and the roughly planned VO are then passed to Partner Search and Suggestion and Negotiation wizard tools for selection of the partners and agreement negotiation.

The aim of the tool is to be a simple web-based application for enabling an easy-to-model approach for the VO planner. Thanks to a wizard like architecture, the modeling phase is relatively simple. By using a unique underlying Reference Model (XML schema), which unifies heterogeneous data sets and applications, the so called VO Model, an innovative aspect of the tool is the provision of a neutral data format and import/export functions for integrating legacy applications: ProJect Management Model (PJMM). Other innovative assets provided by the tool are the support to both the Resource-driven and Activity-driven management, and support to legacy applications. Fig. 5 shows one user interface for the module.

Figure 5 – CO Characterization and VO Rough Plan tool

6   PARTNERS SEARCH AND SUGGESTION

The partner search and suggestion (PSS) process is decomposed in four functionalities, namely, Suggestion Criteria Identification, Partners Search, Generation of Suggested VOs, and Sensitivity Analysis. Fig. 6 presents the whole PSS process including both the information and control flows.

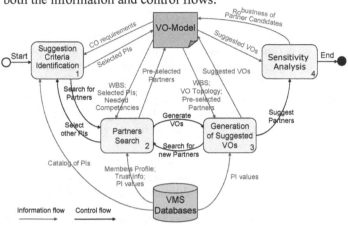

Figure 6 – Partners Search and Suggestion process

The suggestion criteria identification is the first stage in the PSS process. It comprises the selection of the most suitable performance indicators (PIs) used to measure organization's performance. In order to perform such process, it is assumed that the VBE has a well-defined set of PIs used to measure performance among those organizations that belong to it. The approach to identify the proper PIs is the utilization of information extraction techniques to annotate and indexing the information that describes the PIs. Using this indexed information combined with the VO's requirements, the entire set of PIs can be filtered and hence just the suitable ones are selected.

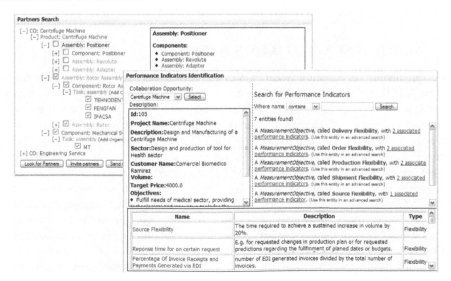

Figure 7 – Examples of interfaces of the PSS tool

The partners search is performed using as main input the CO decomposition. This decomposition means the fragmentation, in elementary parts, of either a product or a service that must be produced or provided by a VO. The aim of partner search is to find the right organizations inside the VBE that can fit the required competencies assigned to the parts of the CO decomposition, as well as to fulfill the required partners' performance identified in the previous step.

The generation of suggested VOs identifies good VO configurations based on multi-criteria optimization models. Among others, the approach takes into account costs, risks, earlier performance, and even inter-organizational dependencies [10]. The generation of suggested VOs, combined with the sensitivity analysis functionality, allows the user to explore Pareto-efficient configurations and further modify and evaluate them. The VBE manager of a test case [9] was particularly satisfied with the model's capability of highlighting inter-organizational dependencies; for a decision maker it is difficult to intuitively see the total synergies of different configurations.

Table 1 presents an example of outcome provided by the generation of suggested VOs. The optimization routines identified five good configurations, on which the decision-maker can perform different kinds of sensitivity analysis.

Table 1 – Five suggested configurations and their performance on three criteria (all criteria are minimized).

#	Bending of pipes	Engin-eering	Gear milling	Grinding	Project mgmt	Cost	Risk	Collab oration
1	SMA	Schuler	Okey	Brunner	VF AG	131000	0,25	86
2	SMA	Schär	Okey	Brunner	VF AG	133000	0,25	85
3	SMA	Schär	Okey	Brunner	Schär	132000	0,75	73
4	SMA	AE&P	Okey	Brunner	VF AG	123000	0,75	83
5	SMA	AE&P	Okey	Brunner	AE&P	122000	1,25	70

For instance, Configurations 1 and 2 are less risky, whereas Configuration 5 is less expensive and the partners have better collaboration history. Moreover, SMA, Okey, and Brunner seem to be robust partner candidates, since they perform the same task in all the suggested configurations. The tool's novelty lies in its ability to account for risks and inter-organizational dependencies.

7   AGREEMENT NEGOTIATION WIZARD

The agreements' negotiation wizard (WizAN) runs in parallel to all the other tools of the VO Creation Framework, and is aimed at assisting human actors during negotiation processes towards the VO establishment. The full negotiation process involves a number of elementary negotiations in order to reach the necessary agreements with the purpose to accomplish VO internal agreement. Given so, the internal consortium agreement is the result or synthesis of all agreements established among the participants of the VO being created and that will regulate their collaboration [6]. The main inputs for WizAN are collected along the various steps of the VO creation process as illustrated in Figs. 1 and 2. These inputs shall come from the other tools previously described; for instance, the coFinder tool will provide WizAN with the CO identity, the "client" and other relevant data about the CO; the COC-Plan tool provides WizAN with the structure of the process, the suggestion of the needed competencies, etc.; finally, the PSS tool provides WizAN with a suggested list of the most suitable configuration of partners to fulfill the CO requirements.

In order to properly answer to the identified requirements, WizAN comprises four main functionalities:

- CTR (Contract Templates Repository) that is a collection of agreement templates and clause templates to support the agreement creation;
- CE (Contract Editor) that uses the CTR and agreed negotiation topics to add new clauses to agreements;
- VNR (Virtual Negotiation Room) that is a virtual "place" where the negotiation participants can access the various negotiation topics and can "discuss" in order to reach the necessary agreements (Fig. 8);
- SAE (Support for Agreement Establishment) with facilities for agreement signing and notification of relevant parties, and repository/archive for its storage (a kind of e-notary).

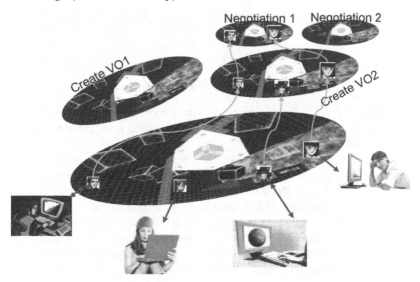

Figure 8 – Virtual negotiation rooms

There are two different situations where a negotiation might be required: (i) to select the best partners to compose the VO, and (ii) reaching agreement on the details of the VO. The WizAN is then intended to provide facilities for both, being the main result of it an agreement where all the related issues of the VO are covered.

Fig. 9 illustrates a rough flow of the negotiation during a VO creation process. Also in this figure, the relationship between WizAN and the other tools that are part of the VO Creation framework is depicted.

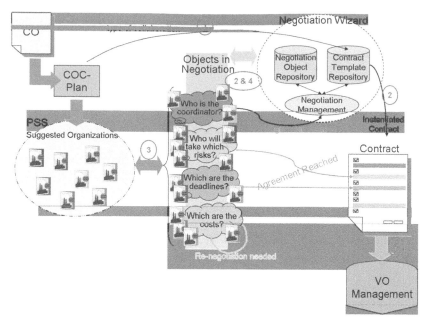

Figure 9 – WizAN usage scenario illustration.

1. First of all, it is necessary to know the type of collaboration that a specific CO requires. That kind of information is essential to conduct the rest of the negotiation;

2. With this information the WizAN can select the right template and also instantiate some general negotiation topics for that specific type of CO;

3. In parallel with the negotiation, the partner search and suggestion process is performed. It is important to synchronize the partner search and selection according to the negotiation. For instance, when it is identified that is necessary to reach some agreements during the partner selection, this process shall be suspended and the execution should be handed over to WizAN until the agreement is reached;

4. After finishing the partners search and suggestion process, another bunch of negotiation steps should start. At this point, it is necessary to reach agreements concerning rights, duties, responsibilities, etc.;

5. Compilation of those agreed negotiation topics in order do build the so called "Contract" or consortium agreement. At this point, tools to support the collaborative writing of documents, as well as e-notary functions can be used;

6. Although all these tools suggest certain configurations for the VO creation, it is important to remark that final decisions are always subject of human interaction.

In Fig. 10 some of the developed interfaces of the WizAN tool are illustrated.

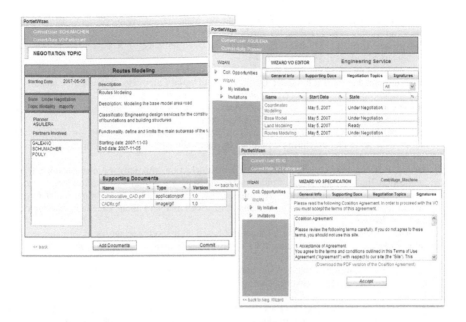

Figure 10 – Example of WizAN Interfaces

8 CONCLUSIONS

The time and amount of resources consumed during the VO creation process whenever a business/collaboration opportunity is acquired, give a good indication of the level of agility of a collaborative network. The effectiveness of this process mainly depends on the availability of adequate information about potential partners and their level of preparedness for VO involvement. The existence of a VO breeding environment facilitates the fulfillment of these requirements and thus enables truly dynamic VOs.

The ECOLEAD approach to VO creation is developed under such assumption, and proposes a detailed process covering all required steps from the identification of the collaboration opportunity till the actual launching of the VO that will exploit that opportunity. A set of tools are proposed to support an iterative decision-making process in which the final decisions are made by the broker/VO planner.

Acknowledgements. This work was supported, in part, be the European Commission through the ECOLEAD project. The authors also thank the contribution of their partners.

9 REFERENCES

1. Afsarmanesh, H., & Camarinha-Matos, L. M. (2000). Future smart organizations: A virtual tourism enterprise. Proc. of WISE 2000 -1st ACM/IEEE International Conference on Web Information Systems Engineering, Hong Kong.
2. Afsarmanesh, H., L. M. Camarinha-Matos (2005). A framework for management of virtual organization breeding environments. In: Collaborative Networks and their Breeding Environments, pp. 35–48, Springer, Boston.
3. Angelov, S., P. Grefen (2003). The 4W framework for B2B e-contracting. Int. J. Networking and Virtual Organizations, 2, No. 1, 78–97.

4. Boon, B. H., Sierksma, G. (2003). Team formation: Matching quality supply and quality demand, European Journal of Operational Research, vol. 148, pp. 277–292.
5. Camarinha-Matos, L. M., H. Afsarmanesh (2003). Elements of a base VE infrastructure. Computers in Industry, 51, Issue 2, 139-163.
6. Camarinha-Matos, L. M., Oliveira, A. I. (2006). Contract Negotiation Wizard for VO Creation. Paper presented at the 3rd Int. CIRP Conference on Digital Enterprise Technology, Setúbal.
7. Camarinha-Matos, L. M., Silveri, I., Afsarmanesh, H., & Oliveira, A. I. (2005). Towards a Framework for Creation of Dynamic Virtual Organizations. In Collaborative Networks and theirs Breeding Environments (pp. 69-80): Springer.
8. Ip,W. H., Yung, K. L.,Wang, D. (2004). A branch and bound algorithm for sub-contractor selection in agile manufacturing environment, International Journal of Production Economics, vol. 87, no. 2, pp. 195–205.
9. Jarimo, T., I. Salkari, S. Bollhalter, (2006). Partner selection with network interdependencies: An application. In: Network-Centric Collaboration and Supporting Frameworks, Springer, Boston.
10. Jarimo, T., U. Pulkkinen (2005). A multi-criteria mathematical programming model for agile virtual organization creation. In: Collaborative Networks and their Breeding Environments, Springer, Boston.
11. Kaihara, T. (1999). Supply chain management based on market mechanism in virtual enterprise. In: Infrastructures for Virtual Enterprises - Networking Industrial Enterprises Kluwer Academic Publishers, Boston.
12. Kaihara, T., S. Fujii, S. (2006). Game theoretic negotiation strategy for virtual enterprise with multiagent systems. In: Network-centric Collaboration and Supporting Frameworks, Springer, Boston.
13. Ko, C. S., Kim, T., Hwang, H. (2001). External partner selection using tabu search heuristics in distributed manufacturing, International Journal of Production Research, vol. 39, no. 17, pp. 3959–3974.
14. Li, Y., B. Q. Huang, W. H. Liu, C. Wu, H. M. Gou (2000). Multi-agent system for partner selection of virtual enterprises. In: Proceedings of 16th IFIP World Computer Congress 2000, Vol. ITBM, Publishing House of Electronics Industry, Beijing.
15. Meyer, J. J., R. J. Wieringa (1993). Deontic Logic in Computer Science: Normative System Specification. John Wiley and Sons, 1993.
16. Mikhailov, L. (2002). Fuzzy analytical approach to partnership selection in formation of virtual enterprises, Omega, vol. 30, pp. 393–401.
17. Rabelo, R.J., L. M. Camarinha-Matos (1994). Negotiation in Multi-Agent based dynamic scheduling. Int. Journal on Robotics and CIM, 11, N. 4, 303–309.
18. Rabelo, R. J., L. M. Camarinha-Matos, R. V. Vallejos (2000). Agent-based Brokerage for Virtual Enterprise Creation in the Moulds Industry, E-business and Virtual Enterprises (pp. 281-290): Kluwer Academic Publishers.
19. Rocha, A., E. Oliveira (1999). An electronic market architecture for the formation of virtual enterprises. In: Infrastructures for Virtual Enterprises - Networking Industrial Enterprises, Kluwer Academic Publishers, Boston.
20. Sha, D. Y., Che, Z. H. (2005). Virtual integration with a multi-criteria partner selection model for the multi-echelon manufacturing system, The International Journal of Advanced Manufacturing Technology, vol. 25, no. 7-8, pp. 793–802.
21. Shen, W., & Norrie, D. H. (1998). An agent-based approach for distributed manufacturing and supply chain management. In Digital Communications Era of the 21st Century. Boston: Kluwer.
22. Wu, N., Su, P. (2005). "Selection of partners in virtual enterprise paradigm," Robotics and Computer-Integrated Manufacturing, vol. 21, pp. 119–131.

| 18 | COLLABORATION OPPORTUNITY FINDER |

Damjan Demšar[1], Igor Mozetič[1], Nada Lavrač[1,2]
{damjan.demsar, igor.mozetic, nada.lavrac}@ijs.si
1 Jožef Stefan Institute, Ljubljana, SLOVENIA
2 University of Nova Gorica, Nova Gorica, SLOVENIA

We have designed and implemented a software tool coFinder – a collaboration opportunity finder - aimed at facilitating the work of an opportunity broker in Collaborative Networked Organizations. It crawls the web to find potential collaboration opportunities (calls for tenders) and compares them with the actual competencies of companies from a Virtual organization Breeding Environment (VBE). The coFinder tool then structures, aligns and matches textual descriptions of calls for tenders with competencies and suggests a list of potential collaboration opportunities to the broker.

1   INTRODUCTION

A Virtual organisation Breeding Environment (VBE) (Camarinha-Matos and Afsarmanesh, 2003, Plisson et al., 2007) is a long-term association of organisations and related supporting institutions with the potential and willingness to cooperate. A Virtual Organisation (VO) is a short-term alliance of organisations from a VBE with a specific goal of acquiring and fulfilling a business opportunity.

We have designed and implemented a software tool, coFinder, which helps the VO broker in identifying appropriate business opportunities from public Calls for Tenders (CfT). The coFinder tool is aimed at facilitating the work of a VO broker. It uses the same approach that is usually carried out manually by the broker: comparing potential collaboration opportunities (CfTs) with the actual competencies of the VBE, stored in the Profiling and Competency Management System (PCMS, which is part of the VBE Management System VMS) (Ermilova et al., 2005). In order to automate this process, the coFinder tool needs comparable structure of information contained in both sides. These structures can then be aligned and matched with each other in order to detect similarities and consequently detect possible collaboration opportunities. The matching in the coFinder tool is based on the comparison of textual descriptions of tenders and VBE competencies. Like the broker, the tool is able to browse public CfTs available on the web and extract tenders' descriptions from the relevant web pages. Similarly, competencies are also described in web pages or can be manually entered in text format within the coFinder tool. Eventually, coFinder will interact with the PCMS in order to get the competencies. Once the tenders' descriptions and competencies have been provided, coFinder is able to compute their similarity in order to estimate the interestingness of tenders and identify the most promising ones, and finally to propose them to the broker as potential collaboration opportunities. The output of the system is a list of potential collaboration opportunities stored in an XML document. The structure of the document follows the directives imposed by an XML schema specified by the VMS.

In Section 2 we describe the overall architecture of coFinder. A detailed description of the collaboration opportunity identification is in Section 3. An

Demšar, D., Mozetič, I., Lavrač, N., 2007, in IFIP International Federation for Information Processing, Volume 243, Establishing the Foundation of Collaborative Networks; eds. Camarinha-Matos, L., Afsarmanesh, H., Novais, P., Analide, C.; (Boston: Springer), pp. 179–186.

example of using coFinder is given in Section 4. Section 5 presents the results of a recent evaluation of coFinder on scenarios with real-world collaborative networked organizations. In conclusion we show the planned integration of coFinder with other software tools for management of virtual organizations.

2   THE ARCHITECTURE

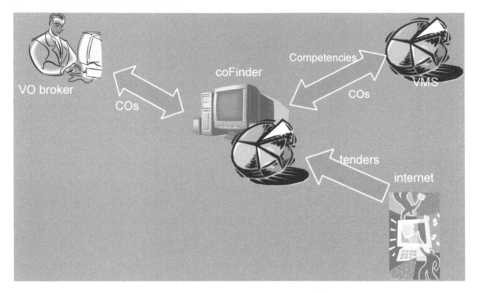

Figure 1: the architecture of coFinder (CO denotes a collaboration opportunity)

The architecture of coFinder is shown in Figure 1. The tool is accessed through a web interface by the VO broker. The coFinder tool accesses internet to collect the data from specified tender servers. It also accesses the VMS (PCMS) to gather competencies data, and returns the selected COs to the VMS.

Implementation-wise, coFinder is a set of PhP tools around a local MySQL database. The most important tools are crawler, parser, browser, and the CfT server template set up tool. The CfT server template set up tool is used to help the user to set up a template, which is used to separate CfTs from other web pages and collect the information from CfT web pages. Additional simple tools are used to collect other information needed to run coFinder.

Some of the tools are used only during the set up (for example the CfT server template set up tool), other tools run on a regular schedule (like crawler and parser), and the rest are used as an interface between the user and the database (for browsing and searching the data). The information always flows through the database. The initial set up data (along with the addresses of the CfT servers and templates for each of the servers) is stored in the database. It is then collected by the crawler and used to gather all new information (web pages) from each of the CfT servers. Web pages are again stored in the database, from where they are collected by the parser. Parser uses the templates to sift out the CfT web pages from the rest and to extract the information about the CfT. This information (in an XML form), along with the calculated similarity to the VBE's competencies, is stored in the database. It is used to inform the users about new CfTs and is also available for browsing.

3   THE COLLABORATION OPPORTUNITY IDENTIFICATION PROCESS

The collaboration opportunity process comprises several steps:

1. input of necessary data, such as list of tender servers urls, templates, XML schemas, etc.,
2. crawling tender servers,
3. parsing the crawled web pages,
4. matching the tender descriptions with the VBE competencies,
5. browsing, editing and adding new tender data.

Steps 1 and 5 require user interaction, while steps 2-4 are automated.

In step 1, the user has to provide some information such as a list of tender servers that he intends to use for finding potential collaboration opportunities. In addition, for each server, the user must create a template that is used to help the system identifying tenders' descriptions inside the HTML pages. Indeed, the HTML format itself does not provide any semantics to access this information directly; therefore a template is needed to detect the tender structure and its contents within the HTML page. Usually, the tender pages on the same server are generated automatically and thus share the same structure to represent tenders. Typically, one or two templates suffice to process all tenders of a single server.

There are two possible ways of creating a template:

- automatically, by comparing two existing tenders on the server, or
- manually by editing the HTML code of an existing tender.

In both cases it is possible to refine the template afterwards with one or more existing tenders or again manually by editing the code of the template.

The creation of a template takes another parameter into consideration, namely the XML schema for the output of collaboration opportunities (the CO schema). In order to create the template automatically, the system takes two existing tender pages and compares them. Since they are generated automatically, they have the same structure but different contents. Only the contents, not the form, should change from one tender to another. This makes it possible to figure out where are the variable parts of the page. A tender template is an HTML code with fields in the form of _#_fieldname_#_ representing the position of data in the tender HTML file. Field names must correspond to the field names in the CO schema. All variable pieces of the server provided HTML must be marked as a field, and as much as possible of unchangeable HTML should remain in the tender template. The template is stored along with the server data in a local database.

Another input needed from the user is the competencies of the VBE. Competencies, in the current system, are entered manually by the broker. It is planned to extend the system in the next version so that it can automatically collect competencies from the PCMS. Competencies are organized in two categories: general competencies and specific competencies. When the connection with PCMS is established, competencies will be collected periodically in order to keep track of the changes, for instance if some partners leave or join the VBE. Eventually, additional information, such as synonyms (e.g., found in the Wordnet lexical ontology), will complete existing competencies.

In step 2, after all the above information is provided, the coFinder tool crawls all the servers specified by the user and gathers tender pages. It is possible to schedule this process to retrieve new tenders periodically. The implementation is dependent on the operating system (for instance Scheduled Tasks on Windows, or crontab on Linux).

The next, step 3, is to parse tender pages. The template built previously is used here to extract tenders' descriptions from their web page. The information is then stored in the database using the CO XML schema.

Step 4: Once the tenders' description have been extracted and structured, it is possible to identify potential collaboration opportunities by matching tenders' description with the competencies available. The interestingness factor is computed for each tender. This measure is a weighted sum of the similarity between textual fields describing the tender (description field in XML and the whole XML) and textual fields describing the VBE competencies (e.g., general and specific competencies).

Step 5: To limit the number of potential collaboration opportunities, a threshold is used for the interestingness measure. This threshold is set by the user at the beginning of the process. The VO broker will be notified by an e-mail only about the potential collaboration opportunities that are above this threshold.

It is also possible to browse and search through all the collected tender data, select the tenders suitable for VO creation, or just select the data to be send by an e-mail to the VO broker. Since all needed data is not always available in the tender data supplied by the server, the system offers the possibility to include some data that the VO broker may collect using other methods (phone calls, email correspondence, etc.). Such data can be useful in further steps of VO creation.

The coFinder structure and data flow is shown in Figure 2. CoFinder first crawls each website from the list of servers and stores the web pages in the local database. Then it parses the collected web pages using tender templates created by the user. For the resulting tender data the interestingness measure is calculated (again storing the complete result in XML form in the local database), and finally the VO broker is notified. The VO broker then checks and possibly edits the data and selects the tenders which are suitable as a basis for potential VO creation. The selected tenders (which can now be called collaboration opportunities) are then delivered as the output of coFinder.

4   AN EXAMPLE OF USE

In this section we show an example of the use of coFinder. When the tool is used for the first time, initial data has to be set up. Most of that data is a simple text like VBE competencies, the e-mail addresses for notification, and the URL addresses of CfTs servers. The most important part of the setup is the definition of CfT server templates. The template is usually generated from two or more CfTs on the server, using a tool in coFinder. This tool compares the web pages of CfTs and asks the user to define the meaning of the differences. The tool in use can be seen in Figure 3, a CfT provided as an input to the tool in Figure 4, and the final template in Figure 5.

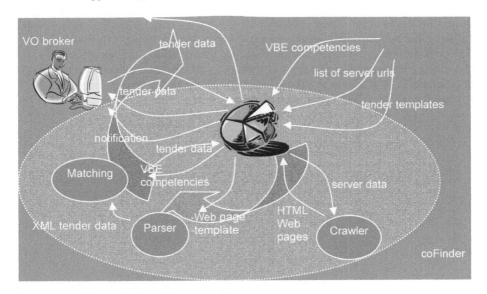

Figure 2: coFinder working procedure

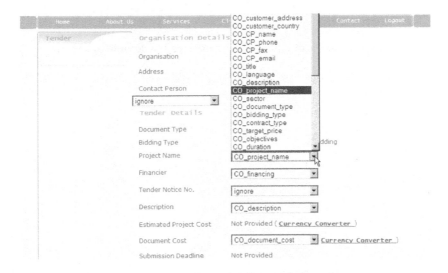

Figure 3: An example of template generation tool in coFinder

After the initial data has been set up, coFinder crawls the specified servers, parses the collected web pages and puts the information about the collected CfTs into the internal database. All CfTs are compared to the VBE competencies as they were set up at the beginning and interestingness factor is calculated. A notification by e-mail is then sent to the specified address, giving information about the best CfTs found on the servers (if any is above the pre-specified interestingness threshold).

The user/broker can use coFinder to browse and search through the collected CfTs (Figure 6). Both, the complete data of the selected call for tender (Figure 7), as well as the original web page can be inspected. The data can also be edited in order to add additional information collected by the broker (e.g., through e-mail, phone calls or other methods) and thereby enrich the data needed during further steps of the VO creation process. To start the process, the broker selects the appropriate CfTs, and marks them as appropriate for VO creation. coFinder then makes the data about appropriate CfTs available to subsequent tools that plan the process needed in VO, suggest the partners, help with negotiation...

Figure 4: An example of Call for Tender from the TerndersInfo.com server

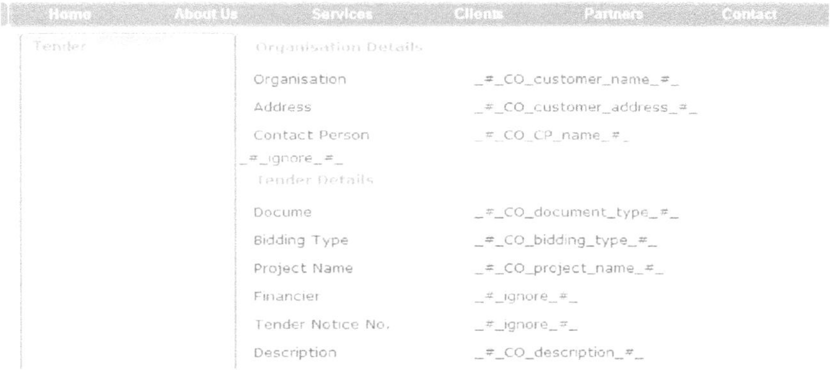

Figure 5: The generated template for the TendersInfo.com server

5   EVALUATION

The coFinder tool was evaluated by three groups of end-users (all from existing VBEs: Swiss Microtech, CeBe Network and ISOIN) after a hands-on exercise. Most of the end-users agree that coFinder is useful in real-life business and will help to save time in their operations. Table 1 shows a part of evaluation questionnaire with answers of one of the end-users. However, most end-users also agree that coFinder should be made easier to use, so we still have to improve on its user interface.

Figure 6: Searching through collected CfTs

Table 1. Part of the end-user questionnaire with answers of one of the test users.

Question	Response
Functionality tested :	Co-Finder
The material objectives are easy to understand	Agree
What makes the comprehension of the material particularly easy ?	CFT are collected automatically
What could be done to increase the comprehension easiness of this material ?	Attach Reference Guide
The material is really useful in your real-life business	Strongly agree
It will help you to gain time in your business	Strongly agree
It will professionalize your activity	Strongly agree
It will increase the trust in your collaborative organization	Agree
It will decrease the risks in your collaborative organization	Disagree
The use of this material will change your business management	Agree
Which are the three parts/functionalities of the material you find particularly relevant ?	Automation of search / Manually create CFT/ Report Status of each CFT
The material is easy to use	Agree
The vocabulary used in the material is relevant and clear	Disagree
The described methodology can be used in your organization	Agree
This template will be applicable in your business environment	Strongly agree
Functionalities are easy to find	Agree
Functionalities are easy to understand	Disagree
Functionalities are easy to handle	Disagree

CO_customer_name	ation Details Organisation CHINA INTERNATIONAL TENDERING COMPANY
CO_customer_URL	
CO_customer_address	CHINA INTERNATIONAL TENDERING COMPANY ROOM 514, JIU LING BLDG. (NORTH WING). NO. 11 XI SAN HUAN BEI LU BEIJING 100089 CHINA Tel : 86-10-68404404 Fax : 86-10-68316696
CO_customer_country	UNKNOWN
CO_CP_name	
CO_CP_phone	
CO_CP_fax	
CO_CP_email	
CO_title	UNKNOWN
CO_language	
CO_Description	SUPPLY OF THE FOLLOWING EQUIPMENTS:- PROFESSIONAL GIS; DESKTOP GIS; GPS; AUTOMATIC WEATHER STATION; AUTOMATIC RAIN-GAUGE; AUTOMATIC RAIN-GAUGE; AUTOMATIC WATER LEVEL; REMOTE SENSING IMAGE; REMOTE SENSING IMAGE; SOFTWARE FOR IMAGE PROCESSING; AUTOMATIC WATER SAMPLER; TDR SOIL MOISTURE METER; ELECTRONIC BALANCE; DRYING OVEN; RAINFALL SIMULATOR; TRANSPORT VEHICLE; COMPUTER; NET SERVER; SWITCH; NOTEBOOK COMPUTER; SCANNER; COPIER; PAGE SETTER; BINDING MACHINE; PRINTER; SLIDE PROJECTOR; PROJECTOR ETC.
CO_project_name	BEIJING ENVIRONMENTAL IMPROVEMENT PROJECT [(LOAN NO.1336) LOAN FUNDED BY THE ASIAN DEVELOPMENT BANK (ADB)]
CO_sector	UNKNOWN
CO_document_type	wbg"> Tender Notice
CO_bidding_type	International Competitive Bidding
CO_contract_type	
CO_target_price	UNKNOWN
CO_objectives	UNKNOWN
CO_duration	UNKNOWN
CO_issuing_date	
CO_opening_date	
CO_due_date	Not Provided
CO_closing_date	
CO_closing_time	
CO_product_description	
CO_volume	UNKNOWN

Figure 7: coFinder parsed data from the call for tender shown in Figure 4

6 CONCLUSION

The coFinder tool is a software tool which can support a Virtual Organization broker in the management of the Virtual Breeding Environment. Its main goal is to help the broker in finding appropriate collaboration opportunities which match the competencies of the VBE. The selected potential collaborative opportunity can be passed to other CO management software tools, such as a tool for collaborative opportunity characterization and rough planning, followed by a tool for appropriate partner search and selection, which can be invoked to suggest a list of potential companies from VBE to actually fulfill the selected collaborative opportunity. In parallel to these activities, there is a negotiation wizard to assist during the negotiation processes of the VO contract.

Acknowledgments

This work was supported by the Slovenian Research Agency programme Knowledge Technologies (2004-2008) and the European 6th Framework Programme project Collaborative Networked Organizations Leadership Initiative (ECOLEAD, IST-1-506958-IP).

7   REFERENCES

1.   Camarinha-Matos LM, Afsarmanesh H. Elements of a base VE infrastructure. Computers in Industry, vol. 51, pp. 139-163, 2003.
2.   Plisson J., Ljubič P., Mozetič I, Lavrač N. An ontology for Virtual Organization Breeding Environments. To appear in IEEE Trans. on Systems, Man, and Cybernetics, 2007.
3.   Ermilova E., Galeano N., Afsarmanesh H., ECOLEAD deliverable D21.2a Specification of the VBE competency/profile management, 2005.

19

AN ONTOLOGY-BASED APPROACH FOR SELECTING PERFORMANCE INDICATORS FOR PARTNERS SUGGESTION

Fabiano Baldo[1], Ricardo J. Rabelo[1], Rolando V. Vallejos[2]
[1]Federal University of Santa Catarina, BRAZIL
baldo@gsigma.ufsc.br
rabelo@das.ufsc.br
[2]University of Caxias do Sul, BRAZIL
rvvallej@ucs.br

In the current fast-paced world, organizations do not have time to postpone ideas due to the lack of suitable technical and scientific supports that can help them in a rapid connection establishment in order to develop collaborative works. This paper presents a methodology that aids the user to find the appropriated performance indicators that may be used to compare and after to suggest a suitable set of organizations to fulfill a specific Collaboration Opportunity. In this work is made an assumption that the Virtual Organization Breeding Environment has a common set of performance indicators that are known and agreed among the involved organizations.

1   INTRODUCTION

In the current fast-paced world, organizations do not have time to postpone colla-boration opportunities (CO), or simply lose them, for the lack of suitable technical and scientific supports that can help them in a rapid connection establishment in order to develop collaborative works. In order to satisfy the organizations' needs of computational and methodological support to collaborate in networks, it was created the research area called "Collaborative Networks". Within the researches provided by this discipline are the studies about "Virtual Organizations". A Virtual Organi-zation (VO) is a dynamic, temporary and logical aggregation of autonomous organizations that cooperate with each other as a strategic answer to attend a given business opportunity or to cope with a specific need, and whose operation is achieved by a coordinated sharing of skills, resources and information, totally enabled by computer networks (Rabelo *et al.*, 2004).

One of the critical aspects concerning the establishment of VOs is how to select the right partners to fulfill a specific CO. This is one of the most discussed problems addressed by VO creation process. However, it was not completely solved, requiring improvements that need to be done in order to reach a suitable level of maturity that can cope with the actual agile requirements claimed by the organizations that desire to collaborate. For example, until few years ago it was supposed that in the creation of a VO partners could be quickly and easily identified and selected from the wide-open universe of organizations. However, nowadays it is known that this is not as simple as it seems to be. Some problems are: How to acquire organizations' infor-mation; How to quickly establish a collaboration infrastructure; How to build trust among organizations (Camarinha-Matos *et al.*, 2005). The more research on VO

Baldo, F., Rabelo, R.J., Vallejos, R.V., 2007, in IFIP International Federation for Information Processing, Volume 243, Establishing the Foundation of Collaborative Networks; eds. Camarinha-Matos, L., Afsarmanesh, H., Novais, P., Analide, C.; (Boston: Springer), pp. 187–196.

creation gained maturity the more it was realized that automatic approaches for that showed unfeasibility. A result of this observation was, for example, that the term "partners selection" has been replaced by "partners suggestion", highlighting the need of more intense involvement of users along the process. Another result is that past approaches stated that costs and delivery dates would be enough to suggest partners. Today is a common sense that is necessary to utilize a well-know, agreed and meaningful set of criteria to more accurately suggest appropriated organizations for VOs. Moreover, each CO and consequently each VO tends to be so particular that suggestion criteria cannot be defined *a priori* or in a fixed way. Instead, the most suitable criteria are necessary to be elected as a way to maximize the VO effectiveness. This is what this paper is about, introducing a methodology to guide in the identification of criteria to suggest partners for the creation of VOs.

This paper is organized as follow. In chapter 2, the problem of finding the right partners for a specific VO is stated. In chapter 3, it is shown the strategy of identifying criteria to suggest partners. Chapter 4 presents in detail the methodology conceived to identify the most suitable set of criteria. Chapter 5 addresses some implementation aspects concerning the development of this methodology. At the end, it is presented the conclusion and future works.

2   CRITERIA IDENTIFICATION FOR PARTNER SUGGESTION

First works related to partners suggestion just considering as suggestion criteria information regarding costs, delivery dates and availability of resources. However, during the last years it was realized that only use these reduced set of generic information is not enough to really ensure the quality of such suggestion. Petersen (2003) emphasizes the importance to select partners using a well defined set of criteria based on a common set of attributes known by every interested organization. Following the idea introduced by Petersen, an alternative of common set of criteria to be applied in partners search and suggestion might be the utilization of the same information used to measure performance either within or among organizations, e.g., SCOR Model, Balanced Scorecard, benchmarks, etc. That is an approach that can be used by those groups of organizations (e.g., VBEs) that already have a common performance measurement model, i.e., they can use these performance indicators (PIs) as criteria for partners search and suggestion. Nevertheless, in order to use measurement models – that are very large in most of the cases – it is necessary to find a way to reduce the number of indicators that are relevant to be applied in such kind of process. Moreover, this filter of indicators should be performed taking into account the type of the CO as well as its requirements and preferences.

How to identify the most important indicators considering the CO's preferences and requirements remains a question under discussion. Some of the studies carried out until now, specially those addressed by Seifert *et al.* (2005), Bittencourt *et al.* (2005) and Grudzewski *et al.* (2005), deal with PIs as criteria to suggest organizations for new VOs. However, these works did not tackle the problem of which PI to use for each particular CO.

Taking into consideration this gap of formalization concerning the identification of PIs for partners search and suggestion, this work presents a strategy to filter the whole set of PIs in order to identify those that can be used to compare and after to suggest organizations for new VOs.

In this work, it is assumed that the suggestion criteria can be represented through organizations' PIs. It means that the VO Breeding Environment has a well-defined set of PIs used to measure performance among its members. A VO Breeding Environment (VBE) represents a long-term association of organizations that are prepared to effectively cooperate, establishing a VO or another form of dynamic collaborative networked organization, in the right time that a CO is identified (Afsarmanesh *et al.*, 2005).

3　APPROACH

The strategy adopted in this work to minimize the set of PIs and thus to find the most relevant ones is described in three general steps.

1.　To get as much information as possible about the description of those PIs that compose the entire set of indicators that are used to measure performance among organizations.
2.　To indeed understand what they mean through the processing of the unstructured textual information and recognition of relevant words that explain what they exactly represent and measure.
3.　To identify the proper PIs for a specific CO applying filters that take into consideration the CO's preferences and constraints.

The filtering of PIs can be seen as a problem of searching for information. The search for information is a field of study of the information retrieval discipline that uses search engines to perform such process. However, only applying a search engine to solve the problem of finding the most relevant PIs is a too simplistic solution that actually does not provide the expected result for this specific problem. This assertion can be supported because different PIs, described in different words, at different organizations, using different models, sometimes can represent the same thing. Yet, different PI implementations of the same model can present different scope and real meaning.

How to represent that similarity of different PIs is something that traditional information retrieval techniques do not support. Therefore, in order to cope with this it is necessary to introduce somehow an additional level of information that can understand the diversity of variation of PIs and thus retrieval the right ones even if they do not have an explicit correlation. A way to do that is using an ontology that can understand the range of variation that a PI can have as well as the similarity among them.

The problem of how to use an ontology to introduce this additional level of information within the PIs' description can be supported by the concept of semantic annotation. Semantic annotation is currently considered the state-of-the-art when retrieval of information is concerned. The term *annotation* refers to the use of auxiliary symbols that are used to modify the interpretation of other symbols (Dorado *et al.*, 2003). Semantic annotation techniques use ontologies to perform the proper annotation of the significant words included in the text. Therefore, in order to semantically annotate the PIs' description it is necessary to specify a comprehensive ontology that describes in a sensible way all the relevant concepts related to PIs' characterization. Although the semantic knowledge, introduced by semantic annotation, can add power and accuracy to information retrieval, the knowledge base needed to perform such process is difficult to obtain. In most cases, the knowledge base is created manually (Riloff *et al.*, 1997). This work fits in this problem, i.e., the ontology as well as the knowledge base used to annotate the information had to be manually encoded using several information sources.

Regarding the input parameters used to filter the whole set of PIs it is used the CO's preferences and constraints. In fact, they are requirements provided during the CO characterization, in a textual matter, and describe the aspects that should be taking into account in order to create the envisaged VO. This requirement can be something as a recommendation, i.e., a *preference*, or something that must be followed, i.e., a *constraint*.

In order to relate COs with PIs and thus to add another level of assistance in the process of PIs retrieval, it was extended the PIs ontology to include the characterization of concepts related to COs, especially those about preferences and constraints and their relationship with PIs. These correlations are the key issues taken into account during the PIs identification.

4   PROPOSED METHODOLOGY

First of all, it is important to keep in mind that the methodology being developed and presented in this work intends to *assist* the user to identify the most appropriated PIs for a given CO instead of doing it automatically, i.e., it supports the user that is who drives the process and takes the final decision.

This methodology is composed of two parts. One that runs just once, called *preparation phase*, and another one that runs whenever a new VO needs to be created to fulfill a certain CO, called *execution phase*. The first part of the methodology comprises the setup of the environment as well as the acquisition of information in order to identify the PIs in the second phase of the methodology. It intends to be as generic as possible to be used for every VBE that has a pre-defined set of PIs applied to measure performance among its members. This methodology uses a specific ontology to perform the PIs identification. This ontology is detailed in the next section. Figure 1 shows the whole methodology that is briefly described below.

Preparation phase:

1. Acquisition of the information related to those PIs (catalog of PIs) that are being used to measure the organizations' processes and activities in a given VBE. It means to obtain information, such as PI name, PI description and PI type.
2. Application of a semantic annotation technique, combined with an ontology that describes PIs, to create annotations in the PIs' information gathered in the previous step. A semantic annotation links a given concept of an ontology to a piece of information inside a text (Kiryakov *et al.*, 2003). After that, these annotations are indexed to improve the retrieval of information.

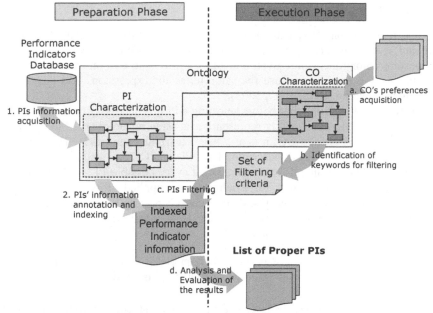

Figure 1 – Performance Indicators Identification Methodology

Execution phase:

a. Acquisition of the preferences and constraints' list that the CO needs to fulfill. This list is required to create a VO that performs the envisaged collaboration.

b. Identification of the CO performance requirements based on the match between the preferences and constraints list and the CO ontology. These performance requirements comprise a list of keywords that will be taken into account for filtering the set of PIs.

c. Search for the proper PIs based on the keywords selected previously. In this step, information retrieval techniques are used to search for PIs indexed in the preparatory phase.

d. Analysis and evaluation of the results in order to ensure whether the PIs are good enough to start the partners search and suggestion. This is a subjective task that should be driven by the human user, who is responsible for taking the final decision considering his expertise about the subject.

Using the methodology described above, the user can perform the partners search and suggestion process with more accurate information to firstly compare the candidates and thus to suggest those that better fit the performance expectation. Besides that, this methodology can be combined with some already developed works in order to improve their results. For instance, Bittencourt *et al.* (2005) applies Analytic Hierarchy Process in the PIs to express the importance of them for the whole CO success. Seifert *et al.* (2005) uses PIs to predict the performance of a set of potential VO partners. Jarimo *et al.* (2006) optimizes VOs' configurations using PIs as optimization parameters. Vallejos *et al.* (2006) proposes a framework to create VBEs and in this framework it is applied a benchmark that can be used as source of PIs for the methodology presented in this work.

4.1   Ontology

The objective of an ontology is to provide a representation of knowledge that can be used and re-used in order to facilitate the comprehension of concepts and the relationships among them in a given domain. By providing definitions, an ontology helps people and machines to use the same terms for expressions and thus better mutual understanding (Khan *et al.*, 2003).

It is reasonable to think that before selecting a PI it is necessary to understand it. A good way to understand PIs is representing it using an ontology. Moreover, to identify the proper PIs for a CO, it is also necessary understand COs. The ontology conceived in this work aims at describing both PIs and COs as well as the relationships between them. It intends to conceptualize every possible PI and CO and also states for each kind of CO which PIs would be better applied. However, to create an ontology manually is not an easy task that can be performed in an ad-hoc way, unlike it is necessary to follow some principles. Here, it was adopted the recommendations proposed by Missikoff *et al.* (2002):

- It was verified if there is any other ontology specified for this specific domain. In fact, it was figured out that there is no ontology specified for this domain.
- It was selected several sources of information that could help the process of understanding the concepts related to that domain. Some of these sources are: performance measurement reference models, benchmarks, PIs cases, etc.
- It was consulted some domain experts in order to realize which are the most important aspects that an ontology that describes PIs and COs should cover. These experts were, in most of the cases, business consultants and economics researchers.

A way to start to evaluate what an ontology will describe is preparing some questions that this ontology should provide answer for. A list of the most important questions is:

- What is a PI?
- What is a CO?
- Which aspects are relevant to classify a PI?
- Which are the correlations between a CO and a PI?

A manner to shortly describe which conceptualization an ontology supports is trying to write statements that represent what this ontology characterizes. For that, both PI and CO definitions must be robust enough to represent them generically and hence to allow the conception of an ontology (figure 2, in a top level) for them. In this work they are defined as:

− A PI, in a general way, has the purpose to measure *something*, with an *objective*, considering a specific *perspective*, applied to a *domain*, using a *calculation rule* and providing results in a certain *measurement unit*.

− A CO is an entity that provides an *outcome*, considering some *technical specifications*, classified according to a *modality* and that has some *requirements*. More specifically, the *performance requirements* require performance of *something*, delimited into a *perspective*, having as target an *objective*, comprising a *specific domain*.

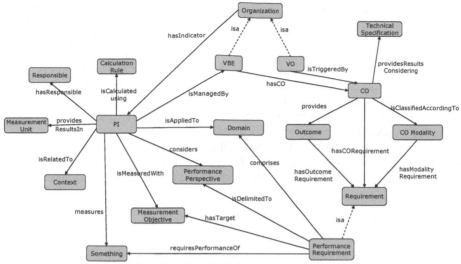

Figure 2 – PI and CO Ontology Top Level

5 IMPLEMENTATION

In order to implement the methodology presented in chapter 4 a prototype is being developed. A list of tools and technologies that provide the necessary features required for the envisaged system have been selected as part of the strategy of taking advantage of using already existing software. The whole environment, presented in figure 3, is composed of:

- The KIM Platform used to semantically annotate, indexing and retrieval information (Kiryakov *et al.*, 2003).
- A web service API that encapsulates the PIs identification programming logic.
- A GUI, developed using the web technology called portlet, where the user can directly access and use the PIs identification system.

The KIM platform was selected mainly because it offers a powerful, well-documented and easy-to-use API for remote access that facilitates the connectivity with other applications. In this particular case, these features are sufficient to implement the PIs identification system.

The tool used to specify the PI & CO ontology was Protégé. This ontology was included as an extension of the ontology provide by KIM. This extension in the KIM's ontology enables KIM to perform the proper semantic annotation of the PIs' description.

The PIs annotation and identification programming logic was coded as a web service API to facilitate other applications to have access to it, for instance Partners Search and Suggestion

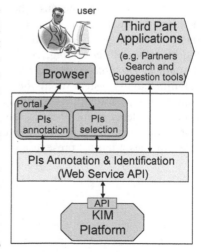

Figure 3 - System Environment

tools, rather then just to provide a predefined GUI as most of the tools used to do. It was decided to follow this approach in order to promote its dissemination as well as because using web service it can be accessed more easily through the utilization of standard web protocols. These API provides services both to annotate and to search for PIs, the former is used during the preparation phase of the methodology, the latter is used in the execution phase of this methology (see Figure 1). The web portal also reflects the approach presented in the methodology. It has two portlets, one devoted to annotate PIs (comprising the preparation phase) and the other one dedicated to select PIs (comprising the execution phase).

The PIs annotation and identification tool is being developed in the scope of the ECOLEAD project (www.ecolead.org). More specifically, it is part of the partners search and suggestion functionality and both belonging to the VO creation system suite.

5.1   Use Case

It can be taken as an example a new CO that arrives in the VBE's domain. This CO has as part of its information some preferences and constraints concerning quality, price and performance. The performance information, stated in a textual manner, serves as input to perform the PIs identification. The process of identification is driven by a human user who is in charge of translating the textual preferences and constraints present in the document that describes the CO in a high-level semantic query. This translation and semantic query construction is supported by the tool. Actually, the tool provides some templates of possible queries where the user just needs to fill in with the keywords took from the textual requirement description. There is a list of templates comprising queries that are more generic, i.e. statements with less parameters, as well as more specific queries, i.e. statements with more parameters. However, if the user prefers to create a semantic query from scratch there is a wizard that guides this process.

For instance, a performance requirement got from the CO description to create a semantic query would be something as: "For a specific CO in the manufacturing industry sector, it is mandatory that the suggested organizations follow the planned schedule of activities, because the deadlines between tasks as well as the time to delivery the final product are short". Instantiating this against the PI definition, the query template generated for that would be: "look for PIs that measure *tasks*, with the objective of *scheduling*, considering the perspective of *responsiveness*, in the domain of *manufacturing industry*". After the user fills this semantic query, it is submitted to the system where the execution phase of the methodology (presented in figure 1) is performed. The resulting PIs will be able to measure things like: the average of delay to fulfill tasks, the percentage of tasks completed on time, etc. At last, with the retrieved PIs, the user can refine this set and thus just to select the most relevant ones. Figure 4 presents a GUI that shows the example explained above.

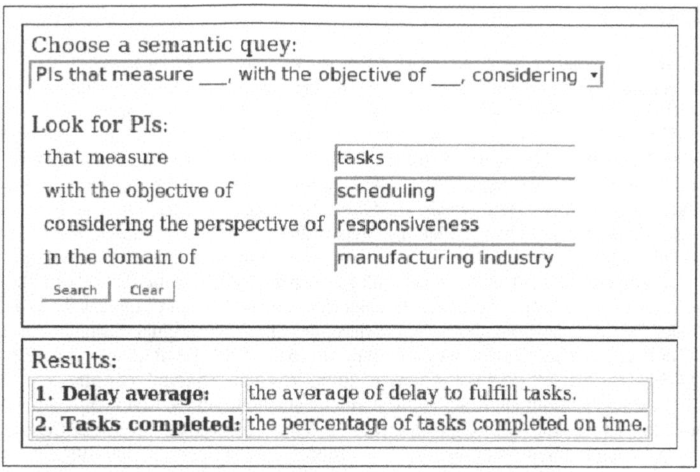

Figure 4 – Screenshot of the tool to identify PIs

6 CONCLUSION

This work has as main contribution the definition of a methodology for PIs identification for VO partners search and suggestion. Actually, it improves the user's decision concerning the selection of organizations giving addition information about what can be used to compare the possible candidates in a more effective way. The user can have different criteria to compare candidates for different types of COs. Hence, he can find better partners comparing them via PIs that better can represent the performance expected in this VO.

Some preliminary tests have pointed out that the methodology works appropriately for, at least, one instance of the manufacturing industry sector. This assertion is based on the fact that part of the information used to test it came from the partners of ECOLEAD project that belong to this sector.

Next short-term goals of this work involves two main actions. The first one refers to the improvement of the wizard semantic query construction with some additional assistance in order to analyze the CO's requirements (in what performance is concerned) and to further generate a list of suggested relevant PIs to select partners for the given CO. The second action consists in the deployment of the system at some project's pilots and hence the application of the methodology in a real case scenario.

Acknowledgements. This work has been partially supported by the CAPES Brazilian Research Agency. It has been developed in the scope of the Brazilian IFM project (http://www.ifm.org.br) and the European IST ECOLEAD project (www.ecolead.org). Special thanks to Mr. Marcus Seifert – from BIBA, Germany – for his substantial contributions concerning the ontology specification.

7 REFERENCES

1. Afsarmanesh, H.; Camarinha-Matos, L. M.; 2005. A Framework for Management of Virtual Organization Breeding Environments. In: 6TH IFIP WORKING CONFERENCE ON VIRTUAL ENTERPRISES (PROVE-05: Sept. 2005: Valencia, Spain). Proceedings. Springer. p. 35-48.
2. Bittencourt, F.; Rabelo, R. J.; 2005. A Systematic Approach for VE Partners Selection Using the SCOR Model and the AHP Method. In: 6TH IFIP WORKING CONFERENCE ON VIRTUAL ENTERPRISES (PROVE-05: Sept, 2005: Valencia, Spain). Proceedings. Springer. p. 99-108.
3. Camarinha-Matos, L. M.; Afsarmanesh, H.; Ollus, M.; 2005. ECOLEAD: A Holistic Approach to Creation and Management of Dynamic Virtual Organization. In: 6TH IFIP WORKING CONFERENCE ON VIRTUAL ENTERPRISES (PROVE-05: Sept, 2005: Valencia, Spain). Proceedings. p. 3-16.
4. Dorado, A.; Izquierdo, E.; 2003. An Approach for Supervised Semantic Annotation. In: Workshop on Image Analysis for Multimedia Interactive Services (WIAMIS: 9-11 Apr. 2003). Proceedings.
5. Grudzewski, W. M.; Sankowska, A.; Wantuchowicz, M.; 2005. Virtual Scorecard as a Decision-making Tool in Creating Virtual Organisation. In: 6TH IFIP WORKING CONFERENCE ON VIRTUAL ENTERPRISES (PROVE-05: Sept, 2005: Valencia, Spain). Proceedings. p. 293-300.
6. Jarimo, T.; Salkari, I.; Bollhalter, S.; 2006. Partner Selection with Network Interdependencies: An Application. In: Seventh Ifip Working Conference on Virtual Enterprises - Network-Centric Collaboration and Supporting Frameworks (Sept. 25-27). Proceedings. Springer. p. 389-396.
7. Khan, L.; Luo, F.; 2003. Ontology Construction for Information Selection. In: 14th IEEE International Conference on Tools with Artificial Intelligence (Washington, DC). Proceedings. p. 122-127.
8. Kiryakov, A.; Popov, B.; Ognyanoff, D.; Manov, D.; et al.; 2003. Semantic Annotation, Indexing, and Retrieval. In: In 2nd International Semantic Web Conference (ISWC2003: 20-23 Oct. 2003: Florida, USA). Proceedings. Springer-Verlag. p. 484-499.
9. Missikoff, M.; Navigli, R.; Velardi, P.; 2002. The Usable Ontology: An Environment for Building and Assesing a Domain Ontology. In: International Semantic Web Conference (ISWC: Sardinia, Italy.). Proceedings.
10. Petersen, S. A.; 2003. Using Competency Questions to Evaluate an Agent-based Model for Virtual Enterprises. In: FOURTH WORKING CONFERENCE ON VIRTUAL ENTERPRISES (PROVE-03: Oct. 2003: Lugano, Switzerland). Proceedings. Kluwer Academic Publishers. p. 261-270.
11. Rabelo, R. J.; Pereira-Klen, A.; Klen, E. R.; 2004. Effective Management of Dynamic Supply Chains. International Journal of Networking and Virtual Organizations.
12. Riloff, E.; Shepherd, J.; 1997. A Corpus-Based Approach for Building Semantic Lexicons. In: Second Conference on Empirical Methods in Natural Language Processing. Proceedings. p. 117-124.
13. Seifert, M.; Eschenbächer, J.; 2005. Predictive Performance Measurement in Virtual Organization. In: Emerging Solutions for Future Manufacturing Systems. Springer. p. 299-307.
14. Vallejos, R. V.; Lima, C. P.; Varvakis, G.; 2006. A Framework to create a Virtual Breeding Environment in the Mould and Die Sector. In: Seventh IFIP Working Conference on Virtual Enterprises (25-27 Sept. 2006: Helsinki, Finland). Proceedings. p. 599-608.

José António Crispim,
Universidade do Minho, PORTUGAL
crispim@eeg.uminho.pt

Jorge Pinho de Sousa
INESC Porto, Faculty of Engineering Univ. Porto, PORTUGAL
jsousa@inescporto.pt

A virtual enterprise (VE) is a temporary organization that pools member enterprises core competencies and exploits fast changing market opportunities Partner selection can be viewed as a multi-criteria decision making problem that involves assessing trade-offs between conflicting tangible and intangible criteria, and stating preferences based on incomplete or non-available information. In general, this is a very complex problem due to the large number of alternatives and criteria of different types. In this paper we propose an integrated approach to rank alternative VE configurations using an extension of the TOPSIS method for fuzzy data, improved through the use of a tabu search meta-heuristic. Preliminary computational results clearly demonstrate its potential for practical application.

1   INTRODUCTION

A virtual enterprise (VE) is a temporary alliance of independent and geographically dispersed enterprises set up to share skills or core competencies and resources, in order to respond to business opportunities, the cooperation among the enterprises being supported by computer networks (Camarinha-Matos and Afsarmanesh, 2003). The creation of a VE is usually triggered by a market opportunity, giving rise to a "project" that is usually decomposable in relatively independent sub-projects or activities. The work needed to "fulfil" a project involves a set of collaborative activities. The cooperation relationship can be represented by an activity network, where the participation of each partner in the project can be viewed as a ring in the chain. The problem of partner selection also arises when the VE needs to be reorganized by adding/expelling some members or by re-assigning tasks or roles in order to better cope with new market circumstances. In this work, we study the partner selection problem under a multi-criteria perspective. First, we review the literature about partner selection methods in various research contexts such as supply chain design, agile manufacturing, network design, dynamic alliances, and innovation management, in order to investigate their applicability to the VE case. We then propose an integrated approach to rank alternative VE configurations using an extension of TOPSIS for fuzzy data, improved through the use of a tabu search metaheuristic. The VE configuration process is a difficult problem due to the complex interactions between the different entities and because the expression of their preferences may be based on incomplete or non-available information. To deal with this problem under a multi-criteria perspective, we allow several types of information (numerical, interval, qualitative and binary) in order to facilitate the expression of the stakeholders' preferences or assessments about the potential

Crispim, J.A., de Sousa, J.P., 2007, in IFIP International Federation for Information Processing, Volume 243, Establishing the Foundation of Collaborative Networks; eds. Camarinha-Matos, L., Afsarmanesh, H., Novais, P., Analide, C.; (Boston: Springer), pp. 197–206.

partners. This is an important requirement in practice as the multiplicity of factors considered when selecting partners for a business opportunity, such as cost, quality, trust and delivery time, cannot be expressed in the same measure or scale. A tabu search meta-heuristic is used to compute and reduce the potential VE configurations and the TOPSIS method is then applied to rank those configurations. The remainder of the paper is organized as follows. In Section 2 the problem is described, in section 3 the literature on the domain is briefly surveyed, in Section 4 the method used to solve the problem is presented, in Section 5 an illustrative example is described and finally, in Section 6 some preliminary conclusions are presented.

2   PROBLEM DESCRIPTION

The VE formation process can be described as follows. Assume a network A representing all potential partners (companies) and their relationships. A specific entity is responsible for the VE formation process (this entity is here referred to as the Decision Maker or DM). Companies and relationships are characterised by a set of m attributes, some assigned to the nodes and some assigned to the edges of the network. These attributes will express the criteria used for evaluating solutions (i.e., VE configurations). The first step in this modelling process is to carefully define what attributes are going to be considered in both subsets. The Decision Maker can give weights to the attributes according to his believes about their relative importance for the project under consideration. The network includes a set of n companies (nodes) connected with each other, capable of performing activities and of providing a finite amount of resources, available over specific intervals of time. We also assume that project P involves k activities that demand a specific amount Q of resources and have to be performed within a given interval of time S. These activities have a number of precedence relationships and therefore form an activity network. Then the partner selection problem consists in choosing the best group of companies to perform all k activities of project P taking into account a set of evaluation criteria based on the m attributes established for the network. The main constraints of the problem are *time windows* and the *minimum amount of resources* required.

Partner selection can be viewed as a multiple attribute decision making (MADM) problem (Li and Liao, 2004). In this problem, the alternatives correspond to groups of enterprises that have the resources and skills needed to carry out the project. Given the multi-criteria nature of the problem, there is generally no "optimal" alternative, and a good "trade-off" solution must therefore be identified. In the classic problem formulation (see Cao and Gao, 2006) the objective is to select the optimal combination of partner enterprises for all activities, in order to minimize the risk or the costs of the project. When partner selection is based on multiple criteria, the objective function (1) can be defined as the sum of the scores for the various criteria. The following variables and parameters are defined:

$$x_{ijt} = \begin{cases} 1 & \text{if activity i is contracted to candidate j for period t} \\ 0 & \text{otherwise} \end{cases}$$

M: set of criteria, $M=\{1, 2, ..., m\}$
l_{lj}: score (contribution) of criterion l for candidate j
d_i: processing time of activity i

$S_i=[f_i; g_i]$: time window (interval) to perform activity i
D: due time to perform the project
K: set of activities in the project, $K=\{1, 2, ..., k\}$
Q_i: quantity of resources needed to perform activity i
$V_j =[u_j; s_j]$: interval of time in which candidate j is available
R_j: capacity (available quantity of resources) of candidate j
W_i: set of candidates for performing activity i
B: maximum investment for the project (budget)
b_{ij}: cost of performing activity i by candidate j

Then, the problem can be modelled as follows:

$$\text{Max} \sum_{l}^{L}\sum_{i}^{k}\sum_{j}^{w_j} l_{li} x_{ijt}, \qquad \forall t \in T \tag{1}$$

$$\text{s.t.} \quad \sum_{i}^{k}\sum_{j}^{w_j}\sum_{t}^{d_i} x_{ijt} b_{ij} \le B \tag{2}$$

$$\sum_{t}^{d_i}\sum_{j}^{w_j} x_{ijt}(f_i + d_i) \le \sum_{t}^{d_k}\sum_{j}^{w_k} x_{kjt} f_k, \qquad \forall i, k \in K \tag{3}$$

$$d \le D, \quad \text{with} \quad d = max\{\sum_{j}^{w_j}\sum_{t}^{d_i}(f_i + d_{ij}) \times x_{ijt}\} \tag{4}$$

$$\sum_{j}^{w_j}\sum_{t}^{d_i} x_{ijt} = 1, \qquad \forall i \in K \tag{5}$$

$$u_j \le g_i - d_i, \qquad \forall i \in K, \quad \forall j \in W_i \tag{6}$$

$$s_j \ge f_i + d_i, \qquad \forall i \in K, \quad \forall j \in W_i \tag{7}$$

Constraint (2) states that the sum of costs is not larger than the global budget for the project. Constraints (3) impose the precedence relationships between the activities. Constraint (4) ensures that the project is completed no later than the project deadline. Constraints (5) impose that for any given activity, only one candidate (or group of enterprises working as an individual element) can be selected. Finally constraints (6) and (7) ensure that the interval of time when the resources of candidate j are available fits the "time window" for activity i. Other constraints related to third party logistics (3PL) might be included but, as an alternative, these aspects can be covered by the objective function through the attributes considered by the decision maker. In this work, we start by identifying potential non-dominate VE configurations, and accordingly we explicitly consider multiple objectives:

$$\text{Max} \; z_1 = \sum_{i}^{k}\sum_{j}^{w_j} l_{li} x_{ijt}, \qquad \forall t \in T \; and \; m = 1 \tag{8}$$

$$\ldots$$

$$\text{Max} \; z_m = \sum_{i}^{k}\sum_{j}^{w_j} l_{li} x_{ijt}, \qquad \forall t \in T \; and \; m = M \tag{9}$$

3   LITERATURE REVIEW

A review of the literature about partner selection methods in various research contexts (such as supply chain design, agile manufacturing, network design, dynamic alliances, and innovation management) has been performed in order to investigate the distinct approaches used to tackle this problem. We have concentrated this survey on research based on mathematical or quantitative decision-making approaches published in the last years (since 2001), and have grouped those approaches according to the methodology adopted. The survey included 41 papers covering quite different perspectives. Three classification criteria have been adopted for categorising the reviewed articles: Research context (Virtual enterprise/dynamic alliance, manufacturing, and supply chain/network; Methods used to solve the problem (almost all the research papers we found use hybrid algorithms), and Criteria/factors on which the partner selection is based. From the 41 papers reviewed, we can summarise our findings as follows.

- Around 74% of the papers were published in the last two and a half years.
- In terms of research context, around 50% of the papers are on virtual enterprises, 25% on manufacturing, and around 25% on supply chains. Although there is a large number of papers published in this last area (supply chain, network design), many of them have not been considered in the survey because they do not tackle partner selection as an isolate problem, but try rather to optimize or create a chain/network configuration considering questions such as localization, inventory management and/or transportation.
- Although around 90% of the papers describe hybrid methodologies, the quantitative approaches to partner selection can be grouped into three main categories: optimization models (exact and heuristic algorithms) – 56%; multi-criteria decision aiding (such as AHP, MAUT, fuzzy set theory) – 32%; and other methods such as simulation or clustering – 12%. Genetic algorithms are very popular within heuristic approaches (85%), and only 2 in 13 articles use tabu search as an alternative method. The "main" algorithm is often combined with contributions from fuzzy set theory. In MADM, the combination of fuzzy numbers with AHP is the most frequent.
- Criteria may be grouped into two main classes: a) risk (e.g., political stability, economy status of the region, financial health, market fluctuations, competency), costs and time factors (around 46%); and b) other attributes (such as trust, technology level, capacity resources, organization structure, financial status, past performance, quality, etc.). In this last group: a) around 54% use quantitative information expressed by numbers, percentages or performance indices; b) around 27% use numerical scales; c) around 9% use fuzzy numbers to deal with the vagueness of the DM preferences; and d) around 9% use linguistic terms to facilitate the expression of DM preferences.

From this survey[1], it is also possible to draw some useful indications about the main research trends for partner selection in a virtual enterprise context, namely: an enormous concern about optimising the solution, i.e., to select the right partner; need to obtain complete and diversified information (multiple attributes) about each potential partner; subjectivity in the data; need to facilitate the expression of the decision maker's assessments about the potential partners; concern with dynamic aspects (e.g., time).

4   DEVELOPED APPROACH

The classic model based on risk and cost factors is a 0-1 integer programming with nonlinear objective and several inequality and equality constraints (Cao and Gao, 2006). Due to the complexity and the nonlinearity of the model, it cannot be efficiently solved by conventional methods. With exact algorithms it is in general impossible, for large problems, to obtain a satisfactory solution in a reasonable computational time. Metaheuristics assume therefore an important role in solving this kind of problems.

4.1   Metaheuristics

Metaheuristics are approximate methods designed to solve hard combinatorial optimisation problems (Reeves, 1993). In this work, we have implemented a TS metaheuristic (see e.g., Glover and Laguna 1997). The main components of TS are: the objective function, the initial (starting) solution, the neighbourhood structure and the tabu list.

We are basically looking for a set of nondominated alternative solutions. A solution (i.e., a potential VE configuration) is represented by a set of companies in the network, associated to the different project activities, along with the corresponding attribute values. In implementation terms, the set of initial solutions is generated through the following simple process: create a *table of enterprises, activities and constraints* (e.g., capacities). A given activity may be performed by a group of enterprises if, for example, separately they do not have enough resources. In this case, the group of enterprises is added to the network as a single unit and the attribute values associated to this unit result from the attribute values of the different enterprises. Following, by scanning that table, a candidate solution (set of enterprises) is created that optimizes each criterion separately considered. This means that this initial set is composed by as many solutions as criteria.

A multi-start improvement strategy was adopted, with these starting solutions. The improvement of a solution is then done by local search, with a neighbourhood structure that consists in swapping, for each activity, an enterprise in the current solution with an enterprise outside the solution (from the *table of enterprises*). The activities are explored by the order they have been defined in the project. In this way, the search starts by attempting to bring into the solution an alternative enterprise that can do the first activity. If this replacement leads to a non-dominated alternative, this new set of enterprises is saved in the *table of alternatives*. Then this process is repeated with the other activities. The best solution found is kept as the new current solution since the strategy used in the neighbourhood search is the "best improvement". Two tabu lists are used: the first forbids the utilization of the enterprises recently chosen, and the second forbids the choice of the last activity selected. The tabu tenure of the first tabu list is determined randomly from a given interval (in our case, [number of nodes/10; number of nodes/2]). This exploration of the neighbourhood is repeated until the search cannot reach any alternative solution (i.e., non-dominated alternative) during a constant number ξ of consecutive iterations. The search only accepts feasible solutions. An intensification strategy is adopted after a given number of consecutive dominated solutions is found and consists of re-starting the procedure with one of the non-dominated start solutions kept.

Algorithm
Generate initial solutions $X=\{1,...,i\}$
Randomly choose one solution from the set of initial solutions, as current solution $X^*=X_i$
Initialise tabu-list
Set aspiration criterion (neighbour solution dominates current solution)
While stopping criterion not met
      Generate n neighbours of X_i
      Choose Y the best neighbour of X_i, that is not in the tabu-list or
         that satisfies the aspiration criterion
      If f(Y) is better than f(X*)
         X*=Y
      Update tabu-list
Return X*

4.2   Multi-attribute decision-making

Multi-attribute decision-making (MADM) is the general process of evaluating and selecting alternative options, characterized by multiple, usually conflicting, attributes or criteria. Many multi-attribute decision-making methods have been proposed in the literature (MAUT, SAW, AHP, TOPSIS, ELECTRE, PROMETHEE, ...). TOPSIS (a technique for ordering preferences by similarity to an ideal solution), one of known classical MADM methods, first developed by Hwang and Yoon (1981), is based on the idea that the chosen alternative should be as "close" as possible to the positive ideal solution and, on the other hand, as "far" as possible from the negative ideal solution. TOPSIS is very easy to implement but assumes the satisfaction of the following requirements: a previous assignment of weights to the attributes by the DM, and a fixed, pre-defined number of alternatives. (Shih et al., 2004). In real-world decision problems we have to handle information that is uncertain, incomplete and/or missing (Li and Lao, 2007). Furthermore, there are many decision situations in which the attributes cannot be assessed precisely in a quantitative form, due to their particular nature (e.g., trust) or because either information is unavailable or the cost of their computation is too high. In these situations an "approximate value" may be acceptable and so the use of a qualitative approach is appropriate (Herrera et al., 2004). "Linguistic variables" will represent qualitative aspects, with values that are not numbers but words or sentences in a natural language, thus making it easier to express preferences. *The linguistic term set*, usually called S, comprises a set of linguistic values that are generally ordered and uniformly distributed. For example, a set S of five terms could be defined as follows: S = {s_0 = very low; s_1 = low; s_2 = medium; s_3 = high; s_4 = very high}, in which $s_a < s_b$ if a < b. The semantics of the elements in the term set (the meaning of each term set) is given by fuzzy numbers defined on the [0, 1] interval and described by membership functions. For the same attribute, the cardinality of S may vary depending on the DM's knowledge about the enterprises under analysis (it may be more detailed in some cases or vaguer in others). Since, fuzziness is inherent to most decision making processes when linguistic variables are used to describe qualitative data, we will use an extension of the TOPSIS procedure for fuzzy data (see e.g., Jahanshahloo et al., 2006). This procedure has the following steps:1. Identify the evaluation criteria; 2. Generate the alternatives; 3. Evaluate alternatives in terms of the criteria (i.e., compute the fuzzy values of the criterion functions); 4. Identify the weights of the criteria; 5. Construct the fuzzy decision matrix; 6. Compute the normalized fuzzy decision matrix; 7. Construct the weighted normalized fuzzy decision matrix; 8. Identify a fuzzy positive ideal solution and a fuzzy negative ideal solution; 9. Compute the distance between each alternative i and the fuzzy positive ideal solution (eq. 10, 11); 10. Compute the "closeness coefficient" to determine the ranking order of all alternatives (eq. 12)

$$\tilde{d}_i^+ = \sum_{j=1}^{n} d(\tilde{v}_{ij}, \tilde{v}_{ij}^+), \qquad i = 1,...,m \qquad (10)$$

$$\tilde{d}_i^- = \sum_{j=1}^{n} d(\tilde{v}_{ij}, \tilde{v}_{ij}^-), \qquad i = 1,...,m \qquad (11)$$

where $\tilde{v}_{ij}^+ = (1, 1, 1)$ is the fuzzy positive ideal solution and $\tilde{v}_{ij}^+ = (0, 0, 0)$ is the fuzzy negative ideal solution for each criterion (benefit or cost criterion).

$$\tilde{R}_i = \tilde{d}_i^- / (\tilde{d}_i^+ + \tilde{d}_i^-), \qquad i = 1,...,m \qquad (12)$$

4.2.1 Differences to the standard procedure

To construct the fuzzy decision matrix we first need to transform the numerical values, interval values and linguistic terms into fuzzy sets (see Herrera et al., 2004) by using equation (11). Due to the incommensurability among attributes, to do this transformation we previously need to normalize the values of the attributes (thus not requiring to do step #6 above). Each solution involves a given number of enterprises for the same project activities, and to evaluate that solution we take the values of each attribute considered for each enterprise separately. To avoid the loss of information caused by the aggregation of values we consider some artificial attributes that characterize the solution itself. In this way, for a given project with k activities and a network of enterprises characterized by m attributes, the solution includes the enterprises that will perform the k activities ($m \times k$ attributes). Following this principle we do not need to perform any aggregation and we keep all the information of all enterprises in the solution.

Our approach is slightly different from those in the literature because we do not use fuzzy numbers in the fuzzy decision matrix. Instead we use fuzzy sets since we want to give more autonomy (through the use of different and more extensive cardinality ranges in linguistic attributes) to the DM. A fuzzy subset of a set S is a mapping from S into $[0, 1]$, where the value of the mapping for an element of S represents the 'degree of membership' or 'membership value' of the element in the fuzzy subset. So instead of using distance formulas for fuzzy numbers (see Li and Yang 2004) we have to use distance formulas for membership functions (see Balopoulos et al., 2007). For any two fuzzy sets $A, B \in FS(X)$, with membership functions μ and v, respectively, we use the following normalized euclidean distance:

$$d_{nE}(\mu, v) = \sqrt{\frac{1}{n} \sum_{i=1}^{n} (\mu(x_i) - v(x_i))^2} \qquad (13)$$

5   ILLUSTRATIVE EXAMPLE

Assume we would like to form a VE to perform two projects decomposed in 6 activities each (Table 1).

Table 1: Projects data

Project 1						Project 2					
Activities (code)	Precedent activities	Duration	Earliest start time	Latest finish time	Quantity of resources	Activities (code)	Precedent activities	Duration	Earliest start time	Latest finish time	Quantity of resources
7	-	36	64	217	400	4	-	99	131	274	362
8	-	62	147	241	604	2	-	56	180	218	206
3	-	67	188	350	528	9	-	30	102	338	135
5	7	16	217	281	275	6	4	41	274	361	116
4	8	25	241	274	368	9	2	32	218	358	282
8	5	43	281	365	304	8	4	44	274	339	221

Suppose a network where 10 different activities can be performed, and composed by 100 enterprises characterized by: enterprise code; activity; interval time about availability of resources; capacity; plus 8 evaluation attributes (Table 2). The attribute type may be: linguistic, numerical and interval. We may want to maximize the attribute (benefit attributes) or minimize it (cost attributes). If the attribute is linguistic, the scale cardinality has to be defined. Figures have been randomly generated. For the linguistic variables we have assumed triangular membership functions with three possible cardinalities of 3,5 or 7, with the following term sets: {none, more or less, perfect}, {none, low, more or less, high, perfect}, {none, very low, low, more or less, high, very high, perfect}. The duration are randomly defined in the correspondent intervals: activities [30, 100], the *earliest start time* [0, 365 - duration], the *latest finish time* [earliest start time, 365], the *quantity of resources* [100, 1000].

Table 2: Description of attributes

Attributes	c1	c2	c3	c4	c5	c6	c7	c8
Type (N - numerical; I - interval; L – linguistic)	L	N	I	I	L	N	N	L
max (+) / min (-)	+	+	-	-	+	+	-	+
cardinality (for linguistic)	7	-	-	-	3	-	-	7
weight(%)	20	23	2	7	19	13	13	2

By applying the Tabu Search procedure we have obtained 20 non-dominated alternatives shown in Table 3. Each row contains the VE composition for the project activities (i.e. the companies assigned to the activities). E.g. solution VE1 for project 1 includes companies 21, 81, 14, 31, 24 and 81, respectively for activities 1, 2, 3, 4, 5 and 6.

Table 3: Non-dominated alternatives

	Project 1 (*Activities*)							Project 2 (*Activities*)					
	1	2	3	4	5	6		1	2	3	4	5	6
VE1	21	81	14	31	24	81	VE1	24	59	27	76	27	81
VE2	35	22	41	79	75	22	VE2	75	59	27	4	27	22
VE3	21	97	14	26	75	97	VE3	75	59	109	86	109	97
VE4	21	81	14	13	102	81	VE4	77	36	25	51	25	81
VE5	74	44	30	55	12	44	VE5	12	2	25	76	25	44
VE6	74	44	48	55	57	44	VE6	57	2	110	34	110	44

VE7	42	44	41	79	39	44	VE7	39	98	27	56	27	44
VE8	83	3	30	79	65	3	VE8	65	2	109	51	109	3
VE9	100	97	48	90	104	97	VE9	108	98	110	99	110	97
VE10	35	44	41	79	39	44	VE10	105	98	27	56	27	44
VE11	35	44	41	79	24	44	VE11	105	2	27	56	27	44
VE12	21	44	41	79	24	44	VE12	24	2	27	76	27	44
VE13	74	44	41	79	24	44	VE13	24	2	27	76	27	22
VE14	74	81	30	79	24	44	VE14	24	36	27	76	27	22
VE15	74	3	30	79	24	44	VE15	24	59	27	76	27	22
VE16	74	3	30	79	57	44	VE16	24	2	27	76	27	22
VE17	74	81	30	79	57	22	VE17	24	36	27	76	27	22
VE18	74	3	30	79	57	22	VE18	24	59	27	76	27	22
VE19	74	94	30	79	57	22	VE19	24	2	27	76	27	22
VE20	74	6	30	79	57	22	VE20	24	36	27	76	27	22

By applying the fuzzy TOPSIS approach, we have obtained the ranking of the non-dominated alternatives set shown in table 4.

Table 4: Closeness coefficients/Ranking of the alternatives

	Project 1					Project 2		
Rank		$\tilde{d}_i^+$	$\tilde{d}_i^-$	$\tilde{R}_i$	Rank		$\tilde{d}_i^+$	$\tilde{d}_i^-$	$\tilde{R}_i$
1	VE16	308.615	188.746	0,057634	1	VE6	867.903	513.326	0,055843
2	VE6	308.508	188.321	0,057531	2	VE2	868.596	510.457	0,055506
3	VE20	308,63	188.368	0,057523	3	VE3	868.094	50.667	0,055147
4	VE13	308,68	187.654	0,057309	4	VE10	868.516	505.683	0,05502
5	VE18	308.636	187.623	0,057307	5	VE20	868.311	504.037	0,054863
6	VE7	308.671	187.493	0,057264	6	VE11	868.499	503.047	0,05475
7	VE5	308.634	186.476	0,056977	7	VE18	868.379	497.232	0,054159
8	VE15	308.659	185.693	0,056747	8	VE16	868.353	496.773	0,054113
9	VE10	308.766	18.493	0,056509	9	VE7	868.606	490.278	0,053429
10	VE11	308.748	18.477	0,056466	10	VE13	868.591	487.449	0,053138
11	VE2	308.831	184.436	0,056355	11	VE5	868.544	486.387	0,053031
12	VE19	308.743	176.865	0,054182	12	VE15	868.501	485.601	0,052952
13	VE17	308.809	175.964	0,053909	13	VE9	868.304	485.115	0,052913
14	VE14	308.832	173.938	0,053318	14	VE17	868.615	482.308	0,052605
15	VE3	308.695	173.427	0,053192	15	VE19	868.585	476.417	0,051998
16	VE9	308,72	170.573	0,052359	16	VE8	868.701	470.816	0,051411
17	VE8	308.849	168.091	0,051616	17	VE14	868.737	470.453	0,051372
18	VE12	308.925	166.468	0,051131	18	VE12	868.925	455.494	0,049809
19	VE4	309.147	147.143	0,045434	19	VE4	869.238	436.086	0,047772
20	VE1	309.091	145.427	0,044936	20	VE1	869.303	407.918	0,044822

6   CONCLUSIONS

The selection of partners is a critical issue in the formation of a virtual enterprise, the basic problem consisting in choosing the entities to be involved in an emergent business opportunity, according to their attributes and interactions. The work presented in this paper is in line with the key trends we have identified in a comprehensive literature survey, by namely considering: a) multiple attributes to describe/structure the decision problem; b) different types of "variables" in order to facilitate the expression of the preferences of the decision-maker; c) the subjectivity of information that leads to the use of a "fuzzy" approach; d) an optimization perspective through the use of metaheuristics; and e) the dynamic aspects occurring when various projects take place simultaneously. In this paper we have presented a formal description for the selection partner problem, consisting in a mathematical formulation based on a multi-attribute perspective. The developed approach can be viewed as a 2-phase algorithm where we first determine a set of potential VE configurations, and then generate a ranking list of potential VEs through the use of a fuzzy TOPSIS based procedure. This efficient quantitative tool seems to provide an adequate support to simulate different alternatives in VE formation or re-organization (through the introduction of different attributes or values/perceptions about the characteristics of the enterprises). Therefore, the final decision is taken by the decision maker. As future work we intend to improve the algorithm to cope with situations where the product is not known or structured in advance.

[1] The complete survey will be presented in a paper to be soon submitted for publication in an international journal.

7   REFERENCES

1.   Balopoulos V, Hatzimichailidis AG, Papadopoulos BK. Distance and similarity measures for fuzzy operators. Information Sciences. In press, Corrected Proof, Available online 16 july 2004.
2.   Camarinha-Matos LM, Afsarmanesh H. Elements of a base VE infrastructure. Computers in Industry 2003; 51: 139–163.
3.   Cao H, Gao Y. Penalty Guided Genetic Algorithm for Partner Selection Problem in Agile Manufacturing Environment. Intelligent Control and Automation June 2006. WCICA 2006-The Sixth World Congress: 3276 – 3280.
4.   Chen T-Y, Chen Y-M, Chu H-C, Wang C-B. Development of an access control model, system architecture and approaches for resource sharing in virtual enterprise. Computers in Industry 2007; 58; 1: 57-73.
5.   Glover F, Laguna M. "Tabu search". Kluwer Academic Publishers. Boston, USA, 1997.
6.   Hwang, CL, Yoon K. Multiple Attribute Decision Making: Methods and Applications, Springer-Verlag, Berlin (Alemanha) 1981.
7.   Herrera F, Martiinez L, Sanchez PJ. Decision Aiding Managing non-homogeneous information in group decision making. European Journal of Operational Research 2004; 166, 1: 115-132.
8.   Jahanshahloo GR a, Hosseinzadeh Lotfi F, Izadikhah M. Extension of the TOPSIS method for decision-making problems with fuzzy data. Applied Mathematics and Computation 2006; 181: 1544–1551.
9.   Li Y, Liao X. Decision support for risk analysis on dynamic alliance. Decision Support Systems 2007; 42: 2043– 2059.
10.   Lin H-Y, Hsu P-Y, Sheen G-J. A fuzzy-based decision-making procedure for data warehouse system selection. Expert Systems with Applications 2007; 32: 939–953.
11.   Reeves CR, ed. "Modern Heuristic Techniques for Combinatorial Problems". John Wiley & Sons, Inc. NY, USA, 1993.
12.   Shih H-S, Wang C-H, Lee ES. A multiattribute GDSS for aiding problem-solving. Mathematical and computer modelling 2004; 39: 1397-1412.

PART 7

e-CONTRACTING IN COLLABORATIVE NETWORK SCENARIOS

21

FUNDAMENTS OF VIRTUAL ORGANIZATION E-CONTRACTING

Lai Xu, Paul de Vrieze
CSIRO ICT Center, AUSTRALIA, Lai.Xu@csiro.au
Paul@adaptivity.nl

E-contracts have been broadly used to improve business-to-business collaboration. Different e-contracting activities have been identified to support e-contract establishment and e-contract fulfillment. In virtual organization domain, there exist different types of virtual organizations. Each of them has different purposes, missions and goals. As an important step in a virtual organization creation process, how e-contracting activities work in different types virtual organization is still blurred. In this article we examine specific requirements of e-contracting activities for different types of virtual organization.

1   INTRODUCTION

E-contracting has been recognized as an important phase of the Virtual Organization (VO) creation process (Camarinha-Matos et al., 2005). General requirements and needs of e-contract and e-contracting platforms have been described in (Camarinha-Matos & Oliveria, 2005). For different purposes, missions and goals, virtual organizations can be further classified into business oriented virtual organizations and non-business oriented virtual organizations, such as incident management teams and disaster rescue teams.

E-contracts and processes for e-contracting among different virtual organizations certainly have different characteristics. A business oriented virtual organization normally has a specific goal, i.e. achieving maximum profit for a common interest between business partners. To achieve the goal, the business process is optimized, specified and agreed upon by all involved partners. The contract between business partners has specified obligations, permissions and prohibitions for each partner; business activities that are expected to occur and sanctions for any deviation from the prescribed behavior. The contract thus clearly defines the business process. The representation/model of the contract and the monitoring for contract violations are very important for business oriented virtual organizations. On the other hand, a contract between parties involved in an incident management team certainly cannot involve all details of the management process. What, why, and how an incident happens can by definition not be predicted well in advance. Therefore, the contract mainly contains guidelines which are much more abstract than the content in a business process contract. After getting more information, different scenarios will appear. The monitoring of the contract execution and performance of each partner is more important for this type of virtual organization.

In this paper, we will present the specific requirements for e-contracts and e-contracting for different types of virtual organization.

Xu, L., de Vrieze, P., 2007, in IFIP International Federation for Information Processing, Volume 243, Establishing the Foundation of Collaborative Networks; eds. Camarinha-Matos, L., Afsarmanesh, H., Novais, P., Analide, C.; (Boston: Springer), pp. 209–216.

2   VIRTUAL ORGANIZATION AND E-CONTRACTING

Different kinds of virtual organizations cause different requirements for different e-contracting processes. In this section, we will further explain relations between four main collaboration modalities and electronic contracting.

Four main collaboration modalities have been identified (Camarinha-Matos et al., 2005), namely: Collaborative business process model, Project model, Problem solving model and Ad-hoc collaboration model. *A collaborative business process model* can be defined as a set of heterogeneous activities normally distributed in cross-organizational sub-processes. Standards and technologies permit business partners to exchange information, collaborate, and carry out business transaction in a pervasive network environment. Business process collaboration predefines a set of activities or processes of organization through networks to accomplish an explicitly shared business goal. A car insurance case can be seen as an example of collaborative business process. In this car insurance case, garages and a call center will collaborate with a car insurance company to provide the service of repairing the damaged cars of insurants (Xu & Brinkkemper, 2005).

A collaborative project model is defined as the support for multi-projects towards the definition of a work break down structure, composed of sub-projects, work packages, tasks and activities and the support for the human resource management where human resources belong to multi-organizations. The crucial issue for a collaboration project model is to optimize resource allocation, such as changing the planning and rescheduling of resources according to situational factors. For example, a European research project normally involves many project partners. A coordinator has to be appointed to report the process to European research consortia. Each project partner works on sub-projects under a big umbrella project.

In *a collaborative problem solving model*, a mediator is needed to collect and evaluate contributions. Collaboration measurement and reward provides identification of value metrics, rewarding of expert contributing decisively towards the roadmap's goal achievement. An example of this class of collaborations is the case of when a manufacturing company would like to reduce the failure rate of its production process. In order to do this the manufacturer will ask other members within the virtual organization, which have equal or similar production process. Different suggestions will be collected and evaluated for using (Camarinha-Matos et al., 2005).

The *ad-hoc collaboration model* is useful when big organizations, not used to tightly collaborate with one another, are required to join their efforts in order to rapidly give a quick response to an external request. An example is the process of responding to an airplane crash. A Belgian Hercules military airplane crashed at army airbase in Eindhoven, The Netherlands, while carrying 37 members of the Royal Dutch Army brass band and a crew of four. The initial crash caused the passengers or crew no serious harm. However, due to the kerosene fire that followed in combination with errors made during the disaster response 34 persons died and the remaining 7 were seriously wounded. The rescue team was composed of partners such as the air-traffic control, the airbase fire department, the Eindhoven fire department, central post for ambulances and national emergency center. The disaster organization failed due to miscommunications, inefficient collaboration between the airbase fire department and the Eindhoven fire department and insufficient resources (human and material) to cope with the disaster (Abbink et al., 2004). The ad-hoc collaboration model is not like a collaborative business process model where a clear process can be defined in advance. To make involved partners work together efficiently is crucial.

2.1 E-contracting and E-contracts

Although there exist different descriptions for the e-contracting process (Milosevic and Bond,1995) (Goodchild, Herring & Milosevic, 2000), the general e-contracting process includes two stages: contract establishment (contract formation) and contract enactment (contract performance or contract fulfillment) (Xu, 2004) (Angelov, 2005). E-contracting processes and all activities belonging to different e-contracting processes are shown in Figure 1. E-contracting activities such as identifying, checking and validating of contractual parties, negotiation and contract validation, are included in the stage of contract establishment. The contract enactment is further separated into two phases: fulfillment and post-contractual activities (Angelov, 2005). Monitoring of contract fulfillment belongs to the contract fulfillment phase while contract enforcement and compensation may be involved in both the contract fulfillment and post-contractual activities.

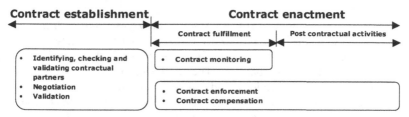

Figure1- E-contracting process and activities

Electronic contracting research focuses on negotiation of the terms and conditions of the contract and the monitoring of contract performance (Lee, 1998). *Contract negotiation* is described as the process in which contractual parties come to a mutual agreement on the contract content. Contract negotiation can be performed with or without the help of a third party. There are three critical aspects in the negotiation of a contract (Burgwinkel, 2002). First, the subject of the contract needs to be defined exactly. Second, the legal validity must be formulated. Third, the price and conditions of each item need to be negotiated in relation to the quality of deliverables and the quality of services and in relation to the legal terms.

Contract monitoring is the process of observing the activities performed by the parties, knowing the state of contract execution and detecting contract violations. It is important for the contractual parties to monitor the performance of the other collaborating parties, especially if the transactions are business critical. This process aims to guarantee that the performed processes are in accordance with the agreed contract. The monitoring of contract performance can be split into two parts divided by the occurrence of an anomalous action (Xu & Jeusfeld, 2003) (Xu, 2004). The part preceding the occurrence of anomalous actions is called the proactive monitoring of contract performance. The part following it is called reactive monitoring of contract performance. The contract monitoring process and activities can be found from Figure 2. In the pro-active monitoring stage, anomalous actions can be avoided and anticipated before contract violation occurrence. In the reactive monitoring stage, anomalous actions can be detected; the partners who are responsible for the violations need to be identified. The relevant partner also needs to be compensated, and unsolvable disputes stored for future human-involved resolution.

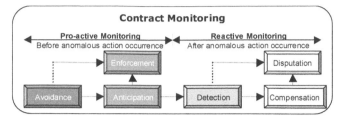

Figure 2 - Contract monitoring processes

Contract enforcement is the process of persuading the noncompliant party to perform corrective actions. The contract enforcement can be done in three ways: pro-actively (through constraints provided in the contract), reactively (via auxiliary corrective measures aiming at minimizing the deviations from the contract), and post-contractually (by constraining future activities of that company in this domain) (Angelov, 2005).

To fulfill contracts automatically, *contract model/representation* brings innovations in collaborative business processes. Existing contract models, such as the e-contracting logic model (Lee, 1998), aim to improve both expressiveness and inferential capabilities of the contracts. The model proposed in (Weigand & Xu, 2001) focuses on task allocations and process co-ordinations. The pro-active monitoring contract model (Xu, 2003, 2004) and multi-party contract model (Xu, 2004b) provide contract models for different objectives. These models are representing trading contracts. To fulfill e-contracts over networks, a contract template is a predefined contract that can be used as a basis for a new contract. It defines the document structure of the contract and has predefined clauses and legal terms (Angelov and Grefen, 2001). To establish contract templates is one possible procedure for managing model contracts.

In order to format and fulfill contracts electronically, e-contracts have to be managed. There are different views at contract management. From a contract platform perspective, *contract management* includes

- a single repository for all contracts, related documents and information to users,
- searching, reporting and reusing capabilities to access all information in contracts and attachments,
- the ability to track and monitor for each contractual partner key performance indicators (KPIs) and performance over the contract execution and use this information to target improvement actions and to determine preferred status, rankings, etc.,
- maintenance of different versions of contracts, automatically reconcile changes to terms and clause language, and compare different versions,
- clause and template library to capture standard and alternate clauses along with guidelines, and
- alerts and reminders to inform contract partners of any upcoming dates, events and milestones.

From one contractual party point of view, both its supplier and customer contracts need to be managed. Moreover, the interrelation between these internal and external obligations, rights, and penalties must be synchronized.

In this section, four collaboration modalities, contract processes, contract negotiation, contract monitoring, contract enforcement, contract model and contract management have been reviewed. The specific needs and requirements of e-contracting for different collaboration modalities will be provided in the next section.

3   E-CONTRACTING FOR VIRTUAL ORGANIZATION

From the aspects of contract negotiation, contract monitoring, contract enforcement, contract model/representation and contract management, we will analyze e-contracting requirements for each collaborative modality of virtual organizations.

3.1   E-Contract for Collaborative Business Process model

After identifying and specifying a new collaboration opportunity, a new virtual organization will be created in response. Contracts or cooperation agreements are defined among the selected partners.

To negotiate the contract, not only the subject of the contract, the terms and conditions of the contract and collaboration business process specification need to be defined exactly, but also representation of the e-contact, such as, it must be decided to specify multi-party involved business collaboration by using a multi-party e-contract or multiple bilateral e-contracts, whether a XML-based contract specification is a suitable representation, etc. The contract is eventually signed after the negotiations are complete.

When the collaboration business process contract is executed, there are three monitoring requirements:

- quality of performance of each party,
- current state of the contract execution,
- contract violation detection.

When collaboration business process is a combination of choreographed business transactions, the quality of each party performance should not be a big concern, because a business transaction is an atomic unit of work that can result in either a success or a failure. If any party fails to perform the transaction, it will be detect as a contract violation. If pro-active monitoring is required, following items need also be included,

- computing what is expected in any state of the business execution
- detecting imminent violations
- reminding the relevant parties to fulfill their obligations

The current state of the contract execution should be monitored in both pro-active and reactive monitoring.

The result of pro-active and reactive monitoring can trigger contract pro-active and reactive enforcement clauses in the contract respectively. Detecting contract violation is certainly important for a collaboration business process virtual organization. Sanctions can be established as a consequence of detection of a contract violation. Furthermore, finding the responsible party or parties for a contract violation is crucial for a collaboration business process virtual organization. All three ways contract enforcement can be useful for a collaboration business process virtual organization. The way of contract monitoring and contract enforcement is performed, such as whether pro-active monitoring or pro-active enforcement is used, will be specified in different constraints. These constrains and calculation of constrains will eventually determine the model/representation of the e-contract.

Contract management, both from a contract platform view and from the point of view of a single contractual party is important for this type of virtual organization.

3.2   E-Contract for Collaborative Project Model

In a collaborative project virtual organization, a coordinator and several project partners are involved and they work together to finish a big project, which no single project partner can finish by itself. Figure 3 shows an example of the contracts between involved members of the virtual organization.

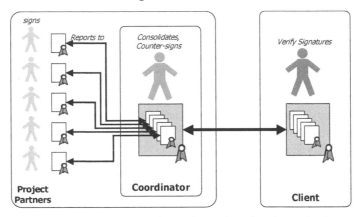

Figure 3 - Contracts in a collaborative project virtual organization

In a collaborative project virtual organization, work can be broken down into multi-projects, tasks or activities, therefore the progress of each sub-project cannot be estimated exactly. Certain parts of contracts or certain parameters should be renegotiable. How much is allowed to be monitored is thus important for the colla-borative project virtual organization. If pro-active contract monitoring is allowed, the accurate process of virtual organization can be known better, the re-planning and re-scheduling can take place properly.

The results of monitoring contract execution can bring great value to this type of virtual organization. Quality of each partner's performance is useful for future colla-boration. Current state of contract execution is the basis of the pro-active contract monitoring. Early detection of contract violations can contribute to the whole process scheduling. In short, the new planning or scheduling can be changed according the results of the pro-active and reactive monitoring.

Contract management is critical for the collaborative project virtual organization. Re-planning, re-scheduling or re-negotiating is often happening in the collaborative project virtual organizations. Different versions of the contract need to be maintained; changes of terms and clauses need to be reconciled; and alerts and reminders should inform involved partners of any upcoming dates and events.

3.3 E-Contracts for Problem Solving Model

In a problem solving virtual organization, a mediator has been assigned. Therefore a central contract platform can be applied in a problem solving virtual organization. It benefits contract negotiation, monitoring and management.

A problem solving virtual organization can only define the scope of the problem, which needs to be solved. After getting experts/contributors for the problems, the content of the contracts needs to be more abstract than going to trivial details. In a problem solving virtual organization, contract negotiation should be relatively easy, even a take-it-or-leave-it contract can be used in this type of virtual organization. An import task for the mediator is to monitor the quality of performance for each partner. The mediator should collect and evaluate contributions from each partner. Mechanisms of collaboration measurement and reward need to be designed. The contract model/representation should facilitate the collection of contributions of each partner.

3.4 E-Contracts for Ad-hoc Collaboration Model

In section 2, we have provided an example for ad-hoc collaboration model virtual organization. Giving a quick response to an unforeseen incident such as a disaster is the characteristic of the ad-hoc collaboration virtual organization. Because the collaboration activities have to rapidly respond to an unknown event, the content of the contracts normally does not have to be negotiated much. The responsibilities or obligations normally have been written in certain documents, e.g. a disaster prevention plan. The way to deal with one specific incident won't be specified. Therefore the content of the contract stays on a meta-level. For contracting in such situation mapping the as-is situation and the to-be scenario with the prevention plan into the procedures will help all partners to deal with confusions, to know exactly what they need to perform. Therefore, contact model/representation and contract monitoring are important. It is a big challenge to design an e-contracting solution that can use contextual information to translate the abstract contract into concrete processes during contract execution.

Table 1 provides summary information of important e-contracting activities for four collaboration model of virtual organizations.

Table 1 – Summary of important e-contracting activities

		Collaborative Business Process VO	Collaborative Project VO	Collaborative Problem Solving VO	Ad-hoc Collaboration VO
Contract negotiation		+	++	+	
Contract model/representation		++	+	+	+++
Contract monitoring	Quality of performance			++	+++
	Current state of contract execution	++	+		+++
	Violation	+	+		++
Contract enforcement		++	+		
Contract management		+	++		++

The numbers of "+" represent the importance.

4   CONCLUSIONS

In collaborative business process virtual organizations, e-contracting is more close to the e-contracting in business-to-business (b2b) collaboration. Although there are still enough challenges in the area, most current research results of e-contracting are mainly in this area. The result of e-contracting research from b2b collaboration e-contracting can be also adopted and be adjusted for collaborative project virtual organizations and collaborative problem solving virtual organizations.

For a collaborative project virtual organization, multiple partners can be involved, in this case the contract with multiple partners can be broken down into multiple bilateral contracts. Therefore, the current result of e-contracting research can still be well applied.

In a collaborative problem solving model of visual organizations, current research on e-contracting can be adopted and adjusted easily. Collection and evaluation of performance quality of each partner are important issues in this area.

However, the issues of ad-hoc collaborative e-contracting certainly are a big challenge in the e-contracting area. To map a meta-level contract/agreement into specific processes during a contract execution stage, many issues need to be solved. Method Engineering is one of the areas which should look at for finding a solution. In short, e-contracting is a still relative new research area. Still many challenges remain.

5   REFERENCES

1.   Angelov, S. (2005) Foundations of B2B Electronic Contracting, Technische Universiteit Eindhoven.
2.   Angelov, S. and Grefen, P., B2B eContract Handling – A survey of Projects, Papers and standards. University Twente, CTIT Technical Reports, 2001.
3.   Burgwinkel, D. (2002) Decision Support in Electronic Contract Management. Procedding of the Interntaional Conference on Decision Marking and Decision support in the Internet Age DSIAGE.
4.   Camarinha-Matos, L. M.; Silveri I.; Afsarmanesh H.; Oliveira A.I. Towards a Framework for Creation of Dynamic Virtual Organizations. In Collaborative Networks and their Breeding Environments, (PRO-VE'05) Springer, Valencia, Spain, 26-28 Sep 2005.
5.   Camarinha-Matos, Luís and Oliveira, A. Contract negotiation wizard for VO creation. In: DET'06 - 3rd International CIRP Conference in Digital Enterprise Technology, 18-20 Sept 2006
6.   Goodchild, A., Herring, C. and Milosevic, Z. (2000) Business contracts for B2B, in Ludwig, H., Hoffner, Y., Bussler, C., and Bichler, M. (eds.) Proceedings of the CAISE*00 Workshop on Infrastructure for Dynamic Business-to-Business Service Outsourcing, ISDO '00, Stockholm, June 5-6, 2000 CEUR-WS.org.
7.   Lee, R. (1998) Towards Open Electronic Contracting, EM – Electronic Markets, 8(3) pp.3-8.
8.   Milosevic, Z. and Bond, A. (1995) Electronic commerce on the Internet: what is still missing? Proceedings of the 5th Annual Conference of the Internet Society, INET'95, Honolulu, Hawaii.
9.   Weigand, H. and Xu, L. (2001) Contracts in e-commerce. In 9th IFIP 2.6 Working Conference on Database Semantic Issues in E-Commerce Systems (DS-9).
10.   Xu, L. and Jeusfeld, M. A. (2003) Pro-active Monitoring of Electronic Contracts , In: The 15th Conference On Advanced Information Systems Engineering (CAiSE 2003). Lecture Notes of Computer Science Volume 2681/2003, Springer-Verlag.
11.   Xu, L. (2004) Monitoring Multi-party Contracts for E-business, Ph.D. thesis, University of Tilburg.
12.   Xu, L. (2004b) A Multi-party Contract Model , In: ACM SIGecom Exchanges Vol. 5, No.1, pages 13-23.
13.   Xu, L. and Brinkkemper, S., Modelling Multi-party Web-based Business Collaborations, In: Proceedings of IFIP WG 2.12 & WG 12.4 Workshop on Web Semantics (SWWS 05). Lecture Notes in Computer Science Volume 3762, Springer Verlag, 2005.

22

INTELLIGENT CONTRACTING: SOFTWARE AGENTS, CORPORATE BODIES AND VIRTUAL ORGANIZATIONS

Francisco Andrade[1], Paulo Novais[2], José Machado[2] and José Neves[2]

[1]*Escola de Direito, Universidade do Minho, Braga, PORTUGAL*
[2]*DI-CCTC, Universidade do Minho, Braga, PORTUGAL*
fandrade@direito.uminho.pt, { pjon, jmac, jneves}@di.uminho.pt

Legal doctrine starts to speak of Inter-systemic electronic contracting, where an important role is played by soft bots, i.e., intelligent software agents, which may be fiction as tools controlled by humans or faced as subjects of electronic commerce, or even seen as legal objects or as legal subjects. The use of software agents in electronic commerce scenarios must be connected with the existence of corporate bodies and Virtual Organizations. The issue to be discussed here is whether there should be Commercial Corporations for the use of Software Agents (as mere tools of the companies) or if the agents themselves can be seen as full and active participants in new types of commercial corporations and Virtual Organizations.

1   INTRODUCTION

In general it may be stated that legal doctrine has established a way of classifying electronic contracts, according to the specific technical way of accomplishing each type of electronic conveying and contracting (Barbagalo, 2001), distinguishing the possibilities of the parties involved to interact through computer devices, where computers are seen as mere communication means, interacting with computer devices and electronic systems, or even considering the case of contracting without human parties interacting at all, leaving all the work to informatics and electronic systems which, in an automatic, and sometimes even autonomous way (according to software developed and put in use on behalf of the contracting parties), produce a sort of "machine only interaction".

Under this distinction, we may speak of different ways of electronically contracting, according to the singularities of human intervention in the contracting process. And it must be faced with the quite interesting, although eventually legally problematic, possibility of inter-systemic electronic contracting.

Inter-systemic contracting can be distinguished from other means of contracting by the degree of human involvement in the process of contract construction. In every conventional means of contracting, through conventional letters, fax, telex (and even in not so conventional ones, as electronic mail), the human intervention always appears at the beginning of any deal (Almeida, 2000; Gentili, 2000; Thoumyre, 1999). However, in inter-systemic contractual relations the whole process of communication and contracting is "between applications" or "between agents" without any human intervention (Elias and Gerard, 1991). The party's computational systems are not only interconnected but are also able to relate among themselves without human intervention. The human beings limit their involvement to organize the computational systems in terms of their necessities of communication and action (Brabagalo, 2001). Henceforth, the machines will act on their own, concluding

Andrade, F., Novais, P., Machado, J., Neves, J., 2007, in IFIP International Federation for Information Processing, Volume 243, Establishing the Foundation of Collaborative Networks; eds. Camarinha-Matos, L., Afsarmanesh, H., Novais, P., Analide, C.; (Boston: Springer), pp. 217–224.

contracts on behalf of the parties involved, either in terms of "automatic inter-systemic electronic contracting", which is classical case of contracting through EDI-Electronic Data Interchange, and "intelligent inter-systemic electronic contracting", where one has soft bots capable of acting, learning, modifying instructions and taking decisions (Allen and Widdison, 1996).

The paper is organized as follows. The following section presents the concepts of agent and organization. Afterwards, it is mentioned the use of agents in e-commerce scenarios and intelligent contracting. We will finish giving an opinion formed after considering the relevant factors or evidence about the proposed model, and point out some directions for future work.

2   AGENTS AND ORGANISATIONS

Agents are computational entities with a rich knowledge component, having sophisticated properties such as planning ability, reactivity, learning, cooperation, communication and the possibility of argumentation (Figure 1) (Novais, 2003). The use of the agent figure is particularly adequate to such problems. The objective is to build logical and computational models, as well as implementing them, having in consideration The Law Norms and Principles (i.e., legislation, doctrine and jurisprudence). Agent societies may mirror a great variety of structured communities of people, such as commercial societies, with an emphasis to the behavioral patterns, or even the more complex ones, with pre-defined roles of engagement, obligations, contractual and specific communication rules.

Figure 1: Agent role

Corporate persons (i.e., an association of individuals which pursue a particular objective), may be understood as real "legal artificial persons", a reason why Emily Weitzenboeck (2001) remarks that "many artificial legal persons are already regarded as person...". Indeed, corporate bodies do not actually have a will of their own ("...legal subjects as collective persons, which really do not hold neither physical characteristics nor will"), being their will formed by the will of the humans (Kemradj, 2002).

Speaking of corporate persons and software agents, we must refer the possibility of the later playing a social role, not only in corporate bodies, but also in the so called Virtual Enterprises (VE), although VEs be understood as "a temporary alliance between globally distributed independent companies working together to improve their competitiveness by sharing resources, skills, risks and costs" (Crispim and Sousa, 2005).

3 INTELLIGENT ELECTRONIC CONTRACTING

One of the possible solutions for considering the issue of consent in electronic intelligent inter systemic contracting, would be treating the whole declarative process as
performed by an human. It would be like establishing a legal presumption (Allen and
Widdison (1996) call it a "legal fiction"), where all the transactions entered into the
computer would be treated as transactions entered by the human trader, thus putting
the intention and the whole risk of the transactions "on the person best able to
control them, i.e. those who program and control the computer".

The acceptance of this theory would have an obvious impact – the risk of
transactions would be entirely put "on the persons who program, control or otherwise
use an electronic agent" (Weitzenboeck, 2001), and these would eventually be
assigned a sort of liability regime similar to the one related to the use of cars or
machines by their owners. "A party may be liable for a damage caused by an object"
(Lerouge, 2000). It is a well known principle of Civil Law's liability regime that "a
person to whose sphere machines can be assigned to, is supposed to be liable for
them. Thus, one shall bear the risk that has the right and ability to control the
machine and to receive a (financial) benefit from its use" (Haentjens, 2002). And
even if the damages to be caused by agents would most surely not be of a physical
order (at least, while it is not considered the existence of robots), but financial and
moral (reputation), the truth is that the financial loss and moral (reputation)
consequences could become quite burdening. Having this in mind, may we make
such an assertion of intention and liability when we are not speaking of machines
that one can control, but of most sophisticated engines whose behavior cannot be
totally predicted? Would it not be a terrible burden to put on programmers and users
– who surely could not be "in such a condition to anticipate the contractual behavior
of the agent in all possible circumstances", and so could not be in position of
"wanting" each and every "contract which the agent will conclude"? (Sartor, 2002)

Another possibility is related to some sort of "personification" or the granting of
legal personality to software agents (Wettig and Zehendner, 2004). But it must be
held clear that "personality" is not a "physical" or "natural" concept (Andrade,
1974), it is rather the capability of being a subject of rights and obligations – being
important to establish "whether or not the entity can and should be made the subject
of a set of legal rights and duties" (Barfield, 2005), its capability of being a centre of
production of legal effects (e.g., constitution, modification, and extinction of legal
relations).

The issue of social roles looks determinant for the attribution of legal personality, maybe even more determinant than intelligence or self-consciousness. Human
beings will (may) play – regardless of the ability to think and learn of each person –
a social role. Legal persons, although instrumental to man interests, also play social
roles. Intelligent software agents may as well, in a near future, engage on a relevant
social role and take active part in many activities reserved, until now, to humans. It
must be questioned which actors intervene in nowadays human societies. Indeed, it
seems obvious that intelligent agents are the newest actors in the global society of
the 21st century, with an impending capability of intervention in the commercial and
legal arenas, and even in producing legal effects.

"As explained by Teubner, the leading theorist on the application of autopoiesis
to law, an autopoietic social system is "a system of actions / communications that

reproduces itself by constantly producing from the network of its elements new communications/actions as elements". As Allen and Widdison (1996) refer, and according to Teubner, "legal persons are entities that are constructed within the legal system as "semantic artefact(s)" to which legally meaningful communications are attributed. In other words, entities are described as legal persons when the legal system attributes legally meaningful communications to them. To put it simply, within the legal system, legal persons are those entities that produce legal acts." Obviously, according to this theory, both natural persons as corporate persons, and even intelligent soft bots, might be considered as legal persons. On the contrary, the so called intelligent animals, although deserving legal protection, have not the referred capacity of producing or generating legal acts.

It is important to remember here the distinction between legal subjects and legal objects. As Wettig and Zehendner (2003) put it, "Legal subjects, usually humans, can be holder of rights and obligations. For legal objects (e.g., things, intellectual property rights) this is not possible. These can only be object of legal owner rights". The issue is whether or not software agents may be seen as mere objects, or if they should be considered as real "subjects". According to their characteristics, they look much like real "subjects".

But can software agents be recognized as legal persons? Many difficulties would certainly arise if we intended that purpose (Andrade et al, 2004). But the most crucial issue will always be the one related to liability for acts practiced by software agents (Wettig and Zehendner, 2004), since these are logical entities (whether or not physical entities) capable of multiple and autonomous intervention in the legal arena, whose personification under the law might be seen as a technical way of responding to a social need – the need for more efficient and reliable ways of undertaking actions that the man alone cannot perform or cannot complete in a sufficiently and economically not long time.

The attribution of legal personality to intelligent software agents would have at least two clear advantages (Andrade et al, 2007). To begin with, by the recognition of an autonomous consent (which is not a fiction at all), it would solve the question of consent and of validity of the declarations and contracts enacted or concluded by electronic agents without affecting more than is desirable the legal theories about consent and declaration, contractual freedom, and conclusion of contracts. Secondly, and also quite important, it would "reassure the owners-users of agents" once, by considering the eventual "agents" liability, it could at least limit their own (human) responsibility in terms of the "agents" behaviour (Sartor, 2003). This solution might look rather convenient in all aspects. But, nevertheless, its adoption will not be without difficulties. A relevant issue concerning the legal personhood of electronic agents is that of its "patrimonial duties". In order to exist, a legal person must have, or at least be capable of having, a patrimony. But does it make any sense to attribute a patrimony to an electronic device? Can we imagine a situation of these electronic devices having "patrimonial rights and also be subject to liability for negligent acts or omissions, just as natural persons would" (Weitzenboeck, 2001)? Is it possible for us to state that an electronic device acted in good faith, in bad faith, with knowledge or ignorance of certain circumstances? And how can electronic agents be sued in Court? How? And will contracts enacted by them be enforceable? (Barfield, 2005) Will specific alternative on-line dispute resolution methods be required for e-commerce acted by software agents? These are undoubtedly major difficulties in the attempt of "personification" of such software agents.

One interesting suggestion of Sartor (2002) in order to overcome some difficulties and to allow the use of software agents in electronic commerce, leads to the creation of companies intended for on-line trading through software agents.

"An easier and less risky way for the agent to make contracts... and to limit the liability of the user (at least, to some extent) is available. This consists in creating companies for on-line trading, which would use agents in doing their business. Such agents would act in the name of a company, their will would count as the will of the company, their legally relevant location would be the company's domicile, and creditors could sue the company for obligations contracted by those agents. The counterparties of an agent could then be warranted by the capital of the company and by the legal remedies available towards defaulting commercial companies" (Sartor, 2002). But under this point of view, software agents are still seen as mere objects, belonging to corporate bodies instead of natural persons. In this view, the software agent is seen as a mere object the corporate body uses. And the consent given by the software agent (a consent that no one will be able to anticipate or control) will be the consent of the corporate body. In this sense, the will of the corporate body will still be formed by the will of its (human) members? Or will it be just the totally aleatory will determined by the action of a software program?

Another interesting possibility is pointed out by Allen and Widdison (1996), making a parallel once again with corporate bodies and speaking of the existence of a hybrid social person, "consisting of a computer and natural person operating in tandem. This "partnership" could exhibit behaviour which is not entirely attributable to either constituent, and yet is the product of their joint efforts. Here we might see something similar to the original idea of the collective of individuals as a single entity possessing social personality (and ultimately legal personality), but the collective would consist of a computer and a natural person".

This suggestion of considering the possibility of a hybrid person, a sort of natural persons and computers (actually software agents), capable of acting a will resulting from the joint efforts of men and software, points out to a new personality composed of man and machine, resulting in an interaction between natural biological (human) intelligence and artificial intelligence, forming thus a different kind of entity with a own will, different from merely human will.

There are interesting views on the constitution of collective entities, integrated not only by humans, but also by corporations and (why not?) by intelligent software (Pacheco, 2001), all this upon the idea that a corporate body never acts directly; it just acts upon the acting of the agents holding a role in its structure. And if human element plays a role in the corporate body, there is apparently no reason why software agents shouldn't also play an important role in a corporation. The question here is to know whether or not we may have not only the above referred hybrid society (constituted by human and by software) but also corporations constituted only by software agents. (Or, in the hypothesis of Sartor (2002), corporations constituted for the use of software agents). These are different possibilities that must be foreseen.

Actually, corporate persons ("an association of individuals which pursues a particular object that is distinct from the human beings which constitute it in such a manner that society starts distinguishing the whole from the individual parts") may be understood as real "legal artificial persons", and that is why Weitzenboeck (2001) notes that "many artificial legal persons are already regarded as persons...". Indeed, Corporate bodies do not actually have a will of their own ("...legal subjects collective persons, which really don't possess neither physical characteristics nor will") (Kemradj, 2002), being their will formed by the will of humans.

The truth is that is must be understood that corporate persons are non natural legal persons (and it is quite accurate that common law doctrine distinguishes natural persons and legal persons or corporations), but also that corporate persons are in fact organizations which may be viewed as "a set of interacting agents (human agents or not)" (Pacheco and Carmo, 2003). It may be assumed (at least the possibility of) that not only natural "persons can act for an organization; there is no reason why software agents ....cannot play some roles". Of course, the participation of software agents under current law is not yet possible, because software agents are not legal persons. On the other hand, participation of software agents in corporations would require not only the attribution of a "patrimony" to the agent, but also the rethinking of the rules of functioning and liabilities of the hybrid corporate person. Probably, a new type of corporation should have to be considered.

Speaking of corporate persons and software agents, we must refer the possibility of the later playing a social role not only in corporate bodies, but also in the so called Virtual Enterprises (VE). Although VEs are understood as "a temporary alliance between globally distributed independent companies working together to improve their competitiveness by sharing resources, skills, risks and costs", (Crispim and Sousa, 2005) and thus must be understood as a "consortium", that is to say that two or more different entities (natural or corporate) "get obliged to undertake certain activities or assuring certain contributions in order to make it possible to achieve certain material or legal acts" (Abreu, 2004), it must be foreseen also the possibility of software agents participating in more stable (not necessarily temporary) organizations. Actually, we must anticipate the possibility of software agents playing a determinant role in corporate bodies, in Virtual Enterprises, in Dynamic Virtual Organizations ("temporary alliances of organisations that come together to share skills or core competencies and resources in order to better respond to business opportunities"), and in Virtual Organisations Breeding Environments ("an association or pool of organisations and their related supporting institutions that have both the potential and the interest to cooperate with each other, through the establishment of a "base" long-term cooperation agreement"), (Camarinha Matos et al, 2005).

4   CONCLUSIONS

Of course further possibilities may be exploited. For instance, to foresee a new legal approach of the contract itself, considering not the agreement of wills but the result of the acts of machines or devices predisposed by human or corporate bodies. Or even to consider informatics systems as instruments capable of a sort of limited personhood, as it happens with some legal "realities" not personified but, for instance, capable of some kind of "procedural legitimacy": capable of being in Court, demanding and being sued, such as it happens with branches, agencies or other commercial establishments or even condominium.

It is obvious that the existing legal norms are not fit for such an endeavouring challenge as the appearance of intelligent electronic agents in electronic relations . The debate about Intelligent Inter-systemic contracting is still beginning. New developments are arising in the field of Artificial Intelligence such as the "embodying" of electronic "conversational agents" (Ball and Breese, 2003). Virtual persons will get more and more sophisticated, but also more identifiable. An dits participation in commercial companies and Virtual Organisations will be unavoidable. An ultimate choice must be made between the fiction of considering agents acts as deriving from human's will and the endeavour of finding new ways of considering the electronic devices own will and responsibility. And maybe in the virtual world – as it happened in the real world about corporate bodies – fictions will definitely be replaced by a more realistic approach considering that the challenging technical possibilities of software agents as new entities definitely require a particular legal approach in order to enhance the use of electronic commerce in a global world.

Acknowledgments

The work described in this paper is included in Intelligent Agents and Legal Relations project (POCTI/JUR/57221/2004), which is a research project supported by FCT (Science & Technology Foundation – Portugal).

5   REFERENCES

1. Abreu JC. Curso de Direito Comercial, Almedina, 2004 (in Portuguese).
2. Allen T, Widdison R. Can Computer Make Contracts?, Harvard Journal of Law and Technology, Volume 9, Number 1, Winter, 1996.
3. Almeida C. Contratos, Almedina, Coimbra, 2000 (in Portuguese).
4. Andrade F, Neves J. Intelligent Electronic Inter-systemic Contracting – Issues on Consent and Contract Formation, ICEIS – Sixth International Conference on Enter-prise Information System Proceedings, vol. 4, pp 403-410, 2004.
5. Andrade F., Novais P., Machado J., Neves J. Contracting Agents: legal personality and represent-tation, Artificial Intelligence and Law, Springer, 2007 (to appear).
6. Andrade F., Novais P., Neves J. Issues on Intelligent Electronic Agents and Legal Relations, Proceedings of the LEA 2004 - Workshop on the Law of Electronic Agents, Roma, Italia, Cevenini C. (ed), Gedit edizioni, ISBN 88-88120-54-8, pp 81-94, 2004.
7. Andrade, MD. Teoria Geral da Relação Jurídica, vol. I Coimbra Editora, 1974 (in Portuguese).
8. Ball G, Breese J. Emotion and Personality in a Conversational Agent, Embodied Conversational Agents, edited by Justine Cassel, Joseph Sullivan, Scott Prevost and Elizabeth Churchill, The MIT Press Cambridge – Massachussets, London – England, 2000.
9. Barbagalo E. Contratos Eletrônicos - Editora Saraiva, São Paulo, 2001 (in Portuguese).
10. Barfield, Woodrow "Issues of law for software agents within virtual environments", Pres-ence, Vol. 14, Issue 6 – December 2005, The MIT Press.
11. Camarinha-Matos L, Afsarmanesh H, Ollus M. ECOLEAD: A holistic approach to creation and management of dynamic and virtual organizations, Collaborative Networks and Their Breeding Environments, Camarinha-Matos L. Afsarmanesh H., Ortiz A., (Eds), Springer-Verlag, ISBN 0-387-28259-9, pp 501-512, 2005.
12. Crispim J, Sousa JP. A multi-Criteria support system for the formation of collaborative networks of enterprises, Collaborative Networks and Their Breeding Environments, Camarinha-Matos L. Afsarmanesh H., Ortiz A., (Eds), Springer-Verlag, ISBN 0-387-28259-9, pp 501-512, 2005.
13. Elias L, Gerard J. Formation of the contract by Electronic Data Interchange, pages 2-3
14. Elias L, Gerard J. Formation of the contract by Electronic Data Interchange", Commission of the European Communities, 1991.
15. Gentili A. L'inefficacia del contratto telematico, in "Rivista di Diritto Civile", Anno XLVI –, Parte I, Padova-Cedam, 2000.
16. Haentjens, Oliver van : "Shopping agents and their legal implications regarding Austrian Law", in http://www.cirfid.unibo.it/~lea-02/pp/Vanhaentjens.pdf , visited 2003/9/8, 2002.
17. Kemradj, A.C. (Кемрадж, А. С.) : "Юридически сила сделок, заключенных через сеть Интернет", in "Правовые аспекты использования Интернет-технологий", Москва, Книжный Мир, 2002.

18. Lerouge JF. The use of electronic agents questioned under contractual law. Suggested solutions on a European and American level, The John Marshall Journal of Computer and Information Law 18(2): 403-433, 2000.
19. Novais P. Teoria dos Processos de Pré-Negociação em Ambientes de Comércio Electrónico, PhD Thesis, Departamento de Informática, Universidade do Minho, 2003 (in Portuguese).
20. Pacheco O, CarmoJ. A Role Based Model for the Normative Specification of Organized Collective Agency and Agents Interaction, Autonomous Agents and Multi-Agent Systems 6(2): 145-184, 2003.
21. Pacheco O. Especificação Normativa de Agentes Institucionais e da Interacção entre Agentes, Ph.D. Thesis, University of Minho, 2002 (in Portuguese).
22. Sartor G. Agents in Cyberlaw, Proceedings of the Workshop on the Law of Elec-tronic Agents (LEA 2002) and "Gli agenti software: nuovi sogetti del ciberdiritto?" in http://www.cirfid.unibo.it/~sartor/sartorpapers/gsartor2002_agenti_software.pdf, visited 2003/9/8
23. Thoumyre L. L'échange des consentements dans le commerce électronique, in Lex Electronica, vol. 5, n° 1, 1999.
24. Weitzenboeck E. Electronic Agents and the formation of contracts. International Journal of Law and Information Technology 9(3): 204-234, 2001.
25. Wettig S, Zehendner E. A legal analysis of human and electronic agents, Artificial Intelligence and Law archive Volume 12 , Issue 1, pp 111-135, 2004.
26. Wettig S, Zehendner E. The Electronic Agent: A Legal Personality under German Law?. A.Oskamp & E. Weitzenböck (eds.), Proceedings of the Law and Electronic Agents workshop (LEA'03), 2003.

23

AGENT-BASED CONTRACTING IN VIRTUAL ENTERPRISES

Claudia Cevenini, Giuseppe Contissa, Migle Laukyte

CIRSFID, University of Bologna, Palazzo Dal Monte Gaudenzi,
via Galliera, 3,Bologna, I-40121, ITALY
Tel: +39 051 277237, Fax: +39 051 260782, Email: {cevenini, contissa,
mlaukyte}@cirsfid.unibo.it

Virtual Enterprises (VEs) use software agents (SAs) to reduce costs, speed up operations, and increase efficiency and competitiveness. Agents can carry out negotiations and make contracts without any human intervention. This makes them useful both in negotiations to set up a VE and in contracting with VE partners. Agents raise legal problems about the relevance and validity of their actions. The law may not always offer a solution to agent-based interactions. This paper investigates whether current laws are suitable to regulating agents and what new rules may need to be introduced.

This paper is partly based on research conducted for the EC project LEGAL-IST (IST-2-004252-SSA, FP6 IST Programme).

1   INTRODUCTION

The use of Software Agents (SAs)—generally in electronic commerce, and particularly by Virtual Enterprises (VEs)—comes with both numerous business benefits and problems to solve. The autonomy of SAs obstructs their application, because this autonomy may result as unpredictability and the actions of SAs may lack legal relevance and may be invalid. The normative framework addresses some of these issues but not all.

Therefore, we point out the questions that remain unsolved by the legal framework. On the one hand, the aim is to integrate the SA's activities within the relevant regulations and, on the other hand, if these regulations hinder agents' utilization and generally cramp the technological development, propose the new ones.

The remainder of the paper is organized as follows. In Section 2 we discuss the basic notions of this paper: VEs and SAs, focusing on how VEs apply SAs. One of the most useful applications is to employ the agents in contractual activities both in negotiation stage during VE's formation, and operation stage of contracting with parties inside and outside the VE. In Section 3 we examine the present legal framework and we question its adequacy to regulate SAs. So in Section 4 we

Cevenini, C., Contissa, G., Laukyte, M., 2007, in IFIP International Federation for Information Processing, Volume 243, Establishing the Foundation of Collaborative Networks; eds. Camarinha-Matos, L., Afsarmanesh, H., Novais, P., Analide, C.; (Boston: Springer), pp. 225–232.

investigate the possibility to introduce new rules which could fill in the gaps in normative framework substituting or integrating the existing regulations on regard. Section 5 concludes the paper with recommendations on possible directions for further research.

2 VIRTUAL ENTERPRISES (VES) AND SOFTWARE AGENTS (SAS): DEFINITIONS AND APPLICATIONS

For the scopes of the paper, we define VE on two perspectives: business and legal one. In a business perspective, VE is a collaboration of legally independent subjects, set up to rapidly and effectively exploit business opportunities and jointly bring products and services to the market. In a legal perspective, VE is a temporary, often cross-border ICT-enabled collaboration (without a separate legal status) between legally independent entities aimed at the joint provision of goods or services, where each partner contributes to particular task and activities.

For our purposes, we will use the definition of (Hayes-Roth, 1995): SA is a computational entity that able to interact with the environment in which it operates, through the performance of three basic capabilities: to perceive its environment, to proceed the information coming from the environment and to perform of actions aimed at modifying its status.

This set of SAs' capabilities explain why VEs use them: these capabilities enable SAs to substantially contribute to reduce costs, to speed up business operations, to increase efficiency and so competitiveness.

In particular, the SAs are applicable in all the spectrum of contractual activities from negotiations to set up the VE, to final contracting with other parties both inside and outside the VE during its operational phase.

The negotiations phase before the setting up of a VE project includes agents which compare the different business structures regulated by national legislation and set up an organization. They match or avoid matching one or more of business structures on the basis of the needs of the initiative. Afterwards, SAs will perform pre-contractual activities on behalf of the partners. Agents have to act in good faith and in a law-abiding manner (Brazier, 2002). Thus the negotiations conducted by agents can become gentlemen's agreements and pre-contractual arrangements with potential partners. (Matskin, 2001) present and (Petersen, 2003) propose to apply *AGORA* multi-agent architecture which is the example of VE formation using SAs.

Prototype PROVE[1] is another example of SAs used to form VE, where agents conduct the negotiations according to the rules coded in them (Szirbik, 2000). Thus the VE partners have to personalize SAs by introducing the rules they want SAs to use during the negotiations or at least review the rules SAs already have.

During VE's operation stage, VE partners may use the agents in all stages of the value chain and in managing both internal and external interactions. The drafting of general VE interchange agreement, which regulates the overall management of the

---

[1] Prototype PROVE makes part of research project ROVE (Reasoning about Operations in Virtual Enterprises) at Eindhoven University of Technology (The Netherlands).

VE (comprising the use of SAs) and the activities of its partners, is made by VE partners themselves. Instead agents could offer substantial support in the execution of minor contracts, especially if the latter are standardized. In fact (Radin, 2000) affirms that contracts stipulated by SAs are the ones which only *offer* a contract on the user's behalf when an opportunity arises: the agent is only offering to trade the contract, stopping short of executing it on its own.

This vast applicability has to consider the legal framework, which regulates the contractual activities, involving the SAs. The following Section 3 addresses the points of intersection between normative regulation and agent's actions in VE.

3 LEGAL FRAMEWORK: STATE-OF-ART

VE partners implementing agent technologies must achieve the compliance of SA's actions with the applicable legal framework. Besides, agents move through open networks which are international by nature, and thus can perform actions which are deemed perfectly legal by some systems and illicit by other ones. In fact, global performance of on line contracts can be problematic. The legislations on contracting and on the use of technical tools van actually be extremely different and contrast with the basic principles that are applied in the legal environment of European Union.

The contract counterpart can be imposed with specific acknowledgements, such as accepting the use of SAs in negotiating and concluding of the contract, and also limiting the liability of the agents' user(s): example of such limitation is the rule which permits to close a contract only to subjects who are resident – or which have their main seat in case of companies – in certain countries or main geographical areas.

In the negotiation and contracting stages, agents are assigned tasks and goals according to which they contact potential contracting parties, negotiate with them and conclude contracts on behalf of the VEs' partners. In performing all these tasks, it is vital that SAs do not infringe other subjects' rights, such as copyright or the right to privacy and that they do not enter protected computer systems without the administrator's authorization.

Article 12(14) of) of "Legal Aspects of Electronic Commerce, Electronic Contracting: Provisions for a Draft Convention," of The United Nations Commission on International Trade Law (UNCITRAL) takes up the question of the "use of automated information systems for contract formation," setting forth the so-called non-discrimination rule, whereby a contract closed by SAs — either fully (both parties to the contract are SAs) or in part (only one of the parties is SA) — "shall not be denied validity or enforceability on the sole ground that no person reviewed each of the individual actions carried out by such systems or [reviewed] the resulting agreement."[2] In other words, these kinds of contracts will be valid even without the

---

[2] Art. 12(14) of "Legal Aspects of Electronic Commerce, Electronic Contracting: Provisions for a Draft Convention," UNCITRAL (2004) A/CN.9/WG.IV/WP. 108, online at http://daccessdds. un.org/doc/UNDOC/LTD/V04/541/06/PDF/V0454106.pdf?OpenElement.

user's acceptance of their terms and conditions. On the one hand, such recognition marks a big step towards legal acknowledgement of SAs as participants in e-commerce; but on the other hand, is SA technology so developed as to ensure there will be little or no risk of the user being held answerable for errors made by the SA? These errors have sometimes been big blunders, and the likelihood of this happening on more than a few rare occasions may discourage the e-community from using agents.

Surely, today we cannot say that nothing can go wrong in the process of contract-making through the use of SAs. There are many consequential errors an SA may make: The SA could sell an item for an incorrect price or pay an incorrect amount for it, or the SA may purchase an incorrect amount of items, or it may make a purchase on conditions harmful to its user. Article 14(16) of UNCITRAL addresses the question of errors, but only *human* error: "if a *person* made an error" (italics added). So there is no legal remedy that the document sets out for errors on the SA's part. The Working Group[3] recognized the complexity in working out legal devices to handle such errors, but haven't yet decided on how to proceed. Thus the question remains open.

The Uniform Computer Information Transactions Act (UCITA, 2002) leaves it to the courts to decide whether an electronic mistake, fraud, or the like, will contribute to a finding that no contract has been concluded.

This UCITA initiative has been widely challenged for enhancing deployment of "poorly understood, and potentially fallible technologies, such as [...] electronic agents" (Fromkin, 1998), thus weakening consumer protection. This is one of the main problems to be solved.

The question of electronic contracts is addressed in the EU Directive on Electronic Commerce (Directive 2000/31/EC),[4] but without specifying the means used for such contracts. Nevertheless, this directive does stress the legal "weight" these contracts carry, and so sets out a duty to remove any obstacles barring their use.

This article, in other words, upholds the legal validity of electronic contracts and encourages the lawmaking bodies of every Member State to write provisions introducing electronic contracts into its national laws on contracts and making their use a legitimate, standard practice.

Article 10 of the same directive requires clearly illustrating to consumers the entire process of contract formation. This requirement contributes to the use of SAs in contract-making, because it makes it mandatory to specify the functioning of SAs.

---

[3] The Working Group took as its model the Uniform Electronic Commerce Act of Canada (1999), which deals specifically with errors made by electronic agents in electronic documents, http://www.ulcc.ca/en/us/index.cfm?sec=1&sub=1u1,

[4] Directive 2000/31/EC of the European Parliament and of the Council of 8 June 2000, on certain legal aspects of information-society services, with particular reference to electronic commerce in the Internal Market (Directive on Electronic Commerce), online at http://eur-lex.europa.eu/LexUriServ/LexUriServ.do?uri=CELEX:32000L0031:EN:NOT.

Failure to clearly explain these matters is one of the main obstacles to building consumer confidence in this technology. Such an explanation of an SA's functioning should not be underestimated: The clearer (and more user-friendly) an SA will be to consumers, more will consumers be inclined trust and use it. The programmers' community should more actively interact with consumer associations, working together to draft a step-by-step explanation of how SAs function, of what they can and cannot do, etc.

Clearly, SAs are very often perceived today as "unknown animals," and the layperson is skeptical about using them, so this requirement to explain the contract-formation process should help SA technology come into wider use in transacting business between consumers and merchants in e-commerce.

If the VE contract counterpart is a consumer, VE partners should bear in mind the rules on consumer protection, in particular those set by Directive 97/7/EC on distance contracts and its amendments introduced in Directive 2002/65/EC on distance marketing of consumer financial services. Furthermore, VE partners should also consider vexatious clauses (for those the reference should be maid to Directive 93/13/EC on unfair terms in consumer contracts). The VE shall, in particular, comply with the duties of information and the right to return the purchased goods. If SAs execute on line contracts, they must be able to provide said information and to enable consumers to exercise their rights. In this context, it is necessary to inform users that they are in fact interacting with a technical device and not with a human counterpart. Additional information may concern technical indications on the functioning of the agent and on the legal framework applicable to contract.

4   NEW RULES: PROPOSALS FOR FILLING IN THE GAPS OF LEGAL FRAMEWORK

We cannot say how will develop SAs in the future, and that is perhaps what is holding back the effort to bring their use under a specific regulatory framework. If the governments will introduce the legislation on SAs, after a while these governments will have to update, rewrite and supplement this legislation.

We already mentioned Directive on Electronic Commerce (Directive 2000/31/EC) as the main law to regulate contractual activities of SAs. This directive makes no specific reference to SAs, but it does not rule out their use in e-commerce, either. Therefore, if this Directive legitimates contracts formed by electronic means, there is no need for a specific legislation: existing law suffices to ensure legal certainty. If new issues will emerge, existing norms could resolve them and there is no need to introduce new legislation.

Thus the main undertaking should be not to introduce new rules on SAs, but to clarify the law already in force, this by putting out recommendations and guidelines, especially on the following points:

(a) offering a clear definition of SA, because the term *agent* itself generates ambiguity with regard to the law of agency. Furthermore, the definitions available today (UCITA, UNCITRAL) fail to reflect the relevant characteristics of SAs, such as autonomy and mobility. We suggest defining a SA a computer program capable of flexible and autonomous action in a dynamic environment, typically an environment in which multiple agents interact;

(b) we should spell out—for users (in this case, VE partners) and developers alike—the risks they face in case a SA malfunctions or oversteps the powers entrusted to it. The main issue is liability, the real sticking point, and if it cannot be clarified, then maybe we do need legislation to cover this specific area. Naturally, if an agent user is liable for the agent's actions, the user will have to be fully informed about what the SA can do. Such information is as yet unavailable.

(c) the parties to SAs-based contracts should have as much latitude as possible in agreeing to terms and conditions, without much interfering legislation going into the details of what can and cannot be done;

(e) at the same time, it would be useful—at least in the early stages—if we had a uniform contractual framework setting out basic rights for the parties engaged in SAs contracting. The best way to solve this problem might be to set up some form of collaboration among all the parties involved (programmers, business, consumers, lawyers) in drafting model contracts: unfortunately, no such initiative that we know of has so far been launched.

The regulation of agents can prove problematic in a non-hierarchical, dynamic organizational structure such as the VE. So the agreements drafted between VE partners can play an important role and be a first step toward the drafting of model contracts that will clearly illustrate the functioning of SAs. These agreements may be a part of a VE interchange agreement. The LEGAL-IST project has created a template for a license agreement for use of software agents, and this template could serve as an example. A special section of the agreement about SAs can be envisaged, in relation to the complexity of these tools and the absence of a specific legal framework. The VE partners not only specify the agents they will use (in other words, VE partners have to agree to use specialized software which permits mobile agents to run on computer system[5] of VE partners), but also identify the trusted third party (Software Agent Common Provider (SACP) to install this software and to take further care of upgrading and testing it (Szirbik, 2000). Furthermore, this agreement can define the actions that an agent shall be allowed to take and set limitations to this purpose. In contracting, these limits can be set on the type of contract or on its monetary value, or, again, on the type of subjects with which the agent is allowed to negotiate and perform contract activities, for example in relation to their nationality.

It may be expected, too, that agents should use digital signatures to strengthen the evidentiary value of contracts and to make for greater confidence, since the digital signature can identify the person who liable for an SA's actions. If so, the interchange agreement should have detailed provisions on the use of digital signatures by SAs. These can concern, *inter alia*, the technical specifications that the signature should comply with, with particular reference to purposes of compatibility; reference can be made to internationally recognized standards[6], as the European Directive on electronic signatures (Directive 1999/93/EC) abstains from imposing any specification on compatibility. The signature certificate can include agreed

---

[5] Also called *Mobile Agent Server* or simply *dock.*

[6] For example, the ones released by International Standard Organisation (ISO), International Electrotechnical Commission (IEC) and International Telecommunication Union (ITU).

limitations on the use of signatures: it is possible to differentiate these limitations as these may depend on specific factors.

Other problems to be addressed in this case is that of different legal requirements different countries have for digital-signature certificates. In Europe the issue is covered under Directive 1999/93/EC, but the problem still remains with regard to the law of non-EU countries.

5   CONCLUSIONS

In this paper initially we have presented the basic notions of discussion: VE and SA, focusing our (and your) attention on the use of SAs by VE in contractual activities, which include both negotiations to contract and contracting itself. We have glanced over the current legal framework and investigated its relevance to regulate these contracts. The legislation applicable to SAs becomes numerous when the contracts closed by SAs involve not only VE partners, but also the consumers. After we have individuated the gaps of SAs' legal regulation and proposed the improvements that should be made to facilitate SAs-based contracting in electronic commerce.

Further steps to be made are to contribute to open standards creation process. VEs are end-users of SAs technologies, which put in practical campus these applications. So their experience can be of great value when identifying the problems and the issues to have in mind while drafting the standards.

The development of standardized contracts for SAs could be the second positive initiative of collaboration between computer science, business and legal fields. Standardized contracts could include several types of contracts: model contract between SA and consumer, model contract between VE partners for application of SAs, model contract between VE partners and trusted third party (SACP) with particular emphasis on role assignment between the parties.

6   REFERENCES

1.   1. Hayes-Roth H. An Architecture for Adaptive Intelligent Systems, in Artificial Intelligence: Special Issue on Agents and Interactivity, 72, 1995, pp. 329-365
2.   2. Brazier F., Kubbe O., Oskamp A., Wijngaards N. Are Law Abiding Agents Realistic?, in Proceedings of the LEA02 Workshop, Bologna, 2002
3.   3. Radin M.J. Humans, Computers and Binding Commitment, in Indiana Law Journal, 2000, http://cyber.law.harvard.edu/ilaw/Contract/Radin_Full.html.
4.   4. Matskin M., Kirkeluten O.J., Krossnes S.B., Sæle Ø. AGORA: An Infrastructure for Cooperative Work Support in Multi-Agent Systems, in Wagner T., Rana O. (eds) Infrastructure for Agents, Multi-Agent Systems, and Scalable Multi-Agent Systems. Springer-Verlag, LNCS, Volume 1887, 2001, pp. 28-40, http://www.springerlink.com/content/hqnm6dktghy35vxf/fulltext.pdf.
5.   5. Petersen S.A., Rao J., Matskin M. Virtual Enterprise Formation with Agents – An Approach to Implementation, in IEEE/WIC International Conference on Intelligent Agent Technology, (IAT), 13-16 October 2003, pp. 527-530, http://ieeexplore.ieee.org/iel5/8789/27820/01241137.pdf.
6.   6. Szirbik N., Aerts A., Wortmann H., Hammer D., Goossenaerts J. Mediating Negotiations in a Virtual Enterprise Via Mobile Agents, in Proceedings of Academia/Industry Working Conference on Research Challenges 2000, 27-29 April, 2000, pp. 237-242, http://ieeexplore.ieee.org/iel5/6809/18271/00843300.pdf.
7.   7. Fromkin A.M. Article 2B as Legal Software for Electronic Contracting - Operating System or Trojan Horse?, http://papers.ssrn.com/sol3/papers.cfm?abstract_id=146908
8.   8. Directive 2000/31/EC on electronic commerce, http://europa.eu.int/eur-lex/pri/en/oj/dat/2000/l_178/l_17820000717en00010016.pdf

9.   9. "Legal Aspects of Electronic Commerce, Electronic Contracting: Provisions for a Draft Con-
     vention", UNCITRAL(2004) A/CN.9/WG.IV/WP.108, available at http://daccessdds.un.org/doc/
     UNDOC/LTD/V04/541/06/PDF/V0454106.pdf?OpenElement;
10. 10. UCITA (Uniform Computer Information Transactions Act, 2002), http://www.law.upenn.edu/
     bll/archives/ulc/ucita/2002final.htm

Michael Conrad
conrad@tm.uka.de, Institut für Telematik, Universität Karlsruhe
Christian Funk
cfunk@ira.uka.de, Institut für Informationsrecht, Universität Karlsruhe
Oliver Raabe
raabe@ira.uka.de, Institut für Informationsrecht, Universität Karlsruhe
Oliver Waldhorst
waldhorst@tm.uka.de, Institut für Telematik, Universität Karlsruhe
GERMANY

While decentralized peer-to-peer market platforms are more suited for trading short-lived or non-material goods (e.g., electrical power, bandwidth-on-demand) due to reduced transaction cost, robustness and scalability, they lack the legal certainty provided by centralized electronic market places operated by a trusted third party. This paper presents a technical framework that, conforming to European regulations, provides legal certainty for distributed market platforms. The framework includes a market-consistent data model representing the facts for the legal subsumption process, maps the European framework for electronic signatures to a distributed system, and comprises solutions for both adducing the reception of electronic documents and their distributed long-time storage. Moreover, it includes an electronic legal adviser for an automatic verification of contracts.

1   INTRODUCTION

In the near future there is a need for markets trading short-lived or non-material goods like, e.g., electrical power (Eßer et al., 2006) or bandwidth-on-demand (Dinger et al., 2006). In addition to a high number of consumers, such markets comprise an equally high number of sellers, each selling only a few items at a marginal price. Centralized electronic market places are not well suited for such scenarios, since, compared to the price of the traded items, the transaction costs are too high. At the same time centralized markets limit the available options of individual contract negotiations.

Decentralized market platforms based on the peer-to-peer (P2P) paradigm reduce transaction costs by eliminating the intermediary. Additionally, P2P systems inherently provide higher robustness and scalability as centralized approaches. While an inter-mediary is missing, a distributed market place can provide higher flexibility for contract negotiations between individual market participants. However, while centralized electronic market places are operated by a trusted third party and, thus, provide a certain level of legal certainty to both consumers and sellers, distributed market platforms lack such certainty since they are operated by a multitude of individuals, which generally cannot establish trust easy to each other and are often legal laities. As a consequence, providing legal certainty is crucial for the acceptance of distri-buted market platforms.

Conrad, M., Funk, C., Raabe, O., Waldhorst, O., 2007, in IFIP International Federation for Information Processing, Volume 243, Establishing the Foundation of Collaborative Networks; eds. Camarinha-Matos, L., Afsarmanesh, H., Novais, P., Analide, C.; (Boston: Springer), pp. 233–240.

In this paper, we present a lawful framework for distributed market platforms, i.e., a technical framework for providing trust and legal certainty conforming to the appropriate European regulations. The framework is based on three building blocks: First, it includes both a market-consistent data model representing the facts for the legal subsumption process and model of juristic expertise as a formal workflow. Second, it provides provableness and verifiability. For this purpose, it maps the European framework for electronic signatures to a distributed system. Furthermore, it includes solutions for both adducing the reception of electronic documents in a distributed system and a distributed long-time storage for such documents. Third, it includes an electronic legal adviser for an automatic verification of the validity of contracts. Consequently selected legal norms are transferred to technical rules and the appropriate state of facts is modeled in a legal ontology.

The proposed framework has been developed in the project "Self-Organization and Spontaneity in Liberalized and Harmonized Markets" (SESAM) (Conrad et al., 2005), which is founded within the priority research program "Internet Economy" by the German Ministry of Education and Research (BMBF). As major application scenario, SESAM considers a virtual power plant with a multitude of participants equipped with small, decentralized facilities for electricity production, e.g., fuel cells, solar panels, and wind power plants. Participants buy required energy or sell surplus energy on a distributed market place implemented by the SESAM platform. For demonstration purpose, SESAM has developed a software prototype, which is currently evaluated in a large distributed setting.

The remainder of this paper is organized as follows. Section 2.1 introduces the data model employed in the proposed framework. In Section 2.2, we show how legal norms are mapped on a contract negotiation process represented by a basic workflow. Section 2.3 shows how provableness and verifiability are provided. As last building block of the framework, the electronic legal adviser is presented in Section 2.4. Finally, concluding remarks are given.

2   LAYOUT FOR A LAWFUL FRAMEWORK

2.1   A Market-Consistent Data Model

As a building block of the lawful framework, a consistent data model is required, which defines a standardized description for electronic document exchange on the distributed market. Besides general technical aspects, also legal and economic requirements have to be considered. For our lawful framework, we propose a data model, which is able to map all required technical, economical and legal aspects into a single object model. The base structure of our data model is shown as UML diagram in Figure 1 in a simplified manner.

The root element of the data model is the class *Object*, almost all other classes inherit from this root element. From economic side, the data model includes the classes *Intention* and *Product*, where each product is described by a set of attributes. The class *Intention* maps the intention of a market participant, where the two attributes outgoing and incoming define which product a participant wants to sell and which one he wants to buy. To reach legal conformity an intention is embedded into the class *Declaration* and *Invitatio*. While the class *Invitatio* only represents an announcement, the class *Declaration* stands for legal binding statement in the contract negotiation process. In addition to the economic attributes, the class *Declaration* includes several legal relevant attributes, for example, person related data, time ranges and consumer protection information as prescribed by the regulation of the Directive 97/7 EC. An even more complicated issue were the requisites for Information Society Services regulated in the Directive 2000/31 EC. The national regulatory implementation is orientated on the classic client-server paradigm. Therefore we mapped this to the specific requirements of the P2P architecture using concepts in the data model.

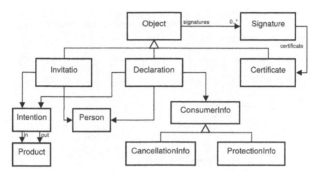

Figure 1: Data Model UML Diagram

Most objects represented by the data model require a guarantee of integrity. Thus the root element includes an attribute signatures of type Signature. Using this attribute, each instance can be secured against modification by applying a digital signature. To prove the identity of the issuer of a signature, the class Certificate is used. This class represents an identity certificate, which binds an identity to a public key. Although certificates typically require a trusted third party, they are issued in a distributed manner as shown in Section 2.3.1.

2.2 Judicial Expertise as Formal Workflow

Electronic Market places that allow negotiation are complex compared to Internet shops offering one click buying. To obtain legal certainty for such market places, it is necessary to embed the negotiation properly into a continental European[1] legal framework. Therefore judicial expertise has been transferred into formal workflow concepts so that automation of formation of contracts can be implemented. We present an easy to understand example of a short negotiation shown in Figure 2 as a UML sequence diagram.

The process starts with an offer[2], which could be based on an *invitatio ad offerendum* (invitation to bargain) previously published. Before being sent, the offer is checked for legal compliance by an electronic legal advisor (see Section 2.4). Optionally, the offer is delivered with a reception confirmation (see Section 2.3.3). A received document is passed automatically to the electronic legal advisor of the offeree. After evaluation the advisor informs the recipient that the document he

---

[1] We analyzed Austrian, French, German and Swiss law. There might be a different outcome for common law systems since the analyzed laws do not recognize concepts such as consideration.

[2] In Austrian, German and Swiss law binding and not revocable after reception or notice, in French law revocable.

received constitutes an offer. The offeree may now generate an acceptance, do not react at all, or (as in our example) create an acceptance conditioned on revisions or supplementary details. In the latter case, the acceptance legally counts for a rejection3 and new offer (sec. 150 German Civil Code, sec. 869 Austrian General Civil Code). The original offeror will be informed about this fact if he checks the incoming document. He now has the same choices as the original offeree, following the description above. In our example he accepts the counter offer. After successful negotiation both can use the distributed archive for long time storage of contracting documents (see Section 2.3.4).

Generally, the workflow will be more complex and dynamic, e.g., due to longer negotiations or auction mechanisms.

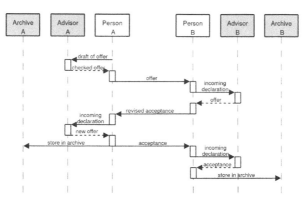

Figure 2: Contract negotiation UML Workflow

2.3 Provableness and Verifiability

Pacta sunt servanda is the root of all contract law. However in case of breach of contract remedies are provided by law and awarded by court. Usually the plaintiff bears the onus of proof for several facts as far as not challenged. Those are:

- identity of contracting parties (usually plaintiff and respondent)
- assignment of declarations, formal requirements (writing, electronic signature)
- reception of declarations (but see article 10 Swiss law of obligations)
- verifiability of declarations

The respondent on the other hand might be interested in being capable to prove the reception of termination notice and the reception time.

Some requirements of the preceding list are subject to the European framework for electronic signatures (as laid out in directive 1999/93/EC), but they are intentionally focused on a trust model with a single trust anchor. This constraint collides with one of the key principles of the P2P paradigm, the independence of centralized instances. After comprehensive analysis of the legal requirements, our framework provides essential functions without central instance in a distributed manner.

---

[3] Upon rejection the offer expires, i. e. it no longer exists (sec. 146 German Civil Code). Consequently it cannot be accepted any more.

2.3.1 Authenticity of Parties

In contrast to contract negotiations in the real world, on an electronic market it is difficult to prove the identities of the parties, since they are not standing vis-a-vis. Undoubtedly, the identities of the parties are important evidence. A common app-roach for establishing the required authenticity of an identity inside the digital world is to use public key infrastructures based on identity certificates. Identity certificates establish a binding between a unique identity and a given public key of an asymme-tric cryptosystem (e.g. RSA). This binding is usually created by a trusted third party (denoted as trust anchor) after a successful verification of the participant's identity. To provide trust relationships among participants, all participants have to trust this dedicated authentication instance and the certificates it issues.

The existence of a single dedicated instance conflicts with the key paradigm of distributed system. On one hand, the whole system can be brought down by attacking this single instance. On the other hand not all participants may trust this dedicated instance. Therefore we propose a distribution of trust anchors across the distributed system. This enables participants to choose a trust anchor out of the available set of trust anchors. The selection of a trust anchor depends highly on the trust relationship and the provided authentication schemes. These authentication schemes are used to prove the participant's identity before a certificate is issued by the trust anchor. All trust anchors issue a certificate of type *Certificate*, described in Section 2.1. Each certificate can be signed by more than one authentication instance, avoiding a high amount of certificates by certifying a participant by multiple trust anchors. To establish a trust relationship between two participants, a subset of identical trust anchors has to be find out by merging the available sets of trust relationships of each participant.

2.3.2 Authentic Legal Declarations

Another important requirement for being able to verify a contract is a provable binding between declarations made by a participant and his identity. Without such binding, a participant can deny the entering into a contract, so that the opposite party is unable to verify the existence of the contract.

To meet this requirement we propose the application of digital signatures for relevant contracting information, building upon the certificates issued by the distri-buted approach described in the previous section. Using the associated private key of the corresponding public key of the participant's certificate, only the owner of the certificate is able to compute a valid signature. The opposite party is able to verify the validity of the signature using the public key from the certificate. In case of dis-putes about contract details, each party is able to evidence declarations made by the opposite party.

2.3.3 Reception of Declarations

In most cases contract law requires for receipt of both offer and acceptance; a mailbox rule is not recognized in German law, nor would be an "electronic mailbox rule", if there exists one at all. On an electronic market, one of the contracting parties can easily deny the reception of declaration. If one party denies a reception it can not be proved easily whether it happened in an action of fraud or bona fide.

So far, this problem has been solved by using a third trusted party supporting the reception of relevant documents and creating a reception confirmation signed by the recipient. However, since on a distributed electronic market such single trusted instance does not exist. Thus, alternative methods are required. Instead of using a dedicated instance, we propose the involvement of other market participants as witnesses, as described in (Conrad, 2006). Key idea of the proposed protocol is a selection of independent witnesses out of the mass of all participants, which support the delivery of contracting documents. The selection is performed by a deterministic function that depends on the chosen document and random information from sender and receiver, preventing a manipulation of the selected witnesses. In addition to the selection process, the protocol contains several features to avoid fraud by sender or receiver. As long as at least a single witness is not corrupted, the reception of a document can be delivered and the delivery can be confirmed by a reception confirmation signed by the witness. We believe that, at least when applying German law, the reception confirmation is sufficient to prove reception. From the point of judicial method this could either be based on an analogy to sec. 175 German Civil Procedure Code or on a prima facie evidence for reception. Here, the German concept of prima facie evidence allows concluding from certain given facts to such ones which usually were to be proven if experience of life states that the one normally leads to the other.

2.3.4   Archiving Contracts

The long term storage of contract documents is an important challenge. Without a backup all documents can be lost in case of a hard disk failure, resulting in a potential lack of evidence before court.

To provide long term storage, our lawful framework includes a distributed user archive, which provides a reliable distributed storage. All documents are secured against modification and unrestricted access by encryption and digital signatures. Due to the distributed storage of documents a breakdown of individual nodes does not infect the storage system at all. At the same time, the user archive acts as electronic mailbox receiving declarations, if the user is off line.

2.4   Legal Evaluation by Electronic Legal Advisors

While sellers and consumers on distributed markets are often legal laities, there is a need for legal assistance while inspecting the contract or negotiating for specific conditions. Thus, our lawful framework includes electronic legal advisors. Recall that the workflow shown in Figure 2 illustrated how automated legal advice is incorporated into an exemplary negotiation process. Due to regulation of legal profession the authorization to give legal advice is restricted. Our framework does not collide with this regulation thus we do not intend to substitute professional legal advice.

2.4.1 Methodology

Legal reasoning is a process that is influenced by numerous factors such as the legal framework, within one operates, or vagueness of a norm. Consequently, we have to begin by deciding on the framework – in our case, it is the Continental European norm-based system of positive law –, on the specificity of the norms, and a few specific legal consequences. This in turn determines a limited set of primary norms from which to start. For automated reasoning we need an abstract model of the legal norms and their classification.

Building a Graph of Norms

Hence, before beginning with legal reasoning it is necessary to find out the norms whose general domain covers the situation, starting from a primary set of norms. Decisions are made by inspecting the norms. Typically, norms determine a legal consequence resulting of one or more states of facts. Other norms may refer to related norms that show alternative routes or exceptions. Based on this set of routes a graph of norms can be built that allows a decision of whether the originally intended legal consequence can be reached or not. Each of these norms must now be inspected in order to determine whether the given real world situation, represented by object instances of the data model (see Section 2.1), matches the state of facts demanded by the norm. This may require to find statutory definitions (norms) or to build own definitions. In other words, we have to see if the individual facts match the states of facts or the (statutory) definitions. This process is called subsumption.

Formalizing the Subsumption Process

There are a number of legal philosophies that try to explain this subsumption process. Our approach is based on the work of Larenz (Larenz, 1991).

We assume that norms in the positive law mostly do not address singular cases but rather cover general classes of real-world situations. On the other hand, the relevant case is a specific real-world situation. Subsumption is an interpretative process. Consequently, to mechanize subsumption the semantics must be considered (Bohrer, 2003), and these should go beyond thesauri. Ontologies constitute a promising approach, because they reflect semantic relationships between terms. These relationships can particularly be defined so that they directly support the subsumption process. Our contribution is to explain the reasoning behind the match in an ontology, which incorporates judicial methodic knowledge. This knowledge summarizes in several steps by textual, historical, systematic and teleological interpretation, and by comparing concrete facts with legal terms that have no direct counterpart in the data model and may thus be subject to judicial opinion.

Ontologies are even more versatile. For example, one could translate some of the statutory definitions into the ontology and thus prune the norm graphs even further. Some related work can be found in (Senn et al., 2006).

2.4.2 Technical Architecture

Under the conditions mentioned before legal reasoning can be modeled as logical inference realized by classical logical rule processing. Therefore, our prototype includes a rule engine where the legal norms and summarized norm graphs are expressed as logical rules in the format required by the rule engine.

For the present implementation, a specific set of legal norms is transformed in logical rules. Those rules have the form *result* **if** *condition*. The states of facts within the condition are fed from user input or declaration instances. The legal reasoning starts from the legal consequence and then works its way backwards to construct a norm graph. Therefore, the rule engine must run a backward chaining strategy, except in some cases where legal obligations must be derived by forward chaining based on given facts. Furthermore, according to legal reasons or to minimize user interaction, the order in which rules are applied is important.

The prototypical implementation of our framework inside the SESAM project depends on the KAON framework (Maedche et al., 2003). The ontology is used to represent our data model and to perform decomposition of indefinite legal terms using the included description logic reasoner.

3 CONCLUSION

In this paper we present essential components to build a lawful framework for distributed electronic markets. Building upon a consistent data model, we proposed a flexible contract negotiation workflow. To provide provableness and verifiability we propose the use of a distributed public key infrastructure. In contrast to classical market scenarios we provide court-proof non-repudiation by digital signatures and a verifiable reception of documents. In addition, our lawful framework includes a distributed long-term storage of contracting documents. Finally, our framework supports legal laities by providing an electronic legal advisor component, which is able to perform an automatic verification of legal statements.

The proposed framework is implemented inside the software prototype of the SESAM project. For the legal subsumption process the rule engine JESS is used. Currently, we are working on a migration to KAON2, mobile phone-based authentication and signature generation.

4 REFERENCES

1. Bohrer, A.: Entwicklung eines internetgestützten Expertensystems zur Prüfung des Anwendungsbereiches urheberrechtlicher Abkommen, 2003
2. Conrad, M., Dinger, J., Hartenstein, H., Rolli, D., Schöller, M., Zitterbart, M.: A Peer-to-Peer Framework for Electronic Markets, in: R. Steinmetz, K. Wehrle (Ed.), Peer-to-Peer Systems and Applications, Lecture Notes in Computer Science 3485, p. 509-525, Springer, Sep 2005.
3. Conrad, M.: Non-repudiation mechanisms for Peer-to-Peer networks, in: CoNext 2006, 2nd Conference on Future Networking Technologies, 4 - 7 December 2006, Lisboa, Portugal, p. 249-250, Dec. 2006
4. Dinger, J., Raabe O., Hartenstein, H.: A Techno-Legal Perspective on Peer-to-Peer-Based Bandwidth on Demand Management, Proceedings of the 1st IEEE International Workshop on Bandwidth on Demand (BoD 2006) in conjunction with IEEE GLOBECOM 2006, p. 73-80, San Francisco, CA, USA, November 2006.
5. Eßer, A., Raabe, O., Rolli, D., Schöller, M.: Eine sichere verteilte Marktplattform für zukunftsfähige Energiesysteme. it- Information Technology, p. 187-192, Aug 2006
6. Larenz, K.: Methodenlehre der Rechtswissenschaft, Springer 1991
7. Maedche, A., Motik, B., Stojanovic, L.: Managing Multiple and Distributed Ontologies in the Semantic Web. The VLDB Journal 12:4 p. 286-302, 2003
8. Senn, A., Schweighofer, E., Liebwald, D., Geist, A., Drachsler, M.: LOIS: Erfahrungen und Herausforderungen bei die Weiterentwicklung mutilingualer Rechtsontologien. In: Schweighofer et al. (Hrsg.): e-Staat und e-Wirtschaft aus rechtlicher Sicht. Boorberg, p. 290-195, 2006

PART **8**

LEARNING AND INHERITANCE IN VO

25

TOWARDS LEARNING COLLABORATIVE NETWORKED ORGANIZATIONS

Leandro Loss, Alexandra A. Pereira-Klen, Ricardo J. Rabelo

Federal University of Santa Catarina, Department of Automation and Systems
GSIGMA – Intelligent Manufacturing Systems Group, BRAZIL
{loss, klen}@gsigma.ufsc.br
rabelo@das.ufsc.br

The concept of Learning Collaborative Networked Organizations merges both the CNO and the LO paradigms. It aims at augmenting the quality of decision-making and of corporate governance taking inter-organizational knowledge into account. The rationale behind the proposal is that CNOs are still lacking research and work for enhancing their agility where rapid decision-making is crucial for achieving their goals. In this paper knowledge management is proposed as an approach for tackling this problem. The paper presents the first step for a framework for gathering information and for generating new knowledge dynamically according to what users need for given situations. The corporate knowledge is retained, organized, shared and re-used to the benefit of individuals and of CNO as well as of their respective members.

1   INTRODUCTION

Emerging markets and the development of new technologies, such as Internet and web search tools are some of the causes for breaking barriers among people, cities, organizations, and even countries in the whole world (Friedman, 2005). Facilitators include the easy and increasing access to communication channels and information, as well as the production of content by and for everybody in a never-ever-thought rate. Manuel Castells (Castells, 2006) points out that the amount of information provided nowadays is changing life styles and the way of making business. In fact, this reveals that in the global market there is a need to be competitive, to be aware about the changes, to be connected to others, to collaborate, and to share knowledge. It means that organizations should monitor their products, clients, suppliers, competitors, as well as the changes occurring in the market in order to be competitive and, as a consequence, to survive. Therefore, it creates a kind of (dynamic) knowledge chain.

Organizations shall improve their competitiveness when they work collaboratively with each other, in a so called Collaborative Networked Organization (CNO) paradigm. According to Camarinha-Matos (2006), a CNO is a network consisting of a variety of entities that are largely autonomous, geographically distributed, and heterogeneous in terms of their operating environment, culture, social capital and goals, which collaborate to better achieve common or compatible goals, and whose interactions are supported by computer networks.

In order to support the collaboration process, challenges such as how organizations should share common goals, build some level of trust, agree on common practices and values as well as inter-operate based on common technological infrastructures, have risen up (Afsarmanesh, 2005). The supporting CNO structure for

Loss, L., Pereira-Klen, A.A., Rabelo, R.J., 2007, in IFIP International Federation for Information Processing, Volume 243, Establishing the Foundation of Collaborative Networks; eds. Camarinha-Matos, L., Afsarmanesh, H., Novais, P., Analide, C.; (Boston: Springer), pp. 243–252.

collaboration among organizations has been called Virtual organization Breeding Environments (VBE). A VBE is an association of organizations and their related supporting institutions, adhering to a long term cooperation agreement, and adoption of common operating principles and infrastructures, targeting the growth of their chances and their preparedness towards collaboration in potential Virtual Organizations (VOs) (Afsarmanesh, 2005). According to Rabelo (2004), VO is a dynamic, temporary and logical aggregation of autonomous organizations that cooperate with each other as a strategic answer to attend to a given business opportunity or to cope with a specific need, and whose operation is achieved by a coordinated sharing of skills, resources and information, totally enabled by computer networks.

The essential rationale of this paper is that current approaches for implementing CNOs and their manifestations (VBEs and VOs) have not so far adequately explored an important aspect for enhancing their agility: they have not been incorporating and effectively using the knowledge generated along the CNO life-cycle. Additionally, there is still a lack of adequate support for managers to consider past experiences, as there is no – or almost none – registering and further dissemination for future use of what has been learned individually and collectively during their life cycle. It is argued that both good and bad experiences (CNO organizational memory), which usually comprise precious information, are simply lost during the CNOs' life time.

In this paper the concept of Learning CNOs (L-CNOs) is introduced by making use of the Learning Organizations (LO) paradigm supported by the Knowledge Management (KM) approach. It represents an extension of the LO concept to strategic alliances based on the knowledge spread over the CNO, where members are usually highly heterogeneous, independent and even competitors of one another. Learning CNO aims at augmenting the quality of decision-making and of corporate governance taking inter-organizational knowledge into account. If a certain CNO is able to learn with its success and failures cases, it can reduce risks and better plan strategically its future. The objective of this paper is to introduce a systematic approach on how CNOs can become L-CNOs, making use of KM and LO philosophies.

The content of this paper is divided as follows: section 2 stresses how learning organizations and knowledge management concepts are combined for supporting a Learning CNO environment; section 3 presents the importance of inherited data, information and knowledge in this process. The supporting tools for the Learning CNO are shown in section 4 and, finally, section 5 provides preliminary conclusions and next steps.

2   LEARNING ORGANIZATION AND KNOWLEDGE MANAGEMENT

As time passes by, different categories of organizations have risen up with different working styles. Figure 1 shows the main characteristics of different kinds of organizations, considering their communication scope, life cycle, decisions styles and knowledge usage. The figure is divided in four quadrants. The lower-left quadrant represents how traditional organizations were structured in the past: there was an intra-organizational communication scope, focusing mostly in operational tasks. Decisions used to be taken without considering neither past information nor knowledge, and both knowledge dissemination and human aspects are low.

The upper-left and lower-right quadrants represent some forms of organizations nowadays. Organizations presented in upper-left quadrant (CNOs) have an inter-organizational communication scope, but they are mainly focused in decisions taken to be applied in operational tasks, similar to the traditional organization view, taking into consideration current data and information, even though they require knowledge. In this quadrant it is possible to observe the improvement of knowledge dissemination and human aspects to an intermediate level. The organizations present in the lower-right quadrant (LOs), however, despite they have been working in a "closed world" due to its focus be an intra-organizational communication scope, they focus on operational, tactic and strategic decision, they are intensive knowledge users and human aspects are relevant.

The last quadrant, upper-right (L-CNO), is how the proposed approach sees future organizations. L-CNOs join the inter-organizational communication scope (CNO) – organizations willing to collaborate – with a knowledge oriented view (LO) making highly intensive use of the knowledge in order to take decisions focused not only in the operational level, but also in tactic and strategic decisions. The processes are based on what has been learned and ameliorated along the time horizon. This paper aims to contribute as a starting point towards establishing stronger theoretical foundations of Learning CNOs.

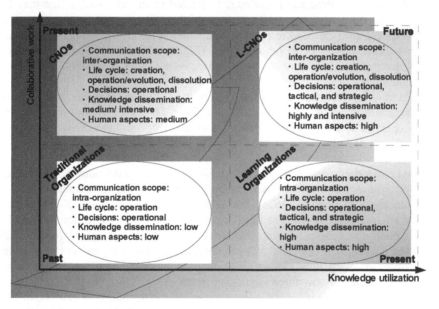

Figure 1- Organizations - past, present, and future views

Peter Senge (2004) explores Learning Organizations concept in a prescriptive view splitting it in five disciplines that he called: systems thinking, personal mastery, mental models, shared vision, and team learning. The first three disciplines have particular application for the individual participant, and the last two disciplines are applied for groups. Senge also argues that the individuals who excel in these areas will be the natural leaders of learning organizations. From another point of view, Nonaka (1995) coined the term of knowledge-creating in companies by the understanding of the dynamic nature of knowledge creation and to manage such a process effectively. It consists of three main elements: i) SECI, that stands for socialization, externalization, combination and internalization; ii) Ba, that can be defined as context in which knowledge is shared, created and used through interaction; and iii) knowledge assets, constituting the inputs, outputs, and moderating factors, of the knowledge-creating process.

LO and KM can complement each other. On the one hand, as defined by Senge (2004), LOs act as human beings cooperating in dynamical systems that are in a state of continuous adaptation and improvement. As such, they need to be fed with knowledge in order organizations can behave like that. On the other hand, KM emerges as the supporting methodology for creating, disseminating, and promoting knowledge use. However, the existence of KM methods and techniques is not enough: CNO's people must be motivated to use the knowledge. In this sense, LO can provide the support to KM activities.

2.1   Learning CNOs

CNOs, as they are nowadays, are mainly focused on daily events, specially during the VO life-cycle. However, past data is extremely important and may be used as source during the learning process. Data collected, stored and not used are seen as *potential knowledge*. Potential knowledge is related to the knowledge that may be extracted from the analysis of a vast amount of data. Data combination, interrogation, and speculation can lead to precious information and gives advantages for the decision making processes in organizations (Figueiredo, 2005). Some techniques available for this extraction are knowledge discovering in databases, intelligent data analysis, among others.

CNOs may have the capacity to learn from their own experiences as well as to use their data in order to become more competitive. On the one hand, in a learning CNO, people are motivated to externalize their knowledge and the LO is responsible for the process of knowledge generation, on the other hand KM offers support for using such knowledge.

Once knowledge is retained and made available as formal documents, procedures and CNO's culture, it should be used not only to improve the operational phases in CNOs' instances (VBEs and VOs), but also in tactic and strategic planning. For example, when a given VO is not fulfilling its deadlines, some decisions should be taken in order to accomplish with the scheduling previously agreed (operational phase). The reasons "why the 'that' VO was delayed" shall be analyzed and, if suitable, VO members must receive a clearer set of instructions or the VO launching process should be re-studied/re-structured (strategic planning).

Considering the definition of CNO presented in the introductory section, in this work, a Learning Collaborative Organization (L-CNO) is defined as a CNO that is able to learn in a dynamic collaborative environment in order to continuously adapt and improve itself. A L-CNO is able to capture CNO knowledge – stored in people's procedures and actions or in databases – and to further organize, formalize, re-store, and make it accessible to its actors in order to make improvements at operational, tactic and strategic levels. This concept is supported by knowledge management and computer systems. The kick-off process for a L-CNO is to be concerned to what has occurred during the CNO life-cycle, it can be done via the inheritance process that is describe in the next section.

3   INHERITED DATA, INFORMATION AND KNOWLEDGE

The basis for a Learning CNO is the use of data, information and knowledge inherited by the CNO – its organizational memory – as well as the preparedness of CNO actors. In order to have a clear picture about inherited content, it is important to frame the nature related to this issue. VOs have temporary and distributed behavior. They are legally and logically dissolved after the product or service be delivered according to the agreed contractual clauses (Rabelo, 2002).

Although CNOs manifestations[1] have a well defined life-cycle comprising the creation, operation/evolution and dissolution (Camarinha-Matos, 2005), the time-horizon varies from short to long-term collaboration depending on its characteristics. Nevertheless, CNO actors are usually able to identify what happened within their enterprises when a VO is running, however they seldom know what happened and the historical performance of other CNO actors. It makes the process of gathering data, information and knowledge a hard task because they are spread over the CNO.

The task of the VO closing/dissolution, aiming to transfer the VO experience and data, especially VO performance history, to the VBE is known as VO Inheritance (VO-I) (Loss, 2006). This process is extremely important and demanding as such, i is facilitated if it is supported by computer systems.

Despite the differences between VOs, VO-I approach gathers relevant data, information and knowledge throughout the CNO and make it easily accessible, no matter its duration. The main users of the knowledge produced by the process of VO-I are the VBE actors. However, VOs actors can also benefit from the knowledge base made available via VO-I.

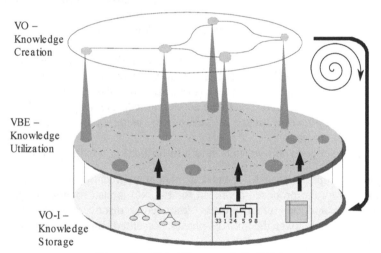

Figure 2 - Global Framework for VO-I

Figure 2 illustrates the overall vision of knowledge flow for VO-I. The top level is seen as an appropriate environment for knowledge creation. VOs are the main producers, because they work dynamically with a diversity of products and services and they are in touch with real and unexpected situations. After the VO dissolution

---

[1] The ones that have relationship like VBE and VOS where a VBE is the facilitator to create of VOs, or between professional virtual communities and virtual teams.

phase, the knowledge produced by VOs shall be properly stored (bottom layer). The storage process may occur either in an electronic/digital way (automatic follow-up operations), or in a traditional way (like in printed reports and memoranda). The VBE (middle layer) appears as the main client of the knowledge. VBE shall use knowledge in order to create value improving its preparedness as well as advertisement campaigns to increase its reputation to the customers. The overall process occurs as a spiral which enhances knowledge time to time flowing through the three layers.

4 SUPPORTING PROCEDURES AND TOOLS FOR L-CNOS

VO-I is more than a sum of pieces of knowledge. It provides a complete framework with experiences, practices and case studies for CNO actors. KM is the approach adopted in order to support the knowledge retained in the VO-I process and that will be used in the L-CNO framework.

The KM model introduced by Nonaka (1995) was the starting point to KM in the academia. Since then many approaches have risen up. Nissen (2000) presented an amalgamated KM model that is used to support the proposal of this paper. This model includes both individual and collective entities. It is arranged in six phases, which are briefly described below:

1. Knowledge *creation* phase involves the discovery and the development of new knowledge. It also includes the knowledge capture where knowledge shall be new to a particular organization or individual.
2. After knowledge be created or gathered it must be *organized*. In order to perform this task, knowledge representational techniques are used, like keyword extraction, thesaurus, and ontologies to interrelate key terms and concepts.
3. The *formalization* process involves the conversion of existing knowledge from tacit to explicit form. It means to validate the knowledge.
4. Knowledge *distribution* phase is related to the dissemination to people and organizations, according to the access rights previously defined.
5. The *application* phase is related to using knowledge for creating competences.
6. Knowledge *evolution* leads in turn to further knowledge creation.

Despite its importance, KM is more a management philosophy than a mechanism. In this way, the proposed approach for L-CNO is also founded in three main pillars: briefing and debriefing process, knowledge discovering, and knowledge search. These pillars cover the six KM phases presented, linking it with the inheritance process.

4.1 Briefing and Debriefing

When dealing with knowledge intensive tasks, like in CNOs, it is important to map data, information and specially knowledge, by adopting a KM practice. There are some available practices like brainstorming, competence maps, brainwriting, heuristic redefinition, and others. This work applies and adapts the *Briefing* and *Debriefing* practices to the CNO context.

VO briefing consists in sharing with general information regarding VO actors. For example, processes to be executed, management procedures concerning the scope of specific VOs, what is expected at the end of the VO when it is dismantled. In summary, it is a general guideline elaborated *a priori* and that describes to the VOs how to proceed and the estimated outcomes. It comprises the *formalization* and *distribution* (overall Figure 2), two out of the six phases described by Nissen (2000). The former appears when the guidelines are official documents that are made available. The latter takes place when the instructions are disseminated among VO actors in a way all VO actors can have access to that knowledge.

During the process of **VO debriefing** VO actors are required to provide feedback regarding the occurrences during the VO life-cycle which will be cross-checked against the original plans (i.e. what was discussed in the *Briefing* phase). VO debriefing comprises three phases related to the KM approach presented by Nissen (2000). The first one is related to *knowledge creation* (Figure 2 top-level). VO actors are motivated to communicate their mental models and visions about the VO. It is donee by sharing ideas and exchanging experiences and formalizing these ideas in working plans, strategies or even rules and, as a consequence, providing the organizational learning in the CNO. Hence, they are *creating* tacit and explicit knowledge. Once knowledge is written down and confirmed by someone else it is *formalized*. If some adjustment is done for the briefing in a further VO, knowledge *evolution* takes place. For example, documents produced by past VOs containing some suggestions about a certain procedure can be used in order to compare and improve processes, like partner search and selection.

Despite VO briefing and VO debriefing do not cover *knowledge application* (Figure 2 middle-top-levels), they provide the source for applying this knowledge. For example, information provided by the debriefing process in, its conclusions as well as the occurrences during the VO life-cycle are refined and, if suitable, used in the briefing process in another VO. This process is repeated for every VO so that VO briefing and VO debriefing are continuously improved. *Knowledge application* (Figure 2 middle-level) is settled when the gained experience (already formalized via documentation) is applied by the CNO.

It is important to emphasize that these processes require the ability to source and integrate information into a suitable format, use effective interpersonal skills to encourage positive contributions, follow up and prepare documentation.

4.2 Knowledge Discovering in Databases

Briefing and Debriefing process deal with tacit and explicit knowledge, but not with potential knowledge. A perspective for dealing with it is to apply techniques of knowledge discovering in databases, such as Data Mining (DM) (performed in Figure 2 bottom-level). DM is the process related to the extraction of knowledge from data repositories aiming to identify valid, new, potentially useful and understandable patterns (Fayyad et al., 1996). Data provided from VO actors, products, schedule, performance indicators, trust indicators, and so forth, when collected, become potential knowledge and this kind of knowledge can be extremely important to the CNO.

The results coming from the DM process shall be shown to the managers as transparently as possible so that they do not need to know details about implementation, data cleaning and even databases. It means that with some mouse clicks and few keywords the manager will have the results of a DM algorithm showing the patterns in data by using an easy-to-use human interface (Google-like). The functionality of knowledge discovering developed to test this concept is called *Mined Knowledge Search* (MKS). It is described in section 5.

If the rules[2] generated by a DM algorithm seem to be interesting to the manager, (s)he may use them or ask for a more detailed and intensive investigation. It allows managers to have dynamic access, to possible solutions. The evaluation and interpretation of results is up to the manager. It is important to highlight that this process guarantee that the results will be neither good nor accurate enough, however they can provide some insights to the managers allowing them to take smarter and better decisions.

4.3   Knowledge Based Information Retrieval

Five of six steps presented by Nissen (2005) were shown until now: creation, formalization, distribution, application and evolution, but the *organization* (Figure 2 bottom-level) of the knowledge is still missing. Knowledge organization is as important as the other steps because there is no reason to have knowledge stored if it is not intended to be retrieved.

Traditionally, managers have access to information by using reports based on databases. However, they barely have an easy access to unstructured data, typically in documents spread around the CNO, such as plain texts, e-mails, chats, or even the reports produced during the process of VO Briefing and VO Debriefing. It is necessary an instrument for retrieving unstructured data in CNOs. It is done by a tool called *K-Search* that is also described in section 5.

Figure 3 summarizes the proposed approach. CNOs can become L-CNOs when the knowledge generated and used during the VBE/VO life-cycle is stored in non-human repositories, made available and incorporated to the CNO as routines, systems, culture, strategies, and so forth. The main support for L-CNO is found in three main pillars described in this paper - briefing and debriefing, knowledge discovering in databases, and knowledge based information retrieval. The overall approach is based in the six aforementioned KM phases.

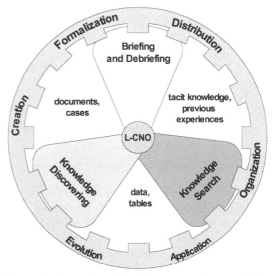

Figure 3 - General model of the proposed approach for L-CNO

---

[2] In this approach the results for DM algorithms are presented as rules (if-then), however there are other forms to represent it (Witten, 2005).

5   IMPLEMENTATION ASPECTS

The assessment of the overall approach has been done through prototypes implementation. The tool developed regarding the perspective of knowledge discovering in databases has been called MKS. MKS is internally divided in two phases. The first one comprises the selection of specific tables and the columns that appear to be relevant to be used by a DM algorithm. Data used in the DM process comes from the VBE database that usually follows a CNO reference model. Once the relevant dataset is made available, the second phase can be started, comprising the execution of a DM algorithm that will produce *Association Rules* (Witten, 2005). Association Rules may predict any attribute and also give the freedom to predict combination of attributes. As so many different association rules can be derived from even a tiny dataset, the interest is restricted to those that apply to a reasonably large number of instances and have reasonably high accuracy on the instances to which they apply to (Witten, 2005). Phase 1 occurs only once, when the DM algorithm is configured. Phase 2 is executed off-line, time to time according to a period settled by each CNO. The results (rules) are stored in a database that is accessible via a web service. Rules are not generated on-line because the process may take several minutes, or even hours, and it is not practical.

An attempt to retrieve unstructured data in CNOs has been developed under the scope of the ECOLEAD project with the *K-Search* functionality. It is a search engine that allows users to perform searches with semantic embedded and in a secure way. The *K-Search* functionality wraps KIM platform (Popov, 2003) which provides infrastructure and services for automatic semantic annotation, indexing, and retrieval of documents (knowledge organization). KIM is equipped with an upper-level ontology and a knowledge base providing extensive coverage of entities of general importance, but it does not cover the requirements for CNOs. An ontology related to the CNOs area (Plisson, 2005) was plugged to KIM in order to support documents related to CNOs and to provide shared meaning of CNO terms into documents. Therefore the *K*-search functionality is able to deal with information related to CNOs Finally, the development of a tool to help the *Briefing* and *Debriefing* is under study.

6   CONCLUSIONS AND NEXT STEPS

This paper has introduced an approach where the concepts of knowledge management and of learning organizations are combined and applied to CNOs. Such approach builds a learning collaborative environment by supporting a more comprehensive decision-making, using data, information and existing knowledge about a CNO.

In order to overcome the necessity of VBE/VO managers in knowing which data, information and knowledge are right and proper, the process is split into three main activities: in the first one there is a transformation from tacit to explicit knowledge and vice-versa as well as the improvement of procedures by applying the processes of VO briefing and VO debriefing. The second one is characterized by the transformation of potential knowledge that is embedded or hidden in CNOs' databases using a data mining tool. The third one allows users to search for unstructured data supported by a tool to retrieve the already stored and semantically treated knowledge.

Most of the prototypes related to the presented approach are already implemented and will be described in details in another opportunity.

The proposed approach is seen as a learning environment where the corporate knowledge is retained, organized, shared, formalized and used to the benefit of CNO's people, CNO's members and CNO as a whole. Next steps include the investigation of the influence of corporate governance in learning, the final implementations as well as examination of how the overall learning process can be used in issues related to logistics in CNOs.

6.1   Acknowledgments

This work has been partially supported by the Brazilian councils of research and scientific development – CNPq and CAPES. It has been developed in the scope of the Brazilian IFM project (www.ifm.org.br) and the European IST FP-6 IP ECOLEAD project (www.ecolead.org). Special thanks also to Mr. Carlos E. Gesser for his help in part of the prototype implementation and Mr. Rui J. Tramontin Jr. for his valuable comments.

7   REFERENCES

1.   Afsarmanesh, H., Camarinha-Matos, L. M.; 2005. A Framework for Management of Virtual Breeding Environments. In: PRO-VE, Proceedings. Valencia, 2005. Spain. p 35-48. Springer.
2.   Camarinha-Matos, L. M.; Afsarmanesh, H.; 2006. Collaborative Networks: Value Creation in a Knowledge Society. In: Proceedings of PROLAMAT'06, Shanghai, China, 14-16 2006.
3.   Camarinha-Matos, L. M., Afsarmanesh, H., e Ollus, M.; 2005. ECOLEAD: A holistic approach to creation and management of dynamic virtual organizations. In: PROVE'06. Proceedings. Helsinki 2006, Finland, p 3-16. Springer.
4.   Castells, M.; 2006. A Sociedade em Rede, volume 1. Paz e Terra, 9a. edição.
5.   Fayyad, U.; Piatetsky-Shapiro, G.; Smyth P.; 1996a. From Data Mining to Knowledge Discovery: an overview. In: Advances in Knowledge Discovery & Data Mining, pp. 1-34.
6.   Figueiredo, S. P.; 2005. Gestão do Conhecimento: Estratégias Competitivas para a Criação e Mobilização do Conhecimento na Empresa. Qualitymark, Rio de Janeiro.
7.   Friedman, T. L.; 2005. The World Is Flat: A Brief History of the Twenty-first Century. Farrar, Straus and Giroux.
8.   Loss, L.; Rabelo, R. J.; Pereira-Klen, A. A.; 2006. Knowledge Management Based Approach for Virtual Organization Inheritance In: PROVE'06. Proceedings. Helsinki 2006, Finland. p 285-294. Springer.
9.   Nonaka, I. e Takeuchi, H.; 1995. The Knowledge-Creating Company: How Japanese Companies Create the Dynamics of Innovation. New York: Oxford University Press, Inc.
10. Nissen, M., Kamel, M., e Sengupta, K.; 2000. Knowledge Management and Virtual Organizations, chapter Integrated Analysis and Design of Knowledge Systems and Process.
11. Popov, B.; Kiryakov, A. ; Kirilov, A.; Manov, D.; Ognyanoff D.; Goranov, M.; 2003. KIM - Semantic Annotation Platform. In: 2nd International Semantic Web Conference (ISWC2003).
12. Plisson, J. Ljubic, P.; 2005. ECOLEAD Deliverable D21.3 – Elaborating Common Ontologies.
13. Rabelo, R. J.; Pereira-Klen, A.; Klen, E. R.; 2004 Effective Management of Dynamic Supply Chains, in International Journal of Networking and Virtual Organizations.
14. Rabelo, R. J.; Pereira-Klen, A. A.; 2002. Business Intelligence Support for Supply Chain Management. In: BASYS02 Proceedings, Cancun 2002 p 437-444.
15. Senge, P. M.; 2004. A Quinta Disciplina. Best Seller, 16a. edição.
16. Witten, I. H.; Eiber, F.; 2005 Data mining: practical machine learning tools and techniques. 2nd Edition, Morgan Kaufmann, San Francisco.

26

IDENTIFICATION OF FORMS AND COMPONENTS OF VO INHERITANCE

Iris Karvonen, Iiro Salkari, Martin Ollus
VTT Industrial Systems, FINLAND
Iris.Karvonen@vtt.fi, Iiro.Salkari@vtt.fi, Martin.Ollus@vtt.fi

Virtual Organizations (VO) are created from a VO Breeding Environment (VBE) or a network, to serve a specific task. In addition to the task-based value the VO and its participants gain valuable experience and create other types of assets. Most often this achieved value is not saved. It is distributed, not managed and sometimes not even identified. The practise of preserving and re-using the common experience and other non-proprietary assets created in the VO is called here "VO inheritance". VO inheritance aims to enrich the VBE "bag of assets", thus improving the preparedness of the VBE for business opportunities. The added value, or the contents of the VO inheritance, is called here "VO heritage".The paper identifies different forms and components of VO heritage. The identification uses previous development of "lessons learnt" in project management field, and a collection of views of SMEs operating in collaborative networks.

1   INTRODUCTION

The concept of Virtual Organization Breeding Environment (VBE) (Camarinha-Matos et al., 2005) aims to establish sustainability and continuity in the environment of one-off or temporary customer deliveries (Virtual Organizations, VOs). Even if the operation as discontinuous VOs may increase flexibility, agility and resource utilization efficiency, it also causes challenges (Karvonen et al. 2004), for example risk of losses of information, knowledge or other values. VO inheritance, defined here as "the practice of storing and passing on the experience and other non-proprietary assets created through collaboration in a VO" (ECOLEAD D33.1 2006)) aims to strengthen the VBE by preserving the common valuable outcome ("VO heritage") from VOs to the VBE. Currently in operating networks a systematic management of VO inheritance is most often missing.

Often VO inheritance is mainly understood as the task of transferring the VO performance history to the VBE. Even if the VO Performance Historical Repository, including both the VO performance models and the related historical data is an important part of VO heritage (ECOLEAD D31.2, 2005), it also includes other types of valuable components which need concern.

In the Project Management field (PMBOK 1996) the inheritance is handled through the activity of "lessons learned" in the project closing phase. Schindler and Eppler (2003) view the learning from project experiences through two groups of methods: process-based methods and documentation-based methods. Also in some specific fields of projects the re-use of information has been discussed, like for engineering projects (Fiatech 2001). These approaches focus on data, information and knowledge, not on other types of assets.

The first step for the systematic preservation of VO heritage is to identify the valuable outcomes to be saved. This is the focus in this paper. The study has been supported by collecting experience, needs as well as priorization of different types of VO heritage from industrial end-users (SME networks).

Karvonen, I., Salkari, I., Ollus, M., 2007, in IFIP International Federation for Information Processing, Volume 243, Establishing the Foundation of Collaborative Networks; eds. Camarinha-Matos, L., Afsarmanesh, H., Novais, P., Analide, C.; (Boston: Springer), pp. 253–262.

The main definitions and objectives of VO inheritance are described in chapter 2. Chapter 3 describes and discusses the main types of VO heritage. The results of the SME network query are summarized in chapter 4 and chapter 5 gives challenges and further development needs.

2 OBJECTIVES OF VO INHERITANCE

2.1 Definitions

Wikipedia (www.wikipedia.org 2007) gives a definition of inheritance of an individual:

"Inheritance is the practise of passing on property, titles, debts and obligations upon the death of an individual."

This definition has been used and adapted to create a first definition of VO inheritance:

"VO inheritance is the practice of storing and passing on the experience and other non-proprietary assets created through collaboration in a VO."

The definition has not been settled yet. Thus VO inheritance is often also used to describe the contents of VO inheritance, that is, what is inherited. In this paper, a specific concept of VO heritage is used:

"VO heritage comprises of the different assets which are inherited from a VO to the VBE."

The VO product/service going to the customer will be the property of the customer after the VO dissolution and is thus not part of VO heritage. That is why the object of inheritance (what is inherited) excludes the assets which belong exclusively to only one partner. Assets with restricted IPR are usually not considered as part of the VO heritage. This does not, however, imply, that all the VO heritage is open for all VBE members.

Management of VO inheritance knowledge and information can be considered as a specific case of Knowledge Management, but VO inheritance management is not only about managing knowledge or information, but also of other types of assets. Thus VO inheritance is not only Knowledge Management.

The given definition refers to assets created in a VO. In general an asset is something that has future value: it can be used to create value. Assets can be both tangible and intangible.

In ECOLEAD D21.4a (ECOLEAD 2006) a concept of "VBE bag of assets" is defined: "The VBE Bag of Assets refers to all valuable elements that different VBE Members may wish to share with others and which are available to all VBE members."

2.2 Benefits of VO inheritance

The objective of a VO is either to perform a specific task or to create a specific product/ service to a customer in an inter-organizational environment. The main focus of VO management is to achieve this goal (ECOLEAD D32.1, 2005). If the need for the VOs is repetitive with sufficient frequency, it is beneficial to develop *preparedness* by creating a Virtual organization breeding environment (network)

(VBE): developing processes, systems, rules and practices which support the collaborative tasks.

When there is a need for a collaborative task, for example a customer request, a VO is created from a VBE for the delivery. After the completion of the task the VO is dissolved and the increased knowledge, experience and other useful outcome should be returned, "inherited" to the VBE (network). Each organization may utilize these assets individually but in addition they can be used to improve the preparedness of the VBE (network). Further, if the VO has been successful, the references and reputation created can be used externally to convince the customers.

Thus VO inheritance is aimed to increase the "bag of assets" of the VBE (ECOLEAD D21.4a, 2006). This benefit may be realized through:

- - improving the preparedness of the VBE: VOs can be created and started faster,
- - making the VOs more effective and reliable both in time and costs, and improving or ensuring the quality,
- - decreasing VO management efforts through increased trust and strengthened relationships,
- - supporting decision-making and tracking of VO problems or deviations,
- - increasing the value of the VBE for the members, for example by increaseing their knowledge and market position,
- - supporting winning in competitive bidding because of customer knowledge and closer customer relationships,
- - supporting the marketing of the VBE services to new customers by offering references of past deliveries.

2.3 Inheritance as the enabler for the VBE feedback loop

In ECOLEAD D32.1 (ECOLEAD 2005) approaches to describe different characteristics of VBEs/networks and virtual organizations have been reviewed. The Globeman21 approach (Pedersen et al., 1999, Zwegers et al. 2003) identifies two kinds of descriptive parameters: Situational factors are environment conditions which cannot be changed or selected, and design parameters are selected parameters.

Virtual Organization Breeding Environment (VBE) and VO have both their own, interdependent descriptive parameters. When a VO is created from a VBE, the characteristics of the VBE (both the situational and design factors of the VBE) are situational factors for the VO. The VO design factors may be decided at the VO creation.

On the other hand, the inherited experience gained in VOs gives back information to the VBE. The VO experience may affect the BE design parameters and be useful in the evolving process of the VBE (Figure 1, Karvonen et al. 2005). As the VBE design parameters are situational factors for the VO, the inheritance enables the effect of VO experience to the preconditions of VOs (VBE). This can further contribute to the success of the VOs. Currently this feedback loop is usually not working.

requirements, experience, inheritance

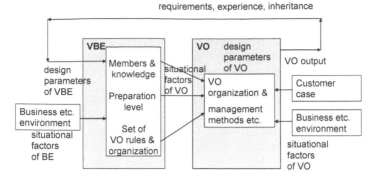

Figure 1. Feedback from VO output to BE design.

3   COMPONENTS OF VO HERITAGE

3.1   Different forms of assets

VO inheritance increases the common VBE Bag of Assets. These assets are not as concrete and visible as the product created to the customer, and thus often the VBE does not even become aware of their existence. To identify the different forms of VO heritage the categorisation of VBE bag of assets can be used. ECOLEAD D21.4a (ECOLEAD 2006) identifies three main types of assets:

1. financial capital: financial resources and values (cash, accounts, physical assets), risky elements
2. intellectual capital: data, information and knowledge, both in tangible and intangible (human) form
3. social capital: also called relational assets; relationships with customers, suppliers and other organizations.

3.2   Inheriting financial capital

Financial capital is typically owned by the independent organizations. However, in principle it is possible that part of the profit created in a VO would be inherited to the VBE. This could be used to pay for the common infrastructure services, development of common procedures and possibly as a reserve fund to reimburse expenses of potential customer complaints.

When discussing inheritance, an important point to solve is also how to take care about the potential risky or negative outcome of the VO:

4. Warranties of the customer product
5. Other obligations and liabilities
6. Inheritance of failed VOs, realized risks

These post-VO liabilities may cause financial expenses and may thus be considered as negative financial heritage. They may require additional work, resources or costs, cause a delay of the customer payment, or decrease the payment.

3.3   Intellectual capital: information assets

The intellectual capital includes all the VO data, information and knowledge, both in databases and documents and in human minds. The information may be both plans and experience about their realization, both of quantitative (for example performance measures) and qualitative type. As it is easier to collect and save quantitative data, in many cases there is a lack of restored qualitative information; for example of reasons behind decisions.

The categorization of knowledge in project management field has been analysed by for example van Donk et al. (2005). He has ended up with a categorization that defines three knowledge aspects of project-based organizations:

7. Entrepreneurial knowledge, which is restricted to project acquisition from markets.
8. Technical knowledge that focuses tightly to technological questions from technological viewpoints.
9. Project management knowledge, which combines aspects of project management know-how and experiences in conducting and managing projects.

In the context of VOs the accumulated entrepreneurial knowledge includes understanding the market conditions, customers' business and value creation to the customers.

Technical knowledge, including the product design and technological solutions, is needed and produced during VO sales, creation and execution phases. The level of detail of the technical knowledge increases along these phases.

Project (or VO) management knowledge is needed and accumulates from sales onwards, through VO planning, execution, monitoring, evolution and dissolution. The VO management knowledge consists of VO management process knowledge, planning and monitoring levels and techniques, partner performances, and knowledge concerning soft issues like trust.

One specific challenge is to manage IPR in collaborative relationships. In most cases IPR belongs to a specific organization, but there may be cases when the VO creates IPR which cannot be considered as the property of one organization. Even if IPR is currently often not considered as part of VO heritage the VBE should define rules how to handle the issue.

3.4 Social/relationship capital

Social/relational VO heritage is nearly linked to the increased knowledge of the collaborating organizations. However, the relational assets do not consist of the knowledge, but of the relationships. It is clear that having even all the knowledge about the relationship has not the same value as having the "living" relationship.

Social and relational capital originates from collaboration. Thus VOs, where the partners collaborate for a common objective, are important contributors to the VBE social capital. Two different types of VO relational inheritance can be distinguished:

1. The increase of relational capital *between the VBE members*: Operating in a VO makes the partners to know each other better both at the personal and organizational level. This means that they know the capabilities, strengths and weaknesses of each other, which makes it more effective to collaborate in the future VOs, and increases the VBE preparedness. VOs also produce tested configurations of partners for specific tasks. Collaboration increases the trust between the partners and contributes to the creation of a VBE "culture". Especially successful VOs increase the *motivation* of partners to work together.

2. The increase of relational capital *with the customers*: Working with the customers contributes to improved customer relationship and understanding the customer needs which is very useful for future business and identification of new business opportunities. Also improved personal relationships and knowledge of customer practices support the preparedness to work for the customer in future. Successful VO deliveries to the customer increase the customer's trust to the VBE. The achieved market position and the references may also be considered as part of VO relational heritage and they are typically very important in order to gain also new customers.

Collaboration is not always successful and all the social relationships do not improve in every VO. It is even possible, that the overall social VO heritage is sometimes negative. In some cases it may even danger the sustainability of the VBE. Thus also mechanisms how to handle these cases, disagreements and disputes need to be considered.

4   VIEWS OF SME NETWORKS OF VO INHERITANCE

4.1   Current practices

To identify the practical needs, opinions and existing practices of VO inheritance a questionnaire was set up for a group of SME networks. The answers were received from eight networks located in different European countries.

All the involved networks identified a need for VO inheritance but they had very few implemented practices to deal with it and no actions planned. Most of the organizations had no practices for systematic collection and saving of experience, but some of them had informal, verbal exchange of experience between managers of similar VOs.

Some partners measured VO performance during the VO for the use of VO management. In some cases the customer required the recording of, for example, quality data. Long-term measurement of partner performance was exceptional. The collection of information from the network was considered difficult, for example, periodic textual questionnaires had not been successful.

Most of the networks had some kind of a platform/portal/server to manage information, but its usability was not always good and in some cases it was only used by the VO manager. Experiences were shared in the networks most often through different events: "cooperation meetings", working groups, discussion forums, workshops, seminars, exhibitions, training programmes, board meetings and round tables with partly business and partly social character. These can be used to share experiences, to introduce new members, present latest news and also to discuss ideas for development.

Mainly the networks had a similar practice for carrying responsibilities after the VO dissolution: the obligations towards the customer are typically carried by one company, which is the company managing the VO. Some of the respondents considered that the customer will never accept a shared responsibility. In some specific cases the risk sharing was defined in the contract, in a MOU (memory of understanding) or in a SLA (service level agreement). In one case it was mentioned that all the VO partners are included in a liability insurance which is placed by the VO manager.

4.2 VO experience: Importance and contents

VO experience, including the information and (also tacit) knowledge is an important part of VO inheritance. The SME networks were asked to estimate the importance of VO experience for different parties operating in collaborative networks:

Most of the networks considered that VO experience is important for all parties, and that most important it is for the partner managing the VO. Customers were seen nearly as important users of the VO heritage. Towards the customer, VO experience gives references and credibility, and thus it can be used as a marketing tool and supporting new business opportunities.

The networks were asked to put the different contents of VO experiences in the order of importance by selecting between experiences of product knowledge, customer relationships and practices, process & management knowledge (needed tasks, actions, resources, schedules, used approaches, templates etc.), faced changes and problems and how they were solved and partners and their performance.

While there are many development actions to collect experience about partner performance, it was interesting to see that the most important experience from the end user point of view was the experience about the customer. Also the process and management experience was nearly as important. The other three types were ranked less important. This may come from the fact that for many networks the main concern is the uncertainty of future business opportunities, inadequacy of customer orders and the instability of business.

The networks were also asked to describe the main contents of each type of experience. The results are reported in ECOLEAD D33.1 (ECOLEAD 2006).

4.3 Other inheritance components

Data, information and (even tacit) knowledge and experience are not all that can be cumulated via VOs. The networks were asked to identify the additional forms of inheritance by setting questions like:

10. -What does a VO/VT give to the participants (except experience and the order & payment)?
11. -How does the state of the VBE differ before and after a VO?
12. -How does a VO affect the social/ relational capital?
13. -What is the effect to customer relationships?
14. -What about obligations and warranties?

For the first question the most commonly identified benefit was that fulfilled VOs contribute to new business opportunities, often also for more extensive responsibilities in the customer delivery. The experience of the fulfilled VOs may influence the strategy of the VBE members, as they learn to know better the resources and competences of other companies of the VBE. Also fulfilled VOs affect updating technology roadmaps and contribute to the creation of new ideas for collaboration.

The state difference of a VBE caused by a fulfilled VO depends on the development stage of the VBE: In a newly created VBE with little experience on collaboration the effect is stronger than in a mature VBE. In a developing VBE starting a VO may "heat up" the whole VBE. In the end, the respondents considered that fulfilled VOs define the quality of the VBE: "the number and size of VOs are the most important performance figures of a VBE".

All the networks thought that successful VOs have the most positive effect to the social capital of the VBE. Fulfilled VOs contribute to trust building, motivation and commitment. The social capital is often dependent on personal relationships. It increases slowly and especial care is needed with partners with similar roles. Also, failed VOs may disturb the collaboration in future, thus, to avoid the negative effects a VO needs to have a certain level of trust before its creation.

Customer relationships are a special form of relational capital. Fulfilled VOs were typically seen as very strong instruments to improve the customer relationships. They contribute to the understanding of customer's future needs, customer's processes, behaviour and price building practices, create and strengthen personal contacts. Typically the customers operate via the interface of a specific company (broker or VO manager), which considers the customer as "their" relation and don't want to share it with the whole network. Thus, to avoid conflicts, the VBE should define rules and practices for customer relationship management.

Most of the customers of the networks do not seem to accept shared responsibility, and they expect that one organization takes the responsibility. Typically this is the VO manager or the one with the biggest share or closest ties to the customer. The VO/VBE may then define how it internally handles the responsibilities. The rules may be different for different responsibilities, like for on time delivery, warranties or other obligations. In collaborative innovation/research projects there is a risk of not obtaining the results, and the rules how to handle the realization of this risk need to be defined.

4.4   Requirements from SME networks

SME networks were also queried about their requirements for VO inheritance. The following are comments from the end-user networks:

1. Contribution to VO inheritance should appear rewarding and beneficial for the actors.
2. The contributions required from VO participants should be made as easy and short as possible. No overloading with sophisticated and laborious procedures will be accepted. Only necessary and really useful information should be saved and shared.
3. Part of the needed data could be created automatically or semi-automatically from the VO monitoring and operation. Collection of VO experience should partly happen as part of the VO management tasks.
4. Templates should be created to capture knowledge in order to allow categorization of information, and facilitate the search based on taxonomy. On the other hand, a sophisticated structure is not as important as easy search.
5. The information has to be easily accessible for all different users.
6. In some cases the amount of data may be a problem for its use, but in most cases the capture is the main problem.
7. Openness of the information is a complex question. In most cases it is unrealistic to have totally "open books". The right level of openness and transparency should be found.
   All networks are not homogeneous; especially when they are in a growing phase. Part of the companies have more experience than the others and don't

need all that information which again may be necessary for newcomers of the network.

5   CONCLUSIONS AND CHALLENGES

5.1   Conclusions

When developing mechanisms to accomplish VO inheritance the first step is to identify its different components and forms. The initial assumption was that the VO inheritance is mainly about storing and re-using the VO and partner performance models and values. The analysis of the VBE assets and end-user views, however, disclosed three specific aspects:

1. Social capital/relational assets are an important part of VO heritage. It is not about the information of the relationships but the relationships themselves. Thus it cannot be stored and treated with only ICT.
2. The relationships to the customers and the information about the customers were considered more important than the relationships to the VBE members. This might be affected by the fact that many of the end-user companies participating in the query operated in a broker role in the network. Management of customer relationship capital has additional unsolved challenges in non-hierarchical networks.
3. The VO heritage is always not only positive. The relational VO heritage may be negative, even in case of a successful VO. (On the other hand, the intellectual capital (experience knowledge) may increase also in an unsuccessful VO.)

VO inheritance aims to bridge the gap between the impermanent VOs. Transforming the VO discontinuity to continuous learning and improvement in the VBE is not an easy task. It requires attention both at the VBE and VO level. In VBEs the rules for the inheritance must be agreed: who is inheriting what, what are the user rights and information openness levels and responsibilities for the inheritance management. How to take care that the inherited information does not cause misuse or decrease of trust? How to refine the gained information for maximum benefit? At the VO level the main thing is to make the inheritance happen and to find inheritance mechanisms which don't require too many resources. In both forms methods and tools to identify the important information or to drag out knowledge from a mass of data or information should be developed. Also best practices to preserve the relational and structural assets of VOs should be found and implemented.

5.2   Acknowledgments

The paper is mainly based on work performed in the Integrated project ECOLEAD funded by the European Community under the Framework programme 6 (IP 506958).

6   REFERENCES

1.   Camarinha-Matos, L., Afsarmanesh, H., Ollus, M., 2005. ECOLEAD: A holistic approach to creation and management of dynamic virtual organizations. In Camarinha-Matos, L., Afsarmanesh, H. & Ortiz, A. (Ed.), Collaborative Networks and Their Breeding Environments (pp 3-16). Springer.
2.   ECOLEAD (EU/FP6 IP 506958) D31.2 VO Performance Measurement approach, performance metrics and measurement process, September 2005. www.ecolead.org.
3.   ECOLEAD (EU/FP6 IP 506958) D33.1 VO inheritance components and mechanisms, September 2006. www.ecolead.org.
4.   ECOLEAD (EU/FP6 IP 506958) D32.1 Challenges in Virtual Organisations Management., www.ecolead.org. March 2005.
5.   ECOLEAD (EU/FP6 IP 506958) D21.4a Characterization of VBE Value Systems and Metrics, www.ecolead.org March 2006.
6.   FIATECH (2001). Guidelines and Drivers for Achieving Plant Lifecycle Data Management. The owner – operator forum. January 2001. http://www.fiatech.org.
7.   Karvonen, I., Jansson, K., Salkari, I., Ollus, M. (2004). Challenges in the management of virtual organizations. In Camarinha-Matos, L. (Ed.), Virtual Enterprises and Collaborative networks (pp 255-264). Kluwer Academic Publishers.
8.   Karvonen, I.; Salkari, I.; Ollus, M. (2005). Characterizing Virtual Organization and Their Management. In Camarinha-Matos, L., Afsarmanesh, H. & Ortiz, A. (Ed.), Collaborative Networks and Their Breeding Environment (pp 193- 204). Springer.
9.   Pedersen, J.D., Tolle, M. Vesterager, J. Final report on Models. Deliverable 1.3 of Esprit 26509 Globeman 21 project. 1999.
10.   PMBOK, 1996. A Guide to the Project Management Body of Knowledge. Project Management Institute Standards Committee. 1996.
11.   Schindler M., Eppler M., 2003. Harvesting project knowledge: a review of project learning methods and success factors. International Journal of Project Management 21 (2003), pp 219-228. Elsevier Science Ltd and IPMA.
12.   van Donk D., Riezebos J., 2005. Exploring the knowledge inventory in project-based organizations: a case study. International Journal of Project Management 23 (2005), pp 75-83. Elsevier Science Ltd and IPMA
13.   WIKIPEDIA: http://www.wikipedia.org, reviewed 28.2.2007
14.   Zwegers, A., Tolle, M, Vesterager J. VERAM: Virtual Enterprise Reference Architecture and Methodology., in Karvonen et al. Global Engineering and Manufacturing in Enterprise Networks (GLOBEMEN), VTT Symposium 224, 2003, p. 17-38.

27 ESTABLISHING AND KEEPING INTER-ORGANISATIONAL COLLABORATION. SOME LESSONS LEARNED

Raúl Rodríguez, Pedro Gómez , Rubén Darío Franco and Angel Ortiz

Research Centre on Production Management and Engineering
Polytechnic University of Valencia
Camino de Vera S/N. Edificio 8G, Acceso D Planta 1°
Tel. (+34) 96.387.96.80/Fax: (+34) 96.387.76.89
{ raurodro | pgomez | dfranco | aortiz}@cigip.upv.es
SPAIN

From a practical point of view, this work focuses on pointing out and providing solutions to some of the most common problems that challenge the establishment and keeping of collaborative inter-organisational practices. These problems are grouped into four main intangible factors: trust, equity, coherence and visibility. Due to the changing nature of these four factors, the concept of dynamic interactions is introduced and illustrated. Dynamic interactions among these four intangible factors make more difficult the monitoring and management of possible problems. Then, some solutions to these problems derived from experience are provided.

1 INTRODUCTION

Over the last years, and mainly due to technological improvements, inter-organisational collaborative practices have become both popular and applicable for organizations in a worldwide basis. In this context, the inter-organisational collaborative process itself implies that at least two entities are willing to collaborate for achieving a common goal, perhaps by sharing resources, perhaps by sharing strategies, but for sure by sharing information. Once the first step of agreeing to collaborate has been given, and when it is time to pass into action, experience says that problems usually arise. Such problems may manifest sooner or later within the collaborative lifecycle but they have really got the potentiality of breaking the whole collaborative process and, extensively, the profits to be achieved by participants. The variety of these problems may be high in both number and nature and their solution usually always involves negotiation processes between the parts. From their experience, the authors think that there are some factors that could be considered the root of many of these problems.

The main objective of the present piece of work is to go through the main of these factors, presenting associated problems and providing at the end some practical solutions that could be taken into account when establishing and keeping inter-organisational collaboration.

Rodríguez, R., Gómez, P., Franco, R.D., Ortiz, A., 2007, in IFIP International Federation for Information Processing, Volume 243, Establishing the Foundation of Collaborative Networks; eds. Camarinha-Matos, L., Afsarmanesh, H., Novais, P., Analide, C.; (Boston: Springer), pp. 263–270.

2   COMMON PROBLEMS

2.1   Intangible factors

The main problems detected from experience came up while carrying out collaborative practices among enterprises. The authors have taken part of collaborative
networks under the form of extended enterprises (EE). An EE span company boundaries and include complex relationships between a company, its partners, customers,
suppliers and market (Browne, Sackett and Wortmann, 1994). Companies in an EE
must co-ordinate their internal systems (intra-organisational activities) with other
systems within the supply chain, being flexible enough to adapt to changes. Several
problems come up when developing collaborating network practices within this
environment: disconformities with assigned roles, disconformities with assigned
tasks, disconformities with allocated resources, unrealistic objectives, etc. Such problems could be grouped into the main four categories, called also intangible factors:

- Trust.
- Equity.
- Coherence.
- Visibility.

As Figure 1 shows, these four intangible factors are directly affecting and making
difficult the collaborative process and will be presented and discussed in the next
points.

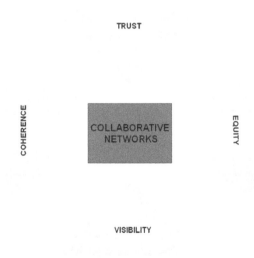

Figure 1 – Intangible factors

From the definition of EE, as well as from experience, it is possible to affirm that
trust between the collaborative parts is essential in order to success in such a
business environment. In the collaborative network context it is essential that the
different members trust each other. This could be stated as a non negotiable starting

point for avoiding later disputes and malfunctions of the collaborative network. But in today's competitive environment trust is not that easy to achieve between organisations. Usually, organisations that are willing to collaborate are those that have known each other for a long time or that have somehow interacted. This lead to the fact that, initially, trust among the members of a collaborative network is a matter of knowing how the others members work. Further, and in the EE context, different flows of both information and material/services are moving within the network boundaries. Such information flows might range from operational information, for instance simple production/facilities data interchange, to strategic information, for instance sharing strategic plans, with the consequent need of trust among the members.

For instance, it is possible to think, in the context of an EE, that the OEM (Original Equipment Manufacturer) creates a collaborative network with one of its first tier suppliers and with one of its first tier distributors for sharing information and working in a much more integrated manner, and achieving then a more agile and flexible network. Focusing on the upstream informational flow, this implies information sharing process between the parts that will not take place in absence of trust.

Therefore, it is possible to conclude that an adequate confidence level or trust among the involved actors is a must for establishing the foundations of collaborative networks.

Once trust among the members of the network has been somehow set, equity is other factor that can potentially hit hard the whole collaborative process. With equity we mean the allocation of tasks and roles between the members of the network. The negotiation process is always a difficult one, as it implies several discussions between the partners and whose main outcome, regarding equity, is the different tasks and roles to be developed by the entire network. Then, it is possible that emerges another problem associated since a conflict of interest among the parts might come up, as they might have different ideas of what applications to develop, what information to share, how to share resources, what the main benefits should be, etc. Then, such an allocation of tasks should be made by taking into account the expected return to be achieved by every member.

Additionally, the allocation of roles might come from the own nature of the collaborative network attending to either win/win or win/lose relationships and also by negotiation. Roles might also be an important source of problems due to individual or collective egos, or to the allocation of concrete roles to the wrong actors; for instance to give a leading role to a member when she does not have either the capabilities or the motivation to execute the pertinent tasks. Therefore, the concept of equity must be carefully handled within collaborative environments.

For instance, and following with the above EE example, if the OEM and its first tier supplier decided, within the collaborative network context, to develop a collaborative demand forecasting tool in order the former would provide the latter with its main future production trends, the allocation of tasks should involve to all the three main actors of the collaborative network: OEM, supplier and distributor, as they all three will benefit of the implantation of such a tool. What it is true is that both the OEM and its supplier should be the ones to lead the development of the tool and should then not rely most of the necessary work to be developed on the distributor's account. Additionally, and regarding the role of allocation, in this particular case, the OEM and its supplier should adopt both the leading roles and take responsibility for the welfare of the tool implementation.

Coherence is other intangible factors to deal with, as it requires that all the objectives (and strategies) defined by the collaborative network will be in accordance and coherent with the initial agreed goals. It is not unusual to set unrealistic objectives for the network that will lead to states of confusion, deception or scepticism. Besides, and regarding coherence purposes, all the components of the network should feel comfortable and agree with the stated objectives of the collaborative network. Unfortunately, in many collaborative environments, even win/win environments, there are members that want or like to play the leader role and sometimes they do not exercise a good management. Moreover, they could even set up objectives that will turn into not being coherent for the rest of the actors of the network.

For our example of the EE, if the collaborative network set as a common objective, for instance, to become as flexible as possible in its deliveries as a network, this may become, if not agreed for all the actors, a non coherent objective of the network. Such an objective implies that the upstream actors of the network must reduce their lead times regarding delivery and production to a maximum that, in most of the real situations, is not possible to reach. This could be a non coherent objective for the network, as it has not taken into account the real capabilities of the network, setting then an unrealistic objective.

Visibility is the last, but nor the least, intangible factor to take into account in our review. Visibility may turn into a problem when some members of the collaborative network want to check other members' work in order to assess whether they are meeting their obligations or not and whether they are doing it as expected: Adequate quality level, in time deliveries, implementations, developments, tasks executed comparing planned and executed tasks, etc. The handling of information within the collaborative network must be defined and agreed from the very beginning, trying always to avoid a complete federated model, where only one member of the network can access and handle the information about the collaborative project.

An illustrative example could be the one when our EE makes the decision of undertaking a project that involves the work of all its members. Then, once all the tasks have been agreed, and the time to develop them comes, some sort of framework should enable visibility for all the members of the network. Then, it could be checked the development of the project and whether all the parts are delivering the accorded work. This example can also be applied for our collaborative network collaborating with others external organisations/networks for carrying out some activities. The exhortation of checking on others' work will probably be stronger in this case so be the need of keeping any type of visibility framework to do so.

Four intangible factors that might potentially impact over the collaborative process have been presented so far. But an important issue has been deliberatively kept apart up to now: The time factor.

2.2   The problem of dynamic interactions

Once trust, equity, coherence and visibility have been presented as the four intangible factors willing to create problems if they are not dealt with properly, the next question is: Do these factors stay still over the lifecycle of the collaborative process? In other words, if a high level of trust has been reached/built among the members of the collaborative network, does this level stay high along the whole lifecycle of the collaboration process? The most intuitive answer is not so is the real answer. All these four intangible factors are dynamic in nature and therefore they do change over time. This fact makes even more difficult to manage them and decision makers from the collaborative network should able to detect such changes and take the appropriate measures to mitigate them.

For instance, and regarding the intangible factor of trust, it is possible to affirm that trust levels develop as managers continually update their expectations and assessments of partners (Wicks et al., 1999); additionally, levels of trust and distrust may change as a result of negotiation processes, partner interactions and external events, and as a result of changes in managerial interpretations and collaborative environments (Doz, 1996). From a practical point of view, trust could be considered as one of the key pillars above which to build a collaborative network and therefore its evolution should be carefully monitored over time. Taking a look at the academic literature, it is possible to find some interesting works (Doz, 1998; Ferrin et al., 2005; Ghoshal and Moran, 1996; Klein Woolthuis et al., 2005; Serva et al., 2005), whose main conclusions are the following:

- Trust evolutions in a more positive and smoother way over time for already consolidated collaborative networks than for external collaborative networks willing to interact with others networks.
- The degrees to which actors of the network trust their partners during initial stages of cooperation leave strong imprints on the development of these relationships in later stages of collaboration.
- There are different trust cycles overtime; among the later the vicious and virtuous cycles of trust are the most popular ones. It is agreed that inter-organisational relationships are willing to take place along these cycles.
- Collaboration processes also occur in the presence of distrust and in the absence of trust.
- Trust is build up and destroying several times overtime as a consequence of the interaction of multiples actors.
- The dynamic interplay between trust and others important factors.

The last of these interesting conclusions lead to think about whether and how the different four intangible factors affect each other. It seems clear that those factors will keep some type of interaction, which make even more difficult their monitorisation, control and management.

There are many real examples that could illustrate the problem of managing dynamic interactions among these four intangible factors. For instance, let think of a collaborative network that is working well on a common project, with a high level of trust among the members and any problems of equity, coherence or visibility. Then, during the lifecycle of the project there are some changes in its scope. Such changes lead to re-organise the man-months originally allocated to the members. This new negotiation process will change in some manner the current levels of these factors. Additionally, this is a perfect opportunity for minor problems to arise. If, for instance, one of the members was thinking that she deserves more incomes for the work that she had carried out, this member will not accept more work for the same income but also will try to get more money from the total budget. This action will lead to diminish the trust towards this member of the rest of the network, which may also result in a closer future monitorisation of the work made by this member in particular and for all the members in general.

This in only one example experimented in a real situation but the domino effect goes beyond the immediate implications of such a re-allocation of resources, it also will highly probably hit negatively in the medium and long term to the whole collaborative network.

3   PROPOSED SOLUTIONS

This point aims to present, based on our experience, some measures that have been proved utile for mitigating negative effects of the four intangible factors of trust, equity, coherence and visibility regarding their dynamic nature and the interactions that may take place between them.

So, Table 1 resumes, for each one of the four intangible factors and more common associated problems, some solutions to be applied.

Table 1 – Proposed solutions

Intangible factor	Problems	Solutions
Trust	Low degree of trust Untrust Vicious cycles of trust	Network committe
Equity	Delivery of tasks Change of roles	Member profile
Coherence	Unrealistic objectives	Working groups
Visibility	Vision of the collaboration process	Visibility framework

For solving any type of problem regarding trust among the members of the network, it should be necessary to create a permanent committee formed by people from all the members of the network. The main goal of such a committee should be to negotiate any issue regarding the collaborative network. For instance, if problems about the contribution of a member arose, such a committee should directly address the point and get on work to solve it as soon as possible. This committee should be established from the very beginning of the creation of the collaborative network and its functions should be well spread within the network.

This solution has proved to be very useful in practice, as it provides, from the starting point of collaboration, a way for members to show their discontent or to make their point regarding conflictive issues that are usually skipped by a network as long as possible, which derives at the end in a much worse situation than the original problem.

For the equity factor, experience says that the roles and task allocation must be clearly defined before the collaborative network get into work. Posterior changes will have to be dealt with carefully. A change in tasks allocations will probably not be as dramatic as a change in the role, especially if the change implies that this member in particular has to play a lower role. In order to better handle all this problems, any change in the tasks and/or the roles within a collaborative network must be approved by all the member of such a network.

Additionally, and as a preventive action, at the beginning of the allocation of tasks and associated roles, a profile with the different roles that could play each member as well as with the different tasks they could carry out should be developed. Such a profile should be agreed by all the parts of the collaborative network and, if changes take place over the lifecycle of the collaborative relationship, there would be an agreed profile from each member, which would avoid lot of discussion and provide a useful resource.

For the coherence factor, in order to avoid the definition of incoherent objectives over time, it would be necessary the creation of a working group forming by people from all members of the network. This people should be well aware their firm's strategy, Then, when setting network objectives up, there would be authorized voices that know to what extend the proposed objectives of the network is realistic, reachable and good for their firms.

Further, these working groups should be the responsible of creating and monitoring a performance management system that would outcome whether the network is achieving the stated objectives or not. Additionally, this working group could hold several meetings where to study the information returned by this system and then decide how good their objectives for the network were, retuning and adjusting them overtime.

Finally, and regarding the visibility factor, the main solution would be to set up an internal visibility framework that would shown all the important information related to the network, specified for each of the members of the network. The possibility of introducing restrained areas and access privileges is an issue to think carefully of. In the past, its introduction has lead to equity problems in different collaborative networks.

Additionally, the solutions illustrated in Table 1 should be supported by IT implementations that would foster and facilitate real time communication and interaction between the parts. For instance, the creation of a visibility framework will imply to design a web space with authorized access to the main members. Further, in some cases it would be necessary to include some sort of restrictions access to the different members according to their privileges of information access. Some networks might also find suitable to make public to all the members the information within the visibility framework. In this case, a single sign-on password could be provided to members in order to facilitate their access.

4   CONCLUSIONS

This paper has presented four main intangible factors, trust, equity, coherence and visibility that have proven to have the potential to break a collaborative network process. These factors are difficult to manage and solve in isolation but, due to its own nature, it is necessary to also consider the dynamic interactions, which make them even more difficult to deal with. Finally, some practical solutions to mitigate them have been presented, highlighting the role of IT practices for supporting them.

5   REFERENCES

1.   Browne, J.; Sackett, P.; Wortmann, H: (1994), Industry requirements and associated research issues in the extended enterprise, Proceedings of the European Workshop on Integrated Manufacturing Systems Engineering, IMSE'94, Grenoble, December 12–14, pp. 9-16.

2.   Doz, Y.L. (1996), The evolution of cooperation in strategic alliances: Initial conditions or learning processes?, Strategic management Journal 17 (Summer), pp. 55-83.

3.   Doz, Y.L. and Hamel, G. (1998), Alliance Advantage. Boston, MA: Harvard Business School Press.

4.   Ferrin, D.L., Bligh, M.C. and Kholes, J.C. (2005), It takes two to tango: An interdependence analysis of trust and cooperation spirals in interpersonal and intergroup relationships. Working paper presented at the 2005 meeting of the Academy of Management.

5.   Ghoshal, S. and Moran, P. (1996), Bas for practice: A critique of the transaction cost theory. Academy of Management Review, 21, pp. 13-47.

6.   Klein Woolthuis,R., K., Hillebrand, R., Nooteboom, B. (2005), Trust, contract and relationship development. Organizations studies, 26, pp. 813-840.

7.   Serva, M.A., Fuller, M.A. & Mayer, R.C. (2005). The reciprocal nature of trust: A longitudinal study of interacting teams. Journal of organizational behavior, 26, pp. 625-648.

8.   Wicks, A.C., Bermen, S.L., and Jones, T.M. (1999), The structure of optimal trust: Moral and strategic implications, Academy of Management Review, 24: 1, pp. 99-116.

PART **9**

ARCHITECTURES FOR COLLABORATION

João Certo[1,2,3], Nuno Lau[1,4], Luís Paulo Reis[2,3]

joao.certo@fe.up.pt, lau@det.ua.pt, lpreis@fe.up.pt
[1] IEETA – Institute of Electronics and Telematics Engineering of Aveiro
[2] LIACC-NIAD&R– Artificial Intelligence and Computer Science Lab, University of Porto,
[3] FEUP – Faculty of Engineering of the University of Porto
Rua Dr. Roberto Frias, 4200-465 Porto, PORTUGAL
[4]DETI –Informatics, Electronics and Telecommunications Dep., University of Aveiro,
Campus de Santiago, 3810-193 Aveiro, PORTUGAL

This paper presents a formal model for a multi-purpose, strategical coordination layer. Based on previous work developed for the RoboCup Soccer simulation, small-size, middle-size, legged leagues and RoboCup Rescue simulation league, a generic coordination model was built that allows the management of collaborative networks of heterogeneous agents. The model uses a multi-level hierarchical approach with the following concepts: strategy, tactics, formations, sub-tactics and roles, from high to low level. Hybrid methods are used to switch formations and tactics. In order to test the model, two strategy instances, for RoboCup Rescue Simulation and RoboCup Soccer, were developed. Strategies are designed with the help of a graphical tool. Results achieved by the team in RoboCup Rescue and Soccer Simulation competitions demonstrate the usefulness of this approach.

1   INTRODUCTION

RoboCup was created as an international research and education initiative, aiming to foster Artificial Intelligence (AI) and Robotics research, by providing standard problems. RoboCup has two main league types: simulation and robotics. Simulation leagues enable research on AI and multi-agent coordination while waiting for the availability of hardware to enable the same type of research.

In RoboCup Soccer leagues two opposing teams play a soccer match, thus creating a dynamic environment. A soccer match provides important scientific challenges, both at an individual level (perception, moving, dribbling, shooting) and at a collective level (strategy, collective play, formations, passing, etc.).

Proposed by Kitano (Kitano, et al., 1999), RoboCup Rescue simulated environment consists of a virtual city, immediately after a big catastrophe, in which heterogeneous, intelligent agents, acting in a dynamic environment, coordinate efforts to save people and property. The agents are of six different types: Fire Brigades, Police Forces, Ambulance Teams and the three respective center agents. Fire Brigades are responsible for extinguishing fires, Police Forces open up blocked routes and Ambulance Teams unbury Civilians. In order to obtain a good score, all these agents work together communicating through supervising center agents.

FC Portugal's research focus is on the development of new coordination methodologies. After successfully developing such methodologies for soccer simulation

Certo, J., Lau, N., Reis, L.P., 2007, in IFIP International Federation for Information Processing, Volume 243, Establishing the Foundation of Collaborative Networks; eds. Camarinha-Matos, L., Afsarmanesh, H., Novais, P., Analide, C.; (Boston: Springer), pp. 273–282.

leagues[1] the team is working on adapting these methodologies to the Rescue Simulation League already with some success[2].

This paper describes the specification and application of a multi-purpose, multi-domain, adaptable, strategical layer on Multi-Agent Systems (MAS). This layer allows the management of homogeneous and heterogeneous agents, the centralized or decentralized management of the strategy. The paper also presents a graphical strategy building tool, compliant with the defined model.

The layer and tools, although generic, were developed with the RoboCup leagues in mind. However, application domains include businesses composed of several parties. Following such a model, Collaborative Networks (Camarinha-Matos and Afsarmanesh, 2005) as well as MAS in general, may be interesting tools for the analysis and congregation of skills that are required to achieve the goal.

The rest of this paper is organized as follows. The next section presents related work. In section 3 the strategic layer is described. Section 4 presents the graphical tool, showing a strategy for a soccer team and a partial strategy for a rescue team. Section 5 concludes this paper and points out to future work.

2   RELATED WORK

Stone et al. (Stone, 2000; Stone and Veloso, 1999) previously defined periodic team synchronization (PST) domains as domains with the following characteristics: "There is a team of autonomous agents that collaborate towards the achievement of a joint long-term goal". The task at hand was decomposed into multiple rigid roles, assigning one agent to each role. Thus each task's component was accomplished with no conflicts among agents in terms of how they should accomplish the team goal. As it was defined, a role consisted of a specification of an agent's internal and external behaviors. The conditions and arguments of any behavior could depend on the agent's current role, which was a function of its internal state.

Due to inflexibility to short-term changes (e.g. one robot is non-operational), inflexibility to long-term changes (e.g. a route is blocked), and a lack of facility for reassigning roles, a formation was introduced as a teamwork structure within the team member agent architecture. A formation decomposes the task space defining a set of roles with associated behaviors. In a general scenario with heterogeneous agents, subsets of homogeneous agents could flexibly switch roles within formations, and agents could change formations dynamically. Formations included as many roles as agents in the team, so that each role is filled by one agent.

The rest of this section explains the concepts and mechanisms developed for soccer simulation leagues usable within the strategical layer.

FC Portugal's team strategy definition extends the concepts introduced by Stone (Stone, 2000; Stone and Veloso, 1999) and is based on a set of player types (roles) and a set of tactics that include several formations for different game situations (defense, attack, etc) (Reis and Lau, 2001). Formations assign each player a positioning (that determines the strategic behavior) and to each positioning corresponds a player type (that determines the active behavior).

---

[1] FC Portugal won several World and European championships in different RoboCup soccer leagues in the past seven years.

[2] FC Portugal rescue simulation team achieved very good results in RoboCup, including winning a rescue European champion using these coordination methodologies.

When Stone defined a situation, the concept was bound to set-plays. A situation was a set of world state conditions that triggered a series of predefined behaviors within the roles. This concept was expanded (Reis, et al., 2001) and situations were redefined as a group of easily identifiable logic conditions set for high-level world state parameters. As such, situations would not suffer a considerable, temporal, variation and could be then associated with formations. However not every situation had to have its own formation, a set of replacement situations could be used.

The Situation Based Strategic Positioning(SBSP) mechanism (Lau and Reis, 2002; Reis, et al., 2001) is used for strategic situations (in which the agent believes that it is not going to enter in active behavior soon). In this system, the agent calculates its base strategic position in the field in that formation, adjusting it according to the ball position and velocity. This enables the team to cover the ball while remaining distributed along the field, just like in real soccer.

The DPRE , Dynamic Positioning and Role Exchange (and Dynamic Covering) (Reis and Lau, 2001), was based on previous work from Peter Stone et al., (Stone, 2000; Stone and Veloso, 1999) which suggested the use of flexible agent roles with protocols for switching among them. The concept was extended and players may exchange their positionings and player types in the current formation if the utility of that exchange is positive for the team.

In the case of communication in single channel, low bandwidth, and unreliable domains the challenge is deciding what and when to communicate. In ADVCOM (Reis and Lau, 2001) (Intelligent Communication Mechanism), agents use communication in order to maintain world states updated by sharing individual world states, and to increase team coordination by communicating useful events (e.g. a positioning swap). The main innovation of this communication strategy is that agents communicate when the utility of their communication is higher than those of their teammates, using mutual modeling to estimate these utilities.

3 MODEL FOR THE STRATEGIC LAYER

The model here depicted provides a structured method of representing, building and managing a strategy in a scenario where a team of agents is used. The terms *scenario* and *agent* should be considered as broader terms. *Scenario* can be a simulation, a game, a virtual organization (Foster, et al., 2001) or any other kind of set where there is an environment, with *agents* who have one or more objectives. Likewise *agents*, besides being software computational entities, can be any kind of independent units like robots, persons or participants of a virtual enterprise (Cardoso and Oliveira, 2005).

This model handles static, dynamic, reactive or nonreactive environments and is designed to manage team strategy and cooperation. A team is an aggregation of *agents* with common goals. When *agents* in a team work together cooperatively they do *teamwork* (Cohen and Levesque, 1991; Tambe, 1997). In this model, homogeneous and heterogeneous *agents* can be used. In heterogeneous environments the term *agent type* is used for differentiation.

3.1 Structure

In order to better explain the model, a top-down approach will be followed. Figure 1 represents the proposed model and depicts the interconnections between the concepts presented in this model, expanding one branch for each concept.

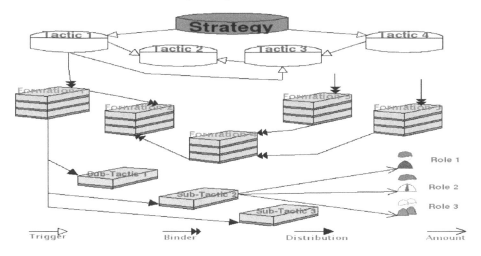

Figure 1 - Schematic of strategic concepts

3.1.1   Strategy

Informally, a strategy is the combining and employment of means in large-scale, long-range planning and the act of directing operations for obtaining a specific goal or result. In this scope, a strategy can be seen as a set of different configurations of collaborative networks or virtual organizations resulting in different approaches to reach the same ultimate goal.

Formally, a *strategy* is a combination of *tactics* used to face the scenario and the *triggers* to change between tactics, where a *strategy* can have several *tactics:*

$$\text{Strategy}=\{\text{Tactics, Triggers}\};\ \text{Tactics}=\{\text{Tactic 1, Tactic 2,...,Tactic t}\},\ \forall\, t \in N \qquad (1)$$
$$\text{Triggers} = \{\text{Trigger 1, Trigger 2, ... , Trigger tg}\}\ ,\ \forall\, tg \in N$$

3.1.2   Tactic

A tactic is an approach to face the scenario in order to achieve a goal. Tactics deal with the use and deployment of agents in the scenario for different, identifiable situations. Tactics specify which resources of the collaborative network should be used to reach the different, partial, goals.

Formally, a *tactic* defines *agents' formations* as the arrangement of *agents, situations* as the combination of scenario conditions that can be seen as a more particular problems and *binder* as the association between a *formation* and a *situation* or between several *situations* and a *formation. Tactics* can optionally also set *tactical parameters,* the default thresholds on which *agents* base their decisions.

A *tactic* should be self-sufficient, i.e., it does not need other tactics to function through all the simulation. There can be only one *tactic* active at one given time.

$$\text{Tactic} = \{\text{Formations, Situations, Binders, [Tactical Parameters]}\} ; \tag{2}$$
$$\text{Formations} = \{\text{Formation1, Formation2, ... , Formation f}\} , \forall f \in N ;$$
$$\text{Situations} = \{\text{Situation 1, Situation 2, ... , Situation s}\} , \forall s \in N ;$$
$$\text{Binders} = \{\text{Binder 1, Binder 2, ... , Binder b}\} , \forall b \in N ;$$
$$\text{Tactical Parameters} = \{\text{Tactical Paramtr1,..., Tactical Paramtr tp}\} , tp \in N$$

In a *situation*, the conditions that make it unique are defined. The *binder* sets the *situations* that lead to a *formation*. Optionally, a *binder* can set the connection between several origin *formations* and a terminus *formation* through *situations*.

$$\text{Situation} = \{\text{Condition 1, Condition 2, ... , Condition cd}\} , \forall cd \in N \tag{3}$$
$$\text{Binder} = \{\text{[Origin Formations], Situations, Terminus Formation}\}.,$$
$$\text{[Origin Formations] , Terminus Formation} \in \text{Formations}$$

3.1.3 Formation

A formation is a high-level structure that aggregates all the agents with the intent of assigning them to specific sub-tactics. The aggregation is either wrought by using agents that belong to the same type, have the same more immediate goals, or both. As such, a formation can be seen as a collaborative network for a pressing goal.

Formally, a *formation* is a specific association of *sub-tactics* with a defined *distribution* that may specify an *agent type*. Only one *formation* can be active at any given time. As such, the *formation* must include *sub-tactics* for all *agents*. The same *sub-tactic* can be used more than once in a *formation*. This allows an implicit definition of *Group*. Let *sub-tactics* be a multiset (Stanley, 1997) where m(SubTactic st) defines the multiplicity of a *sub-tactic*.

$$\text{Formation} = \{ \text{Distribution, Sub-Tactics, [Agent Types]} \} , \tag{4}$$
$$\text{Sub-Tactics} = \{\text{(SubTactic1, m(SubTactic1)), (SubTactic2, m(SubTactic2), ...}$$
$$\text{, (SubTactic st, m(SubTactic st))}\} , \forall st \in N$$

For each element in *sub-tactics* there is a correspondent value in a *distribution*:

$$\text{Distribution} = \{\text{Value1, Value2, ... , Value v}\} , v = \sum m(\textit{Sub-Tactics st}) \tag{5}$$

A distribution specifies absolute or percentage distribution values for each sub-tactic in the formation. These *values* always refer to *agent types* when applicable. In this manner, the total of *values* can surpass 100%, but not for a specific *agent type*.

The association with *agent type* is implicit when a *sub-tactic* can only be applied to one *agent type*. Otherwise, when more than one *agent type* can be used (see section 3.1.5), an *agent type* must be specified for that *sub-tactic*:

$$[\text{Agent Types}] = \{\text{Type1, Type2, ..., Type ty}\} \, , \, \forall \, ty \in N \qquad (6)$$

3.1.4   Sub-Tactic

A sub-tactic reflects the approach to face the scenario of a limited set of agents either partially for a number of situations or during the whole scenario. A sub-tactic can be seen as a limited association of resources, a virtual enterprise or a network.

Formally, a *sub-tactic* is an association of *roles* with one default *amount* of *agents* assigned to those *roles*. Additionally a *sub-tactic* may also have *sub-tactical parameters* to reflect specific thresholds, *agent* parameters, coordination options or other values that are needed to configure the *roles* used on the *sub-tactic*.

$$\text{Sub-Tactic} = \{\text{Amounts, Roles, [Sub-Tactical Parameters]}\} \qquad (7)$$
$$\text{Roles} = \{\text{Role 1, Role 2, ... , Role r}\} \, , \, \forall \, r \in N$$
$$\text{Amounts} = \{\text{ Amount 1, Amount 2, ... , Amount a}\} \, , \, a = \sum role \; r$$

A *sub-tactic* can have one or more *roles* and for each *role* in *sub-tactic* there is an *amount* in *amounts*. Like in a distribution, an *amount* specifies either absolute or percentage values for each *role* in the sub-*tactic*. Percentage *amounts* in a given *sub-tactic* must total 100%.

Sub-tactics can be divided into *Typed Sub-Tactic*s and *Generic Sub-Tactic*s. In a *typed sub-tactic* at least one of the *roles* is associated with an *agent type*, which becomes the *sub-tactic's* type. In order to ease the handling of different *agent types*, it is not possible to use *roles* of different *agent types* in the same *sub-tactic*. As such, *typed sub-tactic* can only use *roles* for one *agent type* together with *generic roles*. As a consequence, to build a *formation* with different *agent types,* there should be at least one *sub-tactic* for each *agent type*.

A *generic sub-tactic* is a particular kind of *sub-tactic* without any association with an *agent type*. Thus, in a generic *sub-tactic,* only *generic roles* can be used. As it was previously stated, if a *generic sub-tactic* is used in a *formation* that contains *sub-tactics* for more than one *agent type*, an *agent type* must be specified. This type is specified together with a *distribution value* when *agents* are assigned to a *generic sub-tactic*.

3.1.5   Role

A role is a normal or customary activity of an agent in a particular environment. In collaborative networks, the role can be seen as the activity pattern of each parti-cipant in a virtual enterprise.

Formally, a *role* is a set of *algorithms* in a defined sequence that describes an *agent*'s behavior. The behavior description is expected to include, when relevant, the specification on how the *agent,* should coordinate with *agents* in the same *role* or in other *roles*. The coordination can be of three different kinds: all *agents* with the same *role* can either act individually, form one *group* or form several smaller *groups* (with a rule specified inside the *role*).

The *role* also defines partial objectives accordingly to the coordination method used. Although *roles* can describe the behavior for an entire scenario, they can also describe the behavior for only a given time frame or *situation*. *Teams* form their *roles* by combining different motion and action mechanisms with partial objectives. The *role* level is the lowest in the proposed model.

As in *sub-tactics*, *roles* can be divided into *Typed Role* or *Generic Role*. A *typed role* is a particular kind of *role* that can only be assumed by one *agent type*. Using heterogeneous *agents* does not necessarily means that *typed roles* or *agent types* will be used in the *strategy*. *Typed roles* are used when, in heterogeneous *agents*, there is a need to employ the different *agent*'s properties or capabilities. A *generic role* is a kind of *role* that can be assumed by any of the *agent types* used in a *tactic*.

3.1.6 Decision, Supervising and Communication

The decision maker depends on the *agents'* organization and types set by the scenario. In teams where there is only a supervisor and all the *agents* are "dummy", the strategical layer will obviously only be applied to the supervisor.

In MAS, the first rule is that all *agents* have full knowledge of the strategical layer being used. Then if all *agents* have a good, shared, world state knowledge, the layer can be used with no extra communication. This is accomplished because all the *agents* switch their *tactics*, *situations* and *formations* based on the same conditions and at almost the same time. When a team already uses a mechanism like ADVCOM (section 2) the strategical layer can also be applied to scenarios where communications is limited and unreliable without extra communication overload.

If *agents* have more limited computational resources but still have good world state knowledge synchronization, the layer can be computed only by a supervising *agent*. This *agent* would only have to communicate a new *formation* whenever declared by the strategical layer. The supervising *agent* is chosen taking into account the *agent* who normally has more computational resources. Some scenarios specifically have supervising *agents*.

3.2 Agent Assignment

The strategical layer defines either absolute or percentage forms for distribution values and role amounts. This possibility is given so that strategies can be built independently from the agent number used in the scenario.

Another possibility of the model is to use both absolute and percentage forms simultaneously. In this model, for both distribution values and role amounts, absolute forms for values take priority over percentage value forms. This means that agents are assigned first to roles in a sub-tactic specified with absolute distribution values and with absolute role amounts in the referred role. Next agents are assigned to sub-tactics with only absolute forms of distribution values. The succeeding priority is assigning agents to roles specified by absolute role amounts in a sub-tactic with a percentage distribution values.

Finally, for the remainder agents that use percentage forms in the mixed method, or when the percentage form is the only assignment method used, the assignment priorities are: first to sub-tactics and then to roles. When converting to absolute numbers, the values are truncated.

If agent types are in use, the previously defined assignment method is applied separately to each agent type. As it is easily concluded the mixed method allows the definition of priority roles in environment where the total agent number is unknown.

The agent assignment methods defined what roles needed to be used, particularly for environments where the total agent number is unknown. In order to assign a specific role to a specific agent, in its simpler form, agents can orderly chose a role based on the environment identification (sequential agent id). Optimal role assignment depends on scenario conditions like proximity to objectives, relative agents' positions, etc.. Based on this fact, the model does not specify a method. In fact, a method like DPRE (section 2.) that uses dynamic role exchanges is strongly advisable. To be noted that the strategical layer is still compatible with dynamic, situation based positioning like SBSP (section 2.). This is accomplished because the positioning systems are specified inside the role.

4   GRAPHICAL TOOL FOR BUILDING STRATEGIES

The graphical tool provides a visual interface for building strategies. By using graphical representations of the strategic layer components, it is possible to interconnect them. The tool exports the edited strategy to an XML file which can be used to implement the layer in *agents*. It also features a C++ code generator still in its early stages. The tool's GUI is provided by Kivio, a flowcharting and diagramming application for the KOffice[3] application suite. A customized, installable, stencil set with the layer objects was also built (Figure 3).

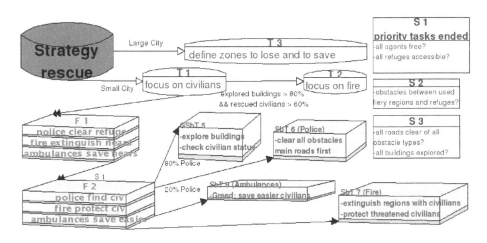

Figure 2 - Partial rescue strategy

Figure 2 depicts a simplified rescue strategy expanded only in one tactic and one formation. In order to fully perceive the strategy some additional knowledge of the rescue simulation league is advisable. On situation S1 formation F1 switches to F2. Note that the *generic sub-tactic* GSbt 5 uses *generic roles* to find civilians. This role can be performed by Fire Brigades, Police Forces or Ambulance Teams.

---

[3] KOffice is an office suite for the K Desktop Environment released under free software/open source licenses. Available at http://koffice.org/.

Using soccer as an example, for a simple strategy, the same sheet can be used to represent the entire layer as seen in Figure 3.

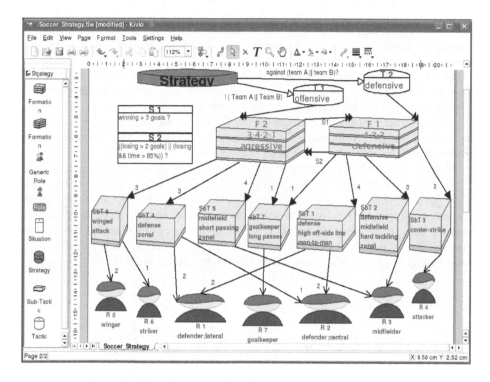

Figure 3 - Screenshot of the graphical tool featuring a soccer strategy

As shown, a trigger can originate in a *strategy* thus defining the initial *tactic*. Likewise a *binder* can originate in a tactic thus defining the initial *formation*. For a more complex *strategy* a multi-sheet is recommended separating *strategy*, each *tactic, formations, situations* and *sub-tactics*. In fact, when defining several *tactics* which use at least one *binder* with no precedence (*origin formation*) a separate sheet for each tactic is mandatory. Figure 2 although only expanding on one strategy branch (not possible under the layer) uses formation F3 and F5 with no precedences.

5   CONCLUSION AND FUTURE WORK

The proposed strategical layer is now fully integrated with our soccer and rescue teams and is successfully being used in our rescue team. The layer also maintains full compatibility with all our RoboCup soccer teams, as the soccer model is a particular case of the specified generic layer. Results in international competitions for both the domains tested, proved the success of the layer.

The model flexibility expands from using it in an environment where a single program manages all homogeneous "dummy" robots, to its collective use in heterogeneous, multi-agent systems. When domains have similar nature like in soccer simulation and soccer robotic leagues, the strategies defined in one, can easily be adapted to the others. This is achieved by only modifying the roles in the existing sub-tactics.

Using the model in areas outside the implemented domains should be straightforward. The layer can be used in areas where there is a need of management of distributed activities like in collaborative environments.

Strategies are easily built through the use of a very user-friendly graphical tool. By using a frequently improved, open source, editor as its base, the developed graphical tool can take advantages of its innovations.

In the future, further development of the graphical tool's source code generator is expected, both in efficiency and language portability. These developments will enable a more generalized use of the strategic layer in the context of RoboCup and in other cooperative domains. Thus, we plan to use the strategical layer, with different instantiations, built using the graphical tool, in all our teams (simulation 2D, simulation 3D, small-size, middle-size, legged, simulation rescue and physical visualization) participating in European and world RoboCup competitions in 2007.

6   REFERENCES

1.   Camarinha-Matos LM, Afsarmanesh H. "Collaborative networks: a new scientific discipline". In Journal of Intelligent Manufacturing, Springer Netherlands, 2005; 16(4-5): 439-452.
2.   Cardoso HL, Oliveira E. "Virtual Enterprise Normative Framework Within Electronic Institutions". In Engineering Societies in the Agents World V, Springer Berlin/Heidelberg, 2005; 3451: 14-32.
3.   Cohen PR, Levesque HJ. "Teamwork". In Noûs, Special Issue on Cognitive Science and Artificial Intelligence, 1991; 25(4): 487-512.
4.   Foster I, Kesselman C, Tuecke S. "The Anatomy of the Grid: Enabling Scalable Virtual Organizations". In International Journal Of High Performance Computing Applications, Sage Science Press, 2001; 15: 200-222.
5.   Kitano H, Tadokoro S, Noda I, Matsubara H, Takahashi T, Shinjou A, Shimada S. "RoboCup Rescue: search and rescue in large-scale disasters as a domain for autonomous agents research". In Proceedings of IEEE International Conference on Systems, Man, and Cybernetics, 1999; 739-743.
6.   Lau N, Reis LP. "FC Portugal 2001 Team Description: Configurable Strategy and Flexible Teamwork". In RoboCup 2001: Robot Soccer World Cup V, Birk, A., Coradeschi, S., and Tadokoro, S., eds. Springer Berlin / Heidelberg, 2002; 2377: 1-10.
7.   Reis LP, Lau N. "FC Portugal Team Description: RoboCup 2000 Simulation League Champion". In RoboCup-2000: Robot Soccer World Cup IV, Stone, P., Balch, T., and Kraetzschmar, G., eds. Berlin: LNAI Springer-Verlag, 2001; 2019: 29-40.
8.   Reis LP, Lau N, Oliveira E. "Situation Based Strategic Positioning for Coordinating a Simulated RoboSoccer Team". In Balancing Reactive and Social Deliberation in MAS, Hannebauer, M., Wendler, J., and Pagello, E., eds. Berlin: LNAI Springer, 2001; 2103: 175-197.
9.   Stanley RP. Enumerative Combinatorics, Cambridge University Press., 1997; ISBN: 0-521-55309-1.
10. Stone P. Layered Learning in Multiagent Systems: A Winning Approach to Robotic Soccer, MIT Press, 2000; ISBN: 0262194384.
11. Stone P, Veloso M. "Task Decomposition, Dynamic Role Assignment, and Low-Bandwidth Communication for Real-Time Strategic Teamwork". In Artificial Intelligence, 1999; 110(2): 241–273.
12. Tambe M. "Towards Flexible Teamwork". In Journal of Artificial Intelligence Research, 1997; 7: 83-124.

29 A PRIVACY-BASED BROKERING ARCHITECTURE FOR COLLABORATION IN VIRTUAL ENVIRONMENTS

AbdulMutalib Masaud-Wahaishi[1], Hamada Ghenniwa[1] and Weiming Shen[2]

[1]*Department of Electrical and Computer Engineering, University of Western Ontario*
amasaud@uwo.ca, hghenniwa@eng.uwo.ca
[2]*Integrated Manufacturing Institute, National research Council, CANADA*
weiming.*shen@nrc.gc.ca*

With the rapidly growing development of applications in open virtual enterprises, privacy is becoming a critical issue. This paper presents an agent-based architecture that provides coordination services, with special focus on capability-based integration as brokering services. These services take into consideration any privacy desires that may be required from various participants in an open, dynamic, and heterogeneous environment. A proof-of-concept prototype system has been implemented to support and provide information-gathering services in healthcare environments.

1 INTRODUCTION

A Virtual Enterprise (VE) is an organization that consists of multiple co-operating autonomous entities (enterprises) that are jointly act in a specified limited domain to fulfill a common enterprise mission. VEs are supported by geographical distribution and heterogeneous entities with no central control. Therefore, building VEs involve dealing with challenges that go beyond traditional integration approaches and design paradigms. The future success of building systems in terms of more sophisticated components, often-entire systems themselves, and integrating them requires an engineering and scientific basis that support high-level of abstraction for connection and interaction in VEs. Although these systems are independently created and administered, they need to collaborate and cooperate to fulfill a desired functionality or service.

A cooperative distributed systems (CDS) approach is a promising design paradigm that is suitable for many virtual enterprises applications; however, coordination is a major challenge in developing cooperative distributed systems in open environments. In a Cooperative Distributed Virtual Environments (CDVEs), entities usually need to work together to accomplish individual or social tasks. However, in open environments, this becomes a challenge where it is no longer feasible to expect designers or users to hardcode, to determine or to keep track of the entities and their capabilities. Brokering is a coordination and cooperation activity among heterogeneous entities in cooperative distributed systems environment that can be used effectively to support integration in VEs.

With the rapidly growing development of applications in open distributed environments, such as e-Business, privacy is becoming a critical issue. Consequently, distributed systems architects, developers and administrators are faced with the challenge of securing the requester's privacy as well as the provider's. In general, requesters and service providers are concerned about their privacy from different perspectives. For example, they may wish to protect their identities from

Masaud-Wahaishi, A., Ghenniwa, H., Shen, W., 2007, in IFIP International Federation for Information Processing, Volume 243, Establishing the Foundation of Collaborative Networks; eds. Camarinha-Matos, L., Afsarmanesh, H., Novais, P., Analide, C.; (Boston: Springer), pp. 283–290.

being used, or decide by whom it will be revealed, and for what purposes, or retain the choice about whether or not to reveal their personal interests or capabilities. This paper presents a novel privacy-based brokering architecture as a capability-based aspect of coordination in CDVEs. The architecture supports ad hoc configurations among distributed, possibly autonomous and heterogeneous entities with various degrees of privacy requirements in terms of three attributes: entity's identity, capability and preferences.

2   AGENT-BASED BROKERING ARCHITECTURE: PRIVACY MODEL

In addition to the dynamic nature of the environment, VEs usually involve complex and nondeterministic interactions, often producing results that are ambiguous and incomplete which requires that the components of these VEs be able to change their configuration to participate in different, often simultaneous roles.

These requirements could not be accomplished using traditional ways of manually configuring software. We strongly believe that agent technology is a very promising design for brokering in cooperative distributed VEs. Here we view agent-orientation as a metaphorical conceptualization tool at a high level of abstraction (knowledge level) that captures, supports and implements features that are useful for distributed computation in open environments. These features include cooperation, coordination, interaction, as well as intelligence, adaptability, economic and logical rationality. An agent is an individual collection of primitive components that provide a focused and cohesive set of capabilities7 [7].

Within this context, we model CDVEs as a distributed group of intelligent, goal oriented, autonomous, and rational agents that act in a cooperative and interactive manner to enable collaboration between various entities. Architecturally, the brokering is viewed as a layer of services where a brokering service is modeled as an agent with a specific architecture and interaction protocol that are appropriate to serve various requests. The architecture allows various entities in the domain to join and benefit from the functionalities provided by the brokering service through a registration and naming service that permits the addition or removal of any agents, service and sources at runtime. The brokering service uses the registration and naming service to build up a knowledge base of the environment in order to facilitate locating and identifying the relevant existing providers that are capable of serving a specific request.

2.1   The Privacy Model

CDVEs users and service providers are concerned about their personal privacy from different perspectives. For example, they may wish to protect their identities from being used, or decide by whom it will be revealed, and for what purposes, or retain the choice about whether or not to reveal their personal interests or capabilities. The objective of the work presented here is correlated mainly with tackling the privacy concerns from the perspective of preserving the identities and capabilities of the various entities that constitute CDVE. Here, we define the degree of privacy in terms of three attributes: the entity's identity, capability and goals. Therefore, an agent can categorize its role under several privacy degrees. Formally, an agent can be represented as a 2-tuple

$$Ag \equiv \langle (RA : Id, G); (PA : Id, Cap) \rangle$$

Where RA and PA refer to the agent role as requester, and provider respectively, Id, G, and Cap refer to the agent's identity, goals and capabilities, which might have a null value. For example an agent might participate with a privacy degree that enables the hiding of its identity as a requester by setting the value of (Id) to null. The challenge in this context is how to architect the brokering layer with the appropriate set of services that enable cooperation across the different degrees of privacy. The interaction protocols represent both message communication and the corresponding constraints on the content of messages. Table 1 summarizes the different brokering scenarios categorized by the possible combination of privacy attributes of the Requester and Provider agents.

Table 1 Brokering Layer Interaction Patterns with Service Requestors

Privacy Attributes				Interaction Patterns	
Case	g(RA)	Id(RA)	Id(PA)	Cap(PA)	With Requesters	With Providers
1	Revealed	Revealed	Revealed	Revealed	Receive request Deliver result	Search for relevant agents, Negotiate and Obtain result
2	Revealed	Revealed	Revealed	Hidden	Receive request Deliver result	Advertise request to known PA
3	Revealed	Revealed	Revealed	Hidden	Receive request Deliver result	PA check for requests PA to reply with results
4	Revealed	Hidden	Provider's privacy attributes are either one of the status shown in (1,2, or 3)		Receive request RA retrieve result	same interaction protocol depicted in any selected case shown in (1,2, or 3)
5	Hidden	Known			Advertise services to RA	
6	Hidden	Hidden			RA to check for services.	

2.2 The Brokering Interaction Patterns

Requesters revealing identities and goals:

Agents playing the role of requestors are required to reveal their identities, and goals to the relevant broker within the layer. The interaction pattern is as follow: Formulating service's requests, Contacting a set of provider-side brokers, forwards, and controls appropriate transaction to achieve the requester's goal; and receive and returns the result of the services to the requester agent as shown in Figure 1.

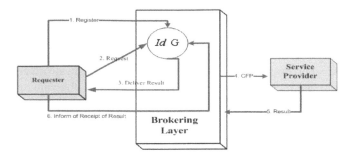

Figure 1 Interaction Pattern for Requesters Revealing Privacy Attributes

Requesters hiding identities

Requesters may wish to access services or seek further assistance without revealing their identities. As shown in Figure 2, requesters are responsible of checking the availability of the service's result. The interaction imposes a significant effort on the performance and efficiency.

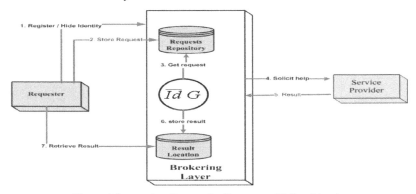

Figure 2 Interaction Pattern for Requester Hiding Identity

Requesters hiding goals:

The layer permits those requestors to check a service's repository for further information or to browse service offerings that have been previously posted as shown Figure 3. The interaction is not restricted only to those service providers who had initiated such advertisements, but it extends to those providers with unknown capabilities, since there might be the case where the same advertised service can be accomplished and achieved as well (for example with better quality or cost).

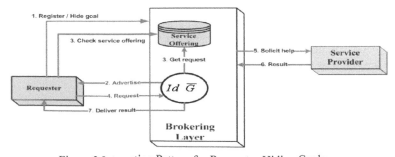

Figure 3 Interaction Pattern for Requestor Hiding Goals

Requesters hiding identities and goals

Requesters would have the possibility to hide their identities and goals from the entire environment; as shown in Figure 4, they have the option either to post their want-ads to the layer's service repository directly, or might check services that would be of an interest. Requesters are responsible to check for the availability of the service's result and hence retrieve it. It is to be noted that a requester with this degree of privacy will have no further dynamic notification in case the service directory becomes unavailable.

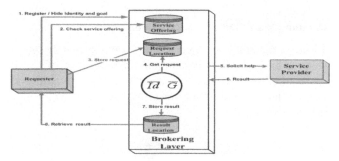

Figure 4 Interaction Pattern for Requestor Hiding Privacy Attributes

Providers revelling identities and capabilities

The brokering layer issues a call-for-proposals (CFP) to available providers informing them of the problem's specifications. Each potential contractor (provider) determines the evaluation parameters (such as goal quality, goal expiration time, and cost) and accordingly submits a bid to the brokering agent, or might reject the proposal. After receiving the bids, the layer selects the most appropriate bid that satisfies with the request's parameters.

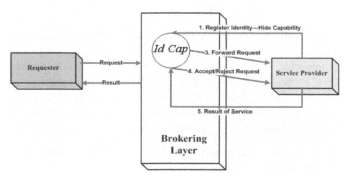

Figure 5 Interaction Pattern for Provider Revealing Privacy Attributes

Providers hiding capabilities

After receiving a request, the layer's interaction protocol with providers will forms requests out to every registered provider with unknown capability.

It is noteworthy that, for every advertised request, providers need to determine whether the request is within its capabilities and/or of an interest, which implies that a considerable elapsed time will be spent on evaluating every single request. Therefore, providers would be deluged by a variety of service requests, which significantly impact performance and efficiency. Figure 6 shows the corresponding interaction pattern.

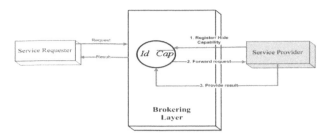

Figure 6 Interaction Pattern for Provider Hiding Capability

Providers hiding identities and capabilities

As shown in Figure 7, the brokering layer's functionality is mainly seen as a directory service, in which a brokering agent maintains a repository of service's requests along with any required preferences. Providers will have the ability to browse this repository and accordingly determine relevant requests that might be of an interest and within their capabilities.

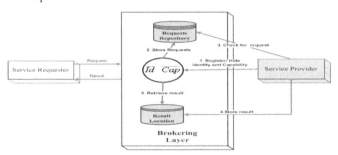

Figure 7 Interaction Pattern for Provider Hiding Privacy Attributes

3   IMPLEMENTATION GUIDELINES

Due to page limitation, we describe the implementation guidelines of one pattern associated with a requestor and provider; both are hiding their identities. The protocol is represented using the FIPA-ACL performatives. All interactions utilize the Contract Net Protocol as a negotiation mechanism. The brokering agent (acts as a manager) issues a call-for-proposals (CFP) to those all available registered providers (under different privacy degrees) in the environment informing them of the problem specifications. The protocol is represented as follow:

- Requester   to store: **(Request)** – a service request is stores in the service location (repository)
- Broker to **Query-If** for posted services' requests
- Broker to store the **(CFP)** in a special repository to be browse by the Provider
- Provider to store **(Propose),** a service proposal for a particular request or **(Refuse)** – provider might decline the service request
- Broker to **Query-If** – for possible service proposals
- Broker to store (for potential providers)
- **(Accept-Proposal)** – an acceptance notification or **(Reject-Proposal)** – or a rejection message is stored in case of not winning
- Provider to **Query-If** for acceptance/rejection of the propose service offerings, **(Accept-Proposal)** or for **(Reject-Proposal)**

- Store(**Confirm**) – Notification of service offering confirmation by the provider
- Store(**Disconfirm**) or Store(**Cancel**) – The Provider stores a cancellation message
- Provider to store (**Inform**) indicating the availability of a service's result
- Broker to **Query-If** for the availability of the service's result
- Broker to retrieve the service' result and to store (**Inform-Done**) indicating the receipt of the result
- Provider to store (**Inform**) (for requester) indicating the availability of a service's result
- Requester to **Query-If** for the received result, retrieve it and to store (**Inform-Done**)
- Broker to **Query-If** for (**Inform-Done**)➔ end of the protocol

A web-based prototype of the proposed system has been implemented using Jade [8] to support and provide information-gathering capabilities to different participants in healthcare environments. Healthcare services are modeled and implemented as CDVEs that consist of a collection of autonomous units that act independently and collaborate in providing services and synergize medical data according to mutual privacy interests.

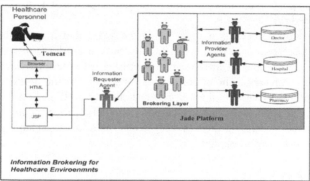

Figure 8 Prototype Architecture

As shown in Figure 8, three relational databases represent various medical data for three distributed locations (hospital, doctors' records, and a pharmacy), each being managed by a dedicated agent (provider). Different brokering agents with different roles are available to domain-specific agent that might play the role of a service provider as well as the role of a requester. Domain agent (requesters and providers) need to register with the brokering layer for which the layer identifies the relevant brokering agent that is appropriate to support the required privacy degree.

4   RELATED WORK AND DISCUSSION

Different techniques were used to enable collaboration in virtual environments including brokering via middle agents [4]. The work in [5] has proposed agent-based mediation approach, in which privacy has been treated as a base for classifying the various mediation architectures only for the initial state of the system. In another approach, agents' capabilities and preferences are assumed to be common knowledge, which might violate the privacy requirements of the participants. Other approaches such as in [10] [11] [9] have proposed framework structures to facilitate coordination between web services by providing semantic based discovery and mediation services that utilize semantic description languages. The work in [6] reviewed and classified the functional requirements that are needed for collaboration in networked virtual organizations. Another recent approach distinguishes a resource brokering architecture that manages and schedules different tasks on various distributed resources on the large-scale Grid [2]. Other initiatives proposed the use of privacy policies along with physical access means (such as smartcards), in which the access of private information is granted through the presence of another trusted authority that mediate between information requesters and information providers in virtual organizations [1]. However, none of the above mentioned approaches has treated privacy as an architectural element that facilitates the collaboration between various entities of cooperative distributed virtual enterprises.

5   CONCLUSION

In this paper we have developed an agent-based brokering architecture that provides seamlessly integrated collaboration and cooperation for different entities within distributed virtual environments. Unlike the traditional brokering, the brokering role is further classified into several sub-roles categorized by the desired privacy attributes of service requesters and providers. Each brokering role is modeled as an agent with a specific architecture and interaction protocol that is appropriate to fulfill a required privacy degree.

The proposed approach is innovative, in the sense that it treats the privacy as a design issue for brokering systems. Different application domains can benefit from the proposed model, such as intelligent cooperative information systems, and agent-based electronic business. The opportunities for exploiting the proposed architecture in building collaborative virtual enterprise are enormous. Based on the level and the amount of information that can be released, virtual enterprise members can securely collaborate while translating their privacy concerns to an applicable privacy degree that suits their desires and objectives.

6   REFERENCES

1. Amin T., Keng P. H.: "Inter-organizational Workflow Management System for Virtual Healthcare Enterprise ", 3rd IFIP Working Conference on Infrastructures for Virtual Enterprises PRO-VE'02, Portugal, May 1-3, 2002.
2. Brook, J. and Fellows, D. "An Architecture for Distributed Brokering on the Grid", 11th International Euro-Par Parallel Processing - Portugal, 2005.
3. Clarke R., "Identification, Anonymity and Pseudonymity in Consumer Transactions: A Vital System Design and Public Policy Issue": at: http://www.anu.edu.au/people/Roger.Clarke/DV/AnonPsPol.html, available as of Feb, 2007
4. Decker K, Sycara K. , and M. Williamson ," Middle-agents for the internet" In IJCAI97 International Joint Conference on Artificial Intelligence, Nagoya, Japan, 1999
5. Decker K., et al., "MACRON: An Architecture for Multi-agent Cooperative Information Gathering", Proceedings of the CIKM '95 Workshop on Intelligent Information Agents, 1998
6. Ellman S. and Eschenbaecher J. "Collaborative Network Models: Overview and Functional Requirements" Virtual Enterprise Integration: Technological and Organizational Perspectives, IDEA Group, Inc, imprints 2005.
7. Ghenniwa, H. and Huhns, M., "Intelligent Enterprise Integration: eMarketplace Model", Creating Knowledge Based Organizations, Idea Group Publishing, Pennsylvania, USA, pp. 46-79, 2004.
8. Java Agent Development Framework: Jade, Home Page: http://jade.cselt.it/
9. Li, L. and Horrocks I., "A Software Framework for Matchmaking Based on Semantic Web Technology", In Proceedings of the 12th International Conference on WWW, Hungary 2003.
10. Motta, E, Domingue, J, Cabral, L, and Gaspari, M. "IRS-II: A Framework and Infrastructure for Semantic Web Services" In Proc. of the International Semantic Web Conference, SA, 2003.
11. Paolucci, M. et al. "Semantic Web Services", AAAI Spring Symposium Series - March, 2004

30	**VIRTUAL POWER PRODUCERS INTEGRATION INTO MASCEM**

Isabel Praça, Hugo Morais, Marílio Cardoso, Carlos Ramos, Zita Vale

GECAD – Knowledge Engineering and Decision Support Group
Institute of Engineering – Polytechnic of Porto
Porto, PORTUGAL
{icp, hgvm, joc, csr, zav}@isep.ipp.pt

All over the world Distributed Generation is seen as a valuable help to get cleaner and more efficient electricity. Under this context distributed generators, owned by different decentralized players can provide a significant amount of the electricity generation. To get negotiation power and advantages of scale economy, these players can be aggregated giving place to a new concept: the Virtual Power Producer. Virtual Power Producers are multi-technology and multi-site heterogeneous entities. Virtual Power Producers should adopt organization and management methodologies so that they can make Distributed Generation a really profitable activity, able to participate in the market. In this paper we address the integration of Virtual Power Producers into an electricity market simulator – MASCEM – as a coalition of distributed producers.

1   INTRODUCTION

The development of new low emission generation technologies (wind generation, solar cells, fuel cells, micro-turbines) leads us to rethink the location of a significant part of the production: distributed generators owned by decentralized players will provide a significant amount of the electricity generation.

With Distributed Generation (DG), electricity is produced near consumers' location and not transmitted over long distances. Thus, it is possible to get lower losses. Moreover, new generation technologies, mainly based on renewable resources, with environmental advantages are a key issue for sustainable development. Investments in this field are encouraged by a favorable regulatory framework and the equipment costs are more attractive every day. At this stage, the main technologies used are micro and hydro turbines, fuel cells, wind generation, and solar cells.

A deregulated market where every single low power rating generation unit sells its power on the market would be optimal for the whole community both economically and technically.

To get negotiation power and advantages of scale economy, these players can be aggregated giving place to a new concept: the Virtual Power Producer (VPP). VPPs are multi-technology and multi-site heterogeneous entities. VPPs should adopt organization

Praça, I., Morais, H., Cardoso, M., Ramos, C., Vale, Z., 2007, in IFIP International Federation for Information Processing, Volume 243, Establishing the Foundation of Collaborative Networks; eds. Camarinha-Matos, L., Afsarmanesh, H., Novais, P., Analide, C.; (Boston: Springer), pp. 291–298.

and management methodologies so that they can make DG a really profitable activity, able to participate in these markets.

In order to operate in an efficient way, VPPs should have adequate decision-support tools. These must be based on the availability and processing of the required information and knowledge concerning producers and market operation. A successful achievement of VPPs' goals requires the use of a mix of adequate technologies for optimizing and supporting their activities.

Agents and multi-agent systems that adequately simulate electricity markets behavior are essential tools to gather knowledge to provide decision-support to strategic behavior.

MASCEM– Multi-Agent Simulator of Competitive Electricity Markets (Praça et al., 2003) was developed to study several negotiation mechanisms usually found in electricity day-ahead markets. In MASCEM market participants have strategic behavior and a scenario decision algorithm to support their decisions. With MASCEM several experiences have already been made, leading us to achieve some conclusions and define future developments. One of the most important goals of MASCEM is the simulation of several different electricity market mechanisms.

With VPP integration into MASCEM, VPP proposals can be effectively evaluated under scenarios considering several different market mechanisms and containing several other producers and consumer entities. With MASCEM, VPP can improve their strategies to face market.

2   MASCEM OVERVIEW

A Pool is a marketplace where electricity-generating companies submit production bids and their corresponding market prices, and consumer companies submit consumption bids. A Market Operator regulates the pool. The Market Operator uses a market-clearing tool to set market price and a set of accepted production and consumption bids for every hour. In Pools, an appropriate market-clearing tool is an auction mechanism.

Bilateral Contracts are negotiable agreements between two traders about power delivery and receipt. The Bilateral-Contract model is flexible; negotiating parties can specify their own contract terms.

The Hybrid model combines features of Pools and Bilateral Contracts (Shahidehpour et al., 2002). In this model, a Pool isn't mandatory, and customers can either negotiate a power supply agreement directly with suppliers or accept power at the established market price. This model therefore offers customer choice.

There are several entities involved in the negotiations; we propose a multi-agent model to represent all the involved entities and their relationships.

MASCEM multi-agent model includes: a Market Facilitator Agent, Seller Agents, Buyer Agents, Trader Agents, a Market Operator Agent and a System Operator Agent. Three types of markets are simulated: Pool Markets, Bilateral Contracts and Hybrid Markets.

The Market Facilitator is the coordinator of the market. It knows the identities of all the agents present in the market, regulates the negotiation process and assures the market is functioning according to the established rules. The first step agents' have to do is the registration at the Market Facilitator, specifying their market role and ser-vices.

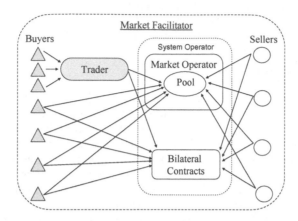

Figure 1 – MASCEM multi-agent model

Seller and Buyer Agents are the two key players in the market. Sellers represent entities able to sell electricity in the market, e.g. companies holding electricity production units. Buyers may represent electricity consumers or even distribution companies. The user, who must also specify their intrinsic and strategic characteristics, defines the number of Sellers and Buyers in each scenario. By intrinsic characteristics we mean the individual knowledge related to reservation and preferred prices, and also to the available capacity (or power needs if it is a Buyer). By strategic characteristics we mean the strategies the agent will employ to reach its objectives.

Sellers will compete with each other, since they are all interested in selling all their available capacity and in obtaining the highest possible market quote. On the other hand, Sellers will cooperate with Buyers while trying to establish some agreement that is profitable for both. This is a very rich domain where it is possible to develop and test several algorithms and negotiation mechanisms for both cooperation and competition.

The System Operator Agent represents the responsible for the transmission grid and all the involved technical constraints. Every contract established, either through Bilateral Contracts or through the Pool, must first be communicated to the System Operator, who analyses its technical viability from the Power System point of view (e.g. feasibility of Power Flow to attend all needs).

The Market Operator Agent represents the responsible for the Pool mechanism. This agent is only present in simulations of Pool or Hybrid markets. The Market Operator will receive bids from Sellers, Buyers and Traders, analyze them and establish the marginal price and accepted bids. The process of determining the accepted bids is done according to the technical validation by the Sys-tem Operator, after, the Market Operator communicates to Sellers, Buyers and Traders the acceptance, or not, of their bids and, optionally, the market price.

The increase in competitiveness creates opportunities for many new players to enter the market; one of these players is the Trader. The introduction of this new entity allows liberalization and competition in the electricity industry to be developed and simplifies the way the whole process works with producers and customers on the market and the relationship with the Market Operator. This entity participates in the market on behalf of customers. It is an intermediary between them, who delegate on the Trader the purchasing of their needs, and the suppliers. The increasing role of this type of entity turn it an important feature of our simulator.

3   MASCEM NEGOTIATION

On the basis of the results obtained in a negotiation period Sellers, Buyers and Traders revise their strategies for the next period. Seller, Buyer and Trader Agents have strategic behavior to define their desired price. These agents have time-dependent strategies, to change the price according to the remaining time until the end of the negotiation period; and behavior-dependent strategies, to define the next period price according to the results obtained in the previous ones.

MASCEM implements four types of strategies to change the price during a negotiation period: Determined, Anxious, Moderate and Gluttonous. The difference between these strategies is the time instant at which the agent starts to modify the price and the amount it changes. Although time-dependent strategies are simple to understand and implement (Morris et al., 2003), they are very important since they allow the simulation of important issues such as: emotional aspects and different risk behaviors. For ex-ample: an agent using a Determined Strategy is a risk indifferent one; while Gluttonous agents exhibit the behavior more risk disposable, since they maintain the same price until very close to the end of the negotiation period, taking the risk of not selling.

To adjust price between negotiation periods, also referred as behavior-dependent strategies, two different strategies were implemented: one called Composed Goal Directed and another called Adapted Derivative Following, see details in (Praça et al., 2005). These are important strategies that use the knowledge obtained with past experiences to de-fine bid prices for next periods.

To obtain an efficient decision support, Seller and Buyer agents also have the capability of using the Scenario Analysis Algorithm.

This algorithm provides a more complex support to develop and implement dynamic pricing strategies since each agent analyses and develops a strategic bid, for the next period, taking into account not only their previous results but also other players results and expected future reactions. It is particularly suitable for markets based on a Pool or for Hybrid markets, to support Sellers, Buyers and Traders decisions for proposing bids to the Pool and accepting or not a bilateral agreement. The algorithm is based on analyzing several bids under different scenarios, constructing a matrix with the obtained results and applying a decision method to select the bid to propose.

Each agent has historical information about market behavior and about other agents' characteristics and behavior. To get warrantable data, each agent uses techniques based on statistical analysis and knowledge discovery tools, which analyze the historical data. With the information gathered agents can build a profile of other agents based on their expected proposed prices, limit prices, and capacities. With these profiles, and based on the agent own objectives, several scenarios, and the possible advantageous bids for each one, are defined. The agent should analyze the incomes that result from bidding its limit, desired prices, and competitive prices—those that are just slightly lower (or higher, in the Buyer's case) than its competitors' prices.

We call a play to a pair bid-scenario. After defining all the scenarios and bids, market simulation is applied to build a matrix with the expected results for each play.

The matrix analysis with the simulated plays' results is inspired by the game theory concepts for a pure-strategy two-player game, assuming each player seeks to minimize the maximum possible loss or maximize the minimum possible gain (Fudenberg and Tirole, 1991).

A Seller—like an offensive player—will try to maximize the minimum possible gain by using the MaxiMin decision method. A Buyer—like a defensive player—will select the strategy with the smallest maximum payoff by using the MiniMax decision method. In Buyers' matrix analyses, they select only situations in which they can fulfill all their consumption needs. They avoid situations in which agents will accept reduced payoff but can't satisfy their consumption needs completely.

The analysis of each period's results will update the agent's market knowledge and the scenarios to study. After each negotiation period, instead of considering how they might increase, decrease, or maintain their bid, agents use knowledge rules that restrict modifications on the basis of other agents' expected behavior.

The knowledge rules update agents' bids in each scenario, but the number of scenarios remains the same. If at the end of a negotiation period the agent concludes — by analyzing market results — that it incorrectly evaluated other agents' behavior, it will fix other agents' profiles on the basis of the calculated deviation from real results.

4   VIRTUAL POWER PRODUCERS

The aggregation of Distributed Generation plants gives place to the new concept of Virtual Power Producers (VPP). VPPs are multi-technology and multi-site hetero-geneous entities, being relationships among aggregated producers and among VPPs and the remaining Electricity Market (EM) agents a key factor for their success. An aggregating strategy can enable owners of Distributed Generation to gain technical and commercial advantages, making profit of the specific advantages of a mix of several generation technologies and overcoming serious disadvantages of some technologies.

Any type of generation unit or load may be included: wind turbines, photovoltaic, mini turbines, micro-turbine, fuel cells, energy storage units, non-controllable loads, controllable loads etc. The typical size of single distributed energy resource units may range from a few kW to some MW.

In the scope of a VPP, aggregated producers (AP) can make sure their generators are optimally operated and that the power that is not consumed in their installation has good chances to be sold on the market. At the same time, VPPs will be able to commit to a more robust generation profile, raising the value of non-dispatchable generation technologies.

Under this context, VPPs can ensure secure, environ-mentally friendly generation and optimal management of heat, electricity and cold and optimal operation and maintenance of electrical equipment, including the sale of electricity to the EM. VPPs should adopt organization and management methodologies so that they can make Distributed Generation a really profitable activity.

VPPs must be flexible enough to use the advantages of its resources (e.g. market-based environmental value in the form of pollution and/or carbon credits, renewable energy credits) and overcoming their problems and limitations.

VPPs must identify the characteristics of each of the AP and try to optimize the selling activity so that each associate delivers the biggest possible amount of energy. However, this is not simple due to uncertainty of generation associated with the technologies that depend from natural resources such as wind, sun, waves or water flows.

So, in order to have VPP able to coexist with other market agents, it is necessary that it gets profits and that has credibility in the EM. This context must be considered in VPPs organization and operation methodologies as their goal is to optimize their APs' profits in this market.

A successful achievement of VPPs' goals requires the use of a mix of adequate technologies for optimizing and supporting their activities. Under this scope agents and multi-agent systems are important technologies to adequately simulate EM behavior and gather knowledge to provide decision-support to strategic behavior.

Taking into account the already described MASCEM characteristics, it can be a valuable framework to test VPP functioning under different market mechanisms and concerning different market strategic behavior. But, how can VPP be integrated into MASCEM model?

4.1   Coalitions in Multi-Agent Systems

Coalition formation is the coming together of a number of distinct, autonomous agents that agree to coordinate and cooperate, acting as a coherent grouping, in the performance of a specific task. Such coalitions can improve the performance of the individual agents and/or the system as a whole. It is an important form of interaction in multi-agent systems.

It has been advocated in e-commerce (where buyers may pool their requirements in order to obtain bigger group discounts), in grid computing (where multi-institution virtual organizations are viewed as being central to coordinated resource sharing and problem solving), and in e-business (where agile groupings of agents need to be formed in order to satisfy particular market niches). In all of these cases, the formation of coalitions aims to in-crease the agents' abilities to satisfy goals and to maximize their individual or the system's outcomes.

Most work on coalition formation in Multi-Agent systems and game theory has focus on payoff distribution, where it is usually assumed that a coalition structure has been formed, and the question is then how to divide the payoff so that the coalition structure is stable. In this con-text, many solutions have been proposed based on different stability concepts. Transfer schemes have also been developed to transfer non-stable payoff distributions to stable ones (while keeping the coalition structure un-changed).

Recently, research is giving more attention to the coalition structure generation (Sandholm et al., 1999) (Dang and Jennings, 2004). The work of Shehory and Kraus (Shehory and Kraus, 1996) considers a somewhat broader environment, where the coalitions can be overlapped but the complexity is reduced by limiting the size of the coalitions.

Some other researchers address both coalition structure generation and payoff distribution in competitive environments. Ketchpel (Ketchpel, 1994) presents a coalition formation method with cubic running time in the number of agents, but his method can neither guarantee a bound from the optimal nor stability. Shehory and Kraus's protocol guarantees that if the agents follow it, certain stability (kernel-stability) is met. In the same paper, they also present an alternative protocol that offers a weaker form of stability with polynomial running time. However, in both cases, no bound from the optimal is guaranteed.

More recent research in coalition formation area has also begun to pay attention to dynamic environments, where agents may enter or leave the coalition formation process and many uncertainties are present (e.g. the coalition value is not fixed, but it is context-based (Klush and Gerber, 2002)).

4.2   VPP Coalition Formation in MASCEM

A negotiation mechanism regarding coalition formation under the scope of a VPP is in fact being included in MASCEM, and strategies will be developed considering the three phases of a coalition's formation process.

VPP needs to have an adequate knowledge of each potential aggregated producer characteristics. We are working on a multi-criteria negotiation protocol.

Some of the most important characteristics are:

- Nominal Power: the sum of nominal power in-stalled in each producer;
- Available Power: the power a VPP can buy to the producer;
- Overload Power: some units may produce overload power for limited periods. The VPP may use this power in critical situations;
- Equipment characteristics: information concerning producers' equipment allows the VPP to know the power characteristic, reliability, maintenance periods, lifetime, relation with external factors, possible variations of the energy price in function of the cost of the primary resources, etc.
- Operating limits: for the units which are dependent from natural resources, it is possible that the primary resource must be below or above of equipment operating limits. This must be considered in risk analysis in the generation forecast. Usually when the resources forecast is near to the minimum machines operating limit the risk is small, but when they are near to the maximum limit the risk can be enormous;
- Grid connection characteristics: This is an important aspect if it is necessary to pay the losses in the lines; also the existence of two or more producers connected to the same electric substation should be considered; etc;
- Historical generation data: the availability of historic generation data can enable the VPP to get useful forecasting tools.

These issues must be carefully analyzed before a new producer enters the coalition. A multi-criteria decision function is being developed. This function must be a dynamic one, since the characteristics weights depends on the lack of already aggregated producers.

Regarding VPP market participation, the same market interface as Seller or Buyer agents will be used. However, there are some preliminary steps to define its proposals and to divide market results among VPP members. First all the capacity available from the different aggregated producers must be gathered, to establish the electricity amount to trade on the market, and the different production costs analyzed to define the interval for acceptable proposals. This means VPP agents will have a utility function that aggregates all the involved units' characteristics. The analysis of received proposals will be done according to each unit capabilities and costs.

Important is the use of previsions, such as climatic ones, to update the database of aggregated producers to forecast more and more efficiently the energy they will be able to provide to the VPP.

5   ACKNOWLEDGEMENTS

The authors would like to acknowledge FCT, FEDER, POCTI, POSI, POCI and POSC for their support to R&D Projects and GECAD Unit.

6   REFERENCES

1.   Dang V. D., Jennings N. Generating coalition structures with finite bound from the optimal guarantees. Proceedings 3rd International Conference on Autonomous Agents and Multi-Agent Systems, Nova York, E.U.A., 2004; 564-571.
2.   Fudenberg D., Tirole J. Game Theory. MIT Press, 1991.
3.   Ketchpel S. P. Forming coalitions in the face of uncertain rewards. Proceedings of the Twelfth National Conference on Artificial Intelligence 1994; 414-419.
4.   Klusch M., Gerber A. Dynamic coalition formation among rational agents. IEEE Intelligent Systems 2002; 17 : 3; 42-47.
5.   Morris J., Greenwald A., Maes P. Learning Curve: A Simulation-based Approach to Dynamic Pricing, Electronic Commerce Research. Special Issue on Aspects of Internet Agent-based E-Business Systems. Kluwer Academic Publishers, 2003; 3:245-276.
6.   Praça I., Ramos C., Vale Z., Cordeiro M. MASCEM: A Multiagent System that Simulates Competitive Electricity Markets. IEEE Intelligent Systems, 2003; 18:6; 54-60.
7.   Praça I., Ramos C., Vale Z., Cordeiro M. Intelligent Agents for Negotiation and Game-based Decision Support in Electricity Markets. Engineering Intelligent Systems Journal, Special Issue "Intelligent Systems Application to Power Systems", 2005; 13:2; 147-154.
8.   Sandholm T., Larson K., Andersson M., Shehory O., Tohme F. Coalition structure generation with worst case guarantees. Artificial Intelligence, 1999; 111: 1-2; 209-238.
9.   Shahidehpour M., Yamin H., Zuyi Li Market Operations in Electric Power Systems: Forecasting, Scheduling and Risk Management. John Wiley & Sons, 2002.
10.   Shehory O., Kraus S. A kernel-oriented model for coalition-formation in general environments: Implementation and results. Proceedings of the Thirteenth National Conference on Artificial Intelligence,1996; 134-140.

31

AGENT-BASED ARCHITECTURE FOR VIRTUAL ENTERPRISES TO SUPPORT AGILITY

Heli Helaakoski
VTT Technical Research Centre of Finland
P.O.Box 3, FIN-92101 Raahe, FINLAND
heli.helaakoski@vtt.fi

Päivi Iskanius
University of Oulu, Faculty of Technology
Department of Industrial Engineering and Management
P.O. Box 4610, 90014 Oulu, FINLAND
paivi.iskanius@oulu.fi

Irina Peltomaa
VTT Technical Research Centre of Finland
P.O.Box 3, FIN-92101 Raahe, FINLAND
irina.peltomaa@vtt.fi

Global competition forces enterprises to concentrate on their core competencies while transforming themselves to participate in emerging inter-enterprise formations following the virtual enterprise (VE) paradigm. VE is a form that offers high flexibility, agility and resilience for enterprises to survive and prosper in the globalized economy. This paper introduces the real world VE that uses agent-based software to support agility. This research is conducted as a case study in the business network, which consist of several small and medium-sized enterprises (SME) and one focal company operating in the steel manufacturing industry in Northern Finland. The new VE, called SteelNet is aiming towards global markets with the support of effective information sharing.

1   INTRODUCTION

The world economy is undergoing a fundamental structural change driven by both globalization and the revolution of information and communication technology (ICT). Cooperation across traditional organizational boundaries is increasing, as outsourcing and electronic business is enabled by the Internet and other modern information-producing and communication-enabling ICT technologies. The Internet enables the use of other supporting technologies, which not only transmit information but also share information based on the intended meaning, the semantics of the data (Davies et al., 2003). One of these technologies is *agent software technology,* which has been considered as an important approach for developing industrial distributed systems (e.g. Jennings et al., 1995; Jennings and Wooldridge, 1998; Shen et al., 2003). Agent technology is seen one of the most promising technologies to enable flexible and dynamic coordination in the business network and support decision-making in every-day logistics activities and operational duties.

When inter-organizational cooperation moves beyond the buying and selling of goods and well-defined services, there is thus a need for flexible infrastructures that support inter-organizational communication, coordination and management. The challenge for the future is to create agile enterprises using modern technologies,

Helaakoski, H., Iskanius, P., Peltomaa, I., 2007, in IFIP International Federation for Information Processing, Volume 243, Establishing the Foundation of Collaborative Networks; eds. Camarinha-Matos, L., Afsarmanesh, H., Novais, P., Analide, C.; (Boston: Springer), pp. 299–306.

organizational forms and people to develop a new virtual form of manufacturing that transcends existing mindsets that are becoming increasingly dominated by the latter manufacturing dogma. *Virtual enterprise* (VE) has become an important business solution during the last decade. VE emphasizes the nature of networking and cooperation and offers high flexibility, agility and resilience. Several well known companies such as Benetton, Dell, Nike and Cisco have organized themselves based on this paradigm (e.g. Cao and Dowlatshahi, 2005; Tatsiopoulos et al., 2002). There is evidence that companies on the basis of network perform very well within their own industries. Network companies are at the moment more common in the fields affected by rapid technological change and growth. Networking is a way to acquire sensitivity and ability to adapt oneself to fast changes. This, however, do not constrain the VEs into high-tech industries. They are applicable to all industries, which are dynamic in nature.

Networking requires information integration, coordination and resource sharing and organizational relationship linkages. The organizational relationship linkages include communication channels between the supply chain members, performance measurement and sharing of common visions and objectives. In rapidly changing business environment, companies should not only be able to form linkages with a wide range of other organizations, but they should be able to form those linkages even more quickly, and be able to dissolve them rapidly and form new linkages as market conditions dictate (Daniel et al., 2005). These linkages are called inter-organizational systems (IOS) that automate the flow of information across organizational boundaries and link a company to its customers, distributors, or supplier.

This paper introduces the real-life VE that considers the use of agent-based solution for forming linkages between companies. The research work is conducted as a case study in the business network, which consist of several small and medium-sized enterprises (SME) and one focal company operating in the steel manufacturing industry in Northern Finland. This paper introduces the requirements for ICT in VE and discusses the suitability of agent technology to meet these requirements. The paper describes the SteelNet agent-based solution which was developed in this research to form lingages and to support mutual activities in case VE. This agent-based solution is called SteelNet system. The research work has been done in close collaboration with case VE and real end users, therefore we have been able to combine the theoretical knowledge and practise. A substantial amount of qualitative material from different sources (single and group interviews, observations, documents, and questionnaires) have been collected and qualitatively analyzed as an entity by the research group, and sometimes also by the company staff.

2   AGILITY SUPPORTING VIRTUAL ENTERPISES

ICT and globalization change the face of manufacturing. Today's globalized manufacturing is exhibiting the following characteristics: networking, meaning that the coordination of these functions makes intensive use of electronic networks and of virtual and geographical clusters of expertise, mass customization, in that methods of production must allow for detailed customization of products to meet the needs of individual markets and customers, and digitization, in the sense that many of these processes are controlled by advanced computer systems, which limit the need for human intervention (Tatsiopoulos et al., 2002). The emerging business paradigm agility is the competitive advantage in the global manufacturing environment. Agility is the ability of an enterprise to rapidly respond to changes in an uncertain and changing business environment, whatever its source - customers, competitors, new technologies, suppliers, government regulation, etc is (Goldman et al., 1995). It is believed that the agility can be realized by dynamically reconfigurable virtual enterprise. *Virtual enterprise* (VE) is commonly defined as a temporary, cooperative alliance of independent companies, who come together to exploit a particular market opportunity (Browne and Zhang, 1999). The idea of VE is meant to establish a dynamic organization by the synergetic combination of dissimilar companies with different core competencies, thereby forming a "best of everything" consortium to perform a given business project to achieve maximum degree of customer satisfaction (Lau et al., 2000). VE companies assemble themselves based on cost-effectiveness and product uniqueness without regard to organization size, geographic location, computing environments, technologies deployed, or processes implemented. They share cost, skills, and core competences which collectively enable them to access global markets with world class solutions that could not be provided by any one of them individually (Browne and Zhang, 1999).

The life cycle of a VE has four stages: creation, operation, evolution and dissolution. When an enterprise has a market opportunity, the enterprise searches potential partners and negotiates with them through the information infrastructure. After contracts are signed, a VE is created for the manufacturing of a product. Then the VE manages the process of the manufacturing of the product. When the product is completed and a new market opportunity is created, the VE can be reconfigured so as to meet the resource requirement. When the mission of the VE is fulfilled the VE is finally dissolved. In other words, VE is characterized by frequent reconfiguration. (Wu and Su, 2005) Ideally, VE companies share capabilities, capacities, costs and risks to fulfill specific customer demands. As an example, project-oriented business typically acts as a VE concept. VE is created in order to manage an individual project, and after the customer order or project is delivered to the customer, also VE is dispersed.

VE form has several advantages, especially for SMEs. Companies in the VE type of business network can be smaller than normally. Because of this, there are less levels of bureaucracy which allows VE to react more quickly. Also, the VE companies can be more specialized to a particular task (i.e. manufacturing, distribution, R&D) and may actually perform better. They concentrate on their core competencies and by networking complement their non-core activities. This specialization may result in improved efficiency and effectiveness. Resources, including money, technology, labor, managerial skills, etc. are utilized more efficiently. SMEs that want to take advantage of a global market opportunity can ally themselves with a company that has expertise or market share in a given region or country. (Strader et al., 1998)

The success of the VE depends on intensive information sharing, which is enabled by sophisticated information technology to make business information transparent, seamless and easily accessible at any time and at any place. It is vitally important for the companies in a VE to share data and information and to communicate with each other effectively. Therefore, it is crucial to have an information infrastructure so that the data can be managed efficiently and inter-operation can be realized. The design and implementation of suitable information management system for VE is complex activity. The software system has to support the distributed design and operation of many activities that are depending on each others and may have time restrictions. Software has to provide access to legacy software or through simple web interfaces. The information sharing and management in VE is a demanding domain that requires the adoption of emerging software solutions.

3   INFORMATION TECHNOLOGY FOR VIRTUAL ENTERPRISE

Due to the rapid development of ICT, the numbers of new IOSs are promising to improve the intensive information sharing. These are Enterprise Resource Planning systems (ERP), web services, electronic hubs and enterprise portals. These systems and technologies may improve the adoption of IOS, but most of these solutions are still insufficient for SMEs. Building such systems require lot of investments, time and knowledge, which SMEs scarcely have in changing business environment. ERPs require additional layers or middleware and WS provides only interface to other information systems, to create such solutions both approaches demand investments and skilled personnel. Electronic marketplaces and enterprise portals are focused for large enterprises due to the high initial costs. For SMEs those systems with external linkages are beneficial, when relationships are constant and the volumes are high in terms of material and costs. The external linkages to other enterprises are beneficial but they also may encumber the personnel of SMEs which are collaborating with several other enterprises via several systems. Hence, SMEs are trying to look for light-weight solutions which provide necessary information management and sharing properties. The design and development of invisible, easy to use and affordable ICT infrastructures is a key prerequisite for the effective large-scale implantation of the collaborative networks paradigm (Camarinha-Matos, 2003).

ICT should support the main business activities of VE by providing 1) network partner management, 2) network management, 3) VE configuration and 4) collaborative time, cost and quality control (Jagdev et al., 2001). Network partner management requires maintaining the capability/capacity information and performance history information. Network management is for storing the project experience data for future evaluation and to maintain collaboration preferences among partners. VE configuration gathers the customer requirements and controls the procurement process of the VE. Collaborative time, cost and quality control mechanism handles the project management concerning scheduling, budget and quality.

In this research, the information management is approached by using an agent-based approach. In a number of research studies, agent technology has been recognized as a promising approach to provide linkages between enterprises (Jennings et al., 2000; Norman et al., 2003; Papazoglou, 2001; Shen and Norrie, 1999) and to overcome the problems of traditional software. The benefits of the agent technology comparing to traditional software are (Jennings et al., 2000):

- flexibility; agents' actions can be based upon the agent's current situation, rather than being prescribed in advance
- agility; new services can be added and configured with minimal effect on other agents

- adaptability; since an agent's choices can be guided by feedback received from previous invocations of particular paths through the business process.

The main advantages of this approach over more traditional counterparts such as management information systems, workflow management, and enterprise integration are that it offers greater flexibility, agility and adaptability. Agent technology provides a better means of building applications in certain domains where other solutions may be too expensive or time-consuming. It is suitable for problems where data, control, expertise or resources are distributed and need to interact with one another in order to solve the problem. Agents are also the most appropriate metaphor for representing a given software functionality when the system is naturally regarded as a community of cooperating autonomous components. Agents can also be used for making legacy components interact with each other, or possibly with new software components, by building an agent wrapper (Genesereth and Ketchpel, 1994).

4   AGENT-BASED SYSTEM FOR THE CASE VIRTUAL NETWORK

The case network structure is stable, but not static: network actors are active, and within the existing network structure, current relationships change, new relationships are formed and some relationships are terminated. In SteelNet system the main emphasis was set to achieve collaborative time, cost, and quality control, which in the same time partly covers network management (stores information about executed projects). Due to the time and resource limits, the network partner management and VE configuration was not implemented complete. There is also a question about maturity of VE, while companies do not want to share sensitive business information like capacity information.

The case network set requirements for the SteelNet system; they required support for following activities:

- sending and receiving request for quotation/quotation/order within VE
- making work order for all VE companies in same time (via Internet)
- the follow-up of project status in real-time
- support for document management concerning projects/deliveries
- resource management of the VE, e.g. services, personnel and machinery
- report on operation in VE, such as amount and time of use, used services, management of changes
- flexible change of quotation to order

The SteelNet system is a multi-agent system in which dedicated agents carry out their tasks in collaboration. SteelNet multi-agent architecture is used at the inter-company level, where each company is represented by a group of agents (Helaakoski et al., 2006; Feng et al., 2007). The agents in one company are responsible for coordinating its actions in the business network by co-operating with each other and communicating with agents in other companies. The agents use FIPA ACL as a communication language, and inter-company communication takes place over the Internet and is protected by SLL encryption (Secure Socket Layer).

At a more detailed level, each company's multi-agent system is a modular system framework that provides core functionality in the form of configurable dynamic module loading, a service registry, agent container services and log services.

Further functionality can be added by implementing new modules. The framework treats agents as extension modules, with the exception that they are attached to the agent container. Modules and agents can provide and utilise services by means of the company-level service registry. At the wider inter-company architecture level an agent can be considered to consist of the agent module and all the internal services it uses.

Figure 1 presents three ways of using SteelNet system: 1) Company A has an agent container which integrates ERP system to SteelNet system, 2) Company B has agent container without integration to own systems, or 3) Company C uses SteelNet system via web.

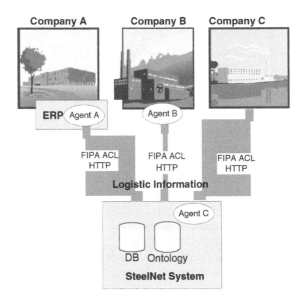

Figure 1 – Agents delivering information in various ways in SteelNet.

The case VE consists of independent companies collaborating with each other, companies that have several autonomous departments and employees. This can be viewed as a three-layer entity, a company, a department and an employee. Each of these layers can be modeled as an agent, since all of them are autonomous and co-operative entities. One agent representing one company would cause complex design inside an agent, as it should be capable of handling all company level activities. On the other hand, one agent per employee would also create very complex and inefficient agent communities. This leads to multi-agent system, where the responsibilities and tasks of the agents are divided by departments or activities, such as sales, management and manufacturing. In SteelNet system each company has several task-specific agents which communicate with their counterparts in the collaborating companies as well as with the agents in their own company.

5   CONCLUSION

This paper gives a real-world example of using agent technology in VE in order to ease the information sharing. Agent technology provides a suitable approach of managing distributed information within business networks, since they offer both flexibility and problem solving services. Task-specific agents can carry out tasks autonomously and release personnel from routine manual work; furthermore the amount and type of agents can be changed. In long-term relationships, the agents can be integrated into company's own ERP system to avoid manual work duplication, and in occasional relationships, the agent system provides a web access into a system.

In this research, the case VE has taken a concrete step towards supply chain integration while SteelNet system gives opportunity for real-time and transparent information sharing among networked company. The ICT infrastructure varies in companies; therefore SteelNet architecture is designed to be flexible by providing several access manners for companies of different size and types. Intensive co-operation between personnel of the companies and research group has guided functionality and the appearance of the system to meet the requirements of every day duties.

The case VE in this research consisted of several SMEs. Thus the system is implemented to be suitable also for SMEs with minimum joining and maintenance costs. The requirements for joining to the VE are minimized for example advanced ERP system is not required. The SteelNet system can be used via web browser, although the system is possible to be integrated with company's own ERP system. The SteelNet system offers possibility for transparent information sharing, but the obtained benefit depends on the usage of the system. The VE has to define mutually accepted rules for sharing and using of information and follow these rules consistently. The prosperity of VE depends on commitment of companies involved in the VE.

The case business network structure was stable, which enabled the development of a common ICT system. Although the case network was committed to developing a common system, there were unsolved issues before the adoption of SteelNet. One of the most important was the role of the service provider, which can be a Third Trusted Party, or else the service can run at the site of the main contractor. Since all the companies in the SteelNet system are able to host projects, a Third Trusted Party as a service provider would be a natural choice. As the numbers of networks and VEs grow in future, collaboration between networks will become a necessity. This was approached by using the FIPA-compliant JADE platform, which theoretically enables collaboration with other FIPA-compliant agents.

6 REFERENCES

1. Browne J, Zhang J. Extended and virtual enterprises – similarities and differences. International Journal of Agile Management Systems 1999; 1(1): 30-6.
2. Camarinha-Matos LM. Infrastructures for virtual organizations - where we are. In Proceedings of IEEE Conference Emerging Technologies and Factory Automation - ETFA '03, 16-19 Sept. 2003, 2: 405-14.
3. Cao Q, Dowlatshahi S. The impact of alignment between virtual enterprise and information technology on business performance in an agile manufacturing environment. Journal of Operations Management 2005; 23: 531-50.
4. Daniel EM, White A. The future of inter-organisational system linkages: findings of an international Delphi study. European Journal of Information Systems 2005; 14(2): 188-203.
5. Davies J, Fensel D, van Harmelen F. Towards the Semantic Web, Ontology Driven Knowledge Management. John Wiley & Sons, 2003.

6. Feng SC, Helaakoski H, Haapasalo H, Kipinä, J. Software agents-enabled systems coalition for integrated manufacturing processes and supply chain management. International Journal of Manufacturing Technology and Management 2007; 11(2): 157-73.
7. Genesereth MR, Ketchpel SP. Software agents. Communications of the ACM 1994; 37(7): 48-53.
8. Goldman SL, Nagel RN, Preiss K. Agile Competitors and Virtual Organizations: Strategies for Enriching the Customer. Van Nostrand Reinhold, 1995.
9. Jagdev HS, Thoben K-D. Anatomy of enterprise collaborations. International Journal of Production Planning and Control 2001; 12(5): 437-51.
10. Jennings NR, Corera JM, Laresgoiti I. Developing Industrial Multi-Agent Systems. In Proceedings of ICMAS'95, San Francisco, 1995, The AAAIpress/The MIT press, 423-30.
11. Jennings NR, Wooldridge M. Applications of Intelligent Agents. In Agent Technology: Foundations, Applications, and Markets, NR Jennings and M Wooldridge, eds. 1998, Springer, 1998, 3-28.
12. Jennings NR, Faratin P, Norman TJ, O'Brien P, Odgers B. Autonomous Agents for Business Process Management. International Journal of Applied Artificial Intelligence 2000; 14(2): 145-89.
13. Helaakoski H, Iskanius P, Peltomaa I, Kipinä J, Ojala K. Agent technology for supporting real-time supply chain management. International Journal of Agile Systems and Management 2006; 1(4): 360-75.
14. Lau HCW, Chin KS, Pun KF, Ning A. Decision supporting functionality in a virtual enterprise network. Expert Systems with Applications 2000; 19(4): 261-70.
15. Norman TJ, Preece A, Chalmers S, Jennings NR, Luck M, Dang VD, Nguyen TD, Deora V, Shao J, Gray A, Fiddian N. CONOISE: Agent-based formation of virtual organizations. In Proceedings of 23rd SGAI International Conference on Innovative Techniques and Applications of AI, Cambridge, UK, 2003, 353-66.
16. Papazoglou M. Agent-oriented technology in support of e-business. Communications of the ACM 2001; 44(4): 71-7.
17. Shen W, Norrie DH. Agent-based systems for intelligent manufacturing: a state-of-the-art survey. International Journal of Knowledge and Information Systems 1999; 1(2): 129-56.
18. Shen W, Kremer R, Ulieru M, Norrie D. A collaborative agent-based infrastructure for Internet-enabled collaborative enterprises. International Journal of Production Research 2003; 41(8): 1621-38.
19. Strader TJ, Lin F-R, Shaw MJ. Information infrastructure for electronic virtual organization management. Decision Support Systems 1998; 23: 75-94.
20. Tatsiopoulus IP, Ponis ST, Hadzilias EA, Panayiotou NA. Realization of the virtual enterprise paradigm in the clothing industry through e-business technology. Production and Operations Management 2002; 11(4): 516-31.
21. Wu N, Su P. Selection of partners in virtual enterprise paradigm. Robotics and Computer-Integrated Manufacturing 2005; 21(2):119-31.

PART 10

MODELLING FRAMEWORKS FOR COLLABORATIVE NETWORKS

32

TOWARDS AN ARCHITECTURE MODELING LANGUAGE FOR NETWORKED ORGANIZATIONS

Duk-Hyun Kim

Sejong Cyber University, KOREA
dhkim@sjcu.ac.kr

Reference models for Collaborative Networked Organizations (CNOs) is under development, but Enterprise Architecture Modeling Languages (EAMLs) for CNOs are very few. Lack of reference models makes it difficult for people to communicate with each other and lack of EAMLs also makes it difficult to implement information systems supporting CNOs. For enrichment of reference models and EAMLs for CNO we develop modeling constructs of an EAML. It supports (1) multi-level modeling based on OMG's Model-Driven Architecture for expressive power and ease of implementation, and (2) multi-focus modeling based on Zachman Framework for completeness of modeling.

1   INTRODUCTION

A *collaborative network* (CN) is 'an alliance constituted by a variety of entities (e.g., organizations and people) that are largely autonomous, geographically distributed, and heterogeneous, but that collaborate to better achieve common or compatible goals, and whose interactions are supported by computer network' (Camarinha-Matos et al., 2006). *Collaborative networked organizations* (CNOs) (e.g., virtual organizations, dynamic supply chains) are manifestations of CN.

Recently, lots of CNOs, networked organizations, or joint ventures appear in industry, government, academia, and society (Camarinha-Matos and Afsarmanesh, 2004; Tapia, 2006). In business sense, it comes from digitization or virtualization of business and organizations for agility against increasing competition in (global) markets. In technology sense, it owes to the rapid development and diffusion of ICT including the Internet and web technology. With the advancement of emerging technologies including ubiquitous computing and networking CNOs will be more popular in all around the world soon.

'A *reference model* is an abstract representation of the *entities* and *relationships* involved in a problem space, and it forms the conceptual basis for the development of more concrete models of the space and ultimately implementations, in a computing context' (refer. www.wikipedia.org). *Enterprise architecture* (EA) is the practice of applying a reference model for describing strategy, business, applications, information/data, technology, and outcomes of an enterprise (e.g., CN or CNO). A *modeling language of enterprise architecture* (EAML) is a conceptual or logical representation of EA. To build an information system for a CNO, an EA of the CNO needs to be developed based on a reference model or an EA framework; and the EA needs to be implemented into information systems through an EAML.

EA frameworks have been developed and applied to many enterprise applications. Examples of EA frameworks include Zachman Framework, GERAM, RM-ODP, Federal Enterprise Architecture, DODAF, TOGAF, Model-Driven Architecture (MDA), etc. EAMLs also have been developed accompanying with EA

Kim, D.H., 2007, in IFIP International Federation for Information Processing, Volume 243, Establishing the Foundation of Collaborative Networks; eds. Camarinha-Matos, L., Afsarmanesh, H., Novais, P., Analide, C.; (Boston: Springer), pp. 309–316.

frameworks. Existing EAMLs can be classified into two groups: one focused on *organization and processes* (e.g., IDEF, NEML, ARIS), the other focused on *technology and applications* (e.g., UML, ACME) (www.telin.nl).

In CN research, reference modeling for CNO has started and a rough model called ARCON is developed in the ECOLEAD project (Camarinha-Matos et al., 2006; Camarinha-Matos and Afsarmanesh, 2006). However, research on EAML for CNO such as NEML (Steen et al., 2002) is very few. Even such research results as ArchiMate (Jonkers et al., 2004) and ARCON show limitations in expressive power and ease of implementation as a language, or in completeness of underlying framework. Lack of reference models for CNO makes it difficult for specialists and non-specialists to understand the problem space, and to communicate with each other. Lack of proper EAML makes it difficult to implement information systems supporting CNO.

The ultimate goal of our research is to develop *an EAML for CNO* (hereafter we'll call it a *CAML*), but in this paper we firstly define and suggest modeling constructs of a CAML. The CAML supports *multi-level modeling* based on OMG's MDA and *multi-focus modeling* based on Zachman Framework. 'Multi-level' means that it includes meta-level models above domain-specific models. 'Multi-focus' means that it includes all six focuses in Zachman Framework. Comparing with existing EAMLs the resultant CAML is self-reflective and has rich modeling constructs, which may raise flexibility and expressive power of modeling as well as implementations. Although this paper is an introductory work, it would help develop information systems as well as reference models for CNO.

The remainder of this paper is organized as follows. In Section 2 we review various modeling aspects in EA modeling research comparing with requirements of a CAML. Section 3 describes modeling constructs of the CAML. In section 4 this paper is concluded with comparison of the CAML with existing research results, and further research.

2   MODELING ASPECTS FOR CNOS

2.1   Requirements of a CAML

CNOs usually have different topology (e.g., star, chain, or network), different levels of cooperation (e.g., information exchange, transaction, and collaboration), stability (i.e., transient or persistent), interdependency (e.g., of resources, cost, IT), and mechanism for coordination (e.g., hierarchy vs. market debate) (Steen et al., 2002). A CNO has much more complex structure and behavior than traditional single or extended enterprises. This comes from the characteristics of CNOs: (1) *distribution* of participants and resources (2) *autonomy* of members, (3) *heterogeneity* of culture, business (strategy and processes), ICT infrastructure, etc. Besides, the elements of CNOs such as members, tasks, products, and rules are varying as time goes. Proper modeling of a CNO can help reduce the complexity and dynamism.

Steen et al. (2002) suggested requirements of a CAML, as follows: (1) appropriateness, (2) ease of use, and (3) general quality criteria. 'Appropriateness' means expressiveness of various concepts in a CNO (e.g., actors, roles, activities, data, systems, protocols). 'Ease of use' means intuitive and graphical support, multi-levels of abstraction, formalism, etc. 'Quality' comprises generality, economy, orthogonality, consistency, coherence, etc. In this research we consider three key requirements: (1) completeness (of the underlying framework), (2) expressive power (of language constructs), and (3) ease of implementation. 'Ease of implementation' means ease of transformation from business (i.e., conceptual-level) model to system (i.e., logical-level) model. A model is in general required both expressive power and ease of implementation, which needs trade-off.

2.2 Modeling Aspects in Existing Research

Camarinha-Matos and Afsarmanesh (2006) classified early contributions to the reference model for CNO into three groups: (1) enterprise modeling, (2) organizational/ management school (e.g., SCOR), and (3) VE/VO ICT-based projects (e.g., PRODNET). We classify existing approaches of enterprise modeling into five categories: (1) EA frameworks for general enterprise, (2) EA frameworks for CNO, (3) EAML for general enterprise, (4) EAML for CNO, i.e., *CAML*, and (5) EA modeling of software. Table 1 shows a summary of some notable research results in each category.

Table 1 – Aspects in EA frameworks for general enterprise

	Models	Aspects or architectural domains
(1)	Zachman Framework	• *views*: scope, business, system, technology, details • *focuses*: what (data), how (process), where (network), who (people), when (time), why (motivation)
(1)	FEA (US Government)	• business (strategy & processes), performance measure, application, information/data, technology
(2)	*ARCON* (Camarinha-Matos et al., 2006)	• *life-cycle of CNO*: creation, operation, evolution, metamorphosis or dissolution • *modeling intent*: general concepts, specific modeling, implementation modeling • *environment characteristics*, i.e., In-CNO, About-CNO a. In-CNO; structural/ componental/ functional/ behavioral dimension b. About-CNO; market/ support/ societal/ constituency dimension
(3)	*'EAML'* (Sarkar & Thonse, 2004)	• views: enterprise, computational, information, engineering, technology (which are aspects in IEEE 1471 & RM-ODP), plus software organization
(3)	*ArchiMate* (Jonkers et al., 2004)	• aspects: information, behavior, structure • layers: business, application, technology
(4)	*NEML* (Steen et al., 2002)	• business, ICT • structure, behavior, artifacts • functional, operational (i.e., platform-independent, platform-specific)
(5)	Model-Driven Architecture (OMG)	• Computation-Independent Model (CIM), e.g., MOF • Platform-Independent Model (PIM), e.g., CWM, UML • Platform-Specific Model (PSM): CORBA, EJB, EDOC • Code
(5)	UML (OMG)	• views: functional (use-case)/ logical (structure & behavior)/ component/ concurrency/ deployment

Categories '(1)' through '(4)' focus on conceptual and/or logical modeling for description, while category '(5)' focuses on logical and/or physical modeling for implementation. Two approaches need to be integrated in a CAML for expressive power and ease of implementation. EA frameworks for general enterprise cover three to five views and up to six focuses; whereas, EAMLs cover relatively few aspects. For example, NEML and ArchiMate cover three views, i.e., business, ICT or technology, and application or system. Regarding the complexity and dynamism of CNOs more modeling aspects need to be adopted to a CAML. An EA framework for CNOs, i.e., ARCON covers too many perspectives and dimensions and has somewhat intermixed *views* and *focuses* in the sense of Zachman Framework, which will be a burden for software engineers to model logical constructs of CNOs using an EAML.

3   MODELING CONSTRUCTS OF THE CAML

3.1   Design Rationale of the CAML

3.1.1   Zachman Framework as the EA framework for CNO

In our approach Zachman Framework is regarded as the EA framework for CNO. It may have some weaknesses that: (1) it is a conceptual framework not to support software engineering in itself, and (2) the distinction between different views or focuses is not so clear or orthogonal. However, it has been widely applied to various problem spaces because of its sufficient modeling perspectives.

In this sense, five *views* and six *focuses* of Zachman Framework are considered in the CAML, as follows.

- Views: scope, business, system, technology, detailed representations
- Focuses: *data* ('what'), *process* ('how'), *link* ('where'), *participant* ('who'), *event* ('when'), and *goals* ('why').

3.1.2   Multi-level modeling based on meta-modeling and MDA

Meta-modeling is a way of representing meta-data and meta-knowledge (Brodie et al., 1989). It helps make software self-reflective for development, maintenance, integration, evolution, reuse of components or resources, and analysis of change impact (Kim and Park, 1997; Thangarathinam, 2004). OMG's MDA is to create an EA modeling capability that analysts and developers can use to describe a company's business and software assets, so it is naturally related with Zachman Framework (Frankel et al., 2003).

In the above sense, the CAML supports meta-level models above domain-specific model. Meta-level models consist of *meta-meta model* and *meta-model*, and domain (-specific) model consists of *business model*, *system model*, and *technology model*. Multi-level models of the CAML provide expressive power and ease of implementation or transformation between different models. The characteristics of modeling constructs at each level will be further explained in this section.

3.1.3 *Multi-focus modeling based on Zachman Framework*

According to Zachman Framework the CAML supports six *focuses* or dimensions of modeling, i.e., data, process, link, participant, event, and goal, which provides completeness of underlying framework and the CAML itself. For example, suppose a CNO is created as a joint venture to develop a new product and it consists of globally distributed suppliers, manufacturers, distributors, and customers. Modeling of common goals, link of participants and resources, and principal events of control is essential for the CNO. In the similar sense, OMG also develops six basic modeling packages for inter- and intra-enterprise integration and collaboration: *business domain* ('what'), *business process* ('how'), *location* ('where'), *business organization* ('who'), *event* ('when'), and *business motivation* ('why') (Hendryx, 2003). Note that most EAMLs usually support *data* ('what'), *process* ('how'), and *participant* ('who'). The characteristics of modeling constructs in the CAML will be further explained in this section.

3.2 Multi-level Modeling Concepts

Table 2 shows modeling concepts at each level of the CAML.

Table 2 – Multi-level modeling concepts of the CAML

Level	Modeling concepts	Remarks
(L0) Meta-meta model	*Entity, Relationship, Property*	CIM in MDA ('M3'), first class constructs
(L1) Meta-model	*Meta-entity*, e.g., data, process, link, participant, event, goal; *Meta-relationship* e.g., composition, generalization, association	PIM in MDA ('M2'), *Scope or context level, Ontology* model
(L2) Business model	*Entity*, e.g., CNO, project, contract; *Relationship*, e.g., is-a, use, etc.	PIM in MDA ('M2'), *Conceptual level*
(L3) System model	e.g., class, attribute, operation, rule, etc.	PIM in MDA ('M2'), *Logical level*
(L4) Technology model	e.g., server configuration, network protocol, etc.	PSM in MDA ('M1'), *Physical level*
(L5) Detailed representations	N/A	Code in MDA ('M0'), *Instance level*

Meta-meta model ('L0') represents the first modeling constructs of the CAML, i.e., Entity, Relationship, and Property, which is compatible with MOF Class, MOF Association, and MOF Attribute in Computation Independent Model (CIM) of MDA. Property type represents structural property (i.e., attribute), behavioral property (i.e., operation), or rule. Meta-model ('L1') represents domain-independent entity types or relationship types, i.e., Meta-entity type and Meta-relationship type that are instances of the types in meta-meta-model. Meta-model is compatible with Platform-Independent Model (PIM) of MDA. The six focuses are subtypes of the *Meta-entity* type. The *Meta-relationship* type represents semantic primitives, e.g., property sharing, existential dependency, cooperation level, multiplicity, etc. (Kim and Park, 1997), detailed explanation of which is beyond the focus of this paper.

Domain model consists of conceptual-level *business model* ('L2'), logical-level *System model* ('L3'), and physical-level *technology model* ('L4'). Each model of domain model supports software engineering phases of requirements analysis, preliminary design, and detailed design. Business model and system model belong to PIM, whereas technology model belongs to Platform-Specific Model (PSM).

3.3   Multi-focus Modeling Concepts

In the following, the characteristics of modeling constructs including attributes and operations in six focuses are explained. Among three domain models modeling constructs in business model and system model are exemplified. Modeling constructs in technology model will be addressed in future papers.

• *Participant* ('who') is for modeling the subject of activities occurring inside or outside of a CNO. In *business model* it represents CNO itself, individual/group/ company member, government, social organization, information system, etc. In *system model* it represents *actor* of processes or agent software.
   - Attributes, e.g., role, responsibility, authority, access right, duration
   - Operations, e.g., join or leave, perform, request or serve
• *Data* ('what') is for modeling the object of life-cycle activities of CNO. In *business model* it represents *information* about product, service, project, contract, document, resource, etc., that are input or output of one or more functions. In *system model* it represents *database schema* defining classes or types, attributes, operations, constraints, etc.
   - Attributes, e.g., type, media, location, access path
   - Operations, e.g., create, manage, use
• *Process* ('how') is for modeling a set of activities. In *business model* it represents function, procedure, transaction, or workflow to accomplish CNO goals. In *system model* it represents *process* that has a sequence of activities and control of flow.
   - Attributes, e.g., start/finish date or time, owner, input/output, flow (i.e., sequential or parallel)
   - Operations, e.g., start, finish, terminate, resume
• *Link* ('where') is for modeling connection between two participants or processes. In *business model* it represents communication/reporting channel, control, interface, collaboration path between two participants. In *system model* it represents interface between two processes or services.
   - Attributes, e.g., online/offline, connected nodes, network protocol, capacity, topology (e.g., hierarchical, horizontal, or network), type (e.g., direct/indirect)
   - Operations, e.g., open/close, connect/disconnect
• *Event* ('when') is for modeling specific time of control for participants, data, processes, and link. In *business model* and *system model* it represents events.
   - Attributes, e.g., time and precondition of invocation, invoking processes
   - Operations, e.g., check, invoke
• *Goal* ('why') is for modeling motivation of participants. In *business model* it represents mission, purpose, strategy, means-ends of participants. In *system model* it represents rules with condition and action.
   - Attributes, e.g., assigned participants, type (e.g., strategic, tactical, operational), duration (e.g., years, months, days), measure of effectiveness
   - Operations, e.g., set/unset, redirect

4   CONCLUSION

On the basis of Zachman Framework and OMG's Model-Driven Architecture (MDA), we suggest a Modeling Language of Enterprise Architecture (EAML) for CNO called CAML. It's an extension of existing research of EA frameworks and EAMLs. As far as we know, inclusion of meta-level models based on MDA is unique in CN discipline. After all, the CAML supports five levels of views and six focuses of modeling, as follows.

• 5 views: meta-model, business model, system model, technology model, and detailed representations,
• 6 focuses: *data* ('what'), *process* ('how'), *link* ('where'), *participant* ('who'), event ('when'), and goals ('why').

Comparing with existing EAMLs the resultant CAML is self-reflective and has rich modeling constructs, which raises flexibility and expressive power of modeling as well as implementations. Modeling constructs in the CAML could be applied to existing EAMLs and/or EA frameworks. For example, adding link, event, and goal to structure ('who'), behavior ('how'), and information/artifacts ('what') in NEML and ArchiMate could enhance modeling power of them. Ten generic dimensions in ArchiMate (Jonkers et al., 2003), i.e., action, process, function, interaction, service, transaction, actor/component, role/interface, collaboration/connector, data object, could be redefined by the six focuses and get more orthogonal perspectives.

As for ARCON we found that (1) 'life-cycle of CNO' can be mapped into *process* and *event* in the CAML, (2) 'modeling intent' can be mapped into three levels of *views,* (3) differentiation of inside and outside of a CNO is not so critical because of ever changing roles of participants, and (4) 'In-CNO' and 'About-CNO', i.e., the 'environmental characteristics' can be mapped into various *focuses.* For example, 'structural dimension' could be mapped into *participants* (e.g., node) and *link* (e.g., relationships), 'market dimension' also could be mapped into *participants* (e.g., customer, competitor, contract), *link* (e.g., interaction with participants), and *goal* (e.g., strategy, mission).

In this paper we only suggest modeling constructs of the CAML. To make the CAML sound and complete we plan to further investigate the following issues: (1) modeling of relationships between suggested modeling constructs in meta-models and domain models, (2) verification of modeling constructs through applying practical examples of CNOs, (3) formal definition of the modeling constructs, and (4) prototyping of the CAML as a modeling language.

5   REFERENCES

1.   Brodie ML, Bobrow D, Lesser V, Madnick S, and Tsichritzis D, Hewitt C. "Future AI requirements for intelligent database systems", In L. Kerschberg (ed), Expert Database Systems, Benjamin Cummings, pp. 45-62.
2.   Camarinha-Matos LM and Afsarmanesh H. "The emerging discipline of collaborative networks", In L. M. Camarinha-Matos (ed), Virtual Enterprises and Collaborative Networks, Kluwer Academic Publishers, IFIP V.149, August 2004, pp. 3-16.
3.   Camarinha-Matos LM, Afsarmanesh H, Ferrada F, Klen A, and Ermilova E. Rough reference model for collaborative networks, D52.2, ECOLEAD, March 2006.

4.   Camarinha-Matos LM and Afsarmanesh H. "Towards a reference model for collaborative networked organizations", In Proceedings of Information Technology for Balanced Manufacturing Systems (BASYS06), Niagara Falls, Canada, September 2006, pp. 193-201.
5.   Frankel DS, Harmon P, Mukerji J, Odell J, Owen M, Rivitt P, and Rosen M. The Zachman Framework and the OMG's Model Driven Architecture, Business Process Trends, White Paper, September 2003.
6.   Hendryx S. Architecture of Business Modeling, OMG document br/2003-11-01, November 2003.
7.   Jonkers et al. "Towards a language for coherent enterprise architecture descriptions", In Proceedings of the 7th IEEE International Enterprise Distributed Object Computing Conference (EDOC), 2003, pp. 28-39.
8.   Jonkers H, Lankhorst M, Buuren R, Hoppenbrouwers S, Bonsangue M, and Torre L. "Concepts for modeling enterprise architectures", International Journal of Cooperative Information Systems, 2004, 13(3), pp. 257-287.
9 . Kim DH and Park SJ. "FORM: A flexible data model for integrated CASE environments", Data & Knowledge Engineering, 22, 1997, pp. 133-158.
10. Sarkar S and Thonse S. "EAML – Architecture modeling language for enterprise applications", In Proceedings of the IEEE International Conference on E-Commerce Technology for Dynamic E-Business (CEC-East'04), 2004, pp. 40-47.
11. Steen MWA, Lankhorst MM, Wetering RG. "Modeling networked enterprise", In Proceeding of the 6th International Enterprise Distributed Object Computing Conference (EDOC), 2002, pp.109-119.
12. Tapia RS. "What is networked enterprise", CTIT Technical Report TR-CTIT-06-23, Center for Telematics and Information Technology, University of Twente, The Netherlands, May 2006.
13. Thangarathinam T, Wyant G, Gibson J, Simpson J. "Metadata management: the foundation for enterprise information integration", *Intel Technology Journal*, 2004, 8(4), pp. 337-344.

33

EVOLVING VIRTUE

Alessandro D'Atri[1], Amihai Motro[2]

[1] CeRSI, LUISS "Guido Carli" University, Roma, ITALY, datri@luiss.it
[2] CS Department, George Mason University, Fairfax, VA, USA, ami@gmu.edu

One of the most attractive aspects of virtual enterprises is their agility: the inherent ability to adapt and evolve in response to changing market conditions. Evolving VirtuE is a formal framework within which such agility can be realized. Through the concepts of enterprise time, activity logging, and log mining, the recent behavior and performance of an enterprise may be studied, and corresponding evolutionary steps can be induced. These steps may be intended to benefit the operation of individual enterprise members, as well the enterprise as a whole. In addition, we examine enterprise creation, a period of rapid evolution that concludes when the enterprise reaches stability and begins transacting its business activities.

1   INTRODUCTION

One of the most attractive aspects of virtual enterprises is their *agility*: the inherent ability to adapt and evolve in response to changing market conditions [6]. This paper presents Evolving VirtuE, a model with capabilities for capturing the *dynamic* aspects of virtual enterprises. Evolving VirtuE incorporates the notions of *time* and *activity logging*. These features enable elaborate measurement of performance, thus providing the rationale for any future evolution of the virtual enterprise. Second, it examines in detail *virtual enterprise creation*, a period of rapid evolution that ends when the enterprise achieves stability. Finally, and perhaps most importantly, it provides a framework for studying the performance and behavior of virtual enterprises, and for evolving them accordingly.

In itself, Evolving VirtuE is an evolution of the VirtuE model [3, 4], a model that formalizes the basic principles and operations of virtual enterprises, concentrating on virtual enterprises that deal with information products (e-products). The purpose of VirtuE was threefold. Others had previously articulated the concept of virtual enterprises; yet, at the time, the literature did not show unanimity with respect to essential principles, precise terminology, or formal definitions. VirtuE was therefore an attempt to establish a uniform platform for virtual enterprises, in which existing concepts could be formalized and standardized. Second, such formal treatment enables deeper (often quantitative) investigation of additional aspects of virtual enterprises, thus advancing the area even further. Finally, a formal model is an

D'Atri, A., Motro, A., 2007, in IFIP International Federation for Information Processing, Volume 243, Establishing the Foundation of Collaborative Networks; eds. Camarinha-Matos, L., Afsarmanesh, H., Novais, P., Analide, C.; (Boston: Springer), pp. 317–325.

essential step before undertaking an implementation of a software system that supports the activities of virtual enterprises.

Yet, the VirtuE model could be described as "static": It provides means for capturing the operations of stable virtual enterprises, but it lacks capabilities for modeling the *dynamic* aspects of virtual enterprises. The model described here seeks to extend the capabilities of VirtuE with various features related to enterprise dynamics.

Evolving VirtuE is described in two sections: In Section 3 we introduce the new features of the model, and in Section 4 we examine virtual enterprise creation, and we outline the framework for learning and evolution. We conclude with a short review of related work in Section 5, and a brief summary in Section 6. We begin with a review of the primary concepts of VirtuE.

2   VIRTUE

Essentially, the VirtuE model defines a distributed environment for virtual enterprises. The model has three principal components. First, it defines a distributed infrastructure with concepts such as members, products, inventories, and production plans. Second, it defines transactions among members, to enable collaborative production of complex products. Finally, it provides means for the instrumentation of enterprises, to measure their performance and to govern their behavior. We retain without modification most of the concepts introduced in earlier papers, and we review here the primary concepts.

2.1   Members

A virtual enterprise-breeding environment (VBE) [1] is a community of business entities that are potential participants in business coalitions. Each virtual enterprise chooses its members from the VBE. The members are independent but have shared interests. They are independent in the sense that they remain autonomous and maintain their own assets. These assets include human, equipment or financial resources, as well as business expertise, such as knowledge about their production and delivery processes. Their shared interests are reflected in that they agree to cooperate with each other to produce joint products that are provided to common clients. After the community had been established, it could evolve because a new member joins or an exiting member departs. This form of evolution provides the virtual enterprise with flexibility and allows it to adapt to new market situations.

2.2   Products

In practice, virtual enterprises may produce many different kinds of products. In VirtuE, we consider only information products, of the type that can be delivered over computer networks. Information products are provided by members of the enterprise to their clients. This provision is the ultimate purpose of an enterprise. Information products are also exchanged among the members of the enterprise in the production phase that precedes the provision of a product to a client. We distinguish between two kinds of information products: content and process. Content is an information item; for example, a specific data table, a specific document, or a specific image. Process is an operation that modifies given content to provide new content; for example, summarization of a data table, encryption of a document, or compression of an image.

2.3 Product dictionary

All products, content as well as processes, are classified into product types. A product type describes the common attributes of all products of that type. For example, all images could be instances of the content type Image, and all compression processes could be instances of the process type Compression. We assume that all intensional information (i.e., types and their attributes) is maintained in an enterprise-wide resource called the dictionary. This global knowledge resource is available to every member of the enterprise. Every product in the virtual enterprise is an instance of a type described in the dictionary. The purpose of the dictionary is to assure semantic consistency across the enterprise.

2.4 Local inventories and global catalog

The products either used or created by each enterprise member are described in a local resource called inventory. Items in the inventory are instances of product types described in the dictionary. Among other information, the inventory specifies the source and target of each product. The source is either native or import: A native product is produced locally, whereas an import product is procured from another member of the enterprise. The target is either internal or export: An internal product is an intermediate product used by this member in the manufacturing of other products, whereas an export product may be delivered to other enterprise members. The product catalog is an enterprise-wide resource that lists the products that are available for procurement from enterprise members; i.e., it is the union of the products marked "export" in all inventories. Each member *publishes* his list of export products in this catalog and is responsible for keeping it updated.[1] Note that products in the catalog are *instances* of the types in the dictionary. Hence, the dictionary *regulates* the catalog.

2.5 Production plans

Another designation of inventory products is whether they are basic or complex. A product is complex if it is derived from other products; otherwise, it is basic. For native complex product, production plans must be provided. A production plan specifies how other contents and processes are combined to derive the new product. In particular, it specifies the dependence of a product on products that must be procured from other members. Production plans are provided for both complex contents and complex processes, and a product may have multiple (alternative) production plans.

---

[1] This is a departure from previous descriptions of Virtue. Previously, each member of the enterprise *distributed* his catalog to a select set of members; this distribution system defined the enterprise procurement channels. This concept of static infrastructure has been deleted from the model; instead, links between arbitrary members are now established dynamically, through the execution of transactions.

2.6   Transactions

Since component products are often obtained from other enterprise members, a procurement mechanism is necessary. Procurement is executed in transactions. A transaction begins when a request for a catalog product (content or process) is sent from one participant to another, and terminates when the request is satisfied. There are two types of transactions in a virtual enterprise. An *external* transaction is a request for a product that is submitted from a client to one of the members of the virtual enterprise. The member processes the request and provides a solution. A member of the virtual enterprise who processes an external transaction acts in the role of a *provider*. To satisfy an external transaction, a provider may decide to purchase products from other members. Such transactions are *internal*. A member of the virtual enterprise who processes an internal transaction acts in a role of a *subcontractor*. The execution of external transactions is the ultimate purpose of the virtual enterprise. Each member of a virtual enterprise may act as a provider on some transactions and as a subcontractor on other transactions.

2.7   Performance indicators and constitutional rules

VirtuE allows the definition of *performance indicators*, which are formulas that capture various quantitative characteristics of the virtual enterprise; for example, the enterprise assets or interdependence levels. Another feature of VirtuE are *constitutional rules*, which are constraints that express behavior standards that are expected. Such rules enable virtual enterprises with different style or flavor; for example, an organization which is without any competition (similar products are not available from different members), or an organization that resembles a free market. Compliance with constitutional rules is monitored and disseminated, but not enforced.

Figure 1 illustrates the relationships among some of the basic concepts. The box indicates an enterprise member m_i. The incoming arrow on the left is a request (via a transaction t) for a product c. The outgoing arrow on the left is the eventual satisfaction of this transaction with the requested product. The circle indicates a production plan that m_i uses for manufacturing product c. This particular plan requires the importation of two component products c_1 and c_2. The two subcontracts are executed in transactions t_1 and t_2.

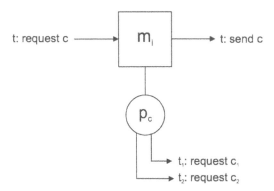

Figure 1: Basic VirtuE interactions.

3   EVOLVING VIRTUE

Evolving VirtuE supplements the features summarized in the previous section with several new concepts, including time, activity logging, internal dissemination of enterprise information, and behavior mining. We begin by introducing the *catalyst*: a privileged member of the enterprise who has specific duties.

3.1   The Catalyst

The launching of a new virtual enterprise begins when a player of the VBE assumes the role of catalyst [2]. The catalyst has a business plan, knowledge of the additional expertise and resources needed to accomplish the business plan, and information on VBE players that can satisfy these needs. The catalyst is a privileged member of the virtual enterprise, with several exclusive roles, such as changing the membership of the enterprise or modifying its goals (i.e., end products). In Evolving VirtuE, the catalyst role consolidates several distinct organizational roles, such broker, planner and coordinator [1].

3.2   Time and Logging

Evolving VirtuE incorporates the concept of *time*. Time is simply a system-wide clock that is stamped on transactions and other enterprise events. The availability of a system clock allows for the introduction of various new performance indicators and constitutional rules. For example, indicators may be defined now to count the number of transactions performed over a period of time, or the average turnaround time. Rules may be established that require members to maintain activity at some minimal frequency, or limit the number of transactions in a given period.

Enterprise events, such as execution of transactions, updates of the catalog, or changes in membership, are now recorded in a *log*. Log records provide essential information on each such event and the time of its occurrence. There are two types of log: local and global. Every enterprise member maintains his own local log, and, in addition, there is an enterprise-wide log. Local logs may be used by members to improve their operations. The global log can be used for studying enterprise-wide performance, as well as for communication among members.

3.3   Information dissemination and behavior mining

Altogether, Evolving VirtuE incorporates four global information resources: the product dictionary, which describes products and types; the product catalog, which lists the products available from members; the log, which chronicles the activities of the enterprise; and the constitution, which establishes the conventions of the enterprise. These resources are managed by the catalyst (who could also designate another member to act as the information manager). It is important to note that the information in these global resources is maintained and processed in a manner identical to any other content.[2] Thus, the catalyst can supply other members with products that calculate performance indicators, or assess compliance with constitutional rules. This information is exchanged using the ordinary transaction mechanism of VirtuE.

The information derived from the enterprise information resources need not be limited to the calculation of performance measures or the validation of constitutional rules. The global log, and to some degree the other information resources, can be subjected to a wide array of data mining techniques. The overall purpose is to study the performance and behavior of the enterprise, and to associate the outcome with various evolutionary decisions. This subject is discussed further in Section 4.

Recall that the dictionary and the constitution describe, respectively, the product types of the enterprise and the restrictions on its behavior.[3] Only the catalyst is allowed to modify the dictionary and the constitution, but all members can retrieve its information. The catalog is the set of products that are available from individual members — it is a union of the individual inventories. Each member can update his own portion of the catalog, and retrieve information on other inventories. The log is updated automatically after various enterprise activities, and can be examined by everyone.

4   CREATION AND EVOLUTION

One notable period of virtual enterprise evolution is the initial stage of its formation. In this period, the new virtual enterprise goes through a period of repetitive refinement, until it acquires stability, at least for a while.

Virtual enterprise creation begins when a VBE player decides to launch a virtual enterprise for some product (or set of products). This participant acts as the *catalyst* of the virtual enterprise, and performs these initial actions:

1. Initialize the four repositories: the constitution, the dictionary, the catalog, and the log. Update the constitution with the enterprise rules, and update the dictionary with the product types and descriptions envisioned for the enterprise. The catalyst has thus set the "charter" for the enterprise: its product line and its business style.
2. Invite other VBE participants to join the enterprise; they become *members* of the enterprise.

Members retrieve information from the dictionary and catalog, and decide the products they wish to manufacture for the enterprise. A member who decides to manufacture a product of a type that appears in the dictionary, defines a production plan for the product and updates the catalog with the new product and its specification. Occasionally, a new production plan may necessitate a product of a new type, not yet in the dictionary. In this case, the member writes the proposed dictionary update to the log. Thereafter, the catalyst examines the log and updates the dictionary appropriately. The member can then complete the definition of the new product.

---

[2] This is analogous to the way database management systems use standard database structures to maintain meta-information such as schema, integrity constraints, and access permissions.

[3] A possible analogy from the area of database management, is to perceive the dictionary and constitution as, respectively, the "schema" and the "integrity constraints" of the enterprise.

This process — in which new products are defined, new production plans are established, and the product dictionary and catalog are updated — is repeated, until stability is achieved: The enterprise is then ready for transacting business.

This process of creation demonstrates how enterprise information sources are consulted continuously for making decisions; in this case, addition of product types and product instances. More generally, Evolving VirtuE provides a framework for studying the behavior of the enterprise and taking corresponding actions.

This activity may be performed by individual enterprise members, who may follow up their conclusions with business decisions, intended to improve their own performance. For example,

- **Whom should I work with?** A member may extract from the global and local sources data on the recent performance of potential transaction partners, and the cost of their services, and use it to improve the turnaround time for his products.

- **Should I make it or should I buy it?** This classical business decision can be resolved based on information mined from the global resources, using data on prices charged and delays incurred (plus estimation of local production and processing costs).

- **Which production plan should I use?** Similarly, recent data on the time and cost required to obtain necessary component products (plus estimation of local production and processing costs) can be used to decide which of alternative production plans to use.

The mining activity may also be performed by the catalyst, who may follow up with more far-reaching conclusions, intended to affect the overall behavior of the enterprise. For example,

- **Improving overall enterprise performance by changing membership.** By analyzing turnaround times for various products, the catalyst may identify members who are overloaded with orders (causing long transaction completion times), and thereby invite new members with equivalent capabilities. Conversely, the catalyst may identify members who are no longer active and dismiss them from the enterprise.

- **Improving overall market responsiveness by changing the product line.** By analyzing log information on external transactions, the catalyst may identify market trends, and modify or expand the product offerings of the enterprise to respond to the new trends. Conversely, the catalyst may delete products for which there is no longer demand. In effect, the enterprise would be evolving its product dictionary.

- **Monitoring enterprise behavior.** The global information sources provide the data for calculating performance indicators and testing compliance with constitutional rules. The results of such monitoring could be associated with triggered actions. For example, warning may be sent to a member who is violating a component of the "charter".

5   BACKGROUND

The literature on virtual enterprises is considerable, and for the sake of brevity we limit our discussion to work that is directly related to the main focus of this paper, which is creation, learning and evolution.

Creation and evolution is strongly dependent on the availability of flexible infrastructures. Camarinha-Matos and Afsarmanesh [5] discuss approaches and trends in architectures for flexible infrastructures and breeding environments.

Experience in building a technological infrastructure for supporting the creation, operation and dissolution stages within the lifecycle of a virtual enterprise is discussed in [8].

Tagg [10] observed three stages in the life of a virtual enterprise: establishment, which focuses on building relationships, a fundamentally iterative activity; business development, when more formal cycles of invitations to tender, joint proposals, cooperative market research are accomplished; and business execution, when processes and workflows are most similar to those of single organizations.

Social Actors Networks (SAN) are used in [9] for modeling collaborations in virtual enterprises. The authors propose SAN analysis to support the identification of the actors involved, their role and importance, and their supplying characteristics (e.g., types of products or delivery performance).

The issue of partner evaluation and selection in considered in [11]. The authors stress the importance of knowing the capability and compatibility of potential partners, and suggest a profile-based approach for measuring these factors.

Issues of selecting business partners, coordinating the distribution of production processes, and the prediction of production problems are studied in [7]. The authors seek to provide decision support for virtual enterprises by using a Neural On-Line Analytical Processing System (NOLAPS). Their system incorporates two components: It uses neural networks for extrapolating probable outcomes based on available patterns of events, and data mining for converting complex data into useful corporate information. The approach has been validated with a prototype system and an example case.

6   CONCLUSION

In this paper we introduced Evolving VirtuE, a model for virtual enterprises with features that support learning and evolution. In particular, it incorporates time, activity logging, and internal dissemination of enterprise information. These create a framework for continuous study of enterprise behavior through data mining techniques. Conclusions from such discoveries are then linked to specific evolutionary actions.

For reasons of space we did not elaborate on various details, including the types of events that are logged and the exact information stored, or particular data mining techniques. Still, much work remains to be done, and we mention here two current research directions.

Work is underway on suitable techniques of mining data from logs of virtual enterprises, and, possibly, on a decision support system that will associate discoveries with specific actions. Also, recognizing that centralized information sources in a distributed environment can cause undesirable bottlenecks, work is underway to decentralize these resources, possibly by adopting a grid architecture.

Acknowledgement

This work was performed within Interop: Interoperability Research for networked Enterprises Applications and Software, European Network of Excellence IST-508011 (http://interop-noe.org), and has been partially supported by the SFIDA-PMI project.

7 REFERENCES

1. Afsarmanesh H, Camarinha-Matos L.M. A framework for management of virtual organization breeding environments. In Proc. PRO-VE 05: Collaborative Networks and their breeding environments, IFIP 6th Working Conf. on Virtual Enterprises, pp. 35–48, Kluwer 2005.
2. D'Atri A. Organizing and managing virtual enterprises: the ECB framework. In Proc. PRO-VE 03: Processes and Foundations for Virtual Organizations, IFIP 4th Working Conf. on Virtual Enterprises, pp. 171–178, Kluwer, 2004.
3. D'Atri A, Motro A. VirtuE: virtual enterprises for information markets. In Proc. ECIS 02, 10th European Conf. on Information Systems; Research Track: Digital Economy - Models for e-Business and m-Business, pp. 768–777, 2002.
4. D'Atri A, Motro A. VirtuE: a formal model of virtual enterprises for information markets. Journal of Intelligent Information Systems, to appear, on-line at http://www.springerlink.com, 2007.
5. Camarinha-Matos L.M., Afsarmanesh H. Elements of base VE infrastructure. J. Computers in Industry, 51(2), pp. 139–163, 2003.
6. Goranson HT. The agile virtual enterprise: cases, metrics, tools. Quorum Books, Westport, CT, 1999.
7. Lau HCW, Chin KS, Pun KF, Ning A. Decision supporting functionality in a virtual enterprise network. Expert Systems with Applications, 19(4), pp. 261–270, 2000.
8. Nayak N, Chao T, Li J, Mihaeli J, Das R, Derebail A, Soo Hoo J. Role of technology in enabling dynamic virtual enterprises. In Proc. Int. Workshop OES-SEO 2001: Open Enterprise Solutions: Systems, Experiences and Organizations, Luiss Edizioni, Rome, 2001.
9. Soares AJ, Sousa JP, Barbedo F. Modeling the Structure of Collaborative Networks: Some Contributions. In Proc. PRO-VE 03: Processes and Foundations for Virtual Organizations, IFIP 4th Working Conf. on Virtual Enterprises, pp. 23–30, Kluwer, 2004.
10. Tagg R. Workflow in different styles of virtual enterprise. In Proc. the Workshop on Information Technology for Virtual Enterprises, ITVE, Vol. 13, pp. 21–28, 2001.
11. Tsakopoulos S, Bokma A, Plekhanova V. Partner evaluation and selection in virtual enterprises using a profile theory based approach. In Proc. PRO-VE 03: Processes and Foundations for Virtual Organizations, IFIP 4th Working Conf. on Virtual Enterprises, pp. 73–84, Kluwer, 2004.

34

BUSINESS MODELLING FOR KNOWLEDGE NETWORKS

André Quadt[1], Heiko Dirlenbach[2]

Research Institute for Operations Management
at Aachen University of Technology
Pontdriesch 14/16
D-52062 Aachen, GERMANY
{qu'\di²}@fir.rwth-aachen.de

Most companies are hardly ready to address current business challenges as far as their knowledge resources are concerned. Instead of making best use of their non-tangible assets they keep their knowledge to themselves. This effect is even stronger in virtual enterprises, which provide value to the user only when they combine their knowledge resources. There is a clear lack of a methodology to turn knowledge resources into profitable goods by a suitable business model. This article presents an approach to address this issue. A case study is presented for the automotive after-sales service sector taken from the European Research project MYCAREVENT.

1 VALUE GENERATION FROM KNOWLEDGE RESOURCES IN ENTREPRENEURIAL NETWORKS

The European economy faces an ever increasing competition by Asian "Tiger States" as well as other emerging economies. Being characterized by rather high wages, economic growth can thus only result from innovative products and especially services making best use of available resources. The European Commission has realized this fact in due time and set out the well-known "Lisbon Objectives". These formulate the political goal to turn Europe into the most dynamic knowledge economy in the world. Following this trend, companies consider knowledge to be a major success factor in today's business environment.

In parallel it can be observed that the complexity of value generation is ever increasing. Customer value is more and more not only delivered by a single company, but a network of partners up to completely virtual organisations. While research has tackled a number of issue which are related to these developments, the implication of business modelling in the area of virtual organisations have rarely been addressed. In order to make best use of their knowledge resources, however, entrepreneurial networks require a systematic guidance on how to *design* their businesses in order to provide customer value based on their knowledge.

This can be observed on numerous industry sectors, but is especially visible in such industries which deal with complex products (which means a high demand for sophisticated knowledge) but are traditionally based on expensive physical goods. Examples are the automotive sector and heavy investment good industries, such as textile machinery.

Quadt, A., Dirlenbach, H., 2007, in IFIP International Federation for Information Processing, Volume 243, Establishing the Foundation of Collaborative Networks; eds. Camarinha-Matos, L., Afsarmanesh, H., Novais, P., Analide, C.; (Boston: Springer), pp. 327–334.

2   CHALLENGES, REQUIREMENTS AND NEED FOR ACTION

Service-oriented virtual enterprises require sophisticated methods to make best use of their combined knowledge resources. In order to successfully develop a business, a dilemma needs to be solved: on the one hand, clear strategic guidelines are required. They ensure a coherent and consistent progress in the business. On the other hand, this must not lead to a static, inflexible organisation, as this would prevent a quick re-adjustment of the business to changes in the market arena and render the idea of a virtual organisation useless. A clear area for flexible development is thus required.

Consequently, a successful business design approach needs to cater for both requirements. In coherence with the concept of integrated management presented by (Bleicher, 2004) this can be achieved by defining a hard (normative) aspects as a static framework and a soft development aspects in each of the design areas laid out above. Service-oriented virtual enterprises require sophisticated methods to make best use of their combined knowledge resources.

3   STATE OF THE ART

In management literature there are various descriptions and definitions of business models (Chesbrough, Rosenbloom, 2002), (Afuah, Tucci, 2001), (Osterwalder, Pingneur, 2002), (Timmers, 1998), (Wirtz, Kleineicken, 2000), (Knecht, Friedli, 2002). Accordingly, there is little common understanding about the term business model. In order to select a suitable starting point for the elaboration of an innovative approach to do business modelling for a networked organisation, a systematic and analytical research of business modelling approaches has been performed. The following criteria were analyzed:

- *descriptive or design oriented:* Is the approach aiming at providing an action plan (how to elaborate a business model) or does it 'only' describe different types or elements of business models?
- *service oriented, production oriented or unspecific:* Business models for services differ from business models for organisations in the production sector. Is the business modelling approach for one of these categories or is it on a more generic level?
- *inter- or intra-organisational:* Does the business modelling approach consider the environment of the organisation (e.g. partners, markets) or does it focus on the internal organisation (e.g. products, services, processes).
- *e-business oriented:* Is the approach especially targeted for e-business issues?
- *micro- or macro-level:* How detailed is the business modelling approach?
- *information/knowledge oriented:* Does the business modelling approach include information and/or knowledge as part of the business model?
- *theory-based or based on empirical data:* is the approach built on well-recognized theories or are there mainly case studies/empirical data to validate the approach?
- which *sub-models* (if any) does the approach include?

Based on the preceding focus categories, different concepts for business models were classified. (Afuah, Tucci, 2003), (Alt, Zimmermann, 2001), (Scheer, Deelmann, Loos, 2003), (Gordjin, Akkermanns, 2001), (Chesboom, Rosenbloom, 2000), (Kim, Mabourgne, 2002), (Knecht, Friedli, 2002), (Kollmann, 2003), (Osterwalder et al., 2004), (Timmers, 1998), (Wirtz, Kleineicke, 2000), (Wölfle, 2000), (Forzi, Laing, 2002). The HVC approach, presented by (Forzi, Laing, 2002), was selected as best fit with the requirements of a virtual enterprise which aims at enabling extended, knowledge based services. This result was mainly based on three arguments:

1. The HVC is design and service oriented. (preceding points 1 and 2)
2. It includes all important sub-models which are discussed within other model-ling concepts and therefore can be seen as a superset of relevant sub-models.
3. It is extendable and adoptable to special requirements for virtual enterprises.

Although HVC being the best fit, extensive enhancements within each sub-model had to be performed to further develop an innovative methodology to support extended products and services for different sectors.

4   RESEARCH APPROACH AND RESULTS

The design of new business models for networked organizations, which are feasible and sustainable is a challenging task. On the one hand, all partners in a virtual enterprise are independent entities taking their own decisions. On the other hand, the network is the perceived entity delivering value to the customer and is thus the body competing on the market. Consequently, business decisions need to be taken on both levels. Considering the sub-models suggested by (Forzi; Laing 2002), these can be defined as "*local* business modelling". Thus, the sub-models are below referred to as the local models. The local business modelling takes into account the fact that a company always only has full control over its internal state. Even companies acting in a network of partners can only enforce decisions which are limited to their own processes and behaviour. Despite this, the companies in the network depend on each other and thus have a strong general interest to foster their common market. Thus, *global* aspects, which cover the network as a whole, also play a crucial role in the modelling of networked businesses. These aspects influence decisions made by the members of the network. Therefore, the local models have to be carefully designed.

Following the approach of (Bleicher 2004), the design of these models is performed by a number of dichotomic positions within the different design areas. Subsequently, these are presented for two example sub-models: the network model and the revenue model.

4.1   Network Sub-Model Design

The HVC network sub-model defines the parameters which are the basis for the interaction of a company in question with its environment. In case of knowledge centred services, these dimensions have been found to be:

- *application of information and communication technology*: This defines whether newest (pioneer) or well-established (follower) technologies are used to interact with others. Pioneers can leverage recent technology potentials, but cannot rely on a general compatibility of their systems with other partners
- *contract negotiation*: All business related activities rely on customer-supplier relationships. This is also true for knowledge centred services. However, as explicit knowledge is immaterial, it can be easily transferred via electronic networks. Consequently it has to be designed, whether any source of knowledge is acceptable ad hoc (dynamic) or only validated, pre-selected sources can be used for customer value generation (static)
- *technical protection of intellectual property*: Recent discussions (Jobs, 2007) have again demonstrated the dilemma between strict technical enforcement of digital rights management as a technical means of intellectual property protection and customer acceptance.
- *application of standards*: Cooperative business requires standards to operate. It is thus necessary to decide whether they are set up making use of existing standards (conformist) or rather define their own standards (trend-setter).
- Figure 1 below shows the design frame for the network sub-model in knowledge centred cooperative businesses:

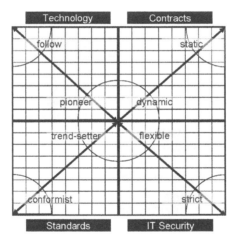

Figure 1: Network sub-model design dichotomy

4.2   Revenue Sub-Model Design

One obvious aspect in designing a business is the consideration of how revenues are generated. Examining the crucial aspects in this field, it was found that four considerations define the design of the respective sub-model:

- *pricing policy*: The price charged for the value created is obviously one of the most decisive factors for the sustainability of any business. It is essential to define a congruent pricing policy. Depending on the market environment, prices can follow a penetration, neutral or skimming approach.

- *granularity:* The value created for the user and thus the achievable turnover needs to cover variable as well as fixed costs. Consequently, a balance has to be found between the sales of large, static packages (e.g. chunks of information, access time intervals) and small, flexible portions provided to the market.
- *degree of dependence*: The generation of values is usually not independent from other resources and other companies which deliver complementary products or services. In some cases, the value of a service is not a direct benefit to the user of the service, but rather an increase in efficiency for another company which can then deliver their products or services more efficiency. In this case it is required, that this company subsidizes the knowledge based service in form a reserve charging.
- *point(s) of sale*: One more crucial aspect for knowledge services, especially in networked environments, is the number of "points of sale". This refers to the number of different (virtual) places from where the user gets invoices. This is especially sensitive in relation to information based services, as these are particularly characterized by ease-of-use. This concept is also expected to be pursued for the invoicing processes. However, this is associated with large hurdles (e.g. due to the lack of standards in this field, company politics, confidentiality reasons, etc.). In the design process for knowledge businesses, this has to be carefully considered.

Figure 2 shows the design dimensions as a diagram:

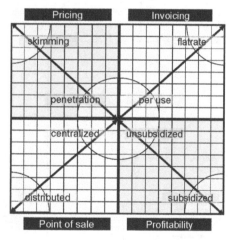

Figure 2: Revenue sub-model design dichotomy

4.3 Global Business Aspects: Business Aspects

Business models for virtual organisations will obviously need to take the (virtual) enterprises' strategy into explicit account, in order to guarantee a sustainable success. This means, that the strategic directives of each individual company, as well as those of the business network as a whole has to set the frame for all business operations.

The "House of Value Creation" as a methodical approach structures and describes all business elements in partial models and thus allows for detailed analysis of companies *and collaborative networks* (Forzi, Laing, 2002). In order to represent the complex business structure of the market a composition/decomposition derivate of the HVC approach is required in order to enable each network partner of the virtual enterprise to plan its business on its own while keeping the overall business structure in mind.

In order to understand business relationships partners these have to be made transparent. In a network like the automotive industry, such relationships are extremely complex and reach far beyond a simple customer-supplier relation. In order to capture these, a business map has been found to be a valuable tool. The business map has been developed to display how changes to the business models of one company have an impact on its environment, i.e. cooperation partners. The different sub models of the relevant companies as defined by the HVC approach are analysed. Subsequently, the business relations are examined and documented on sub model level. The result is a graphical representation of the market relations between different players. This can be either focused on one particular player (as seen in Figure 3) or represent a wider view on all relevant market players. For early analysis of markets it has proven to be helpful to define more generic roles rather than individual companies as the starting ground for the development of business maps. Figure 3 shows an example for a business map focussing on the role of an "application service provider" in a knowledge provision market situation.

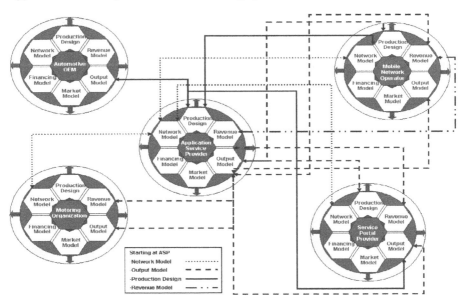

Figure 3: Application Service Provider Business Map

On the basis of these business maps for the different roles or partners within the virtual enterprise, each of the sub-models of the HVC can be adjusted or refined. Therefore, a definition of all valid types of relations between partners for all sub-models and for all interactions within the sub-models is required. On that basis the explicit specification for each of the interactions can be made respecting the overall business structure and at the same time each partners' business strategy.

5 CASE STUDY IN THE AUTOMOTIVE INDUSTRY

The methodology presented above has been used in a European research project to establish not only breakthrough research results, but at the same ensure their take-up by commercial companies. In the MYCAREVENT project (IST – 04402) more than 20 partners develop an infrastructure to provide mechanics and drivers with exactly the required information in situations of vehicle maintenance and breakdowns. In congruence with the previous sections, Figure 4 presents the results of the analysis for the network and pricing sub-model for the entity operating the service portal.

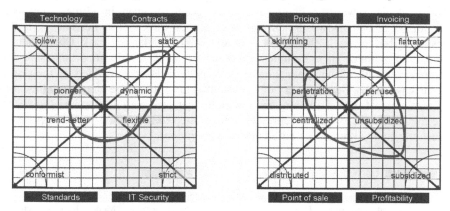

Figure 4: Design results for the portal operating entity of MYCAREVENT

It can be seen, that very clear design decisions have been made to ensure a successful take up of businesses. To further break down this example the cash flow model implemented within the network sub-model for all participants serves as a good case. Figure 5 presents a scenario to provide mobile extended services to the end customer via a central service portal. In this example the applications provided by the application service provider are paid by the service portal provider. The service portal passes applications on to the user, who only pays to the service portal for both services, repair information and application provision (centralized point of sale, see Figure 4). The service portal provider distributes the funds from the user to the service, information and application provider.

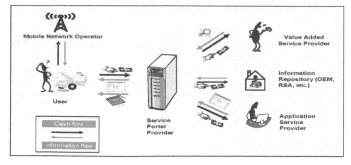

Figure 5: Example for the cash and information flow within MYCAREVENT

Based on the results of these designs an in-depth market analysis has been performed (MYCAREVENT 2005). The businesses which have been designed using this approach have been analysed especially in regards to what customer value can be achieved by their application. The results of this market analysis and sub-sequent business planning exercise were extremely encouraging. It was found that applying the business models as they were laid out, a considerable market potential can be tapped into. Thus, the goal of a knowledge based economy can be argued to be very much facilitated by the approach presented.

6   CONCLUSION

The tendency towards a knowledge based economy even in virtual enterprises cannot be denied. However, during our research work it has become clear that designing businesses in such fields is an extremely challenging task. Consequently, structured methods are a definite requirement to achieve this important goal. The impressive result of the application of such methods is demonstrated by the results of the case study. The discovery of a substantial market volume along with the proof of feasibility of the calculations for a complex network with 20 partners shows that the methodology developed represent a major step to support virtual enterprises to reach the goal of knowledge based business operations.

7   REFERENCES

1.   Afuah, A. & Tucci,C.L. Internet Business Models and Strategies, 2001.
2.   Alt, R. and Zimmermann, H.D. Introduction to Special Section-Business Models. In: EM-Electronics Markets,11(2001)1,1-7.
3.   Bleicher, K. Das Konzept Integriertes Management, 2004
4.   Chesbrough, H. and Rosenbloom, R.S. "The role of the business model in capturing value from innovation: evidence from Xerox Corporation's technology spin-off companies." Industrial and Corporate Change, 2002, vol. 11, no.3, pp. 529-555. Six components for a business model.
5.   Forzi, T.; Laing, P. Challenges for Business Modelling in the New Communication Era. Proceedings of the 31st Annual meeting of the Western Decision Sciences Institute (WDSI 2002),April 2nd -5th, 2002,Las Vegas, NV (USA), 434-436.
6.   Gordijin, J. and Akkermans, H. Designing and Evaluating E-Business Models, Vol. 16, 2001.
7.   Jobs, S. Thoughts on music, Public Letter, 2007 <http://www.apple.com/hotnews/thoughtsonmusic/>
8.   Kim, C. and Mabourgne, R. Knowing a winnning business idea when you see one. Harvard Business Review, Sept.-Oct. 2000, s. 129-138.
9.   Knecht, F. and Friedli, T. Wege zur Intelligenten Positionerung von Industrielieferanten, 2002.
10.   Kollmann, R. Identifying the Quality of E-Commerce Reference Models, 1997.
11.   MYCAREVENT project deliverable "Consolidated User Survey Report" available at http://www. mycarevent.com/Deliverables/DL.2.1.b_Consolidated_User%20Survey_Report_FL_v01.00.pdf, last visit 15. May 2007
12.   Osterwalder, A. et al. e-Business Model Design, Classification and Measurements, 2001.
13.   Scheer, C; Deelmann, T.; Loos, P. Geschäftsmodelle und internetbasierte Geschäftsmodelle - Begriffsbestimmung und Teilnehmermodell. 2003
14.   Timmers, P. „Business Models for Electronic Markets", Journal on Electronic Markets,8(2):3-8; 1998.
15.   Wirtz,B.W. and Kleineicken, A. Geschäftsmodelltypologien im Internet.In: WiSt,Heft 11, 2000.
16.   Wölfle, R. Das E-Business Project im Unternehmen - der Beratungsansatz der Fachhochschule beider Basel, 2000.

PART 11

BUSINESS BENEFITS IN NETWORKS

35

DISTRIBUTION OF NETWORK GENERATED PROFIT BY CONSIDERING INDIVIDUAL PROFIT EXPECTATIONS

Hendrik Jähn[1], Marco Fischer[2], Tobias Teich[3]

[1]*Chemnitz University of Technology, hendrik.jaehn@wirtschaft.tu-chemnitz.de*
[2]*Chemnitz University of Technology, marco.fischer@wirtschaft.tu-chemnitz.de*
[3]*Zwickau University of Applied Sciences of West Saxony, tobias.teich@fh-zwickau.de*
GERMANY

In this contribution approaches for the distribution of profit within networked production structures to the different network members are introduced and discussed. In this context exact rules are indispensable for the success of a cooperation because profits are the main target of all economic activities. In this context three influencing parameters are considered: a fixed share, a value-adding-dependent share and a profit expectation dependent share whereby the last mentioned parameter represents the most important variable.

1   INTRODUCTORY REMARKS AND OVERVIEW

In this contribution possibilities for the distribution of profit in production networks are focused. In that context it is assumed that a product is manufactured in a collaborative network of independent enterprises. The introduced models are of theoretical nature; however the practical relevancy is undisputed. In order to provide suitable solutions for different situations, several models have been elaborated. Basically it is assumed that a central operation and coordination instance operates as a broker for the whole network.

In existent literature hardly any comprehensive models focusing that topic can be identified. As an exception game-theoretic approaches can be identified (Fromen, 2005; Sucky, 2004) but there are no approaches taking into account the macroeconomic approach of the New Institutional Economics (Furubotn, 2005). Thereby, informational asymmetries among the network members, opportunistic behaviour, a limited rationality of actors and the tendency for individual maximisation of utility are the basic assumptions in that context.

The following profit distribution models consider mainly three influence parameters. In addition to a value-adding-independent (fixed) and a value-adding-dependent (variable) part, a profit expectation-dependent component is taken into consideration. The profit share of an enterprise which is determined by this influence factor is called g_i^p. The variable represents the profit expectation-dependent profit share of an enterprise. The individual profit expectation of an enterprise (with regard to the individual value-adding-share w_i) can be indicated as an amount g_i^e or a percentage of the value-adding-share g_i^{ep}. It is stored in a central data base which is neither accessible to the network members nor to the broker instance. There is no "open book" strategy in the network.

In the further modelling three different influence components are taken into consideration. Thereby it has to be differentiated whether the product offer price of the network P^{offer} (respectively the offer profit G^{offer}) correspond to the final sales price P^{sales} (respectively the sales profit P) to the customer. Thus, several possibilities

Jähn, H., Fischer, M., Teich, T., 2007, in IFIP International Federation for Information Processing, Volume 243, Establishing the Foundation of Collaborative Networks; eds. Camarinha-Matos, L., Afsarmanesh, H., Novais, P., Analide, C.; (Boston: Springer), pp. 337–344 of component integration arise for the calculation of the profit shares. The following paragraph 3 will focus that structure. A further approach consists in the introduction of weightings for each component which is discussed in section 4.

In principle, the calculation of the network profit calculated in the offer (G^{offer}) is based on the individual profit expectations of the enterprises g^e_i or g^{ep}_i as was stated before. However, it is imaginable that, after the value adding-process has been carried out, the distributed profit expectation-dependent profit share G^p does not correspond to the complete profit G that can be distributed. This so-called undistributed remaining profit G^{ur} is negative if a too high amount has been distributed already whereas it is positive if a profit share remains and can be distributed. In both cases, measures need to be taken in order to exactly distribute the earned profit. Therefore, either a corresponding revaluation or devaluation by the help of a standardisation parameter or the consideration of the two remaining components are imaginable. While the first mentioned approach will be discussed in paragraph 3.1, the second option will be focussed in paragraph 3.2. For the less complicating case that the offer profit and the realised profit correspond to each other, two different approaches are discussed next in paragraph 2.1 and 2.2.

It has to be stressed that the different approaches for profit distribution presupposes a flat-hierarchical structure with an independent broker. The sensible data are stored centrally for the calculation of individual profit shares in an automated way using the modern information and communication technology.

2   MODELS CONSIDERING NO REMAINING PROFIT

2.1   Enterprise-related profit expectation g^{ep}_i as a basis

In the simplest case, the calculation of the offer price P^{offer} is based on the individual value-adding-shares w_i and the corresponding profit expectations g^{ep}_i an enterprise stated. If the offer including the suggested price is accepted by a customer, the goods are produced and finally finished and delivered. In the usual case, the customer then pays the agreed sales price P^{sales} including the profit G, which is based on the individual profit expectations g^{ep}_i and thus corresponds to the offer price. The achieved profit G can completely be distributed to the single enterprises in the network, no rest remains. The calculation of the enterprise-related profit shares g^p_i is made by multiplying the enterprise-related profit expectation (in per cent) g^{ep}_i with the net value-adding of an enterprise w_i, cf. equation (1).

$$g^p_i = g^{ep}_i \cdot w_i \tag{1}$$

Thus, the enterprises are given their desired profit share without any reductions or supplements. Finally, the distributed (profit-expectation-dependent) profit G^p results from the sum of those individual profit expectation-dependent profit shares g^p_i of all enterprises. This profit expectation-dependently distributed profit G^p corresponds to the offer profit G^{offer} and thus, the complete profit G was distributed. There is no remaining profit G^{ur}.

One problem of this procedure is the initial parameter "individual profit expectation" g^{ep}_i. The enterprises indicate this parameter independent from a certain value adding-process. However, there is the problem of intended incorrect information. For this reason, a parameter should be introduced which eliminates outliers and obviously wrong numbers. This parameter is called the average percentage of the expected profit g^{epd} and it is equal for all enterprises. Thereby, however, we often face the situation that the distributed profit does not necessarily correspond to the profit that can be distributed, anymore. This is also dependent on the calculation methodologies for the g^{epd}. Thus, further distribution mechanisms need to be used which are also valid if a profit G, that can be distributed, was achieved which deviates from the offer profit G^{offer}. These mechanisms are introduced next.

2.2 Enterprise-related average profit expectations g^{epd} as a basis

For calculating the (weighted) average profit g^{epd} (measured in per cent of W), equation (2) can be applied. The individual percentage of the profit expectation g^{ep}_i therefore is weighted by the share of the individual value-adding-process w_i of the complete value-adding-process W. Thereby, it has to be considered that this parameter is enterprise-independent.

$$g^{epd} = \frac{\sum_{i=1}^{n} \left(g_i^{ep} \cdot w_i \right)}{W} \tag{2}$$

In the next step, it is now possible to ascertain the profit expectation-dependent profit share for every enterprise g^p_i. This variable represents the most important component of the complete profit share of an enterprise g_i. It is valid:

$$g_i^p = g^{epd} \cdot w_i \tag{3}$$

Finally, the complete (profit expectation-dependent) profit G^P, that has so far been paid out, results from the sum of those individual profit expectation-dependent profit shares g^p_i of all enterprises. Summing up the profit shares per enterprise is necessary in order to determine the further procedure. Thus, a comparison between the already distributed profit G^P and the profit after the value adding-process, that can in total be distributed, is the next step. By subtracting the already distributed profit from the distributable profit, a non-distributed remaining profit G^{ur} results, which still can be distributed among the enterprises. It is valid:

$$G^{ur} = G - G^P \tag{4}$$

The total profit could be completely distributed based on the (non-weighted) profit expectation (per cent) g^{ep}_i. When applying the profit expectation, that is weighted using the individual value adding-process, it has to be checked subsequently if this condition is fulfilled.

Here, it is significant to stress an effect of the application of the equations (2) and (3). This effect occurs in case the offer profit G^{offer} corresponds to the distributable profit G. This is not unusual because the offer profit G^{offer} is already based on the indications concerning the profit expectation of the enterprises g^{ep}_i. Starting from the enterprise-related percentage of the profit expectations g^{ep}_i (related to the enterprise-related net value-adding-process w_i and unweighted), the profit expectation-dependent profit share g^p_i is calculated as follows:

$$g_i^p = g^{ep} \cdot w_i \tag{5}$$

As opposed to that, equation (3) determined the profit expectation-dependent profit shares g^p_i in dependence of the weighted average percentage of the profit expectation, see calculation in equation (2). This procedure usually leads to different values for g^p_i than equation (5). However, it can be remarked that the distributable profit G will in any case need to be distributed among the enterprises without a remaining profit G^{ur}. This happens independently from the kind of calculation. This effect is especially interesting because thus it is made sure that this procedure provides usable results in a simple way despite of the improved modelling.

It is guaranteed that this approach does not provide any procedure-specific remaining profit. However, those procedure-specific remaining profits must not be changed with the remaining profits, which occur in case the distributable profit G from the sales price P^{sales} is higher than the offer profit G^{offer} in the offer price P^{offer}. This will be the focus of the following paragraphs.

3   MODELS CONSIDERING REMAINING PROFIT

3.1   Solution with a standardisation parameter

In case the distributable profit G differs from the offer profit G^{offer} the balance forms the remaining profit. That amount can be positive $(G>G^{offer})$ or negative $(G<G^{offer})$. In that case, a corresponding distribution mechanism needs to be applied for the non-distributed remaining profit G^{ur}. One possibility for that is the application of a standardisation parameter. With regard to a reference parameter, the individual profit shares g_i are adapted based on a standardisation by the profit expectation dependent profit shares g^p_i.

In the following, the procedure will be described. It is assumed that a certain amount G^d could be distributed which is based on the individual profit expectations. Here, it is of secondary importance whether the distribution took place based on the individual profit expectation g^{ep}_i or on the weighted profit expectation g^{epd}, because it could be shown that the distributed profit is the same in each case.

However, a profit G could be realised which exceeds the distributed profit G^d. This requires an alternative distribution approach. The suggested standardisation parameter is calculated by proportioning the total profit G and the profit expectation-dependent profit share G^P that has already been distributed, cf. equation (6):

$$\gamma = \frac{G}{G^P} \qquad (6)$$

Finally, the profit g^p_i, that has already been distributed, is multiplied with γ for calculating the individual profit share of an enterprise g_i, cf. equation (7).

$$g_i = \gamma \cdot g^p_i \qquad (7)$$

When calculating the model using concrete numbers, it strikes that the profit share of an enterprise of the complete profit corresponds to the value adding-share of an enterprise of the entire value adding-process.

3.2   Distribution by means of a fixed and a variable profit share

A further distribution variant results by the inclusion of fixed and variable profit shares in addition to the profit expectation-dependent profit share. This approach can again be applied for positive as well as negative remaining profits. The distribution of that remaining non-distributed profit G^{ur}, which was calculated using equation (4), is made subsequently by a fixed and a variable profit share. Thus, it is valid as follows for the fixed profit share:

$$g_i^{fix} = \alpha \cdot \frac{G^{ur}}{n} \qquad (8)$$

G^{ur} hereby is divided by the number n of active enterprises of the network and multiplied by the distribution parameter α which weights the fixed share. The remaining profit share is calculated as follows:

$$g_i^{var} = (1-\alpha) \cdot G^{ur} \cdot \frac{w_i}{W} \qquad (9)$$

By applying those equations, a distribution of the profit G to the enterprises that is based on three components is realised. The calculation of the complete profit share g_i of an enterprise results by summing up the profit expectation-dependent profit share $g^p{}_i$, the fixed profit share $g^{fix}{}_i$ and the variable profit share $g^{var}{}_i$ as equation (10) illustrates:

$$g_i = g_i^p + g_i^{fix} + g_i^{var} \qquad (10)$$

It becomes clear that this model applies a distribution parameter α. Several possibilities are imaginable for determining α (Jähn, 2005). That parameter is calculated as a share of the enterprise-related fixed share of the value adding-process. Thereby, it seems to be probable that, after the distribution, the complete profit G still has not been distributed. In that case the standardisation parameter is applied again.

Because on the one hand, the performance-oriented profit distribution is favoured, but on the other hand enterprise with a small value-adding share w_i should not be disfavoured, the profit distribution based on three components and using a variable distribution parameter α_i is recommended in case the numbers are similar.

3.3 Interim Conclusion

The necessity of taking remaining profits into consideration predominantly arises when the offer price and the sales price (and thus offer profit and sales profit) do not correspond. It has to be remarked that the application of α is only obligatory in the second model. In principle, several α could be applied in this connection. Our example, however, is restricted to the application of an individualised distribution parameter. All the further models render α dispensable – a fact that is absolutely desirable because the (only) consideration of the enterprise-related profit expectation $g^e{}_i$ promises a higher rate of being accepted by end-consumers. However this option will increase the complexity of the process.

4 THREE-COMPONENT-APPROACH WITH WEIGHTINGS

4.1 Fundamentals

So far it has been shown that the profit G realised within a value-adding-process can be distributed to the enterprises within a network according to the enterprise-related profit expectations – no matter if weighted or not – in case this amount corresponds to the offer profit G^{offer} or even exceeds it. From that perspective, a distribution with regard to value-adding-dependent and value-adding-independent shares can be neglected. However, because it is aimed at a distribution that is based on several parameters, an alternative modelling, which meets this requirement, will be introduced in the following. Thereby the distributions are made according to the stated profit expectations G^e_i as well as to the number n of participating enterprises in the network and the value-adding-share of an enterprise w_i.

4.2   4.2 Selection of Weightings

Here, weightings v_j for the three components (distribution parameters) are introduced. The determination of the weightings can be made based on established procedures such as the trade-off-procedure (Eisenführ, 2005). According to their relevance, the distribution parameters are given a weighting. The sum of all the weights has to be 1 for standardisation reasons.

The (partial) distributable profit share that belongs to every component can be calculated by multiplying the profit, which must be distributed, G with the corresponding weighting. After that, the several components are treated separately before finally the three calculated partial profit shares are summed up to the complete profit g_i that an enterprise is entitled to. In the following, the single procedures are dealt with.

4.3   Modelling

By multiplying the weight v_1 with the profit G, that can be distributed, the profit share G^{Pe}, that is possible according to the individual profit expectation, can be calculated using equation (11):

$$G^{Pe} = v_1 \cdot G \qquad (11)$$

This calculated value for G^{Pe} is compared to the value for the sum of the profit expectations of the enterprises G^e. Thereby, it is not important whether the pure profit expectation of the enterprises in per cent g^{ep} or the average (weighted) profit expectation in per cent g^{epd} are used for the calculation. The paragraphs 2.1 and 2.2 already illustrated that the same value for G^e results in both cases.

The ascertainment of the value comparison can lead to different alternatives of acting. In case the two values do not correspond to each other, which should be the rule, it has to be cleared up whether the calculatorily possible profit share G^{Pe} or the sum of the profit expectations G^e are used as the basis of the further calculations. Due to the fact that the least value has been assumed as liable in the previous approaches, that means it was always assumed that the enterprises receive their expected profit (if the profit is sufficient), it is now assumed that only the calculatorily possible profit share G^{Pe} is distributed.

This results in the necessity to aim at an adaptation if the two values G^{Pe} and G^e do not correspond. Therefore, the standardisation parameter γ is applied again. Thereby, it is valid that G^{Pe} and G^e are proportioned according to the following equation (12):

$$\gamma = \frac{G^{Pe}}{G^e} \tag{12}$$

The value for γ calculated thereby is subsequently multiplied with the corresponding absolute profit expectations of the enterprises g^e_i. As a result, the (corrected) profit expectation-dependent profit share can be calculated for every enterprise. It is valid:

$$g^p_i = \gamma \cdot g^e_i \tag{13}$$

If all the individual profit expectation-dependent profit shares g^p_i are summed up (as the first component), the complete profit expectation-dependent profit share needs to result according to the weighting G^{Pe}. For this interdependency confer equation (14):

$$\sum g^p_i = G^{Pe} \tag{14}$$

Those coherences can be merged to one single equation as described in the following. If the term from equation (11) is put into the equation (12) for G^{Pe} and this is again put into equation (13) for γ, the following equation (15) for the calculation of the profit share-dependent profit share of an enterprise results for a specific weighting of the three components:

$$g^p_i = v_1 \cdot G \cdot \frac{g^e_i}{G^e} \tag{15}$$

A further detailing of the components in the numerator of the fraction is not necessary because they need to be calculated in advance in order to be able to calculate G^e. Thereby, the calculation rules of paragraph 2.2 are applied.

In the following, the fixed profit share g^{fix}_i that is dependent on the number of the enterprises participating in the network is considered as a further component. According to equation (8) it is valid:

$$g^{fix}_i = v_2 \cdot \frac{G}{n} \tag{16}$$

By multiplying the corresponding weighting v_2 with the profit G, that can be distributed, the partial profit is ascertained which can be distributed within the scope of the second component n (number of totally engaged enterprises in the value-adding network).

Finally, the share of the net value-adding-process of one enterprise in the complete value adding-process has to be considered as a third component. Thereby, it can again be traced back to the already applied equation (9) which only needs to be slightly modified. It is valid:

$$g^{var}_i = v_3 \cdot G \cdot \frac{w_i}{W} \tag{17}$$

The profit, that can be distributed, G is multiplied with the corresponding weighting v_3 as well as the corresponding value-adding share of an enterprise w_i in the complete value-adding-process of the network W.

4.4 Aggregation of the Components

After having considered the single components, it presents itself to develop an equation which allows the calculation of a enterprise-specific profit share g_i based on pre-defined initial parameters. Therefore, equation (18) can serve as the basis. Thus, it is valid as follows for the combination of the equations (15) until (17):

$$g_i = v_1 \cdot G \cdot \frac{g_i^e}{G^e} + v_2 \cdot \frac{G}{n} + v_3 \cdot G \cdot \frac{w_i}{W} \qquad (18)$$

Thereby, the required initial parameters are: the three weightings v_1, v_2 and v_3, the realised profit G that can be distributed, the profit expectations of the enterprises in per cent g_i^{ep} as well as the net value-adding of the enterprises w_i.

The gross value-adding W can again be calculated by summing up from the individual net value-addings w_i of the enterprises. The profit expectation of an enterprise in per cent g_i^{ep} allows the calculation of the total amount of the profit expectation of an enterprise by multiplying that value with the net value-adding w_i. If those values are summed up, the sum of the individual profit expectations of the enterprises G^e results.

Based on equation (18), a simplified equation for the calculation of individual profit shares of the enterprises of a network can be developed by factoring out G and converting the equation. This leads to equation (19):

$$g_i = G \cdot \left(\frac{v_1 \cdot g_i^e}{G^e} + \frac{v_2}{n} + \frac{v_3 \cdot w_i}{W} \right) \qquad (19)$$

It becomes clear that only the individual profit expectation g_i^e (or g_i^{ep}) as well as the individual value-adding w_i need to be available as enterprise-specific influence parameters for the model. This makes allowance for the claim for transparency.

5 CONCLUSION

In this contribution different approaches for the distribution of profit shares under consideration of collaborative network structures are introduced. These models are applicable for the information-technically implementation into highly automated operator concepts for enterprise networks or virtual enterprises because especially the profits can be regarded as a motivation basis for the contractual performance of the network participants. Thereby it has to be considered that the striving for individual maximisation of utility and the tendency to maximise the utility of the entire networks are concurring targets which must be harmonised in the context of the New Institutional Economics.

6 REFERENCES

1. Eisenführ F. Rationales Entscheiden. 4. Auflage. Berlin, Heidelberg, New York: Springer, 2003.
2. Fromen B. Faire Aufteilung in Unternehmensnetzwerken. Wiesbaden: DUV, 2004.
3. Furubotn EG, Richter, R. Institutions and Economic Theory: The Contribution of the New Institutional Economics. 2nd ed. Ann Arbor: University of Michigan Press, 2005.
4. Jähn H, Fischer M, Zimmermann M. An Approach for the Ascertainment of Profit Shares for Network Participants. In Collaborative Networks and their breeding Environments. Camarinha-Matos L.M. et al., eds. New York: Springer, 2005; 257-264.
5. Sucky E. Koordination in Supply Chains – Spieltheoretische Ansätze zur Ermittlung integrierter Bestell- und Produktionspolitiken. Wiesbaden: DUV, 2004.

36

AN ESTIMATION MODEL FOR BUSINESS BENEFITS IN HORIZONTAL COLLABORATIVE NETWORKS

Grégory Piot, Michel Pouly, Naoufel Cheikhrouhou and Rémy Glardon

Ecole Polytechnique Fédérale de Lausanne (EPFL)
Laboratory for production management and processes, Station 9, 1015 Lausanne,
SWITZERLAND
gregory.piot@epfl.ch, michel.pouly@epfl.ch,
naoufel.cheikhrouhou@epfl.ch, remy.glardon@epfl.ch

Nowadays, the advantages of virtual enterprises and collaborative networks are well known by scientists and professional communities. Despite the advantages, only a few networks continue running businesses after stopping the governmental subsides. One of the reasons is the lack of a model that evaluates the benefit from the firm's point of view. The objective of this work is to develop a model that estimates the business benefits in horizontal collaborative networks. We propose a method for evaluating the benefits for a firm to be enrolled in a collaborative network. This method can also be extended to the selection of partner. The approach is based on a combination of a product realisation graph and core competencies model.

1   INTRODUCTION

Several works have been carried out for the identification of the advantages of taking part in virtual enterprises and collaborative networks (Varamäki E. 2006). Many of them have focused more on the performance evolution than on the financial business aspects. The current estimation models then focus more on the End User performances and none of them really estimates the benefits from firms' point of view. This is even true in the case of horizontal (H) collaborative networks, for which this work is dedicated.

Aiming to build and to maintain Virtual Organisations (VO), we develop an estimation model for business benefits in horizontal collaborative networks. This paper gives first an overview of the current modelling techniques and proposes in a second step a new approach for estimating the benefits for a firm considering its involvement in a new opportunity for the H VO. The developed model is simple and can also be used for partners' selection during the set up of a new VO.

The benefit model might help in strengthening the mechanism of trust building among the organisations and in focusing on some common objectives.

2   MODELLING BUSINESS ACTIVITIES AND PERFORMANCE EVALUATION IN COLLABORATIVE NETWORKS

The previous developed models were focused on "Vertical networks" or "Hub and spoke networks" (Katzy, 2003). Few of them were oriented on "Horizontal networks" due to their complex dynamics. However, this kind of network exists and there is

Piot, G., Pouly, M., Cheikhrouhou, N., Glardon, R., 2007, in IFIP International Federation for Information Processing, Volume 243, Establishing the Foundation of Collaborative Networks; eds. Camarinha-Matos, L., Afsarmanesh, H., Novais, P., Analide, C.; (Boston: Springer), pp. 345–352.

a need for benefit estimation model in order to estimate the best opportunity configuration based on cost optimisation.

In the literature, there are two orientations of research; one is focused on the management of a network and the other one is more oriented on how to set up the virtual enterprises through the breeding environment. In the first orientation, the developed models measure the past performance of the network, based on balanced scorecard. These works focus mainly on the End User (Bourgault et al. 2002)

Camarinha-Matos and Abreu (2005) build up a different model for the quantification of advantages in a horizontal network. This model is based on benefits that can be self benefit, received benefit or contributed benefit. This decomposition allows a better understanding of how the network runs and which firm is the most beneficiary. On the other side, it is quite hard to measure these different benefits due to information privacy.

The aim of the second orientation of research is to find a predictive method for evaluating the performance of different alternatives. Some authors have defined different modelling approaches for designing value chain in Virtual Enterprises. Kim et al. (2003) consider an approach that combines enterprises modelling and simulation modelling in "Hub and spoke networks". A similar approach can be found in a model based on SCOR approach where particular key performance indicators are proposed (Seifert and Eschenbaecher 2004). Confessore et al. (2006) develop a model for supporting the potential decision of getting new business opportunity. This model is based on competencies and activities. Even if this approach is interesting, it is not appropriate for H networks. In a H network, the core competencies are almost the same for all firms and the selection of different alternatives can not only be evaluated from this point of view. Despite that, the idea of core competencies will be used in our model. Chu X. et al. (2002) develops a model that permits to set up a preferential alternative; this model is based on Group Technology. The drawback of this method is the long audit time to determine what kind of component companies can produce. This approach is more oriented for assembly business and takes a lot of resources to estimate the advantages to set up a VE. Furthermore, the iterative process composed of a Product requirement Analysis, Product Function Design, Product Layout, Partner type Synthesis and partner Instance synthesis will be partly integrated in our model.

Wu and Sun (2002) have developed a different approach based on activity grouping to identify the core competencies needed to develop a new product. They identified two types of activities for grouping activities: key activities that require core competencies, and non-key activities that can be performed by all the members of a breeding environment.

In this review, we draw the conclusion that none of the developed models permit to estimate the benefits of being part of a horizontal collaborative networks in terms of financial optimisation.

3   PROPOSED MODEL FOR BUSINESS BENEFITS ESTIMATION

The proposed model is based on four different phases (see Figure 1). The first phase consists of the estimation of the opportunities that can be generated by the network; the second phase is the construction of product realisation graph for each opportunity and its related operations. The third part is the research of the best combination of firms to realize a customer's order. The last one is a summation of earnings for all members of the networks.

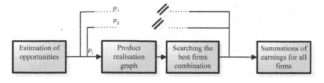

Figure 1: General model

3.1   Estimation of opportunities

There are three kinds of opportunities:

- Product introduction in new markets
- Increasing sales in actual markets for a given product
- Introduction of new product

These opportunities can be generated through the network which brings some advantages like the increase of renown, know-how, flexibility, production capacity and so on. For each opportunity, related to a product, we determine a production volume.

3.2   Product realisation graph

The product realisation graph is built for each opportunity. This graph is composed by activities, arcs and linguistic variables (Wu and Sun 2002). An arc represents the antecedence link between two activities. There are two different kinds of activities, the key activities and the non-key activities. A key activity is an activity that requires a core competency to be performed. A non-key activity is activity that doesn't require any core competency and that can be performed by every member of the considered network. To take into account the importance that two consecutive activities have to be performed by the same company, we introduce for each arc a linguistic variable. This latter can take one of the five values: {none, weak, medium, strong, absolute}. The weak term means that two consecutive activities can be easily performed by two different companies. The strong term mean that the link between the two activities is strong and it will be difficult to perform them by two different companies. The absolute mean that it will be impossible to perform the two activities by two different companies.

In order to reduce the complexity of the problem, we merge non-key activities to key activities. The merging mechanism is the following (see Figure 2):

1. First, we merge all non-key activities (represented by circles), which are at the beginning or at the end of the product realisation graph with the next, respectively following or previous, key activities (represented by ellipses).
2. In the second step, we merge all the remaining non-key activities. For merging activities, we use the value of the linguistic variable of each arc. We merge non-key activity which has the weakest link and so on.

We stop to merge activities when all the remaining activities are the key activities. This graph is called simplified product graph.

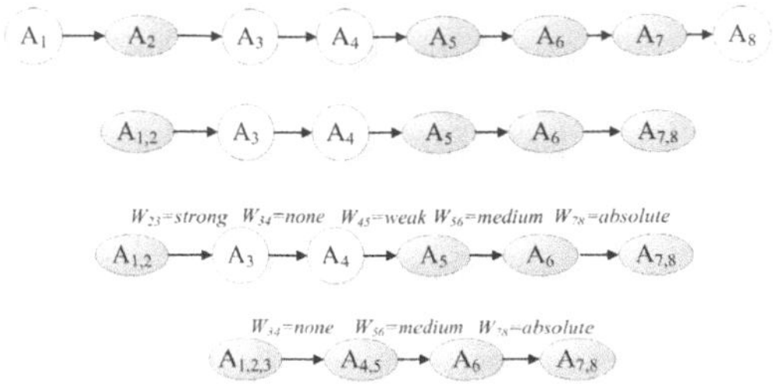

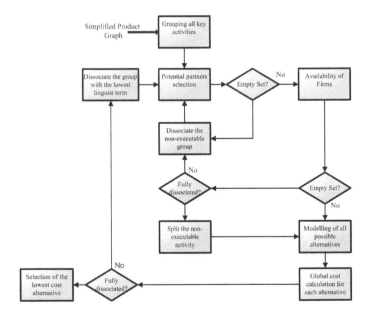

Figure 2: Product realisation graph

3.3   Searching the best firms combination

The third part of the model is the search of the best firms' combination to realize a customer's order. The Input for this part of the model is the Simplified Product Graph and the output will be the best alternative and its global cost (see Figure 3).

Figure 3: search of the best configuration

The first step consists of grouping all the activities together. This step means that all the activities will be performed by one firm. The second step is the potential partner selection based on core competencies of each firm. These core competencies have to match the competencies needed to perform an activity.

Among this set, we identify firms which have the availability to perform the activity or the group of activities. Among this sub set, we set all the possible alternatives to realise the product. For each alternative, we estimate the global cost of the full process. If during one of these previous steps an empty set is detected, the model dissociates the group of activities, which are unsolved. If there is still no solution when a model is totally dissociated, the unsolved activity is split in order to perform this activity in two different companies. Once we have obtained the global costs of alternatives, the model dissociates the group of activities with the lowest linguist term. This iterative procedure stops once we obtain the simplified product graph. Among all alternatives, we consider the best alternative as the alternative with lowest global cost. The calculation of the global price is the sum of the prices of realization of the activities or groups of activities and some additional costs which depend on the network.

3.3.1 Realisation costs of the activities and groups of activities

The cost of realisation of an activity is firm and volume dependent.

$$
\begin{aligned}
TRP(alt_y) &= tr\left(\mathbf{Pr} \cdot (\mathbf{A}^y)^T\right) \\
&= tr\left(
\begin{bmatrix}
Pr_{F1A1} & Pr_{F1A2} & \cdots & Pr_{F1Aa} \\
Pr_{F2A1} & Pr_{F2A2} & \cdots & Pr_{F2Aa} \\
\cdots & \cdots & \cdots & \cdots \\
Pr_{FnA1} & Pr_{FnA2} & \cdots & Pr_{F_nAa}
\end{bmatrix}
\cdot
\begin{bmatrix}
A^y_{F1A1} & A^y_{F1A2} & \cdots & A^y_{F1Aa} \\
A^y_{F2A1} & A^y_{F2A2} & \cdots & A^y_{F2Aa} \\
\cdots & \cdots & \cdots & \cdots \\
A^y_{FnA1} & A^y_{FnA2} & \cdots & A^y_{FnAa}
\end{bmatrix}^T
\right)
\end{aligned}
\tag{1}
$$

Where:

TRP	Total realisation price for the alternative y alt_y	$\mathbf{A}^y$	Matrix of distribution activities among partners
Pr	Matrix of realisation prices	tr	Trace of a matrix
n	number of partners	a	number of activity groups

The matrix $\mathbf{A}^y$ is a repartition of the activities among partners. The value of a component normally is 0 or 1, but if an activity is split among partners, the component A^y_{FxAz} can be of any value between 0 and 1. The only condition is that the sum of a column is equal to one.

3.3.2 Additional costs

The additional costs are the transport costs, administrative costs and knowledge transfer costs. The transport costs are dependent of the two partners involved; we assume that is time constant. The administrative costs depend on the trust between the two partners enrolled; this parameter can change with the evolution of the network. The knowledge transfer costs depend on the stage of activities, and we assume that these costs do not depend on the partner involved. All of these parameters are represented by some matrices in the aim of computation resolution (Piot 2007).

$$AC(\text{alt}_y) = \text{tr}\left(\mathbf{TpC} \cdot (\mathbf{T}^y)^T\right) + \left(\overrightarrow{KC} \cdot \vec{t}\right) + \alpha \cdot \text{tr}\left(\mathbf{Trust} \cdot (\mathbf{T}^y)^T\right)$$

$$= \text{tr}\left(\begin{bmatrix} 0 & TpC_{F1F2} & \dots & TpC_{F1Fn} \\ \text{Sym.} & 0 & \dots & TpC_{F1Fn} \\ \text{Sym.} & \text{Sym.} & \dots & \dots \\ \text{Sym.} & \text{Sym.} & \text{Sym.} & 0 \end{bmatrix} \cdot \begin{bmatrix} T^y_{F1F1} & T^y_{F1F2} & \dots & T^y_{F1Fn} \\ T^y_{F2F1} & T^y_{F2F2} & \dots & T^y_{F2Fn} \\ \dots & \dots & \dots & \dots \\ T^y_{FnF1} & T^y_{FnF2} & \dots & T^y_{FnFn} \end{bmatrix}^T\right)$$

$$+ \left(\left(KC(A_1 A_2); KC(A_2 A_3); \dots; KC(A_{a-1} A_a)\right) \cdot \left(t(A_1 A_2); t(A_2 A_3); \dots; t(A_{a-1} A_a)\right)\right)^T \quad (2)$$

$$+ \alpha \cdot \text{tr}\left(\begin{bmatrix} 0 & \text{Trust}_{F1F2} & \dots & \text{Trust}_{F1Fn} \\ \text{Trust}_{F2F1} & 0 & \dots & \text{Trust}_{F2Fn} \\ \dots & \dots & \dots & \dots \\ \text{Trust}_{FnF1} & \text{Trust}_{FnF2} & \dots & 0 \end{bmatrix} \cdot \begin{bmatrix} T^y_{F1F1} & T^y_{F1F2} & \dots & T^y_{F1Fn} \\ T^y_{F2F1} & T^y_{F2F2} & \dots & T^y_{F2Fn} \\ \dots & \dots & \dots & \dots \\ T^y_{FnF1} & T^y_{FnF2} & \dots & T^y_{FnFn} \end{bmatrix}^T\right)$$

where:

AC	Additional costs	$\vec{t}$	Vector of activities separation
TpC	Transport costs	α	Value of the average
T	Matrix of interaction between		administrative cost for an invoice
	partners	**Trust**	Matrix of trust among partners
$\overrightarrow{KC}$	Vector of knowledge transfer costs		

The interaction matrix changes for each alternative. The range of variation of a component T^y_{FxFy} is between 0 and (a-1). Each component of the trust matrix varies between 0 and 1.

4   APPLICATION OF THE MODEL TO VIRTUAL SWISS MANUFACTURING NETWORK

The model is applied to the "Virtuelle Fabrik Nordwestschweiz-Mittelland" (Göckel M. 2001). The concept of this network was established by the 'Institut für Technologie-management' of the University of St-Gall. The network was built in 1997 and now is containing 19 firms (Fi, i=1…19) and 2 public institutes. The aim of this network is to create high-value product, which integrate the following competencies: design, engineering, manufacturing, assembly, control and commissioning. Most of the companies are manufacturers, some of them are in the engineering field and a few of them are consulting partners.

Few products have been developed up to now, namely a-turning assembly table, a dustbin, and some others. We have done an application of our model for the dustbin product (Litter Shark). The dustbins are developed by a partnership with some firms of the network. Without this partnership, none of the firm would have been involved in this opportunity. The requirement of the client is to have only one interlocutor. Actually, this product is one of the leader products developed by the network, and its worldwide commercialisation is bringing some new profits.

5   RESULTS

We apply our model to the dustbin product. The first step is to build the product realisation graph. To summarize the development only the simplified product graph will be displayed. It is composed of fives key activities, in order, design (A1), engineering (A2), sheet metal working (A3), painting (A4), and assembly (A5). The obtained simplified product graph is represented in figure 4.

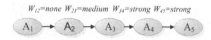

Figure 4 - Dustbin simplified product graph

The first iteration of the model evaluate that none of the firm can perform all the five activities. The second iteration, which is based on a graph composed by the activity A1 and a group G1 of the four remaining activities, evaluate that one alternative (alt1) is possible. The alternative alt1 enrol two firms, Quadesign Partner AG (F14) for the activity A_1 and Brüco Swiss AG (F_5) for the group G_1. The global costs of this alternative is estimated to be 71.7 kCHF (Table 2)

The third iteration, which is based on a graph composed by the activities A1, A2 and a group of activities G2 (A_3, A_4, A_5), evaluates four possible alternatives (Table 1 which gives the firms combinations for each alternative). In this case, there are no transport costs because there is no physical product between activities A_1, A_2 and G_2. The global costs of alternatives, estimated using equations 1 and 2 are shown in the Table 2.

Table 1 – Alternatives Table

Activity	Firm	Alt$_i$ 2	3	4	5
A_1	F_{14}	1	1	1	1
A_2	F_2	1	0	0	0
	F_5	0	1	0	0
	F_6	0	0	1	0
	F_{11}	0	0	0	1
G_2	F_5	1	1	1	1

Table 2 - Global costs of all alternatives

Alternative	Global cost
Alt$_1$ =Alt$_3$	**71.7 kCHF**
Alt$_2$	**68.8 kCHF**
Alt$_4$	**74 kCHF**
Alt$_5$	**78.3 kCHF**

The results of further iterations are not interesting enough to be displayed and the global costs of these alternatives are more expensive due to the knowledge transfer costs and the administrative costs. As we see, the alternatives alt$_1$ and alt$_3$ are the same, only two firms are involved.
The best alternative for the model is the alternative Alt$_2$, which involves the firms (F14, F2 and F5). If we compare the results to the reality only two firms (F_{14} and F_5) were involved in realizing the product. The reality matched the alternative Alt$_1$, which is the second best alternative for our model. The reasons might be that the network did not look for the optimal alternative; the additional costs were underestimated or personal reasons for the firm F_2. Furthermore this solution is still acceptable and we arrive with few resources to estimate the benefit for the firm to be part of one

network. The application and the result analysis have been approved and validated by the network. The model can be used without generating privacy or autonomy problems among the future network's participants.

6 CONCLUSION AND FUTURE WORK

An estimation model for business benefits in horizontal collaborative networks is presented and developed. As a conclusion, the selection can not be only based on core competencies. Other criteria are then considered as the global price or the availability. In the future, our goal will be to continue the development of the model by introducing the delays and the risks related to the alternatives. Further test for managing opportunities on the operation level could be done using the model.

7 ACKNOWLEDGEMENT

The authors thanks the valuable contribution of their partners Swiss Microtech, especially Mr Beeler, and the Virtuelle Fabrik, especially Mr Plüss as well as the Commission for Technology and Innovation of the Swiss Federal Government, which funded this research.

8 REFERENCES

1. Bourgault M. , Lefebvre E., Lefebvre L.A., Pellerin R., Elia E.; Discussion of metrics for distributed project management: Preliminary Findings; Proceedings of the 35th Hawaii International Conference on System Sciences; 2002
2. Camarinha-Matos L.M , Abreu A.; Performance indicators based on collaboration benefits; PROVE 2005; Lisbon; 2005
3. Chu X., Tso S.K., Zhang W.J. and Li Q.; Partnership synthesis for Virtual Enterprises; Advanced Manufacturing Technology; London; 2002
4. Confessore G.,Liotta G., Rismondo S.; A new model for achieving value added goals in a collaborative industrial scenario; Network-centric collaboration supporting frameworks, Springer; Helsinki; 2006
5. Göckel M.; La Fabrique virtuelle; http://fr.experience-online.ch/ cases/experience.nsf/summary/ vituelle_fabrik_f; 2001
6. Katzy B.R., Löh H.; Virtual Entreprise Research State of the Art and Way Forward; 2003
7. Kim C.-H., Son Y.-J., Kim T.-Y., Kim K.; A modeling approach for designing value chain of VE; Virtual Enterprises and collaborative Networks, Kluwer Academic Publishers; Toulouse; 2004
8. Piot G.; Master thesis, Développement d'un modèle et d'une métrique pour des réseaux collaboratifs d'entreprises, Laboratory for production management and processes EPFL; 2006
9. Seifert M., Eschenbaecher J.; Predictive performance measurement in virtual organisations-Emerging solutions for future manufacturing systems; Springer; 2004
10. Varamäki E.; Operationalising A Network-level Performance Measurement System for SME Networks; Tampere; 2006
11. Wu N., Sun J.; Grouping the activities in virtual enterprise paradigm; Production Planning & Control Vol 13, N°4, P407-415; 2002

37

EXAMINING THE ANTECEDENTS TO INNOVATION IN ELECTRONIC NETWORKS OF PRACTICE

Eoin Whelan, Brian Donnellan and Gabriel Costello

National University of Ireland, Galway
IRELAND
Email: [eoin.whelan, brian.donnellan, gabriel.costello]@nuigalway.ie

The way in which firms innovate ideas and bring them to market is undergoing a fundamental change. Useful knowledge is increasingly dispersed outside the firm's boundaries and the exceptionally fast time to market for many products and services suggest that some very different organising principles for innovation are needed. These developments have led to an increased interest in the electronic network of practice concept to facilitate innovation. This paper argues that innovative behaviour in electronic networks of practice is determined by three interacting systems – individual motivations, network communication structure, and the social context of the network. The theoretical position of the interactive process theory of innovation is used to support this claim.

1   INTRODUCTION

The current environment for organisations is one that is characterised by uncertainty and continuous change. This rapid and dynamic pace of change is forcing organisations that were accustomed to structure and routine to become ones that must improvise solutions quickly and correctly. To respond to this changed environment, organisations are moving away from the structures of the past that are based on hierarchies, discrete groups and teams and moving towards those based on more fluid and emergent organisational forms such as networks and communities. Employees are no longer constrained by the role of formally prescribed relationships in organisations. More work is being done through informal networks and "supporting collaboration and work in these informal networks is increasingly important for organisations competing on knowledge and an ability to innovate and adapt" (Cross and Parker 2004). With the global penetration of internet technologies, individuals may now cross organisational boundaries to exchange their knowledge

Whelan, E., Donnellan, B., Costello, G., 2007, in IFIP International Federation for Information Processing, Volume 243, Establishing the Foundation of Collaborative Networks; eds. Camarinha-Matos, L., Afsarmanesh, H., Novais, P., Analide, C.; (Boston: Springer), pp. 353–360.

with others in various networks of practice regardless of time and space. These developments have led to an increased interest in the electronic network of practice (ENoP) concept to facilitate innovation. ENoPs are computer mediated discussion forums focused on problems of practice that enable individuals to exchange advice and ideas with others based on common interests (Wasko and Faraj 2005). In essence, ENoPs are inter-organisational collaborative knowledge management systems. Tuomi (2002) suggests that the network of relationships that develop in an ENoP, the inner motivation that drives them and the knowledge they produce, lead to the creation of an environment that is rich in creativity and innovation.

Even though ENoPs are becoming an integral facilitator of new knowledge creation, we still have a limited understanding of the antecedents to innovative behaviour. All indications are that any organisation expecting to compete on knowledge and innovation will have to exploit collaborative IT systems. Technologies such as Web 2.0 are dramatically reducing the costs of sourcing external knowledge for the average knowledge worker. In their recent book 'Wikinomics', Tapscott and Williams (2006) argue that we are only beginning to see how the internet can be used for mass collaboration and gathering innovative knowledge. With the internet being so engrained in the everyday lives of today's youth, we will really only see these advances come to fruition when this 'Net generation' moves into industry. Thus, it is vital that we now begin to understand what drives innovation in ICT supported communities. This paper asks the question - What are the antecedents to innovative behaviour in ENoPs? The theoretical positions of the interactive process theory of innovation are used to examine this question. This paper presents a conceptual model which will be tested by gathering data from the R&D labs of three Irish high technology companies.

2   THE ANTECEDENTS TO INNOVATION

To advance innovation we need to understand the antecedents to innovative behaviour. The causes of innovation in organisations have been a major theme in studies of innovation. Three theoretical perspectives as identified by Slappendel (1996) are used to map out this literature on innovation in organisations (Table 1). These are referred to as the individualist perspective, the structuralist perspective, and the interactive process perspective. The earliest innovation studies assumed that single individuals are the main source of innovation in organisations. In this individualist perspective, their actions are not seen to be constrained by external factors; instead, they are understood to be self-directing agents who are guided by the goals they have set. In this view, individuals are rational and make decisions in order to maximise value or utility. This 'trait' approach assumes that some individuals have personal qualities which predispose them to innovative behaviour. Consequently, individual characteristics, such as age, sex, educational level, values, personality, creativity and cognitive style, define the antecedents for innovation. Likewise, concepts such as leader, champion, entrepreneur, innovator and change agent, are of central interest in this perspective.

Table 1 - Main Features of the Three Perspectives (Adapted from Slappendel 1996)

	Individualist	Structuralist	Interactive Process
Basic assumptions	Individuals cause innovation	Innovation Determined by Structural characteristics	Innovation produced by the interaction of structural influences and the actions of individuals
Conceptualisation of an innovation	Static and objectively defined objects and practices	Static and Objectively defined Objects or practices	Innovations are subject to reinvention and reconfiguration. Innovations are perceived.
Conceptualisation of the innovation Process	Simple linear, with Focus on the adoption stage	Simple linear, with focus on the adoption stage	Complex process
Core concepts	Champions Leaders Entrepreneur	Environment Size Complexity Differentiation Formalisation Centralisation Strategic type	Shocks Proliferation Innovative capability Context
Research methodology	Cross-sectional Survey	Cross-sectional survey	Case studies Case histories
Main authors	Rogers March and Simon	Zaltman et al.	Van de Ven et al.

The structuralist perspective assumes that innovation is determined by objective organisational characteristics. Of all the potential influences on innovativeness, organisational variables have been the most widely studied, and some authors have pointed to their primary importance as determinants of innovation (Kimberly and Evanisko 1981; Damanpour 1991). Researchers within this perspective have hypothesised on the relationships between innovation and a range of organisation structural variables including size, complexity, differentiation, professionalism, formalisation and centralisation. Slappendel (1996) believes that the advantage of this approach is that it overcomes the narrow concern with the organisation itself by drawing attention to the interrelation of organisation and environment. However, the disadvantage is that this view is too objective - it treats organisational features as objective realities whose factual character is unchallenged. Furthermore, the relationships between organisational variables and innovation are complex and often contradictory.

The individualist and structuralist perspectives (when applied in their purist forms) have major disadvantages in that they place undue emphasis on particular causal factors and so may lead to errors of attribution (Slappendel 1996). These concerns have resulted in the emergence of a third perspective on innovation in organisations, referred to as the interactive process perspective. This perspective views innovation as a dynamic, continuous phenomenon of change over time in which various factors have a mutual impact on each other. The individualist and the structuralist perspectives have seen innovation as *either* being caused by individual actions *or* by objective structures. In the *interactive process* perspective, the actions of innovative individuals cannot be divorced from either the activities of other individuals or from the organisational structures within which they operate. Thus, innovation is viewed as the result of the continuous *interrelation* of individual actions and structural influences.

3   A CONCEPTUAL MODEL

Theories of innovation generally assume that either financial incentives or need based incentives drive innovative activity. ENoPs are exemplars of a fundamentally different organisational model for innovation. Open source software communities are one example of an ENoP and these communities have been the subject of much scholarly attention in recent times. Open source projects such as Linux, Apache and Gnome have achieved remarkable success and have on occasion, displaced commercially produced software. This model of innovation is based on the open, voluntary, and collaborative efforts of users – a term that describes enthusiast, tinkers, amateurs, everyday people, and even firms that derive benefit from a product or service by using it (Shah 2006). This model extends well beyond the domain of software. ENoPs have been influential in fields as diverse as astronomy (Ferris 2002), law (Wasko and Faraj 2005), IT consultancy (Teigland and Wasko 2003), public health (Vaast 2003) and sports products (Franke and Shah 2005) thus making the study of ENoPs of prime interest for researchers and practitioners.

This research is firmly located within the 'interactive process' perspective of innovation which advocates that innovation is produced by the interaction of structural influences and the actions of individuals (Slappendel 1996). By combining the NoP, knowledge management and organisational innovation literatures, this research proposes that innovative behaviour in ENoPs is the outcome of three constructs; individual motivations, network communication structure, and the social context within which the network operates (Figure 1). The arrows between the three constructs indicate that these variables interact together to influence innovative behaviour. It is believed that this research is the first to study ENoPs through the interactive process lens. Future research will involve testing the proposed relationships illustrated in the model.

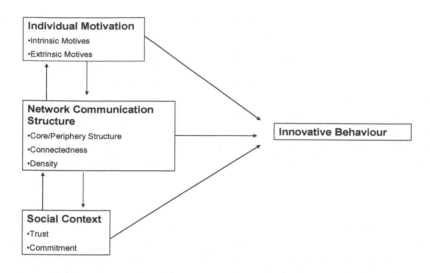

Figure 1 - A Conceptual Model

3.1 Individual Motivations

According to Monge, Cozzens et al. (1992) "The effectiveness of any system for generating innovations depends on many things, one of which is the individuals who find, invent, or propose useful innovations. In a formal organisational setting, intentional innovation requires motivated individuals". Some organisational positions, such as those in R&D groups, are defined such that individuals in these positions are expected to develop innovations. In these cases, the individuals are presumably motivated by the various rewards and punishments associated with an employees expected performance; for example, job security, wages, promotions etc. What motivates individuals to contribute to voluntary communities? Previous research has found that both intrinsic and extrinsic motivations drive participation in ENoPs.

This research proposes that individual motivations to participate will have a significant relationship with innovative behaviour in ENoPs. Early empirical works have suggested a number of competing and contentious theories. Some argue that participation is driven by users desire to satisfy their own needs, career concerns, learning, status, enjoyment, creativity. Shah (2006) states that there is some evidence to support all of these motives, "However, research has yet to devise a coherent explanation for these findings, connect these motives to the social structure, and understand how differences in social structure affect participation and vice versa."

3.2 Network Communication Structure

In the field of social psychology, an important tradition of study on networks is that of social network theory. The power of social network theory stems from its difference from traditional sociological studies, which assume that it is the attributes of individual actors that matter. Social network theory produces an alternate view, where the attributes of individuals are less important than their relationships and ties with other actors within the network. It suggests that at least some properties and outcomes of a social network are a function of its complete structure and are not reducible to either an individual actor or a single link (Degenne and Forse 1999).

The structural properties of the social network help determine the networks usefulness to its individuals. When talking about the structural properties, what is meant is the impact of group communication structure on collective performance outcomes. Structural properties refer to concepts such as density, connectedness, centrality, core/periphery structure, coreness, symmetry, closeness etc. For the purposes of this study, the relationship between three structural properties (i.e. core/periphery structure, connectedness, density) and innovative behaviour will be developed.

3.3   Social Context

Previous research provides a great deal of evidence that individual behaviours are embedded in a social context, and decisions to engage in inter-personal exchange are influence by perceptions of social relations (Granovetter 1973). Social capital theories propose that people are influenced by their social and organisational context. Whether people engage in interpersonal knowledge exchange not only depends upon the individual, but also depends upon characteristics of the social context (Nahapiet and Ghoshal 1998). Therefore, this research proposes that peoples' innovative behaviour in ENoPs are determined by individual factors, network communication structure, as well as the social context of the network. An example of social capital could be the voluntary participation of the members over the lunch break to discuss various social/organisational aspects which benefits all the participants.

Following the approach of Wasko (2002), social capital is operationalised in this study through two variables; commitment and generalised trust. Mowday, Steers and Porter (1979) define organisational commitment as "the relative strength of an individual's identification with and involvement in a particular organization". Wasko (2002) extends this definition to include on-line organisations including ENoPs. Identification reflects the overlap between an individual's identity and that of the larger collective. Specifically, identification allows a party to understand, appreciate, and feel invested in what others want and need. Identification with a collective enhances concern for the collective processes and outcomes (Kramer and Tyler 1996). In addition, identification enhances the frequency of cooperation and provides a better explanation than self-interest approaches for understanding cooperative behaviour (Lewicki and Bunker 1996). Therefore, people who identify with the collective are more likely to engage in cooperative action in order to sustain the community.

4   CONCLUSION

While traditional face-to-face networks within organisations (i.e. communities of practice) have received increasing attention, we know much less about the dynamics underlying ENoPs and the electronic knowledge exchange supported by these computer networks (Teigland and Wasko 2003). A review of the literature has shown that little consideration has been paid to the drivers of innovation in electronic communities. This paper argues that innovative behaviour in ENoPs is determined by three interacting systems – individual motivations, network communication structure, and the social context of the network. Future research will involve testing this model by gathering data from the R&D labs of three high technology Irish companies. The ENoPs used to support to work of these labs will be examined. In order to determine the network communication structure of each ENoP, social network analysis (SNA) will first be conducted. SNA is a technique which maps and measures of relationships and flows between people, groups, organisations, computers or other information/knowledge processing entities. The nodes in the network are the people and groups while the links show relationships or flows between the nodes. SNA provides both a visual and a mathematical analysis of complex human systems. Following the SNA, in-depth interviews with a sample of the discussion forum participants will be conducted. The interviews will tease out how the participants' motivations, trust and commitment impact their innovative behaviour.

5   REFERENCES

1. Cross, R. and A. Parker. The Hidden Power of Social Networks. Understanding How Work Really Gets Done in Organizations. Boston, Harvard Business School Publishing. 2004.
2. Cummings, J. and R. Cross. "Structural Properties of Work Groups and their Consequences for Performance." Social Networks 25. 2003. 197-210.
3. Damanpour, F. "Organisational innovation: A meta-analysis of effects of determinants and moderators." Academy of Management Journal 34(3). 1991. 555-590.
4. Degenne, A. and M. Forse. Introducing social networks. California, Sage Publications. 1999.
5. Ferris, T. Seeing in the dark: How backyard stargazers are probing deep space and guarding earth from interplanetary Peril. New York, Simon & Schuster. 2002.
6. Franke, N. and S. Shah. "How communities support innovative activities: an exploration of assistance and sharing among end users." Research Policy 32. 2005. 157-178.
7. Granovetter, M. "The Strength of Weak Ties." American Journal of Sociology 78. 1973.
8. Kimberly, J. and M. Evanisko. "Oranizational innovation: The influence of individual, organisational, and contextual factors on hospital adoption of technological and administrative innovations." Academy of Management Journal 24(4). 1981. 689-713.
9. Kramer, R. M. and T. R. Tyler. Trust in Organizations. Thousand Oaks, CA, Sage Publications. 1996.
10. Lewicki, R. J. and B. B. Bunker. Developing and maintaining trust in work relationships. Trust in Organizations. R. M. Kramer and T. R. Tyloer. London, Sage Publications. 1996.
11. Monge, P., M. Cozzens, et al. "Communication and motivational predictors of the dynamics of organizational innovation." Organization Science 3(2). 1992. 250-274.
12. Mowday, R. T., R. M. Steers, et al. "The measurement of organizational commitment." Journal of Vocational Behavior 14. 1979. 224-247.
13. Nahapiet, J. and S. Ghoshal. "Social capital, intellectual capital, and the organizational advantage." Academy of Management Review 23(2). 1998. 242-266.
14. Roberts, J., I.-H. Hann, et al. "Understanding the motivations, participation, an performance of open source software developers: A longtudinal study of apache projects." Management Science 52(7). 2006. 984-999.
15. Schenkel, A., R. Teigland, et al. Theorizing Structural Properties of Communities of Practice: A Social Network Approach. Academy of Management Conference, Washington DC, Organisation and Management Division. 2001.

16. Shah, S. "Motivations, goverance, and the viability if hybrid forms in open source software development." Management Science 52(7). 2006. 1000-1014.
17. Slappendel, C. "Perspectives on Innovation in Organizations." Organization Studies 17(1). 1996. 107-129.
18. Tapscott, D., and A. Williams. 2006. "Wikinomics: How Mass Collaboration Changes Everthing." Portfolio Hardcover. New York.
19. Teigland, R and Wasko M. Integrating Knowledge Through Information Trading: Examining the Relationship between Boundary Spanning Communication and Individual Performance. Decision Science, 32(2). 2003. 261-287.
20. Tuomi, I. Networks of Innovation. Oxford, Oxford University Press. 2002.
21. Vaast, E. The use of intranets: The missing link between communities of practice and networks of practice. Knowledge networks; Innovation through communities of practice. P. Hildreth and C. Kimble. London, Idea Group Publishing. 2003. 216-229.
22. Wasko, M. M. Why should I share? Examing knowledge contribution in networks of practice. Faculty of the Graduate School, University of Maryland. 2002. 150.
23. Wasko, M. M. and S. Faraj. "Why should I share? Examining social capital and knowledge contribution in electronic networks of practice." MIS Quarterly 29(1). 2005. 35-57.

PART 12

PROFESSIONAL VIRTUAL COMMUNITIES

Willy Picard

Department of Information Technology
The Poznań University of Economics
ul. Mansfelda 4
60-854 Poznań, POLAND
picard@kti.ae.poznan.pl

Support for human-to-human interactions over a network is still insufficient, particularly for professional virtual communities (PVCs). Among other limitations, neither adaptation capabilities of humans, nor social aspects related to leverage are taken into account in existing models for collaboration processes in PVC. This paper presents a model for adaptive human collaboration. A key element of this model is the modeling of power during the adaptation of collaboration processes modeled as social protocols.

1   INTRODUCTION

Enterprises are constantly increasing their efforts in order to improve their business processes. A main reason for this may be the fact that enterprises are exposed to a highly competitive global market. Among the most visible actions associated with this effort towards better support for better business processes, one may distinguish the current research work concerning Web services and associated standards: high-level languages such as BPEL or WS-Coordination take the service concept one step further by providing a method of defining and supporting workflows and business processes.

However, it should be noticed that most of these actions are directed towards interoperable machine-to-machine interactions over a network. Support for *human-to-human interactions* over a network is still insufficient and more research has to be done to provide both theoretical and practical knowledge to this field.

Among various reasons for the weak support for human-to-human interactions, one may distinguish the following two reasons: first, many *social elements* are involved in the interaction among humans. An example of such a social element may be the roles played by humans during their interactions. Social elements are usually difficult to model, i.e. integrating non-verbal communication to collaboration models. There-fore, their integration to a model of interaction between humans is not easy. A second reason is the *adaptation capabilities* of humans which are not only far more advanced than adaptation capabilities of software entities, but also not taken into account in existing models for collaboration processes.

The insufficient support for human-to-human interactions over a network is a strong limitation for a wide adoption of *professional virtual communities (PVCs)*. As mentioned in (Camarinha-Matos, 2005), "professional virtual community represents

Picard, W., 2007, in IFIP International Federation for Information Processing, Volume 243, Establishing the Foundation of Collaborative Networks; eds. Camarinha-Matos, L., Afsarmanesh, H., Novais, P., Analide, C.; (Boston: Springer), pp. 363–370.

the combination of concepts of virtual community and professional community. Virtual communities are defined as social systems of networks of individuals, who use computer technologies to mediate their relationships. Professional communities provide environments for professionals to share the body of knowledge of their professions [...]". According to (Chituc, 2005), little attention has been paid to the social perspective on Collaborative Networks (CN) business environment, including obviously professional virtual communities in which social aspects are of high importance.

This paper is an attempt to provide a model for human-to-human interactions within professional virtual communities. The proposed model addresses, at least to some extent, the two characteristics of the interactions between humans. It should however been kept in mind that the results presented here are a work in progress and therefore they are not claimed to be neither sufficient nor exhaustive.

The rest of this paper is organized as follows. In section 2, the concept of *social protocol*, used to model collaboration processes, is presented. Section 3 then expands on *adaptation* of social protocols. Next, support for *power* as an important social aspect in adaptation of social protocols on PVCs is discussed. Finally, section 5 concludes this paper.

2   STRUCTURING COLLABORATION IN PVCS

Support for human-to-human collaboration in PVCs should obviously take into account the characteristics of PVCs as social environments. From an information system approach, at least two characteristics of PVCs should be distinguished: PVCs are heterogeneous and dynamic environments. Therefore, these two characteristics should be supported by a model for interactions within PVCs.

2.1   PVCs as Heterogeneous Environments

As defined by (Ekholm and Fridqvist, 1996), "a human *sociosystem* has a composition of human individuals, its structure is the social behaviour repertoire, i.e. interaction among human individuals". In professional virtual communities, the sociosystem is highly heterogeneous. The heterogeneity of PVCs exists at various levels of granularity within PVCs.

At a high level, a PVC consists usually of many different "sub-communities". Each sub-community is different from other coexisting in the same PVC sub-communities in terms of goals, intentions, knowledge, processes, members, etc. Additionally, some sub-communities may be overlapping, as they may share some members, allowing knowledge to be transfered from one sub-community to another. Other sub-communities are isolated. The lifetime of sub-communities may vary from a few hours – e.g. for short document translation – to many years – e.g. in open source development.

At a lower level, one may notice that the structure of a sub-community is usually complex and heterogeneous. The roles played by the sub-community members, their skills, their competences usually present a high level of diversity.

2.2   PVCs as Dynamic Environments

PVCs are not only heterogeneous environments, they are also usually highly dynamic. Similarly to the heterogeneity of PVCs , the dynamics of PVCs exists at various levels of granularity within PVCs.

At a high level, the set of sub-communities that the PVC consists of evolves in time: new sub-communities are created to answer new needs and opportunities, unnecessary sub-communities are dissolved, existing sub-communities changes as new members enter and leave the community, etc. The dynamics of PVCs may hardly, not to say cannot, be foreseen at design time, as changes of a given PVC are naturally related to changes in its business environment (which is usually not a deterministic system).

At a lower level, the structure of a sub-community is evolving in time: some members may have a job promotion, the skills of the members usually evolve (improve) in time. Additionally, it may be noticed that members of a given sub-community may face new situations implying the development of new solutions, new ways of collaboration, etc.

2.3   Modeling Group Interactions with Social Protocols

Support for human-to-human collaboration in PVCs should obviously take into account the characteristics of PVCs presented in the two former subsections, i.e. heterogeneity and dynamics.

A first model for group interactions within a PVC has been presented in (Picard, 2005). The proposed model is based on the concept of *social protocol*. Social protocols model collaboration at a group level. The interactions of collaborators are captured by social protocols. Interactions are strongly related to social aspects, such as the role played by collaborators. The proposed model integrates some of these social aspects, which may explain the choice of the term "social protocols". Hetero-geneity of PVCs at the sub-community level is then at least partially addressed by the social protocol approach.

A social protocol aims at modeling a set of collaboration processes, in the same way as a class models a set of objects in object-oriented programming. In other words, a social protocol may be seen as a model which instances are collaboration processes. Within a given PVC, various social protocols may be used to control interactions within different sub-communities. Therefore, one may state that social protocols address at least partially the high level heterogeneity of PVCs.

A *social protocol p* is a finite state machine consisting of $\{ S_p, S_p^{start}, S_p^{end}, T_p \}$ where S_p is the set of states, $S_p^{start} \subset S$ is the set of starting states, $S_p^{end} \subset S$ is the set of ending states, $S_p^{start} \cap S_p^{end} = \varnothing$, T_p is the set of transitions from states to states.

In a social protocol, collaborators – as a group –move from state to state via the transitions. A transition may be triggered only by a collaborator labeled with the appropriate role. A transition is associated with the execution of an action. Execution of an action means the execution of remote code. SOAP or CORBA are examples of technologies that may be used to such remote code executions.

A set of *group actions* have been identified to support *group dynamics*, i.e. the dynamics of PVCs at a high level. A group action is a special action that may be executed to modify the set of sub-communities that the PVC consists of. A group action may for instance allow a collaborator to split a group in two or more groups, or to merge two or more groups into a single group. Group dynamics may be modeled by a set of group actions.

A formal definition of the proposed model has been already presented in (Picard, 2006a), while an algorithm for structural validation of social protocols has been presented in (Picard, 2007).

3   ADAPTIVE SOCIAL PROTOCOLS

Social protocols address heterogeneity of PVCs at both high and low level, and dynamics at high level. However, the need for support for dynamics of PVCs is still only partially addressed at the sub-community level. Social protocol adaptation is proposed here as a mean to support dynamics of PVCs at the sub-community level.

3.1   Run-time vs. Design-Time Adaptation

In the workflow management literature, information required to model and control a collaboration process has been classified according to various perspectives.

In (van der Aalst et al., 2003), five perspectives have been presented:
  ➢ the *functional perspective* focuses on activities to be performed,
  ➢ the *process perspective* focuses on the execution conditions for activities,
  ➢ the *organization perspective* focuses on the organizational structure of the population that may potentially execute activities,
  ➢ the *information perspective* focuses on data flow among tasks,
  ➢ the *operation perspective* focuses on elementary operations performed by applications and resources.

A sixth perspective has been added in (Daoudi and Nurcan, 2003): the *intentional perspective* focuses on goals and strategies related to a given process.

One may easily notice that all six perspectives presented above focus on elements that evolve in time, for instance:

  ➢ in the *functional perspective*, new activities may be identified and some activities may be suppressed by new information systems and/or robots,
  ➢ in the *process perspective*, execution conditions for activities may change as some new activities may be required,
  ➢ in the *organization perspective*, the organizational structure of the population that may potentially execute activities may evolve, as some employees are promoted or are fired,
  ➢ in the *information perspective*, data flow among tasks may need to be defined among new tasks,
  ➢ in the *operation perspective*, a newly introduced information system may perform various operations that used to be performed by a legacy system,
  ➢ in the *intentional perspective*, changes in the business environment, e.g. the collaboration of two concurrent professionals, may lead to a redefinition of goals and strategies of a third professional on the same market, which may imply changes in business processes.

In typical workflow management systems, two parts may be distinguished: a design-time part allows for definition of workflow schemas while the run-time part is responsible for execution of workflow instances. A main limitation of typical workflow management systems is the fact that once a workflow schema has been instantiated, the execution of the workflow instance must stick to the workflow schema till the end of the workflow instance execution. This limitation is not an issue if the lifespan of workflow instances is short in comparison with the time interval between successive requests for changes of the workflow schema. When the lifespan of workflow instances is long in comparison with the time interval between successive requests for changes of the workflow schema, a high number of workflow instances has to be executed with an ``incorrect'' workflow schema (i.e. that does not take into account required changes) or has to be cancelled. As a consequence, typical workflow management systems are not flexible enough to support collaborative processes in two cases: *highly dynamic, competitive markets/environments* and *long lasting collaboration processes.*

In highly dynamic and competitive markets/environments, situations which have not been foreseen in the workflow schemas are highly probable as business actors may appear and disappear from the market, the apparition and removal of products and services are frequent, the turnover among employees may be high, etc.

In long lasting collaboration processes, the workflow instance is supposed to run for years, e.g. production workflows. In long lasting collaboration processes, the occurrence of unforeseen situation is highly probable too: new knowledge – e.g. robot reliability – or new situations – e.g. legal restrictions about privacy – may appear many years after the workflow schema has been designed.

In the case of highly dynamic, competitive markets/environments and long lasting collaboration processes, there is a strong need for the modifications of a workflow instance at run-time, denoted here *social protocol adaptation.* Such modifications are usually needed to deal with situations which have not been foreseen nor modeled in the associated workflow schema. Social protocol adaptation refers to the possibility to *modify a running social protocol instance* to new situations which have not been foreseen and modeled in the associated social protocol.

3.2   Negotiation-based Adaptation

While social protocols support, at least to some extent, the integration of some social elements (such as roles) to models of interactions among humans, the adaptation capabilities of humans are not taken into account into social protocols. There is however the need to provide adaptation mechanisms to social protocols. Indeed, interactions among humans are often a context-aware activity. In this paper, context-awareness refers to the capabilities of applications to provide relevant services to their users by sensing and exploring the users' context (Dey, 2001; Dockhorn, 2005). Context is defined as a "collection of interrelated conditions in which something exists or occurs" (Dockhorn, 2005). The users' context often consists of a collection of conditions, e.g. the users' location, environmental aspects (temperature, light intensity, etc.) and activities (Chen, 2003). The users' context may change dynamically, and, therefore, a basic requirement for a context-aware system is its ability to sense context and to react to context changes.

In (Picard, 2006b), negotiations have been proposed as a mean for adaptation of social protocols. Negotiation of social protocols has been presented as "an attempt to weaken constraints usually limiting the interaction between collaborators, so that the adaptation capabilities of humans may be integrated in the life of a social protocol".

The idea of using negotiations as an adaptation mean for social protocols comes from the fact that social protocols rule the interactions of all collaborators in a given group. Therefore each modification of the social protocol may influence all collaborators. As a consequence, the decision to modify a social protocol should be consulted and approved by many collaborators. Negotiations are a classical way to make collaborative decision and to reach an agreement in situations where expectations and goals of collaborators may be in conflict.

1. Power-enabled Adaptation

3.3   Definition(s) of Power

Negotiations of social protocols would allow collaborators to establish cooperatively a new version of the social protocol that 1) is acceptable by all collaborators; 2) allows collaborators to collaborate in a way which is better adapted to the current situation they are facing. We propose to integrate the concept of *power* to model social interactions influencing the negotiation process.

Power is often considered as a synonym for "capacity to influence". Power has been defined by Deutsch (Deutsch, 1973) in the following way: "an actor ... has power in a given situation (situational power) to the degree that he can satisfy the purpose (goals, desires, or wants) that he is attempting to fulfill in that situation. Power is a relational concept: it does not reside in the individual by rather in the relationship of the person to his environment. Thus, the power of an actor in a given situation is determined by the characteristics of the situation as well as by his own characteristics". Lewicki, Saunders and Minton (Lewicki, 2000) proposed the following three main sources of power:

> ➢ *Information and expertise*: the accumulation and presentation of data intended to change the other person's point of view or position on an issue; and (for expertise) an acknowledged accumulation of information, or mastery of a body of information, on a particular problem or issue;
> ➢ *Control over resources*: the accumulation of money, raw material, labor, time and equipment that can be used as incentives to encourage compliance or as punishments for noncompliance;
> ➢ *Location in an organizational structure*: power derived from being located in a particular position in an organizational or communication structure; leads to two different kinds of leverage:

> • Formal authority, derived from occupying a key position in a hierarchical organization.
> • Access to or control over information or supply flows, derived from location within a network.

3.4   Modeling Power in Social Protocols

Support for power in negotiation of social protocols requires a model of power based on information available during the collaboration process. Some information may be implicitly available, while other information are tacit knowledge.

As a first attempt to model power of collaborators in collaboration processes driven by social protocols, we propose the following criteria based on implicitly available information:

> *Collaborator's involvement in the collaboration process*: measurable as the number of actions executed by a *given collaborator* during the whole negotiation process. This criterion may be normalized by dividing the number of actions executed by a given collaborator by the total number of actions executed by all collaborators.

> *Role rate of occurrence*: this criterion measures the "importance" of a *given role* with regard to other roles in the social protocol. A role rate of occurrence is measured as the number of potential transitions associated with a given role divided by the total number of transitions.

> *Locality and role*: when the negotiation of a given social protocol starts, the group is in a given state. From the current state, various actions may be performed by collaborators playing different roles. A collaborator playing a role which allows him/her to execute many actions from the current state has potentially more leverage than a collaborator playing a role which does not allow him/her to execute many actions. This may be extended to a broader locality, i.e. to actions that may be executed not only directly from the current state but close to it (two or more transitions away from the current state).

Other criteria require either some extensions of social protocols, or transformation of tacit knowledge into implicit knowledge:

> *Locality and competences*: social protocols should be extended to integrate the notion of competences with potential actions, e.g. the action record an invoice could be associated with accounting and bookkeeping competences. Similarly, collaborators should also be associated with labels describing their competences. Based on competence information of both collaborators and actions, a measurement of the matching of competences of a given collaborator and competences associated with local actions may be processed to measure the power of a given collaborator derived from being competent in the current state.

> *Organizational position*: as the power derived from the organization position of collaborators "cannot function without obedience, or the consent of the governed", we propose that each collaborator assigns to every collaborator a value representing their consent to accept decisions taken by the former.

4   CONCLUSIONS

The introduction of the concept of power in adaptation of social protocols is an attempt to provide collaborators with support for social aspects influencing their decisions during adaptation. The main innovations presented in this paper are 1) the characterization of PVCs as heterogeneous and dynamic sociosystems at various levels, 2) the idea of a support for power in the negotiations of social protocols, 3) a set of criteria that could be used to model collaborators' power in collaboration processes ruled by social protocols. The proposed concepts are currently under implementation as extensions to the DynG protocol, a social protocol-based platform. The list of criteria proposed to model power is obviously not exhaustive and additional research has to be done for a more accurate modeling of power in negotiation of social protocols. Additionally, the contribution of each criteria to the global evaluation of a given collaborator's power in a given situation remains an open issue.

5   REFERENCES

1.   [van der Aalst 2003] W. M. P. van der Aalst, M. Weske, and G. Wirtz. Advanced topics in workflow management: Issues, requirements, and solutions. Journal of Integrated Design and Process Science, 7(3), pp. 49 – 77, 2003.
2.   [Camarinha-Matos 2005] L.M. Camarinha-Matos, H. Afsarmanesh and M. Ollus, "ECOLEAD: A Holistic Approach to Creation and Management of Dynamic Virtual Organizations", In L. Camarinha-Matos, H. Afsarmanesh and A. Ortiz, Eds, Collaborative Networks and their Breeding Environments, Proceedings of the 6th IFIP Working Conference on Virtual Enterprises (PRO-VE 2005), Valencia, Spain, September 26-28, 2005, Springer, pp. 3 – 16, 2005.
3.   [Chen 2003] H. Chen, T. Finin and A. Joshi, "An Ontology for Context-Aware Pervasive Computing Environments.", Knowledge Engineering Review, Special Issue on Ontologies for Distributed Systems, Vol. 18, No. 3. Cambridge University Press, pp. 197 – 207, 2003.
4.   [Chituc 2005] C.M. Chituc, A.L. Azevedo, "Multi-Perspective Challenges on Collaborative Networks Business Environments", In L. Camarinha-Matos, H. Afsarmanesh and A. Ortiz, Eds, Collaborative Networks and their Breeding Environments, Proceedings of the 6th IFIP Working Conference on Virtual Enterprises (PRO-VE 2005), Valencia, Spain, September 26-28, 2005, Springer, pp. 25 – 32, 2005.
5.   [Daoudi 2007] F. Daoudi and S. Nurcan. A benchmarking framework for methods to design flexible business processes. Special Issue on Design for Flexibility of the "Software Process: Improvement and Practice Journal", 12(1), pp. 51 – 63, 2007.
6.   [Deutsch 1973] M. Deutsch. The Resolution of Conflicts. New Haven, CT: Yale University Press, 1973.
7.   [Dey 2001] A. K. Dey, D. Salber and G. D. Abowd, "A Conceptual Framework and a Toolkit for Supporting the Rapid Prototyping of Context-Aware Applications.", Human-Computer Interaction, 16(2-4), pp. 97 – 166, 2001.
8.   [Dockhorn 2005] P. Dockhorn Costa, L. Ferreira Pires and M. van Sinderen, "Designing a Configurable Services Platform for Mobile Context-Aware Applications", International Journal of Pervasive Computing and Communications (JPCC), 1(1), Troubador Publishing, 2005.
9.   [Ekholm 1996] A. Ekholm and S. Fridqvist, "Modelling of user organisations, buildings and spaces for the design process". In Construction on the Information Highway. (Ed. Ziga Turk). Proceedings from the CIB W78 Workshop, 10-12 June 1996, Bled, Slovenia, 1996.
10. [Lewicki 2000] R.J. Lewicki, J. Minton and D. Saunders. Essentials of Negotiation. Second Edition. McGraw Hill/Irwin, 2000.
11. [Picard 2007] W. Picard, "An Algebraic Algorithm for Structural Validation of Social Protocols", Proceedings of the 10th Int. Conference on Business Information Systems, Lecture Notes in Computer Science, 4439, Springer, pp. 570–583, 2007.
12. [Picard 2006a] W. Picard, "Adaptive Human-to-Human Collaboration via Negotiations of Social Protocols". In A. Witold and H.C. Mayr, Eds, Technologies for Business Information Systems, Proceedings of the 9th Int. Conference on Business Information Systems in cooperation with ACM SIGMIS, Klagenfurt, Austria, May 31 – June 2, 2006, Springer Verlag, pp. 193 – 203, 2006.
13. [Picard 2006b] W. Picard. Adaptive Collaboration in Professional Virtual Communities via Negotiations of Social Protocols. In L. Camarinha-Matos, H. Afsarmanesh, and M. Ollus, Eds, Network-centric Collaboration and Supporting Frameworks, Proc. of the 7th IFIP Working Conference on Virtual Enterprises (PRO-VE 2006), Helsinki, Finland, Sept. 2006. Springer, pp. 353 – 360, 2006.
14. [Picard 2005] W. Picard, "Modeling Structured Non-monolithic Collaboration Processes", In L. Camarinha-Matos, H. Afsarmanesh and A. Ortiz, Eds, Collaborative Networks and their Breeding Environments, Proceedings of the 6th IFIP Working Conference on Virtual Enterprises (PRO-VE 2005), Valencia, Spain, September 26-28, 2005, Springer, pp. 379 – 386, 2006.

39

UNDERSTANDING USERS' RESPONSE TO ONTOLOGY BASED SYSTEMS IN THE CONTEXT OF AN ENTERPRISE SPONSORED VIRTUAL COMMUNITY

Carla Pereira[1,4], Manuel Silva[1,3], Joana Fernandes[1,3], António Lucas Soares[1,2]

[1]INESC Porto, [2]Fac. Engineering Univ. Porto, [3]ISCAP-IPP, [4]ESTGF-IPP, PORTUGAL
cpereira@estgf.ipp.pt, mdasilva@iscap.ipp.pt, joanaf@iscap.ipp.pt, asoares@inescporto.pt

This paper aims at presenting the preliminary results of a research work that seeks to understand the users' response to semantic based technologies, in the context of enterprise sponsored virtual communities. The research follows a qualitative methodology based on an action research approach. It particularly focuses on the socio-cognitive processes that underlie users' learning and acquisition methods when training and interacting with a new knowledge management approach based on semantically enabled technologies in a collaborative, and sometimes virtual, learning/working environment. The outcomes of this research are expected to provide an assessment framework for a deeper level understanding of the cognition process in what concerns the evolution of individual's knowledge, opinions, beliefs, and thoughts about ontology based systems.

1   INTRODUCTION

Building and construction companies have to continuously renew their working habits in order to face an increasing competitive environment where flexibility and adaptability to change are the obliged route to success. Particularly SMEs, have to act quickly on redefining the ways for the achievement of their business objectives. The main challenge is to provide a cost-effective solution for the two main problems: 1) Construction industry (particularly SMEs) urgently needs radical improvements of communication with customers in order to provide better product support and services. The innovative forms of communications and relationships among SMEs and their customers are increasingly important in order to improve the market share and/or survival chances in the "new economy era". 2) To respond to ever increasing customer requirements it is increasingly necessary to establish a closer co-operation (particularly among SMEs) within this sector, aiming at assembling alliances of SMEs into integrated teams that will genuinely align with challenging performance targets.

As the community paradigm is winning space among more established inter-organizational interaction forms such as chains or networks, complementing them in some cases, and taking into account the needs described above the KNOW-CONSTRUCT (KC) EU project[1] developed an Internet Platform for Knowledge-based

---

[1] COLL-CT-2004-500276 – KNOW-CONSTRUCT – www.know-construct.com

Pereira, C., Silva, M., Fernandes, J., Soares, A.L., 2007, in IFIP International Federation for Information Processing, Volume 243, Establishing the Foundation of Collaborative Networks; eds. Camarinha-Matos, L., Afsarmanesh, H., Novais, P., Analide, C.; (Boston: Springer), pp. 371–380.

Customer Needs Management and for Support to Knowledge Communities of SMEs in the Construction Industry. It intends to improve the effectiveness of the Construction Industry (CI) SME's by improving and extending the relationship with their customers through an innovative support regarding information and knowledge about products, processes and associated issues. This is achieved through specifically developed tools, supporting in particular the formation and operation of SME's knowledge communities in the context of Industry Association Groups (IAG). More specifically, these objectives aim (i) to provide a platform to support the creation and management of a community of CI SME's, coordinated by an association, fostering collaboration and knowledge sharing among its members and (ii) to provide problem-solving support to the individual IAG member's customers, as well as addressing other related problems such as legislative issues, safety issues, among other possibilities. A large set of professional associations of the sector were involved in the process, which will now provide the environment for the dissemination of the innovative solutions and for the development of a knowledge community support (KCS) system in order to acquire a wider and deeper technical and professional competence shared by the SME's community, obtained through closer co-operation and knowledge exchange.

Based on the typology of virtual communities proposed by Porter [3] where the communities are classified under two levels - establishment and relationship orientation - the KC community, named as *Construction Industry Knowledge* (CIK) Community is classified as an organization-sponsored community relatively to type of establishment and as a commercial community relatively to the relationship orientation having the following characteristics: (i) the goal is to develop and exploit knowledge about civil construction sector; (ii) there are continuous interactions between participants to meet these goals, (iii) information and communication processes are continuously made explicit, (iv) it adds value to the participants (professionals within the sector and customers alike), the on-line meeting place that is usable, (v) the culture focuses on the participants' needs as the route to high performance; involvement and participation create a sense of responsibility and ownership and, hence, greater commitment, and (vi) the context is highly complex and constantly evolving and the Construction Industry Knowledge (CIK) Community will have to continuously cope with the expectations of its participants and their context of use of the system.

Enterprise sponsored virtual communities (ESVC) are emerging as serious business schemes fostering collaboration and knowledge sharing both intra and inter-organizations. This community will, thus, have key stakeholders and/or beneficiaries (e.g. customers) that will play an important part in sponsoring the community's mission and goals. Being an organization-sponsored community, it will foster relationships both among members (e.g. professionals belonging to the associations of the project partnership) and between individual members (e.g. customers) and the sponsoring organizations (associations of the project partnership).

2   TRAINING ON KC METHODOLOGY AND SYSTEM

ESVCs are complex socio-technical systems, difficult to design and maintain, needing multi-disciplinary approaches for their development. In order to assure its functioning and to assure a highly productive usage of the system by end-users it is of utmost importance to organise optimal adoption of the system by them. In addition to participation of end users in the system concept creation and testing, what assured an initial creation of awareness on system characteristics, a final training is to be organised for familiarisation of the end-user with the full system functionalities and advantages to be achieved through its usage. An appropriate planning, including the training methods selection and training materials creation is crucial for the success of the training. Thus a training plan and training sessions were devised, which aim at (i) assuring maximal acceptance of the Know-Construct system through creation of a full awareness on the system characteristics and advantages it will bring to the end user companies; (ii) ensuring that all the SMEs fully understand the concepts involved with KC methodology and ICT system; (iii) providing familiarization of the future system users with all related aspects, primarily related to knowledge gathering, structuring within the system and presentation; (iv) assuring, through common "hands on" training sessions for the groups of users for all involved employees in SMEs and Associations, an efficient deployment of the future system for all planned functionalities.

The methods used for the training have been adapted to the needs of training on the KC Methodology and System, following the most appropriate teaching approach for the targeted audiences. The approaches include introductory lectures, coached "hands-on" training and application of e-learning tools. The training courses will be carried out through the following forms: a) In IAGs for groups of belonging SMEs as courses organised and coached by the system experts; b)In individual SMEs as courses organised and coached by the system experts; c) In individual SMEs as e-learning courses; whereby the e-learning form can be used also in all other suitable occasions and places. In order to maximize acceptance of the solutions delivered, it is essential to consider also the "human factors" such as the detailed identification of the targeted trained population, including the starting skill level and technical prerequisites if necessary. The scope and methods of the training will, thus, be adapted to the user requirements evolution (up to the training start and later for each new course and system upgrade) and different education levels.

The initial training on the KC system usage occurred during the early prototype testing by the end users, which were encouraged to work individually on the system. This initial training has resulted in an improved system understanding and has also facilitated the formal training activities. The methods to be applied for the formal training on the KC system usage have been selected assuming that all participants at the System Training sessions have attended the training on KC Methodology sessions and are basically familiar with KC system functionalities. The main part of the training will be the "hands-on" training through testing of different system application scenarios described in the use-cases, emphasizing specific interests of each group of trainees. The concluding part of the methodology training will comprise basic presentation of the practical usage of the KC system, structured according to the system-user groups.

Looking at professional development as the process of continually developing knowledge, skills and attitudes of professionals by means of formal and informal learning in the course of practice, the use of on-line knowledge communities for this purpose implies that an on-line knowledge community has to support this process. As a CIK community member, professionals in the construction sector will have a place for continual professional development that gives them individualized, flexible and easy access to a coherent and up to date knowledge domain, a range of opportunities to interact with like-minded persons and a range of opportunities to develop and exploit the knowledge domain. An example of this is: applying knowledge, learning from it, guiding others, disseminating ideas and results or doing research, embedded in a professional network. Our premise is that the membership of professionals of an online knowledge community will have positive effects on their continuing development, expressed not only in competences like knowledge, skills, experiences and attitude, but also in the acquisition of organizational knowledge assets expressed in the growth and elaboration of professional knowledge, applicability of knowledge and legitimacy of knowledge.

Due to the different participants/targets and in order to meet the needs of the project, KC will be based on a *Project-based learning* approach. This approach, which is a comprehensive instructional approach that engages trainees in a sustained and cooperative learning experience, fostering the idea of community, will use small projects/activities as a starting point for each session. These projects have two essential components: 1/A driving question/problem or case-study that serves to organize and determine various activities, which taken as a whole amount to a meaningful project. 2/Culminating product(s) or multiple representations as a series of results or consequential tasks that meaningfully addresses the driving question (Campione & Brown, 1994). In this approach, the driving question that is anchored in a real-world problem/case-study and ideally uses multiple content areas is presented in order to lead to: 1/opportunities for trainees to make active investigations that enable them to learn concepts, apply information, and represent their knowledge in a variety of ways; 2/collaboration among trainees, teachers, and others in the community so that knowledge can be shared and distributed among the members of the "learning community"; 3/the use of cognitive tools in learning environments that support trainees in the representation of their ideas: cognitive tools such as hypermedia and graphing applications (Blumenfeld et al., 1991).

3   METHODOLOGY FOR THE TRAINING RESULTS ANALYSIS

Most methodologies for analysing enterprise environments are supposedly user-centred. However this can be rather vague, for subjects have both explicit objective knowledge and knowledge that is more implicitly understood. Such tacit knowledge is among the most difficult to articulate, but it entails perhaps the most interesting and valuable information. Furthermore, such a framework implies an engagement in a qualitative inquiry, which is certainly a major risk, because one must be committed to spending extensive time in the field. Within the ESVC presented context and for the correct implementation of KC system it is vital to understand the cognitive processes that underlie users' learning and acquisition methods when training and interacting with new knowledge management approaches based on semantically enabled knowledge technologies in a collaborative learning/working environment, in order to correctly assess the evolution of individual's knowledge, opinions, beliefs and thoughts about the new technology working/sharing environment.

Therefore, an empirical study to identify the main difficulties faced by users was planned. As the particular focus of this investigation is on how the user accepts the ontology of the construction industry sector, it seems vital to carry out a naturalistic inquiry into the opinions, beliefs and experience of enterprise/community members. This was done by collecting data through interview and think-aloud protocol elicitation methodologies, as the record and analysis of the verbal reports produced by the community members will provide a way to understand cognitive processes that underlie users' actions.

To evaluate the KCS use we decided to use the action research approach, seen here as a collaborative and iterative evaluation method that allows a continuous improvement of the solution presented to the community, as described by (Carr et al., 1986), who state that first a project takes the form of social practice; secondly, the project proceeds through a spiral of cycles of planning, acting, observing and reflecting, with each of these activities being systematically implemented; thirdly, the project involves those responsible for the practice in activity, including those affected by the practice. We share the vision of Hult and Lennung (1980), cited in (Fowler et al., 1998), to whom action research simultaneously assists in practical problem solving and expands scientific knowledge, as well as enhances the competencies of the respective actors, being performed collaboratively in an immediate situation using data feedback in a cyclical process aiming at an increased understanding of a given social situation, primarily applicable for the understanding of change processes in social systems and undertaken within a mutually acceptable framework.

It is thus a collaborative approach that requires and fosters a strong interaction between the researchers and the practitioners (Avison et al., 1999). Considering the knowledge community support (KCS) system requirements defined in the scope of Know-Construct project, this approach, as seen in the picture bellow, leads to the acquisition of results about the social acceptance of semantic resources and leads to the continuous improvement of the system functionalities provided to the community, thus generating an efficient response to the requirements of the SME community.

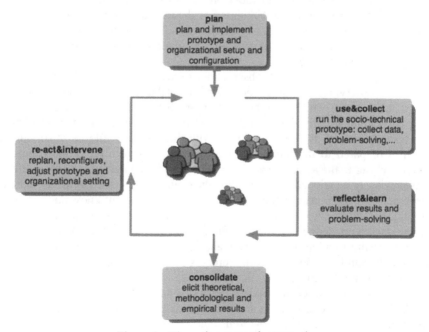

Figure 1 – The action-research approach

3.1   KC approach to the grasping of user's cognition

As a reflective and cyclical process, action research is concerned with social practice and change that leads to improvement. Thus, if the researcher wants to act in order to improve something, he needs first to find out a way to understand and examine thought and action of the social actors he is concerned with. There are many different possibilities for data collection. Among them, and as mentioned above, interviews and think-aloud protocol analyses are methods of research that have been widely used both in social and cognitive sciences for many years (Creswell, 1997). If carried out in natural environment, interviews and protocols can capture the context/scenario of the subjects' interaction. The researcher may take notes and video or audio-record whilst observing the subject. Interviews, together with thinking aloud, can provide a detailed insight into the activity or process being observed.

Think-aloud protocols were originally presented by (Ericsson et al., 1985). The purpose of this method is to understand cognitive processes by trying to capture thoughts as they are in short-term memory. Therefore, the researcher collects verbal representations of thoughts, which will be later analysed. Protocol analysis provides a means for extracting subjects' thoughts while they are performing a task. Scenarios are collected by asking subjects to solve the specific problem and verbalize their decision process by stating directly what they think. The elicited information is structured later when the researcher analyses the protocol. Here the term scenario refers to a detailed and somehow complex sequence of events or more precisely, an episode.

A different orientation is suggested by (Boren et al., 2000). To them protocols are regarded as speech acts, rather than as brain dumps. Their approach presents several advantages over the model above present. First, the listener and speaker roles are acknowledged and set in the beginning of the user test. Subjects are established as the work domain experts and primary speakers. The researcher takes the role of the listener and he can intervene at various parts. Interventions will consist of neutral language to avoid biased results.

Another possibility is on-site observation, or action protocol. This is a process that involves observing, recording, and interpreting subjects' problem-solving process while it takes place. The researcher does more listening than talking; he avoids giving advice and usually does not pass his/her own judgement on what is being observed and most of all, does not argue with the subject while he is solving the problem. Compared to the process of interviewing, on-site observation brings the researcher closer to the actual steps, experience and procedures used by the subject.

As previously mentioned, understanding the cognitive processes by which subjects retrieve new information and manipulate it to produce coherent knowledge seems to be a vital step within the current project. Thus, such an approach requires the access to users' tacit knowledge combined with qualitative data gathering tools. It was therefore our aim to adopt the interview and the think-aloud protocol elicitations in order to understand the user's cognition process before and after using the prototype.

Thus, the general aims of the elicitation procedures to be undertaken are: 1/ To understand cognitive processes underlying users' terminology research; 2/ To ask for task descriptions related to the use of semantic resources; 3/ To measure users' performance after being taught how to use the prototype; 4/ To assess the cognition process: the evolution of individual's knowledge, opinions, beliefs, thoughts and performance after using the prototype; 5/ To evaluate the change of attitudes and beliefs toward the use of the ontology after training; 6/ To evaluate the change of attitudes and beliefs toward the notion of community; 7/ To evaluate the usefulness of the knowledge represented in the ontology.

The research carried out comprises a naturalistic approach into the opinions, beliefs and *modus operandi* and changes in the learning behavior of users, which will seek to be as conversational and reflective as possible. Using as source the model adapted by (O'Brien, 1998), primarily presented by Gerald Susman (1983) we propose a methodology for evaluating information systems with semantic resources.

The former states that each cycle of the action research process is composed by five phases: diagnosing, action planning, taking action, evaluating and specifying learning. Initially the research questions are identified and data is collected for a more detailed diagnosis. This is followed by a collective postulation of several possible solutions, from which a single plan of action emerges and is implemented. Data on the results of the intervention is collected and analyzed, and the findings are interpreted in light of how successful the action has been. At this point, the questions are re-assessed and the process begins another cycle. This process continues until the research questions are answered, as described in the picture below.

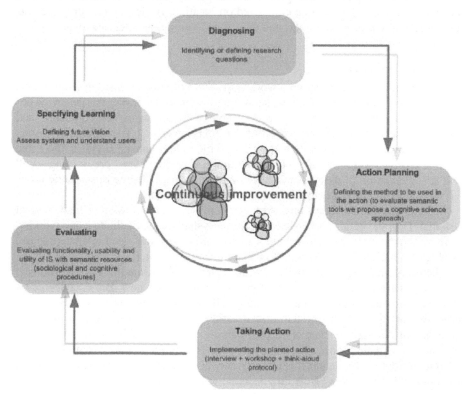

Figure 2 – Methodological approach

3.1.1   Diagnosing

The first step consists of the definition of the team that will conduct the investigation. This team comprises the authors of this paper, whose first task is to define the starting questions. Here are some of them: How do results obtained through the use and management of information based on semantically enabled tools correspond to the stakeholders/users' expectations? Does this new approach/vision collide with the conventional well-known and established one? What sort of learning/interacting problems and difficulties does this tool pose? How do users react to the use of semantic tools presented through an ontology format? To what extent do experts and non-experts accept the conceptual structure entailed by the system? What sort of interacting problems and difficulties does the notion of community pose? What sort of metaphors and image schemas do users verbalize to express their views? Depending on the type of user and organizational context, how is the use of these tools valued? What advantages/disadvantages do the users recognize?

3.1.2   Action planning

The second step requires carefully drafting the format of the interview and designing the think-aloud procedure. A naturalistic inquiry is particularly suited to settings that are dependent on individual interpretations and perceptions. Following the spirit of a naturalistic inquiry, they will be conducted on location. A clear micro-structure was developed in order to set out goals and questions to guide the interview plan.

3.1.3   Taking action

Action was taken by carrying out a workshop where the plan defined in the previous phase is implemented. The following steps were taken: 1/ To ensure that interviewees understand the questions and are comfortable with our aims; 2/ To record and transcribe interviews, with permission of the interviewees. 3/ To analyze the results and propose the necessary system revision. This action can be divided into three moments: pre-training, training and post-training. The first step - pre-training - will be a first evaluation of users' expectations and knowledge degree of semantic tools. We wanted to urge the user to think in terms of the following:

Pre-training sample questions: Are you familiar with knowledge management systems? Do you believe knowledge sharing systems will facilitate your working routine? What aspects of your behavior do you think you will need to change to use ontology? What sort of difficulties do you expect to encounter?

The users' training is then performed in which the functionalities of the information systems are presented. In the third part - post-training - new data is collected by using the think-aloud protocol methodology allowing a comparative and contrastive evaluation relatively to the system classification by the users (in terms of usability, utility and functionality). Some of the post-training questions will be: What is unique or innovative about this tool? What limitations did you encounter? What challenges did you face during the training? Is learning how to use this tool very time-consuming? What did and didn't work? How do you agree with the semantic resources?

3.1.4 Evaluating

Considering the data collected in pre and post-training moments, an evaluation of the system and a new working session was carried out. If the action is successful the necessary information to answer the initial questions will have been collected. The evaluation of the information systems in terms of usability, functionality and utility can then be accomplished. Considering the data collected in the previous phase, it is necessary to consider the perspective of continuous improvement, the changes that should be made and new functionalities to be developed so that the system is fully and successfully implemented. These changes will be established in the next cycle of the process.

3.1.5 Specifying learning

The action research cycle continues considering the results of the evaluation accomplished in the previous phase. This is the moment to define the future vision and to evaluate the need to execute another cycle. If the results obtained in the previous phase are satisfactory, the process will stop during one month. At the end of this period, using direct observation, a new observation in the context of the working place and a new evaluation of the system's acceptance and usage will be performed. The results will determine whether there is a need to extend research to a new cycle of the process.

4   CONCLUSION AND FUTURE PERSPECTIVES

Being an experimental approach, the authors are aware that the quality of the study and the accuracy of the steps to be taken need careful evaluation. The outcomes of this research are being analysed and are expected to provide a deeper level of understanding of how CIK community members respond to the prototype and to assess their cognition process, namely to understand their attitudes toward the use of the ontology; to know how they evaluate the usefulness of the knowledge represented in the ontology and to measure users' performance when using/testing the prototype.

5   REFERENCES

1.   Avison D, Lau F, Myers M, Nielsen P. Action research. Communications of the ACM, 42(1), 1999, 94-97.
2.   Baskerville RL. Investigating Information Systems with Action Research. Communications of the Association for Information Systems, 2 (19), October 1999.
3.   Blumenfeld P, Soloway E, Marx R, Krajcik J, Guzdial M, Palincsar A. Motivating project-based learning: Sustaining the doing, supporting the learning. Educational Psychologist, 26 (3 & 4), 369-398, 1991.
4.   Boren MT, Ramey J. Thinking aloud: Reconciling theory and practice. IEEE Transactions on Professional Communication, 43(3), 261-278, 2000.
5.   Campione, JC, Brown AL. Guided learning and transfer: Implications for approaches to assessment. in N. Fredericksen, R. Glasser, A. Lesgold & M. G. Shafto (Orgs.), Diagnostic monitoring of skill and knowledge acquisition (pp. 141-172). Hillsdale: Lawrence Erlbaum, 1990.
6.   Carr W, Kemmis S.Becoming critical: education knowledge and action research. London: Falmer Press, 1986.

7.   Creswell J. Qualitative Inquiry and Research Design. Chosing Among Five Traditions, United Kingdom, Sage Publications, 1997.
8.   Ericsson KA., Simon HA. Protocol Analysis: Verbal Reports as Data. Cambridge, MIT Press, 1984.
9.   Fowler D, Swatman P. Building Information systems Development Methods: Synthesising from a Basis in both Theory and Practice, Australian Software Engineering Conference, pp. 110-117, IEEE Computer Society, Adelaide South Australia, 1998.
10. O'Brien R. An Overview of the Methodological Approach of Action Research. Faculty of Information Studies, University of Toronto, 1998.

40

CONTINUOUS MANAGEMENT OF PROFESSIONAL VIRTUAL COMMUNITY INHERITANCE BASED ON THE ADAPTATION OF SOCIAL PROTOCOLS

Willy Picard
Department of Information Technology
The Poznań University of Economics
ul. Mansfelda 4
60-854 Poznań, POLAND
picard@kti.ae.poznan.pl

Support for human-to-human interactions over a network is still insufficient, particularly for professional virtual communities (PVC). Among other limitations, adaptation and learning-by-experience capabilities of humans are not taken into account in existing models for collaboration processes in PVC. This paper presents a model for adaptive human collaboration. A key element of this model is the use of negotiation for adaptation of social protocols modeling processes. A second contribution is the proposition of various adaptation propagation strategies as means for continuous management of the PVC inheritance.

1   INTRODUCTION

Enterprises are constantly increasing their efforts in order to improve their business processes. A main reason for this may be the fact that enterprises are exposed to a highly competitive global market. Among the most visible actions associated with this effort towards better support for better business processes, one may distinguish the current research work concerning Web services and associated standards: high-level languages such as BPEL or WS-Coordination take the service concept one step further by providing a method of defining and supporting workflows and business processes.

However, it should be noticed that most of these actions are directed towards interoperable machine-to-machine interactions over a network. Support for *human-to-human interactions* over a network is still insufficient and more research has to be done to provide both theoretical and practical knowledge to this field.

Among various reasons for the weak support for human-to-human interactions, one may distinguish the following three reasons: first, many *social elements* are involved in the interaction among humans. An example of such a social element may be the role played by humans during their interactions. Social elements are usually difficult to model, i.e. integrating non-verbal communication to collaboration models. Therefore, their integration to a model of interaction between humans is not easy. A second reason is the *adaptation capabilities* of humans which are not only far more advanced than adaptation capabilities of software entities, but also not taken into account in existing models for collaboration processes. A third reason is the *learning-by-experience capabilities* of humans, i.e. the capabilities to extract know-how and knowledge from previous experience and reuse it in similar situations.

Picard, W., 2007, in IFIP International Federation for Information Processing, Volume 243, Establishing the Foundation of Collaborative Networks; eds. Camarinha-Matos, L., Afsarmanesh, H., Novais, P., Analide, C.; (Boston: Springer), pp. 381–388.

The insufficient support for human-to-human interactions over a network is a strong limitation for a wide adoption of *professional virtual communities (PVCs)*. As mentioned in (Camarinha-Matos et al., 2005), "professional virtual community represents the combination of concepts of virtual community and professional community. Virtual communities are defined as social systems of networks of individuals, who use computer technologies to mediate their relationships. Professional communities provide environments for professionals to share the body of knowledge of their professions […]". According to Chituc and Azevedo (2005), little attention has been paid to the social perspective on Collaborative Networks (CN) business environment, including obviously professional virtual communities in which social aspects are of high importance.

This paper is an attempt to provide a model for human-to-human interactions within professional virtual communities. The proposed model addresses, at least to some extent, the three characteristics of the interactions between humans. It should however been kept in mind that the results presented here are a work in progress and therefore they are not claimed to be neither sufficient nor exhaustive.

The rest of this paper is organized as follows. In section 2, the concept of *social protocol*, used to model collaboration processes, is presented. Section 3 then expands on *adaptation* of social protocols. Next, the continuous management of PVC-inheritance based on adaptation propagation strategies is discussed. Finally, section 5 concludes this paper.

2   STRUCTURING COLLABORATION IN PVCS

2.1   PVCs as Heterogeneous and Dynamic Environments

As defined by Ekholm and Fridqvist (1996), "a human *sociosystem* has a composition of human individuals, its structure is the social behaviour repertoire, i.e. interaction among human individuals". The sociosystem of professional virtual communities is highly *heterogeneous* and *dynamic*.

The heterogeneity of PVCs exists at various levels of granularity within PVCs. At a high level, a PVC consists usually of many different "sub-communities". Each sub-community is different from other coexisting in the same PVC sub-communities in terms of goals, intentions, knowledge, processes, members, etc. At a lower level, one may notice that the structure of a sub-community is usually complex and heterogeneous. The roles played by the sub-community members, their skills, their competences are usually presenting a high level of diversity.

Similarly to the heterogeneity of PVCs, the dynamics of PVCs exists at various levels of granularity within PVCs. At a high level, the set of sub-communities that the PVC consists of evolves in time: new sub-communities are created to answer new needs and opportunities, unnecessary sub-communities are dissolved, existing sub-communities change as new members enter and leave the community, etc. The dynamics of PVCs may hardly, not to say cannot, be foreseen at design time, as changes of a given PVC are naturally related to changes in its business environment (which is usually not a deterministic system). At a lower level, the structure of a sub-community is evolving in time: some members may have job promotion, the skills of the members are usually evolving (improve) in time. Additionally, members of a given sub-community may face new situations implying the development of new solutions, new ways of collaboration, etc.

2.2   Modeling Group Interactions with Social Protocols

Support for human-to-human collaboration in PVCs should obviously take into account the characteristics of PVCs as sociosystems presented in the former subsection, i.e. heterogeneity and dynamics.

A first model for group interactions within a PVC has been presented in (Picard, 2005). The proposed model is based on the concept of *social protocol*. Social protocols model collaboration at a group level. The interactions of collaborators are captured by social protocols. Interactions are strongly related to social aspects, such as the role played by collaborators. The proposed model integrates some of these social aspects, which may explain the choice of the term "social protocols". Heterogeneity of PVCs at the sub-community level is then at least partially addressed by the social protocol approach.

A social protocol aims at modeling a set of collaboration processes, in the same way as a class models a set of objects in object-oriented programming. In other words, a social protocol may be seen as a model which instances are collaboration processes. Within a given PVC, various social protocols may be used to control interactions within different sub- communities, addressing at least partially the high level heterogeneity of PVCs.

Formally, a *social protocol p* is a finite state machine consisting of $\{\,S_p,\,S_p^{start},\,S_p^{end},\,Tp\,\}$ where S_p is the set of states, $S_p^{start} \subset S$ is the set of starting states, $S_p^{end} \subset S$ is the set of ending states, $S_p^{start} \cap S_p^{end} = \varnothing$, T_p is the set of transitions from states to states.

In a social protocol, collaborators – as a group –move from state to state via the transitions. A transition may be triggered only by a collaborator labeled with the appropriate role. A transition is associated with the execution of an action. Execution of an action means the execution of remote code. SOAP or CORBA are examples of technologies that may be used to such remote code executions.

A set of *group actions* have been identified to support *group dynamics*, i.e. the dynamics of PVCs at a high level. A group action is a special action that may be executed to modify the set of sub-communities that the PVC consists of. A group action may for instance allows a collaborator to split a group in two or more groups, or to merge two or more groups into a single group. Group dynamics may be modeled by a set of group actions.

A formal definition of the proposed model has been already presented in (Picard, 2006a), while an algorithm for structural validation of social protocols has been presented in (Picard, 2007).

3   ADAPTIVE SOCIAL PROTOCOLS

Social protocols address heterogeneity of PVCs at both high and low level, and dynamics at high level. However, the need for support for dynamics of PVCs is still only partially addressed at the sub-community level.

3.1 Run-time vs. Design-Time Adaptation

In the workflow management literature, information required to model and control a collaboration process has been classified according to various perspectives.

In (van der Aalst et al., 2003), five perspectives have been presented:

> ➢ the *functional perspective* focuses on activities to be performed,
> ➢ the *process perspective* focuses on the execution conditions for activities,
> ➢ the *organization perspective* focuses on the organizational structure of the population that may potentially execute activities,
> ➢ the *information perspective* focuses on data flow among tasks,
> ➢ the *operation perspective* focuses on elementary operations performed by applications and resources.

A sixth perspective has been added in (Daoudi and Nurcan, 2003): the intentional perspective focuses on goals and strategies related to a given process. One may easily notice that all six perspectives presented above focus on elements that evolve in time.

In typical workflow management systems, two parts may be distinguished: a *design-time* part allows for definition of workflow schemas while the *run-time* part is responsible for execution of workflow instances. A main limitation of typical workflow management systems is the fact that once a workflow schema has been instantiated, the execution of the workflow instance must stick to the workflow schema till the end of the workflow instance execution. This limitation is not an issue if the lifespan of workflow instances is short in comparison with the time interval between two requests for changes of the workflow schema. When the lifespan of workflow instances is long in comparison with the time interval between two requests for changes of the workflow schema, a high number of workflow instances has to be executed with an "incorrect" workflow schema (i.e. that does not take into account required changes) or cancelled. As a consequence, typical workflow management systems are not flexible enough to support collaborative processes in two cases: highly dynamic, competitive markets/environments and long lasting collaboration processes.

In the case of highly dynamic, competitive markets/environments or long lasting collaboration processes, there is a strong need for the possibility to modify a workflow instance at run-time. Such modifications are usually needed to deal with situations which have not been foreseen nor modeled in the associated workflow schema. *Social protocol adaptation* refers to the possibility to *modify a running social protocol instance* to new situations which have not been foreseen and modeled in the associated social protocol.

3.2 Negotiation-based Adaptation

While social protocols support, at least to some extent, the integration of some social elements (such as roles) to models of interactions among humans, the adaptation capabilities of humans are not taken into account into social protocols. There is however the need to provide adaptation mechanisms to social protocols. Indeed, interactions among humans are often a context-aware activity. In this paper, context-awareness refers to the capabilities of applications to provide relevant services to their users by sensing and exploring the users' context (Dey et al., 2001; Dockhorn et al., 2005). Context is defined as a "collection of interrelated conditions in which something exists or occurs" (Dockhorn et al., 2005). The users' context often consists of a collection of conditions, such as, e.g., the users' location, environmental aspects (temperature, light intensity, etc.) and activities (Chen et al., 2003). The users' context may change dynamically, and, therefore, a basic requirement for a context-aware system is its ability to sense context and to react to context changes.

In (Picard, 2006b), negotiations have been proposed as a method for adaptation of social protocols. The idea of negotiation of social protocol has been presented as "an attempt to weaken constraints usually limiting the interaction between collaborators, so that the adaptation capabilities of humans may be integrate in the life of a social protocol". The idea of using negotiations as an adaptation mean for social protocols comes from the fact that social protocols rule the interactions of all collaborators in a given group. Therefore each modification of the social protocol may influence all collaborators. As a consequence, the decision to modify a social protocol should be consulted and approved by many collaborators. Negotiations are a classical way to make collaborative decision and to reach an agreement in situations where expectations and goals of collaborators may be in conflict.

4   ADAPATION OF SOCIAL PROTOCOLS IN PVCS

In the context of PVCs, adaptation leads to support for dynamics of collaboration processes at the group level. Additionally, decisions taken during adaptation of social protocols may be reused by other groups facing similar problems.

4.1   Adaptation Propagation Strategies

Adaptation of a social protocol in a given group leads to the creation of a new version of the social protocol ruling collaboration within this group. Let assume that the adaptation of a given social protocol P1 in a given group G leads to the creation of a new social protocol P1'. In the context of a PVC, various strategies may be used to manage the change caused by the adaptation of a social protocol:

> ➢ *Local adaptation strategy*: Other groups ruled by the social protocol P are not affected by the adaptation and are still ruled by P. The social protocol P' is only used by group G and is not available for future groups.
> ➢ *Global propagation strategy*: Other groups ruled by the social protocol P are not affected by the adaptation and are still ruled by P. The social protocol P' is used by group G and is available for future groups.
> ➢ *Instant propagation strategy*: Other groups ruled by the social protocol P are affected by the adaptation, as they are now ruled by P'. The social protocol P' replaces P in the whole PVC.

It should be noticed that the instant propagation strategy may not always be used as the changes provided by the adaptation of the social protocol may be in conflict with the current state of some collaboration processes.

4.2   Adaptation Propagation in a VO-Inheritance Management Perspective

The concept of virtual organization inheritance (VO-I) has been defined in (Loss et al., 2006a) as "the set of information and knowledge accumulated from past and current VOs along their entire life cycle. *Virtual organization inheritance management* (VO-I-M) corresponds to the VO activity that manages what has been inherited about given VOs, usually supported by computer systems".

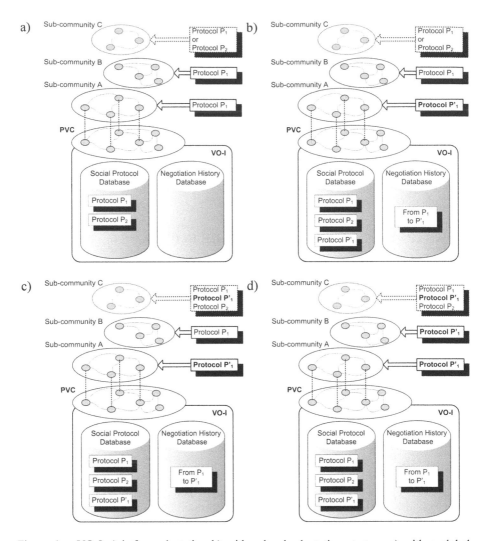

Figure 1 – VO-I a) before adaptation b) with a local adaptation strategy c) with a global propagation strategy d) with an instant propagation strategy

In a VO-I-M perspective, adaptation of social protocols may be seen as part of the VO-I, as presented in Figure 1. In the PVC presented in Figure 1a), two protocols are available – P1 and P2 – and two sub-communities – A and B – are ruled by P1. A new sub-community C may be created with either protocol P1 or protocol P2. It is then assumed that the sub-community A has adapted the protocol P1, which leads to the protocol P'1. Figure 1b) (respectively 1c) and 1d)) illustrates the state of the PVCs after the adaptation in the case of a local adaptation strategy (respectively global and instant adaptation strategy). In Figure 1b), the newly created protocol P'_1

rules the sub-community *A* but is not available to sub-communities *B* and *C*. In Figure 1c), the newly created protocol is available to the new sub-community *C* but the sub-community *B* is still ruled by P_1. In Figure 1d), P'_1 is available to the new sub-community *C* and the sub-community *B* is now ruled by P'_1.

The newly created social protocol P'_1 embeds knowledge about an alternative way to collaborate. The social protocol P'_1 models the additional knowledge and expertise which have been required to react to situations which have not been unforeseen nor modeled in the social protocol P_1. Information about the negotiation process that leads from P_1 to P'_1 is available from the negotiation history database, as presented in Figure 1. One should notice that these knowledge and expertise should not necessarily been directly reused, but could be used for consultation about what has happened in similar cases and the solution found. Obviously, privacy should be taken into account. Collaborators that negotiated the social protocol P_1 should explicitly agree to publish negotiation-related information before such information is available to other sub-communities.

The global propagation strategy would allow collaborators of sub-communities to consult and eventually reuse the VO-I of sub-communities in which a social protocol has been adapted. The instant propagation strategy would enforce the reuse of newly-created knowledge by other sub-communities in a normative way: the adapted social protocol "overwrites" the original social protocol.

Finally, the proposed adaptation propagation strategies provide means for *continuous VO-I-M*. A classical issue in VO-I-M is the frequency of VO-I capturing. A briefing-debriefing technique has been presented by Loss et al. (2006b), proposing to capture VO-I by comparing the results of two interview meetings: usually the first interview meeting takes place before the VO is created, while the second one (the debriefing) takes place after VO dissolution or metamorphosis. The briefing-debriefing technique may be used "to double-check the plans, fine tune the assignments of tasks, rehearsal the actions and also to exchange lessons learned, evaluate the actions against the plans and to register explicitly the knowledge acquired, respectively". Therefore, the briefing-debriefing technique may capture more elements of the VO-I, than just those related to social protocols. On the second hand, information about adaptation of a social protocol would be captured by the briefing-debriefing technique during the debriefing session, while the adaptation propagation strategies make information about adaptation of a social protocol accessible by other VOs just after the adaptation. Therefore, propagation strategies may enable continuous VO-I-M of social protocols, while the briefing-debriefing technique is less agile but may capture more elements of the VO-I.

5   CONCLUSIONS

The introduction of adaptation of social protocols and adaptation propagation strategies to provide computer support to management of PVC-inheritance related to collaboration processes. To our best knowledge, it is the first attempt to support continuous management of VO-inheritance, even if the proposed solution is limited to PVC-inheritance elements related to collaboration processes.

The main innovations presented in this paper are 1) the rational for adaptation of social protocols in PVCs as heterogeneous and dynamic sociosystems, 2) three strategies for adaptation propagation, 3) the proposition of adaptation of social protocols and adaptation propagation as means for continuous management of PVC inheritance. Among future works, a formal model of propagation strategies presented in this paper should be established and validated by experiments.

6   REFERENCES

1.   van der Aalst, W.M.P., Weske, M. and Wirtz, G. (2003) Advanced topics in workflow management: Issues, requirements, and solutions. J. of Integrated Design and Process Science, 7(3), pp. 49–77
2.   Camarinha-Matos, L.M., Afsarmanesh, H. and Ollus, M. (2005) ECOLEAD: A Holistic Approach to Creation and Management of Dynamic Virtual Organizations. In Collaborative Networks and their Breeding Environments, Proc. of the 6th IFIP Working Conf. on Virtual Enterprises (PRO-VE 2005), Valencia, Spain, Sept. 26-28, 2005, Springer, pp. 3–16
3.   Chen, H., Finin, T. and Joshi, A. (2003) An Ontology for Context-Aware Pervasive Computing Environments. Knowledge Engineering Review, Special Issue on Ontologies for Distributed Systems, 18(3) Cambridge University Press, pp. 197–207
4.   Chituc, C.M., and Azevedo, A.L. (2005) Multi-Perspective Challenges on Collaborative Networks Business Environments. In Collaborative Networks and their Breeding Environments, Proceedings of the 6th IFIP Working Conf. on Virtual Enterprises (PRO-VE 2005), Valencia, Spain, Sept. 26-28, 2005, Springer, pp. 25–32
5.   Daoudi, F. and Nurcan, S. (2007) A benchmarking framework for methods to design flexible business processes. Special Issue on Design for Flexibility of the "Software Process: Improvement and Practice Journal", 12(1), pp. 51–63
6.   Dey, A.K., Salber, D. and Abowd, G. D. (2001) A Conceptual Framework and a Toolkit for Supporting the Rapid Prototyping of Context-Aware Applications. Human-Computer Interaction, 16(2-4), pp. 97–166
7.   Dockhorn Costa, P., Ferreira Pires, L. and van Sinderen, M. (2005) Designing a Configurable Services Platform for Mobile Context-Aware Applications. Int. J. of Pervasive Computing and Communications (JPCC), 1(1), pp. 27–37
8.   Ekholm, A. and Fridqvist, S. (1996) Modelling of user organisations, buildings and spaces for the design process. In Construction on the Information Highway, Proceedings from the CIB W78 Workshop, Bled, Slovenia, June 10-12, 1996
9.   Loss, L., Pereira-Klen, A.A. and Rabelo, R.J. (2006a) Knowledge Management Based Approach for Virtual Organization Inheritance. In Network-centric Collaboration and Supporting Frameworks, Proc. of the 7th IFIP Working Conf. on Virtual Enterprises (PRO-VE 2006), Helsinki, Finland, Sept. 2006. Springer, pp. 285–294
10. Loss, L., Rabelo, R.J. and Pereira-Klen, A.A. (2006b) Virtual Organization Management: An Approach Based on Inheritance Information. In: Global Conference on Sustainable Product Development and Life Cycle Engineering, São Carlos, SP, Brazil, Editora Suprema
11. Picard, W. (2007) An Algebraic Algorithm for Structural Validation of Social Protocols. In Lecture Notes in Computer Science, 4439, Springer, pp. 570–583
12. Picard, W. (2006a) Adaptive Collaboration in Professional Virtual Communities via Negotiations of Social Protocols. In Network-centric Collaboration and Supporting Frameworks, Proc. of the 7th IFIP Working Conf. on Virtual Enterprises (PRO-VE 2006), Helsinki, Finland, Sept. 2006. Springer, pp. 353–360
13. Picard, W. (2006b) Adaptive Human-to-Human Collaboration via Negotiations of Social Protocols". In Technologies for Business Information Systems, Proc. of the 9th Int. Conf. on Business Information Systems, Klagenfurt, Austria, May 31 – June 2, 2006, Springer Verlag, pp. 193–203
14. Picard, W. (2005) Modeling Structured Non-monolithic Collaboration Processes. In Collaborative Networks and their Breeding Environments, Proc. of the 6th IFIP Working Conf. on Virtual Enterprises (PRO-VE 2005), Valencia, Spain, Sept. 26-28, 2005, Springer, pp. 379–386

PART **13**

CUSTOMER INVOLVEMENT IN NETWORKS

41   VIRTUAL CUSTOMER COMMUNITIES: AN INNOVATIVE CASE FROM THE MEDIA INDUSTRY

Miia Kosonen and Hanna-Kaisa Ellonen

Lappeenranta University of Technology, School of Business, FINLAND
miia.kosonen@lut.fi, hanna-kaisa.ellonen@lut.fi

Online communication technologies enhance the ability of firms to engage in on-going dialogue with their customers and leverage valuable knowledge. However, there is little formal research on virtual customer communities. The aim of this paper is to offer new insights of the different customer roles and business benefits of virtual customer community-based collaboration in product development. We present a case study from the media industry, and demonstrate how the roles and interactions have been integrated into a novel form of a virtual customer community, supporting continuous product development with a large base of paying customers.

1   INTRODUCTION

Several authors have noted how online communication technologies enhance the ability of firms to engage in on-going dialogue with their customers, and thus leverage valuable knowledge (Sawhney and Prandelli, 2000; Nambisan, 2002; Füller et al., 2006; Chan and Lee, 2004). Customer participation may take many forms, ranging from using especially designed customer toolkits (Dahan and Hauser, 2002) to voluntary participation in online customer communities (Franz and Wolkinger, 2003). In general, virtual communities are *groups of people who use communication technologies for repeated social interaction to meet certain needs* (cf. Preece, 2000). An increasing number of these communities are sponsored by commercial organizations (Porter, 2004). Yet, there is little formal research on virtual customer communities and how they may benefit businesses.

Researchers (e.g. Nambisan, 2002; Thompke and von Hippel, 2002; Dahan and Hauser, 2002; Jeppesen and Molin, 2004; Fuller et al., 2006; Sawhney et al., 2005) argue that customer participation in both the front end (idea generation, concept) and the back end (design and testing) phases of new product development enhances innovation and thus creates more value. We note, however, that customer interactions have mainly been investigated from the new product development (NPD) viewpoint, where customers have eventually played a limited and mostly passive role (Nambisan, 2002). We argue that current research fails to acknowledge the potential of customer collaboration to support *continuous* (existing) product development and *on-going* interactions.

In our understanding, the value of virtual customer communities (VCC's) is truly revealed with *continuous creation products,* such as most media products (cf. Picard, 2005), that involve the continuous creativity and improvement every day or week. For these products, it is impossible – both for the time and cost associated – to use

Kosonen, M., Ellonen, H.-K., 2007, in IFIP International Federation for Information Processing, Volume 243, Establishing the Foundation of Collaborative Networks; eds. Camarinha-Matos, L., Afsarmanesh, H., Novais, P., Analide, C.; (Boston: Springer), pp. 391–398.

traditional customer research methods, such as focus groups and surveys, every time a new issue is planned. Prior literature implies that virtual customer communities have the possibility of creating value in the media context, e.g. within the newspaper industry (Boczkowski, 2004) and the magazine publishing industry, by enabling firms to perceive weak signals from the audience and fulfill the needs of customer when improving the service (Ellonen and Kuivalainen, 2006). However, current research still lacks examples and systematic approaches on how to integrate virtual customer communities into the product development.

The aim of this paper is to offer new insights of the different customer roles and business benefits of virtual customer community-based collaboration in product development. We present a case study from the media industry, and demonstrate how the product development and customer interactions have been integrated into a novel form of a virtual customer community.

The rest of the paper is structured as follows: We start by presenting literature on virtual customer communities. Thereafter, we describe our research design and methodology. In the empirical part of the paper, we start by presenting our case – the dieting community – and then describe and analyze the ways in which customer interactions support the product development. We conclude with a discussion of the lessons learned and relate our findings to the theory.

2   VIRTUAL CUSTOMER COMMUNITIES

The market has become more open for public criticism, and consumers have taken the role of competitors in creating value (Prahalad and Ramaswahy, 2000; Chan and Lee, 2004). Foray (2004) suggests collaboration among users and doers as one outstanding model of innovation. Collaboration takes two particular forms: firstly, businesses create organizational systems through which users are able to make adjustments and develop the product, and secondly, user cooperatives can be organized as sector-defined communities where users voluntarily interact, develop product and freely share their ideas. These novel forms of social communities, often referred to as virtual communities, support customer-based value creation and provide a way to interact, learn, conduct transactions, and share knowledge.

Virtual community relationships vary in depth and nature. For instance, open source (OS) software development is rooted in loosely coupled communities kept together by common values and norms. At the other end of the continuum there are tightly knit groups of people sharing personal experiences and affections and also developing interpersonal relationships, such as in patient support communities. In any case, communities are rooted in social relationships. Thus interactions must be considered based on the sociological perspectives on knowledge and value creation (Nambisan, 2002), and not focusing solely into the supportive communication systems and technologies. It is particularly important to make user status transparent, which may strengthen collective invention and trust building (Prahalad and Ramaswamy, 2000). Trust is considered both as an antecedent for virtual community participation, and as a dynamic process which maintains sense of community among members (Ellonen et al., 2007).

According to Füller et al. (2006), virtual interest groups typically possess high levels of knowledge about a specific domain. Virtual customer communities can benefit firms, as their members show high product interest and typically high presence on the Web. Online discussions represent a source of feedback on a continuous and natural basis, also with drastically lower costs than in offline environments. Interaction can take place on two levels: one between the firm and its customers, and the other among customers who help and support each other. Virtual communities have been applied by companies for various purposes, such as building brands (McWilliam, 2000), collecting feedback from customers (Williams and Cothrel, 2000), supporting product use (Moon and Sproull, 2001), and enhancing quality management (Finch, 1999).

In particular, VCCs enable firms to establish distributed product development and modification through various customer roles. Firstly, customer can be involved as *buyers* of the product. Secondly, as *users*, customers may contribute into product testing, and provide product support to peer users. Thirdly, customers can be seen as valuable *resources* providing information to companies and supporting innovation processes. Finally, customers may take the role of *co-creators*, contributing into the design and development of new products. (Nambisan, 2002)

In the media context, communities have primarily seen as a cost effective way to update website content, thus giving customers a voice and an opportunity to express themselves. Nevertheless, current research fails to address the question how the media companies can *hear* the voice of customers and build on customer interactions in order to adopt to the changing environment, and make changes and modifications. This is the purpose of our case study. We now present our methodology and case study from the media industry.

3   CASE STUDY

Nambisan (2002) suggested that detailed case studies of virtual customer communities could be conducted to collect rich descriptive data on the design and evolution on these communities in different product development contexts. Given the scant number of prior studies on the subject and our goal to gain new insights on the subject, we chose to conduct a single case study. According to Yin (2003), the objective of a case study is to understand a phenomenon in its natural context. Eriksson and Koistinen (2005) emphasize the importance of describing and understanding the context, as it makes the case understandable and partly explains it. In particular, our research goals are linked to Dyer and Wilkins (1991) who consider "good stories" to be the ultimate result of case studies: good stories may make us see new theoretical relationships and question old ones.

Our data-collection methods were a theme interview and observation. Theme interviews involve the implementation of a number of predetermined questions and special topics, but allow the interviewers freedom to digress (Berg, 2004) and latitude in terms of how the questions are asked and in what order (Shank, 2006). The interview themes covered the implementation history, community functionality and the related innovations, incorporating users into the development work, building sense of community, and connections to other media products. The interview was conducted face-to-face in November 2006, and it lasted for 45 minutes. The interviewee has been a central actor in both planning and implementing the community as the community producer. The interview was audiotaped with the participant's consent and transcribed in full.

In addition, following the suggestion by Kendall (1999) to include observation as a method when studying online communities, the community was observed for a six week period to explore the discussion forums and evaluate the functionality of the site in general. A field diary was kept on the observations and messages collected from the discussion forums. This totaled a textual dataset of nearly 70 pages. The collected data was then analyzed thematically (cf. Auerbach and Silverstein, 2003). The unit of analysis in this case study is the product.

In order to increase the validity (cf. Yin, 1989), three tactics were used: using multiple sources of evidence, establishing a chain of evidence with the coding, and having the key informant review the research report drafts. Having presented our methodology, we now proceed to describe our case.

3.1   Case description

The case study concerns a novel form of a virtual community within the media context. The community is targeted at customers willing to lose weight, and it was launched in Spring 2006. During the first half year of its existence, the community had attracted over 20,000 unique visitors. There are over 10 discussion boards, covering topics such as food, exercise, physical looks, success stories, and feedback to the hosting team.

From a social viewpoint, a dieting peer group is not a new phenomenon, but large-scale weight-watching virtual communities applying usage fees have only recently emerged in Finland. Two different community sites hosted by rival media companies were launched almost simultaneously. Companies thus were able to identify an emerging customer need to be fulfilled. Therefore, our case community could be considered an innovation in itself. We see both the software product and the social community as integral parts of the case product concept, and in this paper we use the term "product development" to cover the development of the whole concept the customers pay for.

3.2   Community functionality and support services

The dieting community guides the member to enhance the quality of his of her diet instead of focusing on the amount of calories. Technically, the community employs a novel piece of software to help customers in achieving their personal goals. In practice, it simplifies the customer's daily input about his or her diet and physical exercise so that users do not have to understand nutrition-specific details. Instead, it gives guidance simply in the form of color code –based "quality marks", functionally resembling the logic of traffic lights: green light signals that all values are in balance, while red and orange lights point out where the user has to repair his or her nutrition or amount of exercise. Guidance on how to repair them is then provided. The program also learns about an individual member by employing a recommendation system where users may rate the provided dishes to get further recommendations and tips for their daily use.

In addition to the program functionality, members are supported by community staff (company internal) and a group of external experts who participate in interesting discussions and write articles about the related topics. They also have an important role in motivating and encouraging members through personal letters.

Customers pay participation fees for using the weight management program, excluding the one week test period that is free. The program is has been developed and modified throughout the process. It is used in a context of a social community, where customers interact and support each other in their weight-losing efforts by conducting discussions through web-based discussion boards, and also engage in message exchange with the community staff and experts. These interactions are closely conjoined; discussions are initiated and maintained equally by customers, experts and staff team. In the following, we will discuss the different forms of customer interactions utilized in the product development of the dieting community.

3.3 Community in product development

The development of the original software product was done in close collaboration with external partners, namely, subcontractors responsible for coding and layout of the site. Customer were involved only after launching the service, yet their feedback proved valuable for modifying and improving the site functionality in particular.

All customer feedback was openly available in the early phases of the implementation, and provided valuable insights for developing the community and adding new features, such as own topics for senior users and members' personal diaries. The feedback also helped in pinpointing the related technical problems without additional workload:

"In the beginning, we had technical problems, but now it is more like general development... As all user feedback was openly there, we did not receive masses of complaints about the same problem, and we could work and 'close the case' out."

At present, members may provide feedback either by using the specific form or share their ideas freely in any of the discussion forums. Since the community has grown larger and the amount of discussion threads has increased in line with the member base, most frequently asked questions are then organized into a separate topic with the community staff's responses.

Based on our data, it seems that hosting a community in the early stages of its life cycle allows more freedom in doing slight modifications. In particular, new communicative features and tools can be easily incorporated into the site. Following the metaphor of the community producer, the development work is like building a house that will never become ready. Thus it is particularly important to engage in collaboration with customers.

"The focal player is the community. We promote members' feelings of belonging by hearing their stories and reacting to their ideas. The more influence, the more commitment."

Using Nambisan's (2002) classification of customer roles, we note that in this case, customers are involved in all four roles. Firstly, they only become members of the community as *a buyer*, since they pay a monthly fee for using the service. Secondly, as *users,* customers use the software and help each other e.g. in technical issues. Thirdly, customers are seen as an important *resource* that supply information and, accordingly, support continuous innovation. This type of activity not only takes place when prompted by the community staff, but customers take an active role in providing feedback. The staff also "rewards" active participants, thus acknowledging their role in the community.

"It does not have to be any major thing but small baits. The quality of the service is improved gradually, due to the community, as well. — One of these baits is that some members become 'messengers'. They are mentioned in community newsletters and thus become testimonials for the product: this is something that truly works."

We also argue that customers play to role of *co-creators*. In our view, this involves a more intense customer-firm relationship than the three earlier mentioned roles. They contribute by reading and submitting messages to the forums and thus make the community more valuable and inviting. While customers do not have a direct access to the software, they initiate or participate in designing and developing new features and customized services that create more value. Examples of the personal diaries and senior discussion forums were described above. Rather than being co-creators of the software, we see the customers as co-creators of the social community and the whole business model.

Thus, we conclude that customer interactions have enabled the continuous development and improvement of this particular product, both in terms of *software functionality* and *social actions* serving as a "continuous test laboratory". We will now discuss the lessons learnt from this case.

3.4   Discussion

There are three specific attributes in the case community that we would like to emphasize: Firstly, customer interactions have played a focal part in the *continuous product development*. For instance, new topics of interest have been added based on customers' feedback. In our view, one of the salient strengths of the community has been the hosting team's openness and the ability to react quickly, which has given them credibility in the eyes of customers and has allowed incorporating them into the development work. This, in turn, increases efficiency from the firm side e.g. by removing overlapping feedback, and gives customers more opportunities and self-esteem (cf. Nambisan, 2002). From the company's perspective, the community has also the potential to support the product development of other media products of the company.   For instance, there has been a growing interest to transfer personal success stories from the community into print media products.

Secondly, the product development of the community relies on interactions *with paying customers*, not just a purposefully collected research sample of them, which is the case in most priorly described examples (cf. Jeppesen and Molin, 2004; Füller et al., 2006). Also, Franz and Wolkinger (2003) have observed that the introduction of membership fees in virtual communities often fails. They speculated that users would not be willing to pay a fee for "nice chat". Our case demonstrates that it is possible to have a commercial, user-fee funded virtual community. Yet, we agree with Franz and Wolkinger that in order to succeed in this endeavor, the community should offer something the customers truly need and value, as our case community clearly does.

We note that product development with paying customers naturally also involves risks for the customers and for the company. On the customer side, it seems that openness in community development, fair practices, and strong personal intention have built trust among members (cf. Radin, 2006; Shankar et al., 2002) and willingness to carry the risk of paying usage fees beforehand. In our view, to build and maintain this type of trust requires true commitment from the community staff. From the trust building perspective the key issue is not to make every modification the customers ask for, but rather to communicate openly with the customers and show respect to their contribution and involvement. At best, this benefits the company, as committed customers spread information about the community through word-of-mouth (cf. Srinivasavan et al. 2002; Wang et al. 2006).

Thirdly, as described above, customers have *several roles* in the case community – those of buyer, user, resource and co-creator (cf. Nambisan, 2002). We propose that the empowerment of customers may help them to commit to the community and pay the usage-fee since their contribution is visibly noted and valued by the community organizer. Also, Cothrel and Williams (1999, 59) state that the informal roles of community members are a good indicator of the health of a community;

when members are willing to serve the community in various roles, it indicates that the community is something people value and want to be part of. In our view, one of strengths of the case community is the integration of customers in all these roles simultaneously. This mode of operation clearly supports both the continuous product development and customer commitment.

4   CONCLUSIONS

Virtual customer communities provide companies with new avenues to create value through customer relationships, by incorporating enthusiastic users that would be difficult to reach without the support of communication technologies. At the same time, communities may themselves become innovations when applied in novel ways.

In this paper, we examined virtual customer communities and the related customer roles based on a case study from the media context. We pointed out how the virtual community has potential to support *continuous product development* with a large base of *paying customers*, simultaneously in line with everyday participation and interactions. It may thus combine commercial purposes, novel forms of supporting software, and Internet-enabled social innovation. This mode of operation both supports continuous iteration of the product to match current customer needs and helps the customers to commit to the community since their contribution is noted and valued by the community organizer.

The main limitation of our study is that it is based on a single case. The case product is a combination of software and social community, and therefore it might be a special type of product in terms of its convertibility. Future studies should explore these issues with different types of products to generate more generic findings. Also, this study only focused on different types of customer roles and their associated business benefits as research variables. However, we hope that our efforts to underline the opportunities for continuous product development and capturing various customer roles simultaneously will provide avenues for more generic theorization and empirical research.

5   REFERENCES

1.   Auerbach, Carl, Silverstein, Louise. Qualitative Data. An introduction to coding and analysis. New York: University Press, 2003.
2.   Berg, Bruce. Qualitative Research Methods for Social Sciences. Boston: Pearson Education, 2004.
3.   Boczkowski, Pablo. Digitizing the news – Innovation in online newspapers. Cambridge, MA: MIT Press, 2004.
4.   Chan, T., Lee, J. "A comparative study of online user communities involvement in product innovation and development". A paper presented in the 13th International Conference on Management of Technology (IAMOT), Washington D.C., April 3-7, 2004. Retrieved December 15, 2006 from http://opensource.mit.edu/papers/chanlee.pdf
5.   Cothrel, J., Williams, R. On-line communities: helping them form and grow. Journal of Knowledge Management, 1999; 3(1): 54-60.
6.   Dahan, E., Hauser, J. The virtual customer. The Journal of Product Innovation Management, 2002; 19: 332-353.
7.   Dyer, W., Wilkins, A. Better stories, not better constructs, to generate better theory: A rejoinder to Eisenhardt. Academy of Management Review, 1991; 16(3): 613-619.
8.   Ellonen, HK, Kuivalainen, O. "The development of an online success story: A case from the magazine publishing industry." In Managing Information in the Digital Economy: Issues and Solutions, Khalid S. Soliman, ed. 2006, pp. 90-98. Proceedings of the 6th International Business

Information Management Association (IBIMA) Conference, 19-21 June 2006, Bonn, Germany.
9. Ellonen, HK., Kosonen, M., Henttonen, K. The development of a sense of virtual community. International Journal of Web Based Communities, 2007; 3(1): 114-130.
10. Eriksson, P., Koistinen, K. Monenlainen tapaustutkimus [Diverse Case Study]. Kuluttajatutkimuskeskuksen julkaisuja 4/2005 [National Consumer Research Centre, publications 4/2005], Helsinki, Finland.
11. Finch, B. Internet discussions as a source of consumer product customer involvement and quality information: an exploratory study. Journal of Operations Management, 1999; 17: 535-556.
12. Foray, D. "New models of innovation and the role of information technologies in the knowledge economy". In Transforming Enterprise. The Economic and Social Implications of Information Technology, W. Dutton, B. Kahin, R. O'Callaghan and A. Wyckoff, eds, pp. 113-130. Cambridge, MA: MIT Press, 2004.
13. Franz, R., Wolkinger, T. Customer Integration with Virtual Communities – Case study: The online community of the largest regional newspaper in Austria. Proceedings of the 36th Hawaii International Conference on System Sciences (HICSS'03), 2003. Retrieved February 12, 2007 from http://csdl2.computer.org/comp/proceedings/hicss/2003/1874/07/187470214c.pdf
14. Füller, J., Bartl, M., Ernst, H., Mühlbacher, H. Community based innovation: How to integrate members of virtual communities into new product development. Electronic Commerce Research, 2006; 6: 57-73.
15. Jeppesen, L., Molin, M.. Consumers as co-developers: Learning and innovation outside the firm. Technology Analysis and Strategic Management, 2003; 15(3): 363-383.
16. Kendall, L. "Recontextualizing 'cyberspace': methodological considerations for on-line research". In Doing Internet Research - Critical Issues and Methods for Examining the Net, Steve Jones, ed, pp. 57-74. California: Sage Publications, 1999.
17. McWilliam, G. Building stronger brands through online communities. Sloan Management Review, 2000; 41(3): 43-55.
18. Moon, J., Sproull, L. Turning love into money: How some firms may profit from voluntary electronic customer communities. In The e-business handbook, P. Lowry, J. Cherrington and R. Watson, eds. Boca Raton, FL: St. Lucie Press, 2001.
19. Nambisan, S. Designing virtual customer environments for new product development: toward a theory. Academy of Management Review, 2002; 27(3): 392-413.
20. Picard, RG. Unique characteristics and business dynamics of media products. Journal of Media Business Studies, 2005; 2(2): 61-69.
21. Porter, CE. A typology of virtual communities: A multi-disciplinary foundation for future research. Journal of Computer-Mediated Communication, 2004; 10(1).
22. Prahalad, C., Ramaswamy, V. Co-opting customer competence. Harvard Business Review, 2000; 78(1): 79-87.
23. Preece, Jenny. Online communities. Designing usability, supporting sociability. Chichester: Wiley, 2000.
24. Radin, P. 'To me, it's my life': Medical communication, trust, and activism in cyberspace. Social Science & Medicine, 2006; 62: 591-601.
25. Sawhney, M., Prandelli, E., Communities of creation. Managing distributed innovation in turbulent markets. California Management Review, 2000; 42(4): 24-54.
26. Sawhney, M., Verona, G., Prandelli, E. Collaborating to create: the Internet as a platform for customer engagement in product innovation. Journal of Interactive Marketing, 2005; 19(4): 4-17.
27. Shank, Gary. Qualitative Research. A personal skills approach. New Jersey: Pearson Education, Upper Saddle River, 2006.
28. Shankar, V., Urban, G., Sultan, F. Online trust: a stakeholder perspective, concepts, implications, and future directions. Journal of Strategic Information Systems, 2002; 11: 325-344.
29. Srinivasan, S., Anderson, R., Ponnavolu, K. Customer loyalty in e-commerce: an exploration of its antecedents and consequences. Journal of Retailing, 2002; 78: 41-50.
30. Thomke, S., von Hippel, E. Customers as innovators. A new way to create value. Harvard Business Review, April 2002; 74-81.
31. Wang, HC, Chia-Yi, MH, Pallister, J., Foxall, G. Innovativeness and involvement as determinants of website loyalty: II. Determinants of consumer loyalty in B2C e-commerce. Technovation, 2006, in press.
32. Williams, R., Cothrel, J. Four smart ways to run online communities. Sloan Management Review, 2000; 41(4): 81-91.
33. Yin, Robert. Case Study Research. Design and Methods. Thousand Oaks: Sage Publications, 1989.
34. Yin, Robert. Case Study Research. Design and Methods. 3rd edition. Thousand Oaks: Sage Publications, 2003.

THE IMPACT OF CUSTOMER PARTICIPATION ON BUSINESS ECOSYSTEMS

Garyfallos Fragidis

Department of Business Administration, University of Macedonia & Institute of Technology and Education of Serres, garyf@teiser.gr

Adamantios Koumpis

Research Programmes Division, ALTEC S.A., akou@altec.gr

Konstantinos Tarabanis

Department of Business Administration, University of Macedonia, kat@uom.gr

GREECE

The concept of business ecosystems is a new, powerful metaphor that steps forward the movement towards symbiotic and co-evolutionary business networks. The literature describes business ecosystems as economic communities comprised of a number of business entities that are closely related the one to the other with symbiotic relationships; as a result, they constantly interact and seek to co-operate to fulfill their particular goals and attain mutual benefits. In this paper we discuss the role of customers in business ecosystems. We argue that the concept of business ecosystems is focused on the needs and the roles of the producers and neglects the customers, especially the end-customers. We analyse the impact of customers' participation as active members in business ecosystems and suggest that it intensifies their co-evolutionary character and increases their dynamism. We discuss technological aspects of customer participation in business ecosystems.

1   INTRODUCTION

The purpose of the business enterprise, as defined in the literature of business strategy, is to create value. The traditional thinking about value creation is based on the industrial organisation theory and the concept of the value chain: the enterprise belongs and operates in some industrial sector; strategy is primarily pre-occupied with positioning the enterprise in the right place on the value chain, so that it performs the right value-adding activities that promise to offer the biggest profit. The competitive advantage derives by disaggregating the value creation process of the business enterprise into discrete activities, which create a basis for differentiation. In the marketplace, the business enterprise selects the products that fit better to its value-adding activities and places them in the right market segments, that correspond to large enough customer bases.

Today, however, a variety of trends, such as globalisation, the development of the digital economy and the increased importance of information technology, services and knowledge, change dramatically the business context and open up new ways of value creation. The term "new economy" launched about the end of the previous century to denote the radical change that was taking place in the business world, the economy and -more broadly- the modern society. The key point of this term is that the economy as we knew it has changed and now it operates in a new, different way (OECD, 2000).

Fragidis, G., Koumpis, A., Tarabanis, K., 2007, in IFIP International Federation for Information Processing, Volume 243, Establishing the Foundation of Collaborative Networks; eds. Camarinha-Matos, L., Afsarmanesh, H., Novais, P., Analide, C.; (Boston: Springer), pp. 399–406.

In this modern business environment, the fundamental logic of business strategy and value creation is changing and new models are emerging. Network structures and concepts of collaboration have been developed as effective means to cope with the needs and challenges of 21st century. The development of business networks, alliances and virtual organisations question the traditional organisational and strategic business models. Value creation in not considered anymore a linear business function, but a collaborative and co-evolutionary process. The focus of the strategic analysis is not on the company itself or even on the industry, but on the whole value-creating system, within which business partners, allies, suppliers and customers work together to co-produce value. According to Normann and Ramirez (1993), the key strategic task in the new business environment is the reconfiguration of roles and relationships among this constellation of economic actors in order to mobilize the creation of value in new forms and by new players. The underlying strategic goal is to create an ever-improving fit between business competencies and customer needs.

In this new setting, the concept of "business ecosystems" has emerged as a new strategic paradigm for business enterpises. Based on concepts and insights from biological systems and complexity theory (Moore, 1996, p. 9-10), it is a powerful metaphor that steps forward the movement towards symbiotic and co-evolutionary business networks. Business ecosystem consists of a large number of participants that can be business firms and other organisations, which are interconnected to each other, in a sense that they have an affect on each other. The concept of business ecosystems proposes a holistic way to examine the business enterprise and its relationships with its environment, showing concern for all the stakeholders.

In this paper we concentrate and discuss the role of customers in business ecosystems. In section 2 we present the concept of business ecosystems; we argue it is focused on the needs and the roles of the producers and neglects the customers, especially the end-customers; based on this argument, we explain the shortcomings and negative aspects of it entails. In section 3 we analyze the need for customer participation in the processes of business ecosystems. In section 4 we present the general aspects for customer participation in business ecosystems and discuss the technological aspects of this endeavor.

2   QUANTIFYING THE ROLE OF THE CUSTOMER IN BUSINESS ECOSYSTEMS

During the 1990s, technological developments and new managerial trends (e.g. focus on core competencies and outsourcing) boosted the growth of networks of business collaboration. The focus of strategic analysis has moved from the single company to different forms of business networks, such as *business constellations* (Normann and Ramirez, 1993), *extended enterprises* (Prahalad and Ramaswamy, 2003), *value nets* (Bovet and Martha, 2000) and *strategic networks* (Jarillo, 1988).

The concept of business ecosystems is a recent addition in the literature of business networks. A business ecosystem is "an economic community comprised of a number of interacting organisations and individuals, including suppliers, producers, competitors, customers and other stakeholders, that produces goods and services of value for the customers" (Moore, 1996, p. 26).

The concept of business ecosystems has several advantages over other forms of business networks (Fragidis, Tarabanis and Koumpis, 2007a). For example, business ecosystems concentrate large populations of different kinds of business entities. They transcend industry and supply chain boundaries and assemble a variety of organisations that can complement each other and synergistically produce composite products. Interdependence and symbiotic relationships are inherent attributes in business eco-systems; as a result, the participants counter a mutual fate and co-evolve with each other. But in parallel, members compete with each other for the acquirement of resources and the attraction of customers.

The evolution of our research should drive us in identifying the lead markets, i.e. those areas that exhibit a highly active profile in terms of innovations for new services that involve customer participation and experiences as an integral part of their structure. Our final sample comprised 254 enterprises – public or private. More specifically, we followed a five step methodology as described below:

STEP 1: We chose 3 parameters which can be easily determined from publicly disclosed data that is available

- **ATOG** = Average Turn-over Growth over a 5-year period 2000 to 2005 (for ~ 12% of the data we had to undergo a projection to cover the entire 5-year period using the average growth of the years before or after)
- **PUBEXCM** = Average Public expenditure on customer participation related areas of investment over the same period
- **BEXCM** = Average Business expenditure on customer participation related areas of investment over the same period

The following were considered as expenditures on customer participation related areas of investment for an enterprise: (i) expenditures for tangible or intangible (immaterial assets) related with the introduction of new products or services except from costs or expenses dedicated to R&D or production lines; (ii) expenditures for improving the relationships with customers in all aspects related with access-to-products or services, costing factors, improvement of existing and development of new communication channels; (iii) expenditures related to the creation of customer relationship management applications and systems, staffing costs for the previous two types of costs, and maintenance.

STEP 2: We computed the average of these figures for all enterprises involved in our study (both public and private).

STEP 3: We then computed the performance of each identified 'cluster' on these indicators. In each case performance is designated by a 1 or 0 corresponding to performance above or below the mean.

STEP 4: The enterprises have been categorised based on their performance in each of these indicators; Each category is referred to as a 'box'; Each box is labelled 1 to 8; This process allows us to define lists of enterprises for each category.

STEP 5: The next step was to rank the enterprises within each list. This last step is not presented here as it needs more attentions as much of the variance comes from the particular business domain and market segment that an enterprise is active in. This enables us to derive the following categories:

Table 1 – Enterprise categories

Category	Description
1	Below average performance on all 3 indicators
2	Above average ATOG growth but below average investment in customer participation related areas by both public and private sectors
3	Above average public investment in customer participation related areas but below average investment by industry and below average ATOG performance
4	Above average ATOG performance, above average public sector investment in customer participation related areas but below average investment by industry.
5	Below average ATOG performance, below average public sector investment in customer participation related areas and above average investment by industry.
6	Above average investment in customer participation related areas by industry, above average ATOG performance and below average public investment in customer-related areas
7	Above average investment in customer participation related areas by both public and private sectors but below average ATOG growth
8	Above average performance on all 3 indicators

Below we summarise the results of the empirical study.

Table 2 – Populated categories for the identified enterprise clusters

BOX	1	2	3	4	5	6	7	8
ATOG	0	1	0	1	0	1	0	1
PUBEXCM	0	0	1	1	0	0	1	1
BEXCM	0	0	0	0	1	1	1	1
Total	48	70	24	20	16	13	43	20

However, it may also be that comparisons between types are perhaps even more useful. In particular because we have 2 inputs (public and private sector expenditures in customer participation related investments) and 1 output (ATOG growth) it is sensible to see how enterprises are able to deliver above or below average growth with the same combination of inputs.

So it seems that the most interesting questions arise (in order of importance) when we consider the following duets of enterprises:

1. Enterprises of boxes 2 and 7. This will answer the question 'what are the factors that enable enterprises of category 2 to grow much faster than these of box 7 even though both have low levels of public and private expenditures in customer participation related areas of investments? This may identify factors apart from expenditures in customer participation related expenditures that enable rapid growth or how to utilise R&D money most effectively.

2. Enterprises of boxes 3 and 4. These both have low levels of private investment and high levels of public investment, yet 3 underperforms economically

and 4 over-performs. Clearly 4 is able to utilise its public investment much more effectively than 3. Furthermore 4 achieves this despite having little private sector investment - this will show how to utilise innovation in a cluster with little existing private sector investment

3. Enterprises of boxes 5 and 6. These are enterprises where high levels of private investment occurs and little use is made of public funds. Yet 6 prospers and 5 does not. This will tell us how to make best use of private investment funds as they are not deployed to get subsidy from the public sector.

4. Enterprises of boxes 1 and 8 do not tell us so much as it is harder to discern cause and effect here, so these should be considered as out of the scope of this paper.

The evidence we collected is in harmony with the approach we present in Section 4 for a conceptual and a business model for the development of "customer-centric business ecosystems" that builds on both business and public administration ecosystems. More over it is easy to identify that if both public and private expenditures in areas of customer participation co-exist, then the success options for business ecosystems are high.

3 GENERAL ASPECTS OF CUSTOMER PARTICIPATION IN BUSINESS ECOSYSTEMS

In most cases, customer participation in business processes is governed by the business needs and is devoted to serve the benefits of businesses. For example, the customer's role is acknowledged to be important in decreasing the development time and improving the effectiveness of the product development process. In this context, customer participation is usually restricted in providing new concept ideas, evaluating quality of the products or helping business firms learn and improve their productivity. Customers seldom participate to resolve their own problems, by participating in the configuration of the goods and services they receive. On the contrary, business firms usually perceive and interpret customer needs through marketing processes into fixed or customizable product and services. Nevertheless, customizable product can usually only approximate customer needs, but hardly can really meet them.

This kind of customer participation is submissive to the needs of business enterprises. Customers can only receive benefits indirectly, say from the better quality of the products, the improved coordination achieved among the business enterprises and the reduced transaction cost.

The concept of business ecosystems promises the development of more participative business schemata and more collaborative business processes, in which the customer can participate to collaborate with the business partners in the configuration and co-production of products and services. This way, the customer and the businesses benefit mutually: the former from the opportunity to meet his/her unique needs and the latter from the opportunity to learn from the customer, come closer to him/her and co-develop innovations. Notice that customers are not interested in single products, but on complete solutions, that are developed by the direct or indirect collaboration of a variety of producers. Customers combine usually single offers from different suppliers to create valuable outcomes for themselves (Prahalad and Ramaswamy, 2004, p. 10).

The need for customer participation is genuine and well documented in the literature. Normann and Ramirez (1993) use the manufacturing metaphor to describe customers' function: customers use a wide range of inputs in order to create value. It is the customers, therefore, not the business enterprises that have value-adding activities. For Sawhney, Balasubramanian and Krishnan (2003) customers seek particular outcomes and engage in activities to achieve them; these activities can be mapped along a customer-activity chain, which represents end-to-end sequences of related activities that often crosses industry and market boundaries.

The recent success of Web 2.0 is another example that supports the prospect of customer participation in business processes (Fragidis G., Tarabanis K. and Koumpis A, 2007b). The message of the Web 2.0 with regard to business strategy seems to be clear: "give people the opportunity to participate". The most well-known success stories of the Web 2.0 (e.g. Wikipedia, MySpace, YouTube, etc.) are based on the concept of user participation. In all these cases, instead of business-generated content we see user-generated content; the users contribute directly or indirectly and collectively co-create content or experiences. The users are not only consumers, but also co-developers; they do not expect passively the fulfillment of their needs and wants by the business firms, but actively participate in the development of the products and services that meet their needs. Their motives for participation are related with their needs to be heard by business firms, to configure products, services and places that fulfill their needs, to tailor offers according to their preferences, to experiment, learn and gain experiences, to contribute to the community, to offer to their peers and communicate and share with the others.

In previous work we (Fragidis G., Tarabanis K. and Koumpis A, 2006, 2007a) proposed a conceptual and a business model for the development of "customer-centric business ecosystems", that is business ecosystems that are developed having in mind customer participation in configuration and production process. The conceptual model analyses customer participation in business ecosystems, while the business model illustrates the operation of customer-centric business ecosystems.

The business model is depicted in figure 1. It is based on an information platform that mobilizes customers to participate in value creation and empowers them to synthesize composite products. Customer needs can sometimes be so much hetero-geneous that a single business firm or even a single business ecosystem cannot address them. Customer needs can, therefore, be satisfied only by the dynamic constellation of business firms, business ecosystems and other organisations, such as public agencies, in new formations we call "customer-centric business ecosystems".

For instance, viewing the business ecosystem of the automobile firms mentioned in section 2 from the customer's perspective, we perceive it is shaped by the customer's need (suppose) to buy a new car. Certain needs and action that derive from this are related with the recycling of the old car (which may involve transportation to recycler's establishment, multiple transactions with various public administration agencies, etc.), the issue of driving licence, the issue of car insurance, etc. As a result, the customer-centric automobile ecosystem can involve the car producer's business ecosystem (notice that Moore (1996) restricts his interest in it), the recycler's business ecosystem, the insurance company (which can be part of an insurance/financial services business ecosystem) and the public administration business ecosystem, which regulates or supports the whole process. Connections among business entities are flexible and temporary and dissolve after the fulfilment of the customer needs. If the car buyer is to drive the new car soon, all these ecosystems have to collaborate closely.

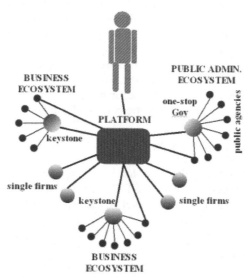

Figure 1: The business model for customer-centric business ecosystems

The platform is the "keystone entity" of the customer-centric business ecosystem. It offers the mechanism for customer participation and leverages recourses and capabilities offered by business entities. It is the customer's agent, it is neutral towards the business enterprises; it is not a retailer of products and services and does not possess the offers. It sets the technological and business standards for the interactions, coordinates them and controls their technical aspects.

Service-oriented architectures (SOA) and web services (WS) technologies, which have both received significant attention in e-business recently because they can provide a flexible environment for the interaction and economic exchanges between business enterprises and with customers, can be used for the development of the business model of customer-centric business ecosystems. The OASIS Reference Model for Service Oriented Architecture (2006) describes SOAs as a paradigm for organizing and utilizing distributed capabilities that may be under the control of different ownership domains. W3C (2004) describes services as abstract resources that represent capabilities of performing tasks and operations and web services as software systems designed to support interoperable interaction over a network.

4   CONCLUSIONS

A customer-centric business ecosystem comprises hubs to both private and public entities – all of which are equally important and can have a substantial impact in the transactions of the individual with the ecosystem as a whole. A buying experience from an internet portal is not exciting at all if part of the transaction cannot be executed in real time because of e.g. shortage of the payment clearing party. This issue directly relates to the value and value creation. Though there is a worryingly growing body of research literature in the area of value creation, it is not bad at all to examine a very basic bottom line: how much do public or private enterprises invest in customer participation related assets – both tangible or intangible. A project for modernising the communication channels with customers of a public entity (e.g. Ministry of Labor) in terms of organising the ecosystem of employment agencies linked with the pool of employers posting their job offerings and the pool of available job-seekers as part of a whole, may substantially increase the growth in the area under consideration. Therefore, it is of great importance the contributions that can have to our study field empirical data we collected that sheds light in the growth related aspects of enterprises – public or private – that have exhibited above the average expenditures in customer participation related activities.

5 ACKNOWLEDGEMENTS

Part of the work reported in the paper has been supported financially by the European Commission in the context of the IST Project PANDA for Collaborative Process Automation Support using Service Level Agreements and Intelligent dynamic Agents in SME clusters.

6 REFERENCES

1.   Bovet D. and Martha J. Value nets: reinventing the rusty supply chain for competitive advantage. Strategy & Leadership, Vol. 28, No 4, 2000, pp. 21 – 26.
2.   Fragidis G., Tarabanis K. and Koumpis A. Value creation in dynamic customer- centric networks. Proceedings of the IEEE International Conference on E-Business Engineering (ICEBE), Shanghai, 24-26 October, 2006.
3.   Fragidis G., Tarabanis K. and Koumpis A. Conceptual and Business Models for Customer-Centric Business Ecosystems. IEEE Inaugural International Digital Ecosystems and Technologies Conference (DEST), Cairns Australia, 21-23 February, 2007.
4.   Fragidis G., Tarabanis K. and Koumpis A. Strategic Opportunities in the Web 2.0: The Development of Customer-Centric Environments. 7th International Conference of the International Academy of E-Business, Vancouver, Canada, 5-8 April, 2007.
5.   Jarillo J. C. On Strategic Networks. Strategic Management Journal, Vol. 9, No. 1, 1988, pp. 31-41.
6.   Moore J.F. The Death of Competition: Leadership and Strategy in the Age of Business Ecosystems. J. Wiley & Sons, Winchester, England, 1996.
7.   Normann R. and Ramirez R. From value chain to value constellation: designing interactive strategy. Harvard Business Review, Vol. 71, Iss. 4, 1993, pp. 65 – 77.
8.   OASIS Committee Specification, Reference Model for Service Oriented Architecture 1.0, 2006, http://www.oasis-open.org/committees/ tc_home.php?wg_abbrev=soa-rm
9.   Organisation for the Economic Cooperation and Development (OECD). Is There a New Economy? OECD, Paris, 2000.
10. Prahalad C.K and Ramaswamy V. The new frontier of experience innovation. Sloan Management Review, Vol. 44, No.4, 2003, pp. 12 – 18.
11. Prahalad C.K and Ramaswamy V. The Future of Competition: Co-creating Unique Value with Customers. Harvard Business School Press, Boston, Massachusetts, 2004.
12. Sawhney M., Balasubramanian S. and Krishnan V.V. Creating growth with services. Sloan Management Review, Vol. 45; Iss. 2, 2003, pp. 34 – 44.
13. W3C Working Group, Web Services Architecture, 2004, http://www.w3c.org

43 SUPPORTING COLLABORATIVE WORK THROUGH WIRELESS TECHNOLOGIES SUPPORT IN PATIENT CENTRIC VIRTUAL ORGANIZATIONS (PCVOS)

[1]Mohyuddin, [1]W.A. Gray, [2]Hazel Bailey, [2]Dave Morrey

[1]*Department of Computer Science, Cardiff University, Cardiff, UK*
[2]*Clinical Information Unit, Velindre NHS Trust, Cardiff, UK*
Mohyuddin@cs.cf.ac.uk, W.A.Gray@cs.cf.ac.uk
Hazel.Bailey@velindre-tr.wales.nhs.uk, Dave.Morrey@velindre-tr.wales.nhs.uk

The paper presents a Virtual Organization (VO) framework which incorporates wireless technologies support at the point of care in the clinical healthcare environment. It reflects the move to patient-centric healthcare given by multi-disciplinary care team collaborating in the patient's treatment. The work sheds light into how VOs incorporating wireless technologies can meet the needs of the care team. It describes technical factors of Virtual Organizations and discusses their role in a clinical environment. It identifies how existing virtual infrastructures in the healthcare literature relate to the development of Patient Centric Virtual Organizations (PCVOs). It addresses the issues and results determined by a case study. These results inform the design, development and evaluation strategy of the pilot project to achieve sustainable collaborative working of care teams for possible improvements in patient care infrastructure.

1   INTRODUCTION

In this paper we present a Virtual Organization (VO) framework as a Patient Centric Virtual Organization (PCVO) incorporating wireless technology support at the point of care. A PCVO provides support for collaborative working of care team members involved in a patient's care. It incorporates a Wireless Point of Care System (WPoCS) to address some of the point of care issues. The pilot project is a case study at Velindre Hospital, the South East Wales Cancer Centre. The pilot involved the secondary and tertiary care level in the cancer domain and was carried out using anonymized data in the Clinical Information Unit. It identified the communication and coordination functional requirements of multi-disciplinary care team members for patient care. A PCVO is based on a patient and supports multi-disciplinary care team members having varied skills involved in the care of that patient. It provides sustainable collaborative working to these care team members with the aim of improved patient treatment and care. In our study, the stakeholders are clinicians, nurses and therapists who play a key role in the patient care process. They need to access information from a variety of patient information resources and work together to achieve the common goal of improved patient care.

An analysis of current patient information resources and working practices of the care team members determined the issues which affect the patient care process. It

Mohyuddin, Gray, W.A., Bailey, H., Morrey, D., 2007, in IFIP International Federation for Information Processing, Volume 243, Establishing the Foundation of Collaborative Networks; eds. Camarinha-Matos, L., Afsarmanesh, H., Novais, P., Analide, C.; (Boston: Springer), pp. 407–414.

suggested how to organize patient information at the point of care and support enhanced integrated working of the care team members. A PCVO harmonizes well with the clinical settings and utilizes existing decentralized and distributed information resources in a structured development. This paper presents the technical aspects of VOs which make the base for the PCVOs in the clinical environment and presents an overview of the pilot project which identified the care team's point of care tasks and looked at their suitability for the WPoCS. This showed that a better organization of the care team's daily routine work can be achieved by performing suitable tasks using handheld devices. It can facilitate the understanding of the role of other members and improve collaboration as tasks become more visible.

2   NEED OF VO DEVELOPMENT IN THE CLINICAL ENVIRONMENT

Several survey, exploratory and technical studies have been conducted which analyze the current problems in the healthcare sector. Some of the major issues identified by McKnight (McKnight et al. 2002), Coiera (Coiera & Tombs 1998), Wickramasinghe (Wickramasinghe & Goldberg 2004), Imhoff (Imhoff et al. 2001), and Embi (Embi 2001) include medication errors; insufficient information structure for patient information management; inconsistent and delayed communication patterns among team members; lack of feedback for patient care; interruptions in the internal communication process; poor provision of information support for team based communication; inappropriate use of communication facilities; and unavailability of required information from decentralized and distributed data resources.

Availability of patient information at the right time and right place is a basic requirement for patient care team members. Thus patient information management at the point of care is important for the smooth running of the technical infrastructure of the hospitals/health institutions (Imhoff et al. 2001). For rapid patient information access, quick and relevant information resources and IT based solutions are required in hospitals McKnight (McKnight et al. 2002). Incorporation of wireless technology applications into existing information resources can meet this need of information provision at the point of care and on the move (Mohyuddin et al. 2006). These technologies utilize previous experience of computerized information systems and harmonize well with mobile workflow of care team in the clinical environment (Grasso 2004).

Although clinical information systems are considered a major information source for patient information, they are not the only way of meeting this need. Currently most patient information is still recorded in patient notes, manual charts, observation charts and other paper based records during the treatment process (Fitzpatrick 2004, Bardram & Bossen 2005). Often care team members have a limited and superficial understanding of each other's work and close coordination is not possible (Bossen 2002). The task repetition and overlapping occurs due to lack of mutual coordination and communication among these care team workers which consumes their effort and time, and results in data redundancy.

Thus there is a need for a better information communication and coordination infrastructure for care team members. This infrastructure must be capable of providing an integrated work pattern and centralizing care team activities in a single platform where they can access and share work information in a better way. These requirements also emphasize the need to incorporate wireless technologies at the point of care to provide the required information to care team members when needed. These issues are addressed by the proposed PCVO framework, which is based on a patient centric approach and harnesses the power of wireless technologies at the point of care.

3 VO BASICS AND ROLE OF WIRELESS TECHNOLOGIES

In the literature, VOs are used in varied ways according to their features; but VOs can certainly be distinguished from traditional organizations because of their functionality and characteristics. Some of the features which are basic for VOs can be described as: 'working for certain organizational objectives together; formation of teams for accessing and sharing resources; usage of computer and communication technologies; trust, collaboration and cooperation among team members' (Rittenbrunch et al. 1998). The functionality of a VO is very much linked with the working of organizations and applications in which they are used. The VO team members may be dispersed by time (temporally) or space (physically), but they use communication and information technologies to share and access information resources. In the clinical environment, care team members collaborating with a common objective of caring for a patient may form a VO. Looking at the nature of clinical environments in a VO context, we find a synergy of aim as the work practices in the clinical environment can be diverse; healthcare professionals with different skills might be caring for the same patient while working from different locations and at different times; and patient resources may be heterogeneous and dispersed (Bossen 2002).

Usage of technology is one of the important pillars in the VO development. Advanced information and communication technologies have played an active role in changing the organizational structures and processes along with evolution of VOs. In order to determine whether a VO approach is suitable, organizations need to know how to expand their technology infrastructure to support the VO environment. They need to consider collaborative technology tools like personal communication tools, laptops and PDAs (Becker et al. 1999). Suitable technology support is a pre-requisite for VO team members who are separated by time, space and culture. Wireless technologies can play a major role within a VO as an information and communication technology factor. These technologies provide a range of value added services to the members of a VO including coordination and collaboration; information access and retrieval; content access and delivery (Camarinha-Matos et al. 2004). Due to the mobility and portability of wireless devices, VO team members can access and share information and updates when working at different physical locations or in different time shifts.

4 VIRTUAL INFRASTRUCTURES IN HEALTHCARE

A concept of dynamic virtual collaborative healthcare teams dealing with home healthcare utilizing fixed computers, mobile phones, PDAs and internet telephones is presented in enterprise project DITIS (Pitsillides et al. 2004). An idea of virtual patient communities which aim to direct and support the chronic patients having long term disease is presented in (Winkelman & Choo 2003). Grootveld (Grootveld et al. 2004) discussed a VO and ad-hoc virtual team formation approach in a telecare project. It describes a VO for the stroke service which is a regional network of healthcare professionals who access patient records in the emergency room for diagnosis. A project for the integration of Cuban healthcare service market discusses a virtual institutional infrastructure which includes different healthcare services and a linked structure of national networks (C. Seror 2003). In a case study of a prison telemedicine program, a VO and virtual clinic creation strategy for distributed clinical consultations which connects an academic medical centre to a prison hospital is discussed (Turner 1998). A new generation of web-based tools like Wikis, blogs and podcasts collectively called collaborationware, are discussed in (Boulos et al. 2006) for virtual collaborative clinical practice.

The related work has shown the benefits of virtual infrastructures and VO formation in different telecare and homecare projects, but no work has been done to analyze the potential benefits of VO development to support a Patient Centric approach at the clinical level, in particular at the point of care. It can be used to manage and classify the tasks of the care team and can play an important role in their mutual cooperation by improving the understanding of other team member's work. Within this domain even less study has been conducted to find out the benefits of VOs with wireless technologies support. The development of PCVOs harnessing the benefits of WPoCS for patient care task management to provide a collaborative working environment for care team members is the novel aspect discussed in this paper and this area needs to be explored further.

5   PROPOSED APPROACH AND FRAMEWORK

PCVOs are built on the VO approach. They use wireless technology support and are based on the functionality and tasks needed by care team members at the point of care in a clinical environment where these members work together in an integrated way to achieve a common goal, i.e. improved patient care. The Patient Centric approach has patient information as the central entity of the paradigm and the PCVO enables each patient's data to be used in different and improved ways in their care. The framework (Figure 1) shows how different decentralized resources such as patient information databases and patient notes in hospital; and distributed resources available on the internet such as medical, pharmacy and evidence based medicine repositories are incorporated in the PCVO. The PCVO works on top of the existing patient information resources to identify and organize patient information with respect to suitable interface for the care team at the point of care. It incorporates WPoCS in the current setup which enables information gaps to be filled and provide missing functionality thereby giving a more complete support facility. The proposed PCVO framework in Figure 1 shows the categorized tasks as 'existing tasks', 'transferable tasks', 'added tasks' and 'automated tasks'. These tasks are classified with the aim of appropriate information provision at the point of care with respect to patient information resources for care team members discussed in the results section.

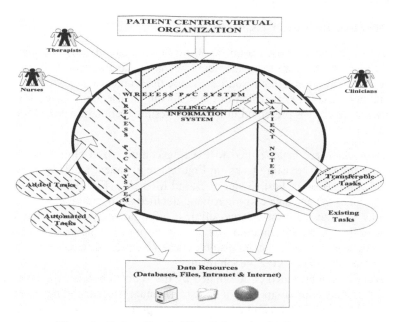

Figure 1 - Patient Centric Virtual Organization Framework

Every PCVO is based on a single patient's information, so different care team members treating that patient become a part of that particular PCVO. Care team members might be working in different time slots and at different physical locations but will always work in a coordinated way for patient treatment under the PCVO platform because patient information structure remains the same.

Because of the distributed nature of clinical work, including the heterogeneity of information resources, and diverse time zones and locations of care team members; we emphasize that wireless technology is a key technology factor for PCVOs. It provides the required communication and coordination among care team for patient care. The steps of a VO roadmap presented in (Camarinha-Matos & Afsarmanesh 2004) show that in general, PCVOs with wireless technologies will provide a roadmap leading to sustainable collaborative care team working for the patient care.

6   STUDY RESULTS

The results of the case study and current work of the pilot project presented in this section were determined by analysis, direct observation, different questionnaires, structured and semi-structured interviews conducted at various levels with different care team members, Information Analysts and IT staff at Velindre Hospital (Burns 1998, Trust 2006). The iterative process of this analysis and design included interviews, discussions and feedback from these stakeholders throughout all the phases of problem discovery, framework approach, suitability and usefulness of task classification, design and modelling of test cases, and continues in the development and evaluation phases. The study identified approximately sixty tasks and is the basis for the next section (Mohyuddin et al. 2007).

6.1   Point of Care Tasks Classification

For improved provision of patient information, PCVOs can identify and classify the point of care tasks for care team members according to the tasks suitability with reference to patient information resources. These three tasks categories are described below and more detailed explanation of the results in tabular forms for each category and care team member is presented in the study results section of paper (Mohyuddin et al. 2007).

1. Tasks which are better suited to existing computerized clinical information systems, are shown as 'existing tasks' in Figure 1, e.g. patient's details on referrals; search and comparison of best Evidence Based Medicine (EBM) cases, X-Ray and large image analysis; and data entry involving detailed keyboard input.

2. Tasks for transfer from existing clinical information systems to the WPoCS due to suitability of the information, are shown as 'transferable tasks' in Figure 1, e.g. accessing summary of treatment history; checking current disease status; checking clinical summary; and checking the lab results.

3. Tasks that can be added or automated by the WPoCS because the tasks do not exist in the current setup or are still done using manual paper based approaches, are shown as 'added tasks' and 'automated tasks' in Figure 1, e.g. accessing vital signs; checking drug details and timings; consulting reference notes; and accessing treatment protocols.

6.2   Collaborative Working Tasks Modelling

A few important test cases have been selected for design and modelling of the clinical collaborative working aspects. These aspects described below are important to collaborative working in a clinical environment, see (Bardram 1996). For each scenario, the current practice structure is compared with the suggested WPoCS design to show how the approach of a PCVO facilitates the collaborative working of care team. These selected collaborative working test cases described below are modelled using Unified Modelling Language (UML) and their detailed explanation with diagrams is given in the results section of paper (Mohyuddin et al. 2007).

1. Sharing of records and material.
2. Communication among care team members.
3. Collaborative problem solving.
4. Care team's task planning for patient treatment.

6.3   Wireless Point of Care System: The Pilot Prototype

A few point of care test cases for the care team members are selected from the tasks list for the WPoCS pilot prototype development. These test cases are verified from the care team members and positive feedback was received. The results of these test cases are to be presented using a Pocket PC Emulator and PDAs. To evaluate the PCVO platform, we will be comparing the proposed working of care team members using WPoCS with the existing practices performed using current information resources. Feedback from the care team members will be used to observe the enhanced collaborative working pattern in their work practices.

7 RESEARCH BOUNDARIES

This pilot prototype utilizes the information resources in the hospital domain but it can be extended for distributed information resources as well. Due to the broad spectrum, some other challenges of administration, management, security and other aspects of PCVOs must be considered if this framework is to be adopted in practice. As wireless handheld devices have limited capabilities, they can only be used for limited information access and are not meant for all information capture and view needs. Finally, using a WPoCS for the collaborative activities is useful for suitable tasks, but it is not a substitute and replacement for computerized systems and all paper based artifacts. It can work in conjunction with these other resources to complement the existing functionality in a clinical environment in a novel way.

8 CONCLUSIONS

This paper presented a PCVO development for a clinical care environment and the potential benefits of using WPoCS in the system. It discussed how a VO is an appropriate foundation for the PCVO framework in a clinical environment as a means of enhancing collaborative working of care team members. It presented the lifecycle of the pilot project including analysis, design, development, implementation and evaluation strategies. The results presented suggest the real and tangible benefits that may be achieved with our framework. The positive feedback from care team members received through discussions and interviews shows the suitability of the results in addressing issues faced during routine clinical tasks. The next step is the development and implementation phase which is in progress. We are also working on qualitative assessment methods for the evaluation phase. The ongoing work is likely to provide useful and practical benefits through patient care improvements in secondary and tertiary cancer care.

9 REFERENCES

1.   Bardram, J. E. (1996), Computer Supported Cooperative Work in clinical practice (doctoral colloquium), in 'Proceedings of the 1996 ACM conference on CSCW', New York, USA.
2.   Bardram, J. E. & Bossen, C. (2005), A web of coordinative artifacts: collaborative work at a hospital ward, in 'GROUP '05: proceedings of the 2005 international ACM SIGGROUP conference on Supporting group work', ACM Press, New York, NY, USA.
3.   Becker, J. D., Ballentine, R. D., Lee, A. & Townsley, C. (1999), Collaborative technology tools for virtual teaming, in 'Proceedings of the Fifth Americas Conference on Information Systems'.
4.   Bossen, C. (2002), The parameters of common information spaces: the heterogeneity of cooperative work at a hospital ward, in 'Proceedings of the 2002 ACM conference on CSCW, New York, USA.
5.   Boulos, M., Maramba, I. & Wheeler, S. (2006), 'Wikis, blogs and podcasts: a new generation of web-based tools for virtual collaborative clinical practice and education'.
     URL: http://www.biomedcentral.com/1472-6920/6/41
6.   Burns, F. (1998), Information for health: An information strategy for the modern NHS 1998-2005 - executive summary, Technical report, Department of Health, UK.
7.   Camarinha-Matos, L. M. & Afsarmanesh, H. (2004), 'A roadmapping methodology for strategic research on VO', Collaborative Networked Organizations Research Agenda for Emerging Business Models.

8.   Camarinha-Matos, L. M., Tschammer, V. & Afsarmanesh, H. (2004), 'On emerging technologies for VO', Collaborative Networked Organizations Research Agenda for Emerging Business Models.
9.   Coiera, E. & Tombs, V. (1998), 'Communication behaviors in a hospital setting: an observational study', BMJ 316(7132).
10. C.Seror, A. (2003), Integrating virtual infrastructures: A sociometry of the Cuban national healthcare system, in 'Academy of Management National Meetings: Democracy in a Knowledge Economy, Technology and Innovation Management Division'.
11. Embi, P. J. (2001), 'Information at hand: using handheld computers in medicine.' Cleve Clin J Med 68(10).
12. Fitzpatrick, G. (2004), 'Integrated care and the working record', Health Informatics Journal 10.
13. Grasso, M. A. (2004), Clinical applications of handheld computers, in 'Proceedings of the 17th IEEE Symposium on Computer Based Medical Systems (CBMS'04)'.
14. Grootveld, M., Swaal, J., Brussee, R., in't Veld, R. H. & Michael-Verkerke, M. (2004), VOs in healthcare: Organization, people and technology, Technical report, Telematica Institute, Netherlands.
15. Imhoff, M., Webb, A. & Goldschmidt, A. (2001), 'Health informatics, Intensive Care Medicine 27.
16. McKnight, L. K., Stetson, P. D., Bakken, S., Curran, C. & Cimino, J. J. (2004), 'Perceived information needs and communication difficulties of inpatient physicians and nurses'. URL: http://www.pubmedcentral.gov/articlerender.fcgi?artid=419422
17. Mohyuddin, Gray, W., Bailey, H., Jones, W. & Morrey, D. (2007), Development of Patient Centric Virtual Organizations (PCVOs) in clinical environment for patient information management, in 'MedInfo 07, Proceedings of the 12th World Congress on Health (Medical) Informatics, Australia'.
18. Mohyuddin, Gray, W., Bailey, H. & Morrey, D. (2007), Collaborative working of multi-disciplinary care teams in Patient Centric Virtual Organizations (PCVOs), in 'HIBIT 07, International Symposium on Health Informatics and Bioinformatics, Turkey'.
19. Mohyuddin, Gray, W. A., Morrey, D. & Jones, W. (2006), Incorporating wireless technology into Virtual Organizations supporting the work of healthcare teams, in 'PERCOMW '06: Proceedings of the Fourth Annual IEEE International Conference on Pervasive Computing and Communications Workshops', IEEE Computer Society, Washington, DC, USA, p. 575.
20. Pitsillides, B., Pitsillides, A., Samaras, G. & Nicolaou, M. (2004), Virtual Teams: Concepts and Applications, ICFAI Press, ch. DITIS: Virtual collaborative teams for improved home healthcare.
21. Rittenbrunch, M., Kahler, H. & Cremers., A. B. (1998), Supporting cooperation in a Virtual Organization, in 'Proceedings of the international conference on Information systems'.
22. Shao, Y. P., Lee, M. K. & Liao, S. Y. (2000), Virtual Organizations: The key dimensions, in 'Academia/Industry Working Conference on Research Challenges (AIWORC'00)'.
23. Velindre NHS Trust annual report (2006): 2003-2006, Technical Report, Velindre NHS Trust, Cardiff, Wales, UK.
24. Turner, J. W. (1998), The integration of new communication technologies to form VOs: A case study of a prison telemedicine program, in 'Pacific Medical Technology Symposium'.
25. Wickramasinghe, N. & Goldberg, S. (2004), How m=ec2 in healthcare, in 'Proceedings of the International Conference on Information Technology: Coding and Computing (ITCC'04)'.
26. Winkelman, W. J. & Choo, C. W. (2003), 'Provider-sponsored virtual communities for chronic patients: improving health outcomes through organizational patient-centred knowledge management.' Health Expect 6(4).

PART 14

SOCIAL NETWORK ANALYSIS

44	# SOCIAL NETWORK ANALYSIS OF TEAM DYNAMICS AND INTRA-ORGANIZATIONAL DEVELOPMENT IN AN AEROSPACE FIRM

Kristie Ogilvie and Dimitris Assimakopoulos
Grenoble Ecole de Management
Europole, 12 rue Pierre Semard, BP127, 38003 Grenoble, FRANCE
profkris7@aol.com, dimitris.assimakopoulos@grenoble-em.com

This research examines results from a dual case study in defining a model for high productivity and performance of cross-functional development teams in an aerospace engineering community. More specifically it explores cohesiveness and team dynamics over an approximate 4-year period in a project team that recently designed and built a highly innovative propulsion system. The 'successful' team delivered this propulsion system ahead of schedule, below cost, and was considered a highly productive team within the researched Aerospace firm. Ucinet is used to map k-cores, month by month, for the entire life cycle of the project. This methodology is then compared to a 'less successful' team to determine those variables responsible for high productivity and overall success of a highly technical research and development team. The results encompass the critical times in networked teams that inclusion in membership of the team is most critical for success.

1   AEROSPACE AND TEAM INTRODUCTION

In the aerospace community, the most common project teams are arranged in an Integrated Product Team (IPT) organization, which is a multidiscipline team approach. This type of organizational structure brings members of functional organizations, otherwise known as " experts" , together to enhance a broad base of knowledge to the organization. Each of these experts brings a core knowledge that must be communicated and maintained throughout the project, and to other projects within the company.

Research has been conducted for integrated product teams, learning within organizations, and innovation, but these studies have gaps in the perspective of the how technology is changing the learning, team environments, and specific operations experienced in today's communities in relation to social network analysis. Aerospace communities share a dynamic like none in any other industry and only limited research has been conducted in this industry. Both the methods and the environmental implications must be explored in tandem, to accurately build a model for learning and innovation to be successful.

In the simplest form, there are two types of contracts within an aerospace company, development and production. Development programs are leading edge projects that usually require one unit, either in experimental form or for a specialized project to its customer. Production programs that are involved in production lines and a large numbers of similar type units that are produced. In production programs,

Ogilvie, K., Assimakopoulos, D., 2007, in IFIP International Federation for Information Processing, Volume 243, Establishing the Foundation of Collaborative Networks; eds. Camarinha-Matos, L., Afsarmanesh, H., Novais, P., Analide, C.; (Boston: Springer), pp. 417–424.

operational aspects and manufacturing practices are key; while in development projects, learning, creativity, innovation, and leading edge technology are the roots for success. In the development projects that require new and state of the art technology to be applied, productivity, and team success is crucial for the success of an aerospace company. Requirements tend to change throughout this process and this makes an additional set of restraints for the organization. Constant team interaction will be the key to enable these changes in the development environment to be compensated and integrated, making the final product robust.

The successful team delivered the propulsion system, ahead of schedule, below cost, and was considered a highly productive team within the organization. After careful analysis of the successful team, the next phase took these best practices and explored their impact in relation to another program similar in size, makeup, and mission. The personnel, especially the core teams, were of the same members of the company, during a different period of time.

2   METHODOLOGY

The overall schedule and methodology was found in the following figure. As illustrated the research project first completed the pertinent literature relating to this study, then moving onto the successful team's strategy and implementation, followed by the less successful team's strategy and implementation. This is followed by the comparative analysis of the two teams, followed by the write up of the findings. The methodology included in depth interviews, social network analysis with UCInet, and statistical analysis. Team A was the successful team, while the Team B designation was the not-as-successful team.

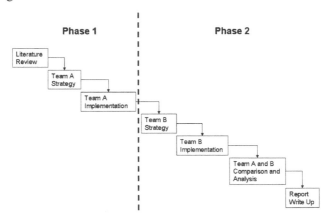

Figure 1: Overall Methodology Process

3   SOCIAL NETWORK ANALYSIS INTRODUCTION

Social network mapping (Hannemann 2001) begins with the conventional rectangular measurement of actors or players within a selected team. Each cell will be assigned either a 0 (in which no relationship or data was transferred between actors), or a 1 (in which a relationship or data was transferred between actors). This creates a table of comparison of actors in their relationship in binary form. The data is captured that could further the relationship from binary form to a strength of tie, but due to the timing constraints and the overall objectives, the binary analysis was sufficient to show the necessary data. This is the foundation data that is used for the mapping portion of the analysis. Network mapping is a special form of conventional data, as it looks at data in a different way. Actors are described by their relations, not by their attributes. This puts an emphasis on the relationships of the actors, not just the individual within the network.

"The major difference between conventional and network data is that conventional data focuses on the actor and their attributes, network data focuses on actors and relations. The difference in emphasis is consequential for the choices that a researcher must make in deciding on research design in conducting sampling, developing measurement, and handling the resulting data." (Hannemann 2001).

The population analyzed is made up of all persons who had vested interest and charged the successful and less than successful team projects. This has made the actors define the population, as well as a demographic approach. In a demographic approach, the criterion is fulfilled for the team members, but in some cases there was no direct interaction with team members. In this case, the actor will be present in the social network map, but not encounter any ties to the team or population. For example, an administrative support person may be forwarded an expense report that needs to have a manager's signature. The support person may charge the work order, including themselves in the population. Since no direct interaction or information was exchanged, no social tie would be made. This would not be considered an interaction in the social network mapping definition, hence no tie will be present.

The collection method for which actors interfaced was a sound methodology for the desired accuracy of the team. The combination of the " full network" approach is one that " yields the maximum information, but can also be costly and difficult to execute" (Hannemann, 2001), hence the snowball method was used. The full network method requires a collection of information from each actor. This enables a full picture, as the entire population has been utilized.

The scale for measurement was a binary measure, as it is the most common, (assigning 0 for no relationship or a 1 where a relationship exists). This enables the network to illustrate whether the relationship existed or not, not the tie between information. This was selected for several reasons. First, it was a starting point for the network analysis. This keeps the illustration simple, and will illustrate the network very clearly. Secondly, and more importantly, the differentiation during the interviews for the core team members *seemed* to indicate that the core members had many more relationships with others in the team, not that there was a differentiation factor of the strength of the ties between the members. This further proves the selection of the binary measurement fit the methodology. The major advantage of the strength illustration in social network mapping is it shows the strength of the given parameter. This can be at the interaction level, frequency of interaction, membership of the team, etc.

4   RESULTS/KEY FINDINGS

A key finding from the successful team was the number of people and interactions were dramatically disproportional during the preliminary design review phase to the critical design review phase, where interaction levels seemed consistent with the efforts of the program. This is the portion of the program in which the design efforts are heightened and the communication process needs to be streamlined and heightened. The following figure shows this trend, which aided in their success. As seen with the less than successful team, the interaction levels were heightened during the conceptual design phase to the preliminary design phase.

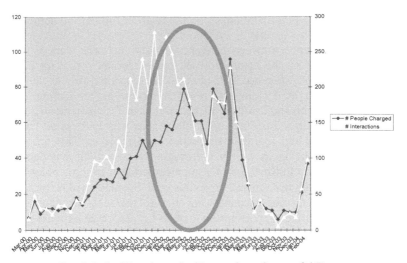

Graph 1: # of People vs. # of Interactions, Successful Team

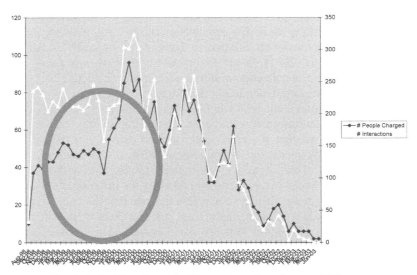

Graph 2: # of People vs. # of Interactions, Less Successful Team

This heightened the interaction level too early for the program task needs. During the conceptual design phase, the requirements are fluid and many team members should work within their discipline to understand their own requirements, where the preliminary design phase begins to bring together the different disciplines and components of the team to ensure overall feasibility of the program.

5   ADDITIONAL SOCIAL NETWORK FINDINGS

As previously discussed, the social dynamics are best captured within the team were not only seen as critical by the team members through primary data collection, but also by the social network analysis conducted.

The next comparison worth noting is the ramp up of the team membership and social network. As seen in month 2 for the successful team versus the unsuccessful team as shown in the following figures.

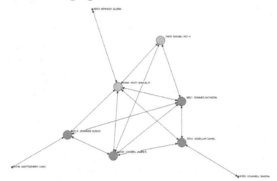

Graph 3: Social Network Analysis, Successful Team

Sept 98

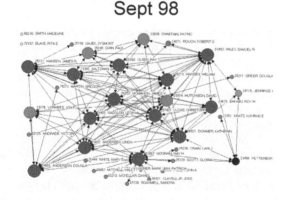

Graph 4: K-Core Social Network Analysis, Not Successful Team

As seen, the successful team was comprised of the core members and only a small number of other team members, as ramp up has not occurred on this team yet. This is not the case with the unsuccessful team, as there are not only the set team members, but membership phase ballooned with many non-core members. As noted in existing research, it takes any new member up to 90 days to become familiar and productive in a new role. With the successful team, the core team is becoming familiar with their role during this time and is focusing their productivity to the team's goals and objectives rather than manage a team before they have a full understanding of the team's requirements.

The ramp up did not occur until month seven, as shown in the following figure. This shows that the core team had been together for over 200 days, and were experts in their given role making their productivity, and in turn the productivity of the team they managed, much more successful. With the less successful team, the ramp up occurred within 30-60 days of contract award.

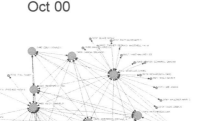

Oct 00

Graph 5: K-Core Social Network Analysis, Ramp up, Successful Team

Next will be a discussion of specific roles and implications in light of the social network findings. First, the systems engineer. This is a role that should have critical importance during the beginning stages of a development program, in that they concrete on defining the requirements and communicating this to the remainder of the team. This role also communicated the different requirements throughout the team and ensures that the different functions changes in these requirements do not conflict with other team tasks, and that the program will meet their overall mission goals. The role then is critical again during the delivery of the unit, as the documentation needs to be updated and submitted. The criticality of the role comes early in the program, and tapers off after design of the unit.

With the successful team, the systems engineer is a Kcore member in months: 1 through 44 of the program and again in months 46-50. The team's goal was to take this person and ensure continued success, so varied the role of this particular person. Though the team member was a systems engineer and provided those function, the person also provided a management role during those times that the systems role was not needed. This prevented turnover and downtime for the team member.

With the less successful team, the systems engineer was a k-core member in months: 1-23, 25-27, and 30. There was no Kcore analysis present or even membership in the later months of the program. This shows the criticality of this role and the strategy of success for the team members to ensure that not only the role, but the particular person throughout the lifecycle of the program is needed for success.

Next, the mechanical engineers one in which the design phase is most critical such that the heightened Kcore analysis should show during the beginning phase to the critical design review. The successful team had mechanical design role (between several people) as a kcore from months 1, 2, 5-8, 11-41, 44-48. Note this role was shared by three members of the team in the same role, based on demand. With the less successful team, the kcores were seen in months: 1-35, 37-44, 56. There does not seem to be any concrete difference between the two roles, only that the successful team was more sporadic with this roles Kcore membership consistently throughout the program.

Next, the manufacturing function is one that is most critical after design and upon build up of the deliverable, making the latter part of the program most critical. The successful team had this role a kcore in months: 7-11, 16-37, 40, 45-50. The less successful team had this role in a kcore in months: 2-40, 42-44. As previously notes with the mechanical team, the successful team was more sporadic in their kcore membership than the unsuccessful team that had consistency of role through a The project engineering role was one in which the kcores for the entire program length, but the role changed from two different person's, with some role confusion and downtime during the transition.

The next variable that is relevant during the social network discussions the turnover of core members. The successful team had no turnover throughout the entire lifecycle of the program. Though members came on and off the team, the role was always filled with the same member. With the less successful team, there were several issues with turnover and change of key roles. First, the core members changed several times throughout the program, and in several instances were not replaced, making the other core members mandated to pick up their role. This made a two fold issue, first the original member who had to pick up the new role was already in another key role and this brought down productivity of the first role, and secondly, the new team members can not have a dual role expertise and this was a weakness with this strategy. It was identified that there were three key members in which the key member either left the program or was reassigned to another program and not replaced immediately. Eventually the role was picked up by other core members. This made role clarity issues and productivity issues.

6 CONCLUSIONS

The conclusions based on the two teams are as follows:
1. Key team members should be introduced to the program between the concept design review (CoDR) and the preliminary design review (PDR), whereby fully integrated onto the team by preliminary design review to critical design review (CDR).

Transition times can make a team encounter lower productivity for up to 4 months. Since this time of interaction with the team is so critical during the time between PDR and CDR, it is important to have the key team members integrated on the team to ensure a successful, highly productive program.
2. Interaction protocols should be heightened between PDR and CDR.

As it has been shown in previous sections of analysis, during the time between PDR and CDR the interaction level should be several times higher than other times in the program. As a result, the interaction protocols should be heightened during this time. The meeting interactions, e-mail communication, and management interface, should all be significant and increased during the time period between PDR and CDR.
3. Roles and responsibilities need to be clearly identified, before PDR with emphasis on focal points of information.

Roles and responsibilities are critical for the success of any team, but as previously stated in the analysis, it is important to maintain productivity and therefore have critical key focal points to facilitate interactions and the flow of information throughout the entire team.

Though these findings have previously been identified, the findings are more robust through the comparative analysis. For example, the interaction levels being heightened during PDR and CDR were derived during the successful team analysis, but the heightening of the interaction level of the less successful team during CoDR to PDR was discovered during the less successful teams analysis. Only when the two teams were compared was it discovered this seemingly small difference, but critical for the success of the project.

There are several areas that need further analysis, as the scope of this research was limited. Specific areas that were seen as significant, but ranged outside of the scope of the project were are as follows. The analysis based on function and interaction levels were an area that was found to be significant and there could be trends that could be analyzed based on function over the lifecycle of the program. This could bring a level of analysis to a management team based on function, which is the make up of many aerospace companies. The interaction levels vary greatly based on function, so exploring a model based on function could be very beneficial and value added both to the industry and to the theoretical perspective. Secondly, the social network analysis was the foundation of this research, but one area that was not analyzed was the strength of the ties between the different members of the team. This would more accurately illustrate the importance of the ties and not a sheer number of interactions between members. Though the number of interactions shows the overall trends, the strength of ties could provide a differing model of what team members had stronger and weaker ties throughout the lifecycle of the program. Additional analysis in the social network analysis area that could further explore the results of this research is to weigh the actors in the social network analysis with the weight of hours that they spent on the program, month to month, over the lifecycle of the program. This would better analyze the contribution and efforts of each team member and fully illustrate the importance of each team member. One could easily argue that the time committed to a program has a direct correlation to the ties that are brought to the team and its members. This additional research methodology would continue to explore the trends and results of this assumption.

7   REFERENCES

1. Barthelemy, J.-F., Waszak, M. R., Jones, K. M., Silcox, R. J., Silva, W. A and Nowaczyk, R.H., " Charting Multidisciplinary Team External Dynamics using a Systems Thinking Approach," AIAA Paper 98-4939, AIAA/USAF/NASA/ISSMO
2. Borgatti, S. & Cross, R. (2003). A Social Network View of Organizational Learning: Relational and Structural Dimensions of 'Know Who'. Management Science, 49 pp. 432-445.
3. Brown Seely, John and Duguid, Paul. " Organizing Knowledge." California Management Review 40, no. 3 (1998): 90-111.
4. Brown, J. S., & Duguid, P. (2000). The social life of information. Boston, MA: Harvard Business School Press.
5. Burt, Ronald S. " Structural Holes Versus Network Closure As Social Capital." Social Capital: Theory and Research (2001): 31-56.
6. Cross, R., Parker, A., Prusak, L. & Borgatti, S.P. " Knowing What We Know: Supporting Knowledge Creation and Sharing in Social Networks." Organizational Dynamics 30, no. 2 (2001): 100-20.
7. Dodgson, Mark. " Learning, trust, and technological collaboration" . Human Relations, New York, Jan 1993, Volume 46, Issue 1, Page 77, 19 pages.
8. Hannemann, Robert A. Introduction to Social Networking Methods, 2001.
9. Powell, W. W., K. W. Koput, L. Smith-Doerr, and J. Owen-Smith. 1999. " Network Position and Firm Performance." pp. 129-59 in Research in the Sociology of Organizations, edited by S. Andrews and D. Knoke, vol. 16, JAI Press.
10. Rothwell, Roy. Towards the Fifth generation Innovation Process;, Science Policy Research Unit, University of Sussexm UK, International Marketing Review Vol 11m No 1, 1994 pp. 7-31 MCB University Press 0265-1335.
11. Wassermann, S. and Faust, K (1994). Social Network Analysis: Methods and Applications. Cambridge: Cambridge University Press.
12. Wellman, B. Networks in the global village: life in contemporary communities. - 1999 - Boulder, Colo: Westview Press.

45

THE TACIT DIMENSIONS OF COLLABORATIVE NETWORK TRAFFIC

Stephen Doak[1], Dimitris Assimakopoulos[2]

[1]*Forensic Scientist, Forensic Science Laboratory, Department of Justice,*
Garda HQ, Phoenix Park, Dublin 8, IRELAND.
sdoak@fsl.gov.ie
[2]*Professor and Associate Dean of Research, Grenoble Ecole de Management,*
Europole, 12 rue Pierre Semard, BP127, 38003 Grenoble, FRANCE.
dimitris.assimakopoulos@grenoble-em.com

We have visualised informal internal and external networks of practicing forensic scientists and now set out to understand how such collaborative networks function. We propose that tacit knowledge acquired through relational mechanisms of social interaction is a major contributor to the functioning of collaborative networks. In our case study on a forensic science community, we examine empirically such tacit knowledge transfer flows at an inter- and intra-organisational collaborative level.

1   INTRODUCTION

Recent research has emphasized the need for a better understanding and characterisation of the basic principles and mechanisms of collaborative networks (Sofia Pereira & Soares 2007). The actors within such networks rely very heavily on their network of relationships to find information and solve problems (Cross, Borgatti, & Parker 2002). A unifying concept of the knowledge and learning gained through participant practice is its construction from 'relations among people engaged in an activity' (Osterlund & Carlile 2005: p. 92). The benefit of these collaborative networks is more than just a conjoining – a synergy is achieved by pooling the thinking of multiple actors and organizations. We propose that the exchange of tacit knowledge (Herbig, Bussing, & Ewert 2001; Polanyi 1966), *mediated* by the *relational mechanisms* of social actors interacting with each other, is a major contributor to the functioning of such collaborative networks.

As networks can by their nature be large, knowledge can become difficult to transfer within, especially where the discussion of ideas can be at the cutting edge and often require specialised expertise, which can be tacit (Bos et al. 2007). In looking at how collaborations function, we have visualised informal internal (Doak & Assimakopoulos 2007b) and external (Doak & Assimakopoulos 2006) networks of practicing forensic scientists and now set out to understand the mechanisms of how such collaborative networks function. We used *social network analysis*, to uncover

Doak, S., Assimakopoulos, D., 2007, in IFIP International Federation for Information Processing, Volume 243, Establishing the Foundation of Collaborative Networks; eds. Camarinha-Matos, L., Afsarmanesh, H., Novais, P., Analide, C.; (Boston: Springer), pp. 425–433.

the structured relational connections shaping tacit knowledge flows between forensic scientists, both in their internal collaborative networks, and outside their homestead, in their inter-organisational collaborative networks. Our analysis took place at the micro-level, where we treated the forensic scientist and his/her network of *advice relations* as the unit of analysis indicative of tacit knowledge exchange.

Organisational learning can be seen as a function of relationships sitting on top of the structural properties within social networks. When viewing the *relational* aspect of social capital it is the nature of the relationships in the social structure that leads to certain benefits for the participant actors. The relational facet 'describes the kind of personal relationships people have developed with each other through a history of interactions (Nahapiet & Ghoshal 1998: p. 244)'. However little is known about the kinds of relationships (in contrast to structural properties) that condition learning and knowledge flows within the networks (Borgatti & Cross 2003). Trust, advice, respect, friendship and social norms are examples of such relational dimensions mediating dyadic knowledge exchanges. These relational factors matter *most* when the exchange involves *tacit* knowledge and indeed the exchange 'relies on the quality of a knowledge seeker's *relationship* with a knowledge source (Levin & Cross 2004: p. 1481)'. Indeed Collins and Hitt, who have examined the 'link between relational capabilities (relational capital) and tacit knowledge transfer' call for 'firms to recognize the importance of inter-personal dynamics involved in the transfer of tacit knowledge' suggesting 'greater attention' is required to be given to the 'relational dimension of social capital (Collins & Hitt 2006: p. 148)'.

Tacit knowledge within a collaborative network umbrella, is both exchanged between actors at a bounded local community of practice level (Lave & Wenger 1991), and is transferred to actors who share a common interest externally outside of an organisation to the open environment through Networks of Practice (Wasko & Faraj 2005). Networks of practice tie in directly with community of practices, where a community from one particular organisation becomes linked through common practices to communities in other organisations. These collaborative networks, where knowledge can flow, cut horizontally across vertically integrated local organisations (Brown & Duguid 2000; Brown & Duguid 2001). The relations among collaborative network members are significantly looser than those within a localised community of practice (Brown & Duguid 2001), who commonly are geographically distributed (Wasko & Faraj 2005). From a network of practice perspective, individuals have practice and knowledge in common but are mostly unknown to each other, whereas from a community of practice perspective, individuals are tightly knit into groups who know each other well and work together directly (van Baalen, Bloemhof-Ruwaard, & van Heck 2006). Networks of practice show their strength in innovation when organizations that do not possess all required knowledge within their formal boundaries, must rely on linkages to outside organizations and individuals to acquire knowledge (Anand, Glick, & Manz 2002).

Professions are a good example of collaborative networks, where similar practitioners, by virtue of their practice, are able to share professional knowledge through conferences, workshops, and web/email contact (Brown & Duguid 2001). The sharing of knowledge is an important aspect of these technical professional communities (Bouty 2000). Such inter-organisational relations while implied in the literature, have rarely been examined empirically (Swan, Scarbrough, & Robertson 2002; Wasko & Faraj 2005). In our case study on a forensic science community, the

Forensic Science Laboratory (FSL) Ireland, we examine empirically such tacit knowledge exchange, mediated within a relational environment at an inter-organisational collaborative level. Our micro-level case study provides an informative insight into the process of how tacit knowledge flows within and between collaborative networks, and how relations between social actors are an integral factor in the mechanisms of such networks.

2   METHODS

2.1   Network visualisation of tacit knowledge transfer within/outside FSL

FSL is the Republic of Ireland's forensic examination and analytical service for all criminal casework encompassing drugs, arson, DNA, toolmarks, paint and glass, explosives, firearm residue, fibre transfer and other trace-type cases. At the time this research was undertaken FSL employed over 43 forensic scientists at the one headquarters. Previous research, established the presence of four local collaborative communities of practice within FSL, comprising forensic scientist experts in the specialist areas of: Biology, DNA, Chemistry and Drugs (Doak & Assimakopoulos 2007a; Doak & Assimakopoulos 2007b). Using *social network analysis* [Pajek (Batagelj & Mrvar 2005) & Ucinet (Borgatti, Everett, & Freeman 2002)] we had uncovered the *advice* relation mediating tacit knowledge transfer between forensic scientists within FSL, and *here* we visualise the tacit knowledge exchanges between forensic scientists in the inter-organisational collaborative networks peripheral to FSL.

Outside of their own inter-organisational collaborative networks, these forensic scientists gain access to knowledge of the tacit nature through their participation in networks of practice, professional associations and peer-attendee conferences. The forensic scientists at FSL are largely influenced by external forensic scientists who practice in fifty-three other forensic science laboratories, distributed over thirty-one European countries, under the umbrella organisation of the European *Network* of Forensic Science Institutes (ENFSI). ENFSI was established in 1995 for the purposes of sharing knowledge, exchanging experiences and coming to mutual agreements in the field of forensic science. Within ENFSI there are sixteen Expert Working Groups including DNA, digital evidence, fingerprints, scene of crime, drugs, fibres, paint & glass, and fires. These working groups comprise the backbone of this pan-european forensic science collaborative network in terms of the scientific knowledge and forensic science policy. We explore the digital evidence ENFSI working group through both through network analysis and participant observation, where the interactions of an FSL forensic scientist with the collaborative group has allowed a nascent digital evidence service to be set up back at FSL. We also view another collaborative group – the International Association of Blood Pattern Analysis (IABPA).

2.2   Personal insights of how Tacit Knowledge is exchanged within collaborative networks

Over the period December 2006 to April 2007 a series of half hour-long, semi-structured interviews were carried out with twenty-eight forensic scientists. The interviewees were all within the local inter-organisational collaborative network (FSL), who were selected through purposeful sampling, using knowledge giving capacities and network position criteria. Although the interviews entailed some degree of variation, the interview questions were selected around elements of tacit knowledge transfer/reciprocation covering the following topic areas: the learning of forensic science practice; the seeking/giving advice; establishment of how knowledge is gained/given; and the exploration of the concept of experience. The questions were developed to directly address the research proposition: that tacit knowledge, acquired through the relational mechanisms of social interaction, is a major contributor to the functioning of collaborative networks.

3   RESULTS & DISCUSSION

3.1   Collaborative Networks – a quantitative view

Previously we mapped relational tacit knowledge flows amongst forensic scientists within/between the intra-organisational collaborative networks at FSL (Doak & Assimakopoulos 2007b). We produced a snapshot of tacit knowledge exchange mediated by the advice relation over a three-day period (see Figure 1).

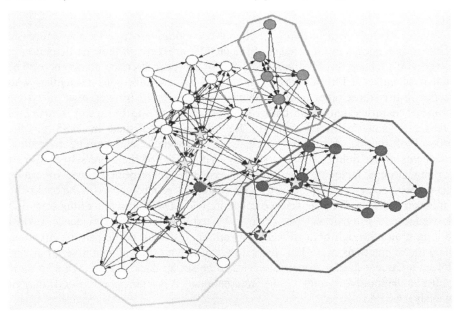

Figure 1. Network map of FSL, recording advices yielding tacit knowledge transfer between forensic scientists over a three-day period within/between four intra-organisational collaborative communities of practice networks. Biology (green), Chemistry (blue), DNA (red), Drugs (pink).

Outside of their own local communities, we show quantitatively how forensic scientists gain access to new tacit insights through their participation in collaborative networks and their subsequent inter-organisational communications. By exploring the participation of scientists in the ENFSI Digital Evidence working group, we have empirically shown how members willingly help other members through giving advice asked of them, where some form of tacit knowledge is transferred (see Figure 2). A FSL forensic scientist, on joining the ENFSI Digital Evidence collaborative network, built up professional relationships through a series of attendances at its annual conferences and resultant inquiritive emails to members who had been socially targeted. A nascent FSL Digital Evidence service was formed as a direct result of the FSL forensic scientist having received advice, from those targeted members of the ENFSI Digital Evidence collaborative network, in the form of tacit knowledge required to operate successfully the nuances of the dense mobile phone interrogative procedures. From participant observations it was found that the majority of knowledge that was required to be able to set up the FSL's digital evidence service was of a tacit face-to-face nature. A proper functioning digital evidence specialty would not have been set up were it not for the attendance of the FSL forensic scientist for a full week at a laboratory in France [FR (1-4), Figure 3] and a full day at a laboratory in the UK [UK5]. At both laboratories there was extensive tacit knowledge captured through intense one is to one face contact. Likewise tacit knowledge from a highly experienced forensic scientist in the UK [UK 2] allowed robust quality assurance attributes to be added to the laboratory protocols, from face to face meetings at the network conferences [UK2a(way)] and through direct contact from a visit by the UK scientist to the local FSL community [UK2h(ome)]. Figure 2 shows the FSL forensic scientist [FSL a(way)] gaining tacit knowledge from members of the collaborative network [country code(n)]. The FSL forensic scientist [FSL h(ome)] brings back the tacit knowledge to set up a nascent digital evidence service and shares this knowledge locally with two colleagues [FSL 2&3].

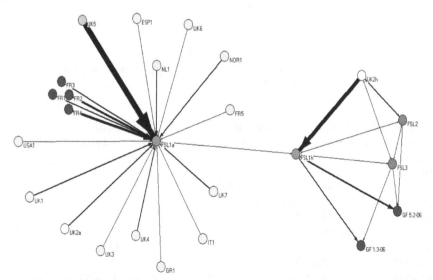

Figure 2. ENFSI Digital Evidence collaborative network [left] – bringing back tacit knowledge to the local FSL nascent digital evidence community [right].

The services made available to the police G(arda S(iochana)] 1&2 were discussed with FSL forensic scientists.

In another collaborative network – IABPA, we show how innovations in blood pattern analysis not available in the local community of practice are brought from the IABPA collaborative network back to the FSL Biology community of practice by a senior FSL scientist [c h(ome) & c a(way)] (Figure 3). We see how four separate innovations from a large wealth of new ideas are chosen to be brought back [blue, green, turquoise, yellow discs]. We capture the interaction of tacit knowledge exchange back at the local community as the new innovations are being brought back. Through participant observation a thorough discussion of one of the four innovations originating from France [Fr 2] was witnessed, where the FSL scientist *c* presented findings to *d*, *e*, and *i* and to the other members of the local community.

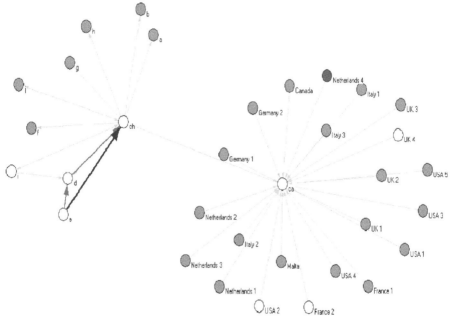

Figure 3. IABPA collaborative network [right] – bringing back tacit knowledge to the local FSL biology community [left].

3.2   Personal insights of how Tacit Knowledge a major constituent of intra-organisational collaborative communication – inside FSL

It was found that all the interviewees, who were asked what was the major contributor as to why they would collaborate with colleagues inter-organisationally, mentioned that there was a need to acquire the tacit dimensions of how to proceed within a certain amount of their processes. We discovered why forensic scientists needed to continually communicate and confer with each other. Although we found that FSL forensic scientists were very adept at examining any piece of evidence that added to the bigger picture through interpretation, where they ultimately compiled a report readied for the prosecution service to present to the courts, they still needed a localised social acceptance recognising that they carried out the correct procedures. A forensic scientist's need is to collaboratively confer with a fellow forensic scientist who is higher in the pecking order, who has already experienced through their own years of practice, the answer to the question that they seek. One explains:

> ... When I have a conflict in my head I suppose is the main thing when I think, Oh it could be this, and that might be the easy one, and that might be the road I would be tempted to go down, but maybe it would be something else, so I really should get somebody else's opinion on it.

or more directly, another admits:

> ... I go out and ask people when I'm unsure myself.

The real need of a forensic scientist is that they are comfortable with their decision, in having made the correct judgement or having expressed fairly an opinion, because their subjectivity will only be tested in the loneliness of the witness box, within the courtroom. A scientist speaks of the journey:

> ...I think because of the adversarial system in the court you really need to be bouncing your ideas and opinions off somebody else because they are always going to be challenged in the long run by somebody else either by a defence scientist or by a defence barrister so you really need to make sure that your opinions are sound all the time.

The adversarial system frames the way another forensic scientist guards herself:

> ...I seek advice...if I'm working in an area and a case that I've had to think out of the box and I want it challenged to check its robustness – then I will go – I will actually pick people that I know will be awkward and difficult and I'd go to them and say right this is how I'm thinking, now, I want you to beat it down.

3.3 The Relational Tacit Dimensions of Inter-Organisational Collaboration – personal opinions from withn FSL to the outside

Qualitatively we examine more indepth how the tacit knowledge trickles from the outside collaborations back to the local networks. The tacit dimensions of collaboration outside the FSL were captured. In essence, as one forensic scientist expressed the function of such groups when serving on a UK/Ireland collaborative network:

> ... the Body Fluids Forum is a great way of gaining knowledge and learning about situations other people have been in and how they have dealt with them. Increasingly we are looking outside...

and another expressed their usefulness:

...I think you get a lot of information from outside, going to meetings and things like that...

and another stated:

... there is a certain amount of knowledge you'll gain by references and literature and by conferences and by networking with other forensic scientists

These personal insights demonstrate how tacit knowledge is brought from the outside back to within the organisation , as is visualised in our network analysis of the IABPA (see Figure 3). The advantage in having been involved in such collaborations is that the forensic scientist feels that they are working on a par with the best practice in Europe, stating:

...now we are as experienced as they are ...

4   CONCLUSION

Our empirical research gives a better understanding of tacit knowledge acquisition, how it is formulated in organisations, and how it is passed on to individual knowledge workers. From the point of view of practice it is possible to understand the flow of tacit knowledge into and within organisations. We see that the transfer of tacit knowledge is linked to social relations and the relationships of social actors developed through shared practice.

We can consider tacit knowledge acquisition and application, as *a function* of participation in collaborative communities of practice (Tschannen-Moran & Nestor-Baker 2004), *present* in the situation (Giroux & Taylor 2002) within a complex social process (Brown & Duguid 2001), and in the flow of practice (Duguid 2005). People in sharing a practice, will share know how, or tacit knowledge (Brown & Duguid 2001). Through qualitative analysis of interviewee comments, we find that tacit knowledge has an implicit richness embedded in the collaborative traffic (Tschannen-Moran & Nestor-Baker 2004). This is a study of the environment in which *tacit knowledge* is created and shared within or across organizational boundaries and communities of practice.

Our future research will include more indepth studies of relationships that yield to the lubrication of tacit knowledge flows, with a purpose to inform the organisational management literature of the importance of the interaction of social actors who feel comfortable within collaboratative groups thereby yielding more knowledge exchange.

5   REFERENCES

1.   Anand, V., Glick, W. H., & Manz, C. C. 2002, "Thriving on the knowledge of outsiders: Tapping organizational social capital", Academy of Management Executive, vol. 16, no. 1, pp. 87-101.

2. Batagelj, V. & Mrvar, A. Pajek 1.03. 2005. http://vlado.fmf.uni-lj.si/pub/networks/pajek/default.htm. Ref Type: Computer Program
3. Borgatti, S. P., Everett, M. G., & Freeman, L. C. 2002, UCINET 6.0 for Windows: Software for Social Network Analysis. Analytic Technologies., Harvard, MA.
4. Borgatti, S. P. & Cross, R. 2003, "A Relational View of Information Seeking and Learning in Social Networks", Management Science, vol. 49, no. 4, pp. 432-445.
5. Bos, N., Zimmerman, A., Olson, J., Yew, J., Yerkie, J., Dahl, E., & Olson, G. 2007, "From shared databases to communities of practice: A taxonomy of collaboratories - art. no. 16", Journal of Computer-Mediated Communication, vol. 12, no. 2, p. 16.
6. Bouty, I. 2000, "Interpersonal and interaction influences on informal resource exchanges between R&D researchers across organizational boundaries", Academy of Management Journal, vol. 43, no. 1, pp. 50-65.
7. Brown, J. S. & Duguid, P. 2000, The Social Life of Information Harvard Business School Press, Boston.
8. Brown, J. S. & Duguid, P. 2001, "Knowledge and Organization: A Social-Practice Perspective", Organization Science, vol. 12, no. 2, pp. 198-213.
9. Collins, J. D. & Hitt, M. A. 2006, "Leveraging tacit knowledge in alliances: The importance of using relational capabilities to build and leverage relational capital", Journal of Engineering and Technology Management, vol. 23, no. 3, pp. 147-167.
10. Cross, R., Borgatti, S. P., & Parker, A. 2002, "Making invisible workvisible: Using social network analysis to support strategic collaboration", California Management Review, vol. 44, no. 2, p. 25-+.
11. Doak, S. & Assimakopoulos, D. 2006, "A Tacit Knowledge perspective on the knowledge dynamics occurring within/beyond communities of practice in a knowledge intensive environment.", D. Bennet et al., eds., Aston Business School, Aston University, Birmingham B4 7ET, United Kingdom and International Association for Management of Technology, University of Miami College of Engineering, Coral Gables, FL 33124-0623 USA, Birmingham UK, pp. 194-205.
12. Doak, S. & Assimakopoulos, D. 2007a, "How do forensic scientists learn to become competent in casework reporting in practice: A theoretical and empirical approach", Forensic Science International, vol. 167, no. 2-3, pp. 201-206.
13. Doak, S. & Assimakopoulos, D. 2007b, "How forensic scientists learn to investigate cases in practice", R and D Management, vol. 37, no. 2, pp. 113-122.
14. Duguid, P. 2005, ""The art of knowing": Social and tacit dimensions of knowledge and the limits of the community of practice", Information Society, vol. 21, no. 2, pp. 109-118.
15. Giroux, H. & Taylor, J. R. 2002, "The justification of knowledge: Tracking the translations of quality", Management Learning, vol. 33, no. 4, pp. 497-517.
16. Herbig, B., Bussing, A., & Ewert, T. 2001, "The role of tacit knowledge in the work context of nursing", J.Adv.Nurs., vol. 34, no. 5, pp. 687-695.
17. Lave, J. & Wenger, E. 1991, Situated Learning: Legitimate peripheral participation Cambridge University Press, New York.
18. Levin, D. Z. & Cross, R. 2004, "The Strength of Weak Ties You Can Trust: The Mediating Role of Trust in Effective Knowledge Transfer", Management Science, vol. 50, no. 11, pp. 1477-1490.
19. Nahapiet, J. & Ghoshal, S. 1998, "Social capital, intellectual capital, and the organizational advantage", Academy of Management.The Academy of Management Review, vol. 23, no. 2, p. 242.
20. Osterlund, C. & Carlile, P. 2005, "Relations in Practice: Sorting Through Practice Theories on Knowledge Sharing in Complex Organizations", Information Society, vol. 21, no. 2, pp. 91-107.
21. Polanyi, M. 1966, The tacit dimension Doubleday, New York.
22. Sofia Pereira, C. & Soares, A. L. 2007, "Improving the quality of collaboration requirements for information management through social networks analysis", International Journal of Information Management, vol. 27, no. 2, pp. 86-103.
23. Swan, J., Scarbrough, H., & Robertson, M. 2002, "The construction of 'communities of practice' in the management of innovation", Management Learning, vol. 33, no. 4, pp. 477-496.
24. Tschannen-Moran, M. & Nestor-Baker, N. 2004, "The Tacit Knowledge of Productive Scholars in Education", Teachers College Record, vol. 106, no. 7, pp. 1484-1511.
25. van Baalen, P., Bloemhof-Ruwaard, J., & van Heck, E. 2006, "Knowledge Sharing in an Emerging Network of Practice: The Role of a Knowledge Portal", European Management Journal, vol. 23, no. 3, pp. 300-314.
26. Wasko, M. M. & Faraj, S. 2005, "Why should I share? Examining social capital and knowledge contribution in electronic networks of practice", Mis Quarterly, vol. 29, no. 1, pp. 35-57.

Peter Weiß, Stefan Klink

Institute of Applied Informatics and Formal Description Methods (AIFB),
University of Karlsruhe (TH), GERMANY
{Peter.Weiss, Stefan.Klink}@aifb.uni-karlsruhe.de

Electronic collaborative networks are a prevailing concept in actual scientific business management literature. Because of the occurrence of newly concepts as "service orientation" and service oriented architectures, electronic networks and business intelligence, has gained momentum and revival. In the paper we look at the conceptual design of a framework for the development of collaborative services to maintain electronic business relationships. The reader gets acquainted with relevant theories and research strands that need to flow into a design framework of collaborative services.

1   INTRODUCTION

During the last decade, along with growing interest and increasing use of electronic networks, society, science and business have been affected by remarkable changes. Electronic networks have had a tremendous impact on the every day and working life changing the way people interact, live and work. In our economy today, networking plays a crucial role in various branches and application domains though there are still numerous barriers to overcome. In this connexion collaborative services are a new paradigm likely to further leverage collaboration and networking among agents, whether humans or machines, in electronic networks.

In focus of this research are social ties between network entities. In electronic networks the linkages of entities (e.g. business partners, employees, experts, etc.) have to be supported by electronic services. Services are designed to overcome identified boundaries for Collaborative Networks (Martin-Flatin et al., 2006). Semantics, self-organisation, security, trust and privacy, awareness and incentives are variables influencing the relational ties between units. However, linkages between agents require the right climate and conditions of a collaboration environment. This environment should provide opportunities for or constraints on individual action in a specific given context. These horizontal dimensions facilitate and catalyse the emergence of relational processes and structures to evolve.

First, the paper overviews briefly the current state of the art of collaborative networks with clear focuses on the aspects of business relationship management. The authors motivate their research by explaining the vision and related challenges of dynamic business ecosystems.

Weiß, P., Klink, S., 2007, in IFIP International Federation for Information Processing, Volume 243, Establishing the Foundation of Collaborative Networks; eds. Camarinha-Matos, L., Afsarmanesh, H., Novais, P., Analide, C.; (Boston: Springer), pp. 435–442.

2 COLLABORATIVE NETWORKS SO FAR

Today, there is a growing community of researchers whose work gravitates towards the topic of Collaborative Networks (Camarinha-Matos et al., 2003, 2004, 2006). The research community has elaborated in the meanwhile a comprehensive knowledge base of Collaborative Networks encompassing theoretical foundations, services, collaboration and innovation environment, and last but not least the analysis of the impact collaborative networks have on daily life and economy. The need of a comprehensive scientific framework of collaborative networks (see Figure 1) is argued facilitating to structure and to align interdisciplinary research activities towards common goals and visions.

From a network perspective, linkages and related relational processes and structures are the subject of analysis. The proposed framework allows to analyse and to conceptualise structures in form of models but also considers the patterns of emerging and evolving relationships among agents (human and machines). Subject of analysis are related interactions at the level of individuals, teams (or groups), organisations, networks and communities. It supports the evolution of dynamic networks and the self-organisation of network entities. The required emergence of relational structures requires specific services within collaborative networks.

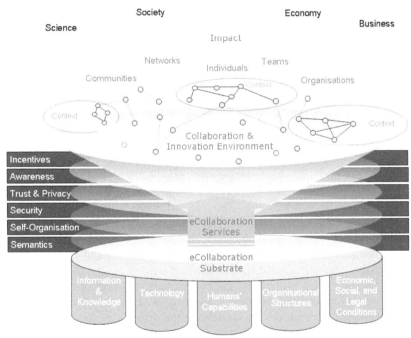

Figure 1 – Framework of collaborative networks' infrastructure

3 OBJECTIVES

Our research thesis claims that organisational structures with demanded abilities to self-manage, self-configure and self-optimise require besides the necessary culture

"[...] semantic-informed self-organizing structures [...]" (Camarinha-Matos et al., 2003, p. 8). Culture and structure are constituted in the collaboration and innovation environment and provides the "breeding environment" for establishing relational ties between agents (e.g., units, actors, etc.). From a network perspective, linkages and related relational processes and structures are subject of analysis. The concept of semantically enriched business partner profiles and sound, proven techniques of information retrieval, data mining, and machine learning, respectively, are combined together to develop the necessary collaborative services environment. In our focus are discovery and matching services respectively because they provide the field for further enhanced services and functionality in collaborative networks.

4   REVIEW OF STATE-OF-THE-ART

4.1   Social Networks and Analysis

The theoretical part is based on the theory of social networks (Wassermann, Faust 1994). Due to the fact that business relationships contains not only people but resources of any kind (material or nonmaterial) common one-mode dyadic networks are not sufficient to represent the given network structure. In our case, we need so called multi-mode social networks described in the following paragraphs.

Basics of Social Networks
    A social network can be seen as a graph $G = (V, E)$ in which the vertices V represent the actors, the edges E the ties between these actors. Clustering describes the situation that if one actor has a tie (of arbitrary origin) to two other actors then it is likely that these two individuals will start a tie as well. This can easily be seen while looking at friends one has and then at the friends they have. It is likely, as Watts (2004) points out that there will be a certain overlap between these two sets of people. If the clustering is advanced and the characteristic path length in a social network satisfies certain conditions, then the observed social network is a specific subtype of network, a so called small world network. In the case of business partners such a small world network is the basis of new algorithms for similarity measurement. The network considered is the business partner network constructed from the database of business partner profiles. The actors are the partners listed in the dataset. A tie between two business profiles is inserted into the graph if the actors are collaborating. The usage of such networks in general is not new in order to find synonyms. However the manner of which and how this information is used is innovative.

Multi-mode Social Networks
    For representing additional information multi-mode networks are needed. In contrast to common one-mode networks with persons as actors and friendship as relation, multi-mode networks are capable to represent relationships of various types. These kinds of networks are also known as affiliation or membership networks where one set of actors (here: business partners) and multiple sets of events (here: contracts, employments, deliverers, developers etc.) are present (Wassermann, Faust, 1994, Chapter 8). Relationships within business partners are manifold and can be listed as a hierarchy with increasing indirection in within several levels.

Social Software & Web 2.0

Social Software supports, extends, or derives added value from human social behaviour (Coates, 2005). It can be used not only for information and identification management but also for relationship management. Social software, e.g. Blogs, Wikis, message boards, social bookmarking/tagging and navigation etc., support to map and to foster current contacts and to endeavour and to tie new contacts. The focus on the web 2.0 lies on the exchange, interaction, and (re)usability of information. It is an easy to use platform for social and collaborative exchange of general information, news, data and services. Web 2.0 applications manipulate the content, the structure and the layout of documents and present all the information in a new combination more or less condensed to the user.

4.2   Business Partner Profiles

The selection of business partners can be identified as key to success and key capability for the realisation of dynamic business ecosystems in near future. Thus, there is a need to conceive business relationships as intangible asset of an enterprise that needs special care. Namely, relational ties are to be maintained continuously through an adequate management. Weiß (2005) proposed a newly approach for business partner management with ontologies in large business communities. This research strived to leverage the capabilities to cope with large numbers of business relationships. New approaches are required to expand the boundaries of electronic networks. A possible solution seems to be support through appropriate services of the ICT infrastructure (Martin-Flatin, 2006). Ontologies offer support for communication processes and complex interactions of business entities in collaborative spaces (Weiß, 2007). The analysis of business relationships and related interactions requires an appropriate analysis framework that allows to investigate and to describe the nature of relational structures and processes.

4.3   Information Retrieval

In standard text information retrieval scenarios, textual queries are compared to a set of documents or a full-text index, respectively to get relevant documents. The same procedure is mostly done in multi-media retrieval for searching for images, videos or music. Recently research is trying to get more out of the query or to put more information into the query for enlargement or for making it more precise. Ontology-based systems try to categorize the users query into a specific ontology entity and then the query is enriched with information stored in the ontology (Klink, 2006).

Another information retrieval approach is to search for similar entities, i.e. not a manually formulated query is given by the user but the user selects an appropriate document, image or piece of music as a query and then the IR-System compares this with all others. More or less sophisticated ranking methods are sorting the results or clustering algorithms are used to categorize the results into various topics. Approaches in the field of Case-Based-Reasoning (CBR) are working analogously. The current (new) case is matched to (known) cases stored in a database and most similar (best matching) cases are retrieved (Bergmann, 2002). In our framework, ontology-based as well as similarity-based approaches are used for discovery and/or matching the BPP mentioned above. Instead of querying business partners by manually formulated queries, our framework is capable for more sophisticated approaches described below.

4.4 Trust in Electronic Networks

Obviously, the increasing dynamics in the interaction of business partners combined with the shortening life-cycle of co-operations contradict the nature and actual needs of business relationships regarding trust and commitment. Both concepts occur over a longer period of time and require stable relationships. Once trust is established it reduces opportunistic behaviour. This is substantiated by existing organisation theories as e.g. transaction cost, principal-agent and property-rights (Picot et al., 2003, p. 45ff.), (Sydow, 1992, p. 130ff.). Trust is the base for a successful business relationship and therefore essential for the success of business endeavours within self-forming networks. The success of virtual organisations depends largely on quality of relational ties between network members. As in social software building and maintaining trust is essential to reduce opportunistic behaviour. Legal contracts might never be totally disappear in real business life though increasing respective transaction costs. Although reducing network efficiency contracts are an appropriate mean to increase the "intensity of linkage" of network structures. Accordingly, advanced collaborative services (e.g. filtering and pre-selection of business partners) aim at establishing zones of trust.

5 CONCEPTUAL MODEL AND FRAMEWORK

In the following, all approaches mentioned above are combined. A conceptual model is developed that serves the identified needs.

5.1 Future of Digital Business Ecosystems

In Figure 2 illustrates the three stages towards a digital business ecosystem. At stage one a centralised model for the business partner profiles (BPPs) is applied. The profiles represent information required to discover, select and integrate business partners preferably dynamic, on demand into emerging or existing value chains. The business partners that can be accessed through the ICT infrastructure are limited to the information stored and accessible through the registry (e.g. in form of an Enterprise Portal). Related work can be found in the area of business registries for web services as e.g. UDDI (Universal Description, Discovery and Integration) and ebXML (Electronic Business XML).

Current research gravitates around the realisation of the scenario shown at stage two. At this stage, a decentralised model is developed. BPPs are no longer stored centrally in an information portal. These profiles are stored decentralised but are created on basis of a shared conceptual model in form of a domain ontology. Business partners maintain latent business relationships solely within the boundaries of the business network they have registered to. The reach of the network are defined by the actual number of registered users.

Whereas, at stage three it is strived for an advanced decentralised model that allows to contact and query business partners as well outside the boundaries of the defined network. For the discovery and selection of business partners desired information needs to be retrieved beforehand through machines (e.g. through agents or web crawlers). Semantics of data stored in a machine-processable form in profiles have to be explicit. In this way, the described approach fulfils the requirements of described application scenario though it has to be further developed. Especially, retrieval of distributed information and heterogeneous data stored in complex data types (e.g. as elements of BPPs) poses interesting questions for future research endeavours (Weiß, 2007).

5.2   Conceptual Framework

In this section, the conceptual framework for the design of collaborative services to maintain electronic business relationships is looked at. Starting from the scenario one described in Figure 2 above, the aim is now to approach the visionary setting displayed at the next stages two and three.

Steps towards a Digital Business Ecosystem

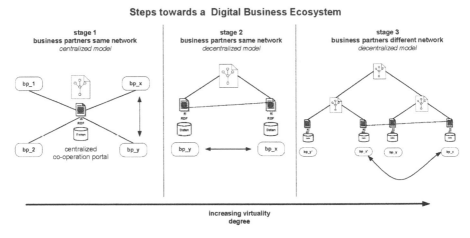

Figure 2 – Steps towards digital business ecosystems (Weiß, 2005)

The work follows the approach to assess decision criteria in order to support the self-formation and self-organisation of adaptive business networks. As a first step, a centralized approach with a shared explicit data model for BPPs as identity or individual "fingerprints" is planned. Profiles are based on an ontology-based model which has been derived from an empirical model for the network analysis encompassing important dimensions for the configuration and description of business relationships (Weiß 2007). BPPs are stored in a central or a distributed database for retrieval and for further analysis.

Complex data structures are required to express the complexity of and formalise business related information. They then can be accessed extracting relevant information from them within a specification of requirements (Field and Hoffner, 2003).

In summary, Figure 3 depicts the overall research approach. The configuration of the business relationship takes place primarily on the organisational layer. To involve the ICT infrastructure collaborative data has to be represented in machine-processable form. This can be realised using ontologies for the structuring and modelling of the BPP. Profiles are a prominent concept for example used by web services to store specified service descriptions (e.g. in WSDL (Web Services Description Language)).

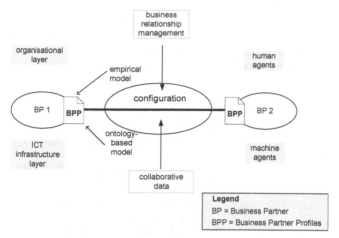

Figure 3 – Design of approach for business partner relationship management with ontologies (Weiß, 2007)

Therefore, this is seen as appropriate way to approach the problem at hand. BPP are anticipated to bridge the existing barrier between the organisational and ICT infrastructure layer. Through the application of ontologies, collaborative services as e.g. for discovery and/or matching of BPP can be used to support the self-reference and emergence of collaborative structure and cultures. Especially zones of trust can be established through filtering of collaborative information and an intensified interaction and information exchange of business entities in forefront of concrete business endeavours (Weiß, 2007).

6   CONCLUSIONS AND OUTLOOK

In the paper we followed the vision to support relational processes within electronic networks. Based on a review of existing state-of-the-art we presented pivotal theories, concepts and techniques that need to flow in an appropriate conceptual model of the management of business relationships. The combination of two strands: namely state-of-the-art data techniques (information retrieval, data mining, social network analysis, machine learning, etc.) and business partner profiling resulted into a novel framework. Though, the framework is not yet ready for implementation we have conceptualised all necessary components and have specified the needed functionality and technologies to develop a demonstrator. At the ICT infrastructure layer collaborative services, namely discovery and matchmaking services, are supposed to handle emergence and evolution of business relationships by processing of collaborative data. Respective data is stored in business partner profiles. Ontologies represent required semantics of data to achieve that both humans and machines can benefit and process the information sets. At the organisational layer the approach requires establishing an appropriate business relationship management. It encompasses mainly appropriate variables and selection criteria as well as a framework to configure respective parameters on which basis business relationships then likely are able to emerge and evolve. The goal is to realise the aspired strong interaction and linking of organisational and ICT infrastructure layer.

It has been pointed out, that presented research is still at stage of research design. Next steps to be taken are to choose and define complex data types in order to implement a prototype so that we gain a huge amount of real-live data for explorative research. On that basis, data techniques will be applied to analyse the data and to set up (personal) recommender supporting the Business Partners. Searching appropriate partners can be automized with agent technologies.

7   REFERENCES

1. Baeza-Yates R, Ribeiro-Neto B. Modern Information Retrieval. Addison-Wesley, 1999.
2. Bergmann R. Experience Management Foundations, Development Methodology, and Internet-Based Applications. LNAI 2432, Springer Verlag, 2002.
3. Bhattacharya I, Getoor L. Iterative record linkage for cleaning and integration. In Proceedings of the 9th ACM SIGMOD Workshop DMKD 2004, Paris, France, June 13, 2004, pages 11-18. ACM, 2004.
4. Camarinha-Matos LM, Afsarmanesh H, Ollus M. Network-Centric Collaboration and Supporting Frameworks. IFIP TC5/WG5.5, Proceedings PRO-VE'06, 2006.
5. Camarinha-Matos LM. Virtual Enterprises and Collaborative Networks. IFIP TC5/WG5.5, Proceedings PRO-VE'04, 2004.
6. Camarinha-Matos LM, Afsarmanesh H. Processes and Foundations for Virtual Organizations. IFIP TC5/WG5.5, Proceedings PRO-VE'03, 2003.
7. Camarinha-Matos LM. Collaborative Business Ecosystems and Virtual Enterprises. IFIP TC5/WG5.5, Proceedings PRO-VE'02, 2002.
8. Field S, Hoffner Y. Web Services and matchmaking. In Intl. Journal Networking and Virtual Organisation, vol. 2, no. 1, 2003.
9. Martin-Flatin, Jean-Philippe; Sventek, Joe and Geihs, Kurt: Self-managed systems and services, in Communications of the ACM, March 2006, vol. 49, no. 3.
10. Klink S. Intelligent Query (Re-)Formulation with Concept-based Expansion. Universität Trier, Dissertation, Dr. Hut-Verlag, München, 2006.
11. Klink S. Improving Document Transformation Techniques with Collaborative Learned Term-based Concepts. LNCS 2956, pages 281-305, Springer, 2004.
12. Klink S, Kise K, Dengel A, Junker M, Agne S. Document Information Retrieval. In Chaudhuri BB, Digital Document Processing: Major Directions and Recent Advances, Springer, 2007.
13. Krystek U, Redel W, Reppegather S. Grundzüge virtueller Organisationen: Elemente und Erfolgsfaktoren, Chancen und Risiken. Wiesbaden, Gabler Verlag, 1997.
14. Picot A, Reichwald R, Wigand, RT. Die grenzenlose Unternehmung. Gabler Verlag, 2003
15. Scott J: Social Network Analysis. Second Edition. London: SAGE Publications Ltd, 2000.
16. Sydow J.: Strategische Netzwerke: Evolution und Organisation. Wiesbaden : Gabler Verlag, 1992.
17. Wasserman S, Faust K. Social Network Analysis: Methods and Applications. Cambridge University Press, 1994.
18. Watts DJ. Six Degrees: The Science of a Connected Age. W.W.Norton&Company, New York, 2004.
19. Weiß P. Management von Geschäftsbeziehungen in virtuellen Organisationsstrukturen. Universität Karlsruhe (TH), Dissertation, Dr. Hut-Verlag, München, 2005.
20. Weiß P.: Towards Adaptive Business Networks: Business Partner Management with Ontologies. In Rittgen P, Handbook of Ontologies for Business Interaction, pp. 24; IDEA GROUP INC., 2007 (to appear).

PART 15

INTEROPERABILITY IN NETWORKS

TOWARDS SEAMLESS INTEROPERABILITY IN COLLABORATIVE NETWORKS

Claudia-Melania Chituc[1,2]
César Toscano[2]
Américo Lopes Azevedo[1,2]
[1]Faculty of Engineering of the University of Porto (FEUP); [2]INESC Porto
{cmchituc, ala}@fe.up.pt, ctoscano@inescporto.pt
PORTUGAL

The goal of achieving full interoperability is still not achieved, despite the high number of tools and infrastructures developed. The objective of this article is to present a framework aiming at supporting seamless interoperability in a business collaborative networked environment. An implementation example from the footwear sector validating the framework proposed is also described.

1   INTRODUCTION

Collaborative Networks'(CNs) paradigm has emerged world wide as a way to increase organizations' efficiency and bring them added value. CNs consist of heterogeneous organizations with different competences but symbiotic interests, which join and efficiently combine their skills and resources to achieve a common objective (Chituc, Azevedo, 2006).

In order to leverage the potential benefits of CNs, it is needed to develop operational infrastructures supporting inter-organizational operations and real time information exchange, so that independent organizations can work as a single integrated unit, while preserving their autonomy (Camarinha-Matos, et al., 1998), (Camarinha-Matos, Afsarmanesh, 2003). Despite the relatively high number of tools and infrastructures supporting (or claiming to support) seamless interoperability in a collaborative networked environment (CNE), this goal is still unachieved (Pollock, 2001) (Camarinha-Matos, Afsarmanesh, 2003a, b).

The objective of this article is to present a framework aiming at supporting seamless interoperability in a CNE. An operational infrastructure from the footwear sector, developed within the scope of a project pursued at national level, validating this framework, is then described.

The rest of the paper is organized as follows. The next section addresses the concept of interoperability. Section three describes the framework proposed towards achieving seamless interoperability. An implementation example from the footwear industry is then described. The article concludes with a section addressing the needs for future research.

Chituc, C.-M., Toscano, C., Azevedo, A.L., 2007, in IFIP International Federation for Information Processing, Volume 243, Establishing the Foundation of Collaborative Networks; eds. Camarinha-Matos, L., Afsarmanesh, H., Novais, P., Analide, C.; (Boston: Springer), pp. 445–452.

2   INTEROPERABILITY AND SEAMLESS INTEROPERABILITY

2.1   Interoperability – a brief overview

Interoperability, in a broad sense, refers to the use of computer-based tools that facilitate inter-organization information flow and coordination of work. It aims at harmonizing the heterogeneous CNE, improve task coordination and real-time information sharing. According to (IEEE, 1990), interoperability represents the capability of two or more systems to exchange information and to use the information exchanged.

Main requirements for interoperability in a networked environment are presented in (Li, 2000); they refer to technical, business and policy interoperability requirements. However, the focus in the area of interoperability continues to be on technological aspects, and research on semantic and business aspects is scarce.

Causes for not achieving yet a fully interoperable infrastructure in a CNE are diverse: e.g., inadequate implementation, poorly managed risks and requirements, human errors, the lack of guiding standards for interoperability, and, as emphasized in (Camarinha-Matos, Afsarmanesh, 2003a), the lack of common reference models and appropriate supporting tools and infrastructures.

2.2   A holistic view on interoperability

Seamless interoperability assures that heterogeneous and geographically distributed entities/systems communicate and make use of the information exchanged (that is meaningful context driven information), and the systems are added or removed without requiring reconfigurations.

Towards seamless interoperability in a CNE, four main views on interoperability have been identified by the authors. They concern **T**echnical aspects (e.g., messaging infrastructure), **B**usiness issues (e.g., strategic, operational and economic aspects), **I**nformation (e.g., information sharing and retrieval, messages exchanged) and **S**emantic aspects (e.g., common dictionary, common set of business documents-BDocs). We argue all these aspects should be tackled by an interoperability framework, and this follows the approach of two EU funded projects: ATHENA (http://www.athena-ip.org) and IDEAS.

Our vision for seamless interoperability relies on a set of attributes to be considered in the development of an interoperability framework and ICT platform. The selection of these attributes is the result of an in depth literature review, analysis of available frameworks, operational infrastructures, independent and industry-specific initiatives, and the experience gained by participation in national and European R&D projects in this field. These attributes are: reliability; time (e.g., to set-up or reconfigurate a CN); cost (e.g., to set-up or operate a CN); openness or extensibility (e.g., the use of open-source software); transparency (e.g., of messages exchanged); scalability, traceability (e.g., collaborative business activities, BDocs exchanged), and other non-functional properties, e.g., security.

2.3 Relevant initiatives

An overview of the current trends towards the establishment of flexible and configurable infrastructure developments is available in (Camarinha-Matos, Afsarmanesh, 2003): layered-based frameworks, agent-based frameworks, and specialized collaborative frameworks.

Important to mention are also advancements of independent (ebXML, http://www. ebxml. org), and industry-specific initiatives, such as RosettaNet (http://www. rosettanet.org) for high-tech and semiconductor industry, papiNet for paper and forest products industry (http://www.papiNet.org).

Concerning semantic interoperability, of relevance are: OASIS's Universal Business Language (http://www.oasiss-open.org) providing a library of XML schemas for common BDocs; the development of industry-specific dictionaries (e.g., RosettaNet Business and Technical Dictionary), and ontologies. However, the use of dictionaries falls short for cross-industry communication, since it would be naïve to believe it is possible to make everybody use the same vocabulary. We strongly support the development of XML schemas for developing common BDocs, which support intra- and inter-industry semantic interoperability.

3 ON THE DESIGN OF A FRAMEWORK FOR SEAMLESS INTEROPERABILITY

3.1 Introduction

Aiming at achieving seamless interoperability in a CNE, a framework comprising **six elements** has been thought: (1) **a messaging service**, responsible for e-communication among organizations, e.g., exchange of BDocs; (2) a **Collaboration Profile/ Agreement Definition and Management** (CP/ADM) service responsible for the definition and management of the organizations' Profile and inter-organization collaboration agreements; (3) a **collaborative business activity** (CBA) service, responsible for the management and integration of the inter-organization BAs; (4) a centralized **Repository** (e.g., storing information on organizations' Profiles, including the description of the products/models produced or supplied; collaborative agreements; messages exchanged); (5) a set of **BDocs** assuring semantic interoperability; (6) a service supporting an **economic analysis**.

The actors involved are: (1) **organizations** (e.g., SMEs), aiming at attaining, for example, shorter negotiation times, faster and cheaper access to new markets and business opportunities, faster and cheaper CN set-up, operation and reconfiguration; (2) a **Business Enabler** (BE)(Section 3.2), (e.g., a Shoe Association in the case of footwear industry) responsible to ease inter-organizations partnerships and agreements setting and management, supporting CNs (and their member organizations) to achieve their goals. Several BEs may exist in a CNE (e.g., one for each industry or services sector).

3.2 Business Enabler for a Collaborative Networked Environment

The framework proposed relies on the concept of BE. Its main responsibility is to enable inter-organizations partnerships and agreements setting and management in a CNE. A BE is an entity within the CNE which is not member of any CN, but it supports CNs (and their member organizations) to achieve their goals, by performing different functions, such as: manage a common Repository; assure reliable and scalable communication among CN members; solve potential conflicts that may occur among CN members (e.g., concerning message repudiation). Depending on each industry or service sector, a BE may support only one or two of the above mentioned functionalities, or may perform additional roles.

3.3   The Messaging Service

The BE assures reliable and scalable communication among CN member organizations. Thus, organizations do not have to set an agreement concerning the communication protocol to be used, that is time and cost consuming and generates errors; the BE is responsible for the secure and reliable transmission of messages/ BDocs among CNE member organizations (e.g., finding an alternative communication way when e-communication fails). In this way, all messages/BDocs sent reach their destination in the time specified. However, some organizations (within the same CN) might choose to communicate on a P2P basis in order to increase their privacy, but this has to be specified in the collaboration agreement.

The messaging service alone is not enough to achieve broad scale interoperability across heterogeneous systems. Research has been pursued to design all the elements of the framework proposed (Section 3.1). As a first step, different business scenarios have been mapped on ebXML. Figure 1 illustrates a high-level overview of two organizations (A and B) conducting e-business according to the framework proposed. The dashed lines illustrate the logical exchange of BDocs, with respect to ebXML scenario, while the actual communication between them (which has been represented with thick arrowed lines) is performed through the BE.

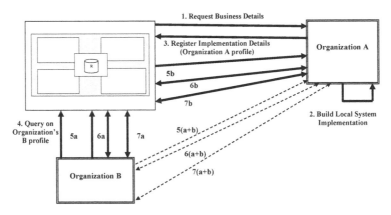

Figure 1. A high-level overview of the interactions of two organizations conducting e-business according to the framework proposed

Seven main steps have been identified: (1) Organization A requests business details from the BE/Repository; (2) Organization A decides to build its own ICT platform-compliant application; (3) Organization A submits its Profile information in the Repository (e.g., by filling in a form in HTML format). The information submitted concerns its capabilities and constraints, information of the products it produces or supplies, the business scenarios and roles supported; (4) Organization B, which already uses an ICT platform-compliant application discovers in the common Repository the Organization's A profile; (5) Organization B contacts Organization A, by sending a first valid draft of a Business Collaboration Agreement document (BCA-Doc). In this way, Organization B asks Organization A if it is interested to engage in a business scenario, by making a first business proposal; (6) Organizations A and B negotiate (e.g., by exchanging different versions of the BCA-Doc) till they reach an agreement. The final BCA-Doc outlines the mutually agreed upon business scenarios, and specific terms; (7) Organizations A and B are now ready to engage in e-business.

3.4 The Collaboration Profile/Agreement Definition and Management Service

This service aims at assuring the definition and management of the collaborative profiles and agreements by supporting different functionalities, e.g., organization's Profile definition, collaboration agreement management; information maintenance. An organization defines and submits its Profile (e.g., capabilities, business scenarios, BDocs and roles supported) to the common Repository through a Portal. This information can be viewed by other organizations (registered in the CNE), and which are searching for potential business partners.

Before organizations actually conduct business with each other, they should define a *business collaboration agreement*, which corresponds to an intersection of their *Profiles* and includes additional results on negotiating variable parameters.

3.5 Collaborative Business Activities

This element of the framework is supported by an activity-oriented view of the several business interactions between CN member organizations (e.g., BDocs exchanged). The inter-organization interactions are, in fact, CBAs. The choreography of these interactions/activities may be globally specified and stored in the common Repository (e.g., allowing the specification of individual and concrete workflow processes, which can be integrated). Some collaborative activities in a given workflow process will need to be integrated with third-party applications in the organization (e.g., ERP solutions). Thus, these organizations will make available a set of Web services whose invocation will be done and coordinated by a CBA integration and coordination service (e.g., which should be able to differentiate human-based from automatic activities, and coordinate their execution).

As a first step, a set of five **operational CBA clusters** has been identified, which define inter-organization interactions in a CNE: *(1) Order Management* (e.g., from price and delivery quotation, Order initiation, till invoicing and payment); *(2) Design and Manufacturing* (e.g., the exchange of information related with the design configurations necessary to manufacture a certain product); *(3) Marketing and Commercialization*, enabling communication of marketing information; *(4) Inventory Management*, enabling inventory management collaboration; *(5) Post-sale Support* (e.g., request warranty claim).

3.6   Centralized Repository

The total set of business scenarios registered in the Repository defines the possibilities of e-business. Each organization may define its capabilities (at the technical and business levels) of a subset of what is possible. The Profiles registered allow other organizations to query on potential business partners Profiles (by accessing a service designed to retrieve information from the common Repository) and on possible ways to conduct business with them.

3.7   The Service Supporting an Economic Analysis

This service aims at providing CNs (and their member organizations) a basis for elaborating an economic analysis (e.g., cost-benefit analysis), as support for their performance assessment. This service can be implemented based on the economic model proposed by (Chituc, Nof, 2007).

4   CONCEPT VALIDATION: AN IMPLEMENTATION EXAMPLE FROM THE FOOTWEAR INDUSTRY

Based on this framework, an ICT platform supporting B2B in the footwear industry is currently being implemented, within the scope of a national project ShoeBiz@PT pursued in partnership between the Portuguese Shoe Technological Center and INESC Porto. It aims at achieving seamless interoperability in this sector.

The footwear industry has a significant delay concerning ICT developments and e-business adoption, compared to other industry sectors, as emphasized in (EC, 2006). Main characteristics of this sector, its requirements, specific scenarios, relevant projects and their main outcomes have been summarized in (Chituc, Toscano, Azevedo, 2007a, b).

Actors. Two main actors are involved in the footwear sector: **(1) SMEs** (e.g., producer, subcontractor, supplier), performing different roles (e.g., buyer, seller, delivery recipient, payer, payee), and which aim at attaining decreasing costs (e.g., for operation), shorter negotiation times, faster and cheaper access to new markets and business opportunities, faster and cheaper CN set-up, operation and reconfiguration; **(2) the Shoe Association**, performing the role of Business Enabler, having the following three main responsibilities: it acts as a communication hub between all SMEs; resolves potential conflicts; manages the Repository.

System architecture. The architecture of the system is illustrated in Figure 2. A **Hub** assures inter-organizations communication, manages the common Repository, and makes available a set of services for the eMail application. The **Connector** is the link with the SMEs' ERP system, keeping track of all BDocs sent and received by the company where it is installed. The **eMail application** is a GUI for information management, supporting human-oriented tasks of BDocs creation, reception and printing. This application works as a regular e-mail front-end allowing users to send/receive BDocs.

Messaging service. After an in depth analysis, the research team has decided to adopt Hermes platform as messaging service. Main reasons for this decision were: it is open-source and in compliance with OASIS ebMS v2; supports any kind of data in the body of the messages exchanged. However, Hermes has been used here in a

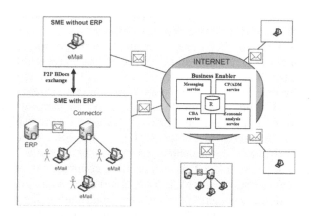

Figure 2. System architecture (footwear industry)

different way: while ebXML encourages communication among SMEs on a peer-to-peer basis, this approach uses a communication Hub allowing a third-party entity (e.g., Shoe Association) to play the role of BE. Elements required implementing this messaging platform are: a messaging service (e.g., ebXML Hermes); a mail service (e.g., ebXML eMail); interfaces (e.g., for to end-users of each organization in order to see the BDocs received/sent).

This element is message-oriented. It supports trading partners to conduct business through a reliable and secure exchange of BDocs. Additional elements (e.g., APIs) may also be present at this level of integration. For example, external applications (e.g., ERP solutions) may use the API to send and receive BDocs from external trading partners.

XML-based Business Documents. Aiming at covering most of the different collaborations and relationships among the actors in this sector, a set of 17 XML-based BDocs has been developed within SHOENET project, and which are used for this implementation. This set of common BDocs assures semantic interoperability among business partners, and supports cross-industry communication.

CP/ADM element has already been designed and it is currently being implemented (by making use of open-source software). **CBA** element is currently being design, considering the *Clusters* identified (Section 3.5) and the specificities of this sector. BPEL will be used for the implementation.

5   CONCLUSIONS AND FUTURE RESEARCH WORK

Although there are available numerous tools and infrastructures supporting interoperability in a collaborative networked environment, this goal is unachieved.

The framework proposed towards seamless interoperability relies on a set of attributes (e.g., reliability, cost, time, traceability) identified by the authors, and four main views on interoperability: technical, semantic, information and business. It comprises six main elements: a messaging service; a Collaboration Profile/Agreement Definition and Management service; a system assuring Collaborative Business

Activities' integration and management; a centralized Repository; a set of business documents; a service supporting an economic analysis.

This framework relies on the concept of *Business Enabler* (e.g., a Shoe Association in the case of footwear industry), which assures communication among organizations, solves conflicts, and manages the Repository. However, some organizations might communicate directly in order to increase the privacy of their communication, but this has to be specified in the collaboration agreement.

Based on this framework, an information and communication technology (ICT) platform is currently being implemented for the footwear sector within the scope of ShoeBiz@PT project pursued at national level in partnership between the Portuguese Shoe Technological Center (CTCP) and INESC Porto. The messaging service has already been implemented, and developments are being pursued to implement the CP/ADM and CBA elements. A common set of 17 XML-based business documents already available is used, assuring semantic interoperability.

This ICT platform represents a significant contribution for the SMEs in the footwear sector by providing them shorter negotiation times; decreased costs; faster and cheaper CN set-up, operation and reconfiguration; faster and cheaper access to new markets and business opportunities; reliable communication among business partners. It assures BDocs reliable delivery, confidentiality, authentication, privacy, non-repudiation, and information integration.

Future work will focus on analyzing the possibility to implement this approach to other industry sectors, and to quantify its impact.

Acknowledgements

The first author acknowledges FCT for PhD grant BD/SFRH/19751/2004.

6   REFERENCES

1. Camarinha-Matos, L.M.; Afsarmanesh, H.; Garita, C.; Lima, C., "Towards an architecture for virtual enterprises". In J. of Intelligent Manufacturing 9, 1998, pp. 198-199
2. Camarinha-Matos, L.M.; Afsarmanesh, H., "Elements of a base VE infrastructure". In Computers in Industry, 51 (2), 2003a, pp. 139-163
3. Camarinha-Matos, L.M.; Afsarmanesh, H.; Rabelo, R.J., "Infrastructure developments for agile virtual enterprises". In Int. J. Computer Integrated Manufacturing 16 (4-5), 2003b, pp. 235-254
4. Chituc, C.-M.; Azeved, A., "Business Networking – the Technological Infrastructure Support". In Knowledge and Technology Management in Virtual Organizations (Eds. Cunha, M.; Putnik, G.), ISBN 978-1599041659, Chapter 16, Idea Group Publishing, 2006, pp. 334-354
5. Chituc, C.-M.; Nof, S.Y., "The Join decision in collaborative networked organizations". In Computers & Industrial Engineering, 2007 (accepted for publication)
6. Chituc, C.-M.; Toscano, C.; Azevedo, A. "Towards the creation of a digital business ecosystem for the shoe manufacturing domain", In Proc. IEEE DEST 2007a
7. Chituc, C.-M.; Toscano, C.; Azevedo, A., "Interoperability in Collaborative Networks: an innovative approach for the shoe up-stream business segment", Proc. I-ESA 2007b
8. European Commission (EC), "ICT and e-Business in the Footwear Industry", Sector impact study no. 2/2006 (retrieved from http://www.ebusiness-watch.org on 12.01.07)
9. IEEE, "IEEE Standard Computer Dictionary: A compilation of IEEE Standard Computer Glossaries", Institute of Electrical and Electronics Engineers, NY, 1990
10. Li, H., "XML and industrial standards for electronic commerce". In Knowledge and Information Systems 2(4), 2000, pp. 487-97
11. Pollock, J.T., "The biggest issues: Interoperability vs. Integration". In eAI Journal, 2001, pp. 48-52

48 | BARRIERS DRIVEN METHODOLOGY FOR ENTERPRISE INTEROPERABILITY

David Chen and Nicolas Daclin
IMS-LAPS, University Bordeaux 1
351 cours de la Libération, 33405 Talence cedex, FRANCE
david.chen@laps.ims-bordeaux.fr

In order to perform enterprise interoperability projects in an organised and efficient way, this paper presents a methodology which aims at helping establishing interoperability in enterprises in a step-by-step manner. A novel barrier-driven approach is adopted. An interoperability framework is elaborated to structure interoperability issues and concerns. An interoperability measurement approach is drafted to characterise the degree of interoperability achieved. A structured approach is defined showing the main phases to follow to use the interoperability framework and interoperability measurement methods.

1 INTRODUCTION

Developing enterprise interoperability in the industrial context is a complex project. Although some fragmented knowledge and solutions for interoperability have been accumulated since years, a complete interoperability methodology is still missing. Existing engineering methodologies such as for example GRAI methodology, CIMOSA, PERA, etc. were developed in the context of enterprise integration rather than interoperability. As part of INTEROP (2003) and ATHENA (2003) initiatives, our aim is to elaborate an enterprise interoperability methodology to help analysing, searching and implementing interoperability solutions in a structured way.

Interoperability is generally defined as the ability for two (or more) systems to exchange information and to use the information that has been exchanged (IEEE, 1990). In the context of enterprises, interoperability refers to the ability of interactions (exchange of information and services) between enterprise systems. Enterprise interoperability is considered as significant if the interactions can take place at least at the three levels: data, services and process, with a semantics defined in a given context (IDEAS, 2003).

Enterprises are not interoperable because there are barriers to interoperability between enterprise systems. Barriers are incompatibilities of various kinds at the various enterprise levels. There exist common barriers to all enterprises. Consequently the methodology we propose aims at a barrier-driven approach to identify the common barriers, measure the importance of the barriers using metrics and search solutions to remove barriers (Chen *et al.*, 2006).

The methodology presented in this paper consists of three main parts: (1) enterprise interoperability framework, (2) structured approach, (3) enterprise interoperability measurement. The paper is structured as follows. Section 2 presents the basic dimensions of the interoperability framework. It defines the domain of enterprise interoperability and structures interoperability concepts, problems and solutions. The framework allows linking interoperability barriers to possible

Chen, D., Daclin, N., 2007, in IFIP International Federation for Information Processing, Volume 243, Establishing the Foundation of Collaborative Networks; eds. Camarinha-Matos, L., Afsarmanesh, H., Novais, P., Analide, C.; (Boston: Springer), pp. 453–460.

solutions for removing the barriers. Based on the framework, section 3 discusses the measurement of degree of interoperability. Three kinds of measures are outlined, namely interoperability potential, compatibility and performance measures. Section 4 defines a structured approach with the main steps to follow and the actors involved in an interoperability project. In section 5 a simplified example will be presented to illustrate the use of the methodology. Future works and conclusions will be given in section 6.

2   ENTERPRISE INTEROPERABILITY FRAMEWORK

The term 'framework' refers to an organising mechanism to structure concepts or 'things' in a certain ways. Recently several initiatives on interoperability have proposed interoperability frameworks to structure issues and concerns in quite different ways. The European Interoperability Framework in the eGovernment domain (EIF, 2004) defines three types of interoperability: semantic, technical and organisational. A similar approach was also proposed in e-Health interoperability framework (NEHTA, 2006) which identified three layers: organizational, informational and technical interpretabilities. In manufacturing area the IDEAS interoperability framework (IDEAS, 2003) defines three main layers (Business, Knowledge and ICT) with two additional vertical dimensions (Semantics and Quality attributes). More recently the ATHENA Interoperability Framework (AIF) proposes to structure interoperability issues and solutions at the three levels: conceptual, technical and applicative (ATHENA, 2003).

Our goal is to tackle interoperability problems through the identification of barriers which prevent interoperability to happen. The Interoperability Framework we proposed (Chen *et al.*, 2006) (INTEROP, 2006) is barrier-driven and has taken into account the basic concepts addressed in the existing frameworks. In particular in the European Interoperability Framework, interoperability is studied from three aspects: Semantic, Technical, and Organisational. In our proposal, these three aspects are considered as problems (barriers) to be tackled rather than interoperability to be established. Consequently three categories of barriers are defined: conceptual barriers (syntax/semantic incompatibilities), technological barriers (additional income-patibility due to the use of computer), and organisational barriers (related to the incompatibilities of method of work, organisation structure,..). In summary the three main framework dimensions we identified are:

- *Interoperability concerns* which defines the content of interoperation that may take place at various levels of the enterprise (data, service, process, business).
- *Interoperability barriers* which identifies various obstacles to interoperability in three categories (conceptual, technological, and organisational)
- *Interoperability approaches* which represents the different ways in which barriers can be removed (integrated, unified, and federated)

Figure 1 shows the interoperability in its simplified form with only two dimensions.

Iop barriers / Iop concerns	CONCEPTUAL	TECHNOLOGICAL	ORGANISATIONAL
BUSINESS			
PROCESS			
SERVICE			
DATA			

Figure 1. Interoperability Framework (here only the first two dimensions)

The focus of the interoperability framework is structuring barriers to interoperability and solutions for removing the barriers. This is important for retrieval and reuses the existing knowledge. For example, PSL (Process Specification Language) allows removing the conceptual barrier (syntactic and semantic barriers) for process interoperability using unified approach. This interoperability framework is partially implemented in Metis modelling tool[1] using the Metis Enterprise Architecture Framework (MEAF). It aims at supporting the search and analysis of available solutions. More details on the framework and the additional dimensions associated to the framework can be found in (INTEROP, 2006).

3   ENTERPRISE INTEROPERABILITY MEASURE

The fact that interoperability can be improved means that there exists metrics for measuring the degree of interoperability. Measuring interoperability allows a company knowing its strengths and weaknesses to interoperate with a third company and to prioritize actions to improve their collaboration ability. To day few methods are developed for measuring interoperability. Existing approaches mainly focus on maturity measure (C4ISR, 1998) (Kasunic, 2004). Maturity can be seen as a kind of interoperability potential. The term maturity model was popularized by the SEI (Software Engineering Institute) when they developed the Capability Maturity Model (CMM) in 1986. Five maturity levels have been proposed (CMM, 2004), namely initial, repeatable, defined, managed and optimizing. Several other models have been developed in different disciplines and focusing on different levels of the enterprise, for example: the Service-Oriented Architecture Maturity Model (Bachman, 2005), the Extended Enterprise Architecture Maturity Model (IFEAD, 2004), the NASCIO (2003) Enterprise Architecture Maturity Model and the Organisational Interoperability Maturity Model (Clark *et al.*, 1999). These models aimed at evaluating processes within organizations and identifying best practices useful in helping them increase the maturity of their processes.

More focused on interoperability issues, the LISI (Levels of Information Systems Interoperability) proposed a maturity model for measuring interoperability in five levels of maturity: isolated, connected, functional, domain, enterprise (C4ISR, 1998). Some similar approaches have been developed based on LISI, for example

---

[1] Troux Technologies, "Metis". http://www.troux.com/products/metis/ (accessed: 2006).

the TENA model identifies six levels (isolated, co-habitable, syntax, semantic, seamless, and adaptive). These maturity models for interoperability were mainly developed for the arm systems of the US department of defence.

Based on these existing maturity models, ATHENA project has elaborated for the manufacturing enterprise the EIMM (Enterprise Interoperability Maturity Model) to address interoperability issues at all levels of the company (ATHENA, 2005). Defining the EIMM involves two tasks: (i) identifying the main areas of concern on which an enterprise need to work in order to achieve interoperability both internally and externally, (ii) defining the maturity levels that describe the improvement path for each area of concern.

In our methodology three types of interoperability measurement are considered: (i) potential measurement, (ii) compatibility measurement, and (iii) performance measurement. This allows going far beyond existing approaches which only consider maturity evaluation.

The interoperability potential measurement is concerned with the identification of a set of characteristics (maturity) that have impact on the interoperability. These measures are performed on one enterprise/system without the necessity to know its interoperation partner. The objective is to evaluate the potentiality of a system to adapt and to accommodate dynamically to overcome possible barriers when interacting with a third partner. For example, an open system has a higher potential of interoperability than a closed system. Our methodology will make use of EIMM to measure interoperability potential of a company.

The interoperability compatibility measurement has to be performed during the engineering stage i.e. when systems need to be re-engineered in order to establish interoperability with a known partner. This measure is performed when the partner/system of the interoperation is known. The measure is done with respect to the identified barriers to interoperability. The highest degree of compatibility means that all the barriers to interoperability are removed. The inverse situation means the poorest degree of interoperability. For measuring the interoperability compatibility, we have developed EIDM (Enterprise Interoperability Degree Measurement) (Daclin *et al.*, 2006) (ATHENA, 2007) based on the interoperability framework.

The performance measurement has to be performed during the operational phase i.e. run time, to evaluate the ability of interoperation between two cooperating enterprises. Criteria such as cost, delay and quality can be used to measure the performance with respect to barriers and concerns during a basic interoperation cycle. Therefore, each type of measurement has to be valued with local coefficients in order to get a global coefficient ranging from "poor interoperability" to "good interoperability". The performance measurement is part of EIDM developed within the frame of ATHENA A8 project. Details about both EIMM and EIDM approaches can be found in (ATHENA, 2007).

4   STRUCTURED APPROACH

The structured approach aims at defining the main phases to follow in a sequential way with possible iterations between the phases. Depending on whether the methodology is being applied to an individual company or a pair collaboration partners each phase will involve the use of the EIMM or the EIDM. Four main phases and activities are identified:

(i) Definition of objectives and needs: It aims at defining the interoperability performance targeted, evaluating the feasibility and cost as well as project planning.

- Define needs of interoperability for each area of concern defined in the EIMM.
- Define needs of interoperability in terms of enterprise level and approach (integrated, unified, and federated) as defined in the EIDM.

(ii) Analysis of existing system: The man goal of this phase is to identify actors, applications and systems involved, and interoperability problems encountered.

- Analyze the as-is situation, define the to-be situation and the gaps between them.
- Identify barriers to interoperability, measure existing interoperability using EIDM (compatibility measurement), analyze strong and weak points.

(iii) Select and combine solutions: It consists in searching and selecting available interoperability solution elements through the interoperability framework.

- Provide recommendation in the form of a conceptual solution (i.e.: standards to be adopted, which solutions to use and where to apply them, etc.).
- Combine and construct a company specific a technical solution taking into account the objective and constraints of the company

(iv) Implementation and test: In this phase, solutions to remove the barriers will be tested and evaluated.

- Implement the technical solutions elaborated.
- Carry out performance measures and compare to the targeted interoperability degree and performance.

The most crucial activity is to identify the barriers to achieve the interoperability degree targeted by the companies. Identifying barriers is only concerned with those 'things' that need to be shared and exchanged between two systems/companies. Interoperability requires a common basis for those elements.

After having identified barriers, solutions need to be searched to remove the barriers. Consequently one needs to map the barriers onto the knowledge/solution repository which is structured according to the framework. Queries can be expressed in terms of barrier types. Solutions found may need to be adapted or combined.

One the solution(s) implemented, a new measurement needs to be done to verify if barriers are removed effectively using the proposed solution(s). In some cases the interoperability is improved but there still exist some incompatibilities. A new iteration is required to adapt the solution or use other solutions till all barriers are completely removed. Performance measures may also be required at the test phase

The methodology is participative and four groups of actors are defined based on the GRAI methodology:

- Project board: the top-level management members of the company. They give the objectives of the project.
- Synthesis group: the main responsible people of the company. They ensure the follow-up of the project and check the results at various stages.
- Specialist group: experts in interoperability and methodology. They give advice to the synthesis group, build various models and perform analysis.
- Interviewees group: company people to be interviewed by specialists. They provide information needed by the other groups.

It is necessary to plan the meetings and tasks to perform. Usually, several iterations are needed to get a validated analysis and models representing the as-is situation of the company.

5   APPLIYING METHODOLOGY

The methodology is partially applied in the frame of the ATHENA A8 project (SME Interoperability in Practice). The case was provided by SAP based on a Carrier-Shipper Scenario (ATHENA, 2007). The study focuses on the application of EIDM to the scenario, where an SME shipper uses the services of multiple larger carriers. It aims at showing how we uncover interoperability barriers, classify interoperability barriers in a coherent framework, classify interoperability solutions in the same framework and use the framework to select the right solutions to each barrier.

The application started by modelling the scenario of interoperation. In the scenario, a set of needs and objectives for new solutions have been defined from the point of view of an SME shipper. For examples, (Semi-) automatic integration of Carrier Services, data and process mapping, user interface, predefined and easy configurable adapters, and configuration etc. The targeted interoperation the all four enterprise levels (business, process, service, and data). Federated and unified approaches are preferred to full integration to keep autonomy/flexibility at the two sides.

During the analysis phase, EIDM was used to identify the barriers between the two companies. Figure 2 shows the process depicted in the scenario and summarises the main barriers that were identified and dealt in the project.

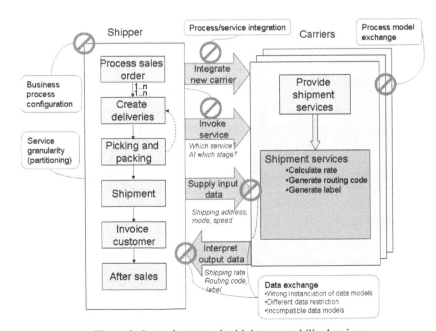

Figure 2. Scenario mapped with interoperability barriers

The barriers identified and presented in figure 2 are mapped to the interoperability framework. For each barrier, a template was used to describe in detail the levels of enterprise concerned, the interoperability problem encountered, the ATHENA solutions identified and possible adaptations necessary to implement the solutions. Table 1 shows an example of data exchange barrier described using the template.

Table 1. Incompatible syntactic and semantic representation of data

Template elements	Description
Enterprise levels concerned	Data, Service
Barriers to interoperability	Conceptual barrier - Incompatible syntactic and semantic representation of data at each interacting partner
Interoperability problem	Different models adopted by the companies makes data exchange difficult as enterprises cannot exchange their data automatically
ATHENA solutions identified	- Conceptual solutions: Annotation of proprietary models according to common ontology to allow data reconciliation - Technical solutions: A3 tools, WSDL Analyzer
ATHENA results evaluation – Relevance to SMEs	- Adoption of the common generic ontology reflecting the business domain - The WSDL Analyzer detects mismatches between data a service expects and provides - Relevant for SME which receive required interfaces of big companies which expect that their smaller business partners adapt to their interfaces
Planned Adaptations	Possibility to manipulate the generated mappings between heterogeneous interfaces.
Remarks	There exist other solutions for data mapping. However, none of them is directly concerned with Web service interface compatibility

During the phase of search of solutions, some ATHENA solutions were selected according to their ability to remove the identified barriers. Each solution is described at the two levels of abstraction: (i) conceptual solution independent of a technology, (ii) technology solution. In the implementation and test phase, a new interoperability measurement needs to be performed to evaluate the gap between the targeted interoperability degree and achieved one.

This case study allows validating the efficiency of the methodology to establish interoperability by identifying the barriers (incompatibilities) between the elements that must be exchanged and shared. More detail on this study can be found in (ATHENA, 2007).

6   CONCLUSIONS

To avoid hazardous demarche in an interoperability project, it is necessary to use a methodology with a structured approach. This paper presented an interoperability methodology which will enhance the interoperability research and development. There are different ways and strategies to deal with interoperability using methodology; our approach is barrier-driven and bottom-up. The strength is its three interrelated components: interoperability framework; interoperability measurement and structured approach. The proposed methodology is particular adapted to SMEs. Typically barrier-driven approach aims at tackle interoperability problems by identifying directly the causes of non-interoperability. This contrasts some top-down or holistic approaches which needs more time and investment to accomplish.

The main advantages of using this methodology are to allow on the one hand, an efficient classification and retrieval of interoperability solutions according to the barriers, promoting reuse of existing solutions; and on the other hand characterising the degree of interoperability from three different aspects and letting a company knowing its strength and weakness.

The proposed methodology applies to both intra and inter enterprise organisation, including extended enterprise, virtual enterprise as well as collaborative and networked enterprises.

Future works are concerned with further identifying and structuring interoperability barriers and solutions in the framework, to implement the framework in a tool to support industry use, and to refine metrics for interoperability measurement. Another work being performed is to define a formal model for describing the proposed concepts as ontology.

Acknowledgement

The author thanks and acknowledges the members of ATHENA A8 project and INTEROP DI (Domain Interoperability) participants for their contributions to the methodology, case study and interoperability framework.

REFERENCES

1. ATHENA. Advanced Technologies for Heterogeneous Enterprise Networks and their Applications, FP6-2002-IST-1, Integrated Project Proposal, 2003
2. INTEROP, Annex1-Description of work, Interoperability Research for Networked Enterprises Applications and Software. INTEROP NoE. Network of Excellence, n°508011, 2003
3. IEEE, A compilation of IEEE standard computer glossaries", standard computer dictionary, 1990
4. IDEAS, IDEAS Project Deliverables (WP1-WP7), Public reports, www.ideas-road map.net, 2003
5. EIF, European Interoperability Framework for PAN-European EGovernment services, IDA working document - Version 4.2 – January 2004
6. Chen, D., Daclin, N., Framework for enterprise interoperability, IFAC EI2N 2006, Bordeaux
7. INTEROP, Enterprise Interoperability-Framework and knowledge corpus-Advanced report, Deliverable DI.2, DI (Domain Interoperability), December 15, 2006
8. C4ISR, Architecture Working Group (AWG), Levels of Information Systems Interoperability (LISI), 30 March 1998
9. Kasunic, M., Anderson, W., Measuring systems interoperability: challenges and opportunities, Software engineering measurement and analysis initiative, 2004
10. NEHTA, Towards a Health Interop Framework, 2006, (http://www. providersedge.com/ehdocs/ .../Towards_an_Interoperability_Framework.pdf)
11. CMM, Carnegie Mellon Software Engineering Institute: SEI Software Engineering Process Management Program, http://www.sei.cmu.edu/organization/programs/sepm/process.html, 2004
12. NASCIO (National Association of State Chief Information Officers). NASCIO Enterprise Architecture Maturity Model, Version 1.3, 2003
13. IFEAD (Institute for Enterprise Architecture Developments). Extended Enterprise Architecture Maturity Model (E2AMM), 2004
14. ATHENA Integrated Project (507849). Framework for the Establishment and Management Methodology, Deliverable DA1.4, 2005
15. Bachman, J. Service-Oriented Architecture Maturity Model, http://www.sonicsoftware.com, 2005.
16. Daclin, N., Chen, D., Vallespir, B.: Enterprise interoperability measurement – Basic concepts, Enterprise Modeling and Ontologies for Interoperability, Luxemburg, 2006
17. ATHENA, Guidelines and Best Practices for Applying the ATHENA Interoperability Framework to Support SME Participation in Digital Ecosystems, Deliverable DA8.2, January, 2007
18. Clark, T., Jones, R., Organizational Interoperability Maturity Model for C2., Department of Defense, Canberra, Australia, 1999

49

AMBIENT INTELLIGENCE AND SIMULATION IN HEALTH CARE VIRTUAL SCENARIOS

António Abelha[1], Cesar Analide[1], José Machado[1], José Neves[1], Manuel Santos[2] and Paulo Novais[1]

[1]*Departamento de Informática, Universidade do Minho, Braga, PORTUGAL*
{abelha,analide,jmac,jneves, pjon}@di.uminho.pt
[2]*Departamento de Sistemas de Informação, Universidade do Minho, Guimarães, PORTUGAL*
mfs@dsi.uminho.pt

The success of change depends greatly on the ability to respond to human needs and to bridge the gap between humans and machines, and understanding the environment. With such experience, in addition to extensive practice in managing change, knowledge sharing and innovation, it would be interesting in offering a contribution by facilitating a dialogue, knowledge café (i.e. bringing in knowledge) on these issues, and how to apply them to new and altering scenarios. When one comes into the area of health care, one major limitation felt by those institutions is in the selection process of physicians to undertake a specific task, where there is a lack of objective, of validated measures of human performance. Indeed, objective measures are necessary if simulators are to be used to evaluate the skills and training of medical practitioners and teams or to evaluate the impact of new processes or equipment design on the overall system performance. In this paper it will be presented a logical theory of Situation Awareness (SA) and discusses the methods required for developing an objective measure of SA within the context of a simulated medical environment, as the one referred to above. Analysis and interpretation of SA data for both individual and team performance in health care are presented.

1   INTRODUCTION

Heath Care Virtual Scenarios (HCVS) allows healthcare workers and professionals to undertake simulated medical practices for patient care, providing a projection of a real unit, using computerized tools to resolve health problems from physical attributes, and simulating conversational dialogue in the area of Medicine. The HCVS offer a wide digital library of cases under supervision allowing the attendance of medical and nursing education courses, in particular in the intensive care arena, integrating highly heterogeneous sources of information into a coherent knowledge base. The system content is created automatically by the physicians as their daily work goes on and students are encouraged to articulate lengthier answers that exhibit deep reasoning, rather than to deliver straight tips of shallow knowledge. The goal is to take advantage of the normal functioning of health care units to build on the fly

Abelha, a., Analide, C., Machado, J., Neves, J., Santos, M., Novais, P., 2007, in IFIP International Federation for Information Processing, Volume 243, Establishing the Foundation of Collaborative Networks; eds. Camarinha-Matos, L., Afsarmanesh, H., Novais, P., Analide, C.; (Boston: Springer), pp. 461–468.

a knowledge base of cases and data for teaching and research purposes. Medical simulation facilitates the widespread acceptance of new techniques in health units and allows the participants to practice diagnosis, medical management and behavioural approaches, with no risk to patient safety. Simulation is a practice where conditions or hypotheses are created in order to study or experience real situations or actions. Learning includes observation (e.g., video watching or book reading), verification (e.g., the accuracy of some information or looking for clues), searching of hypotheses (e.g., diagnostic), induction of rules (e.g., program generation) and problem solving (e.g., deduction). Learning may be built upon a web-based framework and involves lessons or tutorials. Students work on a context-dependent scenario activating a precipitating event and requiring a fast response, and play with possibilities and alternatives making the approximation between simulation and game. In the HCVS, learning should arise from how people learn, naturally.

Beyond the organizational, functional, technical and scientific requisites, it must be taken into consideration ethical and legal issues, as well as data quality, information security, access control and privacy. Indeed, in a HCVS, the collection of vast amounts of medical data will not only support the requirements of archiving but also provide a platform for the application of data mining and knowledge discovery to determine possible medical trends and the real data to support educational training. Knowledge discovery techniques can be applied to identify pathologies and disease trends. The data can also be used for educational and training purposes because maybe one of the unique cases can be identified and used in expert system like applications to advise practitioners.

On the other hand Ambient Intelligence (AmI) is a new paradigm in information technology, in which people are empowered through a digital environment that is aware of their presence and context, which is sensitive, adaptive, and responsive to their needs, habits, gestures and emotions [1]. Indeed, simulators are used to evaluate the skills and training of medical practitioners and teams or to evaluate the impact of new processes or equipment design on the overall system performance.

2   MEDICAL INFORMATION SYSTEMS

Specific interaction and communication based protocols are paramount for the successful implementation, running, and/or management of any medical information system. Indeed, Medical Information Systems have to be addressed in terms of a wide variety of heterogeneous distributed systems speaking different languages, integrating medical equipment and customized by several companies, which in turn were developed by people aiming at different goals. This lead us to consider the solution(s) to a particular problem, to be part of an integration process of different sources of information, using different protocols, in terms of an Agency for the Integration, Diffusion and Archive (AIDA) of medical information, and the Electronic Medical Record (EMR) software, bringing to the healthcare arena new methodologies for problem solving in medical education, computational models, technologies and tools.

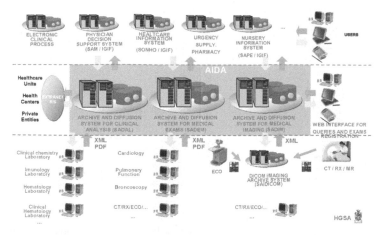

Figure 1: AIDA : Agency for Integration, Diffusion and Archive of Medical Information

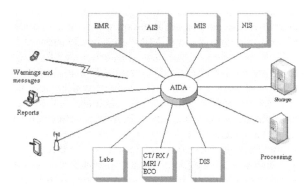

Figure 2: The AIDA modules

AIDA – Agency for Integration, Diffusion and Archive of Medical Information (Figure1) - is an agency that provides intelligent electronic workers, here defined as agents, that present a pro-active behaviour, and are in charge of tasks such as the communications among the different sub-systems, sending and receiving information (e.g., medical or clinical reports, images, collections of data, prescriptions), managing and saving the information and answering to information requests, in time [2][3]. The main goal is to integrate, diffuse and archive large sets of information from heterogeneous sources (e.g. departments, services, units, computers, medical equipments). Under these presuppositions a virtual Healthcare Information System (HIS) is presented (Figure 2), which will be addressed in terms of a virtual Administrative Information System (AIS), which intends to represent, manage and archive the administrative information that is generated during the episode (an episode is a collection of all the operations assigned to the patient since the beginning of the treatment until the end); the virtual Medical Support Information System (MIS),

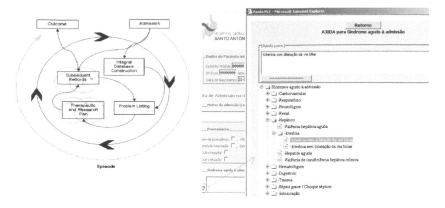

Figure 3: The POMR method   Figure 4: Procedure Registration with EMR

which intends to represent, manage and archive the clinical information during the episode; the virtual Nursing Support Information System (NIS), which intends to represent, manage and archive the nursing information during the episode; the Electronic Medical Record Information System (EMR); and the Distributed Information Systems (DIS) of all the departments or services, in particular of the Laboratories (Labs), Radiological Information System (RIS) and Medical Imaging (PACS - Picture Archive and Communication System), which deals with images in a standard format, the DICOM one. Agents exchange messages which are well-formed formulae of the communication language, performing acts or communicative actions [4].

The "intelligence" of the system as a whole arises from the interactions among all the system's components. The interfaces are based on Web-related front-ends, querying or managing a data warehouse [5]. Such an approach can provide decision support. A context dependent formalism has been used to specify the AIDA system, incorporating facilities such as abstraction, encapsulation and hierarchy, in order to define the system components or agents; the socialization process, at the agent level and the multi-agent one, following other possible way of aggregation and cooperation; the coordination procedure at the agent plane; and the global system behaviour.

3   THE ELECTRONIC MEDICAL RECORD

The Electronic Medical Record (EMR) is a core application which covers horizontally the virtual health care unit and makes possible a transverse analysis of medical records along the several services, units or treated pathologies, bringing to healthcare units new computational models, technologies and tools, based on data warehouses, agents, multi-agent systems and ambient intelligence [6]. Beyond the organizational, functional, technical and scientific requisites, one may have to attend ethical and legal ones, as well as data quality, information security, access control and privacy. An EMR is an assembly of standardized documents, ordered and concise, directed to the register of actions and medical procedures; a set of information compiled by physicians and others health professionals; a register of integral facts, containing all the information regarding patient health data; and a follow up of the risk values and clinical profile. The main goal is to replace hard documents by electronic ones, increasing data processing and reducing time and costs. The patient assistance will be more effective, faster and quality will be improved [7]. The medical training will be based on a rich repository with particular historical cases [8].

Indeed, clinical research and practice involve a process to collect data to systematize knowledge about patients, their health status and the motives of the health care admittance. At the same time, data has to be registered in a structured and organized way, making effective automation and supporting using Information Technologies. For example, from an information repository, one may have collected patient data which is registered in an efficient, consistent, clear and structured way to improve disease knowledge and therapy; the medical processes for registering data are complemented with the information interchange between the different physicians that work around the patient; the clinical data recording are guaranteed in the Electronic Medical Record (EMR) application and procedural context; the protocol to use the EMR is implemented in a secure and efficient way; log files are used to associate physicians to clinical data recording; medical education will be improved.

The process to collect data comes from Problem Oriented Medical Record (POMR) method. This is a format for clinical recording consisting of a problem list; a database including the patient history with physical examination and clinical findings; diagnostic, therapeutic and educational plans; a daily SOAP (Subjective, Objective, Assessment and Plan) progress note. The problem list serves as an index for the reader, each problem being followed through until resolution. This system widely influences note keeping by recognizing the four different phases of the decision making process: data collection; the formulation of problems; the devising of a management plan; and the reviewing of the situation and the revising of the plan if necessary (Figure 3).

Data processing is made taking under consideration organization, structure, systematization and codification. Using concepts and techniques in the domains of knowledge representation and databases, data, objects and structures can be represented. On the other hand, the use of codification systems, scripting and ontologies enable a more natural, automatic, efficient, adaptive and intelligent recording. The system is ubiquitous; i.e. may be used anywhere in the healthcare unit. In Figure 4 it is shown an example of procedure registration using EMR.

4   AMBIENT INTELLIGENCE IN MEDICINE

Ambient intelligence is related with an atmosphere where rational and emotional intelligence is omnipresent. In an ambient intelligent environment, people are surrounded with networks of embedded intelligent devices to gather and diffuse information around physical places, forming a ubiquitous network around an integrated global middleware accepting specific requests and data from hetero-geneous sources, and providing ubiquitous information, communication and services [9] [12]. Intelligent devices are available whenever needed, enabled by simple or effortless interactions, attuned to senses, adaptive to users and contexts, and acting autonomously. High quality information and content may therefore be available to any user, anywhere, at any time, and on any device. Users are aware of their presence and context and digital environments are sensitive, adaptive, and responsive to needs, habits, gestures and emotions [10].

In virtual health care environments, they may not be separated from medical informatics, biomedical informatics or bio-informatics, aggregating electronic health records, decision support, telemedicine, knowledge representation and reasoning, knowledge discovery and computational biology. Radiological films, pathology slides and laboratory reports can be viewed in remote places. Remote robotics is used in surgery [11] and telemedicine is becoming popular. However applications are used for discrete clinical and medical activities in specific areas and services, in particular diagnostics and pathologies.

Each service has small database management systems where specific patient data are registered depending on pathologies or specific interests. This computational tissue generates development problems. However, these applications are used by people with good satisfaction despite they do not allow a transversal vision of the patient data along different services or specialties, they can not grow easily and sometimes they do not attend secure and confident procedures. Running applications in distributed environment is a huge problem when applications have not been developed to share knowledge and actions.

Ambient Intelligence is related with an exponential growth of Internet use on the last few years. New rapid web advancements are emerging, transferring technology benefits sometimes without a solid theoretic underpinning. Although web browsers support many features that facilitate the development of user-friendly applications and allow users to run application anywhere without installing flat software packages in order to run remote applications. Storage and information access over the web encourages the information and knowledge re-use and the offer of global information and resources. The vitality of a web-based system lies in its integration potential, in supporting communities of virtual entities and in the gathering, organization and diffusion of information. Operating on the web means the use of documents or programs that contain images, audios, videos and interactive tools in addition to text. Scripting languages are used to build high level programs improving distribution, as well as information and knowledge sharing, increasing quality software and reducing costs.

5   MODELLING THE SYSTEM

Situation awareness (SA) refers to a person's perception and understanding of their dynamic environment. This awareness and comprehension is critical in making correct decisions that ultimately lead to correct actions in medical care settings. An objective measure of SA may be more sensitive and diagnostic than traditional performance measures. In order to model the system, it is considered an extension to the logic programming language, where a logic program presents two kinds of negation, classical negation "¬" and negation-by-failure "not" [10]. Intuitively, "not a" is true whenever there is no reason to believe "a", whereas "¬a" requires a proof of the negated literal. An extended logic program (program, for short) P is a finite collection of rules r of the form:

c ← a₁, ..., aₙ, not b₁, ..., not bₘ

where the a_i, b_j, and c are classical ground literals, i.e. either positive atoms or atoms preceded by the classical negation sign ¬.

One may now obtain, considering the case's predicates *gender/2*, *age/2*, *isquemic-lesions/2*, *malign-tumor/2*, and *hemorrhagy/2* considering Filipa, the logical theory or program:

gender(female, filipa).
¬gender(X,Y)← not gender(X,Y),not exception$_{gender}$(X,Y).
exception$_{malign-tumor}$(malign-tumor,filipa).
¬ malign-tumor(X,Y) ←not malign-tumor(X,Y), not exception$_{malign-tumor}$(X,Y).
age(24, filipa).
¬ age (X,Y) ←not age(X,Y),not exception$_{age}$(X,Y).
exception$_{isquemic-lesions}$(yes, filipa).
exception$_{isquemic-lesions}$(no, filipa).
exception$_{isquemic-lesions}$(unknown, filipa).
hemorrhagy(yes, filipa).

It is now possible to define a process of quantification of the quality of information that emerges from the logical program or theory referred to above, in terms of a function L_p, and map its extension, when applied to predicates *gender/2*, *age/2*, *isquemic-lesions/2*, *malign-tumor/2*, *hemorrhage/2* and to *filipa*, into the hyperspace, whose dimension is given by the cardinality of the extensions of the predicates under consideration (Figure 5). The above program is now rewritten in terms of the function L_p (being p a predicate), in the form:

$L_{filipa}(gender) = 1$
$L_{filipa}(malign-tumor) = 1/N ≈ 0 \ (N ≫ 0)$
$L_{filipa}(age) = 1$
$L_{filipa}(isquemic-lesions) = 1/3 = 0,33$
$L_{filipa}(hemorrhagy) = 1$

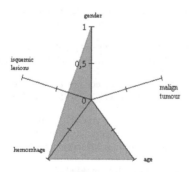

Figure 5: The quality of information about filipa's state of health

It is therefore possible, through the evaluation of a simple area, to measure or quantify the quality of the information that is carried out by the logic program referred to above, whose values are to be taken in the interval [0,1] [10]. Indeed, logic is broadly concerned with studying inference and expressive power of formal languages with well-defined semantics. As a representation, a plan guides the deliberation and action of a case. Plans are more than programs. It is explored a representation of plans as proofs in a logical theory of action, time and knowledge. This view does not only allow plans to be constructed by logical proof-search techniques, but allows plans to be transformed and reused respecting proof-theoretic principles. It was under this umbrella that AIDA was built [3][4][6][7].

6　CONCLUSIONS

Logic is broadly concerned with studying inference and the expressive power of formal languages with well-defined semantics. To implement the health care virtual scenarios, it was used an extension to the language of Logic Programming that incorporates a measure of the Situation Awareness through the function L_p, which operates on an extended repository containing all the information regarding patient health data and following up clinical profiles. They provide the tools for the physician front-end to any simulation training system. Analysis and interpretation of SA data for both individual and team performance in health care were presented.

ACKNOWLEDGEMENT

We are thankful to the Hospital Geral de Santo António, in Oporto, Portugal, for their help to the analysis and development of the EMR system referred to above, which is now being largely used in their premises.

7　REFERENCES

1. Picard, R. What does it mean for a computer to have emotions?; In Trappl, R.; Petta, P.; and Payr, S. (eds) Emotions in Human and Artefacts, 2003.
2. Weiss, G. (ed), Multi-Agent Systems: A Modern Approach to Distributed Artificial Intelligence, Cambridge, M.A., MIT Press, 1999.
3. Machado J., Abelha A., Santos M. and Neves J., Multi-agent Based Problem Solving in Medical Decision Support Systems, in Proc. of the 2nd International Conference on Knowledge Engineering and Decision Support, Lisbon, 2006.
4. Abelha, A., PhD Thesis, "Multi-agent systems as Working Cooperative Entities in Health Care Units" (In Portuguese), Universidade do Minho, Braga, Portugal, 2004.
5. Abelha A., Machado J., Alves V. e Neves J., Data Warehousing through Multi-Agent Systems in the Medical Arena, in Proceedings of the 1st International Conference on Knowledge Engineering and Decision Support, Porto, Portugal, 2004.
6. Machado J., Abelha A., Neves J. and Santos M., Ambient Intelligence in Medicine, in proc. of the IEEE Biomedical Circuits and Systems Conference, Healthcare Technology, Imperial College, London, UK, 2006.
7. Abelha A., Santos M., Machado J. and Neves J., Auditing Agents in the Context of a Telemedical Information Society, in Knowledge and Decision Technologies, Vale Z., Ramos C. and Faria L. (eds), Lisbon, Portugal (ISBN: 972-8688-39-3), 2006.
8. Machado J. and Alves V., Web-based Simulation in Medicine, in Proceedings of the European Simulation and Modelling Conference, MODELLING AND SIMULATION 2005, Feliz Teixeira JM, Brito AEC (eds), Porto, 2005.
9. Grudin, J., Group Dynamics and Ubiquitous computing, Comm. of the ACM, 45, 12, 2002.
10. Analide, C., Novais, P., Machado, J., and Neves, J. Quality of Knowledge in Virtual Entities, in Encyclopedia of Communities of Practice in Information and Knowledge Management, Idea Group Inc., 436-442, 2006.
11. Kaltenborn K. and Rienhoff O., "Virtual reality in medicine", Meth. Inform. Med., 32(5), 407-417, 1993.
12. Björklind, A., Holmlid, S., "Ambient intelligence to go", White paper on mobile intelligent ambience, 2003.

50

COLLABORATION WITHIN THE TOOL-AND-DIE MANUFACTURING INDUSTRY THROUGH OPEN-SOURCE MODULAR ERP/CRM SYSTEMS

Ali Imtiaz
Research Institute for Operations Management (FIR) at Aachen University of Technology, GERMANY
ali.imtiaz@fir.rwth-aachen.de

Jannicke Baalsrud Hauge
Bremen Institute of Industrial Engineering and Applied Work Science, GERMANY
baa@biba.uni-bremen.de

Si Chen
Open Source StrategiesINC
sichen@opensourcestrategies.com

There is a definite trend for European SMEs to form "collaborative networks" based on core competencies to have a competitive advantage in the dynamic global market. This leads to the need of utilising electronic communication for which arrangements for a basic level of technological competence and IT infrastructure have to be established. Currently, the IT infrastructure of many SMEs is based on inappropriate tools, which cannot supports standardised communication within the network. The Tool-East initiative described in this paper is attempting to reduce the technological infrastructure hurdle by providing an open-source ERP/CRM platform to SME participants in the Tool-and-Die making industry. This will be done in the hope that SMEs in this sector will standardise their business process annotation so that they will be able to exchange business documents with each other electronically.

1   INTRODUCTION

Manufacturing has always represented a strong foundation for the European economy, reaching currently at about 28% of the European Gross Domestic Product (GDP), and presents an undoubted source of wealth. A strong manufacturing industry is certainly necessary to create a stable European employment market. From a European perspective, the integration of the production clusters is a very important prerequisite to secure the success of these manufacturing clusters in the global market.

One prominent sector within the manufacturing industry is Tool-and-Die manufacturing. Almost all Tool-and-Die workshops in Eastern Europe are small or medium sized enterprises (SMEs). Low margins and a decreasing market share force most of these SMEs to optimise productivity and structure business processes more efficiently. Furthermore, increasing competition requires professional customer relationship management and better cooperation with other companies in this sector. SMEs need to become more responsive to rapid fluctuation in supply and demand, to assure availability of different materials at the right time and at the right place, and to reduce inventory risks. To achieve these goals, Tool-and-Die workshops must bridge the gap between their order acceptance, inventory, and production processes.

Imtaiz, A., Hauge, J.B., Chen, S., 2007, in IFIP International Federation for Information Processing, Volume 243, Establishing the Foundation of Collaborative Networks; eds. Camarinha-Matos, L., Afsarmanesh, H., Novais, P., Analide, C.; (Boston: Springer), pp. 469–476.

The success of collaboration is not only dependent on finding a partner with the right key competencies, but also about having appropriate ICT tools for seamless information processing and involving the right people to perform the daily collaboration work as well as on the ability of the participating organisations to act in a dynamical environment. Typical ICT tools needed for fast and seamless information processing within a networked environment are ERP and CRM tools. For intra-organisational collaboration, the newest SCM tools also provide some of the required functionalities. Until recently, such tools have been quite expensive to buy and their implementation required a high degree of IT competencies within the company. Even though large industrial enterprises play a dominating role in the European manufacturing industry, SMEs mostly acting as suppliers to larger ones still remain the backbone of the economy, especially in the Eastern European countries. However, if the SMEs intend to survive and to thrive, they need to stay competitive and to increase their productivity; therefore there is a need of a fast, reliable integrating support system at a feasible price fostering collaboration between SMEs. In order to keep the cost and the access on a low level, such a collaboration tool should be open-source based and only offer the needed functionalities. Therefore, the focus from uniform solution for all industries has to be shifted to Tool-and-Die making industry and their specific needs.

2   MAIN RESEARCH CHALLENGES AND APPROACH

Collaborations are complex to handle due to various reasons: different goals among collaborating partners and rapid process changes. In these dynamic and flexible networks, most partners have not collaborated before, which often results in the lack of trust. In addition, European collaboration networks also need to deal with the culture aspect. The above mentioned problems are relevant for almost all colla-borations.

These problems can be classified into three categories:

- Interoperability, management and organisational models
- Sharing culture and technology transfer
- Cheap and effective software solutions based on open-source standards

For Tool-and-Die making workshops, the problems are mainly related to their production management and resource planning, customer relationship management, and especially e-collaboration. Collaboration processes represent a key factor in the competitiveness of Tool-and-Die making clusters. By improving these processes, clusters will be able to strengthen their position as suppliers. Such an improvement can be achieved through the implementation of a collaboration platform utilising emerging, innovative technologies at the lowest possible cost.

The EU-funded Tool-East project aims at developing an integrated solution for the overall supply chain in the Tool-and-Die making industry. In order to integrate a solution in the overall supply chain, the solution will connect all SMEs' existing individual back-end systems. The solution will be augmented with (adaptive) service modules, allowing fast and flexible, standardised interfacing. Different modules will be integrated to develop a synchronised open-source ERP application in close relationship with each SME in the consortium.

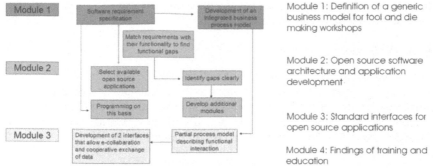

Module 1: Definition of a generic business model for tool and die making workshops

Module 2: Open source software architecture and application development

Module 3: Standard interfaces for open source applications

Module 4: Findings of training and education

Figure 1: Tool East Modules

Module I: Definition of a generic business process model for Tool-and-Die making workshops

Modelling the business process is an essential part of any information-based business networking development process. A survey was performed in the Tool-East project to model the business processes at the participating SMEs in order to develop software requirement specifications. The software requirement specification from the business model is formulated as the basis for software development, which specifies the required behaviour of a system.

The performed survey of suitable process models showed that the Aachner PPC [Luczak, 1999] model is the most suitable for analysing the end user business processes and to collect the user requirements. Based upon the individual business processes of the end-user's places, a semi-generic business process reference model was developed. The idea behind the model is the reduction of time needed for any new SME to analyse whether the Tool-East solution is suitable for them or not.

Module II: Open source software architecture and application development

The project will come up with an enriched open-source ERP/CRM system with additional functionalities. The first objective of the second module is to evaluate and select the best open-source solution available as the foundation for the intended specific development. The second objective is to develop additional modules to support processes described in the business process model. SMEs will be involved from a very early stage, where a first prototype will be available in order to receive a first feedback.

Module III: Standard interfaces for open-source applications

Competitive forces are driving technology efforts towards the information exchange within and across corporate boundaries via intelligent interfaces. Evolving new technologies provide an array of services to effectively design and develop integrated, collaborative solutions that connect different systems like ERP, CRM, or other internal systems between partners, vendors, and other service providers. For SMEs, not only the integration of large systems is problematic, but also the possibility to import existing data stored e.g. in Microsoft Excel files or other individually programmed databases, since this data must be entered manually. The technical possibilities and the latest developments will be examined and evaluated to provide additional functionality via interfaces.

Module IV: Training and education

The findings of the training and education module are critical to develop a methodology to carry out personnel training. The methodology should support the establishment of an appropriate training system between classroom, on-site, and e-learning modules. Furthermore, the educational trainings have to meet the different stakeholder groups' individual requirements and training needs.

3   RESULTS

3.1   Collaboration in SME Clusters

Since SMEs have formed clusters to collaborate more efficiently, the understanding of such clusters and collaboration processes within the clusters is important to the Tool-East project. The approach followed within the Tool-East project analyses the individual SME requirements to support cluster evolution towards collaborative business. The analysis revealed that the development of a collaborative cluster followed an evolutionary path. The evolutionary paths of SMEs in these clusters and the cluster itself have three fundamental stages, represented in Figure 2:

- *Empowerment* - Cluster SMEs are very cost conscious and limit overhead costs, like administration and IT, to a bare minimum. In a first step, SMEs need to be empowered by low cost applications to support their key business processes. As a result of empowerment, reliable business data are available for internal use and for external integration.

- *Integration* - At this stage, the SME is able to open internal business processes to their main supply chain partners, either customers or suppliers. The perspective is still enterprise-centric, i.e. from inside the SME out. This is made possible through the adoption of data interchange standards and tools to support transactional processes for supply chain integration.

- *Awareness* - In the final stage, SMEs are aware that their business processes belong in the bigger picture of the overall cluster. The cluster behaves externally like a single enterprise, as SMEs are able to cooperate in knowledge-intensive and strategic processes like, e.g., sourcing, product development, marketing, and customer relationship management.

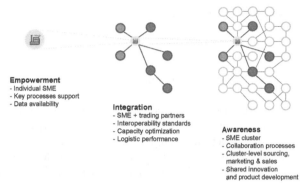

Empowerment
- Individual SME
- Key processes support
- Data availability

Integration
- SME + trading partners
- Interoperability standards
- Capacity optimization
- Logistic performance

Awareness
- SME cluster
- Collaboration processes
- Cluster-level sourcing,
  marketing & sales
- Shared innovation
  and product development

Figure 2: Stages in SME Cluster Evolution

By introducing the Tool-East concept, standardised processes will be introduced, which lead to better data exchange between business partners in electronic format. For the Tool-and-Die making clusters, the standardisation implies that they can take advantage of other e-business tools to support their particular business processes.

3.2 Open Source Platform for Collaborative Software Development

The term "open source" technically refers to software whose source code is made available under a license that permits its use, modification, and redistribution [OSI Definition]. In practice, such a licensing model has created the environment where software is developed collaboratively by a group of users and developers. Open-source software development projects share their source code through a source code repository management system such as Concurrent Versioning System (CVS) or Subversion (SVN), and the users and developers coordinate their efforts via an electronic mailing list, forum, or issue tracker.

Open source creates a collaborative environment in two significant ways. First, open-source development projects are themselves developed in a collaborative manner, with many users and developers contributing. Second, an open-source project can be extended to fit new requirements outside of its original goals. Thus, an open-source project can be thought of as a lump sum contribution by its original developers to a new software package.

In its ideal form, the collaboration between the original open-source project and the new package based upon or "derived" from it can be highly beneficial to both groups. The developers of the derived package can benefit from all the features offered by the original project plus continuous maintenance and enhancements for those core features over time. The original package could benefit from regular enhancements contributed back to it by the developers of the derived package. For this symbiotic relationship to occur, the following conditions must be met:

1. There must be compatible, mutually beneficial, but separate areas of focus and competency between the developers of the two packages.
2. The code of the derived package must be well separated from the original open source project, permitting regular updates.
3. The original project must provide stable releases for use by the developers of derived packages and regular updates for those developers to benefit from future enhancements.

The developers of both packages must be committed to the symbiotic relationship.

3.3   'Opentaps' ERP System as a Collaborative Platform

The Tool-East project is geared towards the extension of restrictive and limited ERP systems to incorporate standardised collaboration processes between SMEs. A Uniform application platform will include features focusing on interoperability and communication required for collaboration. The extension focuses on two points: 1) the development of a strict intercommunication standard for different companies with different ERP systems to communicate, and 2) the flexibility through open-source application allowing the users to further extend the features without altering the company's base application. To extend the features of an ERP system, a modular approach must be taken. Modular ERP systems have open system architectures, which means any module can be interfaced or detached whenever required without affecting the other modules. Furthermore, such modular systems support third party add-ons and multiple hardware platforms for the companies having a heterogeneous collection of systems and support.

As a preferred solution, Opentaps (www.opentaps.org) was selected to be customised according to the requirements of Tool-and-Die makers. Opentaps is an open-source ERP and CRM application suite based upon the Apache OFBIZ framework and is a Java-based application. The software leverages the technically robust Apache OFBIZ framework, which in turn incorporates such well-known open-source projects as Tomcat, Lucene, Derby, and Xerces, to build a complete ERP and CRM application. Like many open-source projects, Opentaps is developed within an open-source community, with the project manager Open Source Strategies, Inc. serving as the hub of the network.

By incorporating Opentaps into an industry-specific ERP/CRM, such as one for European Tool-and-Die making SMEs, the developers of the industry-specific package gain the benefits of collaborating with the users and developers of the Opentaps open-source community. Opentaps offers a technical infrastructure that addresses requirements common to all business applications and a core feature set that is based on international standards. Furthermore, an ongoing process of collaboration with Opentaps should bring continued maintenance and enhancements of both the infrastructure and the applications.

In practice, Opentaps has a modular components-based software architecture that facilitates collaborative development. Opentaps is divided into many smaller applications, each with its own data model, business logic, workflows, and user interface. Because each application component is kept completely separated, Opentaps allows add-on features to be implemented in a separate component with minimal overlap. New tables, business logic, screens, and security permissions can be created separately, and existing workflows can be altered with minimal change to the core code base. A developer of an industry-specific ERP/CRM system using Opentaps could take an existing release and add a new module according to the industry-specific requirements. Such an approach creates a de facto long-term collaboration between the developers of the industry-specific ERP/CRM system and the Opentaps open-source community.

4 EXPECTED BENEFITS FOR TOOL-AND-DIE MAKING CLUSTERS

The results of the Tool-East project are expected to generate benefits for SMEs in the Tool-and-Die making industry by improving the cooperation in industrial clusters through an information platform. Serving as a collaborative platform, the developed ERP/CRM system will integrate the information flows between SMEs within an industrial cluster. This will allow the industrial cluster to reach the awareness stage in the SME cluster evolution. The ability for the cluster to behave externally like a single enterprise will generate a competitive advantage for the involved SMEs over independent SMEs. The expected competitive advantage should be observable through:

1. *Quicker response* to market demands due to a shortened time-to-market through improved communication and collaboration

2. *Improved product quality* through automatic information sharing e.g. CAD drawings and utilisation of the core competence of the individual SMEs

3. *Cost reduction* through optimised collaborative business processes and competence sharing.

5 CONCLUSIONS AND SUMMARY

SMEs in Europe have to develop innovative business strategies, for example, the participation in business networks and clusters, to secure long-term success. ERP/CRM applications and their integration with existing applications are necessary to ensure successful electronic collaboration in the business network. Applications must be extended with modules specifically created for the particular processes carried out in the cluster to enable the e-collaboration of SMEs in industrial clusters. Cost-efficient ERP applications based on existing open-source ERP applications represent a promising approach to foster collaboration in industrial clusters of SMEs. The temporal cluster Tool-East project with Tool-and-Die makers, IT companies and research institutes is exploring, selecting and adapting an open-source ERP application for exactly this purpose. The new adapted and modified ERP application will support the efficient coordination of intra-enterprise order processing and strengthens the competitiveness of Eastern European SMEs.

An enormous potential can be generated for SMEs through the development of an ERP application based on the open-source initiative. The expected benefits include cost advantages through an optimisation of collaboration, fast response to challenges, and a gradual reorganisation and simplification of complex information systems in the network. The benefits from a customised ERP/CRM solution thus improves three major factors for competition: 1) reduction of the time-to-market through improved communication, 2) higher quality through automatic information sharing e.g. CAD drawings, and 3) reduction of costs through optimised business processes.

The systematic and analytic approach used by the Tool-East project is not limited to the Tool-and-Die making industry. Through the generalisation of the approach, the impact can be replicated to different sectors for SMEs. The only prerequisite for applying the Tool-East approach for other sectors is the business process model. Based on the model, the selection and customisation of an ERP application for SMEs is possible. Such an approach is expected to bring similar advantages for SMEs in other industrial sectors.

For the long term success of European SMEs (like the Tool-and-Die making industry) it is essential to focus on knowledge intensive, innovative business strategies to produce goods and services that can compete on dynamic and global markets. Our research highlights the value of a strategy using IT technologies to increase participation in dynamic business networks as a way to achieve this.

6   ACKNOWLEDGEMENTS

This work has been partly funded by the European Commission through IST Project Tool-East: Open Source Enterprise Resource Planning and Order Management System for Eastern European Tool-and-Die Making Workshops (No. IST-FP6-027802). The authors wish to acknowledge the Commission for their support. We also wish to acknowledge our gratitude and appreciation to all the Tool-East project partners for their contribution during the development of various ideas and concepts presented in this paper.

7   REFERENCES

1. [OSI Definition]: The Open Source Initiative: http://www.opensource.org/docs/definition.php
2. [Sherman, 1996]: Sherman, Heidemarie(1996): "Globalisierung: Transnationale Unternehmen auf dem Vormarsch", ifo Schnelldienst, Nr. 23, 1996
3. [Meyer, 2004]: Meyer, M et al(2004): Plug and do Business- ERP of the next generation for efficient order processing in dynamic business networks in: International Journal of Internet and Enterprise Management, p.153 Vol.2, 2004
4. [Luczak, 1999]Holger Luczak, Walter Eversheim: Produktionsplanung und -steuerung: Grundlagen, Gestaltung und Konzepte. 2. Auflage.: Springer-Verlag (1999), ISBN 3-540-65559-X
5. [Oliveira, 2000]: Oliveira et al. (2000) 'SMARTISAN-moving e-commerce to extended product', Helsinki Conference Proceedings.
6. [Scheer, 2002]: Scheer, A.-W., Grieble, O., Hans, S., Zang, S.(2002): Geschäftsprozessmanagement – The 2nd wave. In: Information Management & Consulting, 17, 2002 Sonderausgabe, pp. 9-14.
7. [Sherman, 1996]: Sherman, Heidemarie(1996): "Globalisierung: Transnationale Unternehmen auf dem Vormarsch", ifo Schnelldienst, Nr. 23, 1996
8. [SCC2006)Supply Chain Council: SCOR 7.0 overview booklet. More Information will be found on http://www.supply-chain.org/page.ww?section=SCOR+Model&name=SCOR+Model

PART 16

COLLABORATIVE PROCESS MODELS

51

A CARTOGRAPHY BASED METHODOLOGY FOR COLLABORATIVE PROCESS DEFINITION

Vatcharaphun Rajsiri, Jean-Pierre Lorré
EBM WebSourcing, FRANCE, netty.rajsiri, jean-pierre.lorre@ebmwebsourcing.com
Fréderick Bénaben, Hervé Pingaud
Ecole des Mines d'Albi-Carmaux, Centre de Génie Industriel, FRANCE,
benaben, pingaud@enstimac.fr

This paper presents a methodology dedicated to the specification of collaborative processes. The successful implementation of methodology requires information about partners and collaboration that takes place in network as well as a reference framework. Information is used to characterize collaborative behavior of partners while cartography contributes to describing the field of collaborative processes. To obtain this information, we apply two approaches: 1) direct gathering information from partners by analyzing their requirements in order to understand their expectation on collaboration and 2) extracting observable information from our "6naps" collaborative platform in order to understand how partners have been collaborating. Cartography will then use this information to propose a specific BPMN collaborative process dedicated to the collaborative context.

1   INTRODUCTION

Today companies open up more and more to their partners because of the global market evolution. The capacity of companies to collaborate efficiently with others becomes an important factor for their evolution and their ability to survive.

The basic problem of each partner in a collaborative network is to be able to establish connections with others (Touzi et al., 2007). Interoperability is mandatory to deal with these issues. The interoperability, according to (Konstantas et al., 2005), should not demand any special effort from users. It can be positioned as a way toward the integration concept (Vernadat, 2006) of information systems (IS) of different partners.

EBM WebSourcing business focuses on providing collaborative software dedicated to SMEs clusters. Thus, our goal is not only to develop the collaborative information system (CIS) to deal with the interoperability issues, but also to provide tools and method to facilitate the collaboration design.

A CIS as described by (Touzi et al., 2006), can be seen as a mediator of a collaborative network. Partners can continue using their own IS. The CIS provides its own services for managing the collaborative process, dealing with the partners' applications and transferring the collaboration data.

Since collaborative networks are complex systems, their design requires models' development as a help to better understand the area and as a basis for the development

Rajsiri, V., Lorré, J.-P., Bénaben, F., Pingaud, H., 2007, in IFIP International Federation for Information Processing, Volume 243, Establishing the Foundation of Collaborative Networks; eds. Camarinha-Matos, L., Afsarmanesh, H., Novais, P., Analide, C.; (Boston: Springer), pp. 479–486.

of tools for better decision-making (Chamarinha-Matos et al., 2006, Ivanov et al., 2006). Therefore, we defined a methodology as shown in Figure 1.

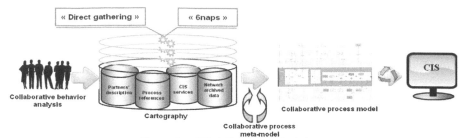

Figure 1 – CIS definition methodology

Our CIS definition methodology is composed of two parts developed separately but dedicated to the same final goal. The first part handles collaborative process model through the cartography. The second part addresses the transformation of collaborative process model using the translator to define a related CIS (Touzi et al., 2006). The collaborative process definition (BPMN based) becomes the link between them. The successful CIS definition requires the full implementation of the methodology.

The objective of this paper is to present the first part of the CIS definition methodology. We will introduce the concept of cartography which is a reference framework for developing two modeling approaches (direct gathering and "6naps"). These two approaches are based on the cartography and will be used as a decision-making tool for building collaborative process models.

2   CARTOGRAPHY: AS A REFERENCE FRAMEWORK

The objective of this section is to discuss about "cartography" which is the core concept of our collaborative framework. In this framework, we will define the references which are used for building collaborative processes.

From the definition of (Dudycha, 2003), cartography includes not only the use of maps as research tools and as sources of information, but also the study of maps as historical documents. This definition fits our vision of cartography which we would like to make as a reference framework. Our cartography tool takes the information about partners and their collaboration perspectives as input and provides collaborative processes (BPMN based) as output. The obtained BPMN should be compliant with the requirements of the partners and the CIS translator. Thus, we have to:

- Understand the collaborative behaviors of all involved partners and use the characterization criteria which have been classified and discussed in (Rajsiri et al., 2007) to analyze the behaviors.
- Integrate the *four modeling elements* in collaborative processes. These elements are actors (partners), exchanged data, collaborative services (provided by partners and CIS) and service orchestration (process).

These bring us to define our reference framework composed of: (1) Collaborative Network Building-up Platform (CNBP) and (2) Knowledge Base (KB), both being designed to support each other as shown below:

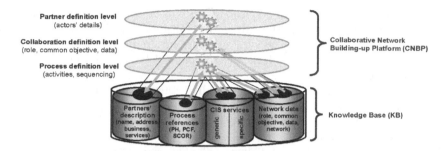

Figure 2 – Cartography with CNBP and KB

2.1 Collaborative Network Building-up Platform (CNBP)

The CNBP is a modeling space used for defining collaborative networks at three levels: partner, collaboration and process. It can perform two operations: supplying and seeking. The arrows in Figure 2 indicate the two directions of information pointing to the KB and CNBP for supplying and seeking respectively.

The *"Supplying operation"* is in charge of providing collaborative behaviors to the related KB. For example, at the Partner definition level where actors of network are identified, it supplies all actors' details for the Partners' description database (KB) while at the Collaboration definition level, we determine common objective of partners, the description of data transmissions as well as their semantic description to be contained in the Network database (KB).

The *"Seeking operation"* is in charge of searching for the desirable information, which concerns four modeling elements, from the KB. This operation focuses on completing collaborative network modeling. For instance, the Process definition level is where we define for example process elements (e.g. activities) by consulting the Process references and the CIS service databases (KB).

2.2 Knowledge Base (KB)

The Knowledge Base is composed of four databases relating to the four modeling elements described previously. It contains different kinds of information which can be filled in the KB and used by the CNBP as described above.

The Partners' description database is where the general descriptions of partners who perform a collaborative network are archived. The descriptions, consisting of company name, size, address, primary business and partners' offering services, will be contained in this database for the whole life cycle of collaborative network. The services contain also their descriptions concerning port, data type, message, etc.

The Process references database contains some generic references, such as the references provided by the Process Handbook[i] (PH), PCF (Process Classification Framework), SCOR (Supply-Chain Operations Reference-Model). These references are classified in business sectors.

The CIS services database is composed of two sub-databases: (1) the *CIS generic service database* which is immediately available and contains the standard services defined by EBM WebSourcing such as send/receive mails, and manage documents (2) the *CIS specific service database* which is an addable database. The last one contains description of services which will be determined upon the needs focusing on completing and supporting the collaboration between partners, for example a "payment validation service" in a customer/supplier process. Once a new CIS specific service is specified, its description will be archived in this base for using afterwards.

The Network database is where all collaboration details including semantic description (ontology concept) of collaboration data, common objectives and role of partners are archived. This database is significant because it offers backtracking possibilities afterwards.

We implement two approaches ("direct gathering" and "6naps") in our cartography tool in order to provide assistance to a consultant of EBM WebSourcing using the collaborative process simulator. We will detail, in the next section, these two approaches which are developed with different modeling methodologies, but both taking into account collaborative behaviors of involved partners.

3   MODELING APPROACHES USING CARTOGRAPHY

This section aims to present two approaches which have been developed on the basis of the CNBP for using as a tool for better decision-making while building collaborative networks. The KB will be introduced according to the CNBP operations (supplying or seeking) as discussed in Section 2. Thus, we focus here on applying these two approaches for analyzing collaborative behaviors by using the reference framework to model a collaborative process related to the partners.

The first approach relies on partners' requirements analysis to understand their expectation on collaboration, while the second one uses tracking information from the running "6naps collaborative platform" to extract automatically knowledge about on-going collaboration behavior.

Before going into detail about these two approaches, we would like to talk briefly about GMF[ii] (Graphical Modeling Framework) technology. GMF is a graphic editor framework built on Eclipse. We develop a simulator with this tool to support our modeling methodology that allows to define and visualize collaborative networks. It is based on the collaborative network meta-model which contains the four modeling elements discussed in the beginning of page 3.

3.1   Direct Gathering from Partners

This approach focuses on how to describe a collaborative network in response to a common business objective. Figure 3 shows the five steps of the collaborative modeling methodology by gathering the information, at the beginning, about partners themselves and their collaboration requirements. We can find also in the figure the application of tools, the KB and the operations of the CNBP (see legends in the figure). We will introduce in each step the description of what we do and corresponding definition levels of the CNBP and database of the KB.

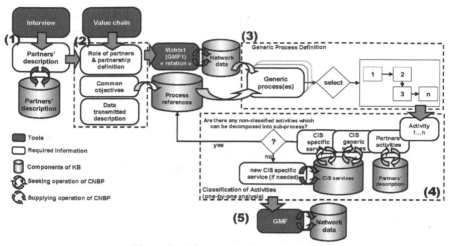

Figure 3 – Direct gathering methodology

Step1 – general description gathering
To collect the details about company name, primary business, address and size, the partners will be interviewed individually. This step addresses the Partner definition level (CNBP). These details will be stored in the Partners' description database (KB).

Step2 – role positioning and common objective defining
The Collaboration definition level (CNBP) starts at this step. We get all partners together in order to gather the information concerning role, relationship as well as common objective. The role and competency of each partner will be identified by means of the value chain of (Porter, 1986). A relationship performed between partners will be also determined pair by pair. Then, a common objective, as same as the transmitted data, will be jointly specified by all involved partners. All of the information will be graphically represented by a GMF based Matrix tool and stored in the Network database (KB).

Step3 – a generic process specifying
We are now at the Process definition level (CNBP). Generic processes will be deduced from the Process references database (KB) by using the common objective defined in Step2. Then, a generic process that fits the most to the common objective will be selected and used for analyzing in the next step.

Step4 – activity analyzing
We are still at the Process definition level (CNBP). From the generic process, the activities will be analyzed one by one. This analysis allows us to classify the activities according to the role of partners and CIS (who is capable to perform them?). The roles have been already defined in Step2 and stored in the Network database. If there are any non-classified activities, we have to redo Step3 but the objective will be changed to how to perform those activities.

For example, if in a buying process we cannot classify a "select supplier activity" to anyone, the new objective "how to select supplier?" is set. Then, we seek from the Process reference database (KB) for a supplier selection activity in order to decompose it into sub-activities. Then, redo Step 3 and loop if needed.

However, if we cannot decompose non-classified activities into sub-activities, we have to create CIS specific services for performing these activities. After the classification has been done, the partners' activities (or services) will be stored in the Partner description database (KB) while the CIS generic and specific services will be stored in the CIS service database (KB).

Step5 – collaborative network representing

The graphical tool will be used again for describing the network that represents all partners' and CIS services as well as data transmitted between services. When all partners have been agreed to an offered network solution, it will be archived in the Network database (KB). However, more than one solution is possible.

Figure 4 presents an example of a group buying network. The common objective of this network is to group similar orders of customers to buy from a selected supplier. We used this common objective to define a generic buying/selling process including all required activities from the Process reference database (KB). After having performed the iterative classification of activities, we obtain the network as follows:

Figure 4 – Network of a group buying (printed screen of the GMF tool)

3.2   "6naps" Collaborative Platform

6naps is a collaborative platform developed by EBM WebSourcing based on the social business network paradigm. It aims to provide a trustable space for members to establish (or not) commercial relations among them.

To be able to access the platform, companies have to subscribe. The companies will be requested to provide during subscription some general descriptions of themselves, their business sector, services offering, etc. These details will be stored in a repository of the platform and are accessible by the members. After subscribing, companies can invite others to join their network, perform the partnerships, visualize their networks, use the services offered by the platform such as shared space, etc.

When collaboration occurs between two or more partners, the platform will record some data (e.g. size of payloads, number of occurrences of transmission) at runtime. Partners can request some services provided by the platform in order to execute their operations, such as send/receive documents, search partners and send/receive mails.

We use this platform in order to extract collaboration information that occurs in reality (see Figure 5) at two stages: subscription and collaboration stages. Some details of extracting and terms of reference (the three definition levels of the CNBP and the four databases of the KB) of the cartography will be introduced in each stage.

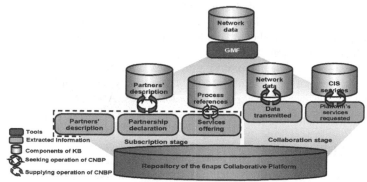

Figure 5 – "6naps" extraction methodology

At the subscription stage, we can extract and store all of the information about partners themselves, their relationships with other members and offering services in the Partners' description database (KB). Semantic relation between offering services and the Process reference database (KB) should be verified before being stored in the Partners' description base. This stage concerns the Partner and Process definition levels (CNBP).

At the collaboration stage, we can extract information from the runtime recording, of collaboration data which occurs between partners and platform's services. These platform's services can be considered as CIS generic services. All transmissions will be stored in the Network database (KB). This stage concerns the Collaboration definition level (CNBP).

After having extracted the information at these two stages, the GMF tool is used to structure that information for showing all transactions taken place between partners in a form of collaborative network. This phase is at the Process definition level (CNBP). The collaborative network that we obtain here describes the real collaboration between partners and will be archived in the Network database (KB).

As shown in the Figure 6, two companies (A and B) perform customer/supplier partnership and start transmitting mails in order to follow up the orders. The "6nap" platform offers send/receive mails service for operating these transmissions. An example of extracted information while transmitting mails is presented as follows:

Figure 6 – Network of mail transmissions (printed screen of the GMF tool)

4   CONCLUSION AND ON-GOING RESEARCH

The output from the two approaches presented in the previous section is a collaborative network described by using the GMF tool. Obtained collaborative networks have to be transformed into collaborative process models (BPMN based). As such a collaborative process model is an input of the CIS translator. Thus, a *meta-model of collaborative process* is needed to be applied for accomplishing this transformation (see Figure 1). The application of the collaborative process meta-model (Touzi et al., 2007) can guarantee that the collaborative process models obtained at the end will be compliant with the translator.

The meta-model of collaborative processes is in progress. Our current work is focused on developing a prototype of cartography and implementing the two modeling approaches to several collaboration cases. After that, we will handle the transformation of collaborative networks into BPMN collaborative processes.

5   REFERENCES

1.   Dudycha DJ. Introduction to Cartography and Remote Sensing: Definition and Scope of Cartography, University of Waterloo, 2003.
2.   Camarinha-Matos LM, Afsarmanesh H. A modeling framework for collaborative networked organizations, PRO-VE'06-7th IFIP Working Conference on Virtual Enterprises, 2006.
3.   Ivanov D, Kaeschel J, Sokolov B, Arkhipov A. A conceptual framework for modeling complex adaptation of collaborative networks, PRO-VE'06-7th IFIP Working Conference on Virtual Enterprises, 2006.
4.   Konstantas D, Bourrières JP, Léonard M, Boudjlida N. Interoperability of enterprise software and applications, INTEROP-ESA'05, Geneva Switzerland, Springer-Verlag, 2005.
5.   Porter M. L'avantage concurrentiel, InterEdition, Paris, 1986, page 52.
6.   Rajsiri V, Lorré JP, Bénaben F, Pingaud H. Cartography for designing collaborative processes, accepted paper for INTEROP-ESA'07, Funchal Portugal, March 2007.
7.   Touzi J, Lorré JP, Bénaben F, Pingaud H. Interoperability through model based generation: the case of the Collaborative IS, INTEROP-ESA'06, Bordeaux France, 2006.
8.   Touzi J, Bénaben F, Lorré JP, Pingaud H. A Service Oriented Architecture approach for collaborative information system design », accepted paper for IESM'07, Beijing China, May-June 2007.
9.   Vernadat FB. Interoperable enterprise systems: architectures and methods, INCOM'06 Conference, St-Etienne, France, 2006.

[i] Process Handbook online: http://ccs.mit.edu/ph/

[ii] www.eclipse.org/gmf

52

INTERACTIVE USER-CENTERED BUSINESS PROCESS MANAGEMENTSERVICES

Roberto Ratti
TXT e-solutions Spa, roberto.ratti@txt.it
Sergio Gusmeroli
TXT e-solutions Spa, sergio.gusmeroli@txt.it

For supporting process interconnection, on top of an existing open-source Business Process Management (BPM) environment oriented to Web Services (modeling module and execution engine, BPEL - Business Process Execution Language - compatible), this paper will propose a support to task-oriented, interactive decisional activities to be performed by CNO (Collaborative Networked Organizations) Actors. At the current status of achievements no standards neither existing solutions are able to provide such feature. These services aim at providing an innovative modeling and execution environments able to manage complex and compound services made of automatic and manual activities.

1   INTRODUCTION

Collaborative Networked Organizations (CNOs) has been considered the discipline in charge of studying all the manifestations of organizations when they work in an inter-linked and organized way (Camarinha, 2004). In order to leverage the potential benefits of collaborative networks, more flexible and generic infrastructures need to be designed and implemented enabling networked organizations to agilely define and set-up relations with other organizations as well as to be adaptive according to the business environment conditions and current organizations' autonomy levels. This is the essential motivation for the development of the ICT-I inside the ECOLEAD project (Rabelo et al, 2006). The goal of this paper is to propose a new way for improving the existing solutions of business processes management by including the human centered aspects inside CNOs.

The current state of the art does not provide any tools or standard language able to manage the two separate domains: human and automatic. Currently, what exists is a support for human based activities, supported by the concept of workflows, and the automatic execution activities, namely business processes. Two different languages are broadly adopted and recognized as standards: XML Process Definition Language - xPDL (Wfmc, 2005), for workflows definition and management, and BPEL (BPEL4WS, 2003), for business process execution and orchestration. What is missing is a combination of the two languages, in order to allow the next generation processes, which involves both human and automatic activities. The aim of this paper is to report the research performed and the preliminary results achieved for introducing an innovative way for modeling and executing complex services made by either automatic or manual activities.

Ratti, R., Gusmeroli, S., 2007, in IFIP International Federation for Information Processing, Volume 243, Establishing the Foundation of Collaborative Networks; eds. Camarinha-Matos, L., Afsarmanesh, H., Novais, P., Analide, C.; (Boston: Springer), pp. 487–494.

2   RESEARCH STATEMENTS AND INNOVATION

This section introduces the research performed in this paper, analyzing the current state of the art in the two main domains, workflows and business processes.

2.1   Research

The ongoing work on the Web Services Business Process Execution Language, version 2.0 (WS-BPEL 2.0, or BPEL for short) focuses on two parts.

The former is the model for executable business processes used to specify automated business processes that orchestrate activities of multiple Web services, and which may be interpreted and executed by compliant engines. The latter is the observable behavior of Web services. The language encompasses features needed to describe complex process control flows, including error handling and compensation behavior. Those constructs are seen and used in multiple process models and are needed to build complex processes, which can be executed by underlying software. However, business processes go beyond the orchestration of activities exposed as Web services. In addition to the orchestration of Web services, the process definition typically incorporates people as an additional possible type of participant, since they can also take part in business processes and can influence the execution of processes. The aspect of how people interact with business processes must be properly modeled.

The BPEL specification focuses on business processes, the activities of which are assumed to be interactions with Web services with no additional prerequisite behavior. But the spectrum of activities that make up general purpose business processes is much broader. People often participate in the execution of business processes introducing new aspects, such as human interaction patterns. Workflow tools already cater for the orchestration of user interactions. User interactions range from simple scenarios, such as manual approval, to complex scenarios where data is entered by the user. Imagine a bank's personal loan process. This process is made available on the internet site of the bank using a web interface. Customers can use this interface to enter the data for their loan approval request and to start the approval process. The process performs some checks, and eventually informs the customer whether his or her personal loan request has been approved or rejected.

Processing is often automatic and does not require any human involvement. However, there are cases that require bank staff to be involved. An example of such a case is if the online check of a customer's creditworthiness returns an ambiguous result. In this case, instead of declining the request automatically, a bank clerk could check the request and determine whether to approve or decline it. Another example would be if a request exceeds the amount of money that can be approved automatically. In this case, a manual approval step is required, in which a member of the "approvers" group either approves or declines the request. User interactions in business processes are not limited to approval steps. They also may involve data. An example of a user interaction that involves data is when an e-mail from an employer is manually attached to the process instance, or when the summary of an interview with an applicant is keyed into the process via a simple form or custom-built application.

On the other hand workflow processes are able to manage just human activities.

The xPDL standard (Wfmc, XPDL) has reached the version 2.0 of the specification, which combines the version 1.0 and BPMN (Business Process Modelling Notation). The XPDL and the BPMN specifications address the same modelling problem from different perspectives.

- XPDL provides an XML (eXtensible Markup Language) file format that can be used to interchange process models between tools.
- BPMN provides a graphical notation to facilitate human communication between business users and technical users, of complex business processes
- It is used for Business Process Modelling activities, where:
- An activity represents work, which will be performed by a combination of resource (specified by participant assignment) and/or computer applications (specified by application assignment). Other optional information may be associated with the activity such as information on whether it is to be started/finished automatically by the process or workflow management system or its priority relative to other activities where contention for resource or system services occurs.
- It also includes (optional) graphical information.

To support a broad range of scenarios that involve people within business processes, a BPEL extension is required.

Currently only a whitepaper had provided some specifications for the merging of the two above approaches. The suggested language, called BPEL4People (IBM-SAP, 2005), introduced a general idea for supporting the identified problems, but the definition process seems now in a suspended state, because no implementation versions have been released at this paper writing time.

2.2 Innovation

The proposed work aims at providing features for managing existing different paradigms.

This issue is recognized as main innovation point of this paper. The result is the definition of a new language specification able to support process interconnection with interactive decisional activities (Ratti, 2007). This means the ability in managing Workflow-oriented decisional tasks with the orchestration of WS (i.e. xPDL with BPEL). The proposed language CBP (Collaborative Business Process) is the extension of the current xPDL and BPEL standards, while waiting for the BPEL4PEOPLE specifications implementation.

The "Figure 1" shows this concept.

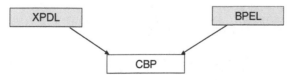

Figure 1 – New paradigm

The analysis performed has highlighted the need of maintaining anyway the semantic of the two languages. This means that the new proposed language shall manage both paradigms without changing radically the structure. For this reason, one language has been chosen as basic (and reference) language, complemented with the tags of the other. So it has been decided to use xPDL as basic language, improved by BPEL constructs which are needed for managing the new approach.

During the integration phase (of the languages) some semantic elements are still the same in the new schema: for instance, transactions, process and basic xPDL activities with BPEL ones. The inherited tags are not changed through the porting process from one language to the other. In the following "Figure 2" the fusion between the two languages is shown.

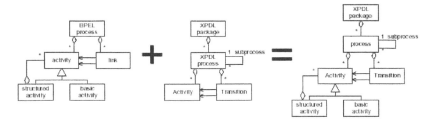

Figure 2 – CBP

As the "Figure 2" shows, the new language contains both the constructs. This is an important issue because the way to access the information tags inside each language will not be changed. In this way the information provided by each standard is still accessible by any parser or by any XQuery (XQuery, 2007) statement, and the existing solutions which currently use xPDL and BPEL remain valid and working.

An example of the resulting schema will contain the above paradigms: it is shown in the following "Figure 3".

```
..
<wSDLs>
    <WSDL Id="newpkg_wp1_1" wSDLpath="wsd1.wsdl"/>
    <WSDL Id="newpkg_wp1_2" wSDLpath="wsdl2.wsdl"/>
</WSDLs>
<partnerLinks>
    <partnerLink myRole="loanService" name="customer"
                 partnerLinkType="loanPartnerLinkType"/>
    <partnerLink name="assessor"
                 partnerLinkType="riskAssessmentLinkType"
                 partnerRole="assessor"/>
</partnerLinks>
..
<Activities Bpel="true">
    <flow>
..
    <Activity Bpel="true" Bpeltype="invoke" Id="newpkg_wp1_act1">
        <invoke inputVariable="request" name="InvokeLoanAssessor"
                operation="check"
outputVariable="riskAssessmentMessage"
partnerLink="assessor" portType="riskAssessmentPT">
        <source linkName="newpkg_wp1_tra1"/>
        </invoke>
    </Activity>
    <Activity Bpel="true" Bpeltype="receive" Id="newpkg_wp1_act2">
        <receive name="ReceiveCustomerRequestforLoanAmt"
                 operation="request" partnerLink="customer"
                 portType="loanServicePT" variable="request">
        <target linkName="newpkg_wp1_tra1"/>
        </receive>
    </Activity>
```

Figure 3 – CBP example

3   THE PROPOSED SOLUTION

This section introduces the identified requirements, functional specifications and developments made for the user centered Business Process management services (iBPM) (Ratti et al., 2007).

3.1   Specifications

From a conceptual point of view, these services consist of two main services: a modeler and an engine. It has to be reminded that some preliminary activities should be performed, for instance the offline creation of the BPEL processes. After this preliminary step a CNO user can start modeling its own iBPM process, by running the editor. Such editor shall provide features for modelling xPDL processes, but it should be also extended in order to include (by means of importing) BPEL processes. The editor shall be able to manage the mapping between the input and output data which goes to / comes from a BPEL process. This is a crucial topic to be considered in the editor, because in this way the complete management of the new generated process will be granted.

Such editor shall provide typical features available for such kind of tools, namely a set of functionalities for managing the storage, retrieval, import and export of processes. The most important feature is the export (and import) into the new format CBP.

In the following, a set of minimal requested functionalities is summarised:

- Import the BPEL process.
- Model manual activities.
- Model the CBP process.
- Save and export the generated CBP file to the engine.
- Once an iBPM process is saved and exported into the new format, it can be invoked by an engine for its execution. The engine should therefore provide at least the following features:
- Load the CBP: it will load the CBP file inside the engine, ready for being executed and managed by the applications which it will interact with.
- Instantiate the CBP process: once the CBP file has been uploaded inside the engine, it shall be instantiated; this means that the process can be invoked by the external applications, in terms of its execution governing.
- Start, pause and stop the process execution: a typical usage of an instantiated process is to start the process and then execute its activities. This means that each activity (either manual or automatic) can be started, paused or finalised through an invocation of the related features.

3.2   Architecture

Two kinds of services should be provided: an editor and an engine. As stated in the previous sections the iBPM services need an environment for modeling the new CBP files and one for executing such processes.

Considering also that a lot of solutions already exists for managing xPDL and BPEL languages, it is not requested to develop from scratch either editor or engine, but it is just needed to extend existing solutions for supporting the here-defined new functionalities. For this reason the iBPM architecture will depend on the extended tools. The proposed solutions are based on two existing software, Jawe and Shark (Together, 2006), two open source editor and engine.

All the original features will still be available: the new architecture will just include the ad-hoc features for supporting and managing CBP file.

3.3   Design

This section reports the use cases which these services should support. The following "Figure 4" shows the main use case, which represents the typical usage of such services.

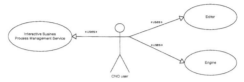

Figure 4 – Main use case

A CNO user will use mainly the features provided by both editor and engine. In the next "Figure 5" the editor use case is shown.

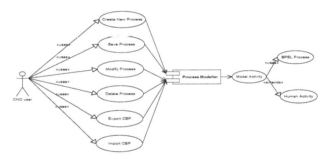

Figure 5 – Editor use case

A CNO user can create new process, save/modify/delete them, and can import/ export the generated process into/from CBP language. During the modeling phase the user can model human activities as well as can import BPEL processes: this is required for supporting the automatic execution. In the next "Figure 6" the engine use case is reported.

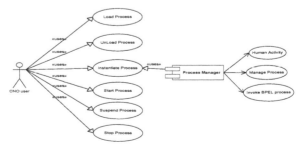

Figure 6 – Engine use case

3.4 A prototype

The research performed in this paper finds a real implementation in a developed prototype (Ratti et al, 2007). This has been based on the extension of two existing tools (Together, 2006), by applying requirements and features suggested by this research, maintaining all the existing functionalities. The two modules are Java client-based applications, which stores information inside XML file (for CBP processes), and are able to store local data inside any relational database management systems. When the editor is loaded the modified version of the Jawe tool is loaded and running. In this way the user can model a normal workflow process (with all the functionalities provided by the tool itself and available inside its user manual), and can improve it by using the new developed features. The main feature is the BPEL import, which allows the user to import a BPEL process inside the workflow. The "Figure 7" shows this new feature and the related box.

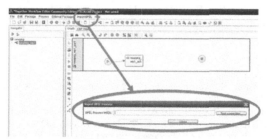

Figure 7 – Editor

The engine is an extension of the existing open source software called Shark, an xPDL engine. The main extension made has just been the possibility to load and execute CBP file.The engine is made by a set of panels where the user can see which are the loaded processes, see the current activities, run and execute the processes.

The "Figure 8" is a screenshot of the proposed engine.

Figure 8 – Engine

4 CONCLUSIONS

The work presented one service provided by the ICT infrastructure (ICT-I) that is being developed in the ECOLEAD Project for supporting CNOs in collaborating and doing businesses. In this scenario, new generation of services should provided and should be managed and dealt with both human and automatic processes. This new discipline requires the definition of new languages, standards and tools able to support both workflows and business processes. The work carried out in this paper presents a roadmap for the definition of a new language and tools which will consider these recommendations.

While also the leading companies in the field of business processes are analyzing this topic (see the BPEL4People specification) the CBP specification could be used as a starting point for the future research activities. This report is intended to provide suggested specifications and a prototypal implementation of this preliminary work. As a next step, similar activities will be analyzed and further researches will be performed. This process could hopefully start a standardization process, this is why it's important to study all aspects involved in such a particular domain.

4.1 Acknowledgments

This work has been partly funded by the European Commission IST Programme through the ECOLEAD project: European Collaborative networked Organizations Leadership Initiative (FP6 IP 506958). The authors wish to gratefully acknowledge their support as well as the contribution of the ECOLEAD project partners.

5 REFERENCES

1. L. Camarinha Matos, H. Afsarmanesh, D51.1Main modeling needs and approaches in CNOs, ECOLEAD project, Sep, 20064
2. R. Rabelo, R, Ratti, M. Rodrigo Castro, P. Gibert, D61.1b First consolidated ICT infrastructure architecture and reference framework for collaboration, ECOLEAD project, May, 2006
3. Process Definition Interface, XML Process Definition Language, Workflow Management Coalition Workflow Standard, October 3, 2005
4. BPEL4WS v1.1, http://www-128.ibm.com/developerworks/library/specification/ws-bpel, May 2003
5. WS-BPEL Extension for People, Whitepaper, IBM, SAP AG, 25 Aug 2005
6. R, Ratti, R. Rabelo, M. Rodrigo Castro, P. Gibert, D61.1c ICT-I Reference Framework (version. 3), ECOLEAD project, Mar, 2007
7. XQuery 1.0, www.w3.org/TR/xquery/, 23 January 2007
8. R, Ratti, R. Rabelo, M. Rodrigo Castro, P. Gibert, S. Mores, D64.1c ICT-I Integrated prototype (version 3), ECOLEAD project, Mar, 2007
9. Together, http://www.together.at/together, 2006

53

WORKFLOW TECHNOLOGY SUPPORTING THE OPERATION OF VIRTUAL ISPS

Klaus-Peter Eckert[1], Jane Hall[1], Henri-Jean Pollet[2]

1Fraunhofer Fokus, GERMANY, {klaus-peter.eckert,jane.hall}@fokus.fraunhofer.de
[2]Perceval Technologies S.A., BELGIUM, hjp@perceval.net

Small Internet Service Providers (ISPs) face many challenges in the world today. One solution for survival is to collaborate in a virtual cluster providing an attractive range of services that can be rapidly composed and deployed. An efficient software infrastructure is required to support such a cluster. The VISP software platform is designed for workflow technologies and will allow the cluster to model, specify, deploy and execute workflows that support the operation of the cluster and the provision of the tailored ISP services that it is offering to customers.

1   INTRODUCTION

An ISP is an organization providing Internet Protocol (IP) enabled internet and communication services to create efficient and innovative solutions that deliver substantial added value to its customers. This paper discusses the challenges facing a small ISP in the world of today and the rationale behind forming a cluster with other small ISPs so that they can compete in the world of tomorrow. It introduces the operating modes of the virtual cluster and considers the technology solutions that are being adopted so that the ISPs in the virtual cluster can offer attractive, competitively priced services that can be rapidly composed and deployed.

There are several definitions in the literature, not only of a virtual organization (Kürümlüoglu, 2005) (Saabeel, 2002) but also of other types of collaborative networks, such as virtual enterprise, dynamic virtual organization, virtual organization breeding environment (Camarinha-Matos, 2005a). The VISP cluster may not be entirely aligned with these definitions as the services offered by an ISP require a longer-term relationship between providers than products that are delivered to customers with no continuing provider involvement after delivery. An ISP service is provided over months, usually years, and so collaboration between cluster partners also lasts years. Unlike a virtual organization, a VISP cluster is not considered a temporary consortium or alliance but a long-living entity, although partners can join and leave. It is not the objective to create and dissolve clusters according to market demands although they will evolve and adapt to changing market conditions.

This paper is structured as follows. In section 2 the rationale behind the development of an ISP cluster and the operating modes of the cluster are presented. In section 3 the VISP software infrastructure comprising workflow technologies and the VISP software platform to support these technologies is introduced together with the business and technical processes that are being developed as workflows for

Eckert, K.-P., Hall, J., Pollet, H.-J., 2007, in IFIP International Federation for Information Processing, Volume 243, Establishing the Foundation of Collaborative Networks; eds. Camarinha-Matos, L., Afsarmanesh, H., Novais, P., Analide, C.; (Boston: Springer), pp. 495–502.

deployment on the VISP platform. Section 4 reports on a validation experiment and in section 5 conclusions are drawn and future work is outlined.

2   WHY VISP?

2.1   The Business Environment

VISP comes from a business pain. A small ISP in a rapidly changing competitive environment with many large, especially incumbent, firms has a constant challenge to survive as a small and medium enterprise (SME) without sacrificing the values held by the company. The ISP market is continually evolving and an ISP has to adapt to meet changing market conditions as well as changing technologies and protocols. The business customers that are being addressed often want services tailored to their specific needs. They also require higher security, higher scalability, higher availability and shorter response times than residential customers as well as greater geographic coverage. No small ISP on its own can provide the geographic coverage and the wide range of complex, specialized services that these customers now want. Small ISPs will have to alter the way they do business to survive, and collaboration with other small ISPs in a VISP cluster is one solution.

Small access ISPs who target business customers are those being addressed in a VISP cluster. The benefits of collaboration that have been recorded in the literature are valid here too (Kürümlüoglu, 2005). In particular, a cluster offers a larger presence in the market. It can create value for ISPs by increasing their attractiveness via a richer offering and so considerably extend their business coverage in terms of possible services. As the number of partners in the cluster increases, the wider the range of services and expertise that is available.

VISP is a term that can be used to represent a range of business models (DIP, 2004). The term is often associated with the reselling of products from a real ISP, where the virtual ISP provides the branding, marketing and sales outlets. This is a different concept from the use of VISP here that refers to real ISPs collaborating in a cluster that behaves as a single business entity providing a wide range of tailored services that can be composed from individual service elements provided by any of the ISPs in the cluster.

2.2   How the VISP Cluster is Organized

The VISP cluster is based on the federation approach; all partners are equals and join in only as much as they want. Each partner is an independent organization with its own resources which it uses to provide services. Figure 1 shows how a VISP cluster may be organized. Two operating modes are foreseen that correspond roughly to the *Internal consortium* (case 2) and the *Partnership* (case 4) types of collaboration in (Camarinha-Matos, 2005b).

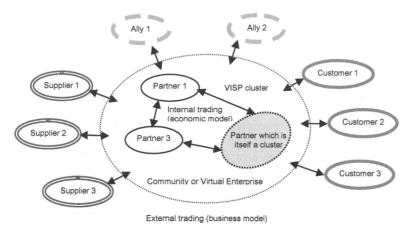

Figure 1 – A VISP Cluster

In the Community operating mode each partner owns its own customers and the cluster is not visible externally. The partner serves its customers and the cluster is used dynamically as a pool of services for subcontracting. The cluster has no assets as these are owned by the individual partners independently of the cluster, but there is a legal agreement defining the cooperation between the partners.

In the Virtual Enterprise operating mode, the cluster is a registered trade organization and all partners share the revenues of the enterprise based on the terms defined in the agreement. The cluster therefore owns the customer relationship, the customer data and the customer transaction. An incoming service request from a customer is dispatched to a partner, which then acts as the cluster mediator and which interfaces with the customer on behalf of the cluster.

3   THE VISP SOFTWARE INFRASTRUCTURE

A virtual organization itself is not a new phenomenon but what is new is the technology now available to support the vision, to overcome the problems and to meet the challenges. The benefits of collaboration in a cluster can only be realized if an adequate infrastructure that can support the operation of the cluster itself as well as the trading of tailored services. The VISP cluster vision is concerned with innovative aspects such as service decomposition and modeling using ontology-based concepts, and business and technical process modeling and workflows. The aim is to provide an automated operating environment that is efficient and agile in providing services to customers, so ensuring the competitiveness of the cluster in the marketplace. The workflow technology approach that has been adopted for the infrastructure is therefore considered key to the success of the VISP vision.

3.1   Workflow Technologies

One of the most significant developments supporting the spread of workflow technologies and business process management has been the emergence of Web services technology and XML in conjunction with expanding Internet use. The loose coupling of Web services enables interoperability between applications on different platforms, and this opens up a range of new possibilities for business models in the ISP market. Integration both within the enterprise as well as between enterprises is not only easier but also cheaper than was the case with locked-in proprietary systems. These developments clearly have an impact on the VISP idea of cooperating roles in a virtual cluster, which requires Internet technologies that automate processes across organization boundaries. Because of the widespread availability of XML and Web services, appropriate technologies have been developed to support such inter-enterprise process systems. This availability is a significant element in realizing the VISP vision.

In the workflow technology area there is a profusion of notations, languages, mappings and tools. Several workflow technologies and associated products were therefore analyzed as to their suitability for VISP's purposes (Eckert, 2006). Other work in the area relevant to the VISP criteria was also considered, for example (Bernauer, 2003), (INTEROP, 2005), (Lippe, 2005), and (van der Aalst, 2003). The BPMN standard (Business Process Modeling Notation, 2006), a business process graphical notation language that can model high-level end-to-end business flows, was selected for choreography modeling with eClarus Business Process Modeler as the tool. BPEL4WS (Business Process Execution Language, 2003), or BPEL for short, models executable business processes based on Web services and was selected as the orchestration language with ActiveBPEL Designer as the tool. BPEL can also be used as a choreography language, as for example in the Astro project (Kazhamiakin, 2004). However, as business analysts prefer to use a graphical notation and as the BPMN standard specifies a mapping from BPMN to BPEL, with tools available to support this mapping, the BPMN-BPEL mapping approach was adopted. The Web Services Description Language (WSDL, 2001) was selected for defining Web service interfaces as it is a widely used standard supported by many tools. Eclipse WTP was the tool selected for editing WSDL files.

Other work in the area of inter-organizational workflows that has been of interest includes that undertaken, for example, in CrossFlow, which based cross-organizational workflow cooperation on contracts between service consumer and service provider, and which used XML but clearly was not able to use the workflow technologies that have been developed subsequently (Grefen, 2000). CrossWork created an architecture for automated workflows in the automotive industry using in particular XRL (eXchangeable Routing Language) (Till, 2005). P2E2 has been developing a platform to support the lifecycle for cross-organizational business processes using the event-driven process chain (EPC) language for top-level modeling and converting the models to XPDL for execution in workflow engines (Walter, 2006). The VISP project is basing its work on standards and open source software wherever possible and has therefore adopted the only currently available standardized mapping between choreography and orchestration languages, i.e., BPMN to BPEL although XPDL was considered a possible execution language.

3.2   The VISP Software Platform

The VISP software platform supports a cluster of small ISPs when modeling, specifying, deploying and executing the tailored services it is offering to customers. It consists of two major parts: the Workflow Modelling and Specification Platform (WfMSP) and the Workflow Execution Platform (WfEP).

The WfMSP is concerned with the modeling and specification of processes that can be deployed and executed as workflows on the distributed WfEP. Three main phases have been identified in order to ensure that an informal textual description of the process that is provided by domain experts for input to the platform emerges as an executable workflow. First, the textual specification provides an informal and then a refined, formalized, specification of the process. Second, the graphical phase takes the textual specification and creates a choreography specification in BPMN, with the required WSDL documents also being defined or imported during this phase. Third, the executable phase takes the choreography specification, maps it to corresponding abstract BPEL orchestration skeletons and refines them to executable orchestration specifications that can be deployed and executed on the WfEP.

The WfEP executes and controls the workflows specified by the WfMSP and it interfaces either directly or through mediation devices with Enterprise Planning Resource (ERP) tools, external applications and network systems and resources. The execution of VISP business processes relies mainly on interactions with the partners' ERP systems and global repositories while the VISP technical processes interact with the network and system components. The workflow engines are the coordinating points of the WfEP and are responsible for executing the workflows. Interoperability between workflows running on diverse workflow engines will enable partners in the cluster to manage their workflows so that they can interact with those of other partners.

3.3   VISP Cluster Processes

Cluster processes are being modeled, specified and executed as workflows of activities in both the business and technical domains in order to cover all service provision related activities. Workflows are needed to operate a complex assembly of resources under the control of the independent partners. They will support cross-application processes, transfer each activity to the adequate resource for manual or automatic execution and deliver the final services. ISP services are continually evolving and so the corresponding workflows need to be specified and implemented in an integrated and standard way so that when a service is modified, the implementation is minimal and automated as much as possible.

The VISP project is providing a consolidated set of business-related workflows able to deal with trading aspects in a dynamic cluster of cooperating partners. The workflows also support the functioning of the cluster and its ability to attract and manage new partners. A set of business processes is being developed using standardized processes wherever appropriate, such as those in the eTOM Business Process Framework (eTOM, 2005) and the OAGIS specifications together with their associated WSDL (OAGIS, 2006). Many specifications, however, assume bilateral relations between partners, often in buyer-seller roles, whereas VISP also requires multiparty business collaboration processes.

A technical process in VISP is any process that interacts directly with network elements. Technical processes cover all technical activities related to the lifecycle of an ISP service in order to instantiate, commission, activate, deactivate and decommission the service. Further administrative activities such as testing, technical location transfer, suspend and resume are also expected to be included. A major challenge of the work is to provide formalized workflow specifications of today's manually executed technical processes to be able to process them automatically in a standardized way as is possible for the business processes mentioned above. Figure 2 shows how the various processes relate to each other.

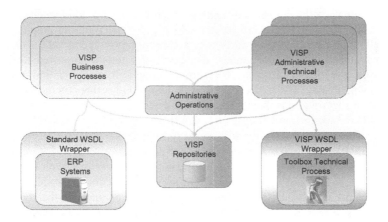

Figure 2 – The VISP Business and Technical Processes

4   VALIDATION

An approach called *goAhead* was undertaken to validate the individual components of the WfMSP as well as the functioning of the platform as an integrated whole. The descriptions of ISP services, the supporting business processes and corresponding technical processes interfacing the service infrastructure required for a typical VISP scenario were developed and refined as they passed through the individual modeling and specification phases. The scenario selected was concerned with the lifecycle of an instance of an ISP service, VoIP, which was considered a typical VISP scenario in that it includes a customer request being received by the VISP cluster, the preparation, negotiation and conclusion of a sales contract, the commissioning, activation and operation of the ISP service and finally its termination.

goAhead was a valuable exercise that enabled several technical details about the individual tools comprising the WfMSP platform and their interoperability to be clarified. It not only validated and refined the functional architecture of the platform but also resulted in an extensive VISP-related evaluation of the selected tools and implementations.

The validation exercise has led to further work aimed at resolving the issues that arose. One issue, for example, concerns the use of asynchronous versus synchronous communication. Many processes are of long duration with execution times in the order of weeks, and often including both manual and automated tasks. For synchronous communication, a BPMN client is modeled as a task of type "service" whereas for asynchronous communication it is modeled as two tasks of type "send" and "receive". The WDSL also has to be modified for asynchronous communication, especially the definitions of "port types", "partner link types" and faults. In synchronous mode the server provides an interface consisting of operations with input, output and fault messages, whereas in asynchronous mode the server provides only operations with input parameters. In asynchronous mode the client also has to provide a call-back interface with operations that explicitly expect responses and faults as input parameters. In BPMN a corresponding exclusive, event-based gateway has to be introduced to separate replies and faults. Although both communication styles can be supported, the modeler has to be aware of the different approaches when deciding which style is appropriate. Interactions with humans also need to be taken into account and many of the processes were redesigned explicitly to reduce the number of such interactions in any one loop.

It was found advisable to establish project-wide conventions for mapping from BPMN, a graph-oriented language supporting processes and sub-processes, to BPEL, a block-structured language. Based on the experience gained in *goAhead* together with other work undertaken in this area, such as (Ouyang, 2006a and 2006b), a set of "best practice" BPMN patterns was defined that map to "good" BPEL code. Conventions for parameter passing also had to be defined as this affects both the WSDL specifications and the BPMN models. Consistency is important in several areas, for example, in ensuring that parameters requested in a bottom-up approach are provided in the corresponding top-down approach. It is also necessary to ensure consistency in error handling mechanisms and compensation activities between the WSDL, BPMN and BPEL models by introducing a common format for all fault messages. Another important requirement resulting from *goAhead* was the development of a consistent information flow for the whole system that connects both the business and technical areas. The resolution of these and other issues are now being input into the next phase of the project work.

5   CONCLUSIONS

The work presented here is a first step towards a long-term vision where workflows enable efficient and seamless collaboration between partners in a VISP cluster so that they can remain competitive in the marketplace. Now that the various components of the platform have been validated in a small experiment, the next phase comprises further work on the specification of workflows and the realization of the architecture to support the workflow specification and execution on a wider scale.

Many of the tools are new and the technology standards are still in flux, so solutions to various issues are not available and have to be created within the project itself. The adoption of workflow technologies to support the automated operation of a cluster of small ISPs in their business is therefore research work that is in progress. There are many challenges in several areas that are being resolved as further experience is gathered. Ongoing work should therefore enable the VISP project to contribute to knowledge about how workflow technology can support virtually organized collaboration.

Acknowledgments.

This work was carried out with partial funding from the EU through the IST project VISP (IST-FP6-027178). The views expressed in this paper do not necessarily reflect those of the VISP project consortium members. Further information on VISP can be obtained from http://www.visp-project.org.

6   REFERENCES

1.   Bernauer B, Kappel G, Kramler G, Retschitegger, W. "Specification of Interorganizational Workflows – A Comparison of Approaches". In Proceedings of the 7th World Multiconference on Systematics, Cybernetics and Informatics (SCI 2003), 2003.
2.   Business Process Execution Language for Web Services, Version 1.1, 5 May 2003, ftp://www6. software.ibm.com/software/developer/library/ws-bpel.pdf.
3.   Business Process Modeling Notation Specification. OMG Final Adopted Specification, February 2006, www.omg.org/docs/dtc/06-02-01.pdf.
4.   Camarinha-Matos LM, Afsarmanesh H. Collaborative networks: a new scientific discipline. Journal of Intelligent Manufacturing 2005a; 16: 439-452.
5.   Camarinha-Matos LM, Silveri I, Afsarmanesh H, Oliveira AI. "Towards a Framework for Creation of Dynamic Virtual Organizations". In Collaborative Networks and Their Breeding Environments (PRO-VE'05), 26-28 September 2005, Valencia, Spain, L.M. Camarinha-Matos, H. Afsarmanesh, A. Ortiz, ed. New York, Springer Science+Business Media, 2005b; 69-80.
6.   DIP Deliverable D8.1, Analysis report: VISP Business Needs, June 2004, http://dip.semanticweb.org.
7.   Eckert K-P, Glickman Y, Hall J, et al. "Workflow Technologies for a Virtual ISP". In Exploiting the Knowledge Economy: Issues, Applications, Case Studies, P. Cunningham and M. Cunningham, ed. Amsterdam: IOS Press, 2006; 1631-1638.
8.   Enhanced Telecom Operations Map® (eTOM), The Business Process Framework. Addendum D: Process Decompositions and Descriptions, GB921D V6.1, Morristown, NJ: TeleManagement Forum, November 2005.
9.   Grefen P, Hoffner Y, Ludwig L. CrossFlow: cross-organizational workflow management in dynamic virtual enterprises. International Journal of Computer Systems Science & Engineering 2000; 15: 277-290.
10.   INTEROP Deliverable D9.1, State-of-the art for Interoperability architecture approaches, December 2005. www.interop-noe.org.
11.   Kazhamiakin R, Pistore M, Poveri M. "A framework for integrating Business Processes and Business Requirements". In Proceedings 9th International IEEE EDOC Conference, 2004.
12.   Kürümlüoglu M, Nøstdal R, Karvonen I. "Base Concepts". In Virtual Organizations: Systems and Practices, L.M. Camarinha-Matos, H. Afsarmanesh, M. Ollus, ed. New York: Springer Science+Business Media, 2005; 11-28.
13.   Lippe S, Greiner U, Barros A. A Survey on State of the Art to Facilitate Modelling of Cross-Organisational Business Processes. 2nd GI Workshop XML4BPM, Karlsruhe, March 2005.
14.   Open Application Group Integration Specification (OAGIS); Business Object Documents, 2006. http://www.openapplications.org/global/intro.htm.
15.   Ouyang C, van der Aalst WMP, Dumas M, ter Hofstede AHM, Translating BPMN to BPEL. BPM Center Report BPM-06-2, BPMcenter.org, 2006a.
16.   Ouyang C, Dumas M, van der Aalst WMP, ter Hofstede AHM, From Business Process Models to Process-oriented Software Systems: The BPMN to BPEL Way. BPM Center Report BPM-06-27, BPMcenter.org, 2006b.
17.   Saabeel W, Verduijn TM, Hagdorn L, Kumar K. A Model of Virtual Organisation: A Structure and Process Perspective. Electronic Journal of Organizational Virtualness 2002; 4 (1).
18.   Till S, Eshuis R, Grefen P. A Workflow Formation Architecture for the Automotive Sector. INTEROP Workshop at EDOC 2005, 19 September 2005, Enschede, The Netherlands.
19.   van der Aalst WMP, ter Hofstede AHM, Kiepuszewski B, Baros AP. Workflow Patterns. Distributed and Parallel Databases 2003; 14: 5-51.
20.   Walter P, Werth D. "Peer-To-Peer-Based Lifecycle Management for Collaborative Business Processes". In Exploiting the Knowledge Economy: Issues, Applications, Case Studies, P. Cunningham and M. Cunningham, ed. Amsterdam: IOS Press, 2006; 1115-1123.
21.   Web Services Description Language (WSDL) 1.1. W3C Note, March 2001, http://www.w3.org/TR/wsdl.

PART 17

PROCESS INTEGRATION AND MANAGEMENT

54 INTRODUCING A COLLABORATIVE BUSINESS MODEL FOR EUROPEAN ERP VALUE CHAINS OF SMES

Ioannis Ignatiadis[1], Jonathan Briggs[1], Adomas Svirskas[2], Kostas Bougiouklis[3], Adamantios Koumpis[4]

[1]Centre for Applied Research in Information Systems, Kingston University, UK
{I.Ignatiadis, J.H.Briggs}@kingston.ac.uk
[2]Department of Computer Science, Vilnius University, LITHUANIA
adomas@svirskas.com
[3]Q-Plan North Greece, Thessaloniki, GREECE
bougiouklis@qplan.gr
[4]Altec, Thessaloniki, GREECE
akou@altec.gr

Similarly to the high-end market segment, a large number of ERP installations in the small and medium market segments also fails or results in time and cost overruns. To overcome those difficulties, a partnership-based e-business model amongst value chain actors is proposed. This model is supported by a platform, which engages and involves local actors in flexible multinational e-collaborations (forming European clusters in the ERP industry), in order to expand and broaden their activities. The envisaged outcome is to improve response times, low cost operations, flexibility towards clients, and provision of high-quality services tailored at end customers, facilitating the whole value chain to act as a single business entity (Virtual Organization).

1 INTRODUCTION

The European ERP market (which is a major part of ICT business applications market in Europe – worth approximately €15 billion) is dominated by large multinational actors, most of them outside the EU, focusing on high-end market segments (ERP solutions for large multinational companies). However, as the high-end market has reached maturity, there is a shift of interest towards small and medium market segments (ERP solutions for small companies and SMEs). This market is currently open to European national large ERP vendors and/or SMEs, with a view to expanding in the future, also due to the enlargement of the EU.

A review (ALTEC-Corporation, 2004) of ERP installations in 3 European countries has in fact shown that more than 85% of ERP projects failed to complete in the assigned time period, whereas 60% of projects exceeded the initially planned costs.

In order to overcome those difficulties, a collaborative business model to facilitate interactions amongst players in the European ERP industry is proposed. Such players include ERP vendors, their national representatives, ERP dealers and consultants. The background of this paper is the EU co-funded project "PANDA" (PANDA-Project, 2006), currently in its implementation phase. PANDA's full title is "Collaborative Process Automation Support using Service Level Agreements and Intelligent Dynamic Agents in SME Clusters". This project aims to provide a

Ignatiadis, I., Briggs, J., Svirskas, A., Bougiouklis, K., Koumpis, A., 2007, in IFIP International Federation for Information Processing, Volume 243, Establishing the Foundation of Collaborative Networks; eds. Camarinha-Matos, L., Afsarmanesh, H., Novais, P., Analide, C.; (Boston: Springer), pp. 505–512.

powerful framework of e-business services, dedicated to addressing current inefficiencies in the European ERP industry of SMEs, as well as facilitating international
e-collaborations based on local actors and alliances. PANDA proposes the development of a new partnership based e-business model using the concept of Request-
Based Virtual Organizations (RBVOs) (Roberts et al., 2005). PANDA also includes
the development of a set of integrated supporting technologies in the form of a platform
that will engage and involve local players in flexible multinational e-collaborations.

In the sections that follow, section 2 reviews relevant literature on the definition
of e-business models, as well as e-collaboration. Section 3 introduces the proposed
collaborative business model for European SME actors in the ERP industry, as
exemplified through the PANDA project. Section 4 concludes this paper, by
discussing other potential applications of the proposed collaborative model.

2   E-BUSINESS MODELS AND E-COLLABORATION

2.1   Business Model Definition

Before discussing the proposed collaborative business model, it is first necessary to
examine the definition of "business model". Although the concept of "business
model" appeared for the first time in an academic article in 1957 (Bellman et al.,
1957), its popularity grew only recently, in the end of the 1990s, mainly due to the
increase of the e-business phenomenon. The number of times the term "business
model" in fact appeared in the past in a business journal, seemed to trace the shape
of the NASDAQ market index, potentially indicating the relationship of the term
"business model" with technology (Osterwalder et al., 2005).

Nevertheless, there is still much disagreement, both in industry and in academia,
on what constitutes a business model, and what its role and potential is. Osterwalder
et al. notice that the term stands for many things, such as elements and relationships
of a model, parts of a business model (e.g. auction model), concrete real world
instances of business models (e.g. the Amazon model), or types of business models
(e.g. business-to-business).

Several definitions of a business model have in fact been given in the literature,
amongst which:

*A description of the commercial relationship between a business enterprise and
the products and/or services it provides in the market. (Hawkins, 2001)*

*An architecture of a firm and its network of partners for creating, marketing and
delivering value and relationship capital to one or several segments of customers
in order to generate profitable and sustainable revenue streams. (Pigneur, 2000)*

*An architecture for the product, service and information flows, including a
description of the various business actors and their roles; and a description of
the potential benefits for the various business actors; and a description of the
sources of revenues. (Timmers, 1998)*

The business model presented in this paper is mainly concerned with defining the interactions and common processes amongst actors in European ERP value chains and the expected benefits to those actors, as exemplified by the real-world application of the PANDA project. The proposed business model is based on e-collaboration, which is presented next.

2.2   E-Collaboration

E-collaboration can be defined as business-to-business interactions among a group of collaborating parties, with the use of Information and Communication Technologies, particularly the Internet. Those interactions go beyond simple buy/sell transactions, and may be better described as relationships, including the sharing of resources amongst partners (Cheng et al., 2006; Johnson and Whang, 2002; Kock et al., 2001).

There are many driving forces behind e-collaboration. Companies are mainly driven by the increasing need of (i) information visibility and sharing along the supply chain, (ii) the efficient communication in a distributed network, (iii) the cost reduction and time compression philosophy, (iv) process automation, (v) increased potential opportunities of partnership, and (vi) the flexibility and adaptability. On the other hand, without the advances of enabling ICT technologies, all above could not be realistically achieved. Thus, the evolution of e-collaboration strongly depends on the developments and adoption of ICT technologies by both businesses and consumers.

E-collaboration tools have progressed from managing simple interactions among individuals to managing complex processes across entire supply chains. Collaboration in the supply chain has been widely discussed in the literature (e.g. Cassivi, 2006; Marquez et al., 2004; Ovalle and Marquez, 2003), and a wealth of concepts is at hand. The origin of supply chain collaboration could trace back to the emergence and promotion of supply chain management philosophy over the last decades, where it is realized that competition no longer takes place between individual businesses, but between entire supply chains. Collaboration can provide the competitive edge that enables all the business partners in the supply chain to act as one in order to achieve a synchronized and seamless supply chain.

Having described e-collaboration, the following section introduces the proposed e-collaboration model in the European ERP industry of SMEs.

3   ONLINE COLLABORATION IN THE EUROPEAN ERP INDUSTRY INDUSTRY OF SMES

Online collaboration for SME actors in the European ERP industry is exemplified through the PANDA project. Part of this project involves the development of a web platform, which is an enabler that helps the ERP actors to flexibly form and manage business relationships. The following sections discuss the target market of the proposed model, the key issues it tries to address and the differentiation of the model, the supported processes and comparison with traditional processes, as well as the innovation aspects associated with the online collaboration of ERP actors.

3.1   Target Market

The proposed business model includes an advanced e-collaboration platform for actors in an ERP value chain (vendors, consultants, dealers, and national represen- tatives), providing them with the capability to locate suitable partners across national boundaries, online manage running projects, and advertise their experiences and expertise. It goes a step ahead from simpler collaboration platforms, by automating many processes (such as searching for partners and monitoring progress) with the use of intelligent software agents (Multi-Agent System).

The platform is mainly addressed at serving large international or interregional ERP projects – demanding the cooperation of at least 2 different service providers – e.g. 2 dealers, 1 national representative and 1 dealer, etc (and not ERP projects with narrow geographical spectrum or small budget – that can be fulfilled by only one dealer). Consequently, the platform focuses on ERP vendors' value chains at the small and medium market segment (ERP solutions for SMEs and/or Medium Enterprises or partially large). It does not envisage competing with large and well established multinational actors that are focusing on the high-end market segments (e.g. SAP, Microsoft, etc).

3.2   Key Issues and Model Differentiation

The problem that the proposed collaborative model tries to solve is associated with the limited partner networks in multinational e-collaborations, the lack of financial and human resources, the risk and uncertainty in expanding in new national markets, the lack of transparency regarding the availability of resources amongst colla- borating partners, as well as the lack of expertise in addressing socio-economic barriers hindering internalization efforts. The impact of those is the difficulty in expanding activities the traditional way (e.g. establishment of branches in a foreign country).

Unlike networks having an own fixed, centrally supported, internationally-wide network of technical subsidiaries, the e-collaboration platform supporting the proposed business model in the European ERP industry of SMEs:

- Can be used by many value chains, supporting either an open source or proprietary product.
- Can be adapted to the particularities of each value chain (with regards to its structure, actor relationships, legal/financial/business issues).
- Is based on the notion of Request-Based Virtual Organizations (RBVOs) (Roberts et al., 2005), referring to a multinational cluster of ERP value chain actors, the cluster being formed ad-hoc upon a request from a value chain actor.
- Employs the use of sector-specific Service Level Agreements (SLAs), serving as the regulating framework of e-collaborations amongst RBVO members.
- Is served by a community of intelligent software agents (Multi-Agent System), developed to automate procedures and operations of RBVOs. Agents represent the intelligent 'back-office' of the platform, aiming at supporting interoperability, distributed peer to peer decision making, robustness, and knowledge sharing/private knowledge disclosure.

3.3   Supported Processes and Benefits

The functionality of the platform to facilitate the envisaged collaborative model in the European ERP industry of SMEs was identified by interviewing actors (such as vendors, national representatives, dealers and consultants) in ERP value chains of European countries (such as Greece, Romania, Bulgaria, Germany, Hungary and Sweden). Most of the interviewed actors were active in their national markets for a number of years, and had an in depth knowledge of the business processes, practices and shortcomings, not only of their own value chain, but also of a large part of the ERP industry in their own and other European countries.

From the interaction with those actors the main requirements regarding the supported processes were elaborated. In general, the business model facilitated by the e-collaboration platform includes the following areas:

1. *Pre-sales activity*: formulation and submission of an offer to an end customer, providing necessary references, such as estimation of time schedule and cost, general conditions for project implementation, etc. This can be supported by data from the platform, e.g. using SLA templates to facilitate the (offline) negotiations with the customer. The benefit is the reduction in time and the standardisation in the submission of offers to customers according to pre-defined SLA templates.

2. *Formation of consortium per ERP project*: searching for potential partners based on a collaboration request, which incorporates major characteristics of the ERP project as well as specific conditions set by the client. This is supported by agent technologies using data from the platform such as partner reputation (see point 4 below), in order to identify the most suitable partners for a project. The benefit is the reduction in time and costs associated with manually identifying potential collaborators.

3. *Overall monitoring/management of the consortium during implementation*: including (if needed) re-planning of the project (e.g. changing tasks) and/or reconfiguration (e.g. adding or removing partners). This is supported by manual and automatic (agent) monitoring of the status of the project. The benefit is the flexibility and time savings in managing the running of the project.

4. *Management of partner profiles*: automatic update of the profiles of all partners-members of a project following project termination. This is supported by automatically recording project results and customer/partner feedback in the platform, which can include rating of partner performance. The benefit is the automatic archiving of the reputation of a partner in the platform, which can be used to measure the partner's suitability for participation in future collaborative projects.

Other benefits of the collaborative business model also include the expansion of geographical activities, as well as the building of new networks and strategic alliances with partners with complementary resources and expertise. Those new networks and strategic alliances can secure new projects for the firm, increasing its profit and market awareness, in its own or other countries. In addition, by using software agents throughout the life-cycle (i.e. partner selection, RBVO formation, operation and termination) of an RBVO associated with an ERP project, the relevant processes are automated, resulting in increased efficiency compared to the manual carrying out of those processes. The next section compares some of the traditional and online collaborative business processes.

3.4   Comparison with Traditional Processes

A comparison between the traditional and the processes associated with the proposed collaboration model is carried out in the table below.

Table 1 – Comparison of traditional and online collaborative processes

Process	Current Solution	Online Collaboration
Partner Identification	Personal contacts and recommendations	Automatic partner identification (from pool of authorised companies) by software agents.
Communication of ERP project's requirements and status	Mostly by telephone and e-mail	Holding of RBVO project data (pre, during and post implementation) in the platform's database, for viewing and maintaining by authorised partners.
Experience sharing from previous similar ERP projects	Mostly personal contacts with relevant actors	Online archival of completed projects, including solutions provided, approaches and issues.
Contracting for international collaborations	Ad-hoc formation of contracts	Storage of SLA templates in the platform, used to guide negotiations with the customer (pre-sales activity), and/or potential partners.
Maintaining a pool of partners	Offline, or other specialized system (Excel, CRM, etc)	Online management (registration, examination, reputation, etc) of companies.

The major innovation aspects of the proposed online collaborative business model are summarized in the next section.

3.5   Innovation Aspects

Innovation in the proposed business model, as facilitated by the e-collaboration platform, lies in the combination of:

1. Process integration (enabled through innovative use of technologies, see point 4 below).
2. Increased business functionality and market responsiveness (through improved structural flexibility (RBVO) and business performance monitoring (SLAs)).
3. Collaborative actions enabled though improved coordination (RBVO model and agent technologies).

4. Innovative use of technologies (such as agent technologies and Service-Oriented Architecture) through an integrated platform to support the collaborative value chain.

The combination of these factors (increased operational capability, tighter process integration coupled with business flexibility and a sound underpinning technical architecture/platform) provides the overall justification, if achieved, to claim that the proposed e-business model provides innovation, resulting in improved business performance (which in the future will be measured and evaluated).

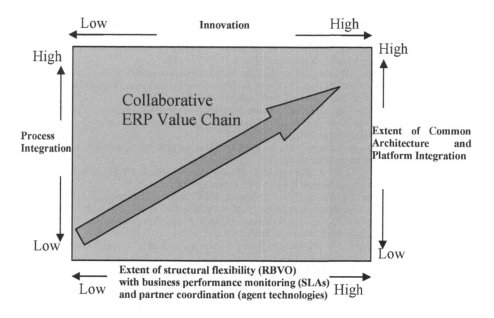

Figure 1 – Innovation aspects of the proposed e-collaboration model

4 CONCLUSIONS

The purpose of this paper has been to introduce a collaborative business model for the (European) ERP industry of SMEs, currently being implemented through the EU co-funded project "PANDA".

The duration of the PANDA project is 30 months, ending in summer 2008. The strategic impact of PANDA lies in its ambition to facilitate the creation of an efficient and integrated European industry on ERP systems. Although the PANDA project is exemplified in the European ERP industry for SMEs, the concepts, business and developed technological aspects could also be applied in other settings where collaborative projects are implemented. This includes practically any business sector where business-oriented software solutions (i.e. software products coupled with value added services to form 'extended' solutions) are used. As such, the

PANDA project is important in serving as a demonstrator and proof-of-concept for future research and development in the area of collaborative e-business environments.

5   ACKNOWLEDGEMENTS

The authors would like to thank members of partner organisations from the PANDA consortium for their valuable input and help in developing the business model.

6   REFERENCES

1. ALTEC-Corporation. ERP Installations: Problems and Inefficiencies (Internal Company Report). 2004.
2. Bellman R, Clark CE, Malcolm DG, Craft CJ, Ricciardi FM. On the Construction of a Multi-Stage, Multi-Person Business Game. Operations Research 1957; 5: 469-503.
3. Cassivi L. Collaboration planning in a supply chain. Supply Chain Management 2006; 11: 249 - 258.
4. Cheng EWL, Love PED, Standing C, Ghavari H. Intention to e-collaborate: propagation of research propositions. Industrial Management & Data Systems 2006; 106: 139-152.
5. Hawkins R. The "Business Model" as a Research Problem in Electronic Commerce. STAR (Socio-economic Trends Assessment for the digital Revolution) IST Project, Issue Report No. 4, SPRU – Science and Technology Policy Research, 2001.
6. Johnson ME, Whang S. E-business and Supply Chain Management: An Overview and Framework. Production and Operations management 2002; 11: 413-422.
7. Kock N, Davison R, Ocker R, Wazlawick R. E-collaboration: A look at past research and future challenges. Journal of Systems and Information Technology 2001; 5: 1-9.
8. Marquez AC, Bianchi C, Gupta JND. Operational and financial effectiveness of e-collaboration tools in supply chain integration. European Journal of Operational Research 2004; 159: 348-363.
9. Osterwalder A, Pigneur Y, Tucci CL. Clarifying Business Models: Origins, Present, and Future of the Concept. Communications of the AIS 2005; 15: 1-43.
10. Ovalle OR, Marquez AC. The effectiveness of using e-collaboration tools in the supply chain: an assessment study with system dynamics. Journal of Purchasing & Supply Management 2003; 9: 151-163.
11. PANDA-Project. EU IST-027169. http://www.panda-project.com, 2006.
12. Pigneur Y. The E-business Model Handbook. HEC Working Paper 2000.
13. Roberts B, Svirskas A, Matthews B. "Request Based Virtual Organisations (RBVO): An Implementation Scenario". PRO-VE'05: 6th IFIP Working Conference on Virtual Enterprises, Valencia - Spain, 2005.
14. Timmers P. Business Models for Electronic Markets. Electronic Markets 1998; 8: 3-8.

55

INTEGRATED CONSTRUCTION PROJECT MANAGEMENT SYSTEM BASED ON IFC AND ISO9001:2000

K. Umut Gökçe & Raimar J. Scherer

Institute for Construction Informatics, Technology University Dresden, GERMANY,
{Raimar.J.Scherer,Umut Gokce}@cib.bau.tu-dresden.de

H. Attila Dikbaş

Project Management Center, Istanbul Technical University, TURKEY,
dikbas@itu.edu.tr

We present a conceptual framework enabling to manage broad set of activities supported by multi-module software application for construction project management. The proposed structure is based on a common building information model (the industry standard IFC Model – ISO PAS 16739), the ISO 9001:2000 Quality Management System, for high-level process specification, and an integrated software infrastructure encompassing the product and process information exchange among the CAD-ERP and Scheduling Systems that support IFC. In this context, we developed Construction Management Phases for Software Interoperability, Organizational and IT Management Processes with using of ARIS methodology in order to implement IFC views. Based on this, we outline a web-based environment enabling to plug in all component tools via a common client, providing a coherent GUI.

1   INTRODUCTION

Today the actors in the construction environment use a great number of different media in an unstructured way which lowers the efficiency of the process and limits access to required information. Therefore, there is a need to describe the building, its parts and the management processes with multiple qualities. To make this description requires common concepts for the definition of standardized building objects, management aspects and relations between them.

In the last years, the aim to achieve higher degree of integration in the design and construction process has led to the development of a number of product and process models and integration architectures. Following early suggestions such as the IRMA model (Luiten et al. 1993), many national and international projects as ATLAS, ToCEE, ISTforCE, ICSS and ARKOS etc. have developed models of increasing complexity, targeting various aspects of interoperability. Supported through these efforts, the industry-driven IFC (industry foundation classes) model was born in the 90s. This model is continuously improving and maturing towards a true standard for cooperative model-based working processes in AEC/FM (Liebich et al. 2006).

Gökçe, K.U., Scherer, R.J., Dikbas, H.A., 2007, in IFIP International Federation for Information Processing, Volume 243, Establishing the Foundation of Collaborative Networks; eds. Camarinha-Matos, L., Afsarmanesh, H., Novais, P., Analide, C.; (Boston: Springer), pp. 513–520.

However, in spite of all achievements for managing the process, product, documentation and communication, the organizational and information infrastructure in the AEC sector is still highly fragmented.

Currently in all industry countries there exist solutions integrating CAD, ERP scheduling and management tools. But, they largely lack generality in terms of data and process interoperability. ICT-supported construction project management (CPM) processes are mainly defined in terms of the used applications, and not on the basis of generalised industry requirements; similarly, integration of product and process information is based on the specific internal data models, and not on generally applicable and hence standardised data structures. All this significantly decreases flexibility, information exchange between the component systems, and last but not least, inter-enterprise cooperation and knowledge transfer.

Based on the determined requirements and acquiescence, to maintain an integrated structure to enable interoperable use of standard data in a generic CPM model in this research, we proposed an IT environment which is based on a formal process methodology, standardized product and process model (IFC), and overall architecture integrating technical (design) work, construction process planning and project management in a web-based structure, enabling to plug in all component tools via a common client providing a coherent GUI.

2   OBJECTIVES

To achieve interoperability in the area of CPM it is necessary to describe the building products, their parts and the related processes with multiple inter-related features. This requires taking into consideration (1) the economic and technical aspects, which can affect the products and processes during their lifecycle, and (2) the different involved discipline domains.

In this context, based on the experience gained from studying state-of-the art systems and best practice examples, the operational objectives for the development of an efficient Integrated CPM solution can be defined as follows:

1.   Generalize and formally describe CPM processes so that interoperability over a broad spectrum of applications is facilitated,
2.   Establish a common information model for CPM, based on the data schemas of the IFC standard (ISO/PAS 16739), thereby providing for the needed integration of product, process, cost and management data,
3.   Provide interoperability methods to integrate legacy systems,
4.   Develop a CPM assistance tool to interactively prove and ensure context-relevant data completeness.

3   APPROACH

The specific requirements, the highly distributed nature of the construction industry, and the independently used systems for management processes provide the rationale for setting up the basic principles of the proposed systems.

In this research, a feasible methodology for interoperability was developed according to: (1) The IFC model of the IAI for a hierarchically structured product model, (2) The ISO Quality Management System (ISO 9001:2000) for the existing real-world process specification for managing CPM requirements of outcome and (3) Web-based integrated methods for encompassing the product and process information exchange within the CAD and CPM systems that support IFCs.

In order to constitute an integrated CPM Model, the Construction Management Phases for Software Interoperability (CMPSI) was formalized with using of IDEF0 modeling methodology according to implied requirements.

ISO9001:2000 Quality Management System Procedures were established subsequently, to support organizational management structure and to establish a control mechanism.

In order to narrow the scope and to better define the CPM aspects, the Bidding Preparation Phase (BPP) of CMPSI was chosen and the overall BPP processes were formalized in two interrelated subsystems using ARIS methodology (1996): (1) Organizational Management Process (OMP) and (2) IT Management processes (ITMP). To provide completeness between these interrelated systems a mapping structure between CMPSI, OMP and ITMP was also obtained.

The OMP provides the core process structure from which ITMP are referenced and coordinated. It was developed based on an implemented Process Lifecycle Model which was formalized according to CMPSI, ISO 9001:2000 Quality Management System Procedures, Procurement Systems, and Software Integration Requirements. The respective technical and support processes were then improved with using of ARIS, eEPC (ARIS, extended Event-driven Process Chain) Model, in order to provide a core/complete CPM model.

The ITMP obtain the guiding process structure, related to interoperability of CAD, ERP and Scheduling Systems which are used for CPM purposes. Using a process-centric approach (based on the ARIS-eEPC), the related services and data resources for each task were identified.

Referencing IFC Model data is provided via formally defined IFC views in the context of the respective tasks. This was achieved with the help of a formal specification using the Generalized Subset Definition Schema (GMSD) (Weise et al. 2003) developed at the TU-Dresden, rules for dynamic run-time filtering, and a dedicated service performing the actual view extraction for the specifically referenced CAD, ERP and Scheduling Systems. IFC schema objects were used as much as possible, with some needed extensions for CPM purposes. However, as the objective is to propose an integrated framework and show how IFC fits into it rather than develop a specific IFC extension model for CPM, this has been done only for selected examples.

Based on the envisaged configurations, an operational framework for CPM will be developed as an integrated client-server environment, enabling to plug in all component tools.

4   INTEGRATED CPM MODEL

Development of an integrated CPM Model requires a holistic approach, taking into consideration management items, software applications, product data descriptions and a web-based system infrastructure.

4.1   Construction Management Phases for Software Interoperability

In order to formalize an integration methodology, encompassing the product and process information exchange within the CAD, ERP and Scheduling Systems which supports IFCs, the phase formalization principles: (1) General Project View, (2) Process Consistency, (3) Phase and Process Reviews etc. were developed. This approach provides the basis for the envisaged structure.

Furthermore, the Construction Management Phases for Software Interoperability which composed of five basic phases as: (1) Design, (2) Bidding Preparation, (3) Planning & Construction, (4) Realization, and (5) Evaluation of Outcome and Feedback was improved with using of IDEF0 modeling methodology. In all phases specific databases and algorithms were used to provide suitable data structures which keep the information about function and content. These obtain re-use of requested information whenever needed. Bidding Preparation Phase of CMPSI was chosen to narrow the scope and to formalize a precise structure in this context.

4.2   ISO9001:2000 Quality Management System CPM Procedures

To establish a concurrent control system in terms of monitoring ongoing activities, there is a need for a generic procedural model. This should include assessment of current work activities which relies on performance standards, rules and regulations for guiding employee tasks and behaviors.

In order to support required aspects and to obtain a generic procedural model, ISO9001:2000 Quality Management System (ISO-QMS) was examined in detail for CPM purposes. To support a conceptual framework, the envisaged CPM structure was basically modeled according to interconnected procedures referencing ISO requirements. Moreover, four main procedures as; (1) General System, (2) Human Resource and Administrative, (3) Customer Relations, and (4) Project Management procedures were formalized. Based on these, the sub-procedures were developed to constitute supporting processes subsequently.

4.3   Integrated CPM Processes

Based on the implemented acquiescence in this research, two inter-related process formalizations as (1) Organizational Management Process (OMP) and (2) IT Management Processes (ITMP) were structured in ARIS-eEPC model. The main aim to use ARIS is to clearly recognize the common functions, events, resources and objects that are used both in OMP and ITMDP. This helps greatly to subsequently formalize the mappings between the different but interrelated data and functional definitions. According to the defined process activities, resources are primarily defined as IFC objects or, where necessary, as suggested new entities within an IFC model extension for CPM.

4.3.1   Process Life Cycle Model for OMP

To complete identified aspects, to develop integrated CPM process patterns and to define a process formalization structure, a Process Life Cycle Model was implemented for OMP formalization purposes. CMPSI, ISO, Procurement Systems and software integration requirements were brought together in this structure, thereby exposing an integrated model which meets the envisaged interoperability.

4.3.2 Organizational Management Process

The Organizational Management Process composed of interconnected processes based on a developed Process Life Cycle Model, was constructed to control whole process sequence.

According to Process Life Cycle Model, (1) initial analysis of bidding preparation phase of CMPSI, related to ISO-QMS procedures, organizational structures, procurement systems, and required services were possessed. This phase is fallowed by (2) a process design phase, during which the overall process structure is engineered, the resulting process model is designed, the resources examined and the mapping methodology is decided. This includes the modeling of organizational structures and services integrations. In the third phase (3) the designed processes were implemented with using of ARIS-eEPC. The main process was defined according to ISO Quality Management System's bidding preparation process which is identified under customer relations main procedure. The supporting processes (six interrelated process) such as job development, design coordination processes etc. under project management main procedure were also defined and used within bidding preparation structure. With bringing together of procurement systems and integration requirements for CAD, ERP and Scheduling Systems, OMP was obtained. After implementation of work flow (4) established processes were checked whether that they are supporting generic integration comprising seamless information flow by using IT systems. The formalized resources consistencies were controlled and the mapping structure was scrutinized in this regard.

4.3.3 IT Management Processes

IT Management Processes (ITMP) are defined in accordance with the CAD-ERP-Scheduling Systems interoperability needs and derived based on OMP. This includes the application sequence of the involved IT tools, their relations to processes, performing actors, input output and control information, and their general systemic interrelations in the IT environment. To show different level of system integration, Bidding Preparation Phase is organized in three subsequent structures as; IT Management (1) Design Process, (2) BOQ Process and (3) Scheduling Process.

4.3.4 Process Mappings

In order to provide a generic concept which identifies workflow participants, in terms of resources that can be addressed by CPM processes, we identified a mapping structure between CMPSI, OMP and ITMP. This helps us to examine IFC views which are used to implement IFC based management approach. The mappings between three structures provide 1-1 mapping (pairing) formalization. The CMPSI phase processes are used as main processes which are referenced by OMP processes as sub-processes. Also CMPSI resources are referenced by OMP resources as sub-resources. The same approach is used within OMP and ITMP mappings.

5   IFC DATA FORMALIZATION

The IFC Object Model (IAI 2005) is essentially a project data model addressing the major data exchange requirements in the highly fragmented construction industry. It encompasses a large set of object definitions so that applications should or can implement only subsets of the full model. Such subsets are called IFC Views or, more generally, Data Exchange Use Cases. For practical use various such subsets are currently being defined applying more or less formal approaches (cf. ProIT 2004).

In this context, to enable interoperable use of IFC data in the General CPM Model and for the CAD-ERP and Scheduling applications the following procedure was applied: (1) The IT Management Processes defined in ARIS were examined with regard to IFC Data Exchange Use Cases that can or should be related to them. An example for such a use case is the data exchange from Architecture to Quantity Take-Off. (2) For each identified use case the relevant IFC objects and their relevant relationships are determined. They are then associated to the relevant organizational entities, and the relevant resource entities in the eEPC model. In the first case these will always be instances of IFC object classes, but in the second case they can be individual objects, property sets or whole model subsets. (3) Whenever model subsets need to be applied, the General Model Subset Definition Schema (GMSD) developed at the TU Dresden was used for the formal specification of the subset content on class level (Weise et al. 2003). (4) Runtime use of the IFC data was then provided via a specialized GMSD client which enables proper extraction of the specifically needed IFC instances in each particular situation. This was done interactively, whereas in the CPM model we provide only some requirements and hints to the user. Figure 1 below illustrates the principal ideas.

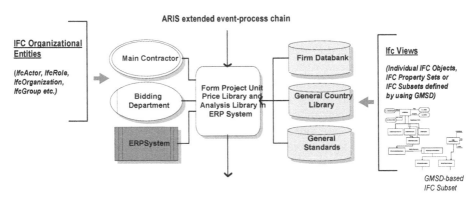

Figure 1. Schematic presentation of the association of IFC data to the CPM Model

6   OPERATIONAL FRAMEWORK

From the operational point of view, interoperability means the ability of the system components to work together in a coherent way for the solution of complex tasks. In this sense, the operational framework has to be structured and established according to a coherent process and information exchange paradigm as shown in Figure 2 below. It is comprised of 4 clearly defined layers: (1) Application Layer, (2) TSD Layer, (3) Management Process Layer, and (4) WPA Layer.

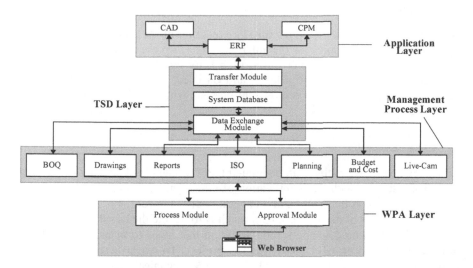

Figure 2. Suggested integrated Web-based CPM solution

6.1 Application Layer

The purpose of this layer is to support different types of value-add project activities, performed with the help of CAD, ERP and Scheduling applications. Typically, such applications are locally installed and used. They may provide some in-built interoperability but the basic input/output to/from them is achieved via the TSD Layer which is their gateway to the Web.

TSD Layer

This layer consists of a Transfer Module, a System Database and a Data Exchange Module. The information obtained from the Application Layer is stored in the System Database. This information covers the identified outcomes of the CAD, ERP and CPM applications. The Transfer Module supports the data exchange between the Application Layer and the System Database. Assuming that IFC data can be exported by the involved applications, this can be done with the help of a general purpose API in some convenient standard format (e.g. using ISO 10303-21 files and/or ifcXML). The stored database information is then processed by the Data Exchange Module which is the coordination module for the below layers, ensuring synchronous and asynchronous information flows in a coherent, standardized way.

6.2 Management Process Layer

The Management Process Layer consists of 7 different modules Drawing Module, Reports Module etc. that can perform and be managed separately and further process the data obtained from the TSD layer. Additionally, a Live-Cam Module can be provided to track the execution on the jobsite, and an ISO Module can be included for process support in accordance to ISO Quality Management procedures.

6.3 WPA Layer

The WPA Layer provides facilities for (1) execution of the management processes and the related applications via the Internet, and (2) presentation of the obtained results to all stakeholders via a common Web Browser. The process workflows can be carried out using a standard schema and on every step the information can be checked and approved by the responsible persons who are attained by the virtual project organization.

7 CONCLUSION

In the above pages we outlined an integrated CPM model based on a logical conceptual schema starting with the specification of management along a number of well-defined steps towards the creation of an operational framework.

The major goals of the suggested approach is to denote the broad set of activities supported by multi-module application software that helps to manage the different work items and processes of a construction project. To reach these goals we have brought together state-of-the-art CAD-ERP-CPM technical interoperability concepts, a novel formalization and integration approach for ISO9001 quality management procedures, advanced IFC-based integration issues. Some clear benefits of the integral treatment of all CPM aspects on the basis of ARIS, ISO9001 and IFC were identified, especially with regard to IFC penetration in practice. Currently IFC use is still modest, mostly for CAD-based data exchange. With the developed CPM model a contribution towards its much broader use in ERP and CPM applications to support collaborative project management in all life cycle phases of the virtual enterprise of a construction project can be accomplished.

After completion of the system requirements, the suggested framework will be prototyped in the name of 'SanTez' (Industry Thesis) Project which is supported by Turkish Ministry of Industry. Subsequently, the prototype will be used within a construction site, in order to revise the necessary developments.

8 REFERENCES

1. IAI (2005): IFC/ifcXML Specifications. © International Alliance for Interoperability(http:/www. iai-international.org/Model/IFC(ifcXML)Specs.html)
2. ISO9001:2000 Quality Management System Requirements. Geneva, Switzerland.
3. Liebich T., Adachi Y., Forester J., Hyvarinen J., Karstila K & Wix J. (2006): Industry Foundation Classes IFC2x3. © International Alliance for Interoperability.
4. Luiten G., Froese T., Björk B-C., Cooper G., Junge R., Karstila K. & Oxman R. (1993): An information Reference Model for Achitecture, Engineering and Construction. In: Mathur K. D., Betts M. P. & Tham K.W. (eds.) The Management of Informations Technology for Construction, World Scientific Publishing, Singapore.
5. ProIT (2004): ProIT: Product Model Data in the Construction Process. (C) IAI International Solutions.
6. Scheer A.-W. (1996): ARIS – House of Business Engineering. Research Report, Heft 133, IWi an der Unversität des Saarlands, Saarbrücken, Germany.
7. Weise M., Katranuschkov P. & Scherer R. J. (2003): Generalised Model Subset Definition Schema. In: Amor R. (ed.) "Construction IT: Bridging the Distance", Proc. of the CIB-W78 Workshop, 23-25 April 2003, Waiheke Island, Auckland, New Zealand.

56

ENHANCING ENTERPRISE COLLABORATION BY USING MULTIFACETED SERVICES

Sodki Chaari[1,2], Loubna Ali[1], Frédérique Biennier[1], Joël Favrel[1], Chokri Ben Amar[2]

INSA de Lyon - LIESP, Lyon, FRANCE
{sodki.chaari, loubna.ali, frederique.biennier, joel.favrel}@insa-lyon.fr
ENI de Sfax – REGIM, Sfax, TUNISIA
Chokri.benamar@enis.rnu.tn

In fast changing markets, dynamic collaboration ability involves establishing and "enacting" business relationships on the fly in an adaptive way. Such dynamic organization relies on interoperable and agile IT solutions. A contemporary approach for addressing these critical issues is the Service Oriented Architecture which can be introduced to implement opened and flexible information system. Accordingly, collaborative processes can be implemented as a chain of services resulting of a service composition process. Nevertheless, combining "directly" elementary IT services from different enterprises may lack of security (as the different enterprises can get information of the partner IS organization) and leads to highly complex system due to the IT service granularity. To overcome these limits, we have developed a service oriented enterprise model which transforms enterprise structure as a set of well defined Virtual Service. Virtual Services are used to orchestrate more elementary IT services and are combined together to form the service chain according to different policies. As contractual relationships between enterprises are concerned, a particular attention must be paid on the service level agreements to support an end to end convenient quality of service level. That is why, we propose to couple the Virtual Service description to a dynamic service level management system, orchestrated thanks to elementary agents.

1   CONTEXT

Nowadays, organizations are more and more centred on their core competencies and outsource secondary tasks. This outsourcing policy leads to stronger inter-organisational relationships often based on service customer/service supplier relationships to adapt and increase continuously the global performance level and gain a competitive advantage. Consequently, enterprises focus has shifted from the improvement of their internal organizational level to the outsourcing strategy and the inter-organizational level. The combination of service consumer and service provider can be seen as global virtual enterprise which can be introduced to a third party as a single entity.

Such collaborative organizations can be more or less stable, depending on the parties contracting conditions and on the environment context which may require more or less flexibility and agility (Kutvonen et al., 2005). This agility constraint, especially in fast changing environments, involves continuous adaptation of both the enterprise internal organization and collaboration partners selection. This context leads to the emergence of dynamic virtual markets in which partners are selected for short or midterm collaboration (Bartelt and Lamersdorf, 2001). Consequently, a highly dynamic approach is required to create or retain a competitive position for

Chaari, S., Ali, L., Biennier, F., Favrel, J., Amar, C.B., 2007, in IFIP International Federation for Information Processing, Volume 243, Establishing the Foundation of Collaborative Networks; eds. Camarinha-Matos, L., Afsarmanesh, H., Novais, P., Analide, C.; (Boston: Springer), pp. 521–528.

such an organization where service consumers dynamically determine which service providers will be selected to support the collaborative business process enactment. We define such a collaborative strategy as dynamic business process collaboration. This paradigm implies dynamic selection, contracting, composition and execution of business services.

Several works have addressed this efficient and fast dynamic business process collaboration: from the structured electronic collaboration between organizations achieved by Electronic Data Interchange (EDI) to frameworks enabling composition, service orchestration, contract enactment, executing and monitoring business services. Nevertheless, as the EDI approach focus on structured data interchange trough electronic transport media (Wob, 2000), it leads to a static connection between partners and not so much on process integration in dynamic business service collaboration. On the other hand, several approaches have been proposed to support inter-organization collaboration, by extending traditional Workflow Management System (WfMS) technology to distributed, Internet-based scenarios. For example the WISE project (Lazcano et al., 2000) proposes an infrastructure to support inter-organizational process: collaboration processes (named virtual business processes) are built thanks to black box services published by potential partners in different registries. Nevertheless as the resulting process consists in the fixed orchestration of "concrete" IT services, it does not exhibit flexibility or agility and a particular attention must be paid on Information System (IS) interoperability.

To support this interoperability requirement, standards are emerging and allow a more dynamic connection between organizations, typically through the use of Internet and XML technology such as the frameworks based on ebXML (Choi et al., 2004) or RosettaNet (Sundaram and Shim, 2001). Nevertheless, these approaches lack of process integration which may lead to inconsistent service chains.

Focusing on process integration leads either on a multiple Workflow management strategy (as the cross flow project) or on a service composition approach (as in eFlow project). Multi Workflow management strategy, as proposed in the CrossFlow project (Grefen et al., 2000) involves the Workflow connection according to a service outsourcing logic. In this case, a service specification is detailed thanks to a contract described in a XML-based specification language. The contract provides the structure of the Workflow which implements the service in combination with other useful ones. The meta-model of both the inter-organizational process and the service structure is the WfMC process meta-model. A service matchmaker (based on the CORBA Trading Service) allows retrieving contract satisfying specific requirements. Services are managed by Workflow management systems and the inter-organization process enactment is performed by Cooperative Support Services (CSS's), which link the different Workflow management systems of the involved organizations through appropriate Proxy Gateways.

On the other hand, the service composition approach as in the eFlow (Casati and Shan, 2001) involves specifying, enacting and monitoring composite e-Services. A composite service is described as a process schema (*i.e.* a graph which combines basic or composite services and defines the order of execution among the nodes in the process). Service heterogeneity is taken into account as eFlow provides adapters for services that support various B2B interaction protocols such as RosettaNet.

Nevertheless, such collaborative strategy relies mostly on the Information System agility and interoperability. These constraints can be partially taken into account thanks to Service-Oriented Architecture (SOA) and particularly the Web service. Such SOA based IS can reinforce a business environment with a flexible infrastructure and processing environment. thanks to independent, reusable automated business process and systems functions (services) to either end-user applications or to other services distributed in a network, via published and discoverable interfaces (Alamri et al., 2006, Alonso et al., 2004, Papazoglou, 2003). Nevertheless, this approach fits well the IT implementation constraint but needs improvements to fit the collaborative enterprise requirements.

Accordingly, we extend this approach to the global enterprise level, and not only to the IT level. The result is a flexible, agile, managed SOA ecosystem that supports dynamic enterprise collaboration. This architecture is based on SOA and extends it to a Service Oriented Enterprise (SOE) (Chaari et al., 2006). Typically, a Service Oriented Enterprise is an enterprise which implements and exposes its business processes through a set of well defined business services. Such services are organized into a multifaceted service called Virtual Services (VS) which bridge the business-oriented world of dynamic business collaboration and the Web service technologies. The main issue of this work consists in improving the IT service structure and functionalities to enable dynamic and flexible business process collaboration through VS composition (section 2) including end to end service level management (section 3).

2   VIRTUAL SERVICE ARCHITECTURE

The central feature of the Service Oriented Enterprise is the alignment of both IT and business sides. In fact, we define two abstraction levels: IT services (i.e. technical services) and business services. On the IT side, Service Oriented Architecture can be built thanks to traditional methods so that a well defined set of IT services can be implemented and orchestrated. Business services are associated to the enterprise business functionalities. They correspond to a set of fine-grained services called business objects and more coarse-grained services called business components. These business components encapsulate the Workflow logic of an activity or the business process they expose. Typically business components are made of business objects which are composed of lower level services, i.e. IT services.

This integration logic aims both at reducing the global complexity (as the Virtual Service orchestrates several concrete services) and increasing the IS security (as the VS encapsulates the lower level IS components and the VS publication is controlled by well defined security policy). As a result, the SOE offers a set of Virtual Services which represent a combination of related IT/Business services to a single logical service. A virtual Service provides no direct business function but offers a global view over those services for customers. Consequently, a Virtual Service can be processed and combined as a traditional Web service, but as its objective is not to define new application programming interfaces (APIs) or new standards; it enhances the Web service concept. The VS builds a higher-level structure which hides the traditional discovery, selection and composition functions so that it simplifies the service deployment by reducing the orchestration complexity. It also provides self-management capabilities related to the service level agreement required.

Consequently, building a service chain relies on the Virtual Service composition process including a multi criteria partner and Virtual Service selection (for example these criteria can be: due date, costs management rules, partner trust, and required service level...) and the concrete service interconnection process. To simplify the VS selection, criteria are gathered in consistent policies described as XML documents. The global orchestration is first achieved by connecting the Virtual Service and then connecting the different IT service chains orchestrated by the different Virtual Services each of them orchestrating the related concrete services. The aggregation of different services belonging to a Virtual Service is achieved through Web service composition languages like BPEL (Andrews et al., 2003). The default model underlying BPEL is that an abstract process is shared among the partners but executable business process remains private to each partner. However, this does not suit the dynamic business process collaboration where service provider wants to provide explicitly information about internal process structure and evolution to partners and enable them to monitor and control an internal process. Developing adapted service monitoring functions involves connecting the service chain to the Service Level Agreements (SLA) chain. Nevertheless, actual SLA frameworks are often limited to elementary technical views and do not fit the service chain constraint. Consequently, we propose to extend the Virtual Service description by adding a Service Level Management (SLM) facet (figure 1), used to orchestrate management agents so that quality of service can be introduced as a key element in the service composition policy.

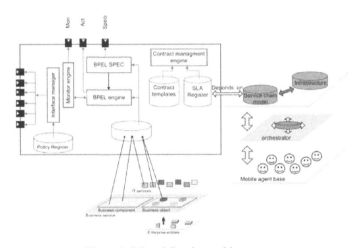

Figure 1: Virtual Service architecture

3 A DISTRIBUTED AND DYNAMIC SLM

While building a service chain, one must introduce a service management facet to control and monitor the global chain execution. Such end to end Service Level Management is a complex task which must be adapted dynamically to the current service chain, infrastructure capability.

SLM is the set of activities required to measure and manage the quality of service provided to end users (Bissel et al., 2000). SLM represents a broader framework for developing and executing Service Level Agreements (Engel, 1999, Verma, 1999). These works are mostly focusing on telecommunication services.

While building the SLA chain describing the QoS requirements, a consistent quality monitoring system must be defined accordingly so that the end to end service level can be monitored.

To set the SLA recommendation of quality of service, Key Quality and Key Performance Indicators (KQI/KPI) are used to measure specific aspects of application or services performance. The global quality of service is described thanks to KQI aggregated in KPI. Then SLA is defined between interconnected services to define KPI goals (TheOpenGROUP, 2004). Consequently, contractual relationships between business application leads to a SLA chain (figure 2).

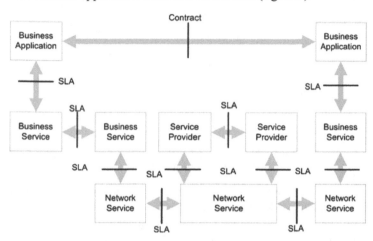

Figure 2: Expanded view of SLA in achieving the End-to-End SLA (TheOpenGROUP, 2004, page 21)

As the global service chain performance level is related to both the organization and the support infrastructure, we propose to include both organizational and operational (i.e. infrastructure related) information in the Service Level Management. Our system consists in three main interconnected parts (Ali et al., 2006): first, the process description area (organizational level), second, the monitoring information area (management level) and lastly the management process or the implementation area (infrastructure level). This architecture leads to a global service chain model (figure 3) used to guide the management service orchestration. As the organizational area is defined by the Virtual Service orchestration, we reduce this description to the distributed business process according to a Workflow organization, coupled to the information system description. Then, the Virtual Services implementation requires IT resources, i.e. concrete services. These resources (presented in the monitoring area), can be associated either to software (mostly application and information parts) or to hardware resources (workstations, servers, communication network equipments...). Consequently, different monitoring information (log files, equipment activity measures...) and convenient SLA patterns can be related to the exact "concrete service chain" (figure 3).

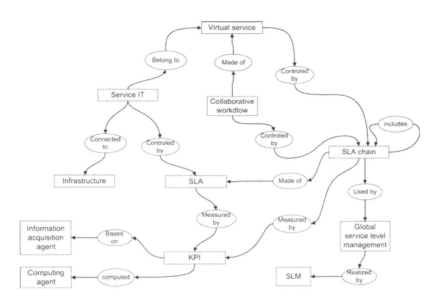

Figure 3: Service chain model

To fit the partner autonomy requirement as well as the end-to-end dynamic service chain requirement, a decentralized management organization must be set. Moreover, due to the agility constraints, an evolving management infrastructure must be implemented. To fit this requirement, we propose a mobile agent architecture including different agent types that can be orchestrated to set adapted management functions dynamically (figure 4).

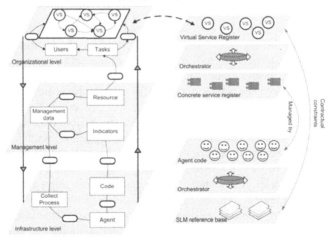

Figure 4: Multi-level monitoring system

Each management unit has to orchestrate the convenient service management agents according to the current context. Management features (both those dealing with the business activity management and those related to the infrastructure monitoring) are based on data collection, indicators building processes and actions (configuration, policy parameter adjustment...). Orchestrating the global management system consists in the convenient combination of three main types of agent instantiated from the agent patterns stored in the SLM reference data base:

- **Itinerary agents** are in charge of the "mobility management»: they have to manage an itinerary (for example a global service chain or a set of similar infrastructure elements), to collect information or to configure parameters on target nodes. After achieving their own process, they have to return the results to the "management node" in charge of the management area (i.e. a particular service chain or a part of the infrastructure). These agents consist in two parts: first an itinerary description and management function and an action part (starting a code agent, installing and starting an action agent...). They are used to collect information on similar infrastructure elements or to get indicator from the different services belonging to a same chain.
- **Code agents** are in charge of running the indicator building programs to set the complex measures computed from the basic data. These processes can be executed in a distributed way on the different nodes. In this case itinerary agents are used to send computing parameters and bring back the computed results to the area manager.
- **Action agents** are used to orchestrate the area management: according to the analysis results, these agents are in charge of setting the convenient itinerary, code and action agents.

4   CONCLUSION

In this work, in order to enhance dynamic inter-enterprise collaboration based on SOA, we introduced a Virtual Service which correspond to a set of related IT and business services. This Virtual Service is associated to a Service Level Agreements (SLA) and offer also capabilities to manage contracts and to monitor related services. We use a dynamic SLM based on mobile agent orchestration to apply the SLA constraints in order to manage and monitor the execution of services.

Further works will integrate more closely the policy-based service composition process with the enactment of the convenient management system so that management patterns could be identified and re-used to improve the system dynamic enactment.

5   REFERENCES

1. Alamri, A., and, M. E. and Saddik, A. E., 2006, Classification of the state-of-the-art dynamic web services composition techniques, International Journal for Web and Grid Services, 2(2), pp. 148–166.
2. Ali, L., Mathieu, H. and Biennier, F., 2006, Monitoring and Managing a Distributed Networks using Mobile Agents, In 2nd IEEE International Conference on Information and Communication Technologies, Damascus, Syria, pp. 3377-3382.
3. Alonso, G., Casati, F., Kuno, H. and Machiraju, V., 2004, Web services Concepts, Architectures and Application, Springer Verlag.
4. Andrews, T., Curbera, F., Dholakia, H., Goland, Y., Klein, J., Leymann, F., Liu, K., Roller, D., Smith, D., Thatte, S., Trickovic, I. and Weerawarana, S., 2003, Business Process Execution Language for Web Services Version 1.1 available at: http://www-128.ibm.com/developerworks/library/specification/ws-bpel/.

5.   Bartelt, A. and Lamersdorf, W., 2001, A Multi-criteria Taxonomy of Business Models in Electronic Commerce, In Second International WorkshopElectronic Commerce (WELCOM), Heidelberg, Germany, pp. 193-205.
6.   Bissel, T., Bogen, M., Bonkowski, C. and Hadamschek, V., 2000, Service level management with agent technology, Computer Networks, 34(6), pp. 831-841.
7.   Casati, F. and Shan, M., 2001, Dynamic and Adaptive Composition of e-Services, Information Systems, 6(3).
8.   Chaari, S., Biennier, F., Benamar, C. and Favrel, J. (2006) In Knowledge Enterprise: Intelligent Strategies in Product Design, Manufacturing, and Management, Shanghai, China, pp. 920-925.
9.   Choi, B., Raghu, T. S. and Vinze, A., 2004, Addressing a standards creation process: a focus on ebXML, International Journal of Human-Computer Studies, 61(5), pp. 627-648.
10. Engel, F., 1999, The role of service level agreements in the internet service provider industry, International Journal of Network Management, 9(5), pp. 299-301.
11. Grefen, P., Aberer, K., Hoffner, Y. and Ludwig, H., 2000, CrossFlow: Cross-Organizational Workflow Management in Dynamic Virtual Enterprises, International Journal of Computer Systems Science & Engineering, 15(5), pp. 277-290.
12. Kutvonen, L., Metso, J. and Ruokolainen, T., 2005, Inter-enterprise collaboration management in dynamic business networks, In International Conference on Cooperative Information Systems (CoopIS2005), Agia Napa, Cyprus, pp. 593-611.
13. Lazcano, A., Alonso, G., Schuldt, H. and Schuler, C., 2000, The WISE approach to electronic commerce, International Journal of Computer Systems Science & Engineering, special issue on Flexible Workflow Technology Driving the Networked Economy, 15(5), pp. 345-357.
14. Papazoglou, M., 2003, Service oriented computing: concepts, characteristics and directions, In the 4th IEEE International Conference on Web Information Systems Engineering, Italy, pp. 3-12.
15. Sundaram, M. and Shim, S. S. Y., 2001, Infrastructure for B2B Exchanges with RosettaNet, In Third International Workshop on Advanced Issues of E-Commerce and Web-Based Information Systems, pp. 110-119.
16. TheOpenGROUP, 2004, SLA Management Handbook, available at: http://www.opengroup.org/pubs/catalog/g045.htm.
17. Verma, D., 1999, Service Level Agreements on IP Networks, Macmillan Technical Publishing.
18. Wob, W., 2000, XML and Meta Data Based EDI for Small Enterprises, In 11th International Conference on Database and Expert Systems Applications (DEXA 2000), London, UK, pp. 357-365.

PART 18

WEB SERVICES AND FUSION

57	# APPLICATION OF THE FUSION APPROACH FOR ASSISTED COMPOSITION OF WEB SERVICES

Spiros Alexakis, Markus Bauer, Albina Pace, Alexa Schumacher
CAS Software AG, Wilhelm-Schickard-Str. 10-12, 76131 Karlsruhe, GERMANY
spiros.alexakis@cas.de markus.bauer@cas.de albina.pace@cas.de
alexa.schumacher@cas.de

Andreas Friesen
SAP Research, CEC Karlsruhe, Vincenz-Prießnitz-Str. 1, 76131 Karlsruhe, GERMANY
andreas.friesen@sap.com

Athanassios Bouras
Institute of Communication and Computer Systems (ICCS),
9, Iroon Polytechniou str., Zografou Campus, 15780 Athens, GREECE
bouras@mail.ntua.gr

Dimitrios Kourtesis
South East European Research Centre (SEERC),
17 Mitropoleos Str., 54624 Thessaloniki, GREECE
dkourtesis@seerc.org

The FUSION approach proposes both a conceptual framework and a system architecture that supports the composition of business processes using semantically annotated web services as building blocks. Results will be validated by supporting collaborative commercial proof-of-concept pilots. The FUSION approach will facilitate trans-national pilot cases having operations spanning the enlarged Europe, in particular: integration of transactions of a franchising firm, provision of career and human resource management services, collaboration of companies in a chain of schools of foreign languages. The paper provides an overview on the FUSION approach and illustrates how it can be applied on one of the pilot cases.

1   INTRODUCTION

Service Oriented Architecture allows systems to be implemented using a wide range of technologies. SOA systems are defined as a set of loosely coupled services. In order to interoperate, services are described using formal definitions such as WSDL. High level languages such as BPEL allow us to define the orchestration for the fine grained services exposed by different systems which then can be incorporated into workflows and business processes implemented in composite applications.

Together these technologies lay the grounds for Enterprise Application Integration; however for systems to be interoperable, inconsistencies at the data and functional level need to be overcome.

FUSION addresses these interoperability issues by proposing a conceptual framework and a system architecture that supports semantically enhanced, reusable business processes through the use of semantic annotations of Web services.

Alexakis, S., Bauer, M., Pace, A., Schumacher, A., Friesen, A., Bouras, A., Koutesis, D., 2007, in IFIP International Federation for Information Processing, Volume 243, Establishing the Foundation of Collaborative Networks; eds. Camarinha-Matos, L., Afsarmanesh, H., Novais, P., Analide, C.; (Boston: Springer), pp. 531–538.

2   FUSION APPROACH OVERVIEW

In order to facilitate the resolution of structural and semantic differences of the input and output messages exchanged between interoperable Web services of a defined process, an Enterprise Integration Ontology (ENIO) is introduced. ENIO is a multi-layered and multi-faceted Ontology. Layering defines the level of abstraction and the level of exposure of the Ontology whereas the facets represent the role of the concepts within the solution. The ontology provides a common reference for data semantics through the data facet; enables search and discovery of Web Services through the functional facet and enables process composition via the process facet. The ontology also introduces an upper layer covering domain independent concepts. The domain dependent extensions are then expressed in the facets (Friesen, 2007).

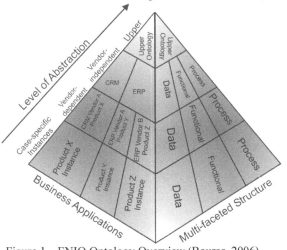

Figure 1 – ENIO Ontology Overview (Bouras, 2006)

2.1   The architecture

The FUSION architecture is made up of the following components:

Semantic Analyzer - Concepts Designer
The Concepts Designer is responsible for handling and managing the multi-layered, multifaceted FUSION Ontology during each phase of the ontology lifecycle.

Semantic Analyzer - Semantic Profiler
The Semantic Profiler is a graphical editor for adding annotations utilizing classes and instances of all the developed facets of the FUSION Ontology through SA-WSDL. It also generates XSLT transformations for up and down-casting functionality, i.e. it provides a mapping from concrete system dependent data types into ontology concepts and vice versa.

Semantic Analyzer - Process Designer
The Process Designer enables the user to reuse Abstract Process Models, discover candidate services automatically, check for and resolve data incompatibilities and

finally, ground the Abstract Process Models to executable BPEL process code using the discovered services.

Ontology Repository
The Ontology Repository module constitutes a fully functional file system, where concepts, classes and instances of the facets of the FUSION Ontology are stored.

Integration Mechanism
The integration mechanism is the execution environment of the FUSION system.

3 PILOT USE CASES

The FUSION approach will be validated in the frame of collaborative commerce proof-of-concept pilots. Each pilot has operations spanning the Enlarged Europe, in particular:

- Germanos: integration of transactions of a franchising firm (Greece, Poland, Romania, Bulgaria, Ukraine, Cyprus and FYROM)
- Interjob: provision of career and human resource management services (Hungary and Germany)
- Pharos: collaboration of companies in a chain of schools (Bulgaria, FYROM, Albania).

These pilots represent different interoperability aspects. While in the Pharos use case all systems have been individually tailored, Germanos only deploys standard software. Processes at Germanos are already automated while the processes of Pharos are performed by mail, phone or fax. Other aspects of complementarity are complexity and intercultural focus. Germanos processes are rather complex, while the exchange of HR information in the Interjob case needs harmonisation due to intercultural differences. In the following, the Pharos case will be explained in more detail.

4 COLLABORATIVE PROCESS BEFORE AND AFTER: PHAROS EXAMPLE

4.1 Scenario

The IT infrastructure of the Pharos network is not homogeneous. Schools in Bulgaria, FYROM and Albania use different variants of *F97*, a custom-built system offering certain core CRM and ERP business functions, customised to support the specific needs of Schools in different countries. On the other hand, the Regional Directorate at Sofia and all Country Headquarters rely on *MIS*, an information management and decision-support system customised specifically for the needs of the Pharos network.

4.2   Demonstration process: student transfer to another school

For the purpose of demonstration of the FUSION approach we have selected the process of a student transfer between schools, as it involves software systems of two schools and one headquarter with bidirectional information exchange.

Before FUSION
A student can be transferred to another school, for example if he moves or if he wishes to visit a different course. In order to change from the old school to the new school, he has to contact the Country Headquarters to initiate the transfer. The Country Headquarter then has to make sure that:

- The student's school and course specific data is retrieved from the old school and forwarded to the new school.
- The student gets properly registered at the new school (provided there are still free places available in the courses the student wants to attend).
- The Country Headquarters internal bookkeeping is updated.

The information exchange necessary for the execution of the steps above is performed by phone, fax or email. System records are edited and updated by hand.

With FUSION:
To improve this situation, an automated process has to be introduced. Its building blocks are Web Services that will be introduced at the schools F97 systems and at the Country HQ MIS. The process consists of the following steps:

1. The user issues a transfer student request, specifying the student's global Customer ID and the IDs of the old school and the new school.
2. Using the Customer ID, the Student's Customer Record is provided by the Country HQ MIS.
3. From the Customer Record, the student's school-specific Student ID (as given and maintained by the old school) is extracted. Using this ID, the school-specific registration data is retrieved.
4. The Student's Registration is then forwarded to the new school. The new school may reject the student, e.g. if there are no places available.
5. If the student is accepted the Country HQ's Customer Record for the student is updated with the new registration information received from the new school.
6. As a last step, the student is unregistered from the old school and the process terminates successfully.

In the next section, we show how Pharos' systems can be prepared to run this reworked process and how the FUSION approach simplifies its implementation.

5   FUSION APPROACH APPLIED TO PHAROS

The FUSION System Lifecycle consists of the following phases: (The process execution is beyond our scope, as it mainly consists of the execution of standard BPEL code.)

5.1   Web service enablement of the involved applications

In FUSION, an enterprise application is called Web Service Enabled, if the relevant functionality is exposed in the form of industry standard web services. FUSION restricts the concept of Web Services to those services that have their interfaces described in WSDL and use SOAP-formatted XML messages (Mitra, 2003).

In the Pharos use case both involved legacy systems do not expose web services. After the identification of relevant business functionality, there are two possibilities for exposing web services. The first approach includes the restructuring of the corresponding source code parts in order to make them run and deploy as Web Servers or as components within Web servers or Web Application containers. Alternatively, adapter components for the legacy functions have to be created.

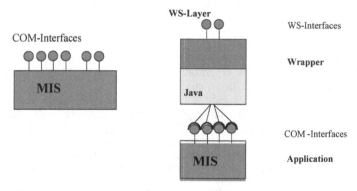

Figure 2 – Possible migration strategies for *the Pharos use case*

The above figure depicts both solutions: on the left a Delphi server component has been enhanced with additional Web Service interfaces, on the right part a Web Service layer in Java communicates with the unchanged server component of MIS through RPCs (remote procedure calls) via DCOM.

For Pharos, the first option has been chosen, as both systems involved have been programmed in Delphi 6. The toolkit from INDY (www.indyproject.org) provides the technical basis for publishing SOAP based Web Services from Delphi Code. Web Services to be published include:

1.   *transferStudent(CustomerID, NewSchoolID)*
2.   *getCustomerRecord(CustomerID)*
3.   *getStudentRegistration (StudentID, SchoolID)*
4.   *registerStudent (studentRegistration, NewSchoolID)*

5.2   Ontology Engineering phase

The Ontology Engineering phase comprises all activities needed for customising the shared semantic model that constitutes the cornerstone of a FUSION EAI solution; the FUSION EAI Ontology. The software tool supporting the user's activities within this procedure is the FUSION Concepts Designer, a visual tool facilitating the creation, extension, customisation, and maintenance of multi-layered and multi-faceted ontologies. In the concrete case the following steps have to be followed:

1. Define a physical location (Web Server Directory with read/write capabilities) in order to deploy the Ontology needed for Pharos, for instance *http://extranet. pharos.bg/ontologies/PharosOntology.owl*
2. For the Functional Facet, examine the operations in the Enterprise Service WSDL file, in order to determine what kind of functional semantics are needed. In the PHAROS case the *setStudentRegistration operation* raises the need for adding a new concept *registerStudent* under *FunctionalFacetEntity*
3. For each Functional Facet concept that is created we must also specify the Input and Output Data Facet Concepts that it relates to.
4. If the Data Facet entity does not exist then it must be created. In the Pharos case *registerStudent* requires as input a *#Student* class. A Student can be considered as a subclass of FUSION's standard concept *#Person* but additional data types and object properties must be added (e.g. *hasGrade*)

5.3   Semantic Uplifting phase

In this phase Web Service descriptions are lifted from the syntactic, to the semantic level, through references to the common semantic model, the FUSION EAI Ontology. The phase consists of the following steps:

1. For each wsdl:portType or wsdl:operation: annotate with the respective functional facet concept, best describing the function being performed

    ```
    <wsdl:operation name="inputSetStudentRegistration">
        <wsdl:input name="inputSetStudentRegistrationRequest
            message="impl:SetStudentRegistration"/>
        <sawsdl:attrExtensions
            sawsdl:modelReference="http://extranet.pharos.bg/ontologies/
    PharosOntology.owl#registerStudent"/>
        </wsdl:operation>
    ```
2. For each wsdl:part: annotate with the respective data concept, best describing the data being transported by the message part
3. For each wsdl:part: define XSLT transformations for translating the data from XSD to the OWL data concept in the previous step, and vice versa
4. Provide the location of the target mediator Web Server, and any other information required for generating and deploying the mediator service
5. Publish the Semantic Profile to the FUSION Integration Mechanism

5.4   Process Design phase

During the process design phase, EAI scenarios involving several "semantically uplifted" business applications are realised. This is supported by the Process Designer which allows instantiating the Abstract Process Models by discovering appropriate services and generates a grounded BPEL4WS model, to be deployed for execution. For the Pharos example in manual composition the phase consists of the following steps:

*   A process model is created in abstract BPEL (using a BPEL editor) and annotated (via comments) with concepts from the functional facet of the ontology. The snippet below shows an invoke activity in BPEL which is annotated with a comment containing a link to the concept *GetCustomerRecord.*
*   <!– function="GetCustomerRecord"

- concept="http://.../FusionOntology#GetCustomerRecord" –>
-- This process model is uploaded to a repository and an instance is created in the process facet of the ontology, with a link to the process model in the repository. This process model may now be reused by other Business Consultants by:
- Browsing through the ontology process facet for the best suited process model. In this case, under the category *Inbound_Outbound_Logistics*, the process model *#Student_School_Transfer_CBPManual*, which has a property hasProcessModel containing a link to the BPEL file http:// *http://extranet.pharos.bg/processes/StudentTransfer.bpel*
- Loading the BPEL file in the process model customizer, which allows the user to view the process graphically, remove optional tasks and invoke discovery, grounding and deployment.

6   RELATED WORK

FUSION aims at simplifying Web service composition with the use of abstract process templates and improves Web service discovery by taking functional semantics into consideration. The idea of replacing abstract functions by executable Web services during runtime was proposed in (Mueller, 2004). FUSION implements this idea by adding semantic annotations to Web services for discovery.

The METEOR-S framework (Verma, 2005) makes use of semantics to describe functional and non functional capabilities of Web services and allows binding of Web services to abstract processes. Data heterogeneities are resolved with the use of proxies. FUSION employs a similar approach, however introduces the concept of optional functions so that abstract processes are customisable and hence reusable. The FUSION ontology also allows for annotation of services such that they may be composed automatically (Friesen, 2007) using planning techniques.

Other research in dynamic workflows such as (Davulcu, 1999) and (Mueller, 2004) are based on homogenous environments and require no mediation amongst services.

7   SUMMARY AND BENEFITS

FUSION addresses the need of many enterprises to implement business processes that involve a number of business partners and information systems. Current software architecture trends (SOA, Web Services and BPEL) support the implementation of these business processes, as they provide a technological solution for the communication between independent systems. However, implementing business processes on the basis of a number of different underlying information systems – even if these expose suitable Web Services – is still a costly and error prone task.

FUSION addresses these issues by defining methodology, architecture and tools that extend the concept of SOA by utilizing Semantic Web Service technologies.

The applicability of the FUSION Approach is demonstrated in the frame of pilots from different application domains, involving organisations of different size and structure. Each pilot benefits by the introduction of automated business processes, which can be cost-effectively implemented by the FUSION EAI Ontology.

Acknowledgements

This paper is supported by the **FUSION FP6-027385 Project**.

8   REFERENCES

1.   Friesen A, Alazeib A, Balogh A, Bauer M, Bouras A, Gouvas P, Mentzas G, Pace A. Towards semantically-assisted design of collaborative business processes in EAI scenarios, INDIN, 2007.
2.   FUSION Consortium. FUSION Deliverable 6.1 – FUSION Initial Exploitation Plan, 2006.
3.   Meyer B. Object-Oriented Software Construction, 2nd ed., Prentice-Hall, 1997.
4.   Mitra N. SOAP – W3C Recommendation, June 2003. http://www.w3.org/TR/soap
5.   K. Verma, K. Gomadam, A. P. Sheth, J. Miller, Z. Wu, The METEOR-S Approach for Configuring and Executing Dynamic Web Processes, 2005.
6.   R. Mueller, U. Greiner, E. Rahm, Agentwork: A Workflow System Supporting Rule-Based Workflow Adaptation, 2004.
7.   H. Davulcu, M. Kifer, L. Pokorny, C. R. Ramakrishnan, I. V. Ramakrishnan, S. Dawson, Modelling and Analysis of Interactions in Virtual Enterprises, 1999.
8.   A. Bouras, P. Gouvas, K. Kalaboukas, G. Mentzas, A Semantic Service Oriented Infrastructure for EAI, 2006.

58

SEMANTIC INTEGRATION OF BUSINESS APPLICATIONS ACROSS COLLABORATIVE VALUE NETWORKS

Athanasios Bouras[1], Panagiotis Gouvas[1], Dimitrios Kourtesis[2], Gregoris Mentzas[1]

[1] *Institute of Communication and Computer Systems, National Technical University of Athens, 9, Iroon Polytechniou Str., 15780 Zografou, Athens, GREECE*
{bouras, pgouvas, gmentzas}@mail.ntua.gr
[2] *SEERC - South East European Research Centre, A Research Centre of the University of Sheffield and CITY Liberal Studies, 17 Mitropoleos Str, 54624 Thessaloniki, GREECE*
dkourtesis@seerc.org

If we try to increase the level of automation in Business-to-Business (B2B) Enterprise Application Integration (EAI) scenarios, we confront challenges related to the resolution of data heterogeneities, service discovery and process composition. In this paper, we propose the Enterprise Interoperability Ontology (ENIO) that provides a shared, common understanding of data, services and processes within B2B integration scenarios. ENIO consists of an Upper Enterprise Interoperability Ontology (Upper ENIO), which is based on the DOLCE-SUMO alignment, with extensions called facets that cover several dimensions of the EAI domain. Each facet contains a relative meta-model that utilizes widely adopted standards. Finally, we demonstrate the utilization of ENIO in a real-world B2B scenario across a franchisor-franchisees collaborative value network.

1   INTRODUCTION

Over the last couple of decades, we have witnessed an enormous increase in competitiveness among companies, leading towards the formulation of new business models and structures, such as virtual enterprises and collaborative value networks. These emerging business-to-business (B2B) formulas constitute alliances of member enterprises that come together to share skills or core competencies and resources to create economic value, which takes the form of knowledge, intelligence, products, or services. Value networks require significant systemic support that actually intends to automate part of the creation process, as well as the operation and the B2B interoperability of these enterprise models (Cardoso & Oliveira, 2005).

The goal of B2B Integration, which could be considered as a specialization of Enterprise Applications Integration (EAI), is to connect enterprises with their trading partners electronically through organized business event exchanges containing business data in order to conduct business between enterprises (Bussler, 2002), based on the integration and streamline of heterogeneous business processes across the collaborative value network.

Bouras, A., Gouvas, P., Kourtesis, D., Mentzas, G., 2007, in IFIP International Federation for Information Processing, Volume 243, Establishing the Foundation of Collaborative Networks; eds. Camarinha-Matos, L., Afsarmanesh, H., Novais, P., Analide, C.; (Boston: Springer), pp. 539–546.

Current industrial EAI, and B2B as well, trends and technologies, like Service-Oriented Architecture (SOA), Enterprise Service Bus (ESB), and Web Services technologies, are up to now quite mature. However, if we try to increase the level of automation in integration scenarios, we confront several problems and challenges, such as a) data and message level heterogeneities between interoperating services, b) insufficient search and discovery of published Web Services in a common registry, and c) inadequate Web Process composition with regard to the desired functionality and the operational requirements. The problem that still exists, which the traditional, syntactic integration technologies are weak to solve, refers to the formalization and the documentation of the semantics related to the interfaces and the data structures of the deployed Web Services. This lack of formal semantics regarding the applications and services to be integrated makes it difficult for software engineers and developers to manually interconnect heterogeneous applications impeding automation within EAI (Haller et al., 2005).

We claim that these needs impose the use and interpretation of semantics in EAI and that a semantically enriched approach will hopefully eliminate the problem of knowing the content and structure of information resources, as well as the structure and architecture of heterogeneous enterprise applications (Friesen et al., 2007).

In this paper, we propose the Enterprise Interoperability Ontology (ENIO), an EAI Ontology that captures and represents formally all entities involved in B2B EAI scenarios, i.e. data, services and processes and tries to address the EAI challenges mentioned above. ENIO comprises a foundational, upper-level EAI ontology, which is based on the alignment of DOLCE and SUMO, with quite a few extensions (which we call "facets") that cover several dimensions of the EAI domain. Each facet contains a relative meta-model that utilizes widely-adopted standards. Finally, we demonstrate the utilization of ENIO in a real-world B2B scenario across a franchisor-franchisees collaborative value network.

The structure of this paper is as follows: in the following section, we present the goals, the role, the structure and the formalism of the ENIO, while, in section 3, we describe the utilization of each facet of the ENIO within the scope of an integration scenario across a franchisor-franchisees collaborative value network. We overview related work in section 4 and conclude with further work and concluding remarks.

2   THE ENTERPRISE INTEROPERABILITY ONTOLOGY

In order to provide formal specification and analysis of B2B integration scenarios, the data, services and processes that exist within an application integration problem should be defined formally and explicitly. The Enterprise Interoperability Ontology (ENIO) that we propose represents an explicit specification of the conceptualization of the EAI domain, and structures and formalizes the procedural and operative knowledge needed to describe and resolve the given EAI problem.

The ENIO Ontology has a three-fold focus: 1) to resolve most message level heterogeneities through the formal definition of the data (-types) in the input and output messages of a service, providing a reference model of data semantics; 2) to enable effective search and discovery of services through the formal representation of the capabilities and the functionality of service operators; and 3) to assist manual process composition through (reusable) process templates (Bouras et al., 2007).

The above-mentioned goals of ENIO constitute the basis for the identification of the dimensions and the structure of the ontology. We have chosen to introduce the model of an upper ontology, which covers generic and domain-independent concepts, with several, domain-related extensions that we call facets. We have developed a three-faceted structure for ENIO: data facet; functional facet and process facet. In the following sections, we present the upper level of ENIO as well as the various facets.

We have decided to define an **Upper Ontology** for ENIO because: a) it provides a reference point and a framework for analyzing, harmonizing, and integrating existing ontologies and metadata standards; b) it provides a starting point, a predefined set of ontological entities and a ontology design pattern for building new, lower-level, domain ontologies; and c) a carefully engineered upper ontology, used as an ontology modelling basis, avoids the typical shortcomings, i.e. conceptual ambiguity and loose design, of commonly built ontologies (Oberle, 2006).

As analytically described in (Bouras et al., 2007), we are using in ENIO an alignment of DOLCE and SUMO that combines their advantages by including a core ontology (based on DOLCE) and a domain-independent ontology (based on SUMO) to establish the basic layers. The implementation of our upper ENIO Ontology is based on Smart SUMO (Oberle et al., 2006). To align SUMO to DOLCE, we pruned the upper-level of the SUMO taxonomy and aligned the remaining concepts to the appropriate DOLCE categories. During the alignment, it became apparent that grasping the intended meaning of SUMO's terms is quite difficult because of the loose merging of several theories in SUMO. Finding the best fitting super-concept in DOLCE for a SUMO term was therefore non-trivial. In addition, the design patterns of DOLCE, such as the design pattern for modelling qualities of endurants via regions, had to be taken into consideration when performing the alignment.

The **Data Facet** of ENIO aims to formally capture the semantics of messages exchanged among collaborative enterprise applications that expose their functionality as web services. The data facet facilitates dynamic data mediation by enabling the design of mappings and XSLT transformations for all service message elements (i.e. inputs and outputs) utilizing the schemaMapping attribute as in (Nagarajan et al., 2006). Two types of mappings between Web Service message elements and semantics have been identified (Nagarajan et al., 2006; Farrell & Lausen, 2006): a) mapping from the Web Service message element to the ontology concept, also called the "up-cast" and "up-level", and b) transformation from the ontology concept to the message element, called the "down-cast" and "down-level". Once the transformations are defined, two collaborative Web Services can interoperate by reusing these mappings, at run-time. As we do not intend to re-invent the wheel, we based the ENIO Data facet on the Core Components Technical Specification (CCTS). CCTS is currently the ISO 15000-5 Technical Specification and is supported and used by more than 50 projects and initiatives (including UBL and RosettaNet). The meta-model of the ENIO Data Facet ontologizes the meta-modelling elements of CCTS, i.e. Core Components (CC), Data Types, Aggregated CC, Basic CC and Association CC. For the population of the Data Facet, we have utilized as knowledge sources the following standards and vocabularies: the OASIS ebXML Core Components Dictionary, the RosettaNet Business Dictionary, the OAGIS specification and the OASIS Universal Business Language (OASIS UBL).

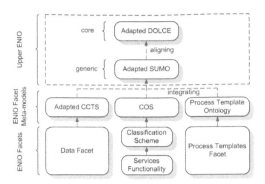

Figure 1 – The ENIO Conceptual Structure

The **Functional Facet** of ENIO defines the capabilities of enterprise services and provides classes for the annotation of services operators with functional semantics. This categorization of the intended functionality of the services combined with ontology-driven match-making algorithms may support efficient and effective discovery of published services in a business services registry. Furthermore, the Functional Facet of ENIO aims to assist manual process design, as the participation of a specific service in a business process composition scenario involves mainly the formal specification and shared understanding of its desired functionality. Our meta-model of the Functional Facet utilizes the Core Ontology of (Web) Services (COS), which is a module of the DOLCE foundational ontology.

The purpose of the **Process Facet** of ENIO is to provide means for defining collaborative business process templates and for annotating the states of Web Services with interior behavioural models that may be utilized in semi-automatic goal-driven composition. For the meta-model of the ENIO Process Facet we developed a process template ontology that follows the MIT Process Handbook methodology (Malone et al., 2003) to compose reusable process templates and includes the definitions of public views of processes and their variants, e.g. the "CRM Sales Order Processing" is a variant of the public process "Sales Order Processing". Moreover, the ENIO Process Facet meta-model classifies each public view of a process under a specific category, associates them with tasks of the Functional Facet and assigns them with exactly one role, e.g. the previously mentioned public process "CRM Sales Order Processing" is classified under the "Sales and Services" category, and is associated to a task variant of the Functional Facet class "Sales" and to the "Sales Representative" role.

Figure 1 gives a bird's eye view of the **ENIO structure**. In this paragraph, we describe the **ontology formalism** we selected for the development of ENIO. As our goal is to provide a general reference ontology for a semantically-enriched B2B EAI solution, a fine-grained axiomatisation is not needed. A semi-formal ontology providing a common vocabulary with a formal taxonomy, but without detailed logical axioms is enough for our purposes. We therefore chose a common denominator of ontology features which are present in all current ontological formalisms, including but not limited to RDFS, OWL, and WSML. The features we use are the following: concepts with formal sub-concept relation, instances with formal instantiates relation, and binary properties with single concept domain and range constraints. We have chosen OWL-DL as our implementation language because it is an already available W3C recommendation and has good tool support. Moreover, other ontology formalisms (including WSML) provide conversion utilities from and to OWL-DL. We therefore expect that ENIO can be (semi-) automatically translated into various other formats in the future, if it is needed by the target application domain.

3 THE ENIO USAGE WITHIN A COLLABORATIVE VALUE NETWORK INTEGRATION SCENARIO

Assuming a typical franchisor-franchisees value-added network, we can identify a complex IT infrastructure in the franchisor headquarters comprising several centralized, corporate systems, i.e. ERP, CRM and WMS, which are required for the coordination of the retail activity, reimbursements, logistics and the pricing policy of the chain of retail stores. On the other hand, the Point-of-Sales (PoS) retail stores should be equipped with an ERP-like Retail System that will allow the collaboration with the franchisor and will facilitate the business activities of the value network.

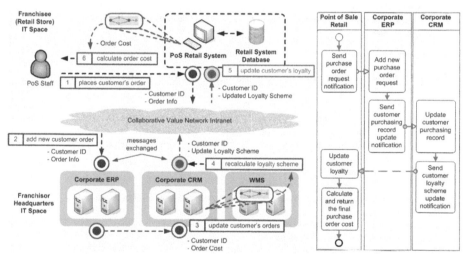

Figure 2 – Update Customer Loyalty Scheme CBP

In this enterprise context, we have identified several Collaborative Business Processes (CBPs) that compose and invoke (complex) services exposed from heterogeneous business systems. We have selected the "Update Customer Loyalty Scheme" CBP, so as to provide paradigms and demonstrate the usage of ENIO in facilitating the smooth integration of business processes in a dynamic environment. The selected CPB involves the calculation of the final cost (e.g. after discount) of a customer's order, based on the customer's loyalty scheme, which is dynamically reconfigured taking into consideration the current order, real time (see Figure 2 for more details).

The realization of the B2B integration scenario comprises two stages: a) the identification and the semantic uplifting of the involved Web Services, and b) the manual composition of the respective business process. A set of four public (non-internal) Web Services have been identified: 1) Place Order (POS Retail), 2) Add New Order (Corporate ERP), 3) Update Customer Order Record (Corporate CRM), and 4) Update Customer Loyalty (POS Retail). Following the SAWSDL annotation mechanisms, i.e. the modelReference, (Farrell & Lausen, 2006), we have introduces semantics in the syntactic description of the Web Services, utilizing the ENIO Data Facet concepts for the semantic uplifting of the Web Services input and output messages and the ENIO Functional Facet concepts for the representation of the services' operators. Tables 1 and 2 depict the semantic annotations of the first two identified services, i.e. Place Order (POS Retail), and Add New Order (ERP).

Table 1 – SAWSDL Annotations for the Place Order PoS Web Service

```
<wsdl:message name="RequestMessage">
<wsdl:part name="custID" element="CustID"
  sawsdl:modelReference="http://.../ENIO/DataFacet.owl#Customer"/>
<wsdl:part name="orderInfo" element="OrderInfo"
  sawsdl:modelReference="http://.../ENIO/DataFacet.owl#OrderInfo"/>
</wsdl:message>
<wsdl:portType name="PlaceOrder">
  <wsdl:operation name="placeOrder ">
    <wsdl:input message="RequestMessage" />
    <sawsdl:attrExtensions
      sawsdl:modelReference="http://......#CustomerPlaceOrder"/>
  </wsdl:operation>
</wsdl:portType>
```

Table 2 – SAWSDL Annotations for the Add New Order ERP Web Service

```
<wsdl:message name="RequestMessage">
  <wsdl:part name="custID" element="CustID"
  sawsdl:modelReference="http://.../ENIO/DataFacet.owl#Customer"/>
  <wsdl:part name="orderInfo" element="OrderInfo"
  sawsdl:modelReference="http://.../ENIO/DataFacet.owl#OrderInfo"/>
</wsdl:message>
<wsdl:message name="ResponseMessage">
  <wsdl:part name="cost" element="cost"
  sawsdl:modelReference="http://.../ENIO/DataFacet.owl#OrderCost"/>
</wsdl:message>
<wsdl:portType name=" AddNewOrder">
  <wsdl:operation name="addNewOrder">
    <wsdl:input  message="RequestMessage" />
    <wsdl:output message="ResponseMessage" />
    <sawsdl:attrExtensions
      sawsdl:modelReference="http://......#CustomerPlaceOrder"/>
  </wsdl:operation>
</wsdl:portType>
```

By the time the semantic uplifting of the involved services is completed and all the relative up- and down- casting, i.e. XSD2OWL and OWL2XSD, XSLT transformations, are created, we utilize the third facet of ENIO, i.e. the Process Template Facet, so as to retrieve and customize a relative process template towards the development of the "Update Customer Loyalty Scheme" abstract process template. For the Abstract Process Template formulation, apart from the flow elements, we utilize concepts of the ENIO Functional Facet to formally define the desired functionality of a service required and concepts of the ENIO Data Facet to specify the interoperable terms exchanged among collaborative services (see Figure 3). To move from the abstract, semantically-enriched process model to the "executable" process, we have to fill in this process skeleton with grounded Web Services that have been already semantically uplifted and meet the "requirements" of the abstract templates in terms of functionality required and input and output message types supported. Finally, as shown in Figure 3, the up- and down- casting transformations are utilized during execution time and facilitate the creation of XSD2XSD transformations among collaborative services, ensuring this way dynamic data mediation during run-time.

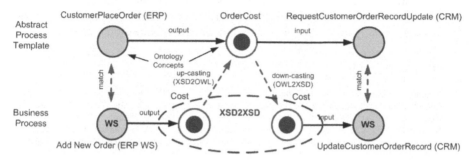

Figure 3 – Update Customer Loyalty Scheme CBP

4   RELATED WORK

There already exist some research initiatives that utilize semantics in EAI. For example, (Haller et al., 2005) have proposed to extend the notion of Service-Oriented Architectures by WSMO-based Semantic Web Services and showed how EAI benefits by it. On the other hand, (Izza et al., 2005) proposes an Ontology-Driven Service-Oriented Integration (ODSOI) that aims to extend the current web services stack technology by a semantic layer offering semantic services that can define the service semantics and also perform semantic mediation in the context of EAI. Finally, (Tektonidis et al., 2005) presents the creation of the ONAR SOA-based integration framework that enriches the semantics of the exchanged information and utilizes web ontologies to create semantic conceptualizations of the business concepts that exist inside an application.

None of these efforts, however, provides an integrated approach and a standards-based ontology to address dynamic data mediation and to facilitate service discovery and composition for business integration.

5   CONCLUSIONS AND FUTURE WORK

In this paper we have proposed an Enterprise Interoperability Ontology (ENIO) which comprises a foundational, upper-level EAI ontology, based on the alignment of DOLCE and SUMO, with extensions that cover several dimensions (facets) of the EAI domain, containing meta-models based on widely-adopted recommendations and research efforts (i.e. CCTS, COS). The upper level of ENIO has 159 classes and 90 properties, the data facet consists of 337 classes and 772 properties and the functional facet is made up of 256 classes. ENIO is available online at: http://www.imu.iccs.gr/projects/fusion/ontology/.

Moreover, we have presented the utilization of all facets of ENIO in a realistic B2B integration scenario within a franchisor-franchisees collaborative value network, comprising complex, heterogeneous systemic infrastructure. In the frame of this scenario, we have demonstrated the dynamic resolution of data heterogeneities at execution time and the semantically-assisted business process composition supported by adequate discovery of exposed enterprise services.

Our current work refers to the use of ENIO with a semantic web service-based framework that facilitates the resolution of data heterogeneity problems and assists in service discovery and manual composition in EAI. Furthermore, we are currently working towards the state-related extensions of the Upper ENIO part that will facilitate the annotation of the internal behavioural model of complex services, which are potentially utilized in semi-automatic process composition scenarios.

6   REFERENCES

1.   Bouras, A., Gouvas, P., & Mentzas, G. (2007). ENIO: An Enterprise Application Integration Ontology. In the Proceedings of the 1st International Workshop on Semantic Web Architectures for Enterprises (SWAE), DEXA'07, 3-7 September, 2007, Regensburg, Germany.
2.   Bussler, C. (2002). B2B integration technology architecture. In the Proceedings of the Fourth IEEE International Workshop on Advanced Issues of E-Commerce and Web-Based Information Systems (WECWIS 2002), Newport Beach, California, USA, June 26-28, 2002.
3.   Cardoso, H. L., & Oliveira, E. (2005). Virtual Enterprise Normative Framework within Electronic Institutions. In M.-P. Gleizes, A. Omicini & F. Zambonelli (eds.), Engineering Societies in the Agents World V, LNAI 3451, Springer, ISBN 3-540-27330-1, pp. 14-32, 2005.
4.   Farrell, J., & Lausen, H. (2006). Semantic Annotations for WSDL. W3C Working Draft.
5.   Friesen, A., A., Alazeib, A. Balogh, et al. M. Bauer, A. Bouras, P. Gouvas, G. Mentzas, A. Pace (2007) Towards semantically-assisted design of collaborative business processes in EAI scenarios, 5th IEEE International Conference on Industrial Informatics, July 23-27 Vienna.
6.   Haller, A., Gomez, J., & Bussler, C. (2005). Exposing Semantic Web Service principles in SOA to solve EAI scenarios. in Workshop on Web Service Semantics, in WWW2005.
7.   Izza, S., Vincent, L., & Burlat, P. (2005). A Unified Framework for Application Integration - an Ontology-driven Service-oriented Approach. ICEIS (1) 2005: 165-170.
8.   Malone, T.W., Crowston. K., & Herman, G.A. (2003). Organizing Business Knowledge: The MIT Process Handbook. Cambridge, MA: MIT Press, 2003.
9.   Nagarajan, M., et al. (2006). Semantic Interoperability of Enterprise Services - Challenges and Experiences. 2006 IEEE International Conference on Enterprise Services
10.   Oberle, D. (2006). Semantic Management of Middleware, volume I of The Semantic Web and Beyond. Springer, 2006.
11.   Oberle, D., Ankolekar, et al. (2006). DOLCE ergo SUMO: On Foundational and Domain Models in SWIntO, AIFB, University of Karlsruhe. July 2006.
12.   Tektonidis. D., Bokma, A., Oatley, G., & Salampasis, M. (2005). ONAR: An Ontologies-based Service-Oriented Application Integration Framework, I-ESA'05, Geneva, Switzerland.

59

WEB SERVICE DISCOVERY IN A SEMANTICALLY EXTENDED UDDI REGISTRY: THE CASE OF FUSION

Dimitrios Kourtesis[1], Iraklis Paraskakis[1], Andreas Friesen[2], Panagiotis Gouvas[3], Athanasios Bouras[3]

[1] *SEERC - South East European Research Centre,*
A Research Centre of the University of Sheffield and CITY Liberal Studies
Mitropoleos 17, 54624, Thessaloniki, GREECE
dkourtesis@seerc.org, iparaskakis@seerc.org
[2] *SAP Research, CEC Karlsruhe*
Vincenz-Prießnitz-Str. 1, D-76131 Karlsruhe, GERMANY
andreas.friesen@sap.com
[3] *Institute of Communication and Computer Systems,*
National Technical University of Athens
Iroon Polutexneiou 9, 15780 Zografou, Athens, GREECE
pgouvas@mail.ntua.gr bouras@mail.ntua.gr

Service-oriented computing is being adopted at an unprecedented rate, making the effectiveness of automated service discovery an increasingly important challenge. UDDI has emerged as a de facto industry standard and fundamental building block within SOA infrastructures. Nevertheless, conventional UDDI registries lack means to provide unambiguous, semantically rich representations of Web service capabilities, and the logic inference power required for facilitating automated service discovery. To overcome this important limitation, a number of approaches have been proposed towards augmenting Web service discovery with semantics. This paper discusses the benefits of semantically extending Web service descriptions and UDDI registries, and presents an overview of the approach put forward in project FUSION, towards semantically-enhanced publication and discovery of services based on SAWSDL.

1   INTRODUCTION

Interoperability among enterprise information systems is key to achieving business agility, especially for enterprises operating within collaborative value networks, as it largely determines their capacity to respond swiftly to changing market conditions and new collaboration opportunities. The paradigm of Service Oriented Architecture (SOA) and its manifestation in the form of Web services promise to alleviate many enterprise application interoperability barriers, thus significantly reducing the effort to establish collaborative business processes. In a SOA environment, the creation of a new business process necessitates the assembly of reusable services exposed by multiple enterprise applications into new compositions. But for services to be composed, they first need to be discovered. Designers of collaborative business processes must search for services able to perform some specific task within a workflow, and compose them to form a complex business process. When searching

Kourtesis, D., Paraskakis, I., Friesen, A., Gouvas, P., Bouras, A., 2007, in IFIP International Federation for Information Processing, Volume 243, Establishing the Foundation of Collaborative Networks; eds. Camarinha-Matos, L., Afsarmanesh, H., Novais, P., Analide, C.; (Boston: Springer), pp. 547–554.

in a pool of resources containing hundreds of Web service descriptions, discovery can become a demanding task.

This is why the Universal Description, Discovery and Integration specification (UDDI, 2002) has emerged as a de facto industry standard. UDDI registries are fundamental building blocks within a SOA infrastructure, serving as central cataloguing services for reusable software components. Nevertheless, conventional UDDI registries (v2 or v3) provide very limited means for automated service discovery (Paolucci et al, 2002), (Colgrave, Akkiraju and Goodwin, 2004). This is because indexing and retrieval in UDDI is not grounded on formal specifications of service capabilities with machine-processable semantics, but on natural language descriptions and categorisations retrievable through keyword-based search. Keyword-based annotation and search cannot be relied upon for automated discovery, because it cannot differentiate between services that have totally different names but equivalent functionality, or services that have identical naming but perform totally unrelated operations. To facilitate efficient service discovery during process design, we need to provide an explicit, formal, unambiguous, commonly comprehensible and machine processable representation of service characteristics.

The aim of this paper is to introduce the approach adopted in project FUSION towards semantically-enhanced publication and discovery of services. FUSION is an EU-funded research project aiming to promote semantics-based interoperability among service-oriented business applications and efficient business process integration among collaborating enterprises (Alazeib et al, 2006). The FUSION Semantic Registry is a semantically extended UDDI registry that is a core part of the FUSION system architecture. The rest of this paper is organised as follows. Section 2 defines a scheme of generic service discovery requirements, setting the basis for the discussion to follow. Section 3 discusses the benefits of adding semantics to Web service descriptions and presents the SAWSDL-based approach adopted in FUSION. Section 4 provides a brief overview of the semantic service publication and discovery procedures, as they take place inside the FUSION Semantic Registry.

2   SERVICE DISCOVERY REQUIREMENTS

A number of solutions for semantically-enhanced service discovery have been proposed in the research literature, each of them satisfying a different set of service discovery requirements. To provide means for comparing with other approaches, and explicating the functionality rationale of the FUSION Semantic Registry, we establish a generic scheme of service discovery requirements. The scheme we present in this section defines the relevance and degree of match between service advertisements and service requests at three distinct levels: (i) functionality-level matching, (ii) message-level matching, and (iii) schema-level matching.

2.1   Functionality-level matching

Functionality-level matching is the most basic interoperability determinant and first aspect of relevance to be considered. Web service descriptions need to categorise a service with respect to some classification scheme, describing the business function being performed. This is one of the factors to be considered in determining if a service advertisement can provide the functionality sought by the service request, or not. Alternative ways to accommodate this type of categorisation and search in conventional UDDI registries (with syntactic means) are quite common in the literature (e.g. for popular taxonomies such as NAICS and UNSPSC, or custom ones). No complex notion of a degree of match exists, since the outcome is boolean.

2.2 Message-level matching

The second aspect of matching we propose is at the level of messages. The goal in this type of matchmaking is to determine the degree to which an advertised service will produce all output data that a business process participant expects to receive, and the degree to which it will accept all input data that a business process participant intends to provide. This involves a comparison between the ontological concepts corresponding to the service messages exchanged by the advertisement, and that of the request. To provide a formalisation of the different degrees of match that could potentially occur at the message level, we provide an intuitive set-theoretic model based on Description Logics (DL), adopted from the work of (Li and Horrocks, 2003), and (Keller et al, 2004).

Table 1 - Set-theoretic model for matchmaking. Advertisement set A is represented with (⊘) and request set R with (⊗)

Degree of Match	Condition	Graphical Representation
Exact Match	The advertisement offers all input and output messages specified by the request, and no irrelevant ones	(sets A and R are equal)
Plugin Match	The advertisement offers all input and output messages specified by the request, and some irrelevant ones	(set A is a proper superset of R)
Subsumption Match	The advertisement offers only some of the input and output messages specified by the request, and no irrelevant ones	(set A is a proper subset of R)
Intersection Match	The advertisement offers only some of the input and output messages specified by the request, and some irrelevant ones	(sets A and R are intersecting)
Non Match	The advertisement offers none of the input and output messages specified by the request	(sets A and R are disjoint)

2.3 Schema-level matching

The situation where an exact match has been established for all requested inputs and outputs is not necessarily sufficient for the request and the advertisement to be considered as matching. When performing matchmaking under the assumption of a shared base ontology (as in the case of FUSION), which any party can extend by subclassing and applying property restrictions in the form of value or cardinality constraints, we need to also consider matching at the message schema structure level. Collaborating partners in a network may choose to extend concepts in a shared ontology in different ways, best expressing the semantics of the Web services that their enterprise application systems expose.

Figure 1 illustrates this through an example: a case in which the concept of *address,* as defined in the FUSION Ontology, could have been extended in different ways through subclassing in order to be used for modelling two different enterprise applications. Although *System1_Address* and *System2_Address* are subclasses of a common concept, their input and output messages cannot always be interoperable. The message schema of *System2_Address* is more specific than that of *System1_Address,* since the first specifies more attributes than the schema of the latter. In fact, if Web services exposed by *System1* were to exchange *address* related messages with Web services exposed by *System2*, *System2* could consume all of the data provided to it, but require some additional data that would not have been provided, thus leading to potential problems during process execution.

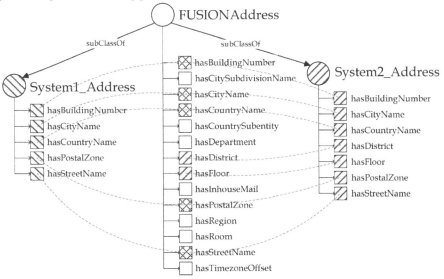

Figure 1 - Different ways to extend a shared ontology concept through subclassing

One could reapply the set-theoretic matchmaking model presented in Table 1 to distinguish among cases where the advertisement message schema is isomorphic to that of the request, more generic, more specific, or has no attributes in common. In the first two cases the match could be considered satisfactory, while in the latter two the match may not be sufficient for seamless message exchange and interoperability.

3   ADDING SEMANTICS TO SERVICE DESCRIPTIONS

Web services are highly reusable, self-contained software components having standardised, platform-independent and implementation-neutral interfaces described using the Web Service Description Language (WSDL) (Christensen et al, 2001). A WSDL description contains the technical information required for invoking a Web service, but does not pronounce anything meaningful about the capabilities or the behaviour of the service itself. The semantics to be added to Web service descriptions should advertise service characteristics in terms of the functionality and intrinsic business value they offer (i.e. functional semantics), the messages they exchange (i.e. data semantics), and the observable behaviour they expose within a complex process execution (i.e. behavioural semantics). This facilitates efficient indexing upon publication to a semantically enhanced service registry, and automated service discovery based on explicit, formal, and unambiguous service characteristics.

Numerous frameworks have been proposed in the recent years for constructing semantic descriptions of services, and several have been promoted for standardisation through W3C member submissions: OWL-S (Martin et al, 2004), WSMO (Bruijn et al, 2005), and WSDL-S (Akkiraju et al, 2005). The implementation of the FUSION Semantic Registry is building upon the most recent development in this area: Semantic Annotations for WSDL (SAWSDL) (Farrell and Lausen, 2007). SAWSDL, building on the same principles as WSDL-S, is a simple and generic mechanism for semantically annotating Web service descriptions taking advantage of the WSDL extension mechanism. SAWSDL defines two types of annotations that can be used for attaching "meaning" to WSDL or XML schema components inside a WSDL file: identifiers of concepts, using modelReference extension attributes, and identifiers of mappings from concepts to XML Schema elements, using loweringSchemaMapping and liftingSchemaMapping extension attributes. SAWSDL supports annotations for both WSDL 1.1 and WSDL 2.0 documents. In this discussion we refer to the use of SAWSDL in conjunction with WSDL 1.1. Table 2 summarises the different type of semantics that must be captured for semantically enriching Web service descriptions, by linking concepts from the FUSION Ontology to WSDL components.

Table 2 - Adding semantics to Web service descriptions

Type of semantics	FUSION Ontology	Annotated WSDL 1.1 component	SAWSDL extension attribute
Functional semantics	Service classification taxonomy	portType	modelReference
Data semantics	Data facet	part	modelReference, loweringSchemaMapping liftingSchemaMapping
Behavioural semantics	State ontology	operation	modelReference

The FUSION Ontology (Bouras et al, 2006) serves as a commonly shared semantic model and interoperability vehicle. It is modular, multi-layered and multi-faceted, and has been created with a view to being easily extended. On one hand, the multiple-layering in the FUSION Ontology reflects hierarchical relationships between entities that are: domain-independent (foundational ontology concepts), vendor-independent (generic concepts in the domain of enterprise applications), vendor-dependent (concepts relating to specific ERP or CRM products) and *case*-specific (concepts relating to a specific installation and customisation of some ERP or CRM product). On the other hand, its multiple-facet structure reflects the different types of such entities, i.e. functionality-related, data-related, and process-related concepts, horizontally pertaining across all abstraction layers.

4   ADDING SEMANTICS TO UDDI

Augmenting a UDDI registry with semantic matchmaking capabilities facilitates automated high-precision retrieval of services to fulfil specific requirements when composing business processes, and constitutes a significant advancement compared to the existing publication and discovery facilities offered in conventional UDDI. The UDDI server module lying at the heart of the FUSION Semantic Registry is a typical implementation of the UDDI v2 specification by OASIS (UDDI, 2002). In order to support concept-driven discovery of Web service descriptions, the FUSION Semantic Registry enhances the purely syntactic search facilities that a UDDI server can offer. This is achieved without any modifications to the UDDI server implementation or the UDDI API, as has been proposed in (Paolucci et al, 2002), and (Akkiraju et al, 2003), but rather, through the incorporation of a number of semantically-enabled processing modules in the FUSION Semantic Registry architecture, such as a publication and a discovery manager with OWL ontology processing and DL reasoning capabilities. As a result, the UDDI server module remains semantics-agnostic, providing FUSION system implementers with UDDI vendor independence. In this section we provide a high-level overview of both publication-time and discovery-time activities in the FUSION Semantic Registry.

4.1   Publication-time activities

Upon delivery to the FUSION Semantic Registry the SAWSDL document is parsed to extract all modelReference annotations attached on wsdl:portType and wsdl:part entities. The concepts that these annotations reference serve as input for creating a new named OWL class definition in an internal index ontology (an extension to the FUSION Ontology), maintained with the sole purpose of assisting in indexing. The registry associates the newly created class with other FUSION Ontology classes to capture functional and data semantics, by assigning concepts from the Service Classification Taxonomy or the FUSION Ontology Data Facet as range values to the newly created class's object properties. Behavioural annotations pointing to State Ontology concepts are not processed since they are only utilised for semi-automated service composition, and not for discovery. The registry uses a DL reasoner to classify the newly created class, computing new subclass relations and identifying superclasses for the newly created concept. The classification information serves as input to an indexing procedure involving SAWSDL to UDDI mapping. The URIs of the inferred superclasses are used as indexing keys for the service in UDDI. The mapping is based on the OASIS Technical Note for WSDL to UDDI mapping (Clément, Colgrave and Riegen, 2004), which we extended and adapted to suit the FUSION Ontology, and SAWSDL annotations for WSDL 1.1 service descriptions.

4.2   Discovery-time activities

As soon as the hybrid UDDI/OWL indexing procedure has been completed, service descriptions are readily discoverable by business process designers and system developers within a collaborative network. The suitability of an advertised service is evaluated based on a discovery query that comprises a URI, pointing to a semantic description of the capabilities sought, and an optional UUID, specifying a target business application offering the service. The registry examines the concept that the discovery URI points to, and determines if it constitutes a generic capability profile based on concepts defined in the FUSION Ontology, or some custom-built capability profile defined in a third ontology, specialising FUSION Ontology concepts by adding restrictions (e.g. by adding an extra object property, or setting some cardinality constraint). The first is the simplest discovery case, since the registry's index has already established associations from service advertisements to all concepts defined in the FUSION Ontology, and can directly seek tModels containing at least one keyedReference with a keyValue equal to the discovery URI. In the second case the registry must classify the custom-built profile against all concepts in its internal index ontology. The DL reasoner computes new subclass relations and reveals the superclasses that the custom-built profile can be classified under. The registry then seeks for service advertisements indexed with respect to the URIs of the inferred superclass concepts.

5   CONCLUSIONS

Collaborative networks have a lot to gain from the adoption of SOA and Web services, for which automated service discovery is a key enabler. To promote interoperability among service-oriented business applications and efficient business process integration among collaborating enterprises, FUSION necessitates the introduction of semantics to all aspects of the service discovery process. In this paper we presented a generic scheme of service discovery requirements, an SAWSDL-based approach for adding semantics to Web service descriptions, and an overview of the FUSION Semantic Registry publication and discovery functionality, augmenting the capabilities of conventional UDDI registries.

6   ACKNOWLEDGMENTS

FUSION (Business process fusion based on semantically-enabled service-oriented business applications) is funded by the European Commission's 6th Framework Programme for RTD (FP6-IST-2004-170835) (http://www.fusion-strep.eu/).

7   REFERENCES

1.   Akkiraju, R., Goodwin, R., Doshi, P. and Roeder, S. A method for semantically enhancing the service discovery capabilities of UDDI. In Proceedings of the IJCAI-03 Workshop on Information Integration on the Web, 2003.
2.   Akkiraju R., Farrell J., Miller J., Nagarajan M., Schmidt M.T., Sheth A., Verma K. Web Service Semantics (WSDL-S). W3C Member Submission, November 2005. Available at: http://www.w3.org/Submission/WSDL-S/
3.   Alazeib A., Bauer M., Bouras A., Dyczkowska M., Friesen A., Gouvas P., Jurkowski G., Jurkowski P., Kalaboukas K., Kourtesis D., Lukacsy G., Martinek P., Mentzas G., Pantelopoulos S., Paraskakis I., Szalai B. FUSION project Deliverable D1.2 - FUSION Approach. July 2006. Available at: http://www.fusion-strep.eu/
4.   Bouras A., Gouvas P., Friesen A., Pantelopoulos S., Alexakis S., Mentzas G. Business Process Fusion based on Semantically-enabled Service-Oriented Business Applications. In Proceedings of

the Second International Conference on Interoperability for Enterprise Software and Applications (I-ESA 2006), Bordeaux France, March 2006.

5. Cardoso, J. Discovering Semantic Web services with and without a Common Ontology Commitment.In Proceedings of the 3rd International Workshop on Semantic and Dynamic Web Processes (SDWP 2006), September 2006.

6. Christensen E., Curbera F., Meredith G., and Weerawarana S. Web Services Description Language (WSDL) Version 1.1, World Wide Web Consortium, 15 March 2001. Available at: http://www.w3.org/TR/2001/NOTE-wsdl-20010315

7. Clément L., Colgrave J., Riegen C.V. Using WSDL in a UDDI Registry, Version 2.0.2 – OASIS Technical Note. Available at: http://www.oasis-open.org/committees/uddi-spec/doc/tn/uddi-spec-tc-tn-wsdl-v2.htm

8. Colgrave J., Akkiraju R., Goodwin R., External Matching in UDDI. In Proceedings of the International Conference on Web Services (ICWS 2004), San Diego, USA, 2004.

9. Farrell J. and Lausen H. (eds) Semantic Annotations for WSDL and XML Schema. W3C Candidate Recommendation, January 2007. Available at: http://www.w3.org/TR/sawsdl/

10. Keller U., Lara R., and Polleres A., Toma I., Kifer M., Fensel D. WSMO Web Service Discovery. Technical Report, DERI, University of Innsbruck, 2004.

11. Lara R., Binder W., Constantinescu I., Fensel D., Keller U., Pan J., Pistore M., Polleres A., Toma I., Traverso P., and Zaremba M. Semantics for Web Service Discovery and Composition. Technical Report, Knowledge Web project, December 2004.

12. Bruijn J.d., Bussler C., Domingue J., Fensel D., Hepp M., Keller U., Kifer M., König-Ries B., Kopecky J., Lara R., Lausen H., Oren E., Polleres A., Roman D., Scicluna J., Stollberg M. Web Service Modeling Ontology (WSMO). W3C Member Submission 3 June 2005. Available at: http://www.w3.org/Submission/WSMO/

13. Li L. and Horrocks I.. A Software Framework for Matchmaking Based on Semantic Web Technology. In Proceedings of the World Wide Web Conference (WWW'03), Hungary, 2003.

14. Martin D., Burstein M., Hobbs J., Lassila O., McDermott D., McIlraith S., Narayanan S., Paolucci M., Parsia B., Payne T., Sirin E., Srinivasan N., Sycara K. OWL Web Ontology Language for Services (OWL-S). W3C Member Submission 22 November 2004. Available at: http://www.w3.org/Submission/OWL-S

15. Paolucci M., Kawamura T., Payne T., and Sycara K. Semantic Matching of Web Service Capabilities. In Proceedings of the First International Semantic Web Conference (ISWC2002), Sardinia, Italy, June 2002.

16. UDDI Version 2.04 API, Published Specification, July 2002. Available at: http://uddi.org/pubs/ProgrammersAPI-V2.04-Published-20020719.htm

PART 19

COLLABORATION ENVIRONMENTS CASES

60

SUPPORTING MOBILE VIRTUAL TEAM'S COORDINATION WITH SOA-BASED ACTIVE ENTITIES

Ruben Dario Franco[1], Andrés Neyem[2],
Sergio Ochoa[3] and Rosa Navarro[4]

[1,4] *CIGIP Research Centre, Polytechnical University of Valencia, SPAIN*
[2,3] *Computer Science Department, University of Chile, CHILE*
dfranco@cigip.upv.es, aneyem|sochoa@dcc.uchile.cl, ronava@cigip.upv.es

The use of IT solutions to support preparedness, response and recovery process has been envisioned as a possible way to improve the support for collaboration among the actors participating in mobile teams operating under constrained scenarios. Software applications supporting mobility have typically been conceived as functional extensions of centralized enterprise systems hosted on corporate servers. However, in this work, we focus on those mobile scenarios which go one step further in terms of interoperability requirements. This proposal aims to support the design, deployment and execution of ad-hoc collaborative business processes (workflows) in mobile networks, operating under constrained conditions and taking advantage of the Active Entity (AE) concept.

1   MOTIVATION

Information and communication technologies (ICT) allow workers to labor outside the office and accomplish their activities while they are on the move. That is, organizations are evolving towards environments where full mobility is a requirement. For instance, one of the most ignored, but urgent and vital challenges confronting society today is the vulnerability of urban areas to "eXtreme" Events (XEs) [7, 1, 3]. These XEs include natural disasters such as earthquakes, hurricanes and floods, as well as accidental and intentional disasters such as fires and terrorist attacks.

One important lesson learned from recent disasters is the need to improve collaboration among organizations or actors involved in those disaster relief efforts [10, 2, 15]. Many pitfalls related to collaboration, such as lack of trust, information sharing, communication and coordination, have been well documented [9, 12, 7, 13].

The use of IT solutions to support preparedness, response and recovery process has been envisioned as a possible way to improve the support for collaboration among the actors participating, for instance, in disaster relief efforts [8]. This work proposes to develop an IT-based platform that allows improving the co-ordination of involved parties.

This paper presents an extension to the traditional workflow models in order to support dynamic settings. Specifically, the scenarios include mobile devices interacting among themselves using a Mobile Ad-hoc NETwork (MANET).

In this paper, we focus on those mobile scenarios which go one step further in terms of interoperability requirements. This proposal aims to support the design, deployment and execution of ad-hoc collaborative business processes (workflows) in mobile networks, operating under constrained conditions and taking advantage of the Active Entity (AE) concept.

Franco, R.D., Neyem, A., Ochoa, S., Navarro, R., 2007, in IFIP International Federation for Information Processing, Volume 243, Establishing the Foundation of Collaborative Networks; eds. Camarinha-Matos, L., Afsarmanesh, H., Novais, P., Analide, C.; (Boston: Springer), pp. 557–564.

In order to describe the strategy to support mobile workflows, this paper introduces a lightweight architecture addressing the challenges involved in such scenarios. Section 2 describes the challenges and opportunities offered by service-oriented computing to support workflows-based collaborations in ad-hoc wireless settings. Section 3 defines the structure of an Active Entity and explains the architecture for executing active entity services. Section 4 presents the conclusions and future work.

2   SUPPORTING DISTRIBUTED PROCESSES IN MOBILE ENVIRONMENTS

Software applications supporting mobility have typically been conceived as functional extensions of centralized enterprise systems hosted on corporate servers. The main design goal of these applications has been to provide a mobile environment within which mobile workers may gather information to be synchronized against a server at a later stage. This issue jeopardizes the collaboration required by mobile workers to execute a workflow process [2, 11].

On the other hand, traditional workflow models offer powerful representations of teamwork activities. These models enable efficient specifications and executions of a business process [2]. The execution of such workflows is designed to work on high-end servers connected by reliable wired connections. Under this approach, the workflow definition and control are kept in a centralized structure. This situation constrains the workflow-based collaboration, particularly in ad-hoc mobile environments, where disconnections occur frequently.

Ad-hoc networking refers to a network with no fixed infrastructure [16]. When the nodes are assumed to be capable of moving, either on their own or carried by their users, these networks are called MANETs. The nodes of the network rely on wireless communication to collaborate with each other [15].

On the other hand, Service-Oriented Computing (SOC) is a new paradigm gaining popularity in distributed computing environments due to its emphasis on highly specialized, modular and platform agnostic code facilitating interoperability of systems [14].

As a summary, high degree of freedom and a fully decentralized architecture can be obtained in MANETs at the expense of facing significant new challenges. MANETs are opportunistically formed structures that change in response to the movement of physically mobile hosts running potentially mobile code. Advances in wireless technologies allow devices to freely join and leave work sessions and networks, and exchange data and services at will, without the need of any infrastructure setup and system administration. Frequent disconnections inherent in ad-hoc networks produce data inconsistencies in centralized service directories. Architectures based on centralized lookup directories are no longer suitable. Thus, the model and techno-logies addressing these issues should consider all nodes as mobile units able to provide and consume services from other mobile units [8].

3   WFMS ARCHITECTURE FOR MANETS

3.1   Active Entities

The architecture supports mobile workflows by enabling distributed workflow execution and taking advantage of the concept of Active Entity (AE), which is a building block used to design abstract models of collaborative business processes. AEs are designed as abstract definitions for each kind of role involved in the process.

For example, in a construction scenario for the electrical inspection process two main roles can be identified: the project manager and the inspector. Both of them need to provide a specific service interface to interoperate to report the results of the designed process. An abstract definition of each role (AE) will include those services belonging to them and, at design time, they will be orchestrated to form a collaborative workflow process.

At execution time, specific instances of each AE are created. Consequently, abstract definitions are instantiated on specific mobile devices being handled by the project manager and electrical engineers acting as inspectors.

In order to simplify process modeling and execution phases, a key architectural decision was made. By wrapping the activities that are part of a workflow process, under services interfaces, it is possible to provide the building blocks needed to compose and execute extended and complex business processes. Although this is an achievement in terms of interoperability and flexibility, the Web service application space needs to be designed and be more useful than just a set of input and output messages. In order to deal with this issue, Yang proposed the service components be organized as an architectural pattern based on a high level self-contained composite service [17]. This architecture presents a public interface and includes a private part comprised of the composition constructs and logics that are required for its manifestation. The public interface definition, provided by a service component, describes its messages and operations. The service component messages and operations can be published and then searched, discovered, and used like any normal web service. The encapsulated composition logic and construction scripts are private (internal and invisible) to a service component.

Following Yang's ideas, AEs can be used as web-based components of business resources (roles), able to be involved in process activities. These AEs can be implemented by an abstract class of web service methods. They make up a mechanism for creating composite services via reuse, specialization, and extension.

3.2   Distributed Processes with Active Entities

A distributed business process may be conceived as a set of activities which are assigned to various roles to be accomplished [6]. An execution unit is a complete piece of work that can be assigned to some entity of the process which has the proper knowledge and capability required for its accomplishment. Thus, Active Entities can be redefined as follows:

Active Entities are service providers which by means of their public service interfaces, are able to accomplish some execution unit, by providing and consuming third-parties (others AE) services. Those services are modeled at design time and, then, they are encapsulated in an abstract class that will be instantiated at each resource of the problem's domain.

From the business process perspective, AE can be used at modeling time to describe patterns of service compositions. Then, each process instance is executed by means of their invocations. Service interfaces are known by them because they are embedded in the entity modeling process. Figure 1 shows the AE structure.

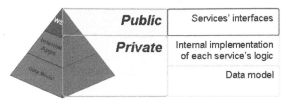

Figure 1. Active entity structure

AEs may represent companies, organizational units, resources or mobile workers. On top of this message-oriented bus (see Figure 2), other applications may also gain access to those services in order to compose value-added functionality. Therefore, the execution model is based on the orchestration of execution unit accomplishments; the execution units are those previously assigned to AEs.

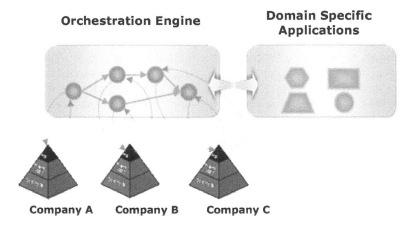

Figure 2. Organizations and organizational resources modeled as active entities

At this level, a business process model can be described as a set of peer-to-peer service invocations among AEs. These relationships are described by means of a Service Level Agreement (SLA) among them (contracts). This model establishes a directed graph of peer-to-peer information exchanges, representing the process flow or path of the task (Figure 3).

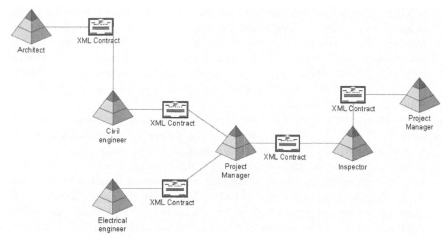

Figure 3. A process can be designed using active service entities and contracts

3.3 The Architecture

The architecture (Fig. 4) consists of a set of components extending traditional server-based workflow engines to be accessible by mobile workers. It has to consider thin clients due to the hardware limitations of mobile devices.

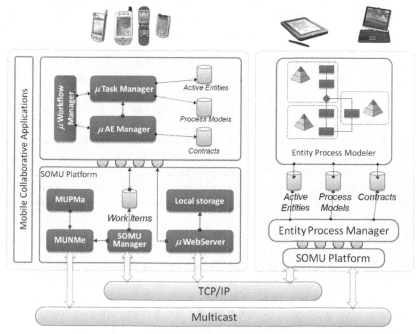

Figure 4. Architecture to support mobile workflows by using AE

- Entities Process Modeler: This component supports the process definition including modeling of activities assigned to active entities, control connectors among AEs, input/output containers and entity contracts. A process is represented as a directed acyclic graph with activities (nodes) and control/contracts connectors (edges). The graph is manipulated via a built-in, event-driven and compliant graphic editor. The entity contracts are specified as XML structures. These structures are described via XML Scheme facilities. The AEs Process Modeler distinguishes two main types of activities assigned to active entities: process activities and blocks. Blocks contain the same constructs as processes, e.g., activities or control connectors.

- • - AEs Process Manager: After the planning stage, this component accepts the plan from the AEs Process Modeler and passes it on to the planner for allocation of AEs. When a process is executed, activity instances are assigned to AE to perform the actions required for the activity. This may be a manual task, such as verifying a legal clause in a contract or a computerized task, such as entering the data status of the electrical facilities at a construction into the database via the program specified for the activity. The identification of the right AE for a mobile worker is based on data running the BP. Thus, roles describe the type of activity the mobile worker performs within the active entity, such as team leader or electrical engineer. The information about the organization and people involved in the process is generally stored in databases. When the process is defined, the AEs Process Modeler defines for each activity, which AE should perform it. Assigning the activity to a role provides significant advantages over the assignment of the activity directly to a mobile worker. It can be replaced without affecting the correct execution of a process. Furthermore, during execution, this component gets regular progress updates in order to monitor active entities distributed among mobile workers.

- • - μWorkflow Manager: This component stores the plan for the active entities assigned to a mobile worker. This Manager uses the μActiveEntity and μTask Manager components to handle the active entities and tasks that have been allocated. This manager needs data about the plan for allocating tasks to determine (1) the active entity from which the inputs for a task are going to come and (2) the active entity to which the results will be returned. The μWorkflow Manager can be updated by the AEs Process Manager when a new plan is entered into the system (on the group leader), or by the group leader via the SOMU Platform [7], when active entities allocations are made.

- • - μActiveEntity Manager: This component handles the active entities assigned to a mobile worker. This component needs status information about the tasks allocation for determining the active entity in order to perform the required actions.

- • - μTask Manager: This component handles the task state transition of an active entity. A task being executed in the disconnection mode may change its state according to the current user's situation. For example, a user may terminate or suspend his/her task according to the surrounding business situation. On the other hand, there is a need to handle predictable task state mismatch when reconnected. The degree of task state mismatch may be higher than one, and it represents the difference of state levels between two task states.

- • - SOMU Platform: The Service-Oriented Mobile Unit (SOMU) is a lightweight platform running on PDAs, TabletPC and notebooks [7]. It enables each mobile computing device to produce and consume Web Services from other peers. Such functionality is implemented on a lightweight Web Server. Thus, the autonomy and part of the interoperability required by mobile workers is supported. SOMU also implements a local storage which is composed of (1) a shared storage space to allocate the files the mobile unit needs to share, and (2) a space to allocate those Web services exposed by the mobile unit. By default, SOMU provides basic

- WS for Web services description and discovery. The SOMU main components are SOMU manager, μWebServer, Mobile Units Near Me (MUNMe) and Mobile Units Profile Manager (MUPMa). The SOMU Manager is the component in charge of creating, storing and dispatching work items when a mobile collaborative application invokes WS exposed by other mobile units. The work items stored in a mobile unit represents the WS invocations that such unit needs to perform. Each work item is composed of a ticket, a mobile universal unit, the WS proxy, WS input and WS output. The ticket is the work item identifier. It is used to inform the results of a WS invocation to a mobile collaborative application. The Mobile Universal

- Identification (MUI) names each mobile unit. The MUI allows the SOMU Manager directly invoke WS running on other mobile units. WS Proxy contains the data needed to coordinate the invocation and the response of WS exposed by other units. WS Input contains the parameters to be sent by the WS Proxy when it invokes the remote WS. WS Output contains the results of a WS invocation. The broker of all interaction between two mobile units is the μWebServer. The MUNMe is the component in charge of discovering and recording the mobile units that are close to the current device. This data is used to decide a good time to start an interaction with a specific unit. This component uses a multicast protocol. It involves discovering the name, MUI and the IP address of the units belonging to the MANET. Since WS are typically accessed from various kinds of mobile devices, interoperability and personalization play an important role for universal access. The MUPMa stores and manages information related to mobile units, such as the MUI, hardware and network capabilities. WS can use this data to provide optimized contents for various clients.

4 CONCLUSIONS AND FURTHER WORK

Workflow-based cooperative technology is promising, but current systems supporting workflow based collaboration (WfMSs) are designed for stable wired networks or nomadic mobile networks. We sought to lay a foundation for WfMSs operating in unpredictable MANET environments without depending on centralized resources or reliable communication links.

We presented an architecture that was implemented to let mobile computing devices expose and consume Web services of AE to perform an activity. This prototype was programmed in C# using the functionality provided by the .NET Compact Framework. However, it could have been implemented using J2ME instead. The type of implementation allows the prototype to run on a wide range of devices from PDAs to desktop PCs.

The prototype provides a basis for the development of mobile collaborative applications based on workflow models. It intends to increase the technical feasibility of solutions in the area and reduce the development effort of MANET-based mobile collaborative applications.

The supporting infrastructure has been used as a basis for mobile workflow that will help electrical engineers to conduct inspections in construction sites. Such application has not been formally tested.

Future work includes experimentation to study the possible contributions and limitations of the proposed strategy. Moreover, the functionality provided by Web services need to be tested to determine if the proposed uncoupled interaction represents a limitation for mobile workers collaborating with ad-hoc communication.

5   REFERENCES

1.   Columbia/Wharton Roundtable. "Risk Management Strategies in an Uncertain World," IBM Palisades Executive Conference Center. April, 2002. (www.ldeo.columbia.edu/CHRR/Roundtable, last visit: Jan-2003)
2.   U. Dayal, M. Hsu and R. Ladin, "Business Process Coordination: State of the Art, Trends, and Open Issues", Proceedings of the Twenty-seventh International Conference on Very Large Data Base, Rome, Italy, Sep. 11-14, 2001, pp. 3-13.
3.   Godschalk, D. "Urban Hazard Mitigation: Creating Resilient Cities", Natural Hazards Review. ASCE. August 2003. pp. 136-146.
4.   G. Hackmann, R. Sen, M. Haitjema, G.-C. Roman and C Gill, MobiWork: Mobile Workflow for MANETs, Technical Report WUCSE-06-18, Washington University, Department of Computer Science and Engineering, St. Louis, Missouri, USA, 2006.
5.   J. Jing, K. Huff, B. Hurwitz, H. Sinha, B. Robinson and M. Feblowitz, "WHAM: Supporting Mobile Workforce and Applications in Workflow Environment", Proceedings of the Tenth International Workshop on Research Issues in Data Engineering, San Diego, California, USA, Feb. 27-28, 2000, pp. 31-38.
6.   R. Khalaf and F. Leymann, "E Role-based Decomposition of Business Processes using BPEL", Proceedings of the IEEE International Conference on Web Services, Chicago, USA, Sep. 18-22, 2006, pp. 770-780.
7.   Mileti, D. Disasters by Design: A Reassessment of Natural Hazards in United States. Joseph Henry Press. Washington D.C. 1999.
8.   National Governors Association (NGA). "Volume Two: Homeland Security – A Governor's Guide To Emergency Management". NGA Center for Best Practices. 2002.
9.   Nigg, J. "Emergency Response Following the 1994 Northridge Earthquake: Intergovernmental Coordination Issues," Disaster Research Center, University of Delaware, Newark, 1997.
10. National Research Council: Board on Natural Disasters. "Reducing Disaster Losses Through Better Information". National Academic Press. Washington, D.C. 1999.
11. A. Neyem, S.F. Ochoa and J.A. Pino, "Supporting Mobile Collaboration with Service-Oriented Mobile Units", Proceedings of the Twelfth International Workshop on Groupware, Medina del Campo, Spain, Sep. 17-21, 2006, LNCS 4154, pp. 228-245.
12. Quarantelli, E. "Major Criteria for Judging Disaster Planning and Managing and their Applicability in Developing Societies," Background paper for the Int. Seminar on the Quality of Life and Environmental Risk. Rio de Janeiro, Brazil, Oct., 1996.
13. Stewart, T. and Bostrom, A. "Extreme Event Decision Making Workshop Report," Center for Policy Research. Rockefeller College of Public Affairs and Policy. University of Albany, and Decision Risk and Management Science Program NSF. June, 2002. (www.albany.edu/cpr/xedm, last visit: Jan-2003).
14. R. Sen, R. Handorean, G-C. Roman and C. Gill, "Service Oriented Computing Imperatives in Ad Hoc Wireless Settings", Service-Oriented Software System Engineering: Challenges and Practices, Stojanovic and Dahanayake (Eds.), Idea Group Publishing, Hershey, USA, 2005, 247-269.
15. I. Stojmenovic and J. Wu, "Ad-hoc Networks", IEEE Computer, 2004, 37(2), 9-74.
16. C. Tschudin, H. Lundgren, and E. Nordström, "Embedding MANETs in the Real World", Proceedings of the Eighth IFIP International Conference on Personal Wireless Communications, Venice, Italy, Sep. 23-25, 2003, LNCS 2775, pp. 578-589.
17. J. Yang, "Web service componentization", Communications of the ACM, 2003, 46(10), 35-40.

61

COLLABORATIVE ENVIRONMENTS WORK: A CASE STUDY OF TEACHER TRAINING

Manuel Meirinhos, António Osório

Instituto Politécnico de Bragança, Universidade do Minho, PORTUGAL
meirinhos@ipb.pt, ajosorio@iec.uminho.pt

In recent years, many research projects related to cooperative and collaborative learning, as well as to learning communities based on these practices, have appeared. Numerous authors have recognised the innovative potential of collaborative networked learning, thus allowing for the growth of research in the field of collaboration connected with education and distance learning. In this paper, through a case study in the context of teacher training, we intend to show that collaborative environments actually work.

1   INTRODUCTION

Collaboration in virtual environments is becoming an increasingly frequent phenomenon and can be looked at as a pedagogical strategy, as well as a philosophy or a lifestyle (Henri & Pudelko, 2003). In the same line, Gros (2004) states that, in the specialised literature, studies on collaborative learning multiply day by day. These studies are giving attention to experiences, usability conditions, types of interaction and point out towards fundamental issues in the learning process. In fact, we can note a predominance of empirical studies related to the creation of virtual environments focusing on collaboration, seen as a learning paradigm *per se* (Develotte & Mangenotte, 2004).

Aiming to collaborate in this process, we conducted an experiment of distance training for teachers trying to better grasp the way training can be developed and the importance collaborative environments can have. We believe that the information to be extracted could be highly relevant in solving some of the problems encountered in teacher training (nowadays so problematic) and in its implementation on a large scale, and in overcoming some space-time contingencies that impose such great limitations on teacher training throughout teachers' lives.

Building on the emergence of the collaborative discourse, we describe briefly the environment that supported the intervention. The findings achieved through the evaluation of all data, are also presented.

2   THE EMERGENCE OF THE COLLABORATIVE DISCOURSE

As Henri & Pudelko (2002) highlight: *the new Internet and Web based collective modes being invented are causing high fascination* (p. 13). In addition, Harasim (2000) also emphasises the importance of collaboration for networked learning: *the principle of collaborative learning may be the simple most important concept for online networked learning, since this principle addresses the strong socio-affective and cognitive of learning in the web* (p. 53).

Meirinhos, M., Osório, A., 2007, in IFIP International Federation for Information Processing, Volume 243, Establishing the Foundation of Collaborative Networks; eds. Camarinha-Matos, L., Afsarmanesh, H., Novais, P., Analide, C.; (Boston: Springer), pp. 565–572.

It is this growing recognition that leads a considerable number of authors to refer to a paradigm change, which has to do with a collaborative paradigm, such as that which is mentioned by Harasim (2000): *The convergence of the computer network revolution with profound social and economic changes has lead to a transformation of education at all levels. The new paradigm of collaborative networked learning is evident in the new modes of course delivery being offered, in the educational principles that frame the educational offerings, the new attributes that shape both the pedagogies and the environments that support them and that yield new educational processes and outcomes* (p. 59).

This new research field is mainly connected with collaborative learning (Henri & Lundgren-Cayrol, 2001) and with the development of virtual communities and all the issues raised by these communities (Henri & Pudelko, 2002). In pedagogical terms, collaboration and virtual communities are concepts that are not easily adjusted to school practices, though they pressupose and inspire the creation of new educational approaches (Dillenbourg *et al.*, 2003). The reason why they are not adjusted to school practices is that the nature, procedures and working style of organisations are insufficient or even contradictory to the demands of new education, social and cultural realities that these new learning environments bring about. In a similar way, Levan (2004) stresses that the practice of collaborative work is still difficult because conditions for the development of this way of working are far from present in the current organisational forms.

The focus on learning, the strengthening of the teacher-student and student-student interactions, the inclusion of collaborative work strategies and learning based on autonomy and reflection: these are the chief aspects that some authors associate with the change in the pedagogical paradigm. At the same time, they provide a suitable background for some of the more conscious approaches to the use of learning environments which meet the current needs for continuing training.

Hence, as Henri & Pudelko (2002) point out, *research shows all the characteristics of a paradigm in emergence, namely: attempts to define the principal concepts, to delimit borders of the studied object, to circumscribe the field compared to the disciplinary camps, to find methodologies suitable.* (p. 20).

The creation of these learning environments demands theoretical and practical knowledge that will provide them with a suitable background and will justify and provide limits for them. Moreover, there are various research projects that prefer one learning theory to another, though some authors take several theories into account to substantiate their collaborative practices. Notwithstanding the contribution given by a variety of theories, collaborative learning feeds on constructivist values, such as autonomy, reflection and active entrepreneurship, and is based on constructivist theories to explain learning mechanisms. According to Coll (2004), since collaborative learning is centred on individual learning, it is rather obvious the importance of theories that establish learning in an environment of mutual help and in the activity of the subject (constructivism), just as are the theories that set up learning on the basis of social interaction (social constructivism).

Collaboration calls on a theoretical underpinning, found in the theory of cognitive flexibility, in the concept of distributed cognition and in andragogy, which permits the establishment of the basic principles of collaborative learning (Depover & Marchand, 2002).

The difference between cooperation and collaboration was well elaborated on by Henri & Lundgren-Cayol (2001), using control and autonomy, the aim to achieve, the task and interdependence as the main aspects to distinguish both.

The first distinctive aspect is the degree of *autonomy* of trainees/learners and the level of *control* of the trainer/teacher. We can then confirm that, in cooperation, there is higher control on the part of the trainer and lower autonomy on the part of the trainee. On the other hand, in collaborative tasks, more autonomy is necessary and, thus, higher cognitive maturity than in cooperation. As a result, the activities in which the trainees possess less maturity should be more structured and contextualised, giving the trainer more control over the learning process. The less developed are the learning strategies for the learner, the more control should there be over the learning process. This control should be carried out in a clear way, in order to gradually develop trainees' autonomy and collaborative capacities: *Collaborative online interaction is best developed with maximum autonomy, without excessive* teacher intervention and control (...) (Tu, 2004, p.14). Consequently, at first sight, collaboration seems to be destined for people with the ability to self-regulate their learning.

Another feature that distinguishes these two concepts is the aim to achieve. Cooperation is based on the distribution of tasks and responsibilities among the members of a team to reach a certain objective, whereas, in collaboration, interaction is negotiated and oriented so as to accomplish a common purpose by means of a consensus. Objectives are expected to be collectively defined and each member is to be individually responsible for attaining the group's objective and not merely his own. In the collaborative process, sharing means "to participate" in order to achieve a common goal, but without the distribution of tasks and responsibilities within the group. As Harassim (2000) mentions, *collaboration or co-laboring means working together to accomplish shared goals; individuals seek outcomes beneficial to themselves and to the other members of the group.*

As far as *the completion of the task* is concerned, and contrary to collaboration, cooperation proposes a task which is distributed among the various members of a working group. In cooperation, emphasis is placed on the completion of the task by the group, based on the sub-tasks for each trainee. Collaborative work does not equal the sum or the juxtaposition of different individual works, rather it is necessary a greater involvement of the group, the establishment of common goals and the coordination of the activity.

Interdependence is a characteristic of both concepts. In cooperation, interdependence must exist, because the contribution of some is not complete without the contribution of others: there is reciprocal interdependence which is necessary for the complementation of the task. On the other hand, in collaboration, interdependence requires a new relational involvement, essential for mutual support and the creation of a common identity. Collaboration is thus found within the interactions of a group, where discoveries are shared and the meaning to be given to work is negotiated, as well as in the validation of new constructed knowledge.

Several authors share the opinion that, instead of separating these two concepts, they should be considered as two ends of a *continuum*: cooperation would represent a highly organised learning process, while collaboration would be a learning process carried out under the responsibility of the trainee. Between one end and another, a range of intermediate situations of group work could emerge depending on the trainee's autonomy, the trainer's degree of intervention and the skills already developed by the trainees. The term 'group' is used in the sense of comprehending the learning processes that include cooperation, collaboration or both in different moments.

Therefore, as an alternative to considering these approaches as dichotomies, one should understand them as part of the above-mentioned continuum that helps trainees to place themselves in the learning process, since collaboration is not a learning procedure that can be achieved immediately, but that previously requires the development of cooperation skills.

3   ENVIRONMENT

On the basis of what was presented above, two training sessions on b-learning mode were chosen, in which the distance component was based on the creation of a platform using a Learning Content Management System (LCMS) and a Groupware. The collaborative learning environment was then established on the ATutor and ACollab platforms, installed in integration, which worked from the same database in an Apache server. These platforms are open source tools with a General Public License (GPL) developed by the University of Toronto (http://www.ATutor.ca).

ATutor is a LCMS that uses SCORM for content development, which in our case was the function we attributed it. On the other hand, ACollab is a collaborative environment (Groupware), i.e. a multi-group Web-based collaborative work environment. It shows a considerably open and flexible structure in the creation and management of groups and in the organisation of collaborative activities, using forums, inboxes, information zones, event scheduling, chats and the joint construction of documents with comments on the work under development. Apart from this, it also includes a library where finished work is made available.

To sum up, we could state that, in this study, ACollab allowed us to form a general group, with all the members of the training, and four smaller groups of four people each, in which some activities were to be completed by the general group and others by the more specific groups.

We chose the b-learning approach with a distance component equal to 2/3 of face-to-face attendances.

The choice for b-learning was due to the fact that:

-   its is highly advisable for users with little experience in the use of computers;
-   it is more sensible for users with little experience in distance training;
-   it takes advantage of the best in face-to-face training and in distance training;
-   it allows for the development of the necessary skills for total distance training.

We cannot neglect the fact that, for those who are not familiar with this type of training and technology, participation in these activities brings about a cognitive overload. B-learning may function as a transition mode for total distance training, while training skills are developed and technologies and distance communication processes are explored.

4   INTERVENTION

The reflection elements of this work come from wider research, using the methodology of case studies, in which two situations of teacher continuous training were analysed with the purpose of understanding how teachers' professional development takes place in collaborative learning environments at a distance. In case studies, the results are very much related to the context. Despite that, we think that the knowledge gained should be taken into account in the implementation of learning environments of the same kind.

The above-mentioned training was given credits by the Scientific and Pedagogical Board for Continuous Training and took place in the Centre of Continuous Training in the Escola Superior de Educação de Bragança (Graduate School of Education of Bragança).

The first workshop (training 1) took place between July and November 2004 and the second one (training 2) between April and July 2005. Training was conducted in the b-learning modality, being that each workshop had a 20-hour in situ component and a 40-hour distance component.

In training 1, there were 16 trainees in which the most representative age category was 36-45 years old (seven people), plus two older trainees than this category and plus another three in the 25-36 category. In training 2, there were 18 trainees and the most representative age category was 25-35 years old (eight people) plus one trainee of more than 45 years old. The age of the participants can be a relevant factor in the implementation of new processes, since age is a question that influences the way teachers act when educational change occurs and necessarily in following these new processes (Hargreaves, 2005).

The teaching level to which trainees belonged was diversified. There was no trainee from kindergarten education; in short, all teaching levels were represented, with the tertiary level included (in training 2).

As far as the Internet use for professional purposes is concerned, all trainees stated that they used it, although some hardly did so. Nevertheless, the majority of them used the Internet quite a lot and several participants said that they used it on a daily basis.

There was also a tendency for teachers to consider that they were capable of using the Internet without considerable difficulties: web navigation, searches, e-mail. Some more advanced tools, such as dealing with forums, videoconference and chats, were reported as being extremely difficult for the greater part of the trainees. The domain of communication technology can influence training success, since good experience with handling communication tools can reduce the effort expended both in tools of communication and the platform work tools.

5   EVALUATION

The platform turned out to be quite useful for distance collaborative work. This statement is based in the analysis of data collected from electronic records of the platform, individual interviews (E), group feedback and a research diary, extracts of which we are using to illustrate a number of findings about the environments and the intervention described (in the quotes below, A1 stands for training 1 and A2 for training 2). The limitations in working collaboratively were not due to the collaborative environment generated by the platform, but rather to a set of conditions independent of the platform and sometimes inherent to the trainees. Thus, the platform *possesses good conditions to establish collaboration, but it was not fully developed* (A2_E6).

I think that [the limitation] *were we teachers, because many had a really basic knowledge of computers (A2_E7). Because if I had explored it more, dedicated myself more, it would have been easier to me. I believe it was a bit my fault* (A2_E5).

(…) I consider it has potential, but it's just that thing we have already mentioned in our training: we need to change the way people think and teachers must have more training in this area. And this is not happening, because when we come to choose a training session, we realise that very often there is only one session to be offered in the area of the Internet or Informatics (A2_E7).

The use of the platform ATutor-ACollab was straightforward and intuitive. The characteristics of the communication system were satisfactorily adjusted to the work developed and showed potential for collaborative work: *(…) it is easy to work with, it is, let's say, functional. Yesterday or the day before, when I was uploading those activities, I was there for 40 minutes and completely forgot to have lunch, because it was being functional and I was verifying a few things* (A1_E1).

Two trainees suggested their use in educational contexts: one of them with children from primary education (from 6 to 9 years of age), enabling work among schools, not forgetting that the teachers' help is indispensable at this level. The other suggested the creation of portfolios which would support face-to-face activities, at the level of secondary education: *It would be rather important to make an experiment with primary education children and, from this point of view, it would be great, because if we could do it with fourth-year children, it would work very well* (A1_E4); *I will immediately attempt to apply the knowledge acquired in this distance training to the classroom, with the network creation of folders, similar to portfolios, in which students will work under my guidance. I believe I shall apply this much more deeply as a trainer* (A1_E1).

Some of the trainees also showed interest in using the platform as trainers, for designing and realising distance training themselves: I got used to the platform and then it was easy. I had never done such work at a distance, but I considered the platform quite reasonable. It was easy to use, though there were a few functions that were not explored and I would have liked to. I would even enjoy, for example, using it for my own purposes [as a trainer] (A1_E2).

The two trainees that demonstrated interest in using the platform as trainers were given permission to access it as trainers themselves and, after two sessions with them, they started creating their own training courses for other teachers in a collaborative environment.

The training environment in the platform offered a set of instruments or tools for working communication, such as the e-mail, chat rooms, forums and tools for group work. By checking which communication tools were the most relevant for interaction and group work, we found that forums and the drafting room stood out, this being the collaborative work tool: Forums. Because… I'm going to give a very simple reason for this – I like to talk and discuss things. Documents are secondary for me, because everything is too theoretical (A1_E3); That was really good, that is what I prefered [drafting rooms], because each one of us completes, updates or gives suggestions so that the colleagues can alter things (A1_E1).

Forums and drafting rooms were the tools mostly used by the trainees for participation in group activities, both in training session 1 as in training session 2. Therefore, 49% and 6% of the participation was developed on forums, in training session 1 and training 2 respectively. The second most used tool was the drafting room with 21% and 29% in training session 1 and training 2 respectively.

The tools that trainees knew the least of before the beginning of training were forums and drafting rooms, though as new work tools they were more used than any others. Chat rooms were not used at all in training 1 and not used much in training 2, owing to the fact that it is a synchronous tool and it demands little group work, as far as we are led to believe. During face-to-face classes, trainees frequently complained that they did not find colleagues in chat rooms (A1_diary log and A2_diary log), which was maximised by the fact that the group was relatively small and there were fewer possibilities of meeting several people at the same time to talk to.

This idea was also recorded by other sources of information: *Once I was about to find the teacher on the chat room, but then I have no idea of what I did, I left the chat room because someone called me and when I returned, there was no one there* (A1_E2); *I thought it was an imperfection at least for me; I couldn't do it. We were few and not everyone could be there at the same time. In my opinion, this would be one of the most important aspects in the exchange of opinions and learning, even for training itself* (A2_E3).

The conversations led in the chat room of training session 2 were mainly established between trainees and trainer, who was concerned with being online as long as possible. Even if a communication tool was favoured over another one, some trainees highlighted the complementary nature and the importance of integration of these tools for group work: *I thought forums were very motivating. (...) But I am of the opinion that all of them were interesting and important as well* (A2_E6); *I considered them all appealing (...) I mean, the drafting room was awesome; it gave us the opportunity to do what we liked the most. Building things, even the activities of the general group and of the smaller group in which we participated... To be able to communicate and to really work and create was fascinating* (A2_E3); *I don't have any preference, they complemented each other in such a way that there is nothing to say. We can't really say that, that one has no value when compared to another. It may have less weight in terms of work, but it is valuable nonetheless. I can use the e-mail fewer times, but it is still there and, whenever I might need it, it is available. This interconnection is of the utmost importance* (A2_E4).

These various tools have particular communicative features that make them more or less appropriate to certain communicative processes for interaction and to the work to be developed. Trainees felt that the communication tools were suitable to the tasks being developed, without identifying any limitations that might influence the completion of the tasks in a collaborative work environment.

6   CONCLUSION

From the intervention described and its evaluation, we can admit that the integration of the ATutor and ACollab platforms generates a "virtual environment" which actually works, providing great potential for communication, interaction and development of distance collaborative work. Through the evidence collected and shared in this paper, we hope to have contributed to the growth of research in the field of collaboration connected with education and distance learning.

7 REFERENCES

1. Coll, C. Las comunidades de aprendizaje. Nuevos horizontes para la investigación y la intervención en psicología de la educación. Paper presented at the IV Congreso Internacional de Psicología y Educación, Almeria, 2004.
2. Depover, C., & Marchand, L. E-learning et formation des adultes en contexte profissionel. Bruxelles: de Boeck, 2002.
3. Develotte, C., & Mangenot, F.: Tutorat et communauté dans un campus numérique non collaboractif. Distances et Savoirs: Enigmes de la relation pédagogique à distance, 2(2-3), 2004.
4. Dillenbourg, P., Poirier, C., & Carles, L. Communautés virtuelles d'apprentissage: e-jargon ou nouveau paradigme? In A. Taurisson & A. Senteni (Eds.), Pédagogies.Net. L'essor des communautés virtuelles d'apprentissage (pp. 11-72). Sainte-Foy: Presses de L'Université du Québec, 2003.
5. Gros, B. S. El aprendizaje colaborativo a través de la red: limites y posibilidades. Congreso Internacional de Educación Mediada por Tecnologías. Octubre 6 al 8 de 2004 - Universidad del Norte Colombia, 2004. Accessed in 22/5/2005 at: http://www.uninorte.edu.co/congresog10/conf/08_El_Aprendizaje_Colaborativo_a_traves_de_la_red.pdf
6. Harassim, L. : Shift happens. Online education as a new paradigm in learning. Internet and Higher Education(3), 41-61, 2000.
7. Hargreaves, A., Educational change takes ages: Life, career and generational factors in teachers' emotional responses to educational change. Teaching and Teacher Education (21), 2005.
8. Henri, F. & Lundgren-Cayrol, K. Apprentissage collaboratif à distance. Pour comprendre et concevoir les environnements d'apprentissage virtuels. Saite-Foy: Presses de l'Univertité du Québec, 2001.
9. Henri, F. & Pudelko, B. La recherche sur la communication asynchrone : de l'outil aux communautés. In Daele, A. & Bernardette, C., (Eds.), Les communautés délocalisées d'enseignants, 2002. Accessed in 3/12/2003, at: http://archive-edutice.ccsd.cnrs.fr/view_by_stamp.php?label=PNER&langue=fr&action_todo=view&id=edutice-00000388&version=1#
10. Henri, F., & Pudelko, B. Understanding and analysing activity and learning in virtual communities. Journal of Computer Assisted Learning (19), 2003.
11. Levan, S. K. Travail Collaboratif sur Internet. Concepts, méthodes et pratiques des plateaux projet. Paris: Vuilbert, 2004.
12. Tu, Chih-Hsiung. Online collaborative Learning Communities. London: Libraries Unlimited, 2004.

A KNOWLEDGE SEARCH FRAMEWORK FOR COLLABORATIVE NETWORKS

Rui J. Tramontin Jr., Ricardo J. Rabelo
Federal University of Santa Catarina, Department of Automation and Systems
GSIGMA – Intelligent Manufacturing Systems Group
Florianópolis (SC), BRAZIL
tramontin@gsigma.ufsc.br
rabelo@das.ufsc.br

Partners in a collaborative network (CN) must interact and share their knowledge. This paper focuses on how the knowledge exchanged in these interactions can be easily and precisely reached by CN partners through an knowledge search framework. In order to improve the search precision, ontologies are used to add metadata (semantic annotations) to documents as well as to provide support for semantic queries. This paper is also concerned to the CN-related requirements not addressed by current information retrieval solutions, like annotations consistency maintenance, multiple ontologies management, ontology mappings management and security issues. The proposed framework is being developed under the scope of the ECOLEAD Project as part of a broader ICT infrastructure for supporting CNs.

1   INTRODUCTION

During the last years, globalization, mass customization, and other new trends have led organizations to focus on new strategies in order to improve their agility, and thus to achieve a competitive advantage in the global market. Such strategies are increasingly based on collaboration forms classified as *collaborative networks*. According to Camarinha-Matos (2005), a collaborative network (CN) is constituted by a variety of entities (organizations and individuals) that are largely autonomous, geographically distributed, and heterogeneous. These entities work together in order to increase their access to business opportunities, share risks, reduce costs and achieve goals not achievable individually, and their interactions are supported by computer networks.

In order to take advantage of the CN paradigm, a number of challenges are faced by partners, coming from multiple perspectives, like technological, semantic, social and business (Chituc, 2005). These challenges include, but are not limited to: maintenance of privacy and visibility levels (security) as CN partners are autonomous; overcoming cultural and legal barriers as they work differently of each other and are placed in different countries; and dealing with semantic and interoperability issues, as partners and systems are heterogeneous. Above all these perspectives, a fundamental issue and challenge is the establishment of mutual trust among partners.

Working collaboratively implies to share information[1], resources and responsebilities among entities that jointly plan, implement, and evaluate a program of activities

---

[1] *Information* is defined as the result of manipulation and organization processes based on data gathered in a given context. *Knowledge* is defined as a complete set of information and its relations that lead people to take decisions and to create new knowledge (Huber, 1991).

Tramontin, Jr., R.J., Rabelo, R.J., 2007, in IFIP International Federation for Information Processing, Volume 243, Establishing the Foundation of Collaborative Networks; eds. Camarinha-Matos, L., Afsarmanesh, H., Novais, P., Analide, C.; (Boston: Springer), pp. 573–582.

to achieve a common goal (Camarinha-Matos, 2006). However, a facet of this is related to the sharing of knowledge, still very low exploited but which has gained relevance as partners realize how much they can benefit with this higher-level of collaboration. *Knowledge sharing* among CN partners is becoming of paramount importance in collaboration, being useful not only at the operational level – helping partners to achieve their goals –, but also at the tactic and strategic levels – helping managers to take decisions and plan future actions.

Collaborative tools, like CSCW[2], provide support to the interactions among partners and so enable knowledge sharing among them. Such tools also store the exchanged knowledge in several information sources, like documents, mailing lists, forums, blogs, etc. On the other hand, CSCW-like tools do not solve the problem of how to access, to search and to filter the knowledge – which is distributed (over CN members) and in diverse formats, sources and has different meanings –, in an efficient and smart way.

This paper proposes a knowledge search framework for CNs. Such framework is supported by ontologies and deals with CN-related requirements not addressed by current information retrieval solutions, like semantic annotations consistency maintenance, multiple ontologies management, ontology mappings management and security issues. The proposed framework is being developed under the scope of the ECOLEAD[3] Project as part of an ICT infrastructure (ICT-I) for supporting CNs. Such infrastructure intends to support general (horizontal) requirements needed by any form of CN: people collaboration, systems interoperation, knowledge sharing, process synchronization, among others, in a secure, transparent, on demand and pay-per use way. The ECOLEAD ICT-I has been developed based on open platform-independent specifications and ICT standards, and in a Web Service Oriented Architecture (Rabelo, 2006).

Although the research on many aspects related to CN is of great value, this work is exclusively concerned with knowledge search aspects, such as semantic and security issues. Issues like trust building or interoperability are out of the scope.

The paper is organized as follows: section 2 describes the problem related to knowledge search in CNs; section 3 presents the envisaged framework; section 4 brings the implementation of a first prototype, and finally; section 5 presents the final remarks and the next steps.

2   PROBLEM DESCRIPTION

This section depicts the characteristics related to the problem of knowledge search in CNs and identifies the supporting techniques as well as the challenges and requirements involved.

2.1   Characteristics

The problem of knowledge search in CNs can be described through three main characteristics:

(I) There are multiple CNs, and each CN has its own shared knowledge available (documents, chat logs, mailing lists, etc.). Hence, **security** aspects should be taken into account in order to avoid unauthorized access from external members of the

---

[2] Computer Supported Cooperative Work
[3] www.ecolead.org

CNs. For example, a post registered in a web forum of a given CN can be only accessible by its partners. Additionally, as CN partners are independent and autonomous, it is also desirable for them to be able to define access levels for the knowledge they are making available. This allows parts of a given document to be kept private for some partners, or even the whole document itself.

(II) CN partners can take part in several CNs simultaneously. As a generalization of the characteristic previously presented, partners are able to have access to knowledge from all CN they are involved in. Here, security mechanisms should again be used to guarantee access as well as to allow partners to perform **federated searches** in the related CNs. Federated search (also known as *distributed information retrieval*) links multiple search engines into a single virtual system (Si, 2005), allowing users to search in multiple systems with a single search request. For example, a partner participating in three CNs, A, B and C, can perform a search in all of them or in just one.

(III) Each CN contains its own way of representing its semantics (domain knowledge). The terms used in a given CN (or even in a single company) may have different meanings in other CNs. This aspect causes some problems when a partner wants to search in all CNs (s)he is involved in. In this case, **semantic translations** should be done in the original search query in order to convert it into different – but equivalent – queries. The results of every query should be translated back to be presented in a unified and understandable format.

2.2   Techniques

As knowledge is explicitly represented (stored in information sources) the application of Information Retrieval (IR) techniques is the most natural approach towards the implementation of a knowledge search framework. IR is a very broad research area and, in general, its main goal is to provide means for searching information in documents or searching for documents themselves. Traditional implementations of these techniques are the Web search engines, notably Google. Search engines are based on keyword queries, meaning that the retrieved documents contain the keywords specified in the query. Although such techniques provide some support for semantics, like search for synonyms and spelling correction, they are not enough to deal with the characteristics of knowledge search in CNs.

From another point of view, one of the new trends in the IR area is the usage of **ontologies** in order to improve the effectiveness of information search (Kiryakov, 2003), (Stojanovic, 2005), (Köhler, 2006), and thus to help retrieving knowledge. Ontologies are being used in a vast range of applications to represent semantics in a formal way. In this regard, one important assumption that is not only related to CNs, but also to the whole IR area, is that information sources express their meaning using a well-defined semantics. In this sense, it is assumed that the domain knowledge of CNs (mentioned in section 2.1, characteristic III) is formally represented by ontologies, whose importance in this context is three-fold:

1. Allows the definition of **semantic annotations** in information sources. With well defined semantics expressed in a machine interpretable way, information sources can be more precisely processed and searched. The idea of annotating document content with semantic information from domain ontologies was proposed

by the Semantic Web[4] initiative (Berners-Lee, 2001), and it has been implemented in a number of applications. Annotations formally identify concepts and relations between concepts and are primarily intended for use by machines. One approach for that is to assign links between the document content and instances of an ontology (Figure 1), as defined by Kiryakov (2003).

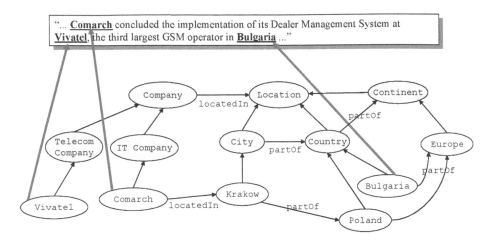

Figure 1 – Semantic annotations pointing to some instances (in white) of an ontology fragment (in grey). [Based on Kiryakov (2003)]

2. Allows the definition of **semantic searches**. Based on ontologies, queries can express precisely what kind of knowledge is going to be searched, which in turn is retrieved based on the semantic annotations previously indexed. A simple example of semantic query is: search for documents that contain *"IT Companies located in a Location called 'Europe'"*, i.e., documents containing annotations related to instances of the class "IT Company" that are located in "Europe", which in turn is an instance of the class "Location" (Figure 1). The result of this query would include the document presented in Figure 1, where "Comarch" is an "IT Company" located in "Poland" (which is part of "Europe").

3. Provides **semantic translation** support during *federated searches*. In this case, the search engine (also called meta-search engine) translates the original query to queries that are based on the ontologies used by the CNs involved in the search. Each new query is then executed in its related CN and the results are translated and presented to the user in a unified way. The query translation among the different contexts can be supported by **ontology mappings**. Ontology mapping (or matching) is a promising solution to the semantic heterogeneity problem, aiming at finding correspondences between semantically related entities of different ontologies, and thus enabling the data expressed in the matched ontologies to interoperate (OntologyMatching, 2006). This research area involves a large number of fields, ranging from machine learning, concept lattices and formal theories to heuristics, database schema and linguistics (Kalfoglou, 2003).

---

[4] http://www.w3.org/2001/sw/

2.3   Requirements and challenges involved

Based on the presented characteristics and the related techniques, some particular requirements of CNs have been identified:

1. Maintenance of multiple ontologies. In order to support semantic translations between CNs, mappings between ontologies should be identified and managed. Semi-automatic facilities are required.

2. Ontology evolution. In a dynamic environment such as CNs, ontologies tend to evolve and so the consistencies of both semantic annotations and ontology mappings should be maintained.

3. Document evolution. In a similar case, when a document evolves, the consistency between this document and its annotations should be assured.

4. Automatic annotation. It is a fundamental aspect considering a large collection of documents, as it occurs in CNs. Automatic or semi-automatic support for annotation can be provided using IE (information extraction) and other related NLP (natural language processing) techniques. Based on the assumption that there will be multiple ontologies, automatic annotation techniques should deal with ambiguities.

5. Usability. The process of search should be easy-to-use for non-technical users. The main drawback of semantic queries is that they are more suitable for specialists that know ontologies than for ordinary users. Additionally, users must know which ontologies they can use and which classes, properties and relations are more appropriate for the search.

6. Security. It is an orthogonal requirement that should be as transparent as possible when controlling the access to ontologies, information sources or the scope of federated searches.

Although some of these requirements are fulfilled by existing solutions, some others still have open research questions or represent significant research challenges. For example, there are several techniques and implementations for automatic annotation of documents; however, as stated by Uren (2006), there is little support for ontology evolution and consistency maintenance. Another relevant challenge is related to the usability of semantic searches, i.e., search queries should be constructed in an easy way. Finally, it is important to highlight that current contributions for each of these requirements were made in isolated areas, not considering the inter-dependencies and integration among them.

3   THE ENVISAGED FRAMEWORK

Based on the problem description presented in the previous section (its characteristics, techniques and requirements) a conceptual framework for knowledge search was envisaged. It provides four main functionalities implemented by one or more services[5]: ontology management (*ontology browser* and *ontology editor* services), document indexing (*document indexer* service), simple search (*search engine*) and federated search (*meta-search engine* and *semantic translator*). These functionalities are detailed below.

1. Ontology management: it is considered a preparatory (off-line) stage for the other functionalities. It is to be used by domain experts to build and to manage

---

[5] In this context the term *service* means a piece of software that provides a given functionality, regardless language and technologies involved on its implementation.

ontologies for representing knowledge in a given CN. This functionality can be divided in two sub-functionalities: *ontology browsing*, to allow read-only operations, like loading classes, properties and instances of ontologies; and *ontology edition*, to add/modify/remove classes, properties and instances. The reason for this division is that edition operations imply on ontology evolution, and consequently the maintenance of consistencies (of semantic annotations and ontology mappings).

2. Document Indexing: this functionality is used by information sources in order allow their documents to be searched in the future. This is provided by the *document indexer* service, which generates semantic annotations automatically, considering the ontologies used by the CN where the information provider is taking part. The annotations are further indexed.

3. Simple Search: using the *search engine* service, CN partners define semantic queries according to the ontologies adopted by the respective CN (provided by the *ontology browser* service).

4. Federated Search: users taking part in several CNs should use the *meta-search engine* service in order to perform federated searches. Users can choose the context of the search (among the CNs they are involved), define the semantic query, and then perform the search. All needed translations are made transparently by the *semantic translator* according to the ontologies of each involved CN, and the search results are translated back to the ontologies used in the original query. Moreover, the *meta-search engine* should use security mechanisms to control the search scope.

Mappings between ontologies must be defined and maintained in order to support automatic semantic translations. This aspect is not specified in this model because it can be implemented in several ways (Freitas, 2005), which has impact on how mappings should be identified and maintained, as well as how the *semantic translator* should work.

Another aspect not covered at the conceptual level is the semantic annotation approach. There are several techniques related to this issue, classified in two broader categories, *pattern-based* and *machine learning-based* (Reeve, 2005). In this sense, the model is not bound to any technique, which should be chosen during its implementation.

Besides the previous aspects, issues related to the *usability* of the semantic search are not covered by the framework. This subject is more related to the implementation level, such as graphical user interfaces.

The architecture of the conceptual framework is shown in Figure 2. Although the services are not bound to any deployment configuration, most of them should be instantiated to specific CNs. The purpose of such distribution is to allow each CN to have its own domain knowledge, documents and indexes managed by dedicated services, and thus allowing searches inside the CN scope (performed by the *search engine* service). Federated searches are provided by the *meta-search engine* and supported by the *semantic translator*. There is a single instance for each one of these services, regardless the number of CNs.

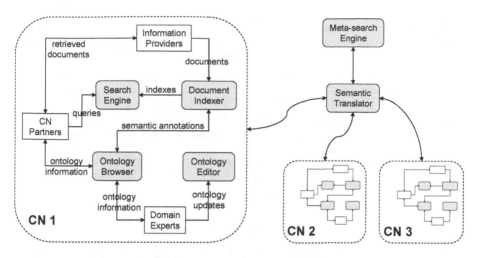

Figure 2 – Architectural view of the conceptual framework.

The services' behavior and their distribution proposed in this framework are just recommendations and can be extended or reconfigured according to specific implementation needs, limitations or by design decisions. Next section presents the implementation aspects of a prototype that is currently being developed.

4   PROTOTYPE IMPLEMENTATION

As mentioned before, the framework proposed in this work has been developed under the scope of the ECOLEAD Project as part of an ICT infrastructure (ICT-I) for supporting CNs in a (Web) Service Oriented Architecture. The implementation of such framework is called Knowledge Search Services (*K. Search*). Following the recommendations applied for the whole ICT-I implementation, these services have been developed on top of existing solutions and some value/innovation for CNs is being added. In this sense, *K. Search* services are built on top of an IR platform called KIM Platform, which provides APIs for automatic (pattern-based) semantic annotation, indexing and retrieval of documents (Popov, 2003). The architecture of *K. Search* is shown in Figure 3.

Besides *K. Search* services themselves (on top of KIM), there are some client applications, namely: information providers for publishing documents; CN applications that perform searches; and an ontology GUI editor for ontology management. There is a special web client used to perform semantic queries upon the *K. Search* services. It is being implemented as a Java portlet that provides an easy-to-use GUI for general purpose searches. This portlet can be extended or customized to be used by particular applications. Figure 4 shows two screenshots of this portlet (showing a query and its matching entities, and the resulting document).

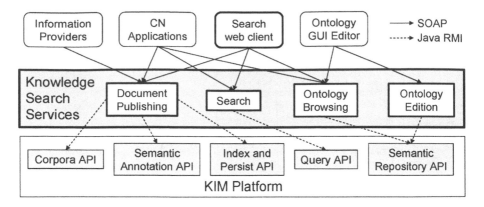

Figure 3 – *K. Search* Architecture.

As the envisaged functionalities should be transparent and easy-to-use, some KIM API functionalities were merged into a single K. Search operation. For instance, the publishing of a document (provided by K. Search) involves storing, annotation and indexing (provided by KIM). The current version of K. Search is limited as KIM Platform covers only a subset of the envisaged requirements: it works only with a single ontology, provides automatic generation of annotations and indexing of them, and it is possible to make semantic queries. These functionalities are being extended in order to cover the remaining requirements. For instance, current K. Search implementation provides a mechanism for consistency maintenance (not provided by KIM), consisting of re-annotating and re-indexing all documents in background. Another improvement regarding *K. Search* services that is under development is the integration with DRACO (Sowa, 2007), a security framework also in development in the scope of ECOLEAD Project.

Knowledge Search

Search for Entities

Where name contains ▾ | yahoo   Search |

2 entities found!

A *Brand*, called **Yahoo!**, present in no document. (Use this entity in an advanced search)

A *PublicCompany*, called **Yahoo! Inc.**, present in 1 document. (Use this entity in an advanced search)

Knowledge Search

Query

1 document found.

Independent News News | Money | Travel | Argument | Advancement | Enjoyment Independent > News > Digital > News Guardian IT joins tech wrecks as warning halves share price By Liz Vaughan-Adams 10 August 2001 Guardian IT, a disaster recovery business, saw its market value halve...

Details...

Figure 4 –*K. Search* portlet screenshots.

5   CONCLUSIONS AND NEXT STEPS

This paper focused on the problem of knowledge search in CNs and proposed a supporting conceptual framework that takes into account requirements and challenges related to CNs. The proposed framework defines some recommendations related to the expected behavior of the envisaged functionalities and can be extended or reconfigured according to implementation needs or limitations.

A first version of a prototype (*K. Search* services) has been developed and it is already available, but it requires a number of improvements in order to cover the identified requirements. This prototype, along with the whole ICT-I, will be evaluated under the scope of the ECOLEAD project in a series of test-cases close to real CNs. Next activities regarding *K. Search* development comprise:

(a) Implementation of the *meta-search engine* service, for allowing federated searches, regarding both security and semantic aspects.

(b) Multiple ontologies management and functionalities for identification of similarities between ontologies and mappings management. MAFRA[6] Toolkit and the system proposed by Sánchez-Alberca (2005) are under evaluation and seem to be good candidates for implementing this feature.

(c) A client Ontology GUI Editor (based on Protégé[7]) will be developed to allow users to manage ontologies. As seen in the implementation architecture, this tool will be the client of the ontology management services (browsing and edition).

(d) Final refinements in the search portlet and in the consistency maintenance mechanism.

Although the conceptual framework is not bound to any implementation model, the further developments under the scope of this work may require future refinements in the conceptual model.

As a final remark, it is important to highlight that the knowledge search task is demanding and complex. Hence, there are many open issues and challenges that require deeper efforts, like natural language processing techniques for interpretation of higher-level queries (defined in natural language), and the automatic identification of similarities between ontologies.

5.1   Acknowledgments

This work has been partially supported by the Brazilian council of research and scientific development – CNPq. It has been developed in the scope of the Brazilian IFM project (www.ifm.org.br) and the European IST FP-6 IP ECOLEAD project (www.ecolead.org). Special thanks also to Mr. Carlos E. Gesser and Mr. Leandro Loss for their contributions during the design and implementation of the prototype.

6   REFERENCES

1.   Berners-Lee, T.; Hendler, J.; Lassila, O.; 2001. The Semantic Web. In: Scientific American, May 2001 issue.
2.   Camarinha-Matos, L. M.; Afsarmanesh; H.; Ollus, M.; 2005. ECOLEAD: A Holistic Approach to Creation and Management of Dynamic Virtual Organizations. In: Proceedings of the Sixth IFIP Working Conference on Virtual Enterprises (PRO-VE'05). pp. 3-16.

---

[6] https://sourceforge.net/projects/mafra-toolkit
[7] http://protege.stanford.edu/index.html

3. Camarinha-Matos, L. M.; Afsarmanesh, H.; 2006. Collaborative Networks: Value Creation in a Knowledge Society. In: Proceedings of PROLAMAT'06, Shanghai, China, 14-16 2006.
4. Chituc, C. M.; Azevedo, A. L.; 2005. Multi-Perspective Challenges on Collaborative Networks Business Environments. In: Proceedings of the Sixth IFIP Working Conference on Virtual Enterprises (PRO-VE'05). pp. 25-32.
5. Freitas, F.; Stuckenschmidt, H.; Noy., N. F.; 2005. Ontology Issues and Applications. In: Journal of the Brazilian Computer Society, Number 2, Volume 11, November 2005. ISSN 0104-6500.
6. Huber, G. P.; 1991. Organizational learning: The contributing processes and the literatures. Organization Science, pp. 88-115.
7. Kalfoglou, Y.; Schorlemmer, M.; 2003. Ontology Mapping: The State of the Art. In: The Knowledge Engineering Review Journal, 2003.
8. Kiryakov, A.; Popov, B.; Ognyanoff, D.; Manov, D.; Kirilov, A.; Goranov, M.; 2003. Semantic Annotation, Indexing, and Retrieval. In: 2nd International Semantic Web Conference (ISWC2003).
9. Köhler, J.; Philippi, S.; Specht, M.; Rüegg, A.; 2006. Ontology based text indexing and querying for the semantic web. In: Knowledge-Based Systems, Volume 19, Issue 8, December 2006, pp. 744-754
10. OntologyMatching; 2006. http://ontologymatching.org/
11. Popov, B.; Kiryakov, A.; Kirilov, A.; Manov, D.; Ognyanoff, D.; Goranov, M.; 2003. KIM – Semantic Annotation Platform. In: 2nd International Semantic Web Conference (ISWC2003).
12. Rabelo, R. J.; Gusmeroli, S.; Arana, C.; Negellen, T.; 2006. The ECOLEAD ICT Infrastructure for Collaborative Networked Organizations. In: Proceedings of the Seventh IFIP Working Conference on Virtual Enterprises (PRO-VE'06). pp. 451-460.
13. Reeve, L.; Han, H.; 2005. Survey of semantic annotation platforms. In: SAC '05: Proceedings of the 2005 ACM symposium on Applied computing. pp. 1634-1638. ACM Press, New York, NY, USA.
14. Sánchez-Alberca, A.; García-García, R.; Sorzano, C. O. S.; Gutiérrez-Cossío, C.; Chagoyen, M.; Fernández-López, M.; 2005. AMON: A Software System for Automatic Generation of Ontology Mappings. In: Workshop on Building and Applying Ontologies for the Sematic Web (BAOSW'05).
15. Si, L.; Callan, J.; 2005. Modeling Search Engine Effectiveness for Federated Search. In: Proceedings of the 28th annual international ACM SIGIR conference on Research and development in information retrieval (SIGIR '05). pp. 83-90. ACM Press, New York, NY, USA.
16. Sowa, G.; Śnieżyński, T.; 2007. Technical Report (Deliverable) D61.4b - Security framework and architecture.
17. Stojanovic, N; 2005. On the query refinement in the ontology-based searching for information. In: Information Systems, Volume 30, Issue 7, November 2005, pp. 543-563.
18. Uren, V.; Cimiano, P.; Iria, J.; Handschuh, S.; Vargas-Vera, M.; Motta, E.; Ciravegna, F.; 2006. Semantic annotation for knowledge management: Requirements and a survey of the state of the art. In: Journal of Web Semantics. 4(1): 14-28 (2006).

PART 20

PRODUCT-ORIENTED COLLABORATION

63

MAINTAINING DYNAMIC PRODUCT DESIGNS TO ENABLE EFFECTIVE CONSORTIUM BUILDING IN VIRTUAL BREEDING ENVIRONMENTS

Marcus Seifert, Klaus-Dieter Thoben
BIBA Bremen, GERMANY, sf@biba.uni-bremen

The potential of a Virtual Breeding Environment (VBE) is the ability to design and to realise innovative, customized products by selecting and integrating for each order the worldwide leading partners. To exploit this potential, it is too late to configure the consortium and to search for partners on the basis of an already specified bill of material: Co-operation has already to take place with the product-idea, where possible contributions to the planned end- product must be identified while concretising the bill of material. Only in this way, the VBE is able to benefit from the expertise of all potential partners and to ensure that the expertise of the planned consortium is also synchronised with the needed capabilities for the requested end-product. In this paper, a method to support the building of consortia within the VBE on the basis of open product designs will be highlighted. The method starts from an end-product and collects possible contributions from potential collaboration partners.

1   INTRODUCTION

Market success under a worldwide competition depends more and more on the ability to provide customised products. The increasing complexity of these products led to the situation that capital intensive, complex investment goods are almost realised in co-operation between many partners. The single partner focuses on its core competencies while the process diversity is ensured by co-operation. Competition does not happen any more between single companies but between consortia (Boutellier 1999, S.66). The ability to form excellent co-operations is an important asset for the today's production and competitiveness.

1.1   Collaboration in virtual organisations

Today's opportunity to have a worldwide access to resources and capacities enables companies to select for each business opportunity the best suitable partners to fulfil highly customised customer orders. By comparing with former times these conditions provide significant and inexhaustible advantages for today's organisations. Companies are not dependent any more on existing relationships or regional suppliers' information and communication technologies. High performing logistics capabilities encourage the global business which means serving worldwide distributed customers on the one hand and benefiting from global resources and capacities for production on the other hand. The commitment of legally independent, coequal companies to take a common advantage of business opportunities to serve the market with specific customer demanded products has been introduced as Virtual Breeding Environment (VBE). This VBE is foreseen to improve the collaboration preparedness of companies to set up Virtual Organisations.

Seifert, M., Thoben, K.-D., 2007, in IFIP International Federation for Information Processing, Volume 243, Establishing the Foundation of Collaborative Networks; eds. Camarinha-Matos, L., Afsarmanesh, H., Novais, P., Analide, C.; (Boston: Springer), pp. 585–592.

Within Virtual Organisations, the capability to optimise existing process chains in a continuous way as required in stable Supply Chains is not any more the main asset. It is rather critical to be able to identify and to select for a certain order the most appropriate partners and to establish in a very efficient way a high performing co-operation (Kemmner 1999, p.33). Today's available approaches to identify and to select partners are mainly focussing on the production phase which means that the search and selection criteria are focussing on a companies' capability to provide excellent processes and to integrate themselves into a networked organisation. Thus the consortium building process is linked with the realisation of an already defined product and founded on an existing bill of material of the desired end-product.

The purpose of these existing approaches can be described as a way to set-up high performing production networks. In consequence, many approaches which have been developed in the past provide a wide range of criteria and key performance indicators (KPIs) which are focussing on the performance of companies and their production processes. KPIs are almost the basis for a structured partner search and evaluation. But the approach to select partners according to their process performance does only consider mainly one phase of the product life cycle which is the production phase. This does always lead to optimisation tasks to select the best performing partners for a pre-defined set of processes to provide already specified components or sub-systems. However a product's lifecycle is characterised by several phases. The other phases of the product life cycle like the conceptual phase or the after sales phases do have completely different requirements for the partner selection. This is due to the fact that each of the phases is characterised by distinctive design of processes, usage of resources and produced outcomes. Identified partners can be excellent for one phase of the product life cycle but may cause detrimental effects at another.

1.2   The conceptual phase as potential for Virtual Breeding Environments

In the VBE, the product life cycle phase with the highest potential is the conceptual phase. Virtual Organisations as concrete instantiation of a VBE do mainly provide complex and customised investment goods (Linde 1997, S.25) which can be described as engineer-to-order products. Considering this aspect, the conceptual phase where the concrete design of the end-product is not defined yet and where the bill of material is rather vague is the phase of the product life cycle with the highest potential for the consortium building: In the conceptual phase, there are still most of the degrees of freedom for the involvement of partners and the design of innovative products.

The chance within VBEs during the conceptual phase is to be able to enrich and improve the product's value to the customer by involving the experience and competencies of all potential partners with the challenge to realise excellent products. Free from long-term contracts with suppliers and static processes, VBEs have the chance to incorporate the worldwide existing expertise into new product designs which enable the network to serve the market with highly customised and reliable products.

This means that it is not the main purpose in the conceptual phase to optimise resources and processes or to identify available capacities but to identify potential beneficial product contributions to the planned end-product and further on, capabilities of possible partnerships. The objective should be to integrate potential partners very early for the concretion of the end-product. Only in this way, possible product innovations can be developed and competencies as well as experiences of all potential partners can be used synergetic in order to concretize the end-product. The chance to get to innovative solutions depends on the ability to gather the knowledge of promising partners already during the conceptual phase.

Today, it can be recognized that many product designs are not developed from scratch. Also, complex "engineer-to-order" products are partly composed of available sub-systems and components which have to be adapted and integrated into the new design. Many companies are providing products which are explicitly meant to become parts of more complex systems. For example today's mobile phones containing touch-screen, GPS, UMTS and wireless-LAN units on a Windows Mobile platform only combine and integrate existing sub-systems and components which are available on the market and therefore normally well described and known. Hence the main task is to identify beneficial sub-systems to develop innovative products and to integrate them into the planned design.

The ability to make use of those available sub-systems, also in complex product designs, enables companies in principle to evaluate potential partnerships already during the conceptual phase of the end-product. Against this background, the ability to identify potential contributions to a planned end-product and to initiate very early commercial relationships becomes a crucial asset for the instantiation of Virtual Organisations.

2 STATE OF THE ART: EXISTING APPROACHES FOR CONSORTIUM BUILDING

The process of consortium building can be divided into two phases which are (1) partner search and (2) partner selection (Mertins, Faisst 1995, p.61ff.). The purpose of the partner search is to identify potential cooperation partners for a specific task within a specific phase of the product life cycle while the objective of the partner selection is to evaluate these potential co-operation partners and to decide for a consortium. Literature and practice provide many methods to support consortium building. In the following, the most important concepts will be highlighted and structured according to the product life. For the product life cycle, the phases requirements, conception, production, usage, maintenance and end-of-life can be distinguished.

2.1 Existing methods for partner search

Each of the product life cycle phases has different degrees of freedom regarding the partner search: The more indefinite the product design, the larger the pool of potential partnerships. While concretizing the product design and the bill of material, the requirements regarding process capabilities of potential partners and component design become more specific. This leads automatically to a reduction of possible choices for partners. Figure 1 shows the interdependency between the potential partnerships and the product life cycle.

According to Zahn, existing relationships between companies are still the main basis for partner search (Zahn 2001, p.60). This means that companies rely on existing co-operations and try to continue the business with well known suppliers. The decision for co-operation almost bases on company representatives' private contacts (Hoebig 2002, p.43). In consequence, the partner selection process cannot be focussed on excellent partnerships but on the maintenance of established bilateral contacts. The advantage of selecting well known partners is the already established trust between the parties. Disadvantage is on the other hand the reduction on a small group of potential partners which makes it improbable to find the best suitable partner and which impedes the consideration of the available potentials to improve the product life cycle processes of a planned product.

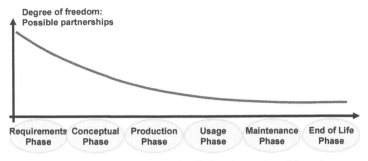

Figure 1: Potential partnerships during the product life cycle

Alternative concepts coming from literature to search for partners in a more structured way are information brokers and co-operation databases (Kramer 1998, Zahn 2001). Co-operation databases make use of the internet and correspond to virtual public market places for partnerships. Companies willing to co-operate are able to enter their profile into these data bases to offer their capabilities or they can search for partners by defining search criteria. Most of these databases are provided by chambers of commerce. Zahn gives a review on co-operation databases in (Zahn 2001, S.63). To improve the search results, Kramer introduces the concept of information broker to identify potential partners by mapping the requested requirements with the offered core competencies.

2.2 Existing methods to select partners

After having identified potential partnerships, the next task is to select the right partners out of this pool. The selection normally bases on an evaluation process using key performance indicators (KPIs). The advantage in using KPIs is to gain common syntax and semantics for the assessment of partners' processes. Today, most of the implemented methods for partner selection are focussing on finding suppliers – nevertheless, there are also approaches available which are able to evaluate the different phases of the product life cycle. The evaluation can be cost-based, quality-based or process-based (Seidl 2002, p. 27). In the following, the most relevant concepts for these three categories to support partner selection are highlighted. Figure 2 maps these concepts in respect of the product life cycle.

Figure 2 shows that there are specific approaches available to evaluate cost, quality and processes during the different phases of the product life cycle. These approaches have been developed almost for traditional Supply Chains. The most relevant process oriented approaches are the Supply Chain Operations Reference Model (SCOR) for Supply Chain processes, the Design Chain Operations Reference Model (DCOR) for design and conception processes, the Value Chain Operations Reference Model (VCOR) also covering the service development and the Balanced Scorecards (BSC). A well known and often used cost oriented approach is the Activity Based Costing (ABC) able to cover in principle almost all activities related to the product life cycle. Finally, Six Sigma and the European Foundation for Quality Management (EFQM) represent the quality oriented approaches to evaluate industrial processes. Dependent on the phase and the perspective, it is possible to select an appropriate approach for evaluating a potential partners' performance.

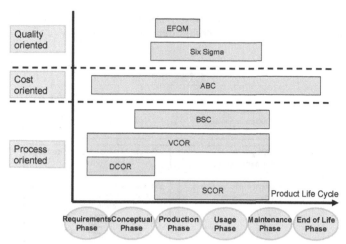

Figure 2: Concepts for the partner selection in the product life cycle (Seifert 2007, p. 39ff.)

3   RESEARCH APPROACH

The proposed approach is structured into two parts: Part one (chapter 3.1) is the collection of company profiles of co-operation willing companies to acquire data on their offered sub-systems and components as potential contributions to any kind of planned end-product. These company profiles are the basis for the partner identification. By applying key performance indicators referring to the different phases of the product life cycle to the profiles, it is also possible to take these profiles in a later step as basis for the partner selection in any phase of the life cycle.

Part two (chapter 3.2) uses these profiles to generate in an iterative way possible product structures for a concrete planned end-product. By searching and combining possible components, different product variants can be developed. Collecting and structuring these potential product contributions, the result are the available alternatives in terms of product structure and partner selection. Following this approach, it is possible to contact and involve potential partners for a new customers' order in a very early phase of the product life cycle. A flexible product design is the main basis for collaborative designs and the derivation of innovative products, because innovation requires the involvement of all available knowledge and experience within a potential network and the structured identification and evaluation of potential solutions.

3.1   Company profiles to acquire potential product contributions

To set up company profiles of VBE members as starting point to generate flexible product designs, it is important to collect information about these potential partners. Beside administrative data, information about the offered products have to be collected and stored in a unified, structured way to enable the iterative generation of bill of materials for the desired end-product. The last aspect to be provided by each partner is the information about their performance to enable, after the partner identification, a partner selection on the basis of their KPIs. To guarantee high quality on potential partners it is proposed to provide specific performance indicators for different

phases of a product life cycle under the auspices of an integrated quality management approach. Figure 3 shows the components of the company profile.

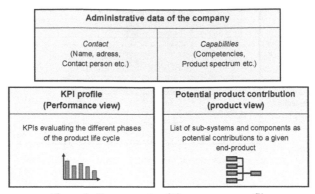

Figure 3: Components of the company profile

The offered sub-systems and components as potential contributions to an end-
product provided by a company have to be described in a way that also the necessary inputs to generate this sub-system have to be defined. Figure 4 shows simple
examples for the description of sub-systems within a company profile.

The sub-systems provided in this example are potential contributions to a bicycle. Each sub-system (e.g. the wheel) is linked with the necessary input to realise
this product which are the in this case rim, casing and tube. Other companies may
offer the same sub-system consisting of different inputs which would lead to alternatives and completely new product designs. Partners providing different variants on
the same level enlarge the networks' capability on a horizontal level. Another company may offer the rim as its own potential contribution to a bicycle consisting of
the specific input. This kind of vertical contribution is called enrichment of the
product scale. Figure 4 shows the difference between horizontal enlargement enabling alternatives and vertical enrichment completing the product structure.

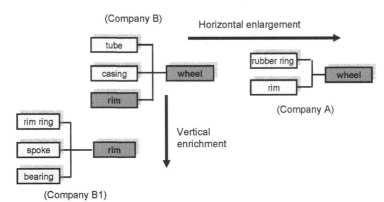

Figure 4: Horizontal enlargement and vertical enrichment of the product scale

All sub-systems and components of all potential partners have to be provided in
this way to be stored in a database. The components are stored within the database
independent from their further usage and independent from a specific end-product.

In the next chapter, it is described how these sub-systems are used to derive complex product designs.

3.2 Iterative generation of possible product structures and derivation of potential partnerships for the Conceptual phase

The generation of possible product structures on the basis of the available company profiles takes its starting point from the desired end-product. By searching in the company profiles, the first vertical level of product contributions is collected and added to the product structure. Different variants of certain product contributions as described in Figure 4 may lead to different potential designs. For each product contribution, the necessary inputs are searched within the available company profiles. Step by step, the alternative product designs can be evaluated and completed. Figure 5 shows the mechanism of the iterative completion with a simple example.

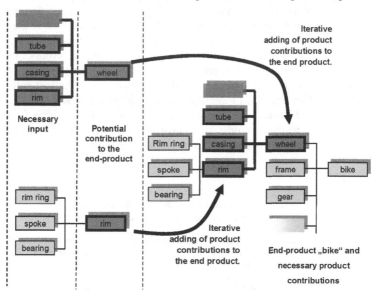

Figure 5: Iterative generation of a product structure by adding possible product contributions

The described iteration loop is executed as long as there are inputs defined for a product contribution. The result is a multi-dimensional tree structure containing all potential product structures provided by the gathered company profiles. On the basis of the performance indicators, it is now possible to evaluate the potential consortia and to select promising partners to realise the requested end-product.

This tree supports VBE not only to identify alternative product designs and to evaluate partnerships. In the case that needed product contributions cannot be covered by the capabilities of the network, these gaps are the impact to concretize the strategic competence development of the co-operation willing partners. Missing competencies and resources can be identified already during the early conceptual phase and suitable additional partners can be searched immediately.

4   CONCLUSION

The presented method demonstrated how different product designs can be evaluated in the conceptual phase of the product life cycle and how these alternatives can support the early involvement of promising partners in the product specification. This approach differs from many approaches in practice which require a concrete product design as starting point for the consortium building. The knowledge about potential product variants and available alternatives in the partner selection is a crucial asset to be able to compensate e.g. a sudden loss of delivery of a certain partner as fast as possible. The preparedness to generate alternative designs and to involve alterative partners is very important for engineer-to-order products where very late design changes may become relevant in case of changing customer wishes or in case of unpredictable technical problems or malfunctions.

The participation of potential partners in the specification phase and the methodological identification of beneficial partnerships enable the consideration of the available knowledge and experience of these potential partners which is the basis for the development of innovative, competitive products and successful offers. Companies having the chance to participate already in the collaborative product design are in a better position to prepare them selves for the order fulfilment which improves the ability of the VBE to place offers. The ability to provide excellent solutions for customer specific demands and to decline leading offers are crucial for the success of a VBE - because the production phase and its optimisation which is an aspect addressed by many research works, can only take place after a successful and accepted offer after the contract negotiation with the customer.

5   REFERENCES

1.   Boutellier, Roman: Konkurrenz der Logistikketten, in Logistik Heute, Ausgabe Mai 1999
2.   Höbig, Michael: Modellgestützte Bewertung der Kooperationsfähigkeit produzierender Unternehmen, Hannover 2002
3.   Kemmner, Götz-Andreas, Gillessen, Andreas: Virtuelle Unternehmen – Ein Leitfaden zum Aufbau und zur Organisation einer mittelständischen Unternehmenskooperation, Heidelberg 1999
4.   Kramer, Peter: Die Virtualisierung der Unternehmung: Prozesse, Strukturen und Instrumente eines "grenzenlosen" strategischen Konzeptes, Basel 1998
5.   Linde, Frank: Virtualisierung von Unternehmen - Wettbewerbspolitische Implikationen, Gabler Verlag, Wiesbaden 1997.
6.   Mertins, Peter; Faisst, Wolfgang: Virtuelle Unternehmen – eine Organisationsstruktur für die Zukunft?, in: technologie+management, Nr.2, 1995
7.   Seidl, Jörg: Business Process Performance-Modellbezogene Beurteilung und Ansätze zur Optimierung, in: HMD Praxis der Wirtschaftsinformatik, Heft 227, S.27-35, Oktober 2002
8.   Seifert, Marcus: Unterstützung der Konsortialbildung in Virtuellen Organisationen durch prospektives Performance Measurement, Bremen 2007
9.   Sydow, Jörg: Strategische Netzwerke: Evolution und Organisation, Gabler Verlag, Wiesbaden 2002
10. Zahn, Erich: Wachstumspotenziale kleiner und mittlerer Dienstleister: Mit Dienstleistungsnetzwerken zu Full-Service Leistungen, Stuttgart 2001

64

DISTRIBUTED DESIGN OF PRODUCT ORIENTED MANUFACTURING SYSTEMS

Sílvio do Carmo-Silva[a], A.C. Alves[a] C., P. Novais[b], M. Costa[c], C. Carvalho[b], J. Costa[b], M. Marques[b]

[a]Centre for Production Systems Engineering (CESP), University of Minho, Campus de Gualtar, 4700-057 Braga, PORTUGAL (scarmo@dps.uminho.pt; anabela@dps.uminho.pt)
[b]Departamento de Informática-CCTC, University of Minho, Campus de Gualtar, 4700-057 Braga, PORTUGAL
(a35288@alunos.uminho.pt; jorgemaiocosta@hotmail.com; marquesmps@gmail.com; pjon@di.uminho.pt)
[c](costamiguel@bragatel.pt)

Manufacturing leanness and agility are requirements of today's manufacturing systems. Leanness call for a best fit of the manufacturing systems to products, therefore requiring product oriented manufacturing systems (POMS). Manufacturing agility can be achieved through easy systems reconfiguration to fit changing manufacturing requirements, which may mean dynamically configuring POMS. For this a suitable design system is required. Due to complexity of this design, and to the need for using suitable design methods, which may not be available locally, distributed sources of design services can be used. This paper presents and describes a prototype of a Distributed Design system for POMS based on a POMS design methodology and distributed suppliers of design services.

1   INTRODUCTION

Industrial companies, nowadays, live in a paradigm of high competition in a market environment of frequently changing product demands. Therefore, manufacturing leanness and agility are requirements of today's manufacturing systems as a means of effectively answer varying market requirements and maintain competitiveness. Leanness call for a best fit of the manufacturing systems to manufacturing require-ments of products. Manufacturing agility can be dealt with by frequently adjusting or reconfiguring manufacturing systems to fit changing manufacturing requirements. Thus apparently, both leanness and agility can be achieved through Product Oriented Manufacturing Systems (POMS). These may be defined as systems interconnect-ting manufacturing workstations or cells, usually involving people, which simul-taneously and in a coordinated manner address the manufacture of a single product or a family of similar products, subject to frequent reconfiguration to be

Carmo-Silva, S., Alves, A.C., Novais, P., Costa, M., Carvalho, C., Costa, J., Marques, M., 2007, in IFIP International Federation for Information Processing, Volume 243, Establishing the Foundation of Collaborative Networks; eds. Camarinha-Matos, L., Afsarmanesh, H., Novais, P., Analide, C.; (Boston: Springer), pp. 539–600.

adapted to changing manufacturing requirements of products or product families (Carmo-Silva et al., 2005).

The design of POMS tends to rely mostly on human expertise and ability for arriving to acceptable system configuration solutions to fit continuously changing product demand. This design approach is slow and ineffective and tends to introduce inefficiency on manufacturing operations activity. Such human based design may be justified when no suitable design system for POMS design, is available. Since, in addition to several methodologies (Suh, 1990, Burbidge, 1989, Black, 1991, Cochran et al., 2002), there are available a large variety of methods and procedures to aid the manufacturing system design function (Suresh and Kay, 1998, Irani, 1999) apparently there is no reason to base POMS design almost exclusively on human expertise. The use of design systems based on computer applications, which implement valid methods under a suitable design methodology, can provide the missing tool required for achieving fast and good reconfiguration solutions of POMS, to fit changing manufacturing requirements. However, not always the methods required are locally available. Due to this, many design functions may have to rely on distributed sources of design services. This paper presents and describes a prototype of a distributed design system for POMS based on a manufacturing system design methodology and distributed suppliers of design services.

The paper presents in section 2 a description of the computer aided design system framework organized around a POMS design methodology. In section 2 the architecture components and prototype of a POMS design system based on a community of servers providing design services is described. In section 4 a conclusion is presented.

2   COMPUTER AIDED DESIGN SYSTEM FRAMEWORK FOR POMS DESIGN

2.1   CADS_POMS Framework

POMS design can be based on a design methodology. One such methodology, named GCD - Generic-Conceptual-Detailed - was proposed by Silva and Alves (2002). It essentially puts forward a hierarchical multilevel and iterative design process for POMS. Important data and restrictions are considered and a range of methods can be used in the POMS design process. Under this methodology the design process is organized in three main phases and includes several design stages and activities.

However important the GCD methodology may be, it can be of little use if not supported by a computer aided design system (CADS). This must address POMS design activities from strategic planning to the POMS organization and production control mechanisms definition. A CADS_POMS framework based on the GCD methodology for POMS design is shown in Figure 1.

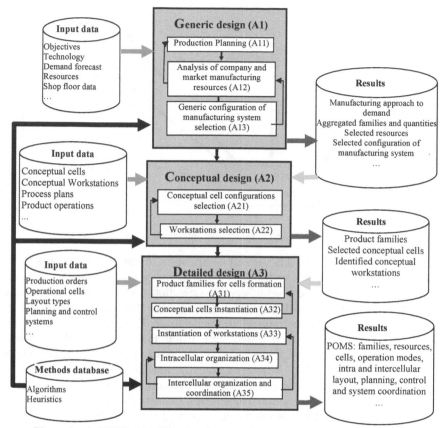

Figure 1 – A CADS_POMS design framework based on the GCD methodology

3 A DISTRIBUTED DESIGN SYSTEM

3.1 System Architecture and Functionalities

Figure 2 illustrates the main components and gives a simplified view of the architecture of the POMS distributed design system that may be seen as an instantiation structure of the CADS_POMS design framework presented in figure 1.

The system is organized around a central POMS database, a POMS design methods database, a distributed set of design methods servers, for aiding POMS design, and a interactive human-computer POMS design application module, with graphical user interfaces, named POMS designer.

Although some design methods and procedures for POMS design may be available locally, many more can be available through several servers distributed globally. These are identified as POMS design methods servers. These servers supply POMS design services requested by the POMS designer to perform design functions or tasks under the CADS-POMS design framework show in figure 1.

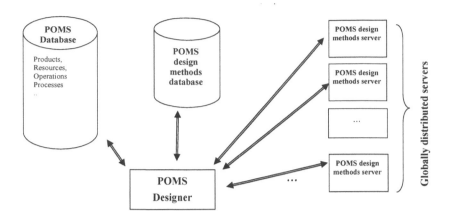

Figure 2 - POMS design system components and architecture

The POMS designer interacts with all components of the POMS design system. It interacts with the POMS system Database in many ways. Initially products, manufacturing resources and a set of generic operations, which can be instantiated by process planning for defining the process plan for each product to be manufactured, are specified or copied into the database. Then, the user can plan the process for manufacturing each product by using the set of standard generic operations which are then parameterized according product processing requirements (Carmo-Silva et al., 2005). Resources, mostly machines that are central to workstations, capable of carrying out product operations, are then chosen according to resource attributes and processing capabilities. Estimates of operation processing times for each resource are also produced. This process is totally under control of user, although some process planning systems may be used to easy this task. These described functions are essential for generating the main data and information required for POMS design. A computer application addressing this process of data generation for POMS design has been already developed (Carmo-Silva et al., 2005). This can be seen as an important part of the prototype of the POMS design system here reported.

Since it is sought frequent system configuration for adapting production systems to changes in product demand, we may refer to this POMS design as POMS reconfiguration.

3.2   Distributed Design Services

POMS reconfiguration relies not only on methods locally available but also on design methods implemented and run at distributed servers. The interaction of POMS designer with the methods database is the first step in the POMS reconfiguration process. This database provides information about the location of servers and the list of methods that are available, and where, for solving specific design tasks or problems, at request of the POMS designer. The methods database also provides information about the data input formats which are used for each method.

The following assumptions were considered in the modeling of the methods database: each method solves a specific problem or design task; each problem relates to a particular design activity in a design phase of the GCD methodology summary illustrated in figure 1; one particular design method may have implementations in more than one server.

The input data for running a method is prepared by the POMS designer and sent to a suitable methods server, which then run the method and send back results to POMS designer in an already known format. The communication process is carried out over the network through the TCP/IP protocols.

3.3 Running Methods on Servers

In an implementation example of the distributed POMS reconfiguration process a methods server application was developed. This, once operating in a methods server that is active, allows the server to accept requests from POMS designer for design tasks. Figure 3 identifies the graphical interface of the methods server application.

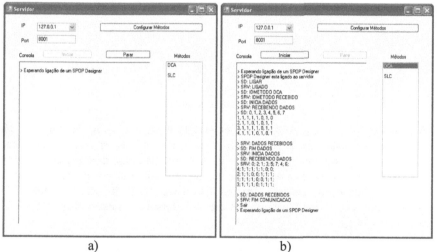

a)   b)

Figure 3 - Methods server application interface: a) waiting for the a request from a client; b) input data from the request and output data sent to the client

It shows the server capability to offer two methods for POMS design tasks, namely the DCA – Direct Clustering Algorithm (Chan and Milner, 1982) and the SLC - Single Linkage Clustering (McAuley, 1972) methods. These are useful for forming manufacturing cells by identifying product families, based on process plan similarities of products. This is part of activity A31 of the detailed design phase A3 (Carmo-Silva and Alves, 2006), as shown in figure 1. Input data sent by the SPOP designer, prepared with basis on a SQL stored procedure for the DCA implementation on the server, is illustrated in the figure 3.

Once there is a need for a design task to be carried out the SPOP designer must choose a suitable method from a methods list provided in the methods database and, additionally, select the server do supply the service.

A request is then generated and stored in a list of requests, figure 4. This list of design service requests by the SPOP designer is generated as a matter of monitoring the answers of servers, and allowing request repetition when for some reason, related for example with communications or server operation, no answer is received from servers.

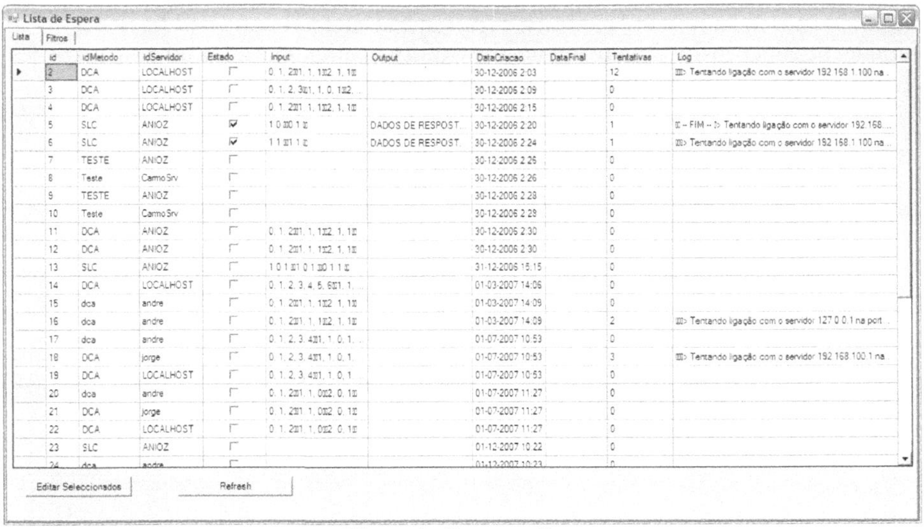

Figure 4 - Requests list

A summary of the request and service supply process is show in figure 5. The need for a design task to be performed in a particular activity of design phase leeds to the choice of a design method listed in the methods database and a selection of the suitable server. This permits a request for the design task after due preparation of the method input data in the correct format. The answer from the server to the SPOP designer request is provided through the methods server application for a of request output, figure 5.

3.4   Managing Distributed Servers Community

The system architecture allows dynamic updating of the community of servers providing design services. Any server that joins the community must be registered. This means supplying its location and specifying the design services that it offers. This is done through the SPOP designer that, in addition to ensuring the POMS design process has also the task of updating the method database. This means adding the new server to the methods' servers list, in the methods database, and specifying the design phase and problem that each new method solves. Moreover, the input data format required by each method, offered by the new server, is also specified. In the actual implementation this is done through SQL stored procedures. The removing of methods and servers from the methods data base can also be carried out.

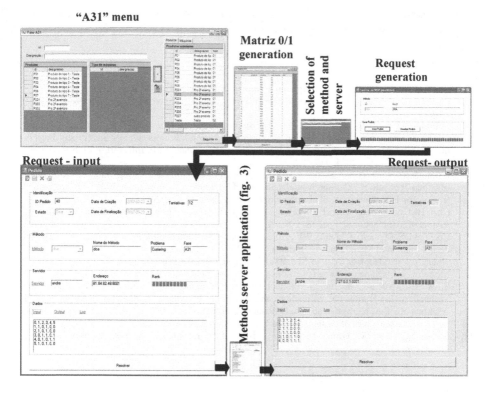

Figure 5 - Forms and menus for the design service request and design results provided

4 CONCLUSION

Frequent reconfiguration for adapting POMS to changing product manufacturing requirements is one way of achieving both manufacturing agility and leanness for gaining competitive advantage in the unpredictable product demand environment of today and tomorrow.

Although in simple manufacturing situations human expertise and ability may be enough to arrive to good POMS reconfiguration solutions, better results are likely to be obtained with a suitable computer aided design systems for POMS. This must be structured around a design framework or methodology which can explore the use of several methods, in different design phases, which have been developed over the years, by many authors, and that can of great value in the POMS reconfiguration process.

The idea of developing an autonomous monolithic POMS design system seems to be unfeasible and not recommended, for many reasons including the difficult of making locally available the necessary POMS design methods which, nevertheless can be accessed through the Internet. Moreover the dynamic up-dating of the system "intelligence" for POMS design, would be a difficult task. Better would be to provide the POMS design system with access to a large community of POMS design service providers. This idea has been explored to develop a computer aided design system, based on a CADS-POMS framework structured under a POMS design methodology and a community of distributed servers providing POMS design services through the Internet. A simple prototype of such a system is described in this paper.

5   REFERENCES

1.   Black JT. The Design of the Factory with a Future", McGraw-Hill, 1991.
2.   Burbidge JL. Production Flow Analysis for planning Group Technology. Clarendon Press, Oxford, 1989.
3.   Carmo-Silva S, Alves AC, Costa M. A Computer Aided Design System for Product Oriented Manufacturing Systems Reconfiguration. Intelligent Production Machines and Systems (Proceedings of the 1st I*PROMS Virtual International Conference), D. T. Pham, E. E. Eldukhri, A. J. Soroka Eds., Amsterdam, Elsevier, 2005: 417-422.
4.   Carmo-Silva S, Alves AC. Detailed design of product oriented manufacturing systems. Proceedings of Group Technology / Cellular Manufacturing 3rd International conference – 2006, J. Riezebos and Ir. J. Slomp Eds., University of Groningem, Holland. 2006: 44, 260-269.
5.   Chan HM, Milner DA. Direct Clustering Algorithm for Group Formation in Cellular Manufacture. Journal of Manufacturing Systems. 1982: 1: 1.
6.   Cochran DS., Arinez, JF., Duda, JW., Linck J. A decomposition approach for manufacturing system design. Journal of Manufacturing Systems, 2001/2002: 20: 6;: 371.
7.   Irani, SA. Handbook of Cellular Manufacturing Systems. John Wiley & Sons, 1999.
8.   McAuley, J. Machine grouping for efficient production. Production Engineer 1972: 51-57.
9.   Silva SC, Alves AC. Design of Product Oriented Manufacturing Systems. In Knowledge and Technology Integration in Production and Services, V. Marik, L Camarinha-Matos and H Afsarmanesh, Eds. Kluwer Academic Publishers, 2002: 359-366.
10.   Suh NP. The principles of Design. Oxford University Press, 1990.
11.   Suresh NC, Kay JM. Group Technology and Cellular manufacturing. Eds., Kluwer Academic Publishers, 1998.

Alexander Mahl, Anatoli Semenenko, Jivka Ovtcharova

Adenauerring 20a, 70131, Karlsruhe, GERMANY

E-mail: { alexander.mahl,anatoli.semenenko, jivka.ovtcharova}@imi.uni-karlsruhe.de

In order to be able to develop new products in a growing competitive environment the modern SMEs face a number of challenges: how best to design and innovate, how to understand constantly shifting customer needs, how to produce the products that meet those needs within tight budget and time constraints. Forming networks through co-operation between different companies (virtual organisations) has become an important business strategy for SMEs to respond to these challenges. The paper discusses new approaches to support cross-domain engineering and cross-enterprise collaborations with help of a modular framework, providing an integrated view of the relevant information. The result of the research carried out is a partly implemented framework for intercultural and cross-domain collaboration, based on the ontology-supported common understanding between the partners within a virtual organisation.

1   INTRODUCTION

The recent trends in development of modern complex products define the development process as cross-domain collaboration between the enterprises. Efficient collaboration over different domains (here: mechanics, electronics and (embedded) software) leads to a much higher competitiveness capability of the enterprises in the distributed and networked information environment. This becomes particular apparent in the industrial sector of the automotive industry which takes a guiding role for future trends in the industry. This brings about the prospect of ad hoc integration of systems across organisational boundaries to support collaborations that may last for a single transaction or evolve dynamically over many years. This sets new requirements for scalability, responsiveness and adaptability that necessitate the on-demand creation and self-management of dynamically evolving virtual organisations (VO) spanning national and enterprise borders, where the participating entities (enterprises or individuals) pool resources, information and knowledge in order to achieve common objectives.

One of the possible ways to respond to these challenges is to use context ontologies. Their wide usage in different application domains is based on their capacity to enable a shared common understanding of a domain between different agents (people, application systems, communities).

2   PROBLEM DEFINITION

Collaboration between companies and enterprises is often initiated only for a certain task and therefore is dynamic and short termed – in other words, this is a virtual organisation. Nevertheless information which has to be shared within the collaboration process gets more complex and is distributed across heterogeneous system environment. This requires methods and tools which allow the management of distributed data and an efficient integration of legacy systems. The main problem addressed by

Mahl, A., Semenenko, A., Ovtcharova, J., 2007, in IFIP International Federation for Information Processing, Volume 243, Establishing the Foundation of Collaborative Networks; eds. Camarinha-Matos, L., Afsarmanesh, H., Novais, P., Analide, C.; (Boston: Springer), pp. 601–608.

the paper is the lack of efficient tools for cross enterprise and cross-domain engineering processes.

There are highly specialised tools available for each engineering domain (e.g. PDM[1]-Systems, E-CAD[2], M-CAD[3], MBS[4] etc.). But existing solutions for bridging between domains are still rare and inefficient. The framework presented in this paper does not aim to replace any specific domain tool but to bridge between the domains. Therefore it is necessary to adapt the existing applications. The highly specialized domain tools overlap only partly over the domains concerning the offered functionality and underlying semantics. There are several software solutions on the market (e.g. PDMConnect (PDMConnect), OpenPDM (OpenPDM, 2005), SAP NetWeaver (NetWeaver, 2005), IBM WebShere (IBM, 2005), MS Bizztalk (Anderson, et al., 2000)) which allow the exchange of product data across the border of enterprises. The focus of these solutions is to exchange data between certain systems of one domain. These solutions do not able to provide an integrated view on the exchanged data, but allow a mapping of data structures between the involved systems. Thus important information is lost within the exchange process within cross domain communication since the target system is not able to "understand" all information needed within the collaboration.

3   OBJECTIVES

The software framework presented in this paper is subject of the research EU funded research project ImportNET[5]. The ImportNET open source framework aims to actively support of cross-domain and cross-enterprise collaborations with focus on SME networks. In order to setup collaboration where engineers of several domains and different enterprises are involved, it is necessary to have a common understanding of the relevant data and processes. An Ontology describes a certain domain and provides a common understanding within that domain. The problem of the use of ontologies (e.g. semantic web) is that there is no "unique ontology" which is valid and describes all relevant facts. The idea within our research is to (semi-) automatically derive an ontology which is valid only within collaboration (collaboration ontology) based on reference ontologies which are available within the internet or standardisation organisations (E.g. STEP[6] (STEP, 2005), IDF[7] (Kehmeier, 2006) etc.). The collaboration ontology describes not only artefacts (data elements) but also processes and services and therewith builds a coherent description of all terms relevant within the collaboration.

In the context of system integration various research prototypes (e.g. A3 module of ATHENA project (Ruggaber, 2005)) have been developed to enable a semi-automatic model matches between systems (Mahl, 2005). This tools use different

---

[1] PDM: Product Data Management
[2] ECAD: Electronic Computer Aided Design
[3] MCAD: Mechanical Computer Aided Design
[4] MBS: Multi Body Simulation
[5] ImportNET: Intelligent modular open source Platform for intercultural and cross-domain SME Networks (see: http://www.importnet-project.org / 6th Framework).
[6] STEP: Standard for the Exchange of Product Model Data. STEP is a synonym for the ISO standard series 10303 "Product Data Representation and Exchange"
[7] IDF: Interchange Definition Format

approaches like neuronal networks, rule bases, etc. (Semenenko, 2004). Up to now the achieved results are not sufficient for commercial use. This is mainly because they attempt to provide "general solutions" independent from the domains. Thus the approach within ImportNET uses background knowledge about the domains of the IT systems to be connected. At the first part the paper outlines a concept of a generic, modular framework which provides an integrated view of the relevant information. The second part of the paper outlines the stages of the setup of a working environment for a collaboration based on the ImportNET framework.

4   IMPORTNET MODULAR FRAMEWORK

4.1   Framework architecture and components

The main result of ImportNET will be a software framework which actively supports following issues:

- Reduction of the complexity of the information to be shared within the collaboration by automatic derivation of the minimal needed collaboration ontology. Setup of the semantic integration of proprietary systems using the collaboration ontology as common semantically basis – setup phase
- Execution of cross domain product development process by providing domain oriented representation of the relevant information (based on the collaboration ontology) – execution phase.

In order to reduce the complexity of the information it is necessary to customize the common ontology according to the need of the collaboration. The ImportNET approach deals with a collaboration ontology (based on reference ontologies) which is valid only within the collaboration. These ontologies will cover the most important concepts of the domains mechanics, electronics, and informatics. The Semantic Application Server (SAS) is the core of ImportNET framework and realises the ontology based access to the information stored in proprietary systems. The general architecture of the framework consists of four main components, described below (see Figure 1).

ImportNET provides a method and a software tool (Ontology Integration Tool (OIT)) which facilitates the specification of the collaboration ontology. The common ontology will be used to automate the development of an adapter of an external system (E.g. PDM system). Therefore a methodology and IT-tool (Intelligent Adapter Generation Tool (IAGT)) will be developed which uses up-to-date approaches of intelligent software applications (e.g. data mining, neural networks etc.) and semantic model matching approaches in order to analyse the API (and underlying data model) of the external system. This will reduce the financial and time consuming manual implementation effort and will speed-up the establishment of collaborations.

The Semantic Application Server (SAS) provides an ontology-based semantic representation of the distributed collaboration data. Thereby the SAS enables an easy development of business applications which have to access distributed data. While the modules OIT and IAGT will be used for configuration issues in order to prepare the collaboration, the SAS manages the IT-support in the collaboration.

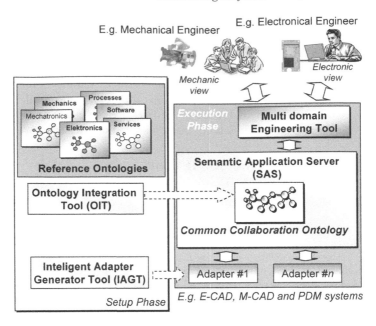

Figure 1: ImportNET framework architecture

The Multi Domain Engineering Tool (MDET) realises an ontology based visualisation of the information that is relevant in the collaboration, corresponding to the engineering domain and cultural background of the user. Information to be visualised could be e.g. product structures, simulation data (multi-body and finite elements), etc. Furthermore, the client will also provide functions for changing the information and trigger new (time consuming) computations. The Multi Domain Engineering Tool represents a generic viewing component which will satisfy requirements resulting from cross engineering tasks (regarding visualisation). Therefore MDET provides a significant improvement of providing cross domain (mechatronic) and cross cultural engineering processes.

4.2   Setup phase of the ImportNET framework

After two or more SMEs have agreed to work together in a cooperation project, there is the need to setup the infrastructure for the collaboration. Within the setup phase two main actions needs to be done (see Figure 2). Firstly the collaboration ontology and therewith the specification of the relevant artefacts (data model elements), services and processes needs to be derived from reference ontologies. This task is provided by the OIT. Secondly the external systems of the collaboration partners need to be connected to the SAS. This is done by implementation of adapters. The implementation of the adapter is partly generated automatically using the Intelligent Adapter Generation Tool (IAGT). The IAGT analyses the semantic models of the external systems and generates source code for the semantically mapping between the external models and the collaboration ontology. If the semantic model of the external system is not available it needs to be derived by analysing the API or defined manually. The rest of this section deals with the question how to derive the collaboration ontology.

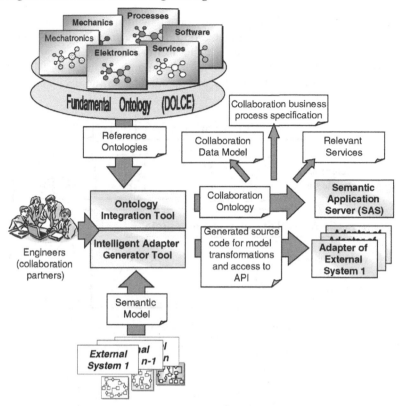

Figure 2: Setup of infrastructure for a collaboration

Figure 3 shows the necessary steps to derive the collaboration ontology and therewith the artefacts (data items), services and processes used within the collaboration. Based on the issues carried out in the collaboration preparation (e.g. specification of business process and initial product structure etc.), the essential concepts on the reference ontology are denoted manually. Subsequently, the collaboration ontology is derived automatically by using semantic hull algorithm (Mahl, 2007). The ontology may be manually extended by concepts that are not available in the reference ontologies. The OIT provides modules for transformation of the collaboration ontology (specified in OWD-DL) into standard representations.

The ImportNET reference ontology uses the task ontology DOLCE (Mika et. al., 2004) as its fundamental ontology. The process domain of the reference ontologies contains a description of reference processes potentially supported by services offered by the ImportNET framework. Thus it is assumed that the transformation between the ontology based representation and a standard representation (here: Business Process Execution Language (BPEL (2003))) is bidirectional. Up to now we did a prototype implementation which allows a bidirectional transformation for a subset of BPEL. The BPEL representation of the process will be used within the workflow engine of the SAS. The SAS implementation does not provide its own domain data model but a meta data model which allows to specify (and modify) the data model on runtime. Based on its XMI representation the data model for the collaboration will be established in the SAS. The (collaboration) data model represents the artefacts of the engineering domains which need to be stored in a data base. The data model is an "implementation oriented semantic model" whereas the collaboration ontology could be seen as "end-user oriented semantic model". Within the transformation towards the data model no semantics will be lost, but the data model will be optimized in the context of implementation (no deep class hierarchy etc.).

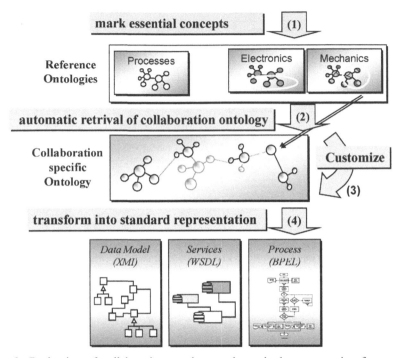

Figure 3: Derivation of collaboration ontology and standard representation for processes, services and data model

That means after the collaboration ontology has been derived semi-automatically by the OIT and experts of the engineering domains a software expert generates the data model using the OIT. The software expert specifies for example which concepts will be represented by an object type and which by an attribute of the object type of its super concept. For example in the collaboration ontology there is the concept "inductor" which is a subconcept of the concept "part". In the data model there will only be an object type "part" with an attribute "type". The attribute may have the value "inductor" (or the name of any other subconcept) in order to indicate that the instance of the object type part is an inductor.

Now we focus on step 1 of the derivation process (see Figure 3) for the collaboration ontology: manual selection of the essential concepts. Since the experts of the involved engineers (domain experts) are usually no ontology modelling experts this task needs be supported by a software tool (OIT) and should not be visible for the engineers.

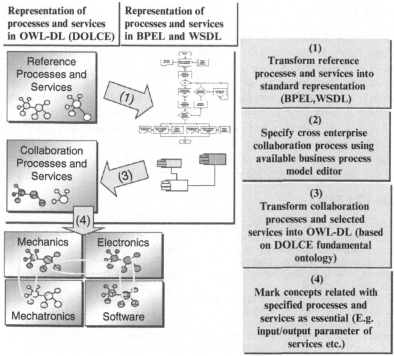

Figure 4: Manual selection of essential concepts by specifying the cross enterprise collaboration process

About 80 percent of the products are developed on former design. The engineer knows in principle the structure of its product (each car consists of four wheels, a chassis, an engine etc.). Thus the OIT provides the functionality to specify the product structure based on pre-defined product structure templates. The engineer specifies the components (e.g. electronic engine, transistor etc.) needed for the product as well as the conceptual structure. Each component has predefined functions and requirements which could be initialized later. For example the electronic engine has got the functions: create power and create heat. Based on the specification of the principle structure a set of concepts is selected as essential. The other concepts are selected during the specification of the cross enterprise business process (see Figure 4).

This approach uses the bidirectional transformation between DOLCE based reference ontology and BPEL. The process domain of the reference ontology contains the specification of reference processes supported by the services of the SAS. Since there are graphical editors for BPEL available the process specification will be transformed into BPEL. Based on the reference processes (and the available services) the business process for the collaboration will be specified. After that the BPEL representation will be transformed back to OWL-DL. Therewith the artefacts relevant for the services or process steps (e.g. input/output parameter for the services or processes) will be marked as "essential". The concepts derived from specification of product structure and business process build a good starting point for the next steps of the collaboration ontology derivation process.

5 CONCLUSION

In the context of dynamic SME networks, the fast installation of virtual enterprises out of the network and the effective and efficient execution of a collaboration network is a critical process for product developing companies. The uniform description of data, processes and services with an approach using ontologies supports the common understanding and builds the base for ontology-based cross-enterprise collaboration process. The cross-enterprise integration framework provides a transparent view on the data, which is relevant within collaboration activities. The platform allows dynamic „on the fly"-integration of external systems. In order to speed up the integration as it was outlined in our approach, we suggest using ontologies to make the integration process more scaleable.

6 REFERENCES

1. Anderson, R.; Birbeck, M.; Kay, M.; Livingstone, S.; Loesgen, B.; Matrin, D.; Mohr, S.; Ozu, N, Peat, B.; Pinnock, J.; Stark, P.; Williams, K.: XML Professionell, Bonn: MITP Verlag, 2000
2. BPEL: Business Process Execution Language for Web Services Version 1.1, http://www-106.ibm.com/developerworks/webservices/library/ws-bpel/ (2003)
3. Bullinger, H.-J.: Innovativer Fahrzeugbau. In magazine: Automobil Produktion, Vol., Edition: April 2004, 2004
4. Champy, J: X-Engineering the Corporation: Reinvent your business in the digital age. London, Hodder and Stoughton General, 2002
5. FAST: Future Automotive Industry Structure 2015 study carried out by Mercer Management Consulting and the Frauenhofer Instituts for production techniques and automation (IPA), 2005
6. WebSphere : N.N.: Business Integration, http://www-306.ibm.com/software/de/websphere/ws-bi.html, Online at: 19.04.2005
7. Kalmbach, R., Kleinhaus, C.: "Zulieferer auf der Gewinnerseite". In magazine: Automobil Produktion, Vol., Ausgabe: April 2004, 2004
8. Kehmeier, David J.: Electrical/Mechanical Design Integration: An Introduction to IDF 4.0 and what it Can Do for You.
9. Mahl A., Krikler R.: Approach for a Rule Based System for Capturing and Usage of Knowledge in the Manufacturing Industry. In: Knowledge enterprise: intelligent strategies in product design, manufacturing, and management. Proceedings of PROLAMAT 2006, IFIP TC5 international conference, 15.-17. Juni 2006, Shanghai China.
10. Mahl A., Semenenko A.: An approach for building intercultural and cross-domain virtual organization. CARV-07, Toronto 2007
11. Machatronic portal: http://www.mechatronik-portal.de
12. Mika, P., Sabou, M., Gangemi, A., Oberle, D.: Foundations for DAML-S: Aligning DAML-S to DOLCE, First International Semantic Web Services Symposium (SWS2004), AAAI Spring Symposium Series, 2004
13. PDMConnect: PDTec Homepage, http://www.pdtec.de, online at 10.04.2006
14. OpenPDM: ProSTEP's CATIA mySAP integration gets SAP certificated, http://www.tenlinks.com/NEWS/PR/PROSTEP_AG/080305_sap.htm, online at 10.08.2005
15. NetWeaver: N.N., NetWeaver, http://www.sap.com/solutions/netweaver/index.epx, online at 30.06.2005
16. Ruggaber, R.: ATHENA – advanced technologies for interoperability of heterogeneous enterprise networks and their applications, 2005
17. Semenenko A.; Krikler R.: Knowledge-based shoe design process, Proceedings of IPD 2004, Magdeburg, Germany, 2004
18. STEP: A Key Tool in the Global Market", UK Council for Electronic Business (UKCEB), 2005

PART 21

ADAPTIVE COLLABORATIVE FRAMEWORKS

Ana Almeida, Goreti Marreiros, Constantino Martins

Knowledge Engineering and Decision Support Research Group - GECAD,
Computer Science Department
Institute of Engineering of Porto, Porto, PORTUGAL
{ana, goreti,const}@dei.isep.ipp.pt

Scheduling is a multi-criteria decision problem in practice, where different schedulers may agree on key objectives but differ greatly on their relative importance in a particular situation. This kind of problems can be tackled with Collaborative approaches, which is the aim of this work. Collaboration supports work being undertaken by dispersed entities allowing the sharing of final results and also the process of obtaining them. This involve a range of activities such as information exchanging, knowledge sharing, argumentation, problem solving strategies, role playing, group mediation, individual training and conflict resolution, among other. Here, we propose a Collaborative framework with an Adaptive behaviour to be used in Manufacturing Scheduling Environments.

1   INTRODUCTION

Today organizations pursue the global objectives of high resource utilization, fast order turnaround and outstanding costumer service. The latter relies on delivery accuracy, i.e., delivering goods on time, with quality and low costs. These are some critical factors of success of an organization, so one of the main aspects for competitiveness and success of an organization is the efficient production managing, particularly in production scheduling which is a complex problem when dealing with multiple criteria sometimes with conflicting goals in dynamic environments with high degree variation factors. This scenario is more problematic because it is known that in reality variables behaviour is not the same as planned, so there is a strong possibility to reformulate the existing plan and the need to change current schedule to adapt to emerging modifications.

Generally, we may say that the present business environment is characterized by the use of groups, working in distributed environments and dealing with uncertainty, ambiguous problem definitions, and rapidly changing information.

Scheduling decisions are often characterized by goals, roles, activities and resources that are dynamically changing, or uncertain. For improved competitiveness scheduling decisions should arise from the integration of different production functions where each participating actor collaborates in achieving a solution.

The purpose of this work is to develop an Adaptive Collaborative Framework that uses Group Decision Support (GDS) and Adaptation concepts to support the scheduling process on manufacturing environments.

This paper is organized as follows. Sections 2 presents a background research giving a general approach to Collaborative Scheduling, Group Decision Support and Adaptive Systems. The architecture and interaction model to support Adaptive Decision Support in Collaborative Scheduling are presented in section 3, and an

Almeida, A., Marreiros, G., Martins, C., 2007, in IFIP International Federation for Information Processing, Volume 243, Establishing the Foundation of Collaborative Networks; eds. Camarinha-Matos, L., Afsarmanesh, H., Novais, P., Analide, C.; (Boston: Springer), pp. 611–618.

illustrative example is provided in section 4. Finally section 5 presents some conclusions.

2   BACKGROUND

An approach to avoid the gap between automatic scheduling and humans is the establishment of Adaptive Collaborative Scheduling Systems, where users and computers collaborate in plans generation, identifying candidate alternatives, thus profiting the better of the two worlds. The user provides intuition, a notion about goals and appropriate trade-off, and refined problem resolution strategies. The computer provides adaptation to user, skill to manage details, to assign and schedule resources and operations, and to analyze quantitatively the suggested choices. These forms of collaboration may provide a very powerful approach to multi-objective decision support in complex manufacturing environments.

2.1   Collaborative Scheduling

Collaborative scheduling integrates multiple problem solving approaches to produce a set of solutions to a single scheduling problem. A wide study on the diversity of scheduling methods can be found in literature (Almeida, 2002; Almeida et al., 2002; Morton and Pentico, 2003). Collaboration can mean interaction between humans, between scheduling methods and between humans and scheduling methods. Through complexity and fashion how production scheduling problems were tackled in the past, we can actually conclude that there is a gap between the way that scheduling systems solve problems and the way human resolves them. While automatic scheduling systems need complete specification of goals and scenario before beginning problem resolution, humans progressively learn with scenario and change their goals during planning and execution. Automatic scheduling quantitatively evaluates plans while persons evaluate them subjectively. While automatic systems focus on one solution at a time, persons compare options and alternatives before decision.

2.2   Group Decision Support

In Collaborative Network Organizations is mandatory to support collaborative work. Collaborative work presupposes that we will have a group of people that has as mission the completion of a specific task (e.g. making a decision) (Camarinha-Matos, 2003). The number of elements involved in the group may be variable, as well as the persistency of the group (permanent or temporary). The group members may be in different places, meet in an asynchronous way (different times), may belong to different organizations. Collaborative work has inherent advantages (e.g. greater pool of knowledge, different perspectives, increased acceptance) but has also disadvantages (e.g. social pressure, domination, goal displacement, groupthink).

The term Group Decision Support System (Huber, 1982; Kull, 1982; Lewis, 1982; Huber, 1984) emerged effectively in the beginning of the eighty-decade. According to Hubber (1984) a GDSS consists of a set of software, hardware, languages components and procedures that support a group of people engaged in a decision related meeting. A more recent definition is from Nunamaker et. al (1997) defining GDSSs as interactive computer-based environment which supports concerted and coordinated team effort towards completion of joint tasks.

2.3   Adaptive Systems

Adaptive behavior focuses on each particular member profile, providing him with appropriate information presented in the most suitable manner. This can limit information requirements and exchanging, and also the number and duration of interactions with the framework, therefore, reduce interaction time and improve transactions' quality and efficiency, enhancing individual members' contribution to the process. This, of course, leads to a significant gain of the collaboration process. In fact adaptation/personalization is becoming one of the main requirements of any system in different application areas, such as manufacturing, education and services. The main objective of Adaptive Systems (AS) is to adequate its relation with the user (content presentation, navigation, interface, etc.) according to a predefined but updatable model of the user that reflects his/her objectives, preferences, knowledge and competences (Brusilovsky, 2001; De Bra, 2004).

The architecture proposed, for example by Benyon (1993) and De Bra (2004), indicate that the AS must have three essential parts: Domain Model (DM), Interaction Model (IM) and User Model (UM).

2.3.1   Adaptive collaborative framework for scheduling

Our proposal considers multiple scheduling objectives in a global multi-criteria collaborative framework (Almeida & Marreiros, 2006). It generates several scheduling alternatives by using autonomous agents which encapsulates different scheduling algorithms. Each scheduling alternative represents a solution regarding an objective such as, accomplishment of deadlines, minimizing throughput times, maximizing profitability, product quality, and minimizing manufacturing disruptions.

This Adaptive Collaborative Decision Support Framework provides decision support considering the negotiation process of a group of users, each one of them with a different perception of the problem, effectively acting as a team to achieve a common and unique solution.

Our framework is an interactive system in which human scheduler's knowledge of organization, customer, and manufacturing issues play the role of an agent in developing a final scheduling solution.

Over many years, customer service and sales personnel have come to know and understand the special requirements of their customers, suppliers, and distributors, but this knowledge is not usually shared with the manufacturing service. A scheduling decision, must take into account the knowledge and experience of different individuals, with different points of view, allowing the consideration of broad issues of the company.

It is impractical to capture too many of the individual special constraints and considerations within the scheduling system itself. Such systems tend to be less efficient, and more brittle. Using the interface, the human, like all agents, decides what to work on, by selecting candidate solutions evaluated according to several important criteria.

To support effective cooperation between the group of humans' decision makers and agents, the scheduling system have an intuitive user-interface allowing the users to manipulate schedules down to the smallest detail.

A better interaction between the human being and the systems is necessary; we intend to achieve this through the construction of Adaptive Environments. This is especially important when we are dealing with Collaborative Decision Support Systems.

The architecture of the system has three essential parts as it can be observed on Figure 1.

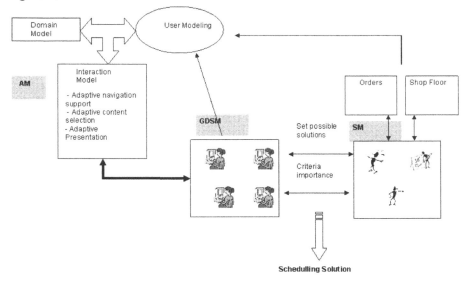

Figure 1- Approach to collaborative scheduling through group decision support

Scheduling module

The Scheduling Module (SM) aims at generate a set of possible solutions for a specific scheduling problem. The SM is composed by several agents, namely:

Scheduling agents that are different autonomous agents each one of them embodying a particular scheduling algorithm;

Information agent, which, in accordance with the type of scheduling problem, sets a time window for the generation of the several scheduling alternatives;

Setting agent which settle on the criteria importance according with the global preferences of the GDS members, in order to cover all the relationships arising from the different departments.

2.4   Group Decision Support Module

One way of enhancing collaboration between agents and humans is to produce not one but many candidate solutions, evaluated with respect to multiple criteria. This allows users to gain important insights into the tradeoffs between multiple competing objectives. They express their preferences by imposing weighting factors for different criteria. The GDSM will support the members of a scheduling meeting and the facilitator. This last one prepares the meeting and invites a group of people to participate, and to exchange different points of view, expertise and information, in order to choice the "best" solution from the set of scheduling solutions proposed by the SM.

The GDSM is composed by the following components (Marreiros et al., 2004):

- Setup, operated by the facilitator during the pre-meeting phase, in several configuration and parameterization activities;
- Management, which supports the meeting in all its phases, sending "notifications" (by e-mail) to the facilitator or to the group members will be also responsible for the communications with the SM;
- Multi-criteria, used by the facilitator to introduce a possible set of criteria;
- Voting, responsible for the emission of "vote bulletins", and for the publication of results;
- Argumentation, where participants argue for the most interesting alternatives or against the worst alternatives, according to his/her preferences.

2.5 Adaptation Module

The Adaptation Module (AM) is defined as a system that monitors user behaviour and adapts its presentation accordingly. User behaviour is mostly defined upon its interaction with the system itself. In our case, system tries to adapt the GDSM interface to the skills of scheduler expert, reorganizing the sequence of content presentation according to the interaction provided. It is composed by three components:

- User Model (UM), that describes user information, knowledge and preferences. This model express, supply and assign conclusions about user characteristics;
- Domain Model that represents concept hierarchies or maps and the related structure for user objective and knowledge level representation, either quantitative, qualitative or probabilistic;
- Interaction Model (IM), represents and defines the interaction between user and application. Usually, this model is composed by some evaluation, adaptation and inference mechanisms.

3 EXAMPLE

To illustrate the proposed framework, we can consider the example of a job shop 5x10, where each job has different routes, due dates and processing times. Applying the SM some criteria are settled and the heuristics respecting those criteria are triggered. The obtained results can be observed on Table 1.

Table 1 – Results from SM

Heuristic	Criteria						
	C_{max}	T_{max}	$\sum U_j$	$\sum C_j$	$\sum T_j$	$\sum w_j C_j$	$\sum w_j T_j$
EDD	406	94	7	2968	301	5329	672
FCFS	347	127	4	2808	219	4666	261
General SB	419	63	7	2819	341	**4343**	445
Local Serach/C_{max}	**306**	67	4	2699	169	4575	224
Local Serach/sum(wT)	346	**12**	2	2679	**22**	4672	**46**
SB/ sum(wT)	317	97	**1**	2610	97	4360	97
SB/ T_{max}	364	12	4	2782	30	4856	66
SPT	422	136	3	**2312**	392	3688	528
WSPT	422	136	3	2312	392	3688	528

At this stage, there are many candidate solutions which must be evaluated with respect to multiple criteria so, experts will reunite to discuss and weigh up results according their preferences, in order to come to a single solution. For instance from the Sales/Costumer service point of view the number of late jobs ($\sum U_j$) and total tardiness ($\sum T_j$) are the most significant criteria, and from the factory floor perspective makespan (Cmax) and total flow time ($\sum C_j$) have higher importance.

The role of the GDSM is to facilitate this process supporting the members of the scheduling meeting and the facilitator. During the pre-meeting phase the facilitator has several configuration and parameterization activities.

Figure 2 - Decision rules for meeting MG11

On Figure 2 we can observe the definition of decision rules for the meeting, namely voting rules, rules for argumentation, single or multiple alternative selection; visualisation (or not) of alternatives values after normalisation, as well as the goal of the meeting.

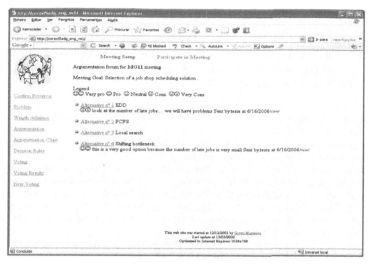

Figure 3 - Initial view of the argumentation forum

On Figure 3 it can be observed the argumentation forum, where each participant will argue for the most interesting alternatives or against the worst alternatives, according to his/her preferences. This component structures the discussion between group members.

As it can be observed on Table 1 EDD is the worst case when referring to the number of late jobs $\sum Uj$, while SB/ sum(wT) presents the best result, This is an argumentation from the Sales/Costumer service which valorise the number of late jobs ($\sum Uj$)

4 CONCLUSIONS

This work addresses the interaction between the scheduling actors through the integration of the different kinds of knowledge in a global view of the system and the potential synergy in association with the collaborative activity of those actors taking in account multiple criteria which can improve the scheduling process. Considering this fact the option for a collaborative model using the concepts of Group Decision Support (GDS) and Adaptive Systems (AS) plays an important role. The practical advantages are evidenced in better performance of managers responsible for production planning, control, adaptability and the consequently increased efficiency and productivity of industrial systems.

We expect a successful deployment of our system resulting in significant savings, new approach and improved customer satisfaction. These positive results arise from improved schedule quality resulting in a global business process improvement.

The application of different adaptive technologies in an integrated way for the development of Adaptive Collaborative Framework for Scheduling will be not only an important alternative, but also a new solution/innovation to support the scheduling process on manufacturing environments.

Acknowledgments

This work is partially supported by ArgEmotionAgents project (POSC/EIA/56259/ 2004 - Argumentative Agents with Emotional Behaviour Modelling for Participants' Support in Group Decision-Making Meetings), which is a project supported by FCT (Science & Technology Foundation – Portugal).

5   REFERENCES

1.   Almeida A and Marreiros G. Toward Collaborative Scheduling. In: Information Technology For Balanced Manufacturing Systems 2006; Springer.
2.   Almeida A, Ramos C and Sílvio C. Toward Dynamic Scheduling of Manufacturing. The International Journal for Manufacturing Science & Production, Freund Publishing House, Ltd. 2002.
3.   Almeida A. Analysis and Development of Mechanisms and Algorithms to Support Product Oriented Scheduling. Doctoral Thesis on Production Engineering, University of Minho, Portugal, 2002.
4.   Benyon D. "Adaptive systems: A solution to Usability Problems". Journal of User Modelling and User Adapted Interaction, Kluwer 1993; 3(1): 1-22.
5.   Brusilovsky P. Adaptive hypermedia. User Modelling and User Adapted Interaction, Ten Year Anniversary Issue (Alfred Kobsa, ed.) 2001; 11 (1/2): 87-110.
6.   Camarinha-Matos L. New collaborative organizations and their research needs, Proceedings of PRO-VE'03 – Processes and Foundations for Virtual Organizations, Kluwer Academic Publishers, 2003.
7.   De Bra P, Aroyo L and Cristea A. Adaptive Web-based Educational Hypermedia. Book chapter in: Web Dynamics, Adaptive to Change in Content, Size, Topology and Use, (Eds.) Mark Levene, Alexandra Poulovassilis 2004; pp. 387-410, Springer
8.   Huber G. Group decision support systems as aids in the use of structured group management techniques. Proc. of second international conference on decision support systems, San Francisco, 1982. in C. W. Holsapple, A. B. Whinston, Decision support systems: a knowledge-based approach (Thomson Learning, inc, 2001).
9.   Huber G. Issues in the design of group decision support systems. Mis Quarteley 1984; 3(8).
10. Kull D. Group Decisions: Can computer Help. Computer Decisions 1982;14(5) in C. W. Holsapple, A. B. Whinston, Decision support systems: a knowledge-based approach (Thomson Learning, inc, 2001).
11. Lewis L. Facilitator: A microcomputer decision support systems for small groups. Ph. D. dissertation, University of Louisville, 1982.
12. Marreiros G, Sousa J and Ramos C. WebMeeting - a group decision support system for multi-criteria decision problems. ICKEDS04, 2004.
13. Morton T and Pentico T. Heuristic Scheduling Systems, John Willey & Sons, Inc, 2003
14. Nunamaker J, Briggs R, Mittleman, D, Vogel, D and Balthazard, P. Lessons from a dozen years of group support systems research: A discussion of lab and field findings. Journal of Management Information Systems 1997; 13 (3).

67

VIRTUAL ORGANIZATIONS FOR MUNICIPALITIES

Malgorzata Pankowska
University of Economics Katowice, POLAND
pank@ae.katowice.pl

The main goal of the paper is to present what virtual organizations are developed to support public administration on municipality level. The virtual organizations are visible through their Web sites. Within the last few years, in Poland a unique opportunity for virtual organizations' development has been created. The Parliamentary Act on Access to Public Information for citizens and business was adopted and the rapid development of the Web sites was noticed. This research has been done for Polish municipalities and the research method covers analysis of the contents of their Web sites. The last part of the paper covers answers the question if the internet is really utilized to improve the governance in the communities i.e. towns and villages.

1   INTRODUCTION

Socio-economic organizations are virtual when producing work deliverables across different locations, at different work cycles and across culture. They are also characterized by the temporality, intensity, reciprocity and multiplexity of the linkages in their networks   (Powell, 1990). A virtual organization is presented as being a network of independent, geographically dispersed units with a partial mission overlap. Within the network, all partners provide their own core competencies and the co-operation is based on semi-stable relations (Phipps, 2000). Generally, virtuality is an ability of an organization to consistently obtain and coordinate critical competences through the design of value-adding business processes and governance mechanisms involving external and internal elements to deliver differential, superior value to the society. In this paper, virtual community and virtual unions are treated as virtual organizations. They are structures consisting of inter-related components oriented towards achievement of common goals. Virtual means something not physically existing as such but made by software. Virtual reality is in fact a pure simulation. The paper is focused on recognition what virtual organizations and virtual reality objects can be developed and what are their roles in eGovernment at municipality level.

2   CHALLENGES OF THE WEB FOR MUNICIPALITIES

Emerging trends in Europe suggest that current thinking on eGovernment is focusing on great quality and efficiency in public services. According to the view, eGovernment needs to be more knowledge-based, user-centric, distributed and

Pankowska, M., 2007, in IFIP International Federation for Information Processing, Volume 243, Establishing the Foundation of Collaborative Networks; eds. Camarinha-Matos, L., Afsarmanesh, H., Novais, P., Analide, C.; (Boston: Springer), pp. 619–626.

networked. New public services will be required by the EU as well as innovative ways of delivering the existing ones. Secondly, technological advances in the miniaturisation and portability of ICTs suggest that in the future, eGovernment will form part of an ambient intelligence environment, where technology will surround people and serve them on their roles as citizens, customers and professionals. eGovernment should have a strategic focus which includes the achievement of the Lisbon goals, the reduction of barriers to the internal market for services and mobility across Europe, the effective implementation of national policies and regional or local development. Providing user-centred services and cutting unnecessary administrative burden require that information is shared across departments and different levels of government.

The vision of eGovernment in the EU in the next decade defines eGovernment as an ICT tool for better government in its broadest sense. It places eGovernment at the core of public management modernisation and reform, where technology is used as a strategic tool to modernise structures, processes, the regulatory framework, human resources and the culture of public administrations to provide better government and ultimately increased public value (Centeno et al, 2004).

By 2010, European public administration will have made public information and services more easily accessible through innovative use of ICT and through increasing public trust, increasing awareness of eGovernment benefits and through improving skills and support for all users. According to the "i2010 eGovernment Action Plan: Accelerating eGovernment in Europe for the Benefit of All" published in April 2006, Member States have committed themselves to inclusive eGovernment objectives to ensure that by 2010 all citizens, including socially disadvantaged groups, become major beneficiaries of eGovernment and European public administrations deliver public information and services that are more easily accessible and increasingly trusted by the public, through innovative use of ICT, increasing awareness of the benefits of eGovernment and improved skills and support for all users.

European Union initiatives have two basic functions i.e. supervising and stimulating. They are to create a socio-economic environment for eAdministration development. However, not only public services online are important. Europeans are to be involved in governmental processes including eDemocracy and eParticipation at national, province and commune levels. In this way, EU initiative creates opportunities for virtual community development and functioning. The "eEurope An Information Society for All, Communication on a Commission Initiative for the Special European Council of Lisbon" paper defines eDemocracy as a conceptual entity with eGovernment as one of its prerequisite components. Citizen action may then be classified in terms of two quite different approaches: 1) the exercise of direct interaction between citizenry and eGovernment, trying to effect changes in laws and administrative systems and 2) the exercise of information exchange and knowledge building and its dissemination among citizens. In a simple sense, citizens are creating an open and on-going town hall meeting where ideas, agendas, personalities, interests, and beliefs may mix dynamically. They are creating online an arena for public expression, development of opinion and accountability.

eParticipation must be seen as relational (i.e. taking place as an evolving set of relations which develops over time). It has to be constructed as an activity that is not cut loose from a workplace context, even though it is a mediated activity, since the activity itself depends on the concept of full participation, not only by the engaged citizens, but also by the staff and politicians who are intended to get involved in preparing, supporting and maintaining the event as such. Methods supporting eParticipation must therefore support a system of relations, including also the work situation, and not solely focusing on the support of a single activity of citizen's participation (Kolsaker & Lee-Kelley, 2006). eParticipation must be rooted in experiences, not just generalised rules, also explaining why it is so important to include work practices in real use and in designing situations of evaluations of eParticipation and in relating those contextual dimensions to future development.

In Poland, where the internet usage by individuals (15+) is 26% (2004) and the internet usage by enterprises of more than 10 employees is 85% (2004), the following Acts adapted by the Parliament (Sejm) were extremely important for eGovernment and eDemocracy development:

- The Act on Computerisation of the Operations of Certain Entities Performing Public Tasks of 17th February 2005. The Act sets up horizontal/infrastructure programmes for all the sectors of public administration and establishes a common interoperability framework for IT systems in the Polish public sector.
- New Law on Public Procurement of 29th January 2004, enabling the development of eProcurement systems for Polish public administrations and allowing the use of electronic auctions for contracts up to €60000.
- ePoland – the Strategy on the Development of the Information Society in Poland for the years 2004-2006 prepared by the Ministry of Scientific Research and Information Technology and adopted by the Cabinet on 13th January 2004.
- The launch of the Public Information Bulletin (PIB) (official electronic journal on public information) in accordance with the Act on Access to Public Information of 6th September 2001. The Ministry of Internal Affairs and Administration is responsible for the PIB.

The right of access to public information constitutes a major component of the democratic standard of open government or openness of public authorities and entities responsible to them. The openness is founded on the transparency of organisations and their operations (Izdebski, 2003).

3   SELECTION CRITERIA AND EVALUATION METHODOLOGY

Cyberspace represents a place in which people can communicate to exchange views and to develop socio-economic and political initiatives. Through the new venues, people can engage in many sorts of economic and political activities, such as joining interest groups, voting in elections or participating in forums to solve joint problems that appeared in their town or province.

Content analysis was conducted of a sample of municipality Web sites to provide empirical validation for the deliberativeness for these new socio-economic spaces. According to the Act on Administrative Division of the country, 2489 municipalities i.e. towns and villages were specified in 2004 in Poland. In research, done from October till December 2006, 130 municipalities' Web sites were analysed. The first research question to be addressed was: To what extent municipalities provide information versus seeking information from citizens? The second research question was: What virtual organizations are developed within municipalities and to what extent do citizen use them to exchange opinions as well as incorporate and respond to others' viewpoints? Content analysis was chosen as the appropriate methodology to address these questions. It is a research technique for making inferences by systematically and objectively identifying specified characteristics within a text. Content of the Web pages and forums' postings comprise a defined context or horizon from which citizen-municipality discussion and collaboration can be evaluated. It is not necessary to know who the participants are to present the conclusions on eAdministration and virtual community development. Content analysis covers Web sites for small communities (i.e. Strykow, 3000 inhabitants, http://www.strykow.pl) as well as for big cities (i.e. Poznan, 570 thousands inhabitants, http://www.wirtualnypoznan. pl/forum/). Full list of the addresses of the analysed Web sites is available upon request.

Resolution of the Act on Access to Public Information of 6th June 2001 caused rapid development of electronic publications named Public Information Bulletin. It is estimated that 98% communities in Poland develop and implement this electronic publication, although only 90% of them have constructed an official Web site for the community. Content of Public Information Bulletin is similar for municipalities, usually it contains important for citizens information on: community authorities, organization of community offices, e-forms of documents, administrative procedures mandatory for citizens and for local businesses, declaration of private properties owned by community authorities, community legal regulations and rules, information on procurements for community, invitations for tenders and auctions, community budgets and land planning. Generally, community Web sites and Public Information Bulletins ensure achievement of eAdministration goals. They enable transfer of top-down administrative information and access to governmental sources of public information, as well as to portals for law interpretation and public administration knowledge dissemination. The citizens have the opportunities to learn about legal acts mandatory for them, to recognize office procedures. They can download forms of documents. They have the possibility to utilize multi-channel communication with Citizen Service Office, where an official can use stationary telephone, mobile, emails. However, citizens still mostly prefer F2F (face-to-face) contacts. The Public Information Bulletins usually ensure investors' and business units' access to databases of tenders considering jobs for public institutions.

4   MUNICIPALITIES WEB SITES RESULTS FINDINGS DISCUSSIONS

The paper titled "eEurope An Information Society for All, Communication on a Commission Initiative for the Special European Council of Lisbon" defines citizen interaction as an approach that does not always aim to change current conditions, but rather encourages activities such as the sharing of concrete, personal experiences, the acquisition of administrative information and the monitoring of the functions of public office. These activities, quite within the existing political, legal and administrative framework, may be carried out both online and offline for mutual support and desirable benefits. As for public administration, the internet is also providing information of two kinds. One is mandatory public information such as pertaining to laws, departmental operation, formal procedure requirements and so on. The other consists of personal experiences that are reported by individuals voluntarily. Public information is provided in the official Public Information Bulletin, but virtual communities can be developed for gathering and exchanging personal opinions and impressions. As it was assumed, virtual community is a form of virtual organization, where citizens are freely involved in participation in discussions.

However, virtual communities are defined in different ways. They can be seen as a local social information infrastructure, providing information over the real community to locals and to visitors of the real community. The virtual community can be interpreted as a communication medium influencing the personal networks of inhabitants of a neighborhood within a municipality. Another view is the virtual community as a tool to improve local democracy and participation; in fact it is the basic idea behind the digital city in Amsterdam (Melis et al., 2000). Virtual community cannot be reduced to any form of electronic commerce or to the provision of online public services as a support of local economic activities. It develops as an experiment with new forms of solving problems and coordinating social life. As a free space to experience and to exchange views, virtual community requires ICT tools as following:

- E-mailing and WWW conferencing;
- Announcement email distribution list;
- Citizens' open discussion forum;
- Newsgroups.

Although people may know themselves, they actively want to maintain community ties. Intensive relations mean for them the belonging to the community. The belonging depends on four systems:

- Civic integration that means being an empowered citizen in a democratic system;
- Economic integration that means having a job and a valued economic function;
- Social integration that means having access to the state support without stigma;
- Interpersonal integration that means having family, friends, neighbours and social networks.

When people chat, get information and find support on the internet, the question is: Do they experience real community or just the inadequate simulacra. The study of the content of the forums allows for the conclusion, that they are not sufficiently well utilized as a medium to involve citizens and officials to act for the community. Within the forum, people need a leader to conduct the discussion, as for example mayor of the town, or a problem which ought to be solved successfully for all the stakeholders involved in the discussion. Shared interests of the people involved in the same virtual community integrate them more than living in the same building. People have strong commitments to their online groups when they perceive them to be long-lasting. There is a danger that virtual communities may develop homogeneous interests. It must be noticed that people do not see that the internet is especially suited to maintaining intermediate–strength ties between people who cannot visit each other frequently. Online relationships are based more on shared interests and less on shared social characteristics. Living in the same non-attractive village is not a sufficient argument for discussion in the forum. The limited evidence available suggests that the ties people develop and maintain in cyberspace are much like most of their real life community. In big city (i.e. Poznan) people noticed the advantage of communication in forum. They got used to communicating online, but in small towns (i.e. Krosno http://www.krosno.pl, Rymanow http://www.rymanow.pl) people know how to use it, but they do not see opportunities for application of forum, chat, blogs. Among the reviewed Web sites 24% have installed forum tool, 8% - chat application, 2% - software for blogging. The internet is still used as a one-way communication channel to inform citizens or to withdraw information from citizens e.g. online questionnaires.

Instead of forum, people ask for photo gallery (e.g. in Rymanow). Films and photo pictures are more impressive and persuasive than text to integrate people around problems or latest events in community. Photo and film galleries seem to be a natural way to integrate citizens in virtual communities. It is worth to notice that the Web derives analytically, not technically from two important stands of media: broadcast media like radio and television and individual communications media like the telephone. As a medium, it holds the potential to incorporate previous focus of mass media - television, audio, radio, text and photography and combine them with the interactivity of the telephone. In comparison with the previous media, the internet has these advantages, that it enables citizens to present themselves and view themselves. The opportunity to see themselves on the internet around the family, neighbours, friends and others more or less known create an irrefutable impression that the entire world has the possibility to view the film or photos. Virtual community focused on photo gallery and the community news develops a potential to stimulate visitors' imagination and interests by engaging in creative communication whilst simultaneously presenting them with a fantastic array of visual and auditory sensations.

15% of the analysed Web sites offer the virtual walk (e.g. the view from the church tower around the town, Niepolomice, http://www.niepolomice.com /pl/nesw.php the view of main street, Chorzow, http://www.um.chorzow.pl) or virtual excursions (Koscielisko http://www.koscielisko.com.pl) mainly for tourists. The camera viewing of non-attractive place (Krosno http://www.krosno.pl) is not a successful tool for encouraging tourists to visit, but the internet camera placed to monitor sea beach, paths in mountains, places near museums or carparks to evaluate how they are crowded is very helpful to steer tourists movement.

There is a distinction between relatively passive broadcasting and interactive communication where information users are also providers. Those who have experienced richness of interactive communications should understand its ability to empower individuals, inspire collaboration, facilitate learning and enhance patterns of access to people and information. Interactive communication is connecting individuals around the world and helping them to reach cast resources of knowledge and information. It should help municipality officers energize citizen participation and bring people together in collaborative efforts to solve the interconnected social problems afflicting those communities. However, in the discussion people need a conductor, which can be the Municipality Chief Officer or an office worker i.e. human or virtual person.

Virtual reality person i.e. interactive agent technology assistant is to create an automated citizen dialogue to increase citizen knowledge on public administration legal regulations, processes and procedures. It has 24/7 availability and enables organizations to decrease cost while improving citizen satisfaction. Interface agent system as virtual reality human is applied as sales advisor or municipality consultant. So far the citizen assistants have been implemented for municipalities of Botkyrka and Malmö (http://www.kiwilogic.com). Botkyrka's assistant, Niklas, was available on the website 24/7. He understood all the common questions of repetitive information character and could turn the conversation over to Botkyrka staff if he didn't know how to answer a question. Now Niklas is changed into Sofia. This was done when Botkyrka renewed their website and image, as well as introducing voice for improving the service availability for minority groups further. Sara is the interactive assistant on Malmö's Web site. She has an extensive knowledge base, which is further developed with Botkyrka's quality, service and assistant work as a base. If Sara can't help the user, she is able to turn him over to customer service through chat. So far, none of the Polish municipality Web sites have interface agent implemented. In 2007 the first implementation of virtual municipality officer is done for Siemianowice (http://www.um.siemianowice.pl). Software agent named Asisso, implemented there, is a virtual adviser from geodesy department for citizens of Siemianowice.

Municipalities are interested in their local integration to better utilize external funds, sponsoring and to better manage local joint investment projects, particularly to reduce the risk of IT innovative projects. eVITA is an example of virtual union of municipalities in rural areas (http://www.witrynawiejska.org.pl/strona.php?p=1173). On January 2004 Partners: Polish-American Freedom Foundation, Cisco Systems and Rural Development Foundation have concluded the Memorandum on joint implementation of "Active Village. Information Society Building – eVITA" programme. Rural Development Foundation became an operator of the programme. The goal of the programme was to stimulate and support civil and economic activity in rural areas using the potential provided by information technologies with a view to facilitate building of exemplary rural information communities in Poland. Practical implementation of the programme took place in 6 rural communities, which were chosen in effect of all-Poland contest. Direct effects of the programme include capacity building of local communities: skills, knowledge, experience and access to ICT, social integration around common tasks, project approach problem solving, increasing knowledge and motivation of local governments to invest in ICT development. Implementation of eVITA pilot program allowed for testing and elaborating the model process of bringing ICT to the village community.

5 CONCLUSIONS

Digital technologies cannot be regarded as the panacea to many of the problems which underline the apparent civic disengagement. The use of information and communication technologies and strategies by democratic actors (government, elected officials, the media, political organizations, citizens/ voters) within political and governance processes, national and the international stage requires long–term education. In Poland, EU initiatives and Act on Access to Public Information cause a tremendous development of Public Information Bulletin as an electronic publication for citizens and investors, but the internet is still used as a one-way communication channel. The lack of implementation of e-signatures for citizens excludes the possibility to upload the fulfilled electronic documents and to send them online directly to municipality departments. Instead of that citizens can only send email or identification number to check the status of the deal at municipality office. So far, there is no intensive feedback and lack of common interchange of information among authorities and citizens. According to the research, two forms of virtual organization for municipalities have been noticed i.e. virtual community and virtual union. The research allows for the conclusion that virtual community integration tools i.e. fun games, blogs, video interviews, chats, forums, interface agents are not sufficient to engage citizens in discussions, creation of social relations and to exchange views. It is not a problem of ICT tool; it is a problem of tradition and culture to be involved in virtual community. Citizens prefer photo and film galleries, eNews and eJournals to be integrated with others in community. They are interested in the development of official as well as unofficial Web sites for community and in publication of eNews. However, citizens have not yet noticed the need to integrate local media i.e. local journals, radio and TV to visualize important municipality problems.

6 REFERENCES

1. Centeno C., van Bavel R. Burgelman J-C. eGovernment in the EU in 2010: Key policy and research challenges. August 2004. http://www.jrc.es/home/publications/publications.html
2. eEurope: An Information Society for All. Communication on a Commission Initiative for the Special European Council of Lisbon 23 and 24 March 2000 (presented by the Commission). COM (99) 687 final, 8.12.1999. http://aei.pitt.edu/3532/
3. i2010 eGovernment Action Plan: Accelerating eGovernment in Europe for the Benefit of All, Policy Strategy paper – 25 April 2006, http://ec.eropa.eu/idabc/en/document/5763/254
4. IDABC eGovernment Observatory, eGovernment in Poland, 2005, http://ec.europa.eu/idabc/servlets/Doc?id=21020
5. Izdebski H. Access to Public Information Act and Open Government Standards, The Polish Yearbook of Civil service, 2003, 113-123.
6. Kolsaker A Lee-Kelley L 'Mind theGap': e-Government and e-Democracy. M.A.Wimmer et al. (2006) Electronic Government 2006, LNCS 4084, 2006, 96-106.
7. Melis I., van den Besselaar P., Beckers D., Digital cities: organization, content and use. Toru Ishida & K.Isbister, Digital Cities: Experiences, Technologies and Future Perspectives, Lecture Notes in Computer Science 1765, 2000, 18-32.
8. Powell W.W. Neither Market nor Hierarchy, Network Forms of Organization. Research in Organizational Behaviour, 12, 1990, 295-336.
9. Phipps L. New communications technologies. Information, Communication & Society, 3:1, 2000, 39-68.

68

A SERVICE INFRASTRUCTURE TO SUPPORT UBIQUITOUS ENGINEERING PRACTICES

Yacine Rezgui and Benachir Medjdoub

Informatics Research Institute, University of Salford, Salford, UK.
School of Architecture, University of Nottingham, , Nottingham, UK
y.rezgui@salford.ac.uk; B.Medjdoub@nottingham.ac.uk

Ubiquitous computing allows users to move between gateways to the information world in ways that are appropriate to their current physical as well as contextual settings. Advanced visualization techniques, including immersive displays and augmented reality, have the potential to address the collocation needs of mobile engineering teams, and enhance their collaboration effectively. The paper explores the use of innovative technologies for implementing a ubiquitous engineering service infrastructure. This comprises a wide range of value-added engineering services that make use of visualization technologies - combined with location tracking techniques - to convey user and context sensitive, semantically enriched, high dimensional multimedia contents.

1   INTRODUCTION

The convergence of ubiquitous computing and visualization technologies is creating unprecedented opportunities for engineering teams to respond more effectively to the increasing demand for sophisticated, customized, and high quality products and services in industry. Ubiquitous computing allows people to move between gateways to the information world in ways that are appropriate to their current physical as well as contextual settings. Visualization related technologies, from immersive displays to Augmented Reality (AR), are today routinely used in industry, with huge potential in engineering, health, heritage and archaeology [1, 2].

Construction is one of the sectors with strong potentials to benefit from these advanced technologies. Over the last few decades it has become increasingly heterogeneous and highly fragmented, depending upon a large number of very different professions ranging from design and engineering firms to component/ product manufacturers, with ever-growing pressures from clients (building owners) to deliver sophisticated facilities on time and on budget. Within the framework of geographical dispersion, the construction industry is characterized by various challenges in terms of working practices [8, 9, 10], including: (a) non co-location of individuals and teams collaborating on projects; (b) the project-oriented nature of the industry, with a tendency for actors to be involved in several projects simultaneously; (c) multi-disciplinary and mobile-working practices; (d) the temporary and often short-term nature of business relationships. In this context, new and novel communication and visualization technologies have the potential to radically change the process of building design and construction, and match more closely the formal aspirations of modern design and engineering teams.

Rezgui, Y., Medjdoub, B., 2007, in IFIP International Federation for Information Processing, Volume 243, Establishing the Foundation of Collaborative Networks; eds. Camarinha-Matos, L., Afsarmanesh, H., Novais, P., Analide, C.; (Boston: Springer), pp. 627–636.

The present research explores the use of innovative technologies for implementing a ubiquitous engineering service infrastructure. This comprises a wide range of value-added engineering services that make use of visualization technologies - combined with location tracking techniques - to convey user and context sensitive, semantically enriched, high dimensional multimedia contents. This is achieved through a variety of display devices ranging from traditional desktop monitors to head mounted display and wearable devices with real time augmented reality capabilities.

2   CURRENT ENGINEERING PRACTICES

Current engineering practices in Construction are diverse and very much influenced by existing information and communication technologies (ICT). Hardware and software infrastructures used to support communication and collaboration within organizations and across projects are most of the time owned or, in some very few instances, leased. Given the dominant SME nature of Construction [8], there is a strong reluctance to invest in ICT infrastructures due to financial considerations. The prevailing model for software provision is licensing. However, the licensed software is rarely exploited to its full potential, as users tend to use a limited range of the available functionality. This, in fact, creates a perception of complexity and can act as a barrier to software adoption.

Software applications often require ad-hoc integration to enable seamless collaboration between individuals and teams on projects. This is however repeated on each project, as partners tend to bring and use their own software [11]. Data and information redundancy are real issues, as information tends to be owned and managed across individuals, teams, and projects with no particular agreed policy. This leads to severe information inconsistency and regulatory compliance problems, resulting in dramatic financial implications.

Practitioners tend to be tied to a physical location (mainly their office) to do their jobs. Software is accessed through desktops and, in very few instances, through laptops on site. Support and maintenance is provided through many points of service representing the different technology licensees.

3   RELATED TECHNICAL AREAS

Several research areas underpin the vision of ubiquitous computing. Three particular ones are relevant for the present research, namely: Service-oriented computing, Location tracking, and Augmented reality.

Service-Oriented Computing (SOC) is becoming the prominent paradigm for leveraging inter and intra enterprise information systems. Web-services have attracted enormous interest from the research community and industry in recent years and have emerged as a serious candidate for deploying service-oriented solutions [10]. Web services are self-contained, web-enabled applications capable not only of performing business activities on their own, but also possessing the ability to engage other web services in order to complete higher-order business transactions [20]. The benefits of web services include the decoupling of service interfaces from implementation and platform considerations, the support for dynamic service binding, and an increase in cross-language and cross-platform interoperability. The challenge of this new form of computing is to move from its initial "Describe, Publish, Interact" capability to support dynamic composition of services into reinvented assemblies, in ways that previously could not be predicted in advance [17].

In terms of location tracking, devices that track in three dimensions the position and orientation of wearable displays, including Head Mounted Displays (HMD), are used to render 3D virtual objects aligned with the physical world. There are a number of different tracking technologies used, varying by the number of dimensions measured and the physical properties used [19]. Relevant technologies include Real-time Kinematic (RTK) GPS, ground–based pseudo-satellite (or pseudolite) technology, and Inertial Navigation System (INS).

Natural interfaces offered by devices such as walk-in displays, body tracking, and haptics allow non co-located people to interact with each other in a natural way. More realistic and faithful models can be visualized thanks to improvements in data capture and display technologies (ranging from digital projectors and plasma screens to wearable devices) and the availability of computing power (offered by commodity graphics cards and GRID technology) capable of rendering such data in real time [13]. On the other hand, Augmented Reality (AR) augments real world experiences by adding computer-generated experiences. AR addresses two major issues with collaboration: (a) seamless integration with existing tools and practices; and (b) enhancing practice by supporting remote and collocated activities that would otherwise be impossible. AR research has developed rapidly over the last decade [1].

4   E-SERVICES IN CONSTRUCTION

Over the last few years, traditional e-commerce is giving way to a new paradigm known as "e-service". E-services include all interactive services that are delivered on the Internet using advanced telecommunications, information, and multimedia technologies [14]. This emerging paradigm represents a coherent point of view that challenges many of the traditional assumptions about how to use the online environment to raise profits (Rust and Lemon, 2001). It is based less on reducing costs through automation and increased efficiency and more on expanding revenues through enhancing service and building profitable customer relationships [15, 16].

As argued by several authors [18], e-services can be classified according to two dimensions: their origin and nature / type of goods supplied (Table 1). The first dimension relates to how well an e-service provider is rooted in the physical world. E-service providers having their origins as a dot.com can be thus distinguished from those having traditional roots. For the latter, the portal site itself is an extension, whereas dot.com starters have always operated in the e-world, while the portal is the original brand. The second dimension concerns the type of products that are supplied. Some e-service providers supply tangible goods or traditional services: the websites mainly function as a distribution channel, an on-line store or an interface with customers. In contrast, other e-service providers offer virtual products, remaining within the borders of the e-world: search functions, communication tools, information, downloadable software etc. Based on the framework depicted in Table 1, there are several variants of the e-Services models in Construction characterized by their intended use. These are categorized below.

Table 1- Classification of e-Services in Construction.

e-Services in Construction		Origin	
		Virtual	**Physical**
Product	**Virtual**	Specialised Portals aiding at selecting the right products taking into account cost, quality and performance parameters	Software manufacturers that have developed service-based solutions of their software products.
			Access to Construction regulations online.
		Access to semantic resources in the Construction domain: thesauri, dictionaries, etc.	Access to construction organization details and yellow pages.
	Physical	Virtual team work and enterprise solutions, e.g. Buildonline, Bricsnet, Buzzsaw, Citadon.	Product / equipment Manufacturers and suppliers.
			Selling Construction Products on line

4.1   e-Services as Enhanced Customer-driven e-Commerce

This is where traditional e-commerce approaches that tended to focus on automating "product selling" practices have been extended to provide a service dimension to the customer using Customer Relationship Management (CRM) techniques. Moreover, there is a difference between conducting basic e-commerce purchases and adopting e-services. In comparison to one-time e-commerce-based purchases, the e-service adoption decision is typically more complex, as it initiates a long-term relationship between the consumer and service provider [4]. E-services can take the form of Consumer and Trading Portals providing advanced market-maker e-services such as reverse auctions and collective bidding. A great deal of services in the Construction sector falling under this category has emerged over the last few years. These are developed mainly in the area of product manufacturers and suppliers.

4.2   e-Services as a new software-licensing paradigm

Increasing complex business processes require the use of a variety of software packages but only a few packages are used on a daily basis. This infrequent usage pattern often does not justify purchasing full licenses and therefore motivates a need for more flexible way to use and pay for usage of software [5]. Although, in the late 1990s, a host of start-ups began offering applications delivered over the Web using a pay-per-use cost model, most of them went out of business, mainly because large corporate customers balked at the idea of allowing untested outsiders to run their most important applications. But in the past couple of years, both corporations and smaller businesses have become more comfortable with this way of buying software [3]. Many software publishers are today reconsidering their software distribution methods. They deliver application software and services (software maintenance, upgrades, staff training, etc.) over the Web on a lease or subscription basis instead of the traditional perpetual licensing model [11]. Several leading software vendors have started adopting this new business model emphasizing cost savings factors. Analysts now estimate that over the next half-decade, as much as half the software sold to corporations will be paid for on a monthly basis, as part of a long-term contract or a monthly rental fee, or even on a pay-per-use basis [3].

This new form of software licensing provides a software service that includes configuration, maintenance, training and access to a help-desk. It enables organizations to rent as opposed to purchase software. This involves using only the functionality directly needed by the user, therefore reducing cost and increasing work efficiency. In the Construction sector, such services include solutions from Bricsnet (http://www.bricsnet.com), Buzzsaw (http://www.buzzsaw.com), BuildOnline (http://www.build-online.com) and Citadon (http://www.citadon.com).

4.3   e-Services as a mean to enable e-Processes

Businesses now have a new opportunity to rethink fundamental aspects of Information Technology (IT). One of the key capabilities within e-services can also be applied to elements of a business' IT infrastructure to facilitate the execution of distributed business processes implemented through a coordinated composition and invocation of web-enabled, service-oriented, corporate Enterprise Information Systems applications. For example, messaging/email can now be provided to the employees of an enterprise using a service-based approach. This frees time and money for the IT organization to invest elsewhere - into areas that can better serve their customers and their partners. The e-services model has been used by some leading organizations to better integrate their in-house legacy as well as commercial software applications, thus becoming ubiquitous and providing better support to mobile users. Some leading construction organizations have started investigating and investing into these technologies [10].

5   CONCEPTUALISATION OF THE UBIQUITOUS ENGINEERING SOLUTION

The underlying conceptualization of the solution is influenced by BPEL4WS as illustrated in Figure 1. A Construction project operates as a Virtual Enterprise [10]. This is assigned a dedicated Workspace environment. In order to reflect the discipline-oriented nature of the sector, a Workspace can involve other Workspaces in a recursive manner. Business processes interact, on a peer-to-peer basis, with a set of Services by invoking one or several of the Methods they support. Methods represent API calls, or functionality, of such services. The way messages are exchanged between the business process and the Service Methods is described through the concept of Activity. The proposed model supports the allocation of such services to Virtual Enterprises and Workspaces within them. Access to Services and Methods from within an individual project is controlled through WorkspaceRoles.

An Actor must hold at least one *WorkspaceRole*, which corresponds to an actual role that is held within a project. This is vital because, whilst it allows the system to capture some semantics about members having performed a task through the *WorkspaceRole*.

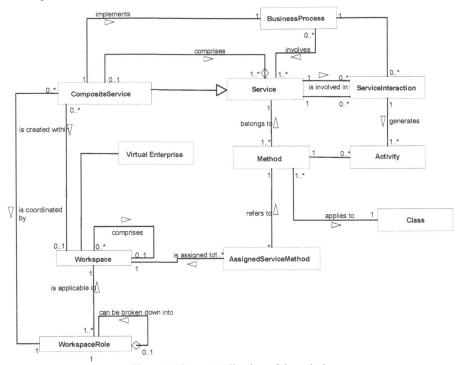

Figure 1- Conceptualization of the solution.

The proposed architecture (Figure 2) makes use of established work, initiatives and standards in the web services domain (including BPEL4WS, WS-Security, WS-Coordination, WS-Transaction). Each layer represents the main building blocks supporting the ubiquitous engineering vision. The service manager box provides access to the API functions necessary for all aspects of invocation, registration and de-registration of services (including web-serviced end-user legacy and commercial design & engineering applications), as well as their publication in a dedicated UDDI registry. The Business Process Specification Layer (BPSL) includes the API functions that enable service composition in order to implement a given business process as described in the previous section. Specialized services are specified in the following layer, including augmented Reality, location tracking, Multi-modal presentation, and user profiling. The business process composition relies on a set of core services concerned with service coordination, transaction, and security. The lower part of the picture represents all web-serviced applications that are ready for invocation and use as part of a service composition exercise in order to implement a business process.

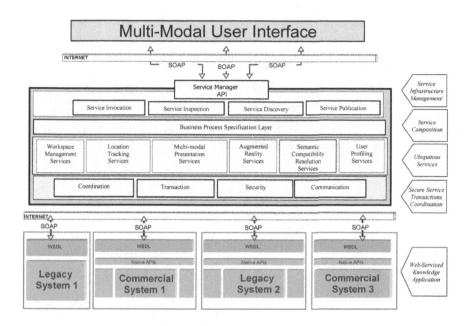

Figure 2 - Architecture of the ubiquitous service infrastructure.

6   CASE STUDIES

To illustrate the main concept described in this paper, two applications (outdoor and indoor augmented reality systems) are presented. These are described below.

6.1   A mobile system for an outdoor augmented visualisation in architecture

Architects design buildings in their offices using a variety of drawings ranging from plans to 3D perspectives. In the best scenario, an architect would use CAD (Computer-Aided Design) software to visualize the building in 2D or 3D, and then superimpose an image of the virtual building on an image of the real site to evaluate his/her design. For any modification, the architect has to (a) go back to the building 3D model, (b) do the necessary modification(s), and (c) produce the image again where the virtual building is superimposed on the real site. In the proposed approach, an on-site real-time augmented visualization system is used to assist architects to visualize/modify/evaluate their design in real time. A dedicated set of functionalities delivered in the form of web-services is invoked through a PDA to manipulate/modify the 3D virtual model of the building. Location tracking techniques (GPS and INS) are used via a see-through head mounted display to visualize the real site (including the existing building) augmented with the virtual extension. The existing site is illustrated in Figure 3a1. The designer invokes a service, Add_Building_Element *()*, to add an overhanging structure to the existing building. This service, in turn, invokes the methods *Superimpose_Models ()* and *Render_Design ()* to deliver the resulting augmented reality design on the designer's head mounted display (Figure 3a2). While assessing the extension, the added building element has triggered automatically, through a service composition procedure, the method *Dimension_Model ()*. The latter identifies a critical structural weakness, due to the length of the overhanging structure, and suggests the addition of two columns to improve the resistance and stability of the overall building (Figure 3a3). Once validated, the *Approve_Design ()* service is invoked, aimed at the lead architect back in the designer's office.

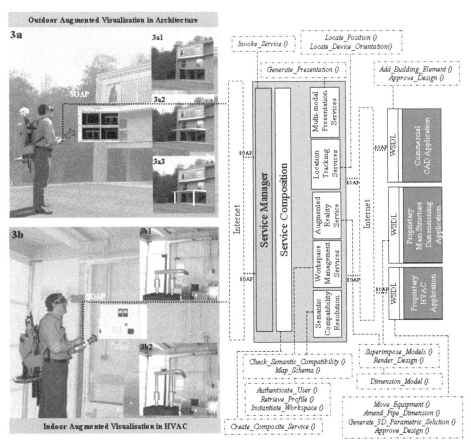

Figure 3 - Ubiquitous access to services in Practice.

6.2   A mobile system for an indoor augmented reality in building services

Currently, the design of heating and ventilation plants is done at work using CAD and simulation software. Thus, starting from the heating load in kW, the building service engineer defines two-dimensional schematic solutions consisting of a set of plans of the building including the equipment location (e.g. boilers, pumps, etc.) and the pipe routing. Through the design process, the engineer has no possibility to check the design on site (plant room space augmented with the virtual 3D solution) and to make the necessary modification(s) if applicable (e.g. an error in the height of the flue pipes). For any design modification, the engineer has to go back to the office and modify the design accordingly.

Through the proposed system, the engineer has the possibility to generate 3D plant room solutions and visualize them on site. A dedicated set of functionality delivered in the form of web-services is invoked through a PDA to generate 3D plant room solutions, including equipment location and pipe routes [6,7]. Motion tracking sensors and a see-through Head mounted display are used to visualize the real site augmented with the virtual 3D solution.

The service-based solution proceeds in the following way. The HVAC engineer invokes a dedicated web-service that generates an optimised 3D parametric solution using Constraint Logic Programming. The service, Generate_3D_Parametric_Solution (), takes the plant room geometry and the heating load in kW as input. First, the standard number and size of modular boilers, pumps, etc., are determined from the heat load. Then, a compatible optimising 3D parametric solution is generated. The novelty of the approach is that it is highly interactive. Modifying the topology of the generated solution is done directly through the graphic interface of the PDA. For example, modifying the position of a boiler is done in two steps. First, the engineer invokes the method *Move_Equipment ()* to specify the new physical location of the boiler. This can also be achieved by a simple dragging routine. The CAD system automatically updates the 3D model including the pipe-routing, while maintaining all the constraints, hence the validity of the design. Once the modification is made, the engineer invokes another web service, *Approve_Design (),* which is submitted to the lead engineer for approval. Only once this is granted can the amendment be made effective.

The scenario illustrated in Figure 3b illustrates an engineer on site invoking a service via SOAP to visualise a plant room solution on his head mounted display (Figure 3b1: 2 Boilers and flue pipes) obtained through *Generate_3D_Parametric_Solution ()* web service. Figure 3b3 illustrates the HVAC application platform graphic interface. Next, the engineer invokes another service, *Amend_Pipe_Dimension (),* to change the height of the flue pipe and visualise the new solution on his HMD in real time (Figure 3b2).

7   CONCLUSION

The research and evaluation of the deployment work has identified (a) a need to have flexible and reusable composite services, and (b) mechanisms to support smart composition of web services to implement a given business process. In fact, web service composition, even when developed using BPEL is not adaptive to change. If the requirements of the application change or need extending, the service composition needs to be re-specified from scratch. It is currently not possible to define and implement a web service composition once and use it in similar designs with some variations in a later stage. A more flexible approach allowing service re-use, extension, and specialization should be supported in a way that is similar to component-based development. Some work has already been done in this area [11]. In relation to aspect (b), web service composition methodologies have a focus on syntactic integration and therefore do not support automatic composition of web services. As highlighted in [12], semantic integration becomes crucial for web services as it allows them to: (a) represent and reason about the task that a web service performs; (b) understand the meaning of exchanged messages; (c) represent and reason about preconditions that are required to use the service and the effects of having invoked the service; and (d) allow intelligent composition of web services to achieve a more complex service. These constitute the current challenges and future directions for research tackled by the authors and the web services community.

8   REFERENCES

[1] Azuma, R.T., Y. Baillot, R. Behringer, S. Feiner, S. Julier, and B. MacIntyre, 2001, "Recent Advances in Augmented Reality", IEEE Computer Graphics and Applications, 21 (6). pp. 34-47.

[2] Burdea, G.C. and Coiet, P.: Virtual Reality Technology. Wiley-Interscience (2003).

[3] Business Week (2004), "Pay-As-You-Go is Up and Running," Business Week, January 12, pp. 93-94.

[4] Featherman, M.S., and Pavlou P.A. Predicting E-services Adoption: A Perceived Risk Facets Perspective, International Journal of Human-Computer Studies, 59, pp. 451–474, 2003.

[5] Fenicle, B., and Wahls, T. A Methodology to Provide and use Interchangeable Services, SAC 2003, Melbourne, Florida, USA, 2003.

[6] Medjdoub, B., Richens, P. and Barnard, B. Generation of Variational Standard Plant Room Solutions, Automation in Construction Journal, 12(2), pp. 155-166, 2003.

[7] Medjdoub, B. and Yannou, B. "Dynamic space ordering at a topological level in space planning", Artificial Intelligence in Engineering, 15(1), pp. 47-60, 2001.

[8] Rezgui, Y. Review of Information and Knowledge Management Practices State of the Art in the Construction Industry, Knowledge Engineering Review, Issue 16(3), pp. 241-254, 2001.

[9] Rezgui, Y., Zarli, A. Paving the way to digital construction: a strategic roadmap, Journal of Construction Management and Engineering (Journal of the American Society of Civil Engineering), 132(7), pp. 767-776, 2006.

[10] Rezgui, Y. Role-Based Service-Oriented Implementation of a Virtual Enterprise: A Case Study in the Construction Sector, Computers in Industry (Elsevier), 58(1), pp. 74-86, 2007.

[11] Rezgui, Y. Exploring Virtual Team-Working Effectiveness in the Construction Sector, Interacting with Computers (Elsevier), 19(2), pp. 96-112 , 2007.

[12] Rezgui, Y. and Nefti-Meziani, S. Ontology-Based Dynamic Composition of Services Using Semantic Relatedness and Categorisation Techniques, ICEIS: 9th International Conference on Enterprise Information Systems, 12-16, June 2007, Funchal, Madeira - Portugal.

[13] Roberts, D., Wolff, R. and O. Otto, "Constructing a Gazebo: Supporting teamwork in a tightly coupled, distributed task in virtual reality," Presence: Teleoperators & Virtual Environments, vol. 12, 2003.

[14] Roth, A.V. Service Strategy and the Technological Revolution, In J.A.D. Machuca, T. Mandakovic (Eds.), POM Facing the New Millennium: Evaluating the Past, Leading With the Present and Planning the Future of Operations, Production and Operations Management Society and the University of Sevilla, Sevilla, 2000, pp. 159–168, 2000.

[15] Rust, R., and Kannan, P.K. E-Service: A New Paradigm for Business in the Electronic Environment, Communications of the ACM, 46(6), 2003.

[16] Ruyter, K.de, Wetzels, M., Kleijnen, M. Customer Adoption of E-Service: An Experimental Study, International Journal of Service Industry Management 12 (2), pp. 184–206, 2001.

[17] Van Den Heuvel, W.J., Maamar, Z. Moving Towards a Framework to Compose Intelligent Web Services, Communications of the ACM, vol. 46, no. 10, Oct 2003, pp. 103-109.

[18] Van Riel, A.C.R., and Ouwersloot, H. Extending Electronic Portals with New Services: Exploring the Usefulness of Brand Extension Models, Journal of Retailing and Consumer Services, 12 (3), pp. 245-254, 2005.

[19] Welch, G. and Foxlin, E. Motion Tracking: No Silver Bullet, but a Respectable Arsenal. IEEE Computer Graphics and Applications, Vol. 22, No. 6, pp. 24-38, 2002.

[20] Yang, J. Web Service Componentization," Communications of the ACM, vol. 46, no. 10, Oct 2003, pp. 35-40.

PART 22

EVALUATION AND MANAGEMENT OF COLLABORATIVE SUPPLY NETWORKS

69

ENGINEERING METHODOLOGY FOR ORGANISATION NETWORKS

X.Boucher[1], A.Zaidat[2], L.Vincent[1]

1-Clermond-Ferrand 1 University, Technology Institute, ali.zaidat@iut.u-clermont1.fr
2-Ecole nationale supérieure des mines de Saint Etienne, G2I, {boucher, vincent}@emse.fr
FRANCE

This paper presents the key features of an engineering methodology dedicated to Organisation Networks. This methodology constitutes one of the elements of a full engineering framework developed through a PhD research thesis. The authors mainly focus hereafter on specifying the "design" and "preliminary engineering" activities of the engineering procedure. The methodology is illustrated on a case study from the sector of metallurgical industry.

1   INTRODUCTION

This paper reports some elements of a PhD research focusing on a modelling architecture and engineering methodology dedicated to a specific cooperative structure: "organisation networks" (Zaidat, 2005). The basic hypothesis and specificities concerning organisation networks, as well as the modeling architecture have been previously published in (Zaidat et al., 2005) (Zaidat et al., 2006).

The objective of an engineering methodology is to specify the procedure required for an engineering objective and to provide the tools (mainly models) necessary for the engineering activities. An engineering methodology can be modelled by a set of activity diagrams or procedures with a detailed description of the various engineering activity tasks. Our proposal for Organisation Networks is based on methodologies from information system engineering (Merise, object oriented methods and methods for open distributed systems), enterprise engineering (IDEF, CIMOSA, PERA, GRAI-GIM, and Zachman methodology), and cooperative structure engineering (Zwegers et al., 2003), (Teleflow, 1998), (Chalmetta, 2003). The engineering framework presented hereafter mainly comes from a specialisation of the two reference frameworks: [GERAM 2000] and VERAM [Zwegers et al. 2003], with the objective to provide a full implementation of GERAM. Indeed, GERAM provides a well-established generic framework, but nearly no complete implementation on any specific area can be found in the literature.

Organisation networks constitute a breeding environment with a long term life cycle [Zwegers et al. 2003], from which partners develop specific "businesses" which represent short term cooperation structures. Thus, this study will refer to two main enterprise modelling entities: "Organisation Network" (ON.) and "Business". For each enterprise entity, an engineering life-cycle and a modelling framework have been specified.

Concerning the life-cycle of enterprise entities, we will refer below to the first four phases defined in the methodology (Zaidat, 2005): (1) Organisation

Boucher, X., Zaidat, A., Vincent, L., 2007, in IFIP International Federation for Information Processing, Volume 243, Establishing the Foundation of Collaborative Networks; eds. Camarinha-Matos, L., Afsarmanesh, H., Novais, P., Analide, C.; (Boston: Springer), pp. 639–648.

Network/Business identification; (2) Organisation Network/Business definition; (3) Design; (4) Preliminary engineering.

Concerning the modelling framework, four modelling views have been specified in (Zaidat et al., 2006). First, to represent the functioning mechanisms, the organisational structure, the resources and flows of a breeding environment or specific business we defined two "content views" called the "functional view" and the "organisational view". In addition, two independent modeling views dealing with the integration issues in the organisation network engineering have been defined: the "application view" and the "knowledge view".

The objective of this communication is to focus on the engineering methodology by presenting some key features of engineering activities specified to build both Organisation Networks and specific Businesses. Section 2 introduces the case study used to illustrate the methodology, and section 3 specifies the engineering activities, putting the focus on the "design" and "preliminary engineering" life-cycle phases.

2   CASE STUDY

The methodology was tested on a case study built from real experiences. The case study "PYRAMICA" presented below, is based on the creation and the operation of two real SME networks working in the sector of metallurgical industry and studied during the GrecoPME project (Grecopme project, 2003).

The creation of the network PYRAMICA has been initiated by two SMEs SURFPAINT (enterprise specialised in painting and surface treatment) and METAGRIT (enterprise specialised in gritting and metal deposits). In a regional context of externalisation from the main contractors, the two SMEs have chosen a strategic vision of collaboration on the market, based on complementary services. Their strategy consists in offering integrated products based on both mechanical and electrical components. They defined four business types in the domain of integrated mechanical and electrical products: (1) Switchgear cubicle; (2) Safety devices for the national markets; (3) Safety devices for the international market and (4) Safety hoods.

SURFPAINT and METAGRIT have decided to develop a vertical cooperation to carry out these businesses. This means first to proceed to the selection of partners in order to get complementary macro-competencies. The selection process led them to choose the three following partners (who gave their agreement to take part in PYRAMICA operations).

-   ROUANESHEET-METAL with macro-competencies in sheetmetal treatment;
-   MACHWIR with macro-competencies in machine assembly and wiring;
-   CPELEC specialised in manufacturing of electrical engineering sub-sets.

The partners have proceeded to some of the most difficult activities of the Organisation Network Engineering Methodology, which consists in applying to PYRAMICA the design and preliminary engineering phases. In this paper, we will describe the application of our methodology on the business "Production and Delivery of Safety Devices for the International Markets" (PDSDIM). This process is described in annexe 1.1. The case study will mainly illustrate the application of the engineering procedure for the design and preliminary engineering.

Our engineering framework has been implemented on the enterprise modelling toolkit ADONIS developed by the Austrian company BOC. The power of Adonis is linked to its strong adaptability provided by a meta-modeling approach. This approach offers the opportunity to develop specific modelling libraries. Adonis also proposes different programming languages – e.g. in order to implement evaluation and simulation methods-.

3 ENGINEERING METHODOLOGY

Engineering activities are distributed among the main engineering phases specified in the Life-Cycle of our modeling framework: Network identification, Network definition, Design and Preliminary engineering. We do not detail hereafter the network identification and definition phases, which are mainly based on the re-use of the TELEfow project results (1998). We specify below the design and preliminary engineering phases.

To support engineering tasks, the methodology uses a large set of models, with the objective to build a full specification of the four modeling views introduced before: Functional, Organisational, Application and Knowledge views. The figure below provides an overview of all the models required, for each modeling view. We illustrate hereafter the progressive building of these models, throughout the engineering procedure (for "Design" and "Preliminary Engineering" steps).

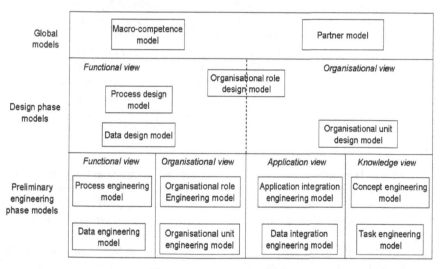

Figure 1 – Engineering Models

3.1 Design

The design phase provides design solutions for the future functioning and organisational structures of the ON and of the different businesses. Figure 2 presents the engineering activities associated with the design phase (detailed below).

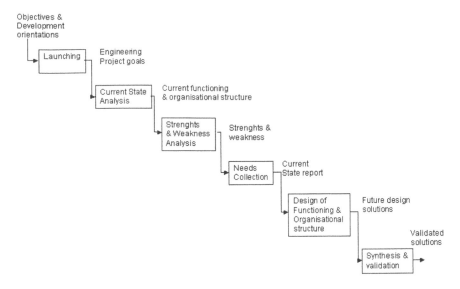

Figure 2 – Engineering activities for the design phase

The goal of the design phase is to define the organisational levels and to give an overall description of the functioning and organisational structures for each decomposed organisational unit. During these engineering activities, the four design models of figure 1 are built (by the tasks described in table1) and they will be later detailed during the preliminary engineering by providing organisational solutions.

Considering that the PYRAMICA Network is under creation, the activities "Current state analysis" and "strengths &weaknesses analysis" are not applied (we just explain them conceptually, without case study application). After "launching" and "needs collection", we are mainly interested by illustrating the results of the "design" activity.

Launching: This activity defines the objectives and development policies related to the organisation network and the specific businesses. Launching increases team projects awareness on the objectives and the importance of the design and preliminary engineering phases. Finally this activity triggers the set up of the ON.

Current state analysis: This analysis concentrates on understanding the current functioning and organisational structures, application integration solutions, concept models, and task models of the ON and of the different businesses. All the modelling views are necessary for the current state analysis, as shown in Table 1.

Strengths and weaknesses analysis: the results of the previous activity are used in order to analyse strength/weaknesses and to collect information relevant to user needs as well as criticism. The analysis of strengths and weaknesses consists in describing the strong points and the weak points related to the Organisation Network global operation. This is an analysis of current state of the ON, the different businesses, and the relationships between them.

Needs collection: The goal of this activity is to collect development needs related to the Organisation Network, the different businesses, and their relationships. This brings the actors to publish a "current state report" gathering the results of analyses related to both enterprise entities ("Organisation Network" and "Business").The current state is analysed in terms of operation, organisational structure, partner participation, etc. This report is the starting point for the next activity of design solution building.

In the case of PYRAMICA, the partners have come up with a considerable set of needs regarding the functioning and organisational structures of the PDSDIM business. Examples of the most general needs:

- The partners will take part in the business operation according to their macro-competencies.
- Each organisational unit has to be specialised on a set of specific missions.
- The authority and the responsibility must be clearly specified for each business.
- The partners will grant data access to technical information from their partners.
- Etc...

Table 1 – Engineering tasks for current state analysis

Modelling View	Engineering tasks
Functional view	Modelling of the organisational roles Modelling of the inter-organisational role processes by describing sub-processes and activities defined in these roles. Modelling of the object views and their relationships. Description of integration solutions related to logistic, culture, etc. These solutions are developed at the process level and they are not taken into account in the integration views.
Organisational view	Modelling of the organisational units, organisational roles, and their relationships. Modelling of resources Modelling of partner participation
Application view	Modelling of the current applications used, their relationships, messages exchanged, and synchronisation actions carried out.
Knowledge view	Description of concept models Description of task models

Design of functioning and organisational structures: at this stage, the specification of the future design solutions is only applied to the content views. Integration solutions will be studied in preliminary engineering, after the processes design activity. Referring to the overall orientations stated in the definition phase, this activity uses the "current state report" to build future design solutions, describing the functioning and organisational structures of the "Organisation Network" and "Businesses". This activity validates the objectives and puts priorities on goals, strong points, weak points and collected needs. The main engineering tasks are listed below. Referring to the modelling approach principles these tasks are applied to each organisational unit and at all the abstraction levels.

Table 2 – Engineering tasks for functional and organisational design

Modelling View	Engineering tasks
Functional view	Design of organisational roles by assigning their missions and objectives Design of inter-organisational processes Design of data models.
Organisational view	Design of the organisational units by specifying their missions and objectives Allocation of the organisational roles to the organisational units Overall definition of partner participations to these units

The application of the design activity to PYRAMICA Network has resulted in several operational models defined in ADONIS modeling environment. Six organisational roles have been specified. Referring to the construct of "organisational role" defined in the methodology (Zaidat et al., 2005), such roles are characterised by the attributes "missions", "rights/obligation" and "performance indicators". In case we refer to decision roles, we add decisional attributes "decision horizon", "decision period". The PDSDIM process of PYRAMYCA Network requires the roles "Business coordinator", "Assembler", "Sheet-metal worker", "Safety mechanism maker", "Surface processor", "Painter". These organisational roles required for the business processes will be taken in charge by five organisational units available among the network members. These organisational units are specified in the organisational view.

The functional view has also led to define inter-organisational processes and a data model. An example of process presented in annexe1.1 describes how organisational units of the PDSDIM cooperate to make and deliver safety devices to the international markets based on the organisational roles introduced above.

Synthesis and validation: the design solutions proposed by the project team are validated by a strategic committee, whose decisions are based on several inputs: current state report; list of priorities on objectives, strong points, weak points, criticisms, and needs; list of design solutions describing the future operation and organisational structure of the ON and of the different businesses. In collaboration with the project team, the strategic committee confirms the development policies of the "Organisation Network" and "Businesses", and validates the design solutions.

3.2 Preliminary engineering

The preliminary engineering step deeper evaluates the potential implementation of a network or a single business, in order to make it possible to compare and/or simulate these solutions. The purpose is to specify the "How" the network should be implemented. Figure 3 presents the engineering activities of this phase.

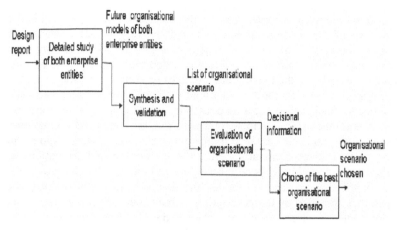

Figure 3 – Engineering activities for the preliminary engineering

Detailed study: For both enterprise entities "Organisation Network" and "Business", the detailed study describes with a sufficient level of precision the processes, inter-organisational roles, resources used, organisational relationships, rights and obligations of partners, etc. In the design phase, we apply a top-down approach with respect to the decomposition principle. The detailed study can use either a top-down or a bottom-up approach. The main engineering activities are summarised in table 3:

Table 3 – Engineering tasks detailed study

Modelling View	Engineering tasks
Functional view	Development of organisational solutions. by defining the macro-competencies required to carry out such sub-processes and activities. Development of a detailed description of resource roles Definition of rights and obligations as well as performance indicators related to sub-processes and activities. Detailed descriptions of federator or integrator elements related to functional, logistic, cultural, semantic … aspects Design of adaptation means (reengineering, migration of partner activities, etc.).
Organisational view	Detailed description of the resources to be used and affectation to resource roles Modelling of the authority and coordination relationships among roles Definition of allocation rules of partners to organisational units, used when several partners can be in charge of a given unit or set of activities. Detailed description of the different modelling concept attributes.
Application view	Description of the treatments managed by the integration system. Modelling of the software applications concerned and of their relationships Modelling of the information flows of synchronisation actions. Definition of the information system urbanisation rules to be used for the development of the future solutions.
Knowledge view	Construction of the future concept models Construction of the future task models

As shown in figure 1, during the preliminary engineering the macro-competency model is detailed and the eight preliminary engineering models are built. Among them, the models of the content view constitute more detailed versions of the design models generated in the previous step, while the models of integration view are created at this stage.

The macro-competency model presents the macro-competencies required for the full execution of the process "Production and delivery of safety devices to the international markets". The macro-competencies are linked to the organisational roles. They can be broken down into more detailed macro-competencies and, later, they can be mapped with the macro-competencies of each organisational unit.

The engineering models for the functional view are more detailed versions of the design models. Each sub-process and activity of the process in annexe 1.1 is specified through the macro-competencies required, the rights and obligation related to their execution, their performance indicators, execution time, transport time, and execution costs. Project teams also define the integration of information, logistic, and cultural aspects, and they specify the inputs and outputs of each sub-process and activity. For the data engineering model, the data classes firstly defined in design step are further specified by the description of their methods and by the enrichment of their attributes. A common semantic class is defined. The engineering models of the organisational view are also more detailed versions of the design models.

A detailed study of the integration view must be done, resulting in various models associated with the integration views. Among these models, annexe 1.2 shows the application integration engineering model underlying notably the software applications taking part in the process, the flows exchanged and the synchronisation actions realized at the level of the process. In this model, a role takes in charge one or several activities; this role is affected to a partner who uses his own enterprise applications, which requires the inter-application synchronisation mechanisms.

Evaluation and selection of organisational scenarios: These activities lead to the choice of the best functioning and organisational solutions. The "scenarios evaluation" activity specifies the information required to compare the scenarios: which descriptive parameters of the organisation network have to be considered and which evaluation criteria are to be used? The evaluation of organisational scenarios has to consider a very large number of variables and factors. In (Zaidat, 2005), we proposed a scientific approach for this evaluation based on complexity-reduction. Our proposal considers notably that the comparison among organisational scenarios can focus at first on the information system dimension.

The "selection" activity consists in integrating all evaluation criteria in an operational evaluation method, applied to choose the best organisational scenario. In our research we refereed on that point to existing decision-aid approaches. Examples of evaluating methods of information systems can be found in (Aubert et al., 2003).

4   CONCLUSION

This paper partially illustrates the specification of an engineering methodology for Organisation Networks. A more complete conceptual specification is provided by (Zaidat, 2006) with more details on the application and the concrete implementation in the modelling toolkit ADONIS. This research demonstrates the feasibility of a complete methodology really dedicated to O.N. engineering. However, further work remains necessary so as to make the method really operational, with the objective to provide a real decision-making environment for O.N. management.

5   REFERENCES

1.   Aubert B.A., Vandenbosch B. and Mignerat M., Towards the measurement of process integration. Scientific series of CIRANO (Centre Interuniversitaire de Recherche en Analyse des Organisations), 2003.
2.   Chalmeta R. and Grangel R, ARDIN extension for virtual enterprise integration, Journal of Systems and Software, 67(3), pp. 141-152, 2003.
3.   GERAM, Generalised Enterprise Reference Architecture and Methodology. The ISO 15704 Requirements for Enterprise Reference Architecture and Methodologies, 2000.
4.   GrecoPME project, under coordination of Burlat P., GRECOPME II: GRoupements d'Entreprises Coopérantes- Potentialités- Moyens-Evolutions, Final report, March 2003
5.   TELEflow project, TELEflow reference architecture, Final Report, 1996-1998.
6.   Zaidat A., Spécification d'un cadre d'ingénierie pour les réseaux d'organisation, PhD thesis, ENSM.SE - Ecole nationale supérieure des mines de Saint Etienne, Sept. 2005.
7.   Zaidat A., Boucher X. and Vincent L, A framework for organisation network engineering and integration, Robotics and Computer-Integrated Manufacturing, 21, pp. 259-271, 2005
8.   Zaidat A., Vincent L., Boucher X. : « A Modeling Framework For Organisation Networks », 12th IFAC Symposium INCOM'06, Saint Etienne, France, May 2006, A. Dolgui, G. Morel, C. Pereira (Eds.), Elsevier Science, 2006, ISBN: 978-0-08-044654-7, vol. 2, pp. 577-582
9.   Zwegers, A., Tölle, M. and Vesterager, J: Virtual Enterprise Reference Architecture and Methodology. Globemen book, Iris Karvonen, VTT Industrial Systems, Finland, 17-36, 2003.

6   ANNEX

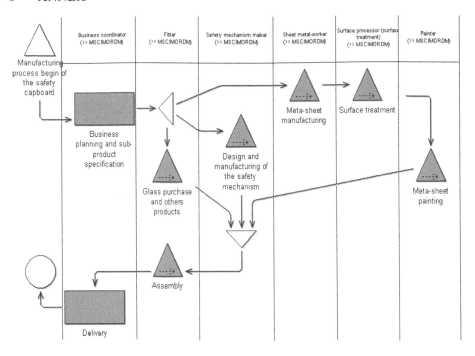

Annex 1.1 - Process design model for PDSDIM

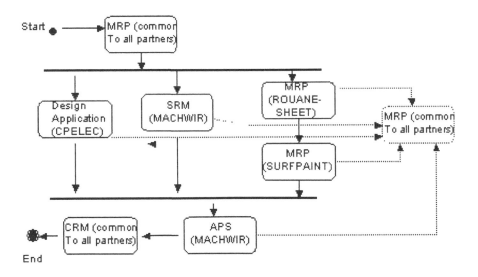

Annex 1.2 - Application integration engineering model

70 | A PROCEDURE FOR THE ANALYSIS OF INDUSTRIAL NETWORKS

Dario Antonelli, Brunella Caroleo, Teresa Taurino
Politecnico di Torino – Corso Duca degli Abruzzi, 24 – 10129 – Torino, ITALY
dario.antonelli@polito.it, brunella.caroleo@polito.it, teresa.taurino@polito.it

This paper gives a presentation of a procedure for the analysis of industrial networks. An appropriate meta-model, specifically dedicated to SME networks, is introduced to describe the interactions among firms. The importance of considering both scientific studies and real industrial systems to make a proper analysis of a network is put in evidence, introducing two significant investigation tools. After a description of a logical arrangement of available information, a procedure useful to fully analyse an industrial network, using both data/information from existing SME networks and technical/scientific reports, is presented.

1   INTRODUCTION

Industrial networks and clusters of Small and Medium Enterprises (SME) represent the European way of aggregating enterprises to compete in a worldwide business market, leaving at the same time autonomy to each SME (Albino and Kuhtz, 2004; Picard and Toulemonde, 2003; Rosenfeld, 1995; Verwaal and Hesselmans, 2004).

Many theoretical contributions have conceptualized the distinctive features of these forms of industrial development, based on affiliation of small and medium sized firms in geographically delimited areas. Firms located in regional industry clusters (called also industrial districts, ID) are generally characterized by some distinctive features: (i) within the district there is a division of labor among firms, which promotes high levels of flexibility and productivity; (ii) high degree of specialization in one or few complementary industries; (iii) horizontal competition and vertical cooperation: the spatial concentration and strong complementarities among different units turn competition into a connective force among agents; (iv) a distinctive milieu that includes the local institutional infrastructure; (v) common marketing strategies.

The academic literature on the performance of ID has been mostly either of qualitative nature or too specific (not looking at the network as a whole).

Some papers concern the comparison of the performances of firms with respect to their belonging to a district. Signorini (1994) compares the financial and economic ratios of some firms belonging to the district of Prato to the average of woolen cloth manufacturers located outside the province. Fabiani and Pellegrini (1998) analyze the profitability and productivity ratios of firms belonging to IDs in comparison with a control sample of similar firms. These and other studies (Molina-Morales, 2001) confirm the hypothesis of positive externalities for SMEs belonging to IDs (in terms of ROE, ROI, etc.), but they are mainly concerning ID performance from economic point of view.

Antonelli, D., Caroleo, B., Taurino, T., 2007, in IFIP International Federation for Information Processing, Volume 243, Establishing the Foundation of Collaborative Networks; eds. Camarinha-Matos, L., Afsarmanesh, H., Novais, P., Analide, C.; (Boston: Springer), pp. 649–656.

ID performance must not be restricted to economic and financial perspective; an industrial district, in fact, is defined as "a socio-territorial entity, characterized by the active co-presence of a community of people and a population of industrial firms" (Becattini, 1990). This is the reason for which it is necessary to consider also the performance of an ID from the social viewpoint, in order to better understand the influence that the district has on the population into which it is immersed and to comprehend the effects on social's welfare. Paniccia (1999) analyses these concepts in her research, focusing on the interactions between the performance of IDs and population's welfare.

Another component it is necessary to take into account is the governance. A comprehensive review of different roles that governance should have in an ID is presented in Alberti (2001). Albino *et al.* (1999) investigate the relationship between the number of leading firms in IDs and the quantity of information shared. Lin *et al.* (2005) examine the relationships between supply chain features and organizational performances, on a qualitative point of view.

Regarding the operational structure component, a wide literature on Supply Chain performance analysis exists (Akif *et al.*, 2005; Abu-Suleiman *et al.*, 2005; Klejinen and Smits, 2003). Furthermore, some ascertained tools can be used, as an example the SCOR model (Supply Chain Council, 2006) or the Balanced Scorecard (Kaplan and Norton, 1992; Kaplan and Norton, 1993; Kaplan and Norton, 1996; Brewer and Speh, 2000). The difficulty of applying these tools to IDs consists in the lack of 'aggregated' KPIs, as those usually disposable from IDs.

In the last years the majority of SME clusters faced a significant reorganization. Among the possible reasons for their crisis there is the lack of investments in innovation, due to the lack of an effective governing board able to boost innovation to SMEs. Except for some cases, industrial clusters have not been able to evolve into "networks". These issues might originate in the problem that SMEs do not know how to operate and effectively manage in a "network of SMEs".

In this context, the Coordination Action CODESNET (CA project n° IST-2002-506673, http://www.codesnet.polito.it) was born with the goal of giving an organization and interpretation of data and information collected from the industrial systems of European countries and concerning networks of enterprises for the sake of improving the ID knowledge about network management.

2   A META-MODEL FOR ANALYSIS OF INDUSTRIAL NETWORKS

In order to give a formulation useful for network analysis and evaluation, a conceptual model of a DESNET (DEmand and Supply NETwork) can be stated in terms of a graph of partially autonomous firms, that means firms which agree to be collaborative together, to have a high rate of reciprocal transactions concerning components and products, to share information and common services, to define together common industrial strategies (as in case of joint projects to search for a new market, to develop either a new technology or a new product, and to organize new logistic services).

In formal terms, a *meta-model* of a DESNET has been proposed (Villa, 2006), where the term 'meta-model' means a model integrating the most important components of a SME network, connected by the critical links and interactions. The meta-model of a DESNET contains the following components (see Figure 1):

1. an **Operation Structure** (OS), representing the graph of the logistic connections among the firms. It refers to the graph of interactions linking the enterprises together, through flows of parts, information & controls, money; each node of this graph is an autonomous enterprise, and plays the role an of individual decision-maker (DM) but included into a group of companion DMs;
2. an **Organization Arrangement** (OA), describing the management architecture which drives the DESNET behavior (i.e., the DESNET governance), and the information pattern which links the firms together;
3. the **Interactions with the Socio-Economic Environment** (ISEE) within which the DESNET operates, that means the interactions with the markets of materials and products, and with the financial market and the labor market. In principle, its scope is to make as strong as possible the presence of the industrial network in the markets of final products, labor, finance, etc.,

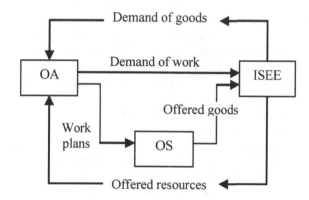

Figure 1 – The conceptual model of a DESNET

To make the above described meta-model an analysis tool, each component must be formally described by specific models, either descriptive or prescriptive.

3   COLLECTED DATA FOR THE ANALYSIS

A useful representation of each meta-model component can be obtained by considering qualitative and quantitative descriptions of existing SME networks, by collecting public data and information on their main features and characteristics, and then by using these data/information representations as examples for an analysis based on comparisons among the several industrial bodies. In the CODESNET approach, since the scope is to offer information both to industrial people and to university researchers, the descriptions of the components must be stated in a standardized form, which must summarize the most important analysis drivers and performance indicators. Two standardized formats represent a way for a conceptual organization of data and information. They have been called V-LIB and V-LAB:

- **V-LIB** (Virtual Library): scientific reports and papers presenting networks' models and discussing problems of network design and management;

- **V-LAB** (Virtual Laboratory): descriptions of existing SME networks, each one presenting a strong characteristic in either the OS, OA, or ISEE.

Each component of the meta-model has been detailed in three main issues that represent some questions that need an answer in order to give a complete and useful description of the ID. This set of typical main issues, concerning SME network management or evaluation, is selected and used as key-driver in the search within the data archive and the model catalogue. Each main issue plays also the role of "analysis viewpoint" for an industrial user.

The main issues representatives of the meta-model have a central role in the interaction of V-LIB with V-LAB and vice versa. Their central position is evident looking at Table 1.

Depending on which main qualifying attributes of the analyzed enterprise network are recognized in the V-LAB format, either proper models (for network simulation, design or performance evaluation) or methods (for network management) or procedures (for network innovation and skill improvement) can be found in some catalogued scientific papers, summarized in V-LIB formats.

Among all V-LIB and V-LAB documents available on CODESNET web portal, a subset of particularly interesting and useful papers has been selected and analyzed. The selection has been done on the strength of the importance and the completeness of information and data available on the documents.

Table 2 and Table 3 show a conceptual organization of the information collected in the V-LIB and V-LAB formats, respectively.

In Table 2, for each selected V-LIB, the numbered Main Issues identified in the scientific paper are described. In the fourth column the type of paper content is specified; the notation introduced is (A) for algorithms and methods, (B) for case study, (C) for survey. In the other columns, the most relevant topics approached in the paper are specified and the related V-LABs are listed.

From the other side, it is also important to have a reverse procedure to connect enterprises networks to one or more papers described through the V-LIB. This reverse path is shown in Table 3, where the list of the selected V-LAB formats is shown. Each V-LAB is associated to one or more CODESNET Main Issues and is summarized by its most qualifying attributes.

These two tables describe the connections between V-LAB and V-LIB lists, which are proposed to the end user when analyzing elements of either the Virtual Laboratory or the Virtual Library. This work has required a logical procedure, which will be explained in Sections 4 and 5 in order to facilitate the understanding and the analysis.

Table 1 – V-LIB and V-LAB correspondence with CODESNET main issues

V-LAB		CODESNET **Main issues**		V-LIB	
Main attributes of an enterprise network	→ ←		→ → ←	**Main topics**	
a. Type b. Logistics	OS	1. how production operations & volumes are distributed among the enterprises	I. Model	
		2. which different skills are employed in the different enterprises		
		3. which logistic network is used		
c. Leading firms d. Governance	OA	4. how management responsibilities are attributed to each enterprise and how information are transferred & managed	II. Organizational chart	
		5. how internal agreements, or control mechanisms, are negotiated		
		6. which organization chart or coordination strategy is selected to assure best efficiency/effectiveness		
e. Personnel skill level f. Innovation programs	ISEE	7. how commercial agreements with external bodies are negotiated for max profit for the network	III. Skill competence profile IV. Innovation plans	
		8. how a network innovation program is decided by partners (and negotiated with financiers)		
		9. which dynamic evolution of the network can be forecast		

4 LINKING V-LIBS AND V-LABS

In order to obtain an accurate association between V-LIBs and V-LABs, a preliminary analysis and classification of V-LIBs is useful. This V-LIBs evaluation is performed according to the informative levels summarized in Figure 2:

1. identifying the main issues among the nine questions;
2. analyzing the paper content, understanding which features the paper discusses;
3. evaluating the completeness and usefulness of information and of data;
4. if they are adequate, the V-LIB can be inserted in the data base; otherwise, the considered V-LIB has to be improved.

Table 2 – Selected list of V-LIB formats, with the most relevant topics

#	Selected V-LIB list	Authors	Main Issue	Type of paper	Most relevant TOPICS					Related V-LAB
					I. model	II. Organiz. chart	III. Skill competence profile	IV. Innovation plans		
9	Collaborative networks: a new scientific discipline	Camarinha-Matos L. M., Afsarmanesh H.	4 , 6	C		X				7, 8, 29, 35
12	Competence Profiling and Problem Solving in Virtual Networks	Edelmann C., Wagner K.	2	C			X			7, 9, 29, 38, 53, 54
13	Constructing a typology for networks of firms based on activities complementarity and competences similarity	Burlat P., Besombes B., Deslandres V.	1	B			X			29, 37, 38, 50, 53, 54
32	Framework for outsourcing manufacturing: strategic and operational implications	Momme J.	5 , 7	A	X					13, 34
33	A framework for comparing outsourcing strategies in multi-layered supply chains	Abdel-Malek L., Kullpattaranitun T.	5 , 7	A	X					13, 34, 66, 68

Table 3 – Selected list of V-LAB formats, with the most qualifying attributes

#	selected V-LAB list	Main Issue	Most qualifying attributes						Related V-LIB
			(a) Type	(b) Logistics	(c) Leading firms	(d) Governance	(e) Personnel skill level	(f) Innovation programs	
7	District 21 - Suzzara	2, 6, 8	2-stage SC 3500 SMEs			Political committee	skills in steeling and manufacturing activities	collaboration with universities	9, 12, 34, 35, 36, 53, 72
13	Automotive District Stuttgart	5, 7, 8	multi-agent	outsourcing	2-3 leading firm (OEM)				16, 32, 33, 52, 56, 96
34	Shoes District of Verona	1, 5, 8, 9	Flexible SC, 524 SMEs	outsourcing		Support agency		collaboration with res. centre, R&D	32, 33, 36, 69, 72, 81
35	BIO cluster district – Bioindustry Park	4, 6, 8, 9	Scientific park 344 companies			Regional system integrator	importance of high competence, skills	innovation	4, 9, 36, 65, 72, 76, 103, 107
37	Evonet	1, 2, 8	flexible SC 6 SMEs			managerial center	different skills in mechanical engineering		13, 20, 27, 34, 48, 69, 70, 76, 77, 96

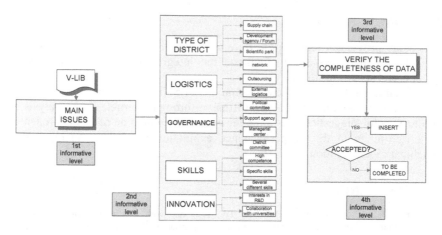

Figure 2 – Steps necessary for V-LIB classification

The most qualifying attributes of each industrial network have been extracted from each selected V-LAB (Table 3). From this information, it is possible to understand the characterizing features of each district. Combining together Tables 2 and 3, it is possible to find for each industrial network its related V-LIBs, looking at the weak and strong points of the district, and associating them proper articles included in the list of the selected V-LIBs.

This association is performed in three steps: 1) consider only the V-LIBs belonging to the main V-LAB issues; 2) among the filtered list of V-LIBs, search for scientific papers having appropriate topics, according to the V-LIB classification; 3) analyze the content of each paper to verify the association.

Let us consider, for instance, the Shoes District of Verona (V-LAB n. 34). It is a flexible supply chain, composed by 524 SMEs. From the logistic point of view, outsourcing is used for the management of the distribution. Coordination is assured by a support agency. There is a relevant cooperation with Universities and other research centers; so, an interest in R&D comes out from this information. The main issues associated to this district are the categories 1, 5, 8 and 9.

The first step for the association consists in filtering V-LIBs, using the four categories the V-LAB belongs to. Among this filtered list, look for scientific papers with appropriate topics. In the Shoes District case, its V-LAB shows as interesting topics: "Model", "Organizational Chart" and "Innovation Plans". Regarding the V-LIB classification, it is necessary to look for papers that relate to: supply chain, outsourcing, support agency, interests in R&D and collaboration with universities. From the list of V-LIBs belonging to the main issues 1, 5, 8, 9 and concerning these topics, some appropriate papers are associated to the Shoes District. Particularly (for the complete list of V-LIBs, see http://www.codesnet.polito.it):

V-LIB n. 32–33: concerning outsourcing;
V-LIB n. 36–81: concerning R&D and innovation;
V-LIB n. 69–72: about coordination and collaboration in a supply chain.

5 CONCLUSIONS

This study provides a logical procedure useful to arrange the available information on industrial networks and to facilitate the integration between actual industrial systems and scientific studies.

Even though the data collected within CODESNET Project are constrained to be public (in order to allow their open diffusion through Internet), their analysis could produce useful suggestions. As a matter of fact, the outcome of this approach could be a starting point for the performance evaluation of IDs management and for benchmark identification.

6 REFERENCES

1. Abu-Suleiman A, Boardman B, Priest JW. A Framework for an Integrated Supply Chain Performance Management System. International Journal of Production Research, 2005; 43(15), 3287-3296.
2. Akif JC, Blanc S, Ducq Y. Comparison of methods and frameworks to evaluate the performance of supply chains, 4th International Workshop on performance measurement implementation of performance measurement systems for supply chains, Bordeaux, June 27-28, 2005.
3. Alberti F. The governance of industrial districts: a theoretical footing proposal. Liuc Papers n. 82, Serie Piccola e Media Impresa 5, January 2001.
4. Albino V, Garavelli AC, Schiuma G. Knowledge transfer and inter-firm relationships in industrial districts: the role of the leader firm. Technovation, 1999; 19: 53-63.
5. Albino V, Kühtz S. Enterprise input–output model for local sustainable development - The case of a tiles manufacturer in Italy, Resources, Conservation and Recycling 2004; 41: 165-176.
6. Becattini G. The Marshallian industrial district as a socio-economic concept. In: F. Pyke, G. Becattini and W. Sengenberger, Industrial Districts and inter-firm cooperation in Italy, Geneva: International Institute for Labour Studies, 1990.
7. Brewer PC, Speh TW. Using the Balanced Scorecard to measure supply chain performance, Journal of Business Logistics, 2000; 21, 1.
8. Fabiani S, Pellegrini G. Un'analisi quantitativa delle imprese nei distretti industriali italiani: redditività, produttività e costo del lavoro. L'Industria, vol XIX, 1998; 4: 811-831.
9. Kaplan RS, Norton DP. Putting the Balanced Scorecard to Work, Harvard Business Review, September - October 1993, 1-15.
10. Kaplan RS, Norton DP. The Balanced Scorecard – Measures that Drive Performance, Harvard Business Review, January - February 1992, 71-79.
11. Kaplan RS, Norton DP. The Balanced Scorecard: Translating Strategy into Action, Harvard Business School Press, 1996.
12. Klejinen JPC, Smits MT. Performance metrics in supply chain mangement. Journal of the Operational Research Society 2003; 54, 5, 507-514.
13. Lin C, Chow WS, Madu CN, Kuei CH, Yu PP. A structural equation model of supply chain quality management and organizational performance. Int. J. of Production Economics, 2005; 96: 355-365.
14. Molina-Morales FX. European industrial districts: Influence of geographic concentration on performance of the firm. Journal of International Management, 2001; 7: 277-294.
15. Paniccia I. The performance of IDs. Some insights from the Italian case. Human Systems Management, 1999; 18: 141-159.
16. Picard PM, Toulemonde E. Regional asymmetries: economies of agglomeration versus unizoned labor markets, Regional Sciences and Urban Economics 2003; 33: 223-249.
17. Rosenfeld S. Industrial strength strategies: regional business clusters and public policy. Aspen Institute, Washington DC, 1995.
18. Signorini LF. The price of Prato, or measuring the ID effect. Papers in Regional Science, 1994; 73: 369-392.
19. Supply Chain Council. Manual of Supply-Chain Operations Reference-model: SCOR 8.0, 2006.
20. Verwaal E, Hesselmans M. Drivers of Supply Network Governance: An Explorative Study of the Dutch Chemical Industry, European Management J, 2004; 22: 442-451.
21. Villa A. Reinforcing Industrial Districts: Need for a Structured Approach. Proceedings of INCOM 2006, 12th IFAC/IFIP Symposium on INformation COntrol problems in Manufacturing, 2006.

71

THE EVALUATION OF COORDINATION POLICIES IN LOGISTICS SERVICES MARKETS

Vito Albino, Rosa Maria Dangelico, Antonio Messeni Petruzzelli[1]
DIMeG, Politecnico di Bari, Viale Japigia 182, 70126 Bari, ITALY

Nowadays, due to the increasing complexity and expansion of supply chains, logistics is becoming a more strategic activity for firms in terms of both time and cost performance. In this paper, the coordination in a logistics services market based on vehicle consolidation policy is considered. In particular, three coordination policies characterized by different levels of collaboration among the actors of a supply stage are identified. Then, a model is developed for evaluating the transportation, coordination, and service lateness costs affecting each coordination policy. Finally, different coordination policies and collaborative relationships among the actors operating in the supply stage of an Italian brickworks company are discussed as a case study.

1   INTRODUCTION

In the current economic scenario, few products for sale in any country are entirely produced by domestic firms making use of domestic inputs only. Then, in order to be customers responsive and costs effective, logistics is becoming more important for firms. Due to the high degree of specialization characterizing nowadays logistics, such activities are generally outsourced to specific actors who make these services their own core-business.

These actors, known as third-party logistics (3PL) providers or logistic service providers (LSPs) (Hertz and Alfredsson, 2003), permit the interconnectedness among the different actors of the supply chain, world-wide located.

In the literature, different types of logistics services carried out by 3PL providers have been identified (see for instance Lai and Cheng, 2004). Among the different types of logistics services, transportation is one of the most important for supply chains efficiency and effectiveness, as empirical researches conducted by scholars and practitioners demonstrated (e.g. Dapiran et al., 1996; Lieb and Bentz, 2004). The importance of transportation for the actual competitive scenario is also highlighted by the effort spent to design and manage effective and efficient transporttation networks, such as point-to-point, corridor, and hub-and-spoke systems (Lapierre et al., 2004; Hesse and Rodrigue, 2006). An effective design of transportation systems involves also problems related to vehicle scheduling, vehicle routing, and lateral transhipments (see for instance Laporte et al., 1988; Dror and Langevin, 1997).

Great attention has been paid in literature to the important role played by coordination as a mechanism by which improving supply chain performance (Colombo and Mariotti, 1998; Xu and Beamon, 2006). A coordination mechanism consists of the informational structure, defining who obtains what information and

---

[1] Corresponding author: a.messeni.petruzzelli@poliba.it

Albino, V., Dangelico, R.M., Petruzzelli, A.M., 2007, in IFIP International Federation for Information Processing, Volume 243, Establishing the Foundation of Collaborative Networks; eds. Camarinha-Matos, L., Afsarmanesh, H., Novais, P., Analide, C.; (Boston: Springer), pp. 657–666.

how uses that information, and of the decision-making process, which helps to select the appropriate action from a set of alternative solutions (Marschak and Radner, 1972). An important matter concerning coordination regards the trade-off between centralized coordination structures and decentralized ones (Malone, 1987). Centralized structures consist of mechanisms based on a single decision maker acting in the interest of the whole system. On the contrary, in decentralized structures each actor selects the most appropriate actions for his own interest. Typical examples of these two coordination structures are represented by hierarchy, where a single actor coordinates the whole network, and market, where the coordination is assigned to market-transactions.

The role of centralized coordination structures seems to be brought into question. In particular, Malone (2004) discusses the opportunity to introduce coordination mechanisms based on market-transactions inside an organisation. In fact, the author introduces the notion of internal markets, used to move information quickly and efficiently in organisations characterised by great units interdependence and operating in dynamic and complex contexts.

Logistics represents a typical activity whose coordination is particularly important for the competitive advantage of supply chains and networks, especially when actors are vertically disaggregated and located in different places. A way in which logistics flows coordination can be achieved is by means of consolidation strategies (Albino et al., 2006), which are the processes of combining different items, produced and used at different locations (spatial consolidation) and/or at different times (temporal consolidation), into single vehicle load (Hall, 1987). Two types of spatial consolidation, namely vehicle and terminal, and one type of temporal one, namely inventory consolidation can be identified.

The aim of the paper is to analyse the role of coordination policies in order to create an organized logistics services market. In particular, vehicle consolidation of products is considered in the transportation service market for a supply stage. To cope with this aim, a model for evaluating the benefits (in terms of reduction of transportation costs) and the costs (in terms of increasing of coordination and service lateness costs) arising from consolidation, in different collaborative contexts, is developed.

The paper is structured as follows. In the next section a brief analysis of the consolidation strategies is provided. In section three the notion of organized logistics services markets is presented and the model is developed. Finally, a case study, based on the supply stage of a brickworks company, is presented and the main findings and results are discussed.

2   CONSOLIDATION STRATEGIES

Consolidation strategies can be analysed taking into account two different dimensions: quantity and time (Newbourne and Barrett, 1972).

Consolidation strategies depend also on the transportation models adopted, as shown by Hall (1995) who examines the interdependence between freight mode and shipment size when they are chosen simultaneously to minimize transportation and inventory costs.

Conway and Gorman (2006) study the benefits arising from a consolidation point (mixing centre). The authors, by means of a simulation of the distribution system of an automobile manufacturer, show that consolidation determines relevant benefits for the whole system, in terms of reduction of inventory holding time, increasing load factors, and reduction of variability of transportation means. However, some drawbacks rise, in particular for customer service. Then, trade-offs have to be considered between system logistics performance and customer service level.

Blanc et al. (2006) study transportation coordination analysing factory gate pricing (FGP) as a means by which achieving orders consolidation. Under FGP, products are collected by the retailer at the factory gates of the suppliers. Then, transportation of logistics flows is completely managed by retailers, because they orchestrate both primary distribution (from supplier to retailer distribution centres) and secondary one (from retailer distribution centre to the shops). Another consolidation strategy strictly related to the concept of FGP is vendor managed inventory (VMI, see for example Cetinkaya and Lee, 2000). Also VMI allows the control of inventory and primary distribution, and sometimes even secondary transportation, to a player in the supply chain. The difference compared with FGP is that in VMI the supplier and not the retailer is in charge of coordination.

3 COORDINATION POLICIES EVALUATION

We define an organized logistics service market as a hybrid organizational system ranging between market and hierarchy where logistics needs are satisfied through the collaboration and the coordination of the different actors involved in the system.

In a supply chain stage, referring to transportation services, three distinct actors are identified: i) suppliers, which have to deliver products to one or more customers; ii) customers, which require products from one or more suppliers; iii) 3PL, which provides the transportation service and coordinates logistics flows between suppliers and customers. Consolidation is then considered as coordination policy.

Two types of vehicle consolidation are distinguished, namely internal consolidation and external consolidation, with only one type of vehicle. Internal consolidation occurs when the 3PL consolidates the products that have to be delivered from one supplier to two or more of its customers. Instead, external consolidation occurs when a 3PL consolidates the products that have to be delivered from two or more suppliers to their customers.

In order to coordinate logistics services market different policies based on collaboration among actors are considered, namely total collaboration, supply-centered collaboration, and no collaboration. In the first policy total collaboration among customers and suppliers occurs and direct trips, internal consolidation, and external consolidation are adopted by 3PL. In particular, direct trips occur only when the total amount of products to be delivered from one supplier to one customer is equal to or greater than the vehicle load capacity. Internal consolidation is eventually adopted to convey the remaining products that have to be delivered from each supplier to its customers. Successively, if some products from more than two suppliers have to be still delivered, external consolidation can be adopted. In the second policy collaboration among one supplier's customers occur and direct trips and internal consolidation are adopted by 3PL, as in the total collaboration policy. However, in this case, if some products have to be still delivered, direct trips instead of external consolidation are adopted. In the third coordination policy, no collaboration among suppliers or customers occurs and logistics flows are managed by 3PL only through direct trips.

To compare these coordination policies a model, based on the Supply Chain Operations Reference[2] (SCOR) model, is developed to evaluate possible solutions in terms of benefits and costs. The benefits are mainly related to the reduction of transportation cost sustained by the 3PL, which depends on the route length of the vehicles. However, to achieve this cost reduction, the 3PL has to face costs, such as a the coordination cost and the service lateness cost. Then, to explore solutions and determine a negotiation between the actors, trade-offs between benefits and costs are needed. Coordination cost is evaluated as the 3PL's effort necessary to work out the service requirements coming from all the actors in order to obtain a specific solution, represented by the route selected to satisfy all the actors service requirements. Then, the coordination cost is strictly related to the number of service requirements, which on turn depends on the number of actors involved in the coordination policies. In fact, a one-to-one relationship between the actors and the service requirements is assumed. Service lateness cost can be related to the delay that can occur for delivering products to a customer adopting supply-centered or total collaboration respect to no collaboration policy.

In the following a heuristic algorithm is developed for a supply chain stage in order to determine the transportation cost sustained by the 3PL in each coordination policy. Then, the coordination cost and the service lateness cost are estimated considering simplified drivers.

Let us assume a supply stage with m suppliers (s_i, i =1,...,m) and n customers (c_j, j=1,...,n) where q_{ij} is the average quantity of products flowing from s_i to c_j, during each time period and $d(s_i c_j)$ is the distance between s_i and c_j.

3.1   Transportation cost evaluation

The transportation cost, TC, in each time period is evaluated as:

$$TC = c_t \cdot L \qquad (1)$$

where L is the total distance covered to deliver products for each time period in the supply stage and c_t is the unitary transportation cost. L depends on the coordination policy adopted and on the following assumptions. The transportation vehicles are always available with load capacity equal to C. When delivery is completed, the transportation vehicle is assumed to come back to the supplier's process from which it started. All products flowing from suppliers to customers can be loaded in the same vehicle and qij can be split out in units of product.

No collaboration
Adopting this policy for each supplier s_i and customer c_j, it results:

$$Y_{ij} = 2 \cdot d(s_i c_j) \cdot \text{int}_{sup}\left(\frac{q_{ij}}{C}\right) \qquad (2)$$

where Y_{ij} represents the distance covered to convey products from s_i to c_j by means of direct trips. In this policy the total distance covered results:

---

[2] The Supply Chain Council has developed the SCOR model for evaluating the performance requirements of partner firms in a supply chain.

$$L = \sum_{i=1}^{m} \sum_{j=1}^{n} Y_{ij} \qquad (3)$$

Supply-centered collaboration
For this policy, a two-step algorithm is proposed.
First step (direct trips)
For each supplier s_i and customers c_j, it results:

$$Y_{ij} = 2 \cdot d(s_i c_j) \cdot \mathrm{int}_{\mathrm{inf}} \left(\frac{q_{ij}}{C} \right) \qquad (4)$$

where Y_{ij} represents the distance covered to convey products from s_i to c_j by means of direct trips with full vehicle load. If $\dfrac{q_{ij}}{C}$ is not an integer number, then for the remaining products that have to be delivered from s_i to c_j internal consolidation applies. The total distance covered in the first step is:

$$L_{DT} = \sum_{i=1}^{m} \sum_{j=1}^{n} Y_{ij} \qquad (5)$$

Second step (internal consolidation)
For each supplier with only one customer remaining to be supplied, direct trips occur. Then, let us consider each s_i with at least two customers to be supplied.

For the internal consolidation, si starts the first trip for supplying the customer farthest from it (cf). If two or more customers are the farthest from si, si starts internal consolidation from the customer with the greatest amount of product to be delivered. Successively, the internal consolidation involves the customer whose needs allow to reach the vehicle load capacity (if it exists) or the closest to cf and so on, until reaching the vehicle load capacity. If two or more customers are the closest to cf, the internal consolidation continues involving the customer with the greatest amount of product to be delivered.

The internal consolidation routine continues since at least two customers have to be supplied, also if the vehicle loading capacity is not reached.

Let $ICD_{s_i c_f}$ be the total distance covered for all the trips needed to supply customers adopting the internal consolidation routine, starting from c_f. Two conditions can hold:

$$\text{If } ICD_{s_i c_f} + d(s_i c_h) \cdot 2A < \sum_{\Gamma_{s_i}} d(s_i c_j) \cdot 2 \qquad (6)$$

then, internal consolidation applies, where c_h is the customer which may remain to be supplied after the internal consolidation routine has been completed, Γ_{s_i} represents the set of customers involved in the internal consolidation routine, $A = \mathrm{int}_{\mathrm{sup}} \left(\dfrac{q'_{ih}}{C} \right)$, q'_{ih} is the quantity of products to be supplied to the last customer once the internal consolidation routine has applied. The quantity of product that cannot be delivered through internal consolidation ($\hat{q}_{ih}$) is delivered through direct trips.

$$\text{If } ICD_{s_i c_f} + d(s_i c_h) \cdot 2A \geq \sum_{j=1}^{h} d(s_i c_j) \cdot 2 \qquad (7)$$

then, only direct trips between s_i and c_f occur. So, repeat the second step considering the remaining customer closest to s_i.

The distance covered in the second step is L_{IC}, which is the total distance covered to deliver products by means of internal consolidation routine and potential direct trips. Then, in the supply-centered collaboration policy the total distance covered results:

$$L = L_{DT} + L_{IC} \qquad (8)$$

Total collaboration

For this policy a three-step algorithm is proposed

First step (direct trips)

The first step is the same as in the supply-centered coordination policy.

Second step (internal consolidation)

The second step is the same as in the supply-centered coordination policy except the quantity of products that cannot be delivered through internal consolidation (q'_{ij}). In fact, in this case, it can be delivered through external consolidation.

Third step (external consolidation)

Let us start the external consolidation routine from the supplier s_i with the greatest q_{ij}. Let us find the suppliers s_k with remaining products q'_{kj} to be delivered to the customer c_j shared with s_i. Among these suppliers let us consider the closest to s_i. The routine may involve two or more suppliers since reaching the vehicle load capacity or consolidating all the suppliers. If it involves more than two suppliers let us consider the supplier closest to s_k.

Let $ECDs_i$ be the total distance covered in order to supply all customers adopting the external consolidation routine, starting from s_i. Two conditions hold:

$$\text{If } ECD_{s_i} + d(s_z c_j) \cdot 2B < \sum_{i \in \Omega_{sc_j}} d(s_i c_j) \cdot 2 \qquad (9)$$

then, external consolidation applies, where Ω_{sc_j} represents the set of suppliers with remaining products to be delivered to c_j after the internal consolidation routine, s_z is the last supplier having to supply c_j, $B = \text{int}_{\sup}\left(\dfrac{q''_{zj}}{C}\right)$, q''_{zj} is the quantity of products to be supplied to c_j by s_z once the external consolidation routine has applied.

$$\text{If } ECD_{s_i} + d(s_z c_j) \cdot 2B \geq \sum_{i \in \Omega_s} d(s_i c_j) \cdot 2 \qquad (10)$$

then, direct trip between s_i and c_j applies. So, repeat the third step considering the second supplier with the greatest q_{ij}. Let us consider the case in which suppliers have no common customer. Then, if

$$d(s_i s_k) + d(c_h c_r) < d(s_i c_h) + d(s_k c_r) \qquad (11)$$

and

$$q_{ij} + q_{kr} \leq C \tag{12}$$

external consolidation routine applies, involving s_i, s_k, c_h, and c_r, where s_i and s_k are the pair of closest suppliers; c_h and c_r are the customers to be supplied by s_i and s_k, respectively; else direct trips apply between s_i and c_h, and between s_k and c_r, respectively.

The distance covered in the third step is L_{EC}, which is the total distance covered to deliver products by means of external consolidation routine and potential direct trips. In the total collaboration policy the total distance covered results:

$$L = L_{DT} + L_{IC} + L_{EC} \tag{13}$$

3.2   Coordination cost evaluation

The coordination cost, CC, is evaluated as:

$$CC = c_c \cdot I_{CE} \tag{14}$$

where I_{CE} is the index of coordination effort and c_c is the unitary coordination cost. I_{CE} can be estimated as:

$$I_{CE} = \sum_{t=1}^{r} \frac{N_{Rt}!}{2! \cdot (N_{Rt} - 2)!} \tag{15}$$

where N_{Rt} is the number of service requirements coming from the suppliers and customers involved in the t-th trip to the 3PL in order to satisfy their needs; r is the total number of trips defined by the 3PL in each coordination policy.

3.3   Service lateness cost evaluation

The service lateness cost, SLC, is evaluated as:

$$SLC = c_s \cdot I_{SL} \tag{16}$$

where I_{SL} is the index of service lateness and c_s is the unitary service lateness cost. I_{SL} can be expressed as:

$$I_{SL} = \sum_i \sum_j \sum_t \left\{ \left[D(s_i - c_j) - d(s_i c_j) \right] \cdot \frac{\Delta q_{ij}}{q_{ij}} \right\}_t \tag{17}$$

where t is the generic trip that takes place when internal or external collaboration occurs; $D(s_i - c_j)$ is the distance covered to deliver products from s_i to c_j, in trip t; Δq_{ij} is the quantity of products delivered from s_i to c_j in trip t.

4   A CASE STUDY

The supply stage of a brickworks company has been considered as a case study. The stage consists of two brickworks production plants (s_1, s_2) supplying four building sites (c_1, c_2, c_3, c_4). The two production plants belong to the same company and each plant produces only one type of bricks. Plants and sites are located in the Southern Italy and the logistics service is managed by only one 3PL.

In Table 1 the distance (expressed in km) between suppliers and customers sites are reported.

Table 1. Distances [km] between suppliers and customers.

	s_1	s_2	c_1	c_2	c_3	c_4
s_1	0	10	80	75	110	90
s_2	10	0	85	90	100	85
c_1	80	85	0	15	30	25
c_2	75	90	15	0	30	35
c_3	110	100	30	30	0	15
c_4	90	85	25	35	15	0

The average quantities of bricks (expressed in pallet) flowing each day from suppliers to customers have been estimated and are shown in Table 2.

Table 2. Average quantities [pallet] of product flowing each day from

production plants to building sites.

	c_1	c_2	c_3	c_4
s_1	15	11	20	10
s_2	7	14	14	20

Transportation, coordination, and service lateness costs of this supply stage are evaluated according to the previously developed model. In Table 3, results are shown for C = 18 pallets.

Table 3. Costs evaluation for different coordination policies.

Coordination policy	Transportation cost	Coordination cost	Service lateness cost	Total cost
No collaboration	$1820c_t$	$8c_c$	0	$1820c_t + 8c_c$
Supply-centered collaboration	$1465c_t$	$12c_c$	$38c_s$	$1465c_t + 12c_c + 38c_c$
Total collaboration	$1365c_t$	$19c_c$	$111c_s$	$1365c_t + 19c_c + 111c_c$

The results show that moving from no collaboration to total collaboration transportation cost decreases. This reduction is due to the adoption of internal consolidation, in the case of the supply-centered collaboration, and of both internal and external consolidation, in the case of total collaboration. Nevertheless, coordination and service lateness costs increase. Then, even if total coordination brings to lower transportation cost, its adoption has to be subordinated to the evaluation of the coordination effort required and to the lack of service responsiveness. Consequently, trade-offs have to be considered. Being the supply stage characterised by specific unitary costs (ct, cc, cs), using this approach the 3PL can evaluate which coordination policy is more suitable to be used in order to organize the market. However, the different coordination policies are based on the collaboration among the actors, which cannot be necessarily achieved. In fact, for instance, actors, such as customers, can decide to do not collaborate, because the service lateness, in terms of lack of responsiveness, can contrasting their own interests. Then, it is important to identify what can occur when customers do not collaborate. In the case study, we compare the costs in the case of total collaboration policy with the case when a single customer affected by service lateness decides to do not collaborate. For these customers, the service lateness related to the delay in delivering products is avoided adopting direct trips. In the total collaboration scenario, assuming no collaboration for only one customer at time, different collaborative scenarios can result. In Table 4 the supply stage costs for each scenario are shown.

Table 4. Supply stage costs in different collaborative scenarios.

Collaborative scenario	Transportation cost	Coordination cost	Service lateness cost	Total cost
Total collaboration without c_1	$1465c_t$	$15c_c$	$35c_s$	$1465c_t+15c_c+35c_c$
Total collaboration without c_2	$1435c_t$	$19c_c$	$82c_s$	$1435c_t+19c_c+82c_c$
Total collaboration without c_4	$1535c_t$	$17c_c$	$109c_s$	$1535c_t+17c_c+109c_c$
Total collaboration	$1365c_t$	$19c_c$	$111c_s$	$1365c_t+19c_c+111c_c$

In these scenarios supply stage's costs change. In particular, the transportation cost increases, the service lateness cost decreases, and the coordination cost is at least the same respect to the total collaboration scenario. Let us consider that the service lateness cost for the not collaborative customers is equal to zero. However, in this case it seems reasonable that the unitary transportation cost will increase for this customer, because of the growing of the supply stage's cost. Then, a customer may decide to be collaborative or not according to the trade-off between ending and rising costs.

5 CONCLUSIONS

In the paper the notion of organized logistics services markets has been provided referring to a supply chain stage. The organization is achieved by means of coordination policies, based on the consolidation of logistics flows and on the collaboration among the actors of the supply stage.

A model for evaluating the trade-offs between the benefits and the costs of the coordination policies (namely no collaboration, supply-centered collaboration, and total collaboration) and the influence of each collaboration level has been developed. This approach permits to explore the opportunities to enhance logistics service performance as the degree of collaboration among actors of a supply chain increases. It is useful to highlight that the model is based on a heuristic algorithm, which has shown to be effective for the examined cases.

In particular, the model has been applied to an Italian brickworks company in order to analyse the transportation, coordination, and service lateness costs for each coordination policy. Moreover, different collaborative scenarios (partial and total) have been investigated and compared. The model suggests which actor of the supply stage can get benefit or cost for not collaborative behaviour. Then, a rational approach for negotiation is provided.

This model can constitute the conceptual base to create the frame of analysis for the designing and managing of logistics services markets.

6   REFERENCES

1.   Albino V, Kuthz S, Messeni Petruzzelli A. Analysing logistics flows in industrial clusters using an enterprise input output model. Intermediate Input-Output Meetings on Sustainability, Trade & Productivity, July 26-28th 2006, Sendai, Japan.
2.   Cetinkaya S, Lee CY. Stock replenishment and shipment scheduling for vendor-managed inventory systems. Management Science 2000; 46: 217-232.
3.   Colombo MG, Mariotti S,. Organizing vertical markets: the Italtel case. European Journal of Purchasing & Supply Management 1998; 4: 7-19.
4.   Conway DG, Gorman MF. An application of interdependent lot size and consolidation point choice. Mathematical and Computer Modelling 2006; 44: 65-72.
5.   Dapiran P, Lieb R, Millen R, Sohal A. Third party logistics services usage by large Australian firms. International Journal of Physical Distribution & Logistics Management 1996; 26: 36-45.
6.   Dror M, Langevin A. A generalized travelling salesmen problem approach to the directed clustered rural postman proble. Transportation Science 1997; 31: 187-192.
7.   Hall RW. Consolidation strategy: inventory, vehicles and terminals. Journal of Business Logistics 1987; 8: 57-73.
8.   Hall RW. Dependence between shipment size and mode in freight transportation. Transportation Science 1995; 19: 436-444.
9.   Hertz S, Alfredsson M. Strategic development of third party logistics provider. Industrial Marketing Management, 2003; 30: 139-149.
10. Hesse M, Rodrigue JP. The Transport Geography of Logistics and Freight Distribution. Journal of Transport Geography 2004; 12: 171-184.
11. Lai KH, Cheng, TCE. A Study of the Freight Forwarding Industry in Hong Kong International Journal of Logistics: Research and Applications 2004; 7: 72-84.
12. Lapierre SD, Ruiz AB, Soriano P. Designing distribution networks: formulation and solution heuristic. Transportation Science 2004; 38: 174-187.
13. Laporte G, Norbert Y, Taillefer S. Solving a family of multi-depot vehicle routing and location-routing problems. Transportation Science 1988; 22: 161-172.
14. le Blanc HM, Cruijssen F, Fleuren HA, de Koster MBM. Factory gate pricing: an analysis of Dutch retail distribution. European Journal of Operational Research 2006; 174: 1950-1967.
15. Lieb, RC, Bentz, BA. The Use of Third-Party Logistics Services by Large American Manufacturers: The 2003 Survey. Transportation Journal 2004; 43: 24-33.
16. Malone TW. Bringing the market inside. Harvard Business Review 2004; 82: 106-114.
17. Malone TW. Modeling coordination in organizations and markets. Management Science 1987; 33: 1317-1332.
18. Marschak J, Radner R. Economic Theory of Teams. New Heaven: Yale University Press 1972.
19. Newbourne MJ, Barrett C. Freight consolidation and the shippers, Part 1-5. Transportation Distribution Management 1972; 12: 2-6.
20. Xu L, Beamon BM. Supply chain coordination and cooperation mechanism: an attribute-based approach. The Journal of Supply Chain Management 2006; winter: 4-12.

72

BUSINESS MODELS FOR COLLABORATIVE PLANNING IN TRANSPORTATION: AN APPLICATION TO WOOD PRODUCTS

Jean-François Audy[1], Sophie D'Amours[2] and Mikael Rönnqvist[3,4]

1 Doctoral Student, Department of Mechanical Engineering, CIRRELT, FORAC Research Consortium, Laval University, CANADA, jean-francois.audy@cirrelt.ca
Professor, Department of Mechanical Engineering, CIRRELT, FORAC Research Consortium, Laval University, CANADA, **SOPHIE.DAMOURS@FORAC.ULAVAL.CA**
3 Professor, Department of Finance and Management Science, Norwegian School of Economics and Business, mikael.ronnqvist@nhh.no
4 The Forestry Research Institute of Sweden, SWEDEN

Transportation is an important part of the wood fibre flow chain in forestry. There are often several forest companies operating in the same region and co-ordination between two or more companies is however rare. Lately, the interest in collaborative transportation planning to support co-ordination has risen since important potential savings have been identified. Even though substantial savings can be realized, it seems that companies' willingness to collaborate is tightly linked to a business model driven by one or many leaders. In this paper, we study a specific business model where one company leads the development of the coalition. The impact of different behaviours of the leading company (i.e. altruistic, opportunistic) is illustrated using an industrial case study of eight forest companies.

1   INTRODUCTION

Transportation is an important part of the wood fibre flow chain in forestry. Large volumes and relatively long transport distances together with rising fuel prices and environmental concerns raise the need for improved transportation planning.

Typically, several forest companies operate in the same region. Harvest areas supply mills that transform the round wood into a basket of end-products (e.g. lumber, veneer) as well as by-products (e.g. chips, sawdust). All of these are then shipped to other mills for further transformation (e.g. engineered wood products or pulp and paper). However, co-ordination between two or more companies is rare, even when supply, demand and mills are evenly dispersed geographically within a region.

Lately, the interest in collaborative transportation planning to support the co-ordination of the wood fibre flow has risen, since important potential savings have been identified, often in the range of 4-7%. Examples of such collaborative

Audy, J.-F., D'Amours, S., Rönnqvist, M., 2007, in IFIP International Federation for Information Processing, Volume 243, Establishing the Foundation of Collaborative Networks; eds. Camarinha-Matos, L., Afsarmanesh, H., Novais, P., Analide, C.; (Boston: Springer), pp. 667–676.

transportation planning that have improved transportation efficiency are found in (Forsberg et al., 2005). In many of the case studies, the savings are defined as the difference between the cost of the collaborative plan (i.e. all companies together) compared with the sum of the cost of each individual plan (i.e. each company alone).

Even though collaboration can provide substantial savings, it seems that companies' willingness to collaborate is tightly linked to the business model driven by one or many leaders. These leaders aim at building the coalition (participants and savings sharing model) that will provide them with the best returns.

In this paper, we first present a general framework for collaborative transportation planning. We discuss how the leadership of the coalition can be assumed, how the participants in a coalition are selected and how the savings are shared. The core of the paper refers to a set of specific business models where one forest company leads the development of the coalition. The impacts of different savings sharing approaches (i.e. altruistic, opportunistic) on the coalition are illustrated using an industrial case study of eight Swedish forest companies.

2   TRANSPORTATION PLANNING

Transportation planning in forestry is done in several steps and is commonly managed according to four time perspective horizons: strategic, tactical, operational and real-time. Decisions at the strategic level often deal with silviculture (defining prescriptions), wood procurement and road upgrade/building/maintenance considerations. Tactical decisions mainly address planning issues from one week to one year. On an annual basis, transportation is often integrated with harvesting planning, deciding on the catchments areas to supply the mills with the right wood assortments (depending on e.g. species and dimensions). A problem which often ranges from one to several weeks is deciding the destination of logs, that is, which supply point(s) should deliver to which demand point(s) in what volume. Operational decisions concern the planning of the entire route schedule for each individual truck for one or many days. Real-time decisions concern the planning of the next route of one truck in the present situation (i.e. when a truck completes a route) instead of the predicted one.

In the case study used below, we will focus on a tactical problem [TP] that deals with transportation of logs from harvest areas/terminals (supply points) to mills/terminals (demand points). A complete description of this problem and its linear programming (LP) formulation is found in (Frisk et al, 2006). In this problem, the savings from collaborative planning derives from two co-ordination opportunities: wood bartering and backhauling. In wood bartering, volumes of some supply points are exchanged between the companies to reduce the total travel distance. Backhauling is used to find better routes by combining transport orders of different companies. The use of backhaulage tours can decrease the transportation cost, savings between 2% and 6% are reported in different case studies, see (Carlsson and Rönnqvist, 1998) and (Gingras et al., 2006).

3   TRANSPORTATION COLLABORATION FRAMEWORK

3.1   Leaders of the coalition

We denote by coalition a set of stakeholders, customer(s) or/and carrier(s), disposed to co-ordinate their wood flow by collaborative planning. We denote by player each of these stakeholders and, consequently, a coalition must include at least two players. To implement the collaborative planning between these players, we need to build a coalition. From a business point of view, one or a set of the players will lead in the creation of the coalition. We identify here six different types of leadership:

#1 A customer leads the coalition: it aims to minimize its transport costs by finding other customers that can provide a good equilibrium (geographical, volume and time) between supply and demand. An example of this, are the forest companies Holmen Skog (HS) and Norra Skogsägarna (NS), who are using the decision support system ÅkarWeb (Eriksson and Rönnqvist, 2003). Via some carriers of the NS player, the leading player, HS, takes advantage of certain backhaulage tours.

#2 A carrier or 3PL leads the coalition: it aims to maximize its profit by a better usage of its carrying capacity. An example is the Swedish forest product carrier Skogsåkarna or the worldwide transporter Ryder in general freight transport.

#3 A fourth party logistics provider, 4PL, leads the coalition: its aims to minimize/maximize the cost/profit of these customers/carriers by finding for each of these customer/carrier the more "compatible" carrier(s)/customer(s). An example of a typical service offered by a 4PL is the e-marketplace of a Nistevo network.

#4 Customers share the leadership of the coalition: they aim to minimize their transportation costs. An example is the regional wood log buyer network of the Canadian wood log supplier Groupe Transforêt, using the decision support system VTM prototype, see (Audy et al., 2006). Another example is the Swedish company Sydved who organizes the purchase and the transport of logs for its owners, the forest companies Stora Enso and Munksjö.

#5 Carriers share the leadership of the coalition: they aim to maximize their profit by a better usage of their carrying capacity. An example is the Canadian TransForce Income Fund that invests in independent carriers and uses its capacities of analysis to implement transport synergies between the carriers. Another example is the Swedish logging and transportation company VSV who collaborates in its transport operations with other carriers.

#6 Carrier(s) and customer(s) share the leadership of the coalition: they aim to minimize their transportation costs by using the carrying capacity of the carriers. No example of this can be found at this present time.

3.2   Building the coalition

If we disregard external business considerations, the basic rule of adding a player p to a coalition c is if the player p increases the *benefit* of the current coalition c. The *benefit* of a coalition c, denoted B^c, is defined as the difference between the value of the collaborative plan including all players in the coalition c, V^c, compared to the sum of the values of the individual plan of each player p in the coalition c, $\sum_{p \in N} V_p$ where N is the set of the players in the coalition c. In a minimization objective context, the benefit refers generally to the savings whereas in a maximization context they refer to a profit. The tactical problem [TP] used in the case study of this paper is in a minimization context, therefore, the values of collaborative and individual plans are defined as costs while the coalition benefit is defined as a saving.

Coalition c' will be created if more benefit can be generated by adding player p' to coalition c. Let's denote $M_{p'}^c$ the marginal increase of the benefit of coalition c when player p' is added to form coalition c'. On the other hand, any player p already in a coalition c who does not contribute to the benefit of this coalition c, should be removed. Let's denote C_p^c the *contribution* of player p to the benefit of coalition c.

Although the addition of a player to a coalition can provide a benefit, it seems that the players' willingness for the collaboration is tightly linked to the business model of the coalition that is driven by one or several leading players. These leading players aim at building the coalition in such a way that they will maximize their returns while providing enough incentives to the others to keep them in the coalition. Let's denote this return by I_p^c, the *incentive* of player p and set the benefit of a coalition as the summation of all its players' incentives.

In this paper, the add/remove rules are therefore based on the benefit to the leading players of the coalition c, BL^c, as opposed to other approaches which could base the rules on the contribution to the benefit of the total coalition B^c. With that perspective, let's denote $ML_{p'}^c$ as the marginal increase of the leaders' benefit when player p' is added to coalition c to form coalition c'. Also, let's denote CL_p^c the *contribution* of player p to the benefit of the leading players in the coalition c.

There remains an exception. Thus, a player who contributes to the benefit of the coalition but not to the benefit of the leading players will be kept in the coalition if and only if its removal reduces the incentive of at least one of the leading players.

3.3   Sharing the benefit of the coalition

Collaboration raises the following question. How should the benefit of a coalition be shared between its players? As suggested by (Frisk et al., 2006), this issue could also be addressed by using a *cost allocation approach* instead of a *saving allocation approach*. In other words, instead of splitting the coalition's benefit (i.e. the saving in the case study used below) among the players, the value of the coalition's collaborative plan (i.e. the cost in the case study) could be split between the players. Thus, the incentive of a player to remain in a coalition is the difference between the player stand alone cost and its allocated cost when a cost allocation approach is used, and the allocated saving when a saving allocation approach is preferred.

The core of this paper refers to the study of a series of business models in which one player, a customer, leads the creation of the coalition. The leader decides, one by one, which player should enter the coalition and when. The leader proposes a method to share the benefits of the coalition among the participants.

In this paper, we explore two different sharing methods for both the cost and savings allocation approaches and show how coalitions may differ, one from another. Thus, in the two allocation approaches, a sharing method is adapted to imitate the altruistic and opportunistic behaviour of the leading player. First, an altruistic behaviour is simulated. For the cost allocation method, the leader shares among all the players the coalition benefit of the new coalition obtained by adding a new player. For the saving allocation method, the leader shares among all the players only the marginal benefit obtained by adding a new player. Secondly, an opportunistic behaviour is simulated. In this case, for both the cost and the saving allocation methods, the leader shares the marginal benefit obtained by adding a new player with the new player only.

In the four sharing methods tested, the cost/saving allocation is based on the stand alone weighted cost of each player in the coalition. This allocation method is easy to understand and to compute. Several cost/saving allocation methods exist in literature, mainly under the term cost allocation methods. An extensive list of literature papers on cost allocation methods based on game theory can be found in (Tijs and Driessen, 1986). The computing and analyze of some cost allocation methods on the case study used below is presented in (Frisk et al., 2006). A new method that allows a proportionally equal incentive to each player is also proposed in (Frisk et al., 2006).

In contrast with these papers, the aim in this paper is to demonstrate through a simple allocation method how under a coalition leader's behavior it can affect the cost/save allocation among the players as well as the development and the size of the coalition. Thus, the cost/saving allocated to a player depends on the business model as well as on the cost/saving allocation method. The same exercise could be achieved with more advanced allocation methods.

3.3.1   Business model 1: altruistic cost allocation method

In this model, each time a new player p' is added to the coalition, the new coalition cost is reallocated to each player of the new coalition. The coalition cost is spilt according to the proportion of the player's stand alone cost on the sum of all the players' stand alone cost in the new coalition. This means that the incentive of the players in the coalition changes as new players enter.

3.3.2   Business model 2: opportunistic cost allocation method

In this model, each time a new player p' is added to the coalition, the cost allocated to the leading players is recomputed. In contrast with the previous model, the cost allocated to a non leading player is computed only once, that is, when it is added to the coalition. This means that, once a non leading player is in the coalition, its incentive remains constant even with the addition of new players.

For each new coalition, the cost allocation is computed in three steps. First, the part of the new coalition' cost that is allocated to the new player p' is computed according to the proportion of the player's p' stand alone cost on the sum of all players stand alone cost in the new coalition. Second, the remaining part of the new coalition cost is calculated by withdrawing the part of the new coalition cost allocated to the new player in the first phase and also all the parts of coalition cost allocated to the non leading players in the previous coalitions. This remaining cost is then divided among the leaders according to the proportion of the leading player alone cost on the sum of all the leading players stand alone cost.

3.3.3   Business model 3: altruistic saving allocation method

In this business model and the following one, instead of using a cost allocation approach as in the two previous business models, we adopt a saving allocation approach. Thus, it is the marginal increase in the benefit (i.e. the saving in the case study used below) of coalition c when player p' is added that is divided among all the players, leader or not, in this new coalition c'. This means that, once a player is in the coalition, its incentive increases each time a new player is added to the coalition. The split of the marginal benefit is computed according to the proportion of player's p' stand alone cost on the sum of all the players' stand alone.

3.3.4   Business model 4: opportunistic saving allocation method

In this business model, the marginal increase in the benefit of coalition c when player p' is added is split between the leading players and the new player p' only. Similar to business model 2, this means that, once a non leading player is in the coalition, its incentive remains constant even with the addition of new players.

The split of the marginal benefit is computed in three steps. First, the part of the marginal benefit given to the new player p' is computed according to the proportion of the player's p' stand alone cost on the sum of all players, including player's p' stand alone cost. Second, the remaining part of the marginal benefit is computed by withdrawing the part given to the new player p'. Finally, this remaining part of the marginal benefit is divided among the leaders according to the proportion of the leading player alone cost on the sum of all the leading players stand alone cost.

4   FORMING SUSTAINABLE COALITION

One of the key issues for the leading players of a coalition is the development of a coalition that will provide the greatest return. In order to study this issue we address the development of a coalition as a step-by-step process where one player at a time is added to the coalition. In this process, it is assumed that all players have the opportunity to join and collaborate in the coalition but it is the leading players who decide which player should be added at which step. Also, it assumes that once a player is in the coalition, it is the leading players only who can decide to remove the player and only one coalition can be created. This step-by-step process allows us to evaluate, for the four business models described above, the impact on the leading players' incentive of the sequence in which the non leading players are added to the coalition.

The leader can develop its coalition in various ways. However, in practice, evaluation of the potential for collaboration is often realized between two companies at one time only (e.g. wood bartering). Each company uses its internal planning system to anticipate the potential benefit of the collaboration without revealing it to the other company and to negotiate a possible collaboration agreement. The main reasons why the information about the potential benefits are not shared are that the information may include sensitive business information and provide insights that could substantially affect the cost/save allocation. It appears realistic to suppose that collaboration with another company can also be evaluated on a "two companies basis" while considering the collaborating companies as one. Then, all the companies can negotiate a new collaboration agreement with the new company with or without modifying the previous collaboration agreements.

We can formulate the development of a coalition as a longest path problem (LPP). Given a network of oriented vectors from node i to node j with each a length value, the objective of the LPP is to find the longest path in the network to reach a sink node 0^* starting by a source node 0. The indexes, sets, parameters and decision variables used in the linear programming formulation are defined in Table 1.

Table 1: Indexes, sets, parameters and decision variables

Indexes	
i	: an arrangement of coalition i
j	: an arrangement of coalition j
0	: the pseudo-player source
0^*	: the pseudo-player sink
Sets	
I	: set of all arrangements of coalition without the pseudo-player sink
J	: set of all arrangements of coalition
Parameters	
$M_{i,j}$	: marginal incentive increase of the leader(s) from coalition i to j
Decision variables	
$X_{i,j}$	: 1 if we develop coalition j from coalition i, 0 otherwise

The problem can be formulated as a LP model :

$$[\text{P}] \quad \text{MAX} \sum_{i \in I} \sum_{j \in J} X_{i,j} M_{i,j}$$

s.t.

$$X_{i,j} - \sum_{j' \in J} X_{i=j,j'} = 0 \quad \forall i \in I, \forall j \in J \tag{1}$$

$$\sum_{j \in J} X_{0,j} = 1 \tag{2}$$

$$\sum_{i \in I} X_{i,0^*} = 1 \tag{3}$$

$$X_{i,j} \in \{0,1\} \quad \forall i \in I, \forall j \in J$$

In this context, a node represents an "ordered" coalition, e.g. the coalition "1,2" is different from the coalition "2,1" even if they have the same set N of players. The sequence in which the players are added to the coalition refers to an arrangement. The vector value represents the marginal increase in the incentive of the leading players to develop a new coalition c' by adding a new player p' in the coalition c. The value of the vector is computed according to a specific business model. All vectors starting from the pseudo-player source or arriving at the pseudo-player sink have a null marginal incentive increase. The objective is to find the coalition arrangement that allows the total maximal incentive to the leading players. The leaders' incentive is the sum of each of the vector values of the path traversed in the network from the pseudo-player source to the pseudo-player sink. The constraints (1) ensure that the development of the coalition is made by adding players to the coalition one by one. The constraints (2) and (3) ensure that only one coalition is created.

5 NUMERICAL RESULTS

The data used has been taken from a case study done by the Forestry Research Institute of Sweden for eight participating forest companies. The case represents a total of 898 supply points, 101 demand points and 12 wood assortments (depending on e.g. species and dimensions). The companies are uneven in volume transported.

For all the *combinations* of coalition of 2 to 8, the tactical problem [TP] has been solved. In contrast to an arrangement, in a *combination* the order of the players in the coalition has no importance. Thus, we obtain the cost (V^c) of 247 combinations of coalitions. To define the stand alone cost (V_p) of each player, the tactical problem [TP] was solved for each company solely. Then, the values of B^c, M_p^c, and C_p^c have been computed for each of the potential coalitions.

For the four business models, the values of BL^c, CL_p^c, I_p^c and ML_p^c have been computed for all the 109 592 possible arrangements of the 247 combinations. This case study is smaller however, since it focusses only on the context where company 2 leads the creation of the coalition. Consequently, the number of combinations considered is 120 while the number of arrangements is 13692.

In business model 1, it is the presence of the player in the coalition which will enable it to have a positive incentive. For business model 1, the leader best coalition brings together all players, except player 1. Thus, by driving the selection of the players in the coalition to its own advantage, the leader obtain an incentive of 9,5% (i.e. a reduction of 9,5% on its stand alone cost, a saving of $1,400,518.81). Player 1 is the big loser of business model 1 even if its addition to the coalition would increase the coalition benefit by 7%. However, it was not chosen because its addition would reduce by 2,2% the incentives of the other players, more specifically player 2 would loose $30,731.89. In a situation in which the excluded player 1 has, for any reason, a strong influence on the leading player 2, it is highly plausible that player 1 will use its influence to join the coalition. To maintain its incentive, the player 2 must negotiate with player 1 by allowing it an incentive equal or smaller to the marginal increase of the coalition benefit. By accepting an incentive equal to the marginal increase of the coalition, the player 1 obtains 76,2% (a loss of 80,819.99$) of the incentive that he would have obtained without the leadership of the coalition by player 2.

In opposition to business model 1, the order in which the players are added in the coalition have an influence on the players' incentive for business models 2, 3 and 4. Thus, the leader best coalition for these models is the arrangement providing the highest incentive for the leader. In order to show the impact of the arrangement, the leader best coalition is compared to the leader worst coalition. The leader worst coalition regroups the same set N of players that found in the leader best coalition but in a different arrangement which results in a lowest incentive for the leader.

Using business model 2, the leader best and worst coalitions have been computed. By following the best coalition arrangement (i.e. player 1, 5, 8, 4, 6, 7 and 3) instead of the worst one (i.e. 3, 7, 8, 4, 1, 6 and 5), the leader obtain an additional saving of 4,5% ($668,752.06) on a total saving of 16,2% ($2,383,787.82). In comparison to the leader altruistic behavior of model 1, the leader opportunistic behavior in model 2 allows the leader to obtain an additional saving of 6,7% ($983,269.01).

In business model 3, the leader best and worst coalitions have been computed. By following the best coalition arrangement (i.e. 3, 7, 8, 4, 6, 5 and 1) instead of the worst one (i.e. 5, 1, 6, 8, 4, 7 and 3), the leader obtain an additional saving of 2,9% ($426,256.47) on a total saving of 15% ($2,201,067.33). In business model 4, the best coalition arrangement (i.e. 4, 1, 6, 3, 8, 7 and 5), instead of the worst one (i.e. 3, 5, 6, 7, 4, 1 and 8), allows the leader to obtain an additional saving of 1,1% ($161,355.49) on a total saving of 22,3% ($3,282,559.05). In comparison to the leader altruistic behaviour of model 3, the leader opportunistic behaviour of model 4 allows the leader to gain an additional saving of 7,4% ($1,081,491.72). In all the tested models, business model 4 is the more lucrative for the leader: he obtain an incentive equal to 83,3% ($3,282,559.05) of the higher coalition benefit which could be obtained by a eight players coalition.

6   CONCLUDING REMARKS

It has been shown that collaboration in transportation can provide savings. There exist decision support systems that can establish the collaborative transportation plans. These systems however raise the question of how to share the obtained benefit? Several business models for the implementation of collaborative planning in transportation were considered in this paper. The leader role for building the coalition is discussed and six different leading approaches are described. Using a case study of eight companies, four specific business models, all driven by one leading company, are tested and numerical results are discussed. The impact of two different behaviours of the leader is studied under two approaches of benefit sharing. The first one is based on the allocation of costs while the second is based on the sharing of the savings.

The business model approach allows the integration of practical considerations (e.g. the leadership position of some players compared to others and their behaviours) in defining the cost/saving allocation method as well as the coalition creation process (e.g. development and size). However, it was shown that in a group of stakeholders, a business model could lead to coalition who is not catching all the economical potential of the group. More research works must be achieved on different coalition building process and business models to study their influence on the leaders' incentive and the achievable of all possible saves. Also, the sustainability of the coalition must be studied taking into consideration the risk for the leaders that one player leave the coalition. Another issue to be addressed relates to temporal aspects and their impact on the development of the coalitions. Finally, the advantage for a company to join more than one coalition by splitting its demand/supply should be investigated.

Acknowledgments

The authors wish to thank Philippe Marier of FORAC Research Consortium for his contribution to this work. The authors would also like to acknowledge the financial support of the Natural Sciences and Engineering Research Council of Canada and the private and public partners of the FORAC Research Consortium.

7   REFERENCES

1. Audy, J.-F., D'Amours, S. and M. Rönnqvist, "Business Models for Collaborative Planning in Transportation: an Application to Wood Products" Proceedings of the ICEB eBRF, 2006, 28 November - 2 December, Tampere, Finland, 7 p.
2. Carlsson, D. and M. Rönnqvist, Tactical planning of forestry transportation with respect to backhauling, LiTH-MAT-R-1998-13, Linköping University, Sweden, 19 p.
3. Eriksson, J. and M. Rönnqvist, "Transportation and route planning: Akarweb - a web-based planning system" Proceedings of the 2nd Forest Engineering Conference, 2003, 12-15 May, Växjö, Sweden, 9 p.
4. Forsberg M., Frisk, M. and M. Rönnqvist, FlowOpt a decision support tool for strategic and tactical transportation planning in forestry, International Journal of Forest Engineering, 16(2), 2005, pp. 101-114
5. Frisk, M., Jörnsten, K., Göthe-Lundgren, M. and M. Rönnqvist, "Cost allocation in forestry operations", Proceedings of the 12th IFAC Symposium on ICPM, 2006, 17-19 May, Saint-Etienne, France, 11 p.
6. Gingras, C., Cordeau, J.-F., and G. Laporte, Un algorithme de minimisation du transport à vide appliqué à l'industrie forestière, INFOR, to be published.
7. Tijs, S. H. and T. S. H. Driessen, "Game theory and cost allocation problems", Management Science, 32(8), 1015-1058, 1986

73

PROVIDING TRANSPARENCY IN THE BUSINESS OF SOFTWARE: A MODELING TECHNIQUE FOR SOFTWARE SUPPLY NETWORKS

Slinger Jansen
s.jansen@cs.uu.nl, Utrecht University, NETHERLANDS
Sjaak Brinkkemper
s.brinkkemper@cs.uu.nl, Utrecht University, NETHERLANDS
Anthony Finkelstein
a.finkelstein@cs.ucl.ac.uk, University College London, UK

One of the most significant paradigm shifts of software business is that individual organizations no longer compete as single entities but as complex dynamic supply networks of interrelated participants that provide blends of software design, development, implementation, publication and services. Understanding these intricate software supply networks is a difficult task for decision makers in software businesses. This paper outlines a modeling technique for representing and reasoning about software supply networks. We show, by way of a worked case study, how modeling software supply networks might allow managers to identify new business opportunities, visualize liability and responsibilities in a supply network, and how it can be used as a planning tool for product software distribution.

1 SOFTWARE BUSINESSES ARE BLENDS

Individual businesses no longer compete as single entities but as supply chains (Lambert, 2002). This holds for the software industry as well, where software products and services are no longer monolithical systems developed in-house, but consist of complex hardware and software system federations (Ghezzi, 2002) produced and sold by different organizations. This development has led organizations to combine their business and components into complex software supply networks (SSNs), from which they supply end-users with integrated products. As these SSNs grow more complex, it becomes harder for the participants of SSNs to make informed decisions on development strategy, responsibility, liability, and market placement (Gartner, 2005; Grieger, 2003). It also becomes harder to manage the risk associated with these decisions (Jansen, 2006A).

A SSN is a series of linked software, hardware, and service organizations cooperating to satisfy market demands. SSN management is different from physical goods supply chain management (SCM) in two ways. First, software is malleable after release and delivery, giving rise to the need for extensive maintenance. Secondly, products delivered to end-users in SSNs are tolerated with much lower quality levels than other products (Baxter, 2001). A result of the difference between conventional supply networks and SSNs is that literature on collaboration in supply networks (Patosalmi, 2003) does not discuss maintenance and how it requires information about the supply chain. The same holds for other work on SCM, such as (Lazzarini, 2001), which groups horizontal ties between firms (such as manufacturers

Jansen, S., Brinkkemper, S., Finkelstein, A., 2007, in IFIP International Federation for Information Processing, Volume 243, Establishing the Foundation of Collaborative Networks; eds. Camarinha-Matos, L., Afsarmanesh, H., Novais, P., Analide, C.; (Boston: Springer), pp. 677–686.

and suppliers), but fails to recognize the importance of leveraging feedback in such networks, or Lambert and Cooper (Lambert, 2002), who provide a conceptual framework for SCM without maintenance.

This paper explores the new field of SSN research by presenting a method for modeling the complex relationships between participants in the supply networks of composite products and services. By conducting a case study of an organization that leverages the SSN we demonstrate that SSN models enable participants in supply networks to reason about business identification, product architecture design, risk identification, product placement planning, and business network redesign. Furthermore we demonstrate that modeling relations in supply networks is the first step in explicitly managing relationships with other participants.

Value chains differ from SSNs in that value chains describe one product only, whereas SSNs specifically address networks of software systems that interact to provide software services. Attempts have already been made to model value chains surrounding large ERP configurations, by Messerschmitt and Szyperski (Messerschmitt, 2003). Their model cannot represent relationships between for instance a component-off-the-shelf (COTS) vendor and an application developer, making their models insufficient to describe a complete SSN. Weill and Vitale's (Weill & Vitale, 2001) value chains describe supply networks best, but lack the accompanying product description required for a software supply network model.

In the following section SSN models are provided, by presenting the participants, the meta-model, a creation method, and an example. In section 3 the case study Tribeka is presented. In section 4 applications of SSN models are presented and discussed. In section 5 a description is provided on how organizations best ready themselves to participate in a supply network.

2   SOFTWARE SUPPLY NETWORK MODEL

Models for SSNs consist of two parts, a product context and a supply network. A **product context** describes the context, in which a software service operates, and the software products, hardware products, and software services that are required to provide the software service. A **supply network** displays all participants in a SSN, the connections between these participants, and the flows describing the type of product that is traded across these connections. **SSN Participants** are any party that provides or requires flows from another participant in the network. The two diagrams are complementary in that the product context shows all products that are traded in their different forms in the supply network.

2.1   Product Context

A software service is the provision of one or more functions by a system of interest to an end-user or to another software service. A software system is a combination of independent but interrelated software services, software components, and hardware components that provides one or more services. There are three types of entities in the product context, being (1) white-box services and their systems, (2) black box services, and (3) software and hardware components making up systems. The main concept for product contexts is that of a software system, which consists of hardware and software components and when combined and activated these components provide a service. A software system requires at least one hardware component, at least one software component, and any number of services. A hardware component can support any amount of services and software components.

When a software component requires other software components (such as libraries and COTS) these are drawn under the software component. When a software component requires software services (such as databases and web servers), these are drawn under the software component as a service. The hardware on which the software components are running is drawn left of the systems. It is assumed that hardware components are complete, and thus do not have dependencies. Systems that provide services are drawn as containers containing the software components and services on which they depend. Please see Figure 2 for an example.

2.2 Supply Network

Supply networks connect participants in the network. Furthermore, these connections are annotated with flows, such as product requirements, product designs, software components, component assemblies, assembled products, assembled deployed systems (hardware and software), and services (provided by these systems). These artifacts all come from decoupling points for software products (see Figure 1), which is the point at which demand and supply meet in a supply network.

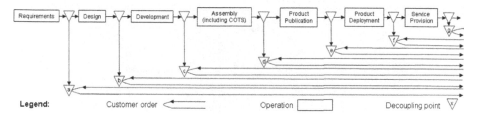

Figure 1 Product Software Decoupling Points

To date, product software is defined as a packaged configuration of software components or a software-based service, with auxiliary materials, which is released for and traded in a specific market (Xu Brinkkemper, 2005). When looking at the product software production pipeline seven decoupling points can be identified. First, a development organization can outsource the requirements engineering process and/or design process (*a, b*). Also, the developer can choose to release their source code, binaries, or assemblies of components (*c, d, e*) to another developing organization who uses these artifacts as a component to their product, or to a publisher who releases the product (common for games, where the vendor is rarely the developer). A software vendor can also choose to release the product itself, either as a package, or as a deployed system (*f*). Finally, a vendor can decide to offer their product to its customer in an application service provider model, where the vendor sells usage of its product instead of the product itself (*g*).

Flows are modeled as labels on the arcs between the participants and are distinguished by different colors and codings. The color indicates whether the artifacts are source artifact collections, compiled binary artifact collections, or complete systems and services. The codings are (in order of creation to usage) **Req** (requirements), **Des** (design), **Comp** (software component), **As** (software component assembly), P (software product), Sys (system, including hardware), HW (hardware),

Establishing the foundation of collaborative networks

and finally Ser (services). It is not uncommon for software products going through iterations of the decoupling points before the product is delivered to a customer. It can be well imagined that a system designer creates a design, sells the design, and the software developer starts at the requirements phase again to see what can be added to the design. To indicate this numbers are used in the codings after the abbreviation, such as Des2.1, which means that this is the second design for product 1. In the supply networks we only make this distinction when two generations of artifacts are produced by different participants.

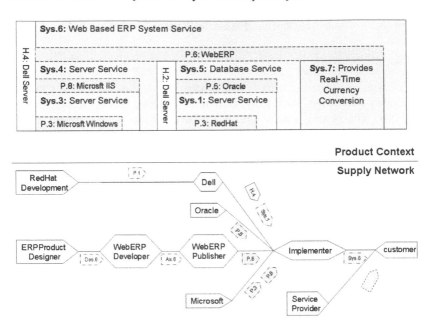

Figure 2 Example of a WebERP SSN Model

In Figure 2 the example models are presented for a customer requiring a Web Enterprise Resource Planning (ERP) service. To supply this service internally, the customer has decided to go with its personal implementer organization who implements a product WebERP on a newly purchased local database server and a local web server. The product context displays that to supply Ser.6, P.6 is required. To run P.6 a server is required that supplies WebERP through a web server application, in this case Microsoft IIS. On the other side a database server (Sys.5) is required that manages all the data for WebERP. Both servers, supplied by Dell, run a different operating system. Furthermore, to provide the WebERP service, a currency conversion web service is required. As products transition from source code to product to system, they generally retain the same number, such as for WebERP; Des.6, As.6, P.6, and Sys.6 are all instances of the same (software) artifacts sold at their different decoupling points.

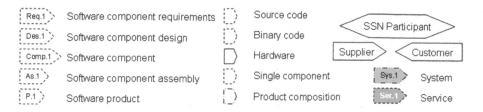

Figure 3 Supply Network Legend

2.3   SSN Model Creation Method

To help define the scope of a SSN model, the product context is created. The product context, which describes the systems that supply software services, must display all products and services that are specifically required for the service(s) of interest. Secondly, the participants must be determined. These participants are all parties that are involved with the products in the product context. The products in the product context will be presented as flows later. Finally, all relationships must be established between the participants. Whenever a product or service is traded between participants, they must be connected by an arc. Once the arc is drawn, it can be annotated with the type of products and services that flow down this arc. Please note that there must be a strict consistency between products in the supply network and the product context. Furthermore, flows are directional, such as software flowing forward to customers and money or feedback flowing back to vendors.

3   A CASE STUDY: TRIBEKA

We use a case study to demonstrate the SSN modeling technique. The company under study is Tribeka (http://www.tribeka.com), an organization that attempts to break through the traditional product software retail supply chain, by delivering assemblies of components to retail outlets that can be burnt, packaged and turned into a finalized product *on-site*. Tribeka, founded in 1996, currently employs twenty five people and has deployed its systems at large retail chains in the United Kingdom, such as WH Smith and HMV. Recently Tribeka has opened four high street outlets where it solely sells software created with Tribeka's SoftWide system.

The Tribeka SoftWide system consists of a server with a large storage memory, an internet connection, a number of CD and DVD burners, and a high quality cover printing facility for boxes, CDs, and DVDs. It is capable of creating between 50 and 100 different shrink-wrapped products per hour. The SoftWide system is not solely a hardware solution, since it is able to deliver the most up-to-date software onto the retail market. On a daily basis software updates are sent to the SoftWide systems deployed in retail stores, including price information. The SoftWide system stores the component assemblies in a coded manner, such that products are only produced when requested and authorized, using a proprietary auditable licensing system.

3.1   Tribeka Models

An SSN model with two different supply networks is presented in Figure 4. At the top level of the figure the product context displays two systems, that provide the "computer use" and "entertainment" services. The entertainment system requires the software service "computer use" and the game product **P.3**. The system **Sys.2** requires a laptop and Microsoft Windows, before it can actually provide the "entertainment" software service.

Traditional software supply is depicted in the ``before Tribeka" section of the figure. Here Microsoft is modeled as a software developer, who delivers its product to Dell. Dell, the hardware manufacturer, deploys the product **P.1** onto the laptop system and delivers **Sys.2** to its retailer, PC Store. PC Store sells the system to the customer, who also purchases a game **P.3** with it. **P.3** is designed by Game Designer and the design is sold to the Game Developer, which actually implements the game. Once game development is finished a collection of source components (**As1.3**) is sent to the game publisher. These source components are then compiled, causing the **As2.3** to be shaded, and sent off to a printing facility. Finally, the game publisher sells the finished products **P.3** to a reseller. The reseller then sells the game to PC Store.

Tribeka takes over from the Game Publisher, the Reseller, and the printing facility, by directly publishing any product from a software developer to retail stores. The Game Developer now passes a compiled set of components directly to Tribeka. Tribeka sends the component assembly to PC Store directly, instead of to a printing facility and then reseller. The component assembly is then assembled into a product at the retail store, enabling the latest possible binding for physically sold software products. Tribeka also has opened three retail stores itself, offering all products offered through the SoftWide system.

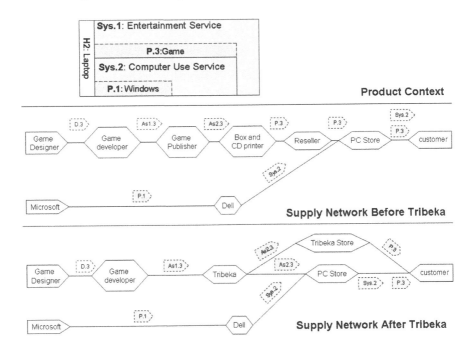

Figure 4. Tribeka Case Study SSN and Product Context

3.2   Tribeka Relationships

The SSN model in Figure 4 shows that Tribeka maintains intensive relationships with the game developer and with retailers. The presented model is slightly simplified because in many cases there will be a publisher in between the developer and Tribeka. As such, Tribeka has three types of participants in the supply network it deals with: retailers, game developers, and game publishers. Tribeka uses its SoftWide system to maintain relationships and transport data between these participants. Publishers and developers send their component assemblies to Tribeka, which are then uploaded into the SoftWide system, including price information, license codes, software artifacts, digital manuals, and images for box covers. These publishers are able to see the status of their products, such as how many sales have been made and what types of licenses have been distributed. On the other side retailers access the SoftWide system through their points of sale, which are used to sell and create software products from the product assemblies supplied by Tribeka.

From Tribeka two lessons can be learnt about SSNs. To be successful in a supply network an organization must explicitly manage relations with the other participants. The second lesson is that an organization must observe opportunities to take part in different parts of the supply network, such as Tribeka's opening of retail stores that only use the SoftWide system.

4   SSN MODEL APPLICATIONS AND USAGE

We have identified five applications of SSN models being business identification, product architecture design, risk identification, product placement planning, and business network redesign. The aim of SSN models is to clarify the blend that is software business. SSN models are thus used by policy makers, software architects, and entrepreneurs. Depending on the application, they must make the SSN model on a regular basis and observe changes, risks, and opportunities. The SSN model can function as an overview diagram for a business plan or even for year end-reports to indicate how a software business made profit.

Business Identification - SSN models show the trade relationships for each participant in the network. These flows can be used to determine the business type for that participant. When, for instance, a participant receives hardware and software components and has one system as output this is an *integrator* (Implementer in the WebERP example). A participant that receives component assemblies and then publishes products is a *publisher* (WebERP publisher in the WebERP example). Another common example is a supplier that has no input but produces a software product (*software product developer*, RedHat in the example). We see that Tribeka (see Figure 4) functions as a *packager* and interestingly enough turns the PC Store into a *software product publisher*. A participant that has the same input as output is a *reseller*. Finally, according to these definitions and due to the absence of a hardware component input Dell is a *hardware producing integrator*. These constructs are commonly encountered in different SSN models.

Product architecture design - In deciding the type of software architecture a software developer must use, the supply network plays an important part. The software architecture decides how a product will depend on other products and services, and this will have far reaching consequences on the future of a software product. SSN models can thus assist in making architectural design decisions.

Risk identification - The SSN model uncovers, for instance, that a product cannot be used without the availability of some component or service. These dependencies on other organizations, though logical, can be disastrous for participants further up the supply network. Such a dependency influences the total cost of ownership of the product, the possibility to internationalize, and even the future when such a dependency can no longer be fulfilled. This calls for diversification and architecting for product dependency variability (Jaring, 2004). The SSN model helps uncover such relations and dependencies. SSN models can be used by customer organizations to uncover whether they are in possession of certain products that are unsupported, or whether they are making use of a service that could easily be terminated. Such investigation is part of portfolio rationalization. A common vulnerability, for instance, is a custom link between two products, built by a software implementation service provider, which stops working after an update for one of the products has been deployed. The SSN models can assist in finding and eliminating such weaknesses for all participants in the supply network.

Product placement planning - A vendor can use the SSN model to determine how to market its product, how to inform customers of product news and releases, and how customers will contact the vendor. The latter is especially important when looking at pay-per-usage feedback and error feedback (Jansen, 2006b). For example, when a bug report is sent from a customer to a participant in the SSN the participant must decide whether to solve this issue or to forward it to another party in the supply network. Software vendors can choose to sell their products as add-ons to other products, in combination with hardware (i.e., navigation systems), and as a service (on-line bookkeeping). Furthermore, software vendors can decide to sell the product through channels they own (their own site), through resellers, through service providers, etc.

Business Network Redesign - Participants of the supply network must identify their business partners and establish different types of relations. SSN models can thus be used to design business information systems that take into account the participants of the supply network with which the business will have regular and even ad-hoc relations. Tribeka for example manages explicitly its relationships with software developers, publishers, and retail outlets and has created different information systems and portals for them.

The SSN model reveals business opportunities and risks by making two types of changes. The first change is to alter the binding times and decoupling points for products and services. Tribeka is a clear example of this, where it takes the role of the traditional reseller, but simply assembles the product at a later stage. This optimization allows resellers to replenish their stock dynamically, saving cost in the area of stock management, delivery, and deployment. The second type of change is seen when a change is made to the participants in the supply network, in the form of acquisitions, split-ups, developers buying new COTS, or customer organizations that become vendors of products or services themselves. An example of this is when Tribeka opens their own SoftWide stores.

5   AD-HOC SOFTWARE SUPPLY NETWORKS

The tendency to integrate components from different developers and manufacturers into new products and components by both customers and integrators has led to a phenomenon of quickly forming and dissolving of ad-hoc supply networks (Zager,

2000). Many organizations, however, are not specifically adjusted to manage relations within such ad-hoc networks. Simultaneously, software vendors and manufacturers are constantly approached by (new) business partners, such as manufacturers, resellers, and service providers, with bugs, feedback, requests for changes, and other communication about their software products.

A coalition between participants in a supply network is where participants rely on each other, yet do not have any of the skills required for collaborative unity (Zager, 2000), such as organizational measures, structured communication, and planned durability. Software organizations can profit from the many opportunities in these ad-hoc supply networks when properly prepared to engage (order of intensity) in conversations, relations, partnerships, and even alliances with other participants. These other vendors are willing to create a user and developer community around a (configuration of) software product(s), which will encourage use of products and create new solutions and opportunities surrounding them. An example of such a relationship between software vendors is when Microsoft sends error messages to product vendors whose products have crashed on Windows. The vendor can opt to resolve the error independently or in different gradients of intensity with Microsoft.

The SSN modeling technique presented in this paper assists a participant in understanding how these coalitions are formed. Secondly, a participant must build a community surrounding its product that unifies external and internal users, developers, implementers, and integrators of the product. Such a community can be built using ontologies, portals, customer days, and partner days. Especially portals, which can be used for the distribution and sharing of knowledge, development and bug finding tools, are an important factor to create a close network of participants willing to add value to the community, and thus increase value of a supply network.

To transform a coalition to collaboration relations must be formalized by the facilitating organization. A clear distinction needs to be made between intensively and loosely coupled alliance partners. By classifying partners in such a way, participants can create different circles of trust with partners and users, which will clarify the different relationships within a supply network considerably for all participants in a network. A participant in the supply network must at all times be aware of opportunities to form coalitions, since each customer question could set in motion the cooperation between multiple participants. The belief that supply networks must be leveraged by software businesses is further strengthened by (Duyster et al., 1999) who claim that to craft successful strategic technology partnerships steps need to be undertaken to strategically position participants, prepare alliance skills, build a business community, and do smart partner selection.

6   CONCLUSIONS AND FUTURE WORK

SSN models provide a novel manner to perform strategic and risk evaluation in the business of software. The Tribeka insights can be realized through experience, but the ability to assess risks a priori is a valuable contribution. This paper presents a modeling method for SSNs to provide insight into supply networks, enabling participants to do risk assessment, strategic decision making, product placement planning, and liability determination. A case study is used for this paper because it is a proven method to introduce a novel research area, such as SSNs.

The decoupling points are a concept taken from physical product development and marketing planning. The combination of supply network with these decoupling points creates a powerful modeling tool that is generalizable to non-software products as well. To be able to do so one must define the decoupling points, the possible range of product decompositions, before creating the supply networks.

Currently we possess a collection of 30+ SSN models from start-ups and medium to large software enterprises. With these models we are hoping to further classify different business models for product software. Furthermore we are experimenting with different flows, such as content, money, and licenses.

7 REFERENCES

1. Baxter, L. and Simmons, J. The software supply chain for manufactured products: reassessing partnership sourcing. In International Conference on Management of Engineering and Technology, 2001.
2. Colville, R. and Adams, P.. It service dependency mapping tools provide configuration view. In Gartner Research News Analysis. Gartner, 2005.
3. Duysters, G., Kok, G., and Vaandrager, M. Crafting successful strategic technology partnerships. In Research and Design management, issue 4:29:343, 1999.
4. Ghezzi, C. and Picco, G. P.. An outlook on software engineering for modern distributed systems. In Proceedings of the Monterey workshop on Radical Approaches to Software Engineering, Venice (Italy), October 8-12, 2002.
5. Grieger, M, Electronic marketplaces: A literature review and a call for supply chain management research, In European Journal of Operational Research, 2003
6. S. Jansen and S. Brinkkemper. Definition and validation of the key process areas of release, delivery and deployment of product software vendors: turning the ugly duckling into a swan. In proceedings of the International Conference on Software Maintenance, September 2006b.
7. S. Jansen and W. Rijsemus. Balancing total cost of ownership and cost of maintenance within a software supply network. In proceedings of the IEEE International Conference on Software Maintenance, Philadelphia, PA, USA, September, 2006A.
8. M. Jaring and J. Bosch. Architecting product diversification - formalizing variability dependencies in software product family engineering. In Fourth International Conference on Quality Software, pages 154–161, Washington, DC, USA, 2004. IEEE Computer Society.
9. Lambert, D. M. and Cooper, M. C., Issues in supply chain management. In Journal of Industrial Martketing Management, 2002.
10. Lazzarini, S. G., Chaddad, F. R. and Cook, M. L.. Integrating supply chain and network analyses: the study of netchains. In Journal on Chain and Network Science. Wageningen Academic, 2001.
11. Messerschmitt, D. G. and Szyperski, C. Software Ecosystem: Understanding an Indispensable Technology and Industry (Chapter 6: Organization of the Software Value Chain. MIT Press, Cambridge, MA, USA, 2003.
12. Patosalmi, J. Collaborative decision-making in supply chain management. In Seminar in Business Strategy, 2003.
13. Weill, P., Vitale, M., "Place to space: Migrating to eBusiness Models", Harvard Business School, 2001
14. Xu, L., Brinkkemper, S., "Concepts of Product Software: Paving the Road for Urgently Needed Research", First International Workshop on Philosophical Foundations of Information Systems Engineering, LNCS, Springer-Verlag, 2005
15. Zager, D. Collaboration on the fly. In AIWORC '00: Proceedings of the Academia/Industry Working Conference on Research Challenges, page 65, Washington DC, USA, 2000. IEEE

AUTHOR INDEX